Cases on Technology Enhanced Learning through Collaborative Opportunities

Siran Mukerji
IGNOU, India

Purnendu Tripathi
IGNOU, India

INFORMATION SCIENCE REFERENCE

Hershey · New York

Director of Editorial Content:	Kristin Klinger
Director of Book Publications:	Julia Mosemann
Acquisitions Editor:	Lindsay Johnston
Development Editor:	Elizabeth Ardner
Publishing Assistant:	Sean Woznicki
Typesetter:	Myla Harty
Production Editor:	Jamie Snavely
Cover Design:	Lisa Tosheff
Printed at:	Yurchak Printing Inc.

Published in the United States of America by
Information Science Reference (an imprint of IGI Global)
701 E. Chocolate Avenue
Hershey PA 17033
Tel: 717-533-8845
Fax: 717-533-8661
E-mail: cust@igi-global.com
Web site: http://www.igi-global.com/reference

Library of Congress Cataloging-in-Publication Data

Cases on technology enhanced learning through collaborative opportunities / Siran Mukerji and Purnendu Tripathi, editors.
    p. cm.

  Includes bibliographical references and index.
  Summary: "The collection of cases in the book analyzes and evaluates how organizations and institutions of learning in the developing and developed world are adapting to technology enhanced learning environments and exploring transnational collaborative opportunities"--Provided by publisher.

  ISBN 978-1-61520-751-0 (hardcover) -- ISBN 978-1-61520-752-7 (ebook) 1.
Group work in education--Computer networks--Cross-cultural studies. 2.
Distance education--Computer-assisted instruction--Cross-cultural studies. 3.
Educational technology--Cross-cultural studies. 4. Education and
globalization--Cross-cultural studies. I. Mukerji, Siran. II. Tripathi,
Purnendu, 1975-
  LB1032.C4 2010
  371.35'8--dc22
                            2009045252

British Cataloguing in Publication Data
A Cataloguing in Publication record for this book is available from the British Library.

Table of Contents

Detailed Table of Contents

Jill Jameson, University of Greenwich, UK

This case study of collaborative e-learning by Jill Jameson reflects on the use of the extended metaphor of the camel in the JISC-funded eLIDA CAMEL and JISC infoNet CAMEL projects in which technological and human adaptability was fostered in a community of practice (CoP). It portrays series of nomadic journeys held in oases provided by partners that enabled honest exchanges amongst a community of 'CAMEL' practitioners, improving e-learning practices. The camel metaphor was formative in stimulating understanding about building communal solutions to sustainability, low-cost innovative engagement and improved cooperation with others.

Deryn Graham, University of Greenwich, UK
Ian Benest, University of York, UK
Peter Nicholl, University of Ulster, UK

The case study aims at improving interaction design for teaching visually impaired students, in an inclusive learning environment with the crux of the problem being the ability to draw and understand diagrams and is motivated by the need to accommodate visually impaired students studying computer science at UK universities.

Francis Bangou, University of Ottawa, Canada
Douglas Fleming, University of Ottawa, Canada

This case by Francis and Douglas looks into the effective use of blogging for teacher for a course in English as a Second Language (ESL) using discourse to explore how teacher candidates use and perceive blogs within a course on ESL teaching methods.

Chapter 4

Birgit Loch, Swinburne University of Technology, Australia
Shirley Reushle, University of Southern Queensland, Australia
Nicola Jayne, Southern Cross University, Australia
Stephen Rowe, Southern Cross University, Australia

This case study attempts to investigate the use of synchronous audiographic web conferencing (Elluminate) as a learning and teaching tool at the two Australian regional universities and compares the issues and challenges relating to software trials in educational environments and provides recommendations for others who may be considering the adoption of similar technologies

Chapter 5

Kathryn Ley, University of Houston Clear Lake, USA
Ruth Gannon-Cook, De Paul University, USA

It is an action research case study describing a successful marketing effort for a Blended University Program to recruit prospective graduate students from a culturally diverse urban and suburban adult non-traditional population.

Chapter 6

Sibongile Simelane, Tshwane University of Technology, South Africa

The need to educate instructors, lecturers and teachers in how to integrate technology into education has been duly emphasized globally, leading to initiatives taken by quite a few higher education institutions by introducing professional development programmes in educational technology to ensure that technology is effectively utilised so as to enhance the quality of the educational practices. This case study portrays the implementation component of the e-TUTO programme in Tshwane University of Technology, South Africa.

Chapter 7

Emmanuel Fokides, University of the Aegean, Greece
Costas Tsolakidis, University of the Aegean, Greece

This case by Emmanuel and Costas portrays issue of road safety education through desktop virtual mode using a 3D video game tested by the students of the last three grades of a primary school in Athens. It simulates the environment of a town with traffic and all of its elements (cars, traffic lights, pedestrian crossings) along with special conditions such as night and rain. It is developed to simulate the walk of a pedestrian and could accommodate many users simultaneously.

Chapter 8

Aleric Joyce Josephs, University of the West Indies - Mona Campus, West Indies

This case study by Aleric discusses teacher education program in Jamaica articulating distance learning and face-to-face modalities and examines the skills needed and the challenges involved in developing a curriculum for teaching History using a blended approach incorporating the available technology and also highlights the challenges and opportunities in blending traditional and technological factors to develop a model teacher education program.

Chapter 9

Christopher T. Miller, Morehead State University, USA

Christopher argues that as the distance grows between the instructor and student within education, it becomes necessary to explore new ways of addressing the instruction that goes into distance education. In this case, he describes a distance-based instructional model, the person-centered model of instruction, as well as a case study implementation of the person-centered model of instruction in a web-based course and discusses the differences in learning of two groups using the person-centered model of instruction and the other one participating in a constructivist learning experience.

Chapter 10

Angelina Khoro, Lesotho College of Education, Lesotho

The author of this case Angelina believes that education practitioners in developing countries like Lesotho, have limited, or no access at all to ICT for supporting instruction, since they still rely heavily on print and tutor/learner meetings as their distance mode of course delivery. She analyses the feasibility of introducing ICT-mediated education for tutors and learners in a Distance Education Programme in Lesotho.

Chapter 11

Wolfram Laaser, FernUniversität in Hagen, Germany

This case illustrates the production and use of DVD-production "Looking for Charisma" in the area of business administration and management training with an emphasis on how real business applications are related to the theoretical knowledge background concepts gained from textbooks.

Chapter 12

Karen Kaun of Knowledge iTrust (KIT) and Payal Arora discuss *Peace Diaries,* a forum where educators, students and their families of diverse cultural backgrounds and discourse groups could gather and submit multi-modal literary works addressing issues of personal, local and global significance. They attempt to explore its enormous potential towards a Global Education Greenhouse, a corporation in formation, which will create a new class of products and services for students in primary and secondary schools/ grades K-12 addressing a void in the current educational system.

Chapter 13

Hamed Fazollahtabar opines that the e-learners are working in isolation with limited or sometimes non-existent human support and thus first impact of any failure in the providers' quality assessment falls on the e-learner. In his case of Fuzzy Logic for Real-time Comprehensive Quality Assessment Model, he discusses that the e-learning development being a team-based activity, the effectiveness or quality of an e-learning program depends on the weakest link in the production chain and e-learning exists at a point of convergence between technology based disciplines and human-centered disciplines.

Chapter 14

Elena Verezub in this case illustrates about a project which aims at designing an e-learning program for students studying within the Department of Horticulture and Environmental Science of an Australian University, with an additional focus on improving students' reading comprehension of hypertexts in the subject-specific context. The case study also discusses STEEP issues concerned with the project.

Chapter 15

In this case, Victor C Wang focuses on technology enhanced learning in China in the light of technology enhanced learning in the USA. He discusses the challenges in the Chinese educational settings due to its dependence upon radio and TV. He further opines that analysis in this case can be considered as a generic one as the issues and challenges are similar to the universities across China's educational settings.

The authors of this case indicate that the many rural schools in the United States have turned to distance education while facing with problems of providing a comprehensive curriculum and qualified teachers. This case examines the use of distance education in the United States through a national survey pertaining to the use of distance education, analysis of barriers to distance education and an experimental study of enhancing distance education by more appropriate training of local facilitators to support students in rural schools.

Getnet Bitew in this case discusses live "plasma" TV as an instructional delivery tool in government secondary schools of Ethiopia and focuses on the problems encountered when the students are not active in the learning process while using this mode. He rationalizes the use of "plasma" TV lessons to be distributed on CDs and its use as a supplementary instructional aid to help the students in developing their creativity, problem solving and critical skills.

This case highlights the transition of an existing distance education program into an interactive fully-online undergraduate degree program of Saint Mary-of-the-Woods College (SMWC). It discusses the rationale behind the design of the program to suit an online community of learners with a format and focus that appeals to net generation (millennial), neo-millennial, and computer savvy non-traditional students, including military personnel.

In this case, the authors outline the challenges of program development, delivering effective course content, using appropriate learning strategies, operating in a cross-cultural context, and working in an organization with limited technological capacities while establishing a joint international masters' program in Instructional Technology in a Central American country. It further discusses the possible opportunities for establishing strong, mutually beneficial relationships with the Central American country, the Central American University (CAU), and the students.

Peter Haber, Salzburg University of Applied Sciences, Austria
Erich Herber, Badegruber & Partner GmbH, Austria
Manfred Mayr, Salzburg University of Applied Sciences, Austria

This case study by Peter Haber, Erich Herber and Manfred Mayr discusses the adaptation and extension of ADDIE Model by Pool2Business (P2B) Consortium to establish a modular online course which addresses on one hand certain specific requirements and qualifications of a company, language and culture specific differences between participants and on the other hand, ensures provision of Project Integrated Training in which the learning outcomes can be immediately used in practical application and thus developing highly qualified project-managers for virtual collaboration.

Foreword

I am very pleased to be able to contribute a Foreword to this important collection of case studies of the changes that the adoption of technology enhanced learning demands of institutions, teachers and researchers, and learners. The volume of essays is important in a number of ways. Firstly, the collection is truly international, and offers case studies from many parts of the world. The substantial international experience of the Editors has brought together a collection that is compelling in its breadth of reference. This is of great value, as the professional understandings of educators must now be international, to reflect the globalising world that they and their students live and work in. It is also the case that for this subject matter in particular- the adoption of new technologies for learning and teaching – the very technologies themselves make international experience both available to us all, and also create an imperative for educational institutions to work more and more across national boundaries.

Two key dimensions of this new age have to be assessed and deployed for the purposes of supporting technology-enhanced learning. These are:

• connectedness
• information and resources

The key to the changes that have been bewildering over the last decade has in fact been the inter-relationship of the two. Most learners now have access to huge resources that have hitherto been locked behind the entrance desks of university libraries in addition to the extraordinary amount of sources and archives that have elsewhere been similarly opened up. This is combined with our ability to discuss these, and provide our own accounts of them, through the development of Web 2.0 tools – blogs, wikis, forums and beyond - which has meant the growth of so much learner-generated information and commentary, of all qualities, on the web. Thus we see communities grow up which are fluid, accepting new members every day at the same time as others leave. This follows directly in some aspects the traditions of distance education which have freed up the learner from the constraints of time and space and accelerated the shift from didactive to facilitative modes of teaching and learning within a constructivist framework.

As a result of this, enquiry and scholarship have become core activities in almost all fields. The new technologies have played an extraordinary part in liberating knowledge from the locally produced and managed to the universally available with contributions from around the world. Enquiry, supported by scholarship in the broader sense, thus stands at the heart of human activity. It is now a form of activity in all its variety of far wider interest than just the world of the University. It has over the last 30 years spread down through the age groups and across organizational types. While 30 years ago enquiry in the sense of independent, even if supported, research was primarily restricted to postgraduate work in universities, it has now spread into baccalaureate or undergraduate degrees, and even into schools, as important practice that learners need to master. It is also at the core of organizational and business practice across all sectors.

The case studies in this volume bring these points out across a range of fields of activity. Finally it is worth saying that the case study approach has its particular merits in this field. It allows learning to be created inductively, from the particular to the more thematic and conceptual concerns to which it may give rise. In this way the Editors have provided space for readers to create their own learning as they reflect on the issues of educational need, pedagogy, policy, and management, all of which are challenged by the continuing fast development of technology-enhanced approaches to learning.

I commend this volume to its readers, and am grateful to the Editors for the contribution it makes to our field of work.

Alan Tait
Pro-Vice-Chancellor, and Professor of Distance Education and Development
The Open University, UK

Alan Tait is Pro-Vice Chancellor for Curriculum and Awards at the Open University UK and was formerly Dean of the Faculty of Education and Language Studies. He is Professor of Distance Education and Development and has a long record of professional practice, publication and the support of professional development in distance and e-learning. He is Editor in Chief of the European Journal of Distance and E Learning (EURODL), and Co-Director of the Cambridge International Conference on Open and Distance Learning. Prof. Tait has worked widely in developing countries for international organisations such as UNESCO, the European Commission and the Commonwealth of Learning and is currently President of the European Distance and E-Learning Network (EDEN).

Preface

This book is, in principal, for an audience of policy makers, planners, distance educators, trainers, teachers and researchers in education, learning and development. With an aim of being developed as a resource book for researchers in ODL, higher education and management and development of education, this book is intended to benefit Educational Technologists and Social Science researchers besides being relevant to social workers also, who will find this volume pertinent due to its analysis and evaluation of educational and technological development environments in respective countries.

The collection of cases in the book analyzes and evaluates how organizations and institutions of learning in the developing and developed world are adapting to technology enhanced learning environments and exploring transnational collaborative opportunities, thus providing prospects for learning, growth and development through a blend of traditional and technological methods. The reader will get a composite and comprehensive perspective of how technologically enhanced learning environments have affected the educational institutions in different countries and vice-versa. An effort has been undertaken to shape this book to provide an international platform to policy makers, educators and trainers, educational administrators and researchers through which they can contribute and share their experiences, ideas, attitudes and perspectives on how institutions in their respective countries are adopting technology and collaborating with partner institutions for addressing the socio-economic issues towards providing education and development opportunities.

A varied array of cases on technology enhanced learning and collaborative opportunities from countries like Australia, Austria, Canada, China, Ethiopia, Germany, Greece, Iran, Lesotho, South Africa, UK and USA is presented in the book. The readers will find illustrative cases of CAMEL (Collaborative Approaches to the Management of e-Learning) metaphorical model, inclusive learning, desktop virtual reality for road safety, person-centered learning, quality assessment model in e-learning, distance education in rural schools, project integrated online learning as well as cases on technology for teacher training and development such as blogging for effective teacher education, blended teacher education program, and professional development through technology enhanced courses. The book also gives opportunity to readers to get acquainted to cases on technology assisted learning in Lesotho, Ethiopia and China. This collection also showcases researches on Global Education Greenhouse, collaborative relationship for blended learning program, innovative online learning, E-learning in Horticulture and Environmental science and comparative tale of universities in using audio-graphic web conferencing.

The first chapter of the book, "An e-Learning Metaphor: The CAMEL Nomadic Community of Practice," is a case study by Jill Jameson, wherein she discusses collaborative e-learning, wherein technological and human adaptability is fostered in a community of practice (CoP). It highlights the CAMEL (Collaborative Approaches to the Management of e-Learning) metaphorical model in a designed community of practice in the light of social and technological issues. The author opines that the camel metaphor was formative in stimulating understanding about building communal solutions to sustainability, low-cost innovative engagement and improved cooperation with others and suggests that this model can provide transnational insights for e-learning development.

In the second chapter "Interaction Design for Inclusive Learning," Deryn Graham, Ian Benest and Peter Nicholl discuss the findings in a case study on improving interaction design for teaching visually impaired students, in an inclusive learning environment with due emphasis on ability to draw and understand diagrams. The findings of the case have led to design criteria and to an application for a large scale project, to produce generic tools and to enable "multi-modal" teaching and learning, with connotations for the support of people with cognitive as well as physical impairments.

This chapter is based on the use of blogs for making teacher education effective in English as a Second Language (ESL) teaching. The authors Francis Bangou and Douglas Fleming in their research conducted semi-structured interviews of teacher candidates in order to explore the ways in which these teacher learners use and perceive blogs within a course directed towards ESL teaching methods, thus, highlighting the issues related to technological integration in teaching and learning and formulating important recommendations for guiding the teacher educators who are working in similar contexts.

The fourth chapter provides a valuable insight into a comparative study of two Australian regional universities towards the effective use of synchronous audiographic web conferencing as learning and teaching tool. The authors Birgit Loch, Shirley Reushle, Stephen Rowe and Nicola Jayne discuss the trials of the web conferencing tool, Elluminate *Live!* (Elluminate) at the two universities and highlight issues and challenges relating to software trials in educational environments. The case suggests recommendations which can be beneficial for those institutions who may be considering the adoption of similar technologies for enhanced access to learning and development.

In the following chapter, Kathryn Ley and Ruth Gannon Cook are concerned about the application of Action Research for Marketing a Blended University Program. The authors describe a successful marketing effort for a blended learning program, which is aimed to be delivered to a culturally diverse urban and suburban adult non-traditional population. The case discusses the core issue of successful marketing process in two phases i.e. renewed effort and measurable success. It also illustrates the marketing of university programs in the light of relationship marketing and how university recruiting becomes marketing. The outcome of the case suggests, the hybrid courses can allay learner fears associated with online courses and can offer more time and place convenience than the traditional courses besides facilitating learners' transition to online courses.

Sibongile Simelane in the chapter "Professional Development Programme in the Use of Educational Technology to Implement Technology-enhanced Courses Successfully," points towards the global realization for the need to provide professional development programmes (PDP) meant to help teachers gain competency in ways of integrating technology into education. The case study highlights the important characteristics of such a PDP, the e-TUTO programme of Tshwane University of Technology in South Africa while exploring the experiences of the participants of this programme and looking at the emerging issues and challenges involved.

The seventh chapter of the book explores the possibility of application of technology for teaching children about road safety using Desktop Virtual Reality. The authors of the case, Emmanuel Fokides & Costas Tsolakidis, believe Virtual Reality can be used for this purpose with effective results. The case elucidates 3D video game based application for simulating the environment of a town with traffic and special conditions such as night and rain and also simulates the walk of a pedestrian while accommodating many users simultaneously.

Thie chapter "Blending Traditional and Technological Factors in Teacher Education in Jamaica," by Aleric Josephs highlights the challenges and opportunities in blending traditional and technological factors in teacher education. While presenting a discussion on how a Bachelor of Education program articulates distance learning and face-to-face modalities and examines the skills needed and the challenges involved in developing a curriculum for teaching History through a blended approach, she suggests readiness of faculty and learner to adopt technology as well as careful consideration of the use of technology is crucial for the success of blended learning in traditional teaching environment.

Christopher Thomas Miller is of the belief that it becomes necessary to explore new ways of addressing the instruction that goes into distance education when the distance grows between the instructor and student within education. The author in this chapter describes a distance-based instructional model, the person-centred model of instruction, as well as a case study implementation of the person-centred model of instruction in a web-based course by focusing on a research to determine whether there are differences in significant learning between a group that used the person-centred model of instruction and a group participating in a constructivist learning experience.

Angelina Khoro, the author of "Distance Education and ICT-Supported Learning in Lesotho: Issues and Evidence" regards Information and Communication Technologies (ICT) as a major contributor to the transforming of distance learning and feels that education practitioners in developing countries like Lesotho, have limited, or no access at all to ICT for supporting instruction, since they still rely heavily on print and tutor/learner meetings as their distance mode of course delivery. This paper is a feasibility study on possibilities of introducing ICT-mediated education for tutors and learners on a Distance Education Programme in Lesotho. The paper specifically focuses on issues, policy initiatives and challenges involved in introducing computer-mediated learning in distance education programmes.

In the eleventh chapter of the book, Wolfram Laaser discusses the effectiveness of DVD technology for management training in higher education. The author illustrates the various issues and concerns on the production and use of DVD-technology for developing training and development sessions for management program through distance education. The case also looks into issues of producing bilingual versions (German/English).

The authors of twelfth chapter, Karen Kaun and Payal Arora, provide a discussion about Global Education Greenhouse towards constructing and organizing online global knowledge. The case covers aspects of the initiative of the *Peace Diaries* project to establish a forum for multi-modal literary works concerning issues of personal, local and global significance and its extension of this initiative into a more synthesized and sustainable online global education portal.

Hamed Fazollahtabar considers assessing quality an obviously key concern for learning, education and training so he questions "why should it be especially crucial in relation to e-learning?" He argues that the e-learners, as with other distance learners, are working in isolation with limited or sometimes non-existent human support which implies that the first impact of any failure in the providers' quality assessment regime falls directly on the e-learner. In this case study, an analysis of different aspects of quality in e-learning is done and then using fuzzy logic approach, a comprehensive assessment model is proposed.

Elena Verezub in the fourteenth chapter of the book is discussing a research project with the aim to design an e-learning program for students studying within the department of horticulture and environmental Science, with an additional focus on improving students' reading comprehension of hypertexts in the subject-specific context. The case also examines the STEEP dimensions associated with the project.

The case "Technology Enhanced Learning in China," by Victor Chunxue Wang brings to the fore various issues and challenges related to implementing technology enhanced learning methods in China based on his study of a typical university of foreign languages in northern China while presenting a comparative analysis with that in the United States of America.

Hannum Wallace, Matthew Irvin and Claire de la Varre in this chapter of the book explicate the application of distance education for extending the educational opportunities in the rural areas. The authors opine that rural schools in many countries face problems in providing educational opportunities to children and youth for a variety of reasons while facing particular difficulties in attracting and retaining qualified teachers. Many rural schools in the United States have opted for distance education due to the problems of providing a comprehensive curriculum and lack of qualified teachers. This case explores the use of distance education in the United States through a national survey of distance education use, analysis of barriers to distance education and an experimental study of enhancing distance education through more appropriate training of local facilitators to support students.

Getnet Bitew explores the case of technological adaptability in the education system of Ethiopia specifically on using live "plasma" TV as a principal mode for instructional delivery in the government secondary schools. In this study, he is of the view that current "plasma" mode of instruction cannot continue in the way it is if it is genuinely intended to help the students develop their creativity, problem solving and critical skills and teachers and students should get enough instructional time in the classrooms for discussion.

The next case study "Building An Interactive Fully-Online Degree Program" by Jennie Mitchell and Daesang Kim focuses transition of an existing distance education program into an interactive fully-online undergraduate degree program at Saint Mary-of-the-Woods College (SMWC) to be launched in 2010. It renders an overview of the program, the process of its development, and technological and organizational concerns related to the design and delivery of this program, and provides a discussion on the Web 2.0 technologies used during the development of this program, meant for net generation (millennial), neo millennial, and computer savvy non-traditional students including military personnel.

In the nineteenth chapter, Ravisha Mathur and Lisa Oliver discuss the challenges of program development, effective course content delivery, using appropriate learning strategies, operating in a cross-cultural context, and working in an organization with limited technological capacities while establishing a joint international Masters' program in Instructional Technology in a Central American country. The case highlights overriding theme of capacity-building in developing this blended learning program so that Central American University is able to take over and manage the program on its own.

The authors Peter Haber, Erich Herber and Manfred Mayr are of the view that new project management skills and processes are prerequisites to meet the challenges of the globalization, and transnational and distributed ICT projects need highly qualified project-managers for virtual collaboration. The case in the final chapter of the book discusses Pool2Business (P2B) project with an objective of establishing a modular online course to address certain specific requirements and qualifications of a company, language and culture specific differences and to ensure that the learning outcomes can be immediately used in practical application. It illustrates that based on extended ADDIE Model, the P2B-Consortium is able to establish the whole curriculum more effectively by having the same strategies, following the same procedures and knowing the next steps to fulfill the target of P2B.

Evidently, more and more institutions across the globe are turning to advancements in technology for enhancing access to learning and development and in doing so, are looking for collaborative opportunities in order to maximize the benefits of technology mix for education. These initiatives are being undertaken not only within the confines of the institutions in developed nations but also in developing countries where there is greater realization and enhanced awareness for exploring the prospects of using ICT for education and overall development.

Here, we as editors of this collection of cases on technology enhanced learning and collaborative opportunities extend our sincere acknowledgement and gratitude to the authors of the case studies who have contributed papers on varied research studies and experiences making this an interesting forum for presenting international perspectives on technology assisted learning, education and development. We hope that this compilation of cases will prove to be an interesting reading for the audience and it will encourage further discussion and deliberation on this important subject area. Finally, we are grateful to the IGI-Global team who have been extremely forthcoming from the very inception of this project and we are thankful for their help, support and cooperation during the development and publication of this book.

Siran Mukerji
Purnendu Tripathi
Editors

Chapter 1
An E-Learning Metaphor:
The CAMEL Nomadic Community of Practice

Jill Jameson
University of Greenwich, UK

ABSTRACT

This chapter describes a case study of collaborative e-learning, in which technological and human adaptability was fostered in a community of practice (CoP). The chapter reflects on the use of the extended metaphor of the camel in the JISC-funded eLIDA CAMEL and JISC infoNet CAMEL projects. Technological and social insights were gained through this use of the camel metaphorical model in a designed community of practice. A series of nomadic journeys held in oases provided by partners enabled honest exchanges amongst a community of 'CAMEL' practitioners, improving e-learning practices. The creation of an intentional e-learning community of practice fostered shared understandings about learning technology innovations. The camel metaphor was formative in stimulating understanding about building communal solutions to sustainability, low-cost innovative engagement and improved cooperation with others. The CAMEL metaphorical model has been validated in numerous other UK e-learning applications from which transnational insights for e-learning development can be drawn.

INTRODUCTION

This chapter applies a case study methodology to examine the phenomenon, or 'case', of the use of an extended metaphor in an e-learning community of practice. A 'case' in social sciences research methodology is 'a unit of human activity embedded in the real world'… which 'can only be understood

DOI: 10.4018/978-1-61520-751-0.ch001

in context'… 'exists in the here and now'… and 'merges in with its context so that precise boundaries are difficult to draw' (Gillham, 2000). A 'case' is therefore a fuzzily bounded entity within the human social world that is investigated in a research 'study' in which the properties of the 'case' are examined and analyzed. In this instance, the 'CAMEL' metaphor is considered as a single or unique case selected for its effectiveness. The instances in which this case is examined in this chapter are in relation to two publicly-funded higher education United Kingdom (UK) e-learning projects: firstly, the eLIDA CAMEL project (e-Learning Independent Design Activities for Collaborative Approaches to the Management of e-Learning) and, secondly, the JISC infoNet CAMEL project.

The unit of analysis for case study (Gillham, 2000; Yin, 1994) in this chapter is therefore the method by which the CAMEL metaphorical model was applied in practical ways in these two e-learning projects. In both projects, the acronym 'CAMEL' was used to describe a shared group approach undertaken to trial a community of practice (CoP) in e-learning. This chapter describes and analyses both projects to draw out a range of transnational insights for e-learning development, including reflections on the use of the 'camel' metaphor for a CoP. The concept of a 'community of practice' has for almost two decades provided an increasingly popular model of knowledge management through collaboration. A CoP involves the bringing together of a group of people who share a concern or passion about a particular 'practice' within a 'domain' of expertise to develop collective knowledge about improvements in that practice, as part of a 'community' (Lave and Wenger, 1991; Wenger, McDermott and Synder, 2002; Wenger and Snyder, 2000). The three basic elements of a CoP: a 'domain', a 'practice' and a 'community', were involved in both projects, although the CoPs discussed here involve 'designed' communities of practice rather than spontaneously self-organizing CoPs.

The first project, the eLIDA CAMEL, was a design for learning (DfL) UK national project comprising several higher and further education partners funded in 2006-07 for £60,000 over eighteen months by the UK Joint Information Systems Committee (JISC) Design for Learning programme. The eLIDA CAMEL was led by the Director of Research and Enterprise at the School of Education and Training of a university based in London, with support from the School of Computing and Mathematical Sciences

(CMS) of the same university. Partners in the project included JISC infoNet, the Association for Learning Technology (ALT), Leeds College of Technology, Loughborough College, Barnet College, Dartford Grammar School, Greenwich Community College, Greenwich Children's Services and Greenwich City Learning Centre. The project was carried out during a period of 18 months in 2006-07, with a further dissemination phase lasting for around two years.

The university in this case is a large modern (post 1992) university in South East London, England, with around 25,000 students, including some 6,900 post-graduates and many international students from around 80 different countries across the world. The eLIDA CAMEL project operated from the main campus of the university

The university has a history of around 110 years, having been founded originally as a polytechnic in Woolwich in 1890. The university has strengths in widening participation, lifelong learning, undergraduate and post-graduate degree programmes across the sciences, social sciences, arts and humanities, and in the training of teachers, further education lecturers, architects, nurses, engineers and numerous other professional groups. The university is led by a Vice Chancellor's Group comprising several top management staff, and an Executive group in which all Heads of Schools are members. Each School, or large higher education faculty/institute, is led by a School senior management team including one Head of School and three Directors, one of which in each case is the Director of Research and Enterprise. The Schools provide higher education degrees, training, research, enterprise and consultancy in particular subject areas. The School of Education and Training is a large School specializing in education programmes in higher education, including initial teacher training, with around 130 staff. The eLIDA CAMEL was a research and enterprise project housed within and managed by this School.

As an eighteen month externally-funded project, the eLIDA CAMEL operated in a more or less stand-alone way alongside the university's routine higher education provision, managed by a director and steering group and responsible to the JISC, the university and the project partners for the management of the project and the expenditure of its allocated funds against a range of pre-planned work packages to produce design for learning innovations and to develop a community of practice amongst its partners. The project carried out its work from May 2006 to December, 2007, successfully producing a range of individual and collaborative case studies and design for learning sequences produced by teaching practitioners within its partner organizations, in addition to a group project report, several survey data collections, a Moodle site, videos, photographs and other media outputs such as powerpoint presentations.

The particular value of the eLIDA CAMEL to the JISC resided in its role as one of nine DfL 'implementation' and evaluation pedagogic e-learning projects. The project was envisaged as a 'seed-bed' within the JISC Design for Learning programme, with a practical focus on trialing innovations development in e-learning and collaboration. The project aimed to glean insights and results from in-depth day-to-day grounded design for learning classroom work carried out by practitioners in its partner institutions. These individuals together shared their attitudes about and practices in teaching and learning using innovative e-learning approaches and tools within the project. The project aimed to feed these results in a 'bottom-up' way back to the JISC, project partners and other stakeholders for dissemination. The 'seedbed', 'hands-on' role and pedagogic community ethos of the group was strongly grounded in the daily practitioner work of e-learning innovation applied in real situations in the classroom. In this respect, the project was different from other projects in the JISC DfL programme which had a more abstract, purely theoretical or technical focus. This 'hands-on' shared community approach of the project was valued for its functionality, and the way in which it connected directly to the sometimes 'messy', difficult situations that teachers can face in applying e-learning with students, in practice, in the classroom.

The eLIDA CAMEL project partners were drawn from several institutions that had previously worked together as part of the second project discussed in this chapter: the JISC infoNet CAMEL (Collaborative Approaches to the Management of e-Learning) project, which was carried out during 2005-06. That earlier CAMEL project was funded for £38,900 by the Higher Education Funding Council for England (HEFCE) Leadership, Governance and Management Fund (LGMF) to trial the setting up of a pilot community of practice in e-learning. The pilot was led by the University of Northumbria-based JISC infoNet group and supported by ALT, the JISC and the Higher Education Academy (HEA) (Ferrell and Kelly 2006; JISC infoNet 2006; Kelly and Riachi 2006; Jameson, 2008). It aimed to explore the development of a community of practice amongst e-learning, IT systems expert and learning technology-focused pedagogic practitioners, all of whom were engaged in promoting lifelong learning and widening participation across their institutions. The innovative CAMEL model for an e-learning community of practice has, since 2006, increasingly gained prominence across the UK in numerous e-learning contexts. The model has been, arguably, outstandingly successful, as it has spawned around 20 new applications of CAMEL since it began to report its results in 2006. Given the generalized popularity and success of communities of practice in education, this is to some extent unsurprising, though, as Chua (2006) notes, the success of CoPs in e-learning (or in fact in any other context) is not inevitable, even in the most apparently favourable of circumstances. Hence there is merit in exploring the attributes that may be likely to lead to effective implementation.

JISC infoNet is an expert e-learning advisory and information service funded by the JISC for managers in the UK post-compulsory education communities. Its organizational remit includes the development of information kits and training on effective strategic planning and the implementation of good practice in e-learning innovations in post-compulsory education. The CAMEL pilot was therefore fortunate in that advanced expert knowledge of and support for the project and its strategic planning processes informed the design of CAMEL from the outset. In addition, its key partners included not only JISC infoNet and the JISC, but also ALT and the Higher Education Academy (HEA), which has a UK-wide role to enhance teaching, learning and students' experiences in higher education. The above agencies and groups therefore comprised the key shapers and designers in CAMEL, who set the project up, guided it and steered it through to completion.

The CAMEL project main institutional participants included four higher and further education institutions who responded to an open competitive call for expressions of interest for a small amount of funding to participate in the pilot CAMEL project in 2005. Four institutional project partners (Loughborough and Leeds Colleges, the Universities of Greenwich and Staffordshire) were selected by JISC infoNet and ALT to participate in CAMEL. The CAMEL concept had originally been designed by Seb Schmoller, Chief Executive Officer of ALT, who had based the idea on a farming self-help community of practice in Uruguay. CAMEL was implemented in 2005-06 and was effective in developing a community of practice that was formed through the process of carrying out structured study visits during the period of one year, each visit being housed in rotation at the venues of the four main partner institutions. The final output of the JISC infoNet CAMEL project was an end of project report describing and evaluating the approach that had been taken, and a series of related outputs such as videos and a CDRom. The project report was prepared by formal external evaluators for the project, who interviewed numerous parties involved and

reported that participants and stakeholders had rated the project as a successful innovation (JISC infoNet, 2006).

The eLIDA CAMEL drew on the sources of expertise in CAMEL to build on the work of the original project and to take the CoP model into a second phase. The eLIDA CAMEL was funded by the JISC, which requires a series of project planning processes to be carried out by all projects, including detailed work-packages with key criteria, outputs and outcomes, milestones and deadlines for completion. A strategic planning process was therefore set up in advance for both projects, despite the complexity of the partnerships involved. The key partners in CAMEL had been selected from institutions making expressions of interest from across the UK, some of whom were already familiar with each other, and they were also all strongly committed to the project. By the time the eLIDA CAMEL was set up, all of the key partners had already worked together for at least a year on CAMEL. These circumstances made the process of planning easily able to be facilitated and negotiated in both projects: they 'hit the ground running' from the start, in terms of ownership by participants and readiness to engage in the work in both formal and informal contexts. This arguably meets a key criterion for success for communities of practice in terms of the nascent community's 'readiness' to become engaged in the establishment of trust (Usoro1, Sharratt, Tsui and Shekhar, 2007).

SETTING THE STAGE

Both projects described in this case study involved a range of partners who had many different kinds of expertise in e-learning and in the use of technology in education in a variety of ways prior to the commencement of the projects. Technology utilization in the leader and partner organizations in the JISC infoNet CAMEL and the eLIDA CAMEL projects had therefore reached advanced levels of innovation before the start of these IT initiatives. JISC infoNet and ALT both play a leading role in learning technology development and innovation across the UK, while ALT, which was founded in 1993, has a formative international role in fostering good practice and collaborative partnership in the use of learning technologies amongst practitioners, researchers and policy makers, as a major academic, professional and learning technology research association (ALT, 2009).

The players involved in both projects also had an open, facilitative, collaborative engagement with the e-learning work carried out, which was publicly funded, non-profit academic development. The management practices and philosophies involved in setting up and maintaining this e-learning work were therefore based on formative, knowledge-sharing, trusting and investigative approaches, in which a mutually shared, harmonious and 'critical practitioner' style of operations was encouraged from the outset. There was no commercial interest or gain to be achieved from rivalry, aggression or competition in these partnerships: this was one of the underpinning ground-rules from the commencement of both initiatives.

A non-profit, charitable, 'grounded' community group focus to the work from the outset meant that some of the tensions that could occur between competing private commercial interests or individual academic rivals aiming to achieve higher profiles were immediately eliminated from the process. Furthermore, the JISC, JISC infoNet, ALT and the partners involved in both projects adopted an ethos in which they agreed they were prepared to tolerate and learn from potential failure: a 'research-informed' investigative attitude regarding reflective practice was encouraged in which the practitioners reported as much on things that were *not* working as those that were. There was an emphasis on authentic, practice-based professional dialogue, collaboration, good planning, critical friendship and honest analysis in both the CAMEL and eLIDA CAMEL. This included explicit project and partner recogni-

tion that collaborative work in a community of practice can sometimes be difficult, can throw up problems and is '… not just about good practice, it's about practice, warts and all – and the warts are more interesting than the practice sometimes' (JISC infoNet 2006). This commitment to honest mutual engagement was an important feature of the CAMEL project, and it was agreed by all participants that discussions in meetings held by the project had to be *'calzon quitao'*, a South American phrase translated as 'with underpants removed'. This meant that, no matter how painful and embarrassing, it was necessary to strive to hold discussions within the community of practice that were nakedly truthful in their attention to both strong and weak points of practice, and for the group both to praise and criticize the practices involved. The farmer uncle who was the source of knowledge about the agriculture group informing the project described this process in the CoP, as reported by JISC infoNet:

'…. you have to put all your cards on the table and hide nothing' from your guests…. 'sometimes there emerged some truths or criticisms which were very painful, and this is what I think helped many to come to terms with reality'. (JISC info-Net, 2006, p. 4)

The individuals who were representing the organizations in both CAMEL projects were also 'champions' of learning technology themselves, occupying a range of roles from chief executive officer, director and senior manager to senior teachers/advisors, lecturers and technicians. The key point that all partner organizations and individuals shared in common was a passion for investigating, sharing and fostering effective practice in e-learning in a community of practice. This collective interest ensured that there was a mutuality of engagement. Therefore, although both projects had a distinct leadership and management organizational structure, with a director and other management staff, overseen by a steering group, all partners were, in addition, tasked with achieving results for the projects through a shared collaborative leadership model in which each partner was the leader for a different area of interest, building on their own preferences and expertise.

Hence, in the eLIDA CAMEL, one partner institution agreed to focus on Moodle course management system, another said they would develop particular interest in LAMS (Learning Activity Management System), a third partner agreed to focus on the interaction between these two e-learning platforms, while other key partners were contracted to concentrate on assisting the project by providing facilitation, critical friendship, advice and administrative support through minute-taking and providing reflective critical comment. An external evaluator for the eLIDA CAMEL was also invited and contracted to deliver an in-depth report on the individual case studies developed by all institutionally-based practitioners in the project. Some findings from these individual case studies are published separately, providing selected detailed results and an outline of pedagogic understandings involved in the classroom-based design for learning activities carried out in the project (JISC, 2009a; Masterman, Jameson and Walker, 2009). The current chapter provides an overview project-level case study that focuses in particular on the metaphor of the camel used in both the eLIDA CAMEL and CAMEL, and its relationship with those projects and their outputs.

PEDAGOGIC FOCUS AND APPROACH

The eLIDA CAMEL project was distinctive for its strong pedagogic CoP focus, in which senior as well as newer teachers in the community shared their extensive knowledge and experience of learning, teaching practices and e-learning development, growing together into new understandings about design for learning activities and processes.

A growth in knowledge sharing and knowledge management took place gradually during the online and offline project activities at partnership visits, in the project team Moodle and project wiki, and within detailed recordings of individual and collective case studies that practitioners contributed to the project (JISC, 2009a). Building pedagogic understanding together in a community of practice focused on design for learning was therefore a key part of the eLIDA CAMEL. The project leadership consciously adopted a pedagogic focus that built on a social constructivist approach. This included understandings derived from Vygotsky's (1978) theories that learning is enhanced, developed and extended through social engagement in shared knowledge-building that can expand the 'zone of proximal development (ZPD)' of individual learners. Partners in the project, being teachers as well as learners themselves, could therefore attain new levels of expert knowledge by engaging in social and professional interactions about e-learning development in a community of practice approach involving 'more capable others'. The project also built on understandings derived from extensive prior theoretical and practical work in communities of practice, in CAMEL and elsewhere, and on the concept of 'legitimate peripheral participation'. By this method, relative newcomers in such communities are accepted naturally as emergent 'apprentices' and inducted into the 'shared repertoire' of understandings and practices of the CoP, as they learn gradually to develop greater levels of expertise from observing the deep knowledge of effective practice demonstrated by old-timers (Lave and Wenger, 1991; JISC infoNet, 2006, 2006a.)

SOME INTERNATIONAL E-LEARNING COMPARATOR PROJECTS

International comparisons can be made between the CoP work done in the JISC eLIDA CAMEL project and that achieved in numerous other past and current e-learning projects that either explicitly or indirectly involve communities of practice within or linked to virtual learning communities. There is an extensive range of such projects across the world, typically focused at local, regional, national and/or continental levels.

These initiatives include the UK JISC Users and Innovations Programme EMERGE project (EMERGE, 2009), the MENON network of more than 20 e-learning projects in Europe (MENON, 2009), including initiatives such as the POLE project (Policy Observatory for Lifelong Learning and Employability: POLE, 2009), funded under the European *Socrates* Programme, the MUVEnation project working on new pedagogical initiatives to increase pupil motivation in active learning using Multi-User Virtual Environments (MUVEnation, 2009) and the former HELIOS European Project (Horizontal E-Learning Integrated Observation System: HELIOS, 2009), which was focused on the ways in which e-learning enables and improves access to learning. HELIOS built a collaboration space involving support from EuroPACE, the Trans-European network of universities and related partners in education and training, the IEA – International Association for the Evaluation of Educational Achievement, the eLearning Industry Group (eLIG), EIFEL- European Institute for eLearning, EENet- European Education Experts Network and The National Unions of Students in Europe (ESIB) (HELIOS, 2009).

Yet another successful European e-learning community initiative was the LEONIE project (Learning in Europe Observatory on National and International Evolution) which noted in its report on *Trends and Drivers of Change in Learning Systems* the emergence of new kinds of online communities, and the benefits as well as the risks that such developments entail (Alfaro et al, 2006). In terms of e-learning projects within specific subject domains, the UK-based Universities' Collaboration in eLearning (UCeL) project is also of interest as a virtual community of practice in professional health education trial-

ing new methods for the sharing of e-learning resources and content creation for professional health education (UCeL, 2009).

Moving wider afield and beyond collaborative projects solely focused on ICT/e-learning, the MERLOT (Multimedia Educational Resource for Learning and Online Teaching) project at the California State University Center for Distributed Learning (CSU-CDL) is a digital peer-reviewed learning content repository that acts as an umbrella for numerous discipline-specific virtual communities, hosting numerous online learning communities who share teaching objects and materials, plus comments regarding pedagogic usage (MERLOT, 2009). MERLOT also hosts an African partnership: the Merlot Africa Network (MAN), which is a networked partnership between educational institutions in Africa and the US. This partnership facilitates communities of e-learning expertise and open education capacity building in Sub-Saharan Africa, developing collaborative innovation projects and meeting bi-annually as part of the *eLearning Africa* conference (MAN, 2009).

In terms of developments elsewhere at a national level, the Taiwan e-Learning and Digital Archives Program (TELDAP), which commenced in 2008, is an exemplar digital archives and e-learning project currently facilitating cultural, social and economic development in Taiwan and promoting virtual international collaboration in cultural exchanges. TELDAP is an umbrella national initiative involving numerous smaller projects focusing on e-learning and digital archive collections. The project has developed international online cooperation with other cultures and nations to extend expertise in Sinology studies, collaborating with, for example, the Getty Research Institute (GRI) and organizing a range of events which engage different communities in its digital cultural archive work in a range of ways, including through its links with the Taiwan News interactive community cultural portal funded by Taiwan's Council for Cultural Affairs (TELDAP, 2009; Taiwan Culture Portal, 2009).

A further transnational online community higher education initiative is the The BRIDGES-LAC project (Building Relationships and Improving Dialogue Geared towards Erasmus Mundus goals - Latin American and the Caribbean), involving 23 academic institutions and research centres developing a virtual community together using a web-based platform to improve collaboration between academics in the EU, Latin America and the Caribbean. While not solely an e-learning project nor yet a community of practice in the stricter senses, BRIDGES-LAC is nevertheless using e-learning in the communities involved in powerful ways to increase knowledge transfer, collaboration and learning amongst different academic partners from several nations spread across the world (BRIDGES-LAC, 2009). Moving wider still in geographical and national terms, the GLOBE project (GLOBE, 2009) is an international e-learning alliance between a range of countries at a global transnational level, involving MERLOT in the USA, the ARIADNE Foundation in Europe, education.au in Australia, LORNET in Canada, the National Institute of Multimedia Education (NIME) in Japan as well as partners in Taiwan, Korea and Latin America.

While some of the national e-learning projects and global alliances described above may not always have attained the status of 'communities of practice' in terms of deeper knowledge-sharing relationships, the growing collaboration between a range of countries in an increasing number of such international online partnerships signifies that recognition of the benefits of online collaborative community knowledge-building is rapidly on the increase worldwide.

The above are a few examples of initiatives from the extensive list of e-learning communities of practice projects or virtual collaboration projects currently operating online and/or face-to-face globally, as a result of successful interactive Web 2.0 technological developments. As Gannon-Leary and Fontainha (2007) observe in their work on *Communities of Practice and Virtual*

Learning Communities: Benefits, Barriers and Success Factors:

Virtual communities of practice (CoPs) and virtual learning communities are becoming widespread within higher education institutions (HEIs) thanks to technological developments which enable increased communication, interactivity among participants and incorporation of collaborative pedagogical models, specifically through information communications technologies (ICTs). They afford the potential for the combination of synchronous and asynchronous communication, access to -and from- geographically isolated communities and international information sharing. Clearly there are benefits to be derived from sharing and learning within and outwith HEIs. There is a sense of connectedness, of shared passion and a deepening of knowledge to be derived from ongoing interaction. Knowledge development can be continuous, cyclical and fluid. (Gannon-Leary and Fontainha, 2007, p. 1)

The virtual communities of practice (VCoP) developments discussed by Gannon-Leary and Fontainha (2007) can for the most part be distinguished from the eLIDA CAMEL project in that eLIDA CAMEL was a 'designed' community of practice involving externally-funded pedagogic collaborative research and enterprise e-learning trials. Both CAMEL and eLIDA CAMEL had important, planned, face-to-face, professional and social elements incorporating visits to partners, rather than being wholly online spontaneous communities developed to share knowledge in informal ways.

Nevertheless, the findings of Gannon-Leary and Fontainha (*ibid.*) are of interest in that the critical success factors (CSFs) they outline for a virtual CoP are similar to those identified in the CAMEL model and those developed in the eLIDA CAMEL project (including usability of technology, good communication, trust, longevity of relationships, a common sense of purpose and sense of belonging in the community, shared values and understandings, etc.). These authors also record an increasing interest in and support for learning communities online and their relationship with e-learning, in this instance, in Europe, outlining the benefits and potential disadvantages of CoPs as well as the utopian views on CoPs of one of their UK respondents:

The potential import of virtual CoPs is recognised by increasing interest in Europe in networked learning and e-learning, as witnessed by the development of organisations engaged in studying and producing data on the topic, e.g. Eurostat, Eurydice, IEA, Eurobarometer, EC projects. (p.7) ………. [An]... academic expanded on her own Utopian vision of a CoP as an updated version of the eighteenth century European 'salon' which provided a base for the discussion of social, artistic and scientific questions: 'Scholarly exchange, the building up of research communities... people really becoming part of a research network in a very active way, even though they're thousands and thousands of miles apart... the democratising potential of that...recreates the conditions, almost, of a mass intellectual salon where people are able to argue and discuss, and be in contact' (UK academic) (p.9). (Gannon-Leary and Fontainha, 2007, p. 9)

The comparison made above between a virtual CoP and a 'mass intellectual' version of the eighteenth century European 'salon' is interesting in terms of the social, professional, cultural and political benefits that knowledge-sharing alliances can have in both local and transnational contexts. Gannon-Leary and Fontainha (2007) also, however, analyze barriers and difficulties in the creation of VCoPs, including reluctance to share knowledge on the part of some academics, difficulties in establishing trust, and problems with communication and technology. Nevertheless, despite identifiable barriers to their creation and difficulties in operation and maintenance, the

overall findings from the literature on the development of communities of practice in e-learning across the world is that this is a growing, buoyant field of work, in which there are numerous international projects.

Having briefly explored the above selected examples from the international literature on communities of practice in e-learning and virtual CoPs, detailed case descriptions for the eLIDA CAMEL and CAMEL projects now follow.

CASE DESCRIPTION

The first case for analysis, the eLIDA CAMEL project, was designed to test the original JISC infoNet CAMEL model of a community of practice for a second time. The main aim was to investigate whether the CoP model would continue to be productive when applied to the work of design for learning pedagogic practitioners in a professional, scholarly and practical context rather than one mainly focused on the institutional management of e-learning. The project effectively completed its main work in December 2007, with a further period of dissemination lasting for the next two years.

The project plan stated at the outset that the aims of the eLIDA CAMEL were to implement e-learning innovations in design for learning, delivering training in DfL for practitioners so that they could develop their own DfL sequences and then share and critique these in a series of collaborative CoP discussions aiming to:

.... train practitioners in principles of design for learning to develop their own design for learning sequences during Phase 1 of the project, in May-October, 2006. During this phase, the project .... set up mentoring teams and a support mechanism for practitioners ..... a key feature of the JISC eLISA which ... worked well: we will now seek to extend this into a CAMEL collaborative model. (JISC Project Plan: eLIDA CAMEL, 2006.)

The project plan included activities in design for learning training workshops, partnership visits at the main venue of each institution involved, design for learning tasks to be carried out by individual teachers in between visits, shared face-to-face meetings of the project team, mentoring and evaluation actions, including collecting feedback in online electronic surveys from all partners and students involved. At the outset, the project trained practitioners in design for learning in two workshops and followed this up by inviting project participants to join in discussions in a Moodle project site that included the materials from the DfL workshops. The project team agreed that the concept of 'design for learning' used in the eLIDA CAMEL would adopt the definition outlined by the JISC (2006), which states that DfL activity-focused learning involves:

.... designing, planning and orchestrating learning activities as part of a learning session or programme [having] a new emphasis on those aspects of the process that can be 'designed' in advance, and articulated and shared across different contexts of practice (JISC, 2006.)

The results from the eLIDA CAMEL project indicated that the CAMEL model worked well for a second time and that the team had not only tested the CoP concept, but had derived from it a series of new findings. The project collected a series of individual practitioner and group case studies, 101 student responses and a DfL data collection that included learning activity sequences, surveys, reports, photographs and video from team members on the implementation and evaluation of tools and systems to support design for learning in post-16/ HE contexts. Design for learning activity sequences and processes were tested by practitioners in different institutions during the project and brought together into a CAMEL community of practice, supported by a critical friend, Professor Mark Stiles of Staffordshire University, to help practitioners reflect on, collect together

and disseminate the DfL developments that had taken place. The project trialed DfL sequences with practitioners in London, the South East of England, Leeds and Loughborough, using LAMS V1.1, V2 and Moodle, with a brief consideration of RELOAD, as planned in the project start-up document. That document had been produced using a strategic planning process, which included the preparation of a detailed project plan with scheduled events, planned outputs and a Project Initiation Document (PID) collaboratively agreed and signed with all partners, echoing the process adopted by the original CAMEL project.

The eLIDA CAMEL project outputs included the final report, final case studies and evaluation report, project plan and work package overview; the Project Initiation Document, Moodle records of virtual discussions and joint work carried out by the project team; collaborative team visits/ activities plans and reports; minutes of meetings and pedagogic interactions between practitioners at the visits; DfL training schedules and materials for practitioners, detailed trials of LD sequences and the DfL materials involved, partner and student evaluation data including quantitative and qualitative feedback and analysis, video clips with verbal feedback from partners, draft individual and collaborative case studies and reflective notes from practitioners on the e-learning, mentoring and support provided to all partners. All of these outputs were achieved successfully and were recorded in the final project report (JISC, 2009).

The second case for analysis, the JISC infoNet CAMEL, was founded on the approach described in the introductory sections above, as designed by ALT and JISC infoNet. As discussed earlier, the project produced at the outset a collaborative PID to establish ground rules amongst the community. The project leaders also organized that recorded minutes of visits would be taken to keep track of outcomes in writing and, further, set up administration and facilitation by an expert for all visits and discussions. The leaders contracted an external agency to carry out a formal evaluation of the project, using a range of measures including observations, interviews and documentary analysis. Within the written PID, it was agreed that there would be an emphasis on tacit knowledge and on the processes by which 'know-how' about practice could be shared so that knowledge was gradually built within the group. Gradually, during the process of just over a year, the CAMEL project set up and tested the model for a community of practice. During this period, the project discovered over a number of visits to partner institutions that the creative and honest processes involved were appreciated by practitioners and that professional learning about effective practice was taking place. At the last CAMEL visit held at the University of Greenwich during July 2006, Seb Schmoller talked about the original farmers' self-help club linked to his uncle that he had observed in 1985 and the way in which the CAMEL model had developed, drawing the attention of the project group to a range of similarities he had found existed between educational practice and agriculture:

I think there is a big parallel between education and agriculture, not in the sense of the technology or process, but in the sense of how being successful at it involves an enormous amount of tactic knowledge and understanding about how many things can work with each other in a coordinated way and the success of it has got a very long time-frame. You can't really look up in a book how to run a good institution: it's a sort of 'know-how' that you acquire over a period of time and there are well-run effective institutions and there are ineffective ones - and that's very similar to agriculture." (Video of Seb Schmoller: JISC infoNet, 2006a)

To articulate and share expert know-how about e-learning practices, using lessons from CAMEL's farming origins, the project group realized that visits should be planned collaboratively in advance of the trip and that the organization of visits should also include documentation to the partners beforehand and afterwards. It was also agreed by all parties that visits should be 'focused on things which mattered; expertly facilitated; formally evaluated' as well as being 'strong in their emphasis on tacit knowledge; focused on making tacit 'know how' explicit' (JISC infoNet 2006). Project participants respected and agreed to this.

An emphasis on authentic processes, practice-based professional dialogue, collaboration, good planning, the inclusion of social as well as formal events, the importance of a nomadic arrangement for visiting partners, critical friendship and honest analysis therefore emerged from CAMEL. This included the recognition, as discussed above, that collaborative work in a community of practice requires awareness and critical recognition of problem areas as well as effective practices (JISC infoNet 2006). As one project participant observed during a video evaluation of the project recorded at the University of Greenwich in July, 2006:

We've actually, ... um... learnt an awful lot from each other in what sort of tools .... technical tools .... that we are using within institutions and we all seem to be using slightly different ones, which means you get a wider understanding of what tools are available to um ... educational institutions and I think that's really useful. And we've also learnt from one another what we've used and what's been good and what's not worked, and so it's allowed us to avoid maybe using things that wouldn't maybe be effective in our institution and that's been good as well. (Video of project participant, JISC infoNet, 2006a)

The final project evaluations by participants were uniformly positive in noting the many benefits that they felt they had derived from CAMEL. A number of these benefits were connected with the meaningfulness that project participants had derived from the adopted metaphor of the 'camel'.

The Unifying Metaphor of the CAMEL

One of the reasons why both e-learning cases considered in this chapter were successful was that they employed a unifying metaphor for sense-making in the project. This acted as an informal mascot in bringing together participant understanding of the nature of the work involved. A metaphor is a powerful figure of speech that compares two things without using the words 'like' or 'as', expressed in a 'phrase which describes one thing by stating another thing with which it can be compared' (Longman, 1978). The purpose of using metaphors is to enliven and focus understanding by stimulating new insights that emerge from otherwise unlikely comparisons, or to concretize abstract concepts by describing these in physical terms. For example, the phrases 'mortgage melt-down' and 'credit crunch' highlight uncomfortable economic truths by envisioning these literally in visual depictions of physical processes. Such metaphors as 'a pitbull in lipstick', 'hairy angel', 'airhead', 'road hog', 'housing bubble' and 'road map to peace' vividly describe familiar concepts compared with initially unfamiliar items, to create new concepts that then acquire a linguistic and cultural history of their own.

Many metaphorical phrases become so familiar (for example, 'world wide web, 'flower bed') that they become 'dead metaphors' and are understood as routine idiomatic sayings rather than as active metaphors, as their original figurative meaning has been forgotten in common usage. The phase is then used as a whole concept in which meta-phorical connotations have been, for the most part, lost. In their still living form, however, metaphors stimulate new ways of thinking about concepts and processes and can give rise to creative under-standings, for example, in relation to professional identity and knowledge (Daley, 2001). As Grey notes, '...metaphors play a vital role in helping us to make sense of unfamiliar situations. To appro-priate an image from Wittgenstein .... metaphor is a ladder of cognitive ascent which can be kicked away after the vista it has exposed is revealed' (Grey, 2000).

Extended metaphors are those which build on an initial metaphorical concept and extend this into other terms and dimensions. For example, in the field of e-learning, the use of the now highly familiar extended metaphor of the 'desktop', is linked to numerous other concepts such as 'icons', 'folders', 'clipboard', 'rubbish bin', 'windows', 'frames' and 'cutting and pasting'. These are used so frequently that they could be regarded as either 'dead' or 'dormant' metaphors, the latter term referring to metaphors whose original figurative meaning has more or less been lost. In 'dormant metaphors', the connective power of the original literal comparison is weakened, but not yet so ossified as to be inaccessible to the generation of new insights. Living metaphors, by contrast, are still inspiring new meanings and understandings, and their conscious use in professional practice can be valuable, as Daly observes:

The major point here is that the metaphor illu-minates connections between learning, context, and professional practice in a way that moves our understanding of these dynamic relationships to a new level and in a way that allows us to compare and contrast relationships for different disciplines. This is more than figurative language. Rather, these metaphors provide a deep conceptual under-standing of the ways in which knowledge becomes meaningful in professional practice and how the context and the nature of the practice provide the schemata by which this meaning-making process happens. (Daley, 2001, p. 329)

The extended 'living' metaphor of the camel was useful in generating professional understand-ings amongst e-learning practitioners regarding the sustainability of low cost 'friendly' solutions for enduring hardship through democratic collabora-tion amongst practitioners stimulated by critical friendship in the 'desert' conditions between, and sometimes within, institutions. This chapter draws on data from the above two UK e-learning projects to highlight the role of the camel metaphor in providing a theoretical 'case' for future transnational learning development and take-up.

In these projects, the paradoxically ugly gracefulness and enduring utilitarian functionality of the camel began to symbolize mutually supportive dialogue and exchange within the professional friendship of a community of practice designed within an e-learning project. The gruelling ride of the long-suffering camel from oasis to oasis across the desert gradually became a 'fit' metaphor for the representation of a collective professional journey in which practitioners shared their attitudes, practices, thoughts, concerns and examples of work in order to improve e-learning practice with partners from other institutions.

In reflecting on the reasons why CAMEL was successful, in comparison with CoP experiments that fail even when both the domain and practice of shared interest is clear and strong, it is helpful to consider the key elements involved in ensuring effectiveness in e-learning CoP innovations. Chua (2006) identifies the criteria that in his view are necessary to establish a successful community of practice (Chua, 2006: 120). Analysis of the CAMEL project indicates that the CAMEL initiative met all of Chua's criteria, in addition to the CoP structuring characteristics identified by Wenger (1998) and McDermott (2001).

Firstly, the concept of CAMEL was coherent, appealing and straightforward. The ingenious acronym 'Collaborative Approaches to the Management of e-Learning' made immediate sense to the project partners. The concept had a likable metaphorical focus on the attributes of the 'camel' as an animal reinforcing not only the nomadic nature of the partnership visits but also the criteria of sustainability, affordability and group survival in harsh, rugged conditions, providing ongoing friendly, reliable support in a group that journeyed together. The concept was designed by a core team with complementary academic and research interests in e-learning

involving the above partners who worked on the original specification of the CoP.

Secondly, the experts involved in shaping CAMEL called together a 'critical mass' of experienced academic and technical experts in e-learning and education, amongst whom were a number of informally influential social entrepreneurs, to support the project. The knowledge and level of social connectivity of this wider group meant that various individuals played the roles of 'mavens' (knowledge experts) and 'connectors' (highly connected socio-professional individuals), who widely disseminated the concept and findings involved in the project. Professional and social connections between several members of the institutional and agency partners supporting CAMEL were proactive and fluid in fostering the kinds of 'weak ties' (making acquaintances easily) and 'bridging ties' (joining others) that Totterdell, Holman and Hukin (2008) observe are characteristic of positional managers and leaders in social networks. The importance of the strength of 'weak ties' has been influential in social network analysis (Granovetter, 1973, p. 1360). Granovetter has demonstrated that weak ties between individuals 'are more likely to link members of *different* small groups than are strong ones, which tend to be concentrated within particular groups' (Granovetter, 1973, p.1376), while numerous other researchers have explored this concept further in relation to social networks (Ryberg and Larsen, 2008). Since the CAMEL project operated independently of institutional and agency main work and comprised a large range of partners, members of the project tended to meet less often than for some other more tightly organized JISC projects, in which all members were part of the same institution. Therefore the 'weak ties' between acquaintances who were individual members of CAMEL were influential in bridging connections between different agencies, institutions and individuals in an open network that supported the project. Arguably, Wenger's model for communities of practice enables the consideration that the CoP model can comprise *both* 'strong and weak' ties and not just the 'strong ties' that Ryberg and Larsen indicate characterize a CoP, in their proposal that 'networked individualism' may be a more useful form of social organization than a CoP (Ryberg and Larsen, 2008, pp. 103-05).

The CAMEL project therefore included a range of leading e-learning experts: arguably, it was the influence of this wider peripheral legitimate network participating and collaborating in knowledge sharing within the CoP, combined with the passion and enthusiasm for e-learning innovations of individual partners, which may have been responsible for the success and multiple take-up of the project. As Chakravorti (2004: 470, 477) observes, 'The role of a network in an innovation's path to market success is crucial, even for the most ingenious innovations..... it is critical to recognize the adoption network surrounding an innovation's journey through market'. The 'adoption network' around the CAMEL was significant in its power and influence, in view of the fact that all agencies involved had weak ties with either all or most higher and further education institutions in the UK and were involved in organizing and running several major conferences and publications connected with e-learning dissemination.

Thirdly, the above factors meant that the 'social capital' created and sustained in the CAMEL project was high in all three dimensions of 'structure', 'relations' and 'cognition' identified by Chua (2006):

Social capital, a salient asset possessed by healthy and thriving communities, may be characterised along three primary dimensions, namely, a perception that individuals are part of a larger network (structural dimension), a sense of trust among individuals (relational dimension) and a shared understanding of the issues facing the organisation (cognitive dimension) (Nahapiet and Ghoshal, 1998).... (Chua, 2006, p. 125).

As described above, the CAMEL project deliberately aimed to build trust amongst all parties, by specifying at the outset the ground-rules for working together in the Project Initiation Document, and arranging social events connected with each visit, to ensure that face-to-face engagement in the project was high. In this regard, CAMEL created a 'genuine' community, rather than a 'pseudo-community' amongst its collaborating members, many of whom are still frequently in touch with and/or working with each other, more than three years after the original project ended. CAMEL was therefore created from partners who were committed and willing to engage in a genuine community around a domain and practice of strong mutual interest. Some of these individuals were also part of a naturally occurring community linked to the interests and activities of ALT, JISC infoNet, the JISC and the HEA, which meant that there was already a shared context in which to nurture the formation of an authentic community in the CoP.

Fourthly, the project ensured its own success in practical but realistic and constrained ways, by ensuring all project participants were paid a small sum of funding to carry out the work and that they also agreed to sign up at the outset to the completion of a small number of key tasks. These were both realistic and well-planned, since at the commencement of the work it was agreed that all partners would organize, for example, a visit to their own place of work.

Fifthly, the project had a distinct leadership and management structure, overseen by a group of supportive interested parties, all of whom were regarded as unquestionably legitimate and authoritative by the wider CAMEL network, on account of the formal and informal expert roles that they had played previously in various e-learning contexts. The leadership structure was also collaborative in involving all partners in organizing visits and sharing knowledge, using a model of co-creation for CAMEL in which each partner's preferences and specialist interests were valued and respected. The CAMEL project was also proactive in utilizing and building informally on the management support of its various interested stakeholders, garnering together a wide range of different interests and resources to support the effective continuation of the work, for example, through later take-up of the CAMEL model in the CAMEL Higher Education Academy Benchmarking and Pathfinder projects.

Finally, the CAMEL project did not focus solely or even mainly on outputs, but emphasized throughout that the *process* of engagement in the face-to-face visits of the project was essential in examining the formation of a community of practice. This focus on process was not at the expense of outputs (although there were indeed a range of useful outputs, including an information kit on the development of a community of practice in e-learning).

Technology Concerns

The technology concerns in the eLIDA CAMEL project had a key emphasis on practitioner pedagogic trials of innovative uses of e-learning in the classroom with students to provide design for learning solutions. This was because the eLIDA CAMEL was funded as a pedagogic e-learning project by the JISC Design for Learning programme: therefore, all technological work carried out in the project had a DfL focus. The project was funded to address theme C in the JISC programme, which was: *Implementing and evaluating learning design tools in the JISC Design for Learning (DfL) pedagogic e-learning programme*. In addressing this theme, the eLIDA CAMEL aimed to:

- Focus its activity primarily on strand (b) carrying out user evaluations on innovative tools with a learning design (LD) functionality
- Train practitioners in using LAMS V1.1, and/or RELOAD, with possibilities of

integration into institutional VLEs, and an option for working with Moodle
- Set up a project team internal forum in Moodle
- For LD-VLE integration, enable practitioners to understand which e-learning practices sit well within a learning design tool/which are best integrated within a VLE
- Train practitioners in principles of design for learning to develop their own sequences during Phase 1 of the project, in May-Oct, 2006. (JISC, 2009)

The technology concerns in the JISC infoNet CAMEL project, by contrast, had a key emphasis on project partners' strategic institutional management of e-learning at a whole-institution level. Therefore the aspect of strategies for the 'management' of technology for the educational institution was highlighted, rather than the pedagogic management and design of e-learning in the classroom. Since the partners had a number of different kinds of e-learning platforms, technologies and tools in operation, the technologies in use were extremely variable. Amongst those items demonstrated or discussed in partner visits were uses of LAMS, Moodle, RELOAD, Horizon Wimba synchronous collaboration tool, personal response systems and interactive electronic voting pads for classroom use.

Technology Components

The technology components in the eLIDA CAMEL project included primarily the tools and resources used by practitioners within LAMS V 1.1 and LAMS V 2 learning activity management system and Moodle course management system. These items included the chat facility, the forums for discussion, e-learning quizzes, the journal tool, the wiki and webpage tools, the upload facility for word documents, image files and powerpoint presentations, the labels and glossaries, as well as the facility to link to external resources. Members of individual partner teams in the project carried out detailed work on the use of innovative e-learning tools in their classrooms across a range of different institutions in the UK. From these elaborated examples of teacher usage of e-learning with students, individual case studies were drawn up over a period of some months, which described in detail the advantages and challenges involved in the work. The individual practitioner case studies are outlined in the final project report and evaluation report, with examples of these provided in the JISC CETIS wiki (see JISC, 2009; JISC, 2009a). However, an overview of the individual case studies and an example of the work done using specific technology components is provided below.

Technology Components in Use: A Case Study Example

The eLIDA CAMEL project produced overall 14 comprehensive teaching practitioner Design for Learning case studies, including five three-part studies and nine two-part studies, in addition to seven studies incorporating video clips on collaborative aspects of the project. These studies included elaborated individual reflections and data on practitioner use of e-learning in the classroom, such as web-based learning materials, considerations relating to collaborative e-learning, notes of reflections about the attitudes and practices of teaching practitioners, designs for learning plans, interviews with team members about the eLIDA CAMEL and CAMEL model, discussions and examples of learning design sequences and student work in developing offline and online learning skills. The eLIDA CAMEL project team investigated both online and offline e-learning to trial pedagogic uses of design for learning, using a project Moodle site to gather together ideas and resources during around eighteen months of ongoing work, including commentary in a project wiki featuring various debates held by the team and also including results from surveymonkey of

student and project team evaluations. Individual case studies considered pedagogic context in relation to practitioners' local situations, including learning and teaching in the classroom, the teachers' pedagogic intentions, design for learning processes, classroom results and the teacher and student evaluations of the trialing of learning design tools with students in the local context. An example is provided below of one of the detailed cases involved:

Alison was one of the eLIDA CAMEL practitioners. She teaches at a post-16 community college in the south-east of London in the United Kingdom. The college has a strong profile in widening participation, particularly for students with prior disadvantages in education and it is committed to use a range of ICT resources and e-learning supported courses to give students greater access to and help with their college studies. As one of the members of the eLIDA CAMEL project, Alison used the course management system Moodle to support and supplement classroom activities for teaching in an accredited Diploma in Childcare course for students aged 16-19 years. Her class was made up of mixed-ability female students, who were already qualified to basic level in IT skills. The college had recently adopted Moodle as a college-wide course management system: both college management and the IT technical staff were supportive of its use. Alison had therefore already had some training in Moodle course management and in course design and she was supported by a college-based mentor who was familiar with Moodle. However, this was her first experience of creating learning activities and resources for a course to be delivered using Moodle. The eLIDA CAMEL project encouraged design for learning activity to be carried out, resourcing the college with additional funding.

The class in childcare that Alison was teaching aimed to develop students' observation skills regarding child development, to teach students about relevant child development theories and to help students understand the difference between subjectivity and objectivity. Alison started her design for learning process in Moodle with the above course aims and related assessment criteria in mind. She discussed her ideas with her mentor at the college: together they worked out the structure of the course to be designed, considering all available e-learning tools that they could use both within and alongside Moodle. Alison's mentor showed her how to adapt existing online e-learning resources so that she could upload these to the college server for use in Moodle, and helped her create some Hot Potatoes quizzes for her class, including images that she could use in her lessons. Her mentor also showed Alison how to create Moodle-based activities using interactive powerpoint presentations with video clips and questions for students. These were intended to be used with students alongside other classroom activities throughout a period of some months.

The eLIDA CAMEL evaluation report (Masterman, 2008) recorded that Alison said she found the process of design for learning using Moodle very enjoyable and she had a sense of achievement when the learning design was completed and demonstrated as a successful example of e-learning to the rest of the college. She did, however, find the process 'quite time-consuming'. She used the interactive powerpoint presentations in class with her students, who watched short video clips and recorded their answers, following which other student class members checked the answers. Alison's students also completed the Hot Potatoes Quiz with a sense of achievement and enjoyment and they scored well in the quiz. Alison reported about the eLIDA CAMEL work that: 'Moodle has added a new dimension to my teaching and has been an enjoyable experience that has made me look at my teaching in a different way. In the future my classes can become more student-centred, as I develop the course to include areas for the students to develop.' The eLIDA CAMEL Evaluation Report noted in relation to Alison's work that:

'It was too early to judge whether the Moodle-based activities would have an impact on .... overall [student] performance. An advantage of Moodle is that the teacher can develop later stages the course while the students are working through the earlier ones. This was allowing Alison to incorporate new tools as she learned about them, including the feedback and assessment tools so that students could submit their assignments online. She also planned to include a glossary for students to create a list of terms relevant to childcare and to set up a number of discussion forums. Alison noted that ... the adaptation of other courses to include a Moodle-based component would have to wait until she had more time. Finally, Alison commented on the gains that Moodle can bring to both students and staff: "As staff you develop additional skills, reflect upon your teaching methods and how to adapt and change them. For the students it can lead to more independent and enjoyable study. So if you have the time I would recommend it, although it does help to have support from an e-guide."

The Learners' Experience

Alison described the students as seeming more motivated by the online environment and the new tools. They were also accessing the resources from home in order to consolidate their classroom learning. Her impressions were reinforced by data obtained from the eLIDA CAMEL. [Regarding the] online student survey, [a]ll six students who responded said they had enjoyed doing the sequence. The key reason for their positive responses lay in the design of the sequence: the combination of theory (presented in PowerPoint presentations with video clips), quizzes and discussions. Five felt that they had learned more than they usually would, primarily because of the "anytime, anywhere" access, and the additional opportunities for practice. Students also perceived a potential across-the-board benefit in using Moodle:

"I really feel that if other subject[s] were put on in this way it would help with the subjects that some students find difficult." (Masterman, 2008).

Alison was one of the eLIDA CAMEL project team who participated proactively in knowledge sharing in project visits, including engaging in collaborative online learning with other project partners, sharing her attitudes and practices as regards teaching and learning design with all teachers in the team. The beneficial development of online learning skills amongst her students was particularly pleasing in her local context, in view of the problems with accessing learning that many of the college students have faced in their lives.

Technology Components in Use: Overview of Components

In addition to their use of Moodle and LAMS, practitioners in the project used a wide range of other technology components, including learning worksheets, NLN objects, flash objects, stand-alone powerpoint presentations, audio podcasts, video, word files and PDF documents, additional hot potatoes quizzes, QUIA quizzes, interactive material from other websites, Camtasia screen capture software, creation of SCORM conformant content, assets from JORUM, images and Quick Topic. Project participants recorded the use of all of the above items in the collective project wiki within the Moodle shared by the eLIDA CAMEL project team. Furthermore, the eLIDA CAMEL project established links with Liverpool Hope University's JISC LD4P project to consider and learn about the use of RELOAD regarding practitioner use of LD/DfL, the comparability of RELOAD with LAMS and the pedagogic trialing of RELOAD to consider the development of IMS LD authoring tools that would be suitable for practitioners to use. Also in use during the project was the online tool surveymonkey to disseminate evaluation surveys and record ongoing detailed feedback from project participants and

students, the use of the project Moodle for meetings and discussions, the use of video and audio recorders as well as digital cameras to collect data for the project, and the use of digital projectors, whiteboards, flipcharts and other practical items to carry out demonstration and training during eLIDA CAMEL project visits.

In the JISC infoNet CAMEL project, as discussed above, the partners used a varied range of kinds of e-learning platforms, technologies and tools to provide demonstrations and discussion items during project visits. Amongst those technologies and tools demonstrated or discussed in partner visits were uses of LAMS, Moodle, RELOAD, Horizon Wimba synchronous collaboration tool, podcasting, the use of institutional VLEs and portals, the use of personal response systems and interactive electronic voting pads with students, the 'taking notes' function of LAMS, the use of digital pens and notepaper to upload information to a PC or mobile phone, the use of chat functions and remote online student support systems, student assessment tools and the use of instant messaging. Also in use during the project was a JISCmail list to send messages to project participants, the use of video recording equipment to record evaluation feedback from project participants, the use of digital cameras to collect data for the project, and the use of whiteboards, flipcharts, digital projectors and other relevant items to carry out demonstration and discussions during CAMEL project visits.

Management and Organizational Concerns

The organizational culture that was nurtured in both the CAMEL and eLIDA CAMEL projects was designed to cultivate an atmosphere of trust. Earlier work had established the importance of creating a trusting environment in which practitioners in a CoP could share knowledge together truthfully in carrying out their work (Jameson, Ferrell, Kelly, Walker and Ryan, 2006). The CAMEL project had implicitly recognized this in the setting up of the design of the original CAMEL model from the work of the Association for Learning Technology (JISC infoNet, 2006; Jameson, 2007).

As noted above, CAMEL had been built from an exemplar that Seb Schmoller, Chief Executive of ALT, had described from a 1985 visit to Uruguay in which he visited his uncle's farming self-help group. This community of practice consisted of eight members, all of them farmers, who met monthly. The farmer participants visited each other's farms regularly on a rotational basis to share their knowledge and to develop improvements in agricultural practice through a collaborative understanding of each others' work. The Uruguayan farming group had gradually evolved into a spontaneously self-organized community of practice in which the farmers' 'know how' about agricultural practices was shared amongst the group, in discussions that were facilitated by an expert. The group had evolved within themselves a community commitment both to collaborative learning and to sharing honest critique about the ways in which to achieve improvements in practice.

This ethos and shared practice had been established over a period of some years, during which each visit was hosted in turn by one of the farmer community members. All partners would tour the farm during the monthly visits and also meet together as a working group, having meals together and sharing each others' company in informal social events. In the course of each visit, the farmers joined in with proactive and exploratory discussions to critique each other's work to help improve agricultural practice on the farm in question. This process was intended to be honestly reflective of both effective and ineffective practice, so that farmers could learn from each other in an atmosphere of trust. Over a period of some years, the farmers found that they had derived many benefits from being part of this community, not only in terms of improvements in

practice, but also regarding their levels of moral support, social connectivity, confidence as regards introducing new farming practices, and awareness of new agricultural systems and tools. The community had therefore achieved much success in helping the farmers to 'grow' new methods, techniques and capabilities.

The management and organizational concerns of the two cases reported here were focused on the particular issue of learning from the above Uruguayan farming experience. Both the CAMEL and eLIDA CAMEL projects aimed to build a CoP to foster improvements in e-learning practice in stable, effective and sustainable ways, building on the prior knowledge not only of the Uruguayan farming model but also from the extant literature on communities of practice and organizational learning. An important feature of both projects is that they were inter-institutional, being situated in a new 'shared space' between all of the organizations and institutions involved. The management and organizational preoccupations that the projects shared were therefore to build best practice in developing an e-learning CoP: the projects were otherwise somewhat abstracted and removed from the daily routine work of the institutions and agencies involved.

The focus on honest communications at all visits was, however, of some concern regarding the potential ethical difficulty of truthful communication about the problems that practitioners might be facing 'at home' in their private lives in the institutions involved: a concern that one member of the CAMEL project group described as 'not wanting to wash your dirty linen in public'. There was therefore some dilemma about the extent to which truthfulness about institutional difficulties could be shared in public without causing embarrassment and damage to the institutions involved. A discussion was held at the outset of the project during the formation of the PID which agreed that, for the effective establishment of trust, it was necessary to apply 'Chatham House Rules' within the project, to protect the institutions and individuals involved. This was recorded in the CAMEL report in the following way:

The Chatham House Rule reads as follows: 'When a meeting, or part thereof, is held under The Chatham House rule, participants are free to use the information received, but neither the identity nor the affiliation of the speaker(s), nor that of any other participant may be revealed'. (JISC infoNet, 2006, p.7)

Once this ground-rule had been established for both the CAMEL and eLIDA CAMEL projects, both project groups were happier to share information freely, in the knowledge that such revelations would be protected by the ethos of mutual respect and confidentiality that had been established by the projects.

CURRENT CHALLENGES FACING THE ORGANIZATION

The main challenges facing the institutions and agencies involved in both the CAMEL and eLIDA CAMEL projects at the completion of these initiatives was how to continue to develop the communities of practice established by these projects once the funding period was over. It was agreed, however, that such continuation was not really possible, and that the projects both needed to recognize that there is sometimes a limited 'life' to communities of practice, which grow, develop and then fade away. The problem of either ending the projects or developing potential renewal and possible sustainability was therefore a preoccupation of project participants for a brief period prior to the ending of both projects, but, in the longer run, all members of the groups involved eventually realized that it was not feasible to continue to work on the project once the external funding had ceased.

A further problem affecting both projects, connected with the issue of sustainability without funding, was the heavy workload of almost all of the members involved. This mitigated against any unfunded continuation and also meant that in some cases there was a short delay in finalizing and publishing results from the projects. Throughout the projects, the group had realized that members of the project teams were heavily taken up with other work and therefore, although project meetings were very well attended, there had to be a realistic timescale for the completion of final outputs such as the detailed case studies completed by individual practitioners. After some delay these were, however, all completed.

Yet another challenge was the question of how to apply the lessons learned in CAMEL and eLIDA CAMEL to the daily work of the institutions and agencies that had taken part in the projects. In some cases, the institutions involved in the project were not, according to participants' views, characterized by the same kind of trusting, positive and creative ethos as members had found in the CoP. At the end of the eLIDA CAMEL, several project partners recorded in the wiki that they would 'miss the building of bonds with members of the team… the encouragement and thanks extended to me and my team for all our work …. feeling our efforts are valued'. Some participants noted that they would not ordinarily receive this kind of support in their own institutions, and therefore they wanted to state that they had appreciated 'the constant support and positive attitudes of partners ….[the].. enthusiasm for using technology to transform teaching and learning, which isn't shared by some senior management within the institution'. Project partners also said that they would also miss the project's '… encouragement to succeed and drive innovation … the acknowledgement and praise of my team's work… [and being guided by] …. an independent voice which raises important questions …. the use of the CAMEL model in this project has been invaluable'. Moreover, one project partner said that they had 'relied on support from the team when my mentees and I had problems' and that this would be missed (Jameson, 2007: p.7). This problem can be partially conceptualized as the challenge of establishing trust within host organizations in which this is not present to the same degree as in these CoP projects, since without the three dimensions of 'competence, integrity and benevolence' that can be said to build trust (Usoro, Sharrat, Tsui and Shekhar, 2007: p.199), it is unlikely that this will be established.

Another problem affecting the projects was the changing educational, policy and e-learning environment involving all institutions and individuals regarding the final project outputs. Institutions, people and e-learning systems changed and moved on in a number of ways after the completion of the projects. Hence the project Moodle site, which had contained all the elements necessary for analysis of the case environment in the eLIDA CAMEL, was transferred to another server shortly after the completion of the project, and this process had resulted in some loss to the functionality of the Moodle, with the result that the re-created collaborative environment was not quite the same as experienced in the project. The analysis completed for post-project disseminations therefore relied more on video recordings, surveymonkey results, photographs, project reports, related documentation and other stable items than on the recorded Moodle site interactions. Further, the member of staff who had completed the web design and hosting of the project web moved on to another institution, causing challenges regarding the upkeep of the website. The above challenges were, however, overcome, with the exception of the problem of members missing the benefits of the project following its completion, which is a challenging issue that relates to particular institutional situations that cannot be easily resolved.

CONCLUSION

The solution to the problem of a lack of sustainability without funding was resolved, albeit somewhat unsatisfactorily, through the recognition that it was not possible to continue these projects without funding. Therefore, a resolution was established that one longer term recommended way of dealing with this issue is simply to gain further funding for the setting up of longer term communities of practice projects along the same lines as those established in the eLIDA CAMEL and CAMEL. Several funding bids to achieve continuation funding for projects linked with CAMEL and eLIDA CAMEL have subsequently been submitted and achieved. For the furtherance of a community of practice pilot such as those developed in these projects, additional funding is recommended, as the aspect of independence and externality is important in ensuring that the project has coherence and authenticity. This solution is recommended also regarding the problem of workload of staff involved, as there is a need for reasonably substantial funding to be obtained to ensure that staff members can have time to be dedicated to the project and to attend face-to-face visits as well as participate in online e-learning project activities.

The question of how to apply the lessons learned in CAMEL and eLIDA CAMEL to the daily work of the institutions and agencies that had taken part in the projects is deeply challenging. This is a variable, complex issue, with, on the one hand, a range of institutions being quite responsive to the concept of establishing and supporting communities of practice, while on the other hand, there are some institutions in which there is no interest or support for this. Some organizations in the project were environments in which there was a high level of trust, while others were not at all characterized by a trusting, positive and creative ethos. Certain members of the project team therefore had difficulty in gaining any management support for a localized follow-on application of CAMEL or eLIDA CAMEL to their work, while other project members found, by contrast, that their local management was keen to apply e-learning innovations to build on CAMEL immediately.

The solution to the problem of a lack of trust has been discussed in detail elsewhere in relation to these and similar projects (Jameson et al., 2006; JISC infoNet, 2006), but in general in the attempt to build trust and thereby effective knowledge-sharing, the recommendations outlined include the establishment of the integrity and authenticity of the community, the assurance of competence in the leadership and management of e-learning innovations and the guarantee of benevolence in behavioral support to the individuals involved in the community of practice. Further, as regards the establishment of competence and integrity, it should be noted that both CAMEL and eLIDA CAMEL project members said that the defining features of the CAMEL model were important as regards the 'sense-making' aspects of the project. The meaningfulness of the metaphor of the camel was a key factor in the generation of insight and innovation in the both projects. It is therefore recommended that some form of unifying theme, name or logo is established for similar projects in the future, to ensure that there is a meaningful common understanding of the identity of e-learning projects and their aims and goals.

As regards the challenge of changes to individuals, institutions and policies affecting projects such as the two e-learning initiatives discussed in this chapter, to some extent there is no real solution to this challenge: such changes happen constantly and there is little if anything that can be done to prevent this. However, despite this, it is recommended that projects develop sustainability and embedding solutions as well as back-up plans for outputs to ensure that archived resources are stored and made available over the long-term. The CAMEL and eLIDA CAMEL projects both featured such plans, as the JISC archival storage

system required these and recommended best practice in this regard to both projects.

ACKNOWLEDGMENT

Financial support for the eLIDA CAMEL project from the JISC Design for Learning Programe is acknowledged and appreciated. JISC infoNet, ALT and the HEFCE LGMF fund are thanked for funding for participation in the JISC infoNet CAMEL project. Thanks to SebSchmoller and Rhonda Riachi of ALT, Sarah Knight, JISC Programme Manager, Jacquie Kelly of JISC infoNet and to all JISC eLIDA CAMEL, eLISA and JISC infoNet CAMEL partners, institutions and agencies for contributing to content forming the data for this paper.

REFERENCES

Alfaro, J. Delrio, C., Dima, G., Dondi, C., Fischer, T., Kastis, N., Koskinen, T., Kretschmer, T., Kugemann, W.F., Lassnigg, L., Rotger, J.M., Szûcs, A., Unger, M., Vasiloglou, A., Vogtenhuber, S., Wermundsen, T., Zarka, D., and Zuheros, A. (2005*). Understanding Change, Adapting to Change, Shaping the Future, Change Drivers, Trends & Core Tensions for European Learning Systems & Educational Policies. In *Learning in Europe; Observatory on National and International Evolution, LEONIE Project, MENON Network EEIG*. Retrieved August 7, from http://www.education-observatories.net/leonie/outputs/LEONIE_Executive_Summary_2006.pdf

Association for Learning Technology (ALT). (2009). *ALT Strategy: February 2008 to January 2011 (revised May 2009)*. Retrieved 14 June 09, from http://www.alt.ac.uk/docs/ALT_2008-2011_Strategy.pdf

BRIDGES-LAC. (2009). *BRIDGES-LAC Project website*. Retrieved August 7, 2009, from http://www.bridges-lac.org/

Chakravorti, B. (2004). The role of adoption networks in the success of innovations: a strategic perspective. *Technology in Society*, *26*(2-3), 469–482. doi:10.1016/j.techsoc.2004.01.007

Chua, A. Y. K. (2006). The Rise and Fall of a Community of practice: A Descriptive Case Study. *Knowledge and Process Management*, *13*(2), 120–128. doi:10.1002/kpm.239

Daley, B. J. (2001). Metaphors for Professional Learning. *Advances in Developing Human Resources*, *3*(3), 322–332. doi:10.1177/15234220122238346

EMERGE. (2009). *JISC Users and Innovations EMERGE project*. Retrieved August 6, 2009, from http://elgg.jiscemerge.org.uk/

Ferrell, G., & Kelly, J. (2006). Collaborative Approaches to the Management of e-Learning (CAMEL). In *European Universities Information Systems 12th International Conference Proceedings* (pp. 333-337).

Ferrell, G., & Kelly, J. (2006). Collaborative Approaches to the Management of e-Learning (CAMEL). In *European Universities Information Systems 12th International Conference Proceedings* (pp. 333-337).

Gannon-Leary, P., & Fontainha, E. (2007) *Communities of Practice and virtual learning communities: benefits, barriers and success factors.*

Gillham, W. E. C. (2000). *Case study research methods*. London: Continuum.

GLOBE. (2009). *The Global Learning Objects Brokered Exchange (GLOBE) alliance*. Retrieved August 7, 2009, from http://www.globe-info.org/en/aboutglobe

Granovetter, M. S. (1973). The Strength of Weak Ties. *American Journal of Sociology*, *78*(6), 1360–1380. doi:10.1086/225469

Grey, W. (2000). Metaphor and Meaning. *Minerva – An Internet Journal of Philosophy*, *4*(4). Retrieved on March 30, 2009, from http://www.ul.ie/~philos/vol4/metaphor.html

HELIOS. (2009). *HELIOS Project website*. Retrieved on August 6, 2009, from http://www.education-observatories.net/helios

Hiltz, S. R., & Goldman, R. (2005). *Learning together online: Research on asynchronous learning*. Mahwah, NJ: Erlbaum.

Jameson, J. (2007). *Investigating Collaborative Leadership for Communities of Practice in Learning and Skills*. Research Report funded and published by Lancaster University Management School: Centre for Excellence in Leadership. Retrieved June 14, 2009, from http://www.centreforexcellence.org.uk/UsersDoc/CollabLeadership.pdf

Jameson, J. (2008, May 6). The eLIDA CAMEL: Designed for Learning by Community. *ALT-N Newsletter Article: Featured Case Study, 12*. Retrieved June 14, 2009, from http://newsletter.alt.ac.uk/e_article001068464.cfm

Jameson, J., Ferrell, G., Kelly, J., Walker, S., & Ryan, M. (2006). Building trust & shared knowledge in communities of e-learning practice: collaborative leadership in the JISC eLISA and CAMEL lifelong learning projects. *British Journal of Educational Technology*, *37*(6), 949–968. doi:10.1111/j.1467-8535.2006.00669.x

JISC infoNet. (2006). *The CAMEL Project: Collaborative Approaches to the Management of E-Learning*. Northumbria University printed and on-line project report. Retrieved on March 21, 2009, from http://www.jiscinfonet.ac.uk/camel

JISC infoNet. (2006a). *Using the CAMEL Model to Build a Community of Practice: Resources: Where did the idea come from?* Retrieved on June 14, 2009, from www.jiscinfonet.ac.uk/camel/camel-model/idea.mov

JISC infoNet. (2007). *Minutes of the final eLIDA CAMEL project meeting.* Unpublished notes in the eLIDA CAMEL project Moodle.

Joint Information Systems Committee (JISC). (2009). *What we Do: Programmes: e-Learning Pedagogy.* e-Learning Independent Design Activities for Collaborative Approaches to the Management of e-Learning (eLIDA CAMEL) Project. Retrieved June 14, 2009, from http://www.jisc.ac.uk/whatwedo/programmes/elearningpedagogy/elidacamel.aspx

Joint Information Systems Committee (JISC). (2009a). *JISC CETIS Design for Learning Projects Wiki, Shared Resources 2: Case Studies.* Retrieved August 7, 2009, from http://DfL.cetis.ac.uk/wiki/index.php/Shared_Resources2

Kelly, J., & Riachi, R. (2006 July). CAMEL train heads for oasis. *ALT-N*, 5. Retrieved March 21, 2009, from http://newsletter.alt.ac.uk/e_article000615315.cfm?x=b11,0,w

Lave, J., & Wenger, E. (1991). *Situated learning: legitimate peripheral participation.* Cambridge, UK: Cambridge University Press.

Leadership Governance and Management Fund. (2009). *Collaborative Approaches to the Management of e-Learning, Leadership, Governance and Management Fund A-Z of Funded Projects.* Higher Education Council for England (HEFCE). Retrieved June 7, 2009, from http://www.hefce.ac.uk/lgm/build/lgmfund/projects/show.asp?id=14&cat=9

LEONIE. (2003). *Trends and drivers of change in learning system.* LEONIE Project Report. Retrieved August 7, 2009 from http://www.education-observatories.net/leonie/outputs/LEONIE__final_trends_of_change.pdf

LEONIE. (2009). *Leonie Project website.* Retrieved August 7, 2009, from http://www.education-observatories.net/leonie

Longman. (1978). *Longman Dictionary of Contemporary English.* Harlow, UK: Longman Group Ltd.

MAN. (2009). *MERLOT Africa Network (MAN) project website.* Retrieved August 7, 2009, from http://man.merlot.org/

Masterman, E. (2008). *Evaluation Report for the eLIDA CAMEL Project.* Unpublished report contributing to the final report of the project to JISC, University of Greenwich.

Masterman, E., Jameson, J., & Walker, S. (2009). Capturing Teachers' Experience Of Learning Design Through Case Studies. *Distance Education Special Issue: Researching Learning Design* . In *Open.* Distance And Flexible Learning.

McDermott, R. (2001) *Knowing in Community: 10 Critical Success Factors in Building Communities of Practice.* Community Intelligence Labs. Retrieved March 20, 2009, from www.co-i-l.com/coil/knowledge-garden/cop/knowing.shtml

MENON. (2009). *Menon project website*, retrieved 6 August, 2009, from http://www.menon.org/

MERLOT. (2009). *MERLOT Project.* Retrieved August 7, 2009, from http://www.merlot.org/merlot/index.htm

MOVEnation. (2000). *MOVEnation project website.* Retrieved August 6, 2009, from http://muvenation.org/about/

POLE. (2009). *POLE: Policy Observatory for Lifelong Learning and Employability project website*. Retrieved August 6, 2009, from http://www.education-observatories.net/pole/reports_html

Ryberg, T., & Larsen, M. C. (2008). Networked identities: understanding relationships between strong and weak ties in networked environments. *Journal of Computer Assisted Learning, 24*(2), 103–115. doi:10.1111/j.1365-2729.2007.00272.x

Taiwan Culture Portal. (2009). *Taiwan Cultural Portal*. Retrieved August 8, 2009, from http://www.culture.tw/

TELDAP. (2009). *Taiwan e-Learning Digital Archives Project (TELDAP) website and collaboration portal*. Retrieved August 8, 2009, from http://teldap.tw/en/ http://collab.teldap.tw/index.php/archives/category/news_en

Totterdell, P., Holman, D., & Hukin, A. (2008). Social networkers: Measuring and examining individual differences in propensity to connect with others. *Social Networks, 30*(4), 283–296. doi:10.1016/j.socnet.2008.04.003

UCEL. (2009). *Universities' Collaboration in e-Learning (UCEL) professional health community of e-learning practice website*. Retrieved August 7, 2009, from http://www.ucel.ac.uk

Usoro1, A., Sharratt, M. W., Tsui, E., & Shekhar, S. (2007). Trust as an antecedent to knowledge sharing in virtual communities of practice. *Knowledge Management Research & Practice, 5*, 199–212.

Vygotsky, L. S. (1978). *Mind in society: The development of higher psychological processes*. Cambridge, MA: Harvard University Press.

Wenger, E. (1998). *Communities of practice. Learning, meaning and identity*. Cambridge, UK: Cambridge University Press.

Wenger, E. C., McDermott, R., & Synder, W. M. (2002). *Cultivating Communities of Practice*. Boston: Harvard Business School Press.

Wenger, E. C., & Snyder, W. M. (2000). Communities of practice: the organizational frontier. *Harvard Business Review, 78*(1), 139–145.

Yin, R. (1994). *Case Study Research: Design and Methods* (2nd ed.). Beverly Hills, CA: Sage Publishing.

ADDITIONAL READING

Ardichvili, A., Page, V., & Wentling, T. (2003). Motivation and barriers to participation in virtual knowledge-sharing communities of practice. *Journal of Knowledge Management, 70*(1), 64–77. doi:10.1108/13673270310463626

Brown, J. S., & Duguid, P. (1991). Organizational learning and communities of practice: toward a unified view of working, learning and innovation. *Organization Science, 2*(1), 40–57. doi:10.1287/orsc.2.1.40

Brown, J. S., & Duguid, P. (2000). Balancing act: how to capture knowledge without killing it. *Harvard Business Review, 78*(3), 73–78.

Cook, S. D. N., & Yanow, D. (1993). Culture and organizational learning. *Journal of Management Inquiry, 2*, 373–390. doi:10.1177/105649269324010

Davenport, T. H., & Prusak, L. (1999). *Working Knowledge*. Boston, MA: Harvard Business School Press.

Dubé, L., Bourhis, A., & Jacob, R. (2004). "Structuring Spontaneity": the Impact of Management Practices on the Success of Intentionally Formed Virtual Communities of Practice. [online] *Cahiers du GReSI no. 04-20*, Retrieved on 19 March 2009, from gresi.hec.ca/cahier.asp

Eisenhardt, K. M. (1989). Building theories from case study research. *Academy of Management Review, 14*, 532–550. doi:10.2307/258557

Glennie, W. P., & Hickok, J. (2003). Meeting critical defense needs with CoPs. *KM Review, 6*(3),16–19.

Hildreth, P., Kimble, C., & Wright, P. (2000). Communities of practice in the distributed international environment. *Journal of Knowledge Management, 4*(1), 27–37. doi:10.1108/13673270010315920

Lave, J., & Wenger, E. C. (1991). *Situated Learning: Legitimate Peripheral Participation*. Cambridge: Cambridge University Press.

McDermott, R. (2001) *Knowing in Community: 10 Critical Success Factors in Building Communities of Practice,* Community Intelligence Labs: Retrieved on 14 June 09, from: http://www.co-i-l.com/coil/knowledge-garden/cop/knowing.shtml

MERLOT. (2009) MERLOT Project website, retrieved 7 August, 2009: http://www.merlot.org/merlot/index.htm

Nahapiet, J., & Ghoshal, S. (1998). Social capital, intellectual capital, and the organizational advantage. *Academy of Management Review, 23*(2), 242–267. doi:10.2307/259373

Orr, J. E. (1996). *Talking About Machines: An Ethnography of a Modern Job*. Ithaca, NY: ILR Press.

Polanyi, M. (1967). *The Tacit Dimension*. New York: Anchor Books.

Storey, J., & Barnett, E. (2000). Knowledge management initiatives: learning from failure. *Journal of Knowledge Management, 4*(2), 145–156. doi:10.1108/13673270010372279

Surowiecki, J. (2004). *The wisdom of crowds: why the many are smarter than the few and how collective wisdom shapes business, economics, society and nations*. London: Little, Brown.

Surowieki, J. (2005). Independent Individuals and Wise Crowds. *The New Yorker:* Audio log Retrieved 21 March 2009, from http://itc.conversationsnetwork.org/shows/detail468.html

Trussler, S. (1998). The rules of the game. *The Journal of Business Strategy, 19*(1), 16–19. doi:10.1108/eb039904

Verenikina, I. (2003). Understanding Scaffolding and the ZPD in Educational Research, Australian Association for Research in Education (AARE) and New Zealand Association for Research in Education (NZARE): *Joint AARE/NZARE Conference*, Auckland 2003, Conference Papers Paper Code: VER03682. Retrieved June 7, 2009 from: http://www.aare.edu.au/03pap/ver03682.pdf

Vestal, W. (2003). Ten traits for a successful community of practice. *KM Review, 5*(6), 6.

Vygotsky, L. S. (1962). *Thought and Language*. Cambridge, MA: MIT Press. doi:10.1037/11193-000

Vygotsky, L. S. (1978). *Mind in society: The development of higher psychological processes*. Cambridge, MA: Harvard University Press.

Wenger, E. (1998). *Communities of Practice*. Cambridge: Cambridge University Press.

Wenger, E. C., McDermott, R., & Synder, W. M. (2002). *Cultivating Communities of Practice*. Boston: Harvard Business School Press.

Wenger, E. C., & Snyder, W. M. (2000). Communities of practice: the organizational frontier. *Harvard Business Review, 78*(1), 139–145.

Winkelen, C. V., & Ramsell, P. (2003). Why aligning value is key to designing communities. *KM Review, 5*(6), 12–15.

Wood, D., Bruner, J., & Ross, G. (1976). The Role Of Tutoring In Problem Solving. *Journal of Child Psychology and Psychiatry, and Allied Disciplines, 17*, 89–100. doi:10.1111/j.1469-7610.1976.tb00381.x

KEY TERMS AND DEFINITIONS

Community of Practice: A group of people who come together to engage in a process of social learning, co-creating improved socio-cultural practices in moving towards common goals.

Metaphor: A powerful figure of speech that compares two things without using the words 'like' or 'as', expressed in a phrase describing one thing by comparing it with reference to another.

Design for Learning: The practices that are undertaken by learning professionals to design, plan and orchestrate learning activities in the classroom, involving the use of technology as part of a learning session or programme.

Chapter 2
Interaction Design for Inclusive Learning

Deryn Graham
University of Greenwich, UK

Ian Benest
University of York, UK

Peter Nicholl
University of Ulster, UK

ABSTRACT

The findings for a case study on improving interaction design for teaching visually impaired students, in an inclusive learning environment, are presented. The crux of the problem is the ability to draw and understand diagrams. The cognitive issues are often underestimated with insufficient attention being given to the use of metaphors, etc. and "one size fits all solutions" are often the norm. The findings of the original seed funded project, which was conducted by three universities in the United Kingdom, have led to design criteria and to an application for a large scale project, to produce generic tools and to enable "multi-modal" teaching and learning, with connotations for the support of people with cognitive as well as physical impairments, especially relevant with respect to an increasingly ageing European population.

INTRODUCTION

The work was motivated by the need to accommodate visually impaired students studying computer science at United Kingdom universities, the adequacies of disability legislation, and an academic interest in multi-modal interaction. The research was conducted at three universities in the UK over a period of a year.

DOI: 10.4018/978-1-61520-751-0.ch002

SETTING THE STAGE

Current interface design for teaching visually impaired students, even when SENDA (Special Educational Needs and Disabilities Act in mainland UK) or SENDO (Special Educational Needs and Disabilities Order in Northern Ireland) compliant, has often neglected the direct involvement of target users in determining the requirements specific for their needs. In particular, there is a lack of awareness of the cognitive issues for the spectrum of users deemed to be visually impaired. The research project funded by the Higher Education Academy (HEA) aimed to determine and produce criteria for the design of interfaces, through the participation of target users from the outset, implementing these criteria in teaching exemplars in computing science at Ulster, and in electronics at York. An important constraint was that these criteria would be inclusive; usable by both sighted and partially sighted students as well as those with other impairments. Furthermore, inclusive design should not impede those without impairments, but potentially give greater variety to the ways in which they could learn or access information. This posed a considerable problem for both the exemplars at York for conveying electronic circuit diagrams and Ulster conveying Unified Modelling Language (UML) diagrams (Graham, Benest, & Nicholl, 2007b).

CASE DESCRIPTION

Methodology

The first activity required is knowledge acquisition. Different authors present methodologies with varying stages of knowledge acquisition, but fundamentally they all involve: the identification and conceptualisation of requirements and problem characteristics, formalising these into some mediating representation scheme, implementation, and final testing and validation (Graham & Barrett, 1997). Knowledge acquisition can be machine-aided or human-labour oriented.

Johnson and Johnson's methodology (1987), enhanced by Graham (1990), proposes a three-stage knowledge acquisition process based around semi-structured interviews.

The first phase is to perform a broad, but shallow survey of the domain. This allows the elicitor to become oriented with the domain, so that a more flexible approach can later be taken. This type of horizon broadening is a standard approach in

social science research. Once this shallow trawl of the domain has been done, the second phase requires that a more detailed task analysis is performed by the elicitor, focussing on the area of interest. The structure of the interview uses a teachback technique to traverse the domain and validate elicitor understanding with the result that the elicitor progressively refines the model of the expert's competence. This model is qualitatively drawn up and uses a mediating representation, Systemic Grammar Networks (SGNs) (Bliss, Monk, & Ogborn, 1983). These are a context free, qualitative representation, which can be used as a tool for the systems design, but their use does not imply the final application of any particular knowledge engineering software or methodology. SGNs have been used in many domains including oncology, printed circuit board (PCB) design, and fault diagnosis. The third phase of this approach is to validate the models drawn up from the expert with the wider expert community. The theoretical predictions of the model are presented to the initial community used in the first phase, and then to a further independent population, to check the appropriateness and validity of the model which has been created.

This knowledge acquisition methodology was adopted and tailored to the needs of the project. The first phase, the Broad and Shallow Survey, was achieved by arranging a telephone survey in conjunction the Royal National Institute for the Blind (RNIB) in London, and with a visually impaired student at the University of Ulster, to complete questionnaires specifically tailored to suit visually impaired interviewees. The second phase, a more detailed task analysis, was achieved through the design of semi-structured interviews with the visually impaired student expert at Ulster. Knowledge synthesis and analysis of survey and interview findings led to design criteria rather than the employment of SGNs which were not considered practical for visually impaired experts. Validation (and verification) was achieved by the evaluation of implemented criteria in exemplars at Ulster and York, for teaching computer science and electronics respectively.

Results

Phase One Results: Broad and Shallow Survey

The results from Phase One were that firstly, current interface design for partially sighted and blind users predominantly includes Tactile User Interfaces (TUIs) or Audio User Interfaces (AUIs) (Benyon, Turner, & Turner, 2005; NCTD, 2006).

The Broad and Shallow Survey conducted at Greenwich with the RNIB resulted in the accumulation of a number of relevant publications, materials and links to appropriate sites (T3, 2006; RNIB, 2006). Whilst extremely useful information was gleaned, the solutions offered were not sufficiently inclusive. A prime example was the use of tactile diagrams and graphs aimed at blind and partially sighted people (NCTD, 2006). For instance, "Tactile and large print maps of three London Underground (LU) Stations" using raised lines. These diagrams were in principle very pertinent, because the concept of the London Underground map was based on an electronics circuit and therefore relevant to the York exemplars. It was initially difficult to see how these diagrams could be made computer tractable. T3, prima facie, appeared to be a solution. The T3 (2006) is a touch sensitive, multi-sensory device which provides instant audio feedback from tactile images. It enables visually impaired people to access graphical information. The T3 is connected to a standard PC or laptop computer via a USB connection and has a bespoke application to understand the diagrams on the tablet. To activate the system, a T3 tactile diagram overlay is placed on the surface of the device and touched by the operator's finger. The T3 is the European version of the Talking Tactile Tablet (TTT) from Touch Graphics, New York. It requires tactile diagrams

(such as the LU maps), so it would be necessary to create every combination and permutation of these for teaching electronics and for them to be marked-up in the T3 software – too numerous to be practical or inclusive. The NCTD (2006) states that Tactile Diagrams are useful when:

- The user is print-impaired and has some tactile ability.
- A novel concept not easily described in words, must be conveyed.
- A real object is unavailable for touching.
- The shape/form/pattern is important.
- Needed to illustrate scale and relationship: biology, maps, technology.
- Used as a reference: once, or as reminder.
- It is necessary to enhance educational experience – variety.

Tactile Diagrams are not good:

- For fine detail.
- When extremely large.
- Without training.
- Without support materials.
- For those who have to spend time creating the metadata and have the diagrams marked-up.

These factors meant that they were not a suitable solution in the electronics domain. The most difficult hurdle was designing an interface that was both computer-tractable and inclusive. The focus on inclusivity distinguished this project from others such as: the TeDub system (2007), a computer-based tool for visually impaired users, and web-based haptic applications that enable blind people to create virtual graphs (Wai, Kangas, & Brewster, 2003). Coping with the number of combinations and permutations for the electronics exemplars also meant that any solution needed to be dynamic.

Guidelines have been suggested by Tiresias (2006) on several aspects of computing for varying disabilities, but were highly specific to web accessibility for instance. The most generic advice was the "User Needs Summary" dealing with each disability in turn. Specific to applications software were "Guidelines for Application Software Accessibility" (NDA, 2006). These guidelines (two priorities) covered application software running under any operating system or runtime environment. Priority one ensures that the application can be used by most people with impaired mobility, vision, hearing, cognition and language understanding, using their assistive technologies. Priority two makes it easier to use and will include more people with cognitive impairments or multiple disabilities. These guidelines were certainly inclusive.

Phase Two Results: Task Analysis

Student Expert

The following results from Phase Two, the task analysis, were conducted with the student expert at Ulster and proved to be most insightful. The student had had a period of being sighted and therefore was able to offer viewpoints with and without a visual and/or haptic memory of things. For example, the student had a visual memory of a grid, but only a haptic memory of resistors and capacitors. The student was therefore able to discriminate between what was meaningful to a visually impaired student who had a visual and/or haptic memory. This proved to be highly significant in terms of metaphors used. For example, when describing the pointer in a linked-list, a statement such as "might be thought of as a door to", is more meaningful (especially for those who have never experienced sight) than the expression adopted by the computing community of "points to".

In relation to the senses utilized by the student expert for using computer interfaces, predictably the main sense used was hearing, however sight was still above smell and taste. For everyday activities, hearing and touch can be interchangeable. The student, perhaps due to the possession of visual memory, still thought in terms of images. This possibly explains why the student placed sight above smell and taste, else the student may simply have been thinking of people who were partially sighted. The student was able to touch-type (learnt whilst sighted) so used standard QWERTY keyboards for input and GUIs (Graphical User Interfaces) with screen readers such as Dream, for audio output. The student was unable to read Braille; this was considered a great disadvantage as there were major gains to be made from using Braille displays and printouts for checking computer programs for example.

The recommendations from the student for interaction design were that: colour contrast can be of great immediate benefit for many partially sighted people; explanations using terms like "door, room, Lego" were meaningful to all; the best input and output devices were "anything tangible", that is, audio or tactile, with touch for orientation, keyboard for input; "hearing is serial, vision is parallel". The student had used examples of raised maps for aircraft flight safety procedures, which were useful provided a reference point was given as to where the student was located in the aircraft or on the map; by itself the map was meaningless. The student had no visual memory of the symbols used to represent AND/OR/NOT gates. The student had some visual memory of programming, namely Visual Basic, prior to losing his sight.

Diagrams

The task analysis proceeded to consider diagrams. A circuit diagram is the result of a design process that begins with a specification and, for analogue circuits, amounts to calculating component values for resistors, capacitors, and so on as appropriate for the selected transistors. By example, students are taught how to analyse and design specific circuits in such a way that they should be able to abstract the analysis and design strategies and then apply them to other circuits. The circuit diagram is central during the teaching and learning process, rather than a supplement or final result. It is used directly during the exposition on how the circuit works, what limits its performance, and how to go about calculating the component values. Analogue circuits are thus an excellent focus for understanding how diagrams can be explained to the visually impaired.

Before students learn to analyse and then design, they need to be able to "see" the artefact on which the exposition is based; for the visually impaired this means that the connectivity must be painted in their mind's eye. A schematic-based circuit (lines interconnecting symbols and annotated with text) is sufficiently semantic to be

automatically converted into a form suitable for a circuit simulator. This being so, a high-level oral description ("spoken" by a text-to-speech synthesiser) can also be generated; the question being: how should it be phrased? It is assumed that, in general, authors of course-ware that includes a spoken narrative would not be familiar with the needs of the visually impaired (including all that needs to be said). So, if possible, this extra information would be generated automatically by the computer.

The circuit diagram used is shown in Figure 1; it is more than suitable for illustrating the problems that the visually impaired would have if a computer spoke the description from its internal storage of that diagram. Three descriptions were created "by-hand", two (Figures 2 and 3) as if they had been automatically generated and a third version (Figure 4) created using a set of "human-empathic" rules and thought to be more difficult to generate automatically.

The three descriptions were presented at the task analysis: "Description by Components Top-to-Bottom, Left-to-Right"; "Description by location and node", and; "Description – Human-orientated" (Figures 2 to 4, respectively). Due to the possession of visual memory, the second description was thought to be "more everyday language", the third "more hierarchical".

The hierarchical structure was deemed to be an aid to cognition, however, the student chose the second description (Figure 3) which was also

Figure 1. Circuit diagram

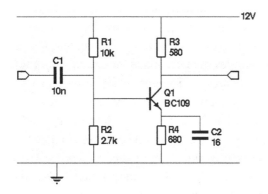

Figure 2. Description by components

This is a common-emitter amplifier consisting of 1 input, 1 output, 2 capacitors, 4 resistors and 1 transistor. There is one power rail and earth. The input is connected to capacitor C1. Capacitor C1 is 10nF and is connected to an input, to resistor R1, to resistor R2 and to the base of transistor Q1. Resistor R1 is 10k ohms and is connected to the 12 volt power rail, to resistor R2 and to the base of transistor Q1. Resistor R2 is 2.7k ohms and is connected to resistor R1, to the base of transistor Q1 and to earth. Transistor Q1 is a BC109. The collector of transistor Q1 is connected to resistor R3 and to an output. The base of transistor Q1 is connected to capacitor C1, to resistor R1 and to resistor R2. The emitter of transistor Q1 is connected to resistor R4 and to capacitor C2. Resistor R3 is 580 ohms and is connected to the collector of transistor Q1, to an output, and to the 12 volt power rail. Resistor R4 is 680 ohms and is connected to earth, to the emitter of transistor Q1 and to capacitor C2. Capacitor C2 is 16uF and is connected to resistor R4, to the emitter of transistor Q1 and to earth. An output is connected to resistor R3 and to the collector of transistor Q1. That's a common-emitter amplifier.

Figure 3. Description by location and nodes

This is a common-emitter amplifier consisting of 1 input, 1 output, 2 capacitors, 4 resistors and 1 transistor. There is one power rail, 12 volts, and earth. On the left is an input connected to C1. On the right is an output connected to R3 and to the collector of Q1. R1 and, to the right, R3 are connected to the power rail at the top. R2, and to the right R4 and C2 are connected to earth at the bottom. R4 and C2 are connected in parallel. On the left is C1 connected to R1, to R2, and to the base of Q1. On the right, R3 is connected to the collector of Q1. R4 is connected to the emitter of Q1. C1 is 10nF, R1 is 10k ohms, R2 is 2.7k ohms, Q1 is a BC109, R3 is 580 ohms, R4 is 680 ohms and C2 is 16uF. That's a common-emitter amplifier.

Figure 4. Human-oriented description

This is a common-emitter amplifier consisting of 1 input, 1 output, 2 capacitors, 4 resistors and 1 transistor. There is one power rail and earth. The input is connected through C1, 10nF, to the base of transistor Q1, a BC109. The base of transistor Q1 is biased by the potential divider provided by R1, 10k ohms, and R2, 2.7k ohms. R1 is connected to the power rail (12 volts) and R2 is connected to earth. Q1's collector resistor is R3, 580 ohms, which is connected to the power rail. Q1's emitter resistor is R4, 680 ohms, which is connected to earth. C2, 16uF, is connected in parallel with R4. The output is taken from the collector of Q1. That's a common-emitter amplifier.

the easier to implement. The interview revealed that the student:

- Did not know about AND/OR gates or appreciate what was meant by a table (of data).
- Used his visual memory of a grid to understand the position of AND and OR gates, and truth tables. People without spatial awareness would be unable to do this, and the grid would be meaningless.
- Understood "gate" to be a meaningful term, but an OR gate posed a problem. An everyday physical gate can be visualised, but not a previously unseen OR gate?
- Only had a tactile memory of resistors and capacitors.
- Having had the first schematic diagram description read to him, the student was lost by the 4th stage (i.e. very early on).

Navigation Advice

The navigation advice from the student was that the following information would be needed for navigating hyperlinked information (and some of these needs are also applicable for navigating schematics):

- Where are you?
- What can you do?
- When do you know you are there?
- How can you get back (not all pages have a home or back button)?
- Best naming convention for Lecture 15, slide 2, would be 15.2.
- Brief reminders of where you are at all times – particularly when moving to somewhere.
- Adopt the Digital Accessible Information System (DAISY), from RNIB, navigation standard as used in their audio books.
- Use spoken descriptions in preference to sound (i.e. do use audio icons).
- The speed of the voice should be controllable, as with Talking books (RNIB), using something like Control+Alt, though this would not be appropriate for those with physical impairments. For example, it would be impossible for a person who used a mouth stick for typing; instead, a special button box would be needed. Arrow keys might be adopted as an alternative.
- Best to keep speaking tone constant.

With the help of a computer science on-line tutorial the student commented that he found:

- Pauses included in the present audio-aided visual presentation were necessary, else the presentation was too fast.
- The presentation could be improved by the use of male and female voices, for example, male for the tutorial facts, female for the details.

Phase Three Results: Validation and Verification

For the follow-up meeting (Phase Three) with the student it was decided to make use of the T3 device to create an example set of UML diagrams. As previously stated in the electronics example, it would be difficult and time-consuming to prepare all detail and levels associated with use-case and class diagrams. This is partly due to the requirement to "register" every diagram for the T3 device, in order to generate a unique key for each diagram. It was hoped that the student's prolonged use of the T3 device in some key examples in a second year module that adopts UML, and also its use on the third year sandwich placement, would reveal more useful information as to the best way to use this device. An alternative and more tactile solution was introduced, based on Lego. The factors to do with colour, size and board boundaries could allow for a more interactive non-computing solution. Could the student work around a diagram? Could they construct a diagram? If two or more boards were available could it represent levels of hierarchy? It was hoped that the validation and verification of the findings from this work over the next six months would prove the use of a more tactile approach, particularly for non-Braille users.

The validation and verification of the UML exemplars (Duplo blocks) identified the following:

- The blocks that were used to represent different symbols, were distinguishable.

- Blocks provide 3D and fully tangible information.
- The student expert could not distinguish between the primary colours used for the blocks, but colours could aid partially sighted users.

For the electronics exemplar, a definition was first given for a teaching object as consisting of one or more visual slides, each with an accompanying aural narrative that is synchronised with any visual changes that occur. They are not videos of live lectures. Each slide (though not the individual changes) were to be provided as "haptic hardcopies". The validation and verification of the exemplars revealed the following aspects of the design.

Having teaching objects available before the live lecture would be useful, because it would enable the user to "get up to speed" before hand. All students should do this, but most, if not all, do not do it. If they did, they would probably get more out of the live lecture. However, most students do buy the booklet of slides before the start of the module.

It is thought that an mp3 player version would be useful for everyone. Designing the narrative with the visually impaired in mind means that it must also be suitable for sighted people with their mp3 players – they should not need (though they might appreciate) the visual support. So for each visual slide, it is necessary to concatenate all the constituent audio files, with suitable delays inserted between each audio file. The delay is currently set to 1.5 seconds, with 4.5 seconds delay at the end of each slide so that the end can be easily recognized when playing. The result is that each slide is equivalent to an audio track and a complete teaching object (on-line lecture) is equivalent to a musical album. Thus students can skip along the play-list and play the slide they want. Experience at York suggests that a 10 credit module-worth of on-line lectures will occupy no more than approximately 150Mbytes in the mp3 format – well within the capacity of a modern mp3 player. Sleeve notes are automatically created giving the title of each slide and its play-time, as well as the lecture's total play-time and disk occupancy.

Most sighted people feel a need to know how long the slide, and the complete teaching object, will take to play and this information is also needed by the visually impaired. For sighted people, this is often provided (thoughtlessly) by a visual ribbon that grows in length as the teaching object plays. Unless the ribbon is tucked out of the way, the movement will distract the eye from the more important animation that is designed to reinforce what is being explained (e.g. how the circuit is drawn to reflect a design). A simple time elapsed/total duration (as with a CD player) placed in a corner somewhere out of the way would be acceptable for sighted people.

For the visually impaired, directions required in the narrative: "I have 5 points to make …. My 4th point is …. My last point is … " These are equivalent to the visual directions in the narrative such as: "…at the top right of the slide…" used to direct the eye visually or virtually.

It will be necessary to judge how long it is before clock watching begins; slides that last longer than that will need the temporal direction (this is likely to be most cases). Unfortunately this is yet another thing to which authors have to attend and they are not used to it.

The animation on the slide needs to be overtly described to the visually impaired and while sighted people can see what is going on, they may still need to have it explained. So in these circumstances users need to be able to turn off the explanation. This implies that some audio files are always played, while others are not, and the software viewer has to be able to differentiate appropriately. This requirement is in addition to the need to differentiate between the spoken narrative and illustrative audio when the system is used in a live lecture. The narrative must be turned off,

but, for example, twenty seconds of Beethoven's symphony might be needed for illustration, or a small part of a great oration ("I have dream…") must be heard in the lecture theatre. The animation should be simply stated for everyone. The "I'll just get rid of clutter" (in the form of a warning to the sighted) is not satisfactory; instead, what is left to view and where that is, needs to be expressed.

The speed with which the narrative is played needs to be variable, but not for the reasons of compensating for a fast or slow lecturer. A fast rate is needed to skim aurally through that material which is already well understood and get (by listening out for keywords) to a position where more attention to detail is required. A slow rate is needed where the user wishes to take notes. For the visually impaired those notes will probably be made on the same computer that is displaying the teaching object. While the use of a pause (in playing the audio) might seem the obvious facility, only if it were foot controlled (for example) would that be acceptable. If, as is the case in the York viewer implementation the space bar is the pause (and pause release), the mouse has to be in the viewer window in order to invoke the pause; the mouse will actually be in the note-taking window. Window swapping will irritate the sighted, and frustrate the visually impaired.

Currently the speed of narration varies from half the original speed (80 to 90 words per minute) to twice the original speed (320 to 360 words per minute) in four steps in either direction. This might be enhanced with experience and feedback from users. The slowest speed must be compatible with a not-very-fast typing rate. Two function keys are used, the left one reduces the speed and the right one increases the speed. It is expected that visually impaired people will count the steps in order to reach their comfortable speed; if the user tries to go beyond the minimum or maximum speeds, a quiet double click is sounded; when arriving back at the originally recorded speed, a single click is heard. The speed can be changed as the system is playing.

In the York viewer the arrow keys move the user forwards or backwards through the linearly organised set of slides (up and down arrow keys are used to step either way through the slide's animation). When the user attempts to go beyond the last slide or back before the first slide, a "bong" is heard. Care must be taken not to over use different sounds in this way, as only the meaning of a few can be easily remembered.

The pause control (space bar) implemented in the York viewer causes the audio to be rolled back to the start of that sentence which was interrupted; so when the pause is released, the audio does not re-start "mid-blurt". The rationale for this is that it quickly reminds the listener of what was being said just before the pause was invoked and that this event would happen when the person was being interrupted by a telephone call or by a colleague. The student expert was adamant that they did not want this roll back and further questioning of the expert is needed; the roll-back feature seems to be an appropriate design decision and currently this is how it has been implemented for all speaking rates. To the authors this mechanism does not appear to impede progress.

Touch is an important sense for the visually impaired and thus should be exploited in order to enhance the system's communication with the user. It is possible to produce "haptic hardcopies" of black and white (no grey) screen dumps. After copying on to special paper and passing it through a heater, the black lines are raised above the surrounding white areas. The black lines can then be felt. Unfortunately the finger's acuity is quite poor so it is difficult to differentiate between, for example an AND gate and a NAND gate by touch alone, as the only difference is a small circle on the output connection. Given that (at York) slides are specified as schematic diagrams in the first place, the symbols can be automatically exchanged for ones that are more haptically visible though still connected in the same position (that is, diagrams are enhanced, not blown up). It must be remembered that an included visually-impaired student must

be able to point to haptic diagrams that are readily understood by sighted students, so the exchanged versions must not be radically different.

While the student expert admitted he could read by feeling text, the aesthetically pleasing proportional spaced fonts were more difficult to read (especially if they were "decorated") than mono-spaced fonts. In any case, characters probably have to be almost one centimeter in height. Converting the text to Braille while simple to perform, would cause the slides to become proportionally very large (Braille also has to be read with haptic senses that have low acuity). Practically speaking this rules out such a conversion. Alternatively, it is possible to lay the haptic hardcopy on to a tablet, inform the system what slide it is, and then let the visually impaired person point to the written text. The system would then speak that text; if a symbol were pointed to, it would say what the symbol was. To identify the haptic hardcopy, it would be necessary to annotate (in Braille and outside of the screen dump area) the module acronym/number, lecture number, and slide number. The position of the slide number around the screen dump would vary according to its value. So the number one would be on the far left, while the maximum slide number would be on the far right. The visually impaired would not need to learn Braille, the position of the number would be sufficient for its recognition. However, the number in Braille might encourage Braille to be learnt. When laid onto the tablet, selecting the acronym, lecture number and slide number would let the system recognize what slide it was and therefore what the text was on the screen dump. The slide text would not be changed to Braille so that sighted people would be able to help the visually impaired. Some means of ensuring that the haptic paper does not move on the tablet needs to be provided. The shirt cuff of a visually impaired person might catch the edge of the paper and the movement not be realised.

The tablet would be carried in a laptop case and plugged into the USB port of a PC. Pointing would amount to the tablet sending an (x,y) coordinate to the viewer. If the viewer were aware of which haptic hardcopy it was, it would readily identify to what the user was pointing. While text-to-speech is tedious when played continuously, it would feel less so because the user was interacting with it. This is similar to a telephone conversation where the poor sound quality only has to be listened to for brief moments, before the listener becomes the speaker. Alternatively, all the text on each slide would have to be recorded by the author of the slide and that is unlikely to be very acceptable to that author.

Of course, last minute updates that are so easy to do with electronic documents, would be less so if the haptic hardcopies also had to be changed. But this might encourage authors to get material correct in the first place!

CURRENT CHALLENGES FACING THE ORGANISATION

The current challenges are faced by all Higher Education establishments within the United Kingdom, but the findings of the case study now described are beyond the present disability legislative requirements and are highly pragmatic.

The distributed cognition of the student expert was mainly acoustic. Understanding diagrams appears to be the crux of the problem. The old (often misquoted) Chinese proverb: a picture is worth more than ten thousand words succinctly expresses the information content that may be contained in a diagram. Furthermore with the ability of the eyes to move at will (with none of the interference of pointing and clicking) the information can be re-presented to the cognitive processes of the brain for further evaluation. The understanding of the information is still serial but because the eyes provide an ability to "look back" and the brain knows precisely what is to be reviewed and can spot it, sight is said to be "parallel". This is particularly apparent when compared

with speech which is inherently serial; it requires physical interaction to move back and forth, and there is no clear indication of where anything is except to rely on a temporal memory of when it occurred. The temporal memory is usually inaccurate, requiring overt physical manipulation, which interferes with the information processing going on in the brain. It is essential that this parallel process of information gathering be accessible in a similar though alternative manner for those who are visually impaired; and this is particularly important where diagrams may be the only reasonable way in which information is conveyed. Learning something like UML for a computer science student would pose a major problem as it involves diagrams and programming code.

Given a haptic interface the hands can provide an alternative to the eyes, although the acuity is quite poor in comparison with normal sight. As the eye would serially follow the connection from a resistor to the collector of a transistor, so would the hands. But while the eye and brain together can quickly recognize symbols such as a resistor, the fingers and brain will be much slower and thus help, in the form of a computer recognizing what the user is touching and expressing what it is, will speed up the user's recognition. Furthermore for example, touching transistor Q5 might also invoke the additional comment that Q4 and Q5 operate as a differential pair – a well-known configuration in electronics that is drawn in a way that it is easily recognizable to those without visual impairment. This means that the diagram must be specified as a schematic; in which all the symbols are uniquely named; and software can interpret circuit fragments and describe them. Such descriptions might also be useful to those learners with normal sight, drawing attention to something they can see, but not readily appreciate. The haptic help needs to be switch-able (on/off). Adopting a touch tablet for user-interaction provides inclusiveness for the visually impaired.

SOLUTIONS AND RECOMMENDATIONS

The criteria identified for interface design for visually impaired students were as follows:

- Solutions should be inclusive (suitable for sighted, partially sighted and blind users).
- Solutions should be computer tractable.

These two criteria above may be diametrically opposite.

- Solutions should be dynamic.
- Metaphors should be meaningful to all ("doors", "rooms", "Lego" not "points to").
- Touch is best for orientation.
- Sound is best for input and output, unlike Braille it is inclusive.
- Colour contrast can help a large range of (but not all) people – different platforms render different colours with different hues and different brightness.
- Inclusion can be aided by multi-modal and multi-media interfaces.
- High-level names which are well understood by all should be adopted, so that an individual's short-term memory limitation (of between five and nine items) are not overly compromised (Benyon, Turner, & Turner, 2005); thus such naming helps to reduce overload (Preece, Rogers, & Sharpe, 2002).
- An emphasis on naming items followed by their use should also help consolidate sighted people's learning.
- Superfluous information or detail needs to be suppressed.

Overall the student expert thought the audio descriptions were "fantastic". Here are some further conclusions from the points made:

- The audio narrative of a lecture would be preferable in advance of the lecture.
- The audio description can be provided asynchronously and Podcast.
- Material needs initially to be given serially ("hearing is serial"), but should be randomly accessible after, so as to reinforce learning and/or provide explanation.
- The student expert felt that a gap between oral paragraphs (an oral paragraph is usually between one and four sentences) should be between one and one-and-a-half seconds, though a facility for customizing pace might be useful in addition to the ability to vary the speaking rate. The danger of course is that the more functions provided, the less likely their position on the keyboard will be remembered; so ideally, pace might change automatically with change in speaking rate.
- For the "haptic hardcopy", the larger version (slightly more than A4) was much better than the A4 version. This implies that the tablet must be large and therefore not very portable. In practice, with the ability to speak the text and help with the diagrams, an A4 size tablet might be acceptable.
- An orientation description of the tactile diagram is required at the start.
- Care must be taken to avoid ambiguity in a description of a diagram that would otherwise be resolved when looking at it.
- Characters in a proportional-spaced font appropriate for reading comfortably in a lecture theatre and printed on to A4 paper cannot be read when felt.
- Ideally, the tablet should be touch sensitive and not require a pen with umbilical chord.
- The student expert was able to follow a haptic slide whilst the audio description was played.
- A haptic diagram adds more information to an audio description.

- Tactile diagrams reduce the cognitive load considerably.
- Blocks could be assigned component descriptions, and with the aid of a board grid, could enable visually impaired students to construct circuit, UML and other diagrams.
- Generic technology could be built to enable component assignment for any diagrams and the output of tactile hardcopies, with optional audio descriptions.
- The additional information for visually impaired people may help sighted people (reinforce learning through multiple encoding). This could be made an option using a toggle switch – to switch on if required.

The final three points listed above are now the focus of a larger research project.

FURTHER READING

As there are no definitive sources in this specific area, the advice for further reading material beyond the references listed here, are publications in the areas of Interaction Design, Human-Computer Interaction, Multi-modal Interaction. For further reading material on disability legislation and current tools, then the web sites given within the references below are recommended. There are likely to be variations of these legislative and charitable organisations in different countries.

ACKNOWLEDGMENT

This work was funded by the Higher Education Academy subject network for Information and Computer Sciences Development Fund. The assistance and information provided by Mr. James Bird at the RNIB is gratefully acknowledged. We reserve our greatest thanks for the student expert at the University of Ulster, Mr Barry Toner, for his tolerance, considerable insight, and in making this project possible. Lego, Daisy, Dream, Duplo and T3, are registered trade marks or names.

REFERENCES

T3. (2006). *T3, RNIB Web Site.* Retrieved December 9, 2006, from http://www.rncb.ac.uk/t3/index.html

Benyon, D., Turner, P., & Turner, S. (2005). *Designing for Interactive Systems.* Reading, MA: Addison Wesley.

Bliss, J., Monk, M., & Ogborn, J. (1983). *Qualitative Data Analysis for Educational Research.* London: Croon Helm.

Graham, D. (1990). *Knowledge Acquisition: A Case Study in Computer Fault Diagnosis and Repair.* Unpublished PhD thesis, Brunel University.

Graham, D., & Barrett, A. (1997). *Knowledge-Based Image Processing Systems.* Berlin: Springer-Verlag.

Graham, D., Benest, I., & Nicholl, P. (2007). Cognitive Issues in Information Visualisation Design for Interaction for the Visually Impaired. In *Proc. of the 11th International Conference on Information Visualisation IV07, IEEE Computer Society*, ETH Zurich, Switzerland, 4-6 July 2007 (pp. 917-920).

Graham, D., Benest, I., & Nicholl, P. (2007a). Interaction Design for Visually Impaired Students: Initial Findings. In *Proc. of the 8th Annual Higher Education Academy Information Sciences HEA-ICS Conference*, University of Southampton, England, 28-30 August 2007 (pp. 116-12).

Graham, D., Benest, I., & Nicholl, P. (2007b). Interaction Design for Teaching Visually Impaired Students. In *Proc. of the International Association for the Scientific Knowledge, IASK E-ALT 2007 International Conference*, Porto, Spain, 3-6 December 2007 (pp. 80-89).

Johnson, L., & Johnson, N. (1987). Knowledge Elicitation Involving Teachback Interviewing. In Kidd, A. L. (Ed.), *Knowledge Acquisition for Expert Systems: a practical handbook* (pp. 91–108). New York: Plennum.

NCTD. (2006). *RNIB National Centre for Tactile Diagrams (NCTD) Web Site*. Retrieved December 9, 2006, from http://www.nctd.org.uk

NDA. (2006). Guidelines for Application Software Accessibility. *Irish National Disability Authority Guidelines Web Site*. Retrieved December 9, 2006, from http://www.acessit.nda.ie

Preece, J., Rogers, Y., & Sharpe, H. (2002). *Interaction Design beyond human-computer interaction*. New York: Wiley.

RNIB. (2006). Using a Computer without Vision and Notetaking. *RNIB Web Site*. Retrieved December 9, 2006, from http://www.rnib.org.uk

TeDub. (2007). The TeDub System (Technical Drawings Understanding for the Blind). *TeDub Web Site*. Retrieved April 23, 2007, from www.tedug.org/tedubsystem_en.html

Tiresias (2006). User Needs Summary. *Tiresias Web Site*. Retrieved December 9, 2006, from http://www.tiresias.org

Wai, Y., Kangas, K., & Brewster, S. (2003). Web-based Haptic Applications for Blind People to Create Virtual Graphs. In *Procs. of the 11th Symposium on Haptic Interfaces for Virtual Environment and Teleoperator Systems, 2003. HAPTICS 2003* (pp. 318-325). Retrieved April 23, 2007, from http://ieeexplore.ieee.org/Xplore/login.jsp?url=/ie15/8472/2296/01191310.pdf

KEY TERMS AND DEFINITIONS

Audio User Interface (AUI): Use of audio (hearing) to interface with a device such as a computer.

Graphical User Interface (GUI): Use of graphics (vision) to interface with a device such as a computer.

Inclusivity: Adopting approaches, methods and technologies which include and accommodate all people, irrespective of their membership of specific groupings, such as the physically impaired.

Interaction Design: Also includes Human-Computer Interaction (HCI). A more generic term, describing the design of interfaces for products, as well as computers.

Learning: An attribute of human cognition requiring the acquisition and internalising of knowledge.

Tactile User Interface (TUI): Use of haptics (touch) to interface with a device such as a computer.

Visual Impairment: Possessing vision outside the "normal" range, not readily correctable by relatively simple means, such as the wearing of spectacles, so that it poses particular difficulties.

Chapter 3
Blogging for Effective Teacher Education Course in English as a Second Language

Francis Bangou
University of Ottawa, Canada

Douglas Fleming
University of Ottawa, Canada

ABSTRACT

Two years ago, as teacher educators, the authors decided to integrate the use of blogs into their practice in order to contribute to the development of an understanding of the knowledge base related to the processes of teaching and learning English as a Second Language (ESL) and provide their teacher candidates with a space to critically reflect collectively and individually on course content. In this chapter, the authors use discourse analysis (Johnston, 2008) of semi-structured interviews conducted with these teacher candidates to explore how they use and perceive blogs within a course specifically focused on ESL teaching methods. This allows the authors to problematize the notion of technological integration in teaching and learning and complexify the notion of blogs as democratic spaces (Kuzu, 2007). On the basis of this analysis, the authors formulate four recommendations to guide teacher educators who are working in similar contexts.

INTRODUCTION

This case study took place at a Faculty of Education in a large Canadian research university. This institution has a history of teacher education excellence going back to the 1800s and has garnered numerous awards for its humanistic approach to education. The Faculty offers diverse undergraduate and graduate programs designed for the development

DOI: 10.4018/978-1-61520-751-0.ch003

of practitioners who are able to critically address current issues in education.

Every year, about 750 students attend the baccalaureate program in education in order to obtain their provincial certification to teach in public schools where English is the language of instruction at the primary and secondary levels. The age range of these teacher candidates is between 23-40 years. Although most of these teacher candidates have no prior teaching experience a significant number have taught abroad or in other jurisdictions within

Canada. The program is focused on developing teacher candidates who are knowledgeable, competent and reflective professionals. It is therefore crucial for teacher candidates to be aware of how to concretely and critically connect theory with their own practice.

The full-time eight-month intensive program of study for this certification consists of 36 course credits and a mandatory ten week practicum (5 weeks in the fall and 5 weeks in the winter). In 2008-2009 the tuition paid by teacher candidates in this program amounts to approximately $6,000 (Canadian) excluding ancillary fees and living expenses.

The course which is the focus of this case was one of the optional classes that teacher candidates could attend. It was a methodology course in English as a Second Language (ESL) worth 1.5 credits. The class met for three and a half hours once a week for 5 weeks. Four sections of the course were offered each year, two in the fall and two in the winter terms. Approximately 35 students enrolled in each. In this study, we report the findings related to three of these sections.

SETTING THE STAGE

In 2005, one of the goals of the university five-year academic strategic plan was to focus on learning that was focused on innovation and excellence. More specifically, one of the objectives was to increase the use of new technologies such as video conferencing, multimedia, and electronic portfolios. Since then, the university has invested a substantial amount of money on the installation of these technologies throughout campus and the provision of necessary technological assistance. There are more than 30 computer labs on campus and over 1,000 computers available to students. Most of the campus is now wireless and there are about 90 multimedia classrooms on campus equipped with Windows and Mac computers, internet connectivity, VHS videocassette players,

DVD players and LCD projectors. In case of emergency, the professors have access to telephones within the classrooms. Professors and students can also easily borrow a variety of multimedia equipments and download a multitude of software from university websites. Workshops and professional development courses focused on technology are also offered on a regular basis. Moreover, professors and students can access online course Web sites as well as other e-learning resources through the University's Virtual Campus.

In step with the rest of the campus, the Faculty of Education has embraced new technologies in significant ways for the last five years. The Faculty is currently expanding the number of multimedia rooms and has installed Smart Board technology in each one of its classrooms and meeting venues. Expertise in technology has become a major criterion in the hiring of professors, who are increasingly expected to integrate it into their course offerings and curricula. This is especially true in terms of on-line teaching innovations. Moreover, professors are increasingly expected to make use of more readily available equipment such as mobile computer cabinets, laptops and LCD projectors through the Faculty Resource Centre.

Information and Communication Technologies (ICT) have changed the traditional thinking about teaching and learning and it is now imperative for teachers to recognize that a new generation of computer literate learners craves intelligent and sophisticated learning resources and support from their instructors (Wang et al, 2008). It is then not surprising that the need for teachers who serve as models in using ICT in the classroom has increased (Kuzu, 2007). It is within this institutional context that we decided to integrate the use of blogs within our teaching practice.

The word weblog was coined by John Berger in 1997. It refers to a web-based tool that enables individuals to create interactive web pages (Rachaël, 2005). Blogs provide a space where writers (e.g. bloggers) can post their ideas and readers can add their comments to the blog content. According to

Kim (2008) it is important to compare weblogs to other Computer Mediated Communication (CMC) applications such as email so that one can make an informed decision regarding its use. The use of blogs in higher education has steadily increased and more research is being conducted around its use by both instructors and students (Nackerud & Scaletta, 2008; Lipka, 2006). A significant survey of 125 undergraduate students conducted by Scaletta (2006), revealed that most students did not write their blogs for large audiences and that most of the students' blogs were password protected. Students in the study communicated with small groups of contacts and used these blogs primarily for social networking and planning such as social event announcements. Another study, conducted by Kerawalla, Minocha, Kirkup and Conole (2009) characterized student behaviour on a blog that was part of an online distance learning course. The study revealed that blogging was an enjoyable experience for most students. They used their blogs primarily to build community, share ideas and find resources and support. The study also found that some students did not feel comfortable blogging. These students felt inadequate and often preferred blogging for themselves instead of interacting with their peers. The researchers in this second study concluded that within their context, it was important to make blogging activities flexible and voluntary to facilitate the appropriation of such tools.

Blogs are usually easily accessible and free. They are more likely to promote social as well as individual learning and since bloggers have control over the content of their entries students feel encouraged to be reflective and make comment (Lin & Yuan, 2006). Because they are so easy to set up and update, in recent years blogs have been extensively integrated into the classroom, notably in higher education. Blogs are often used by instructors as administrative tools that can be used to post information regarding information or facilitate discussion (Downes, 2004). Students may also be required to post their own blog entries

and comments (Krause, 2005). Scaletta (2006), argues that feeling comfortable with public writing takes time and that the benefits of blogging are usually achieved at a very slow pace. This is one reason that measuring associated outcomes soon after the end of a course is often frustrating for both the instructor and the student.

Kuzu (2007) conducted a study that investigated pre-service teachers' views on blog use for instruction and social interaction. The study revealed that a vast majority of the pre-service teachers' views on blog use for instruction and social interaction were positive. Kuzu concluded that blogs have the potential to enhance instruction and social interactions among individuals by transferring in-class activities outside of the classroom. It is now widely recognized that instructional activities mediated by blogs provide democratic space where learners can present their opinions and comment freely (Kuzu, 2007, Wu, 2006). Luehmann (2008), through the case analysis of a science-teacher, argued that blogs can also support teacher professional identity development. Through blogging the teacher in her study was able to reflect on her practice and engage in critical thinking. She concluded that 1) blogs provide learners with the opportunity to be self-directed; 2) to reflect; and 3) to develop one's thinking through interaction with the readers and knowledge brokering.

According to Murray & Hourigan (2008), in addition to the above qualities, blogs are considered to be useful also as language tools because they can be host on multilingual sites, learners can develop a variety of transferable skills, and they provide students with target language sites that can be analysed. Campbell (2003), identified three types of weblogs that are usually used in an English as a Second Language (ESL) classroom — the tutor blog, the learner blog and the class blog. According to Wu (2006), the tutor blog is a weblog that is run by the instructor. It can be used in a ESL class to provide daily reading activities; to explore English web sites; to promote online verbal interactions, or to provide information about the class. The learner blog is usually managed by an individual learner or a small group of learners. According to Wu, it is best suited for reading and writing classes. Finally, the class blog is the product of the collaboration of a class. It can be used as a classroom bulletin-board, or a space for international online exchanges. Weblogs are promising new tools to teach ESL because they are convenient for both teachers and students and can assist students in their learning but one also needs to be aware of issues related to etiquette, privacy, and authorship.

Case Description

As faculty members in this institution, one of our general objectives was to contribute to the development of reflective practitioners who were able to critically address current issues in ESL. As said previously, most of the teacher candidates had no previous teaching experience in the provincial public school context and, in fact, had never before attended a course on ESL methods. One of our biggest challenges was to provide, in a short period of time, the teacher candidates with basic understandings of the very complex field of ESL both in terms of K-12 credit programs and adult non-credit programs, while balancing theoretical and practical content. We wanted to give our students the opportunity to examine and practice fundamental concepts and approaches in a way that would allow them to determine how best to position themselves as ESL teachers. More specifically, at the end of the course, teacher candidates were expected to:

1. Demonstrate a basic understanding of some of the current issues, conceptual frameworks, methods and practices related to the teaching of ESL;
2. Illustrate how these issues influence teaching options for diverse populations of students; and

3. Determine their own orientation in terms of ESL teaching approaches, strategies and methods.

Since we only had five weeks to reach our goals, we thought that a blog would be the perfect medium to easily and inexpensively expand the space and time of the class and give teacher candidates a chance to critically reflect both individually and collectively on the information provided in the course. According to Lin & Yuan (2006), blogs are more likely to promote social as well as individual learning since participants have control over the content of their entries and feel encouraged to be reflective and make comments on the on-line contributions of others. As said earlier in this chapter, because weblogs are so easy to set up and update, in recent years they have been extensively integrated into the second language classroom (Almeida Soares, 2008) and we thought that integrating the blog would also allow us to be models in using a popular technological medium in an instructional context.

Technology Components

There are numerous ways of using blogs in higher education. Nackerud and Scaletta (2008) suggested two types of blogs that are mostly used in academia: *class-based blogs; and blogs by and for students*. According to Nacherud and Scaletta (2008), there are three types of class-based blogs. The first type is the *instructor created blog* that enables the instructor to provide students with relevant information about the class. The second type is *the student created blog* where students are required to create their individual blogs as part of a class assignment. The third type is the *instructors and students managed blog*. It is usually created by the instructor who first registers the students and then allows them to freely create new entries and post comments. As instructors, we decided to use an instructors and students managed blog for each of the section we were teaching. We used *blogger.*

com to design a blog for each section because it was easy to use and most students seemed to be familiar with it. *Blogger.com* is a web site that enables individuals or groups to create their own blog for free. After creating an account one can customize his/her blog by selecting a template and a variety of features related to one's privacy and connection to the audience. For instance, one can choose to make his/her blog invisible to the search engines and password protected. Moreover, one can also allow readers to add his/her blog to their readers account and dashboard. When posting a message one also has the option of adding photos and videos to posts. However, it is not possible to attach a text document. Readers can also easily post a comment after reading a message. Unfortunately, it is not possible to attach a document to a comment. One can also easily follow the interactions and access a message by clicking on the threaded tree that is always visible on the side of the interface.

As part of the course requirements, teacher candidates were expected to post on the blog a minimum of four entries of at least 100 words each. We provided students with the necessary login information to post their entries and make their comments and they were encouraged to post an entry after each class but it was not required as long as at the end of the course the totality of their contributions were posted. As instructors, we suggested in the course syllabus that they could address the following questions:

Did something in the class or readings unsettle, disturb, or otherwise "get to you"? If so, why? Did something disrupt taken-for-granted assumptions? Does it challenge and/or sustain your conception of ESL?

However, specific answers to these questions were not required and the teacher candidates were free to write about anything they wanted as long as it was related to ESL and was written in a professional and respectful manner. Moreover,

teacher candidates were also required to comment on at least four of their colleagues' entries. Each comment had to be at least 50 words long. The teacher candidates were reassured that their entries and comments were not subject to public access and could only be viewed by the professor and their fellow colleagues. Since this assignment was graded, it was crucial that the teacher candidates signed both their entries and their comments. The teacher candidates were strongly encouraged to make the blog their own. As professors, we decided against contributing to the blog ourselves because we did not want to control or influence the subsequent on-line conversations and interfere with the teacher candidates' potential feelings of ownership. We made sure that the teacher candidates knew that we were available to help them, particularly if they were not familiar with such media and provided an alternative assignment for those teacher candidates who did not feel comfortable using blogs.

Technology Concerns

Since this was the first time that we were integrating such tools into this context, it was important to assess if the blog did indeed expand the space and the time of the class and provide teacher candidates with opportunities to critically reflect on the content of the course both individually and collectively. After the course was over and the grades had been posted, we invited the teacher candidates to participate in a study that would allow us to analyse their knowledge base construction related to 1) ESL teaching and learning theories; 2) English Language Learners (ELL); and 3) Teaching. Part of the research focused on the blog contributions to the construction of such knowledge base. Of the approximately 90 teacher candidates enrolled in the three sections of the course, 31 responded to our invitations to share their blog entries: 9 from the first, 6 from the second, and 16 from the third. The blog entries and comments were analyzed using discourse analysis (Johnstone, 2008), a process that allowed us to map out both how the teacher candidates conceptualized the field of ESL and how their participation in the blog contributed to their learning. Moreover, eight of the 31 teacher candidates accepted to participate in a semi-structured interview regarding their experiences in the course and notably with the blog. After the data was collected, it was transferred into QSR qualitative research software, permitting us to look for reoccurring patterns and highlight some of the unique experiences we believe are relevant to the study.

The results revealed that most interview participants viewed using the blog as an enjoyable experience:

"Yeah that was fun."

The participants commonly mentioned that blogging was enjoyable mainly because it was an informal way for the teacher candidates to communicate with their colleagues and become aware of each other's opinions:

"And the blog –it was kind of more informal;"

"It just made me more aware of what other people were thinking."

The majority of the teacher candidates who were interviewed declared that, in contrast to typical classroom settings, they felt safe to express their opinions on the blog in large part because they did not have the pressure of a live audience. One expressed this feeling in this way:

"So, I think the blog gave people a space to do that but also, this may sound so cliché...but a safe space. So they're not, you know, they're not vulnerably standing in front of the class and explaining their experiences."

Another teacher candidate admitted that it was more enjoyable and safer because on the blog they

could direct the conversation the way they wanted without the lead of the professor:

"There's no instructor at the front of the classroom who's guiding your discussion in one direction or another or focusing your discussion."

One of the student teachers declared that contrary to a classroom setting everybody had a chance to express his/her opinion on the blog:

"So the people who maybe didn't talk as much in class were able to talk on the blog without being interrupted or without, I don't know...not being able to say things they want to say..."

Moreover, according to one respondent, the blog provided the teacher candidates with the opportunity to take the time to process the information:

Within the blog postings people would write really thoughtful things and have the time to spell it out, the way they were thinking of it. And then, you had sort of the time as the reader to kind of go through and reflect on it. It kept the thread of learning going.

Most teacher candidates appreciated the fact that the blog was an extension of the class:

"Like the class didn't end after the four hours; you still had to – you still were reading the blog and still writing on the blog, so..."

It was also provided them with additional space and time to further reflect on issues that were raised in class:

So, you know, you never have enough time in class and you say that in teaching as well. Professional development days...you never have enough time to just talk with teachers and hear about what they're doing and their great ideas; and with this class, the blog really kind of opened it up to see what other people had experienced

On the blog the teacher candidates created a community of learning where they were able to do both address issues that were pertinent to them:

"It gives them the opportunity to focus on an aspect that was important to them and pertinent to their own, you know, learning experiences as a student teacher,"

and learn from their colleagues:

The blog itself was wonderful but the blog and what it did in that I was able to get other people's opinions is what enlightened me to the idea that, you know what? Other people's opinions and ideas are very good resources for your teaching practice.

When analyzing the blog entries it becomes clear that learning from the community was appreciated and valued on the blog: Statement such as

"Good Luck this month everyone. I appreciated all of your personal stories and examples from actual ESL classes (especially since I have none of my own)"

*"***I** *think that setting up a natural, low-stress environment for all student evaluations is so important. This way* **we** *will be getting a better representation of what student can really do [emphasizes added]."*

Some students went a step further by systematically making reference to the blog community of learners through greetings such as "Hello classmates" and closures such as

"looking forwards to reading more of everyone's thoughts"

or

"thanks for reading & your comments and responses would be welcome."

Others specifically used the blog community to find more resource on an issue of their own interest:

"Hey everyone. I wanted to explore a bit on appropriate orientation for new ESL students. I'm curious to know if anyone has good strategies for welcoming a new ESL student."

In these cases the blog did contribute to the teacher candidates' learning by providing them with a space where they could reflect in an informal way on the content of the course collectively and individually and at their own pace. Moreover, two student teachers declared that participating in the blog enabled them to learn more about web based communication tools: It added to what people are saying so that added to my learning because I understood maybe more where they're coming from? I think it helped me too, like, to learn more about web resources, I guess? Web tools? Cause then I understood like, what a blog was and that everyone could add to it and now I understand what a wiki is 'cause I'm learning about that. Like, I have to do a class project right now; I have to make a website. Like, those kinds of things, they add because when I go to find a job and I'm like, 'I can create my own website', that's going to help me. Or like, I know what a blog is, 'cause some people might not even know what it is, right? So I think it helped me in that way, for sure.

It seems then that through this experience student teachers developed a better understanding of how ICT could be integrated in the classroom, which was another important goal that we wanted to achieve as members of this institution and as second language educators since it is now imperative for second language teachers to become technologically literate to use computers as an integral part of their teaching (Tognozzi, 2001, Bangou & Waterhouse, 2008).

However, a teacher candidate did admit that the blog wasn't as beneficial as there was an agenda – they had to write something based on the readings and it was mark based; this made him question the validity as he felt some people would be doing it because it was mandatory:

I'll be honest. It wasn't so beneficial...Yeah. And, and the reason is because the blog...there was an agenda for it. Like, the blog...you had to write something based on the readings or something like that. And then you were doing it because that was part of your mark. That was...so there was the motivation for doing it, itself.

This teacher candidate also felt that it was same people who always posted and that few people used it to engage in "critical thinking" and that there was a lot of validating and "piggy backing on other people's comments" rather than starting new conversations and questionings:

The other thing with the blog that I discovered was that it was really...it really was the same people over and over again to contribute. Like there was a few that I don't think ever did contribute, or that wouldn't really...wouldn't really post something that was more of a critical thinking type. It was more like, 'Oh yes. I agree with this.' Not so much of questioning, ahh...you know, 'cause I think there were people who questioned about learning and uh-m, what do you mean...they would say like, 'What do you mean by this?'

He believed the actual sharing "came from a human voice" in the classroom. Although teacher candidates were verbally encouraged to write about anything they wanted as long as it was related to ESL, the following sentence in the syllabus might have led him to think that the blog entries and comments had to be related to the readings:

"Each week you will be expected to make a contribution in a course blog that provides your reflections on the **course material** *[Emphasis added]."*

The course material consisted in part of lectures and readings from a textbook. However, the course relied more heavily on the readings since each week they had to read a chapter at home and we would also read a chapter in class. Moreover, most of the classrooms discussions addressed issues that were raised in the textbook. It seems that most of the teacher candidates might have the same opinion about the assignment since a majority of the blog postings were related to the course readings. Moreover, instead of building their reflection on other supports most teacher candidates relied on the questions provided in the course syllabus. Only few teacher candidates based their reflection on external material, like this teacher candidate who used an article that she found online:

To hopefully clear-up some of the ideas that were throwing around, I found this article online written by a Professor of Linguistics in Finland http://linguistlist.org/ask-ling/biling.html some of the more interesting parts of the article include: concerning teaching children more than one language at an early age

This leads us to also question the validity of our assignment, how committed were the teacher candidates if they approached this exercise mostly as another assignment that they had to complete? It is this question that we address in the next section.

Management and Organizational Concerns

If we consider that technological integration is shaped by the context in which it occurs, it is then impossible to investigate the way that technology is integrated in one's teaching practices without taking into consideration the social context in which it occurs. Technology is "constructed by the interaction between its design and how it is appropriated by its users" (Cutrim Schmid, 2006, p. 50). Therefore, technology is embedded within our everyday social practices that influence the way that it is used and the impact that it has on our lives. According to Feenberg's (1991) adaptation of *critical theory*, values and biases are integrated in the historical development and design of technology. Therefore, technology is not neutral and people cannot use it to perform any task they wish. Technology is, rather, a site of conflict and tension where "individuals and groups can struggle to influence and change technological design, uses and meanings" (Cutrim Schmid, 2006, p. 50). Stereotypes and power relationships that exist in the real world are also reproduced on the Internet (Nakamura, 2000). This is why it is also important to examine the power relationships that mold the way that technology is integrated. Moreover, we believe that in order to understand how technology is implemented within one's teaching practice it is critical to understand how it has been lived by the participants of this process.

As said previously, the Baccalaureate of Education was a very intense one-year program that included one practicum. To be able to attend the program full-time, some teacher educators had to quit their previous employment and take out government-sponsored loans. A few were able to obtain limited scholarships and bursaries. Therefore, the program required a full financial, intellectual and physical engagement. There was a lot at stake. Throughout the course a number of teacher candidates did struggle. Many did not complete their assignments on time and asked for extensions. Within such a context, the teacher candidates were not willing to take any risks that might jeopardize their success, and they developed some strategies to cope with the intensity of the program. For instance, as a time management strategy some teacher candidates decided to rank

the assignments they had to complete in one session and dedicated most of their time to the ones they thought required the most effort and had a higher percentage on their final grade. Once, a teacher candidate said to the first author that she did not complete one of the assignments because she did not have enough time and had to focus on the ones she thought were most critical. The blog contributions were worth 20% of the final grade which was the lowest percentage of the three assignments that they had to complete in the course — the other assignments were each worth 40% of the final grade. Although, the teacher candidates were strongly encouraged to post a blog entry or a comment every week it was not required as long as at the end of the course the totality of the required entries and comments were posted on the blog. A majority of teacher candidates decided to post their blog entries and comments at the last minute:

"I think what happened was a lot of people ended up saving their blogs for the very end so that last week they really hammered out, you know, four or five blogs, or whatever the required amount was."

Only a minority of teacher candidates regularly posted an entry or a comment on the blog and a smaller number did complete more postings than required. We wanted teacher candidates to own the space that we provided them, however, because of the nature of the program for most of them it became an additional constrain that they had to complete, and most of them decided to post their entries and comments at the last minute. To fully participate in the blog discussion and take full advantage of the reflective practice it would have been best if it had been done on a regular basis and not in the hurry at the last minute. As said previously teacher candidates were not willing to take any risk that might jeopardize their success and this is why most of them preferred to rely on what was indicated on the course syllabus.

As second language teacher educators we believe that it is crucial to address issues of equity within the field of ESL, and we made a point in class to talk about issues such as racism and other discriminations. One of our goals as teacher educators was to provide teacher candidates with multiple perspectives on the issue raised in class, and the blog was a medium we thought would allow us to achieve such goal by providing student teachers with the opportunity to confront their own opinion as well as the ones of their colleagues. To be able to do so it was important for teacher candidates to not be afraid to address controversial issues such as racism or sexism. It was also important that they felt comfortable to express their opinion even if it was unpopular. As teacher educators we were aware of the fact that our opinion could be overpowering and we thought that by not intervening on the blog the teacher candidates would feel more comfortable expressing their opinions even if they were contentious. It is true that to some extent teacher candidates were not afraid to disagree with some of the ideas that were expressed in class or on the blog, and statements such as

"some of the ideas are not realistic"

"I will have to disagree with the author…"

"I wholeheartedly agree with the authors about the importance of providing rich and meaningful reading experiences for ESL;" "we need to provide support for them within the pedagogical context of the classrooms."

It might be the reason why a majority of the comments were just validations of what had been said in the entry, like in the following examples:

"Your points are well taken and you're absolutely right,"

or "I liked the same section of chapter 3 as well."

However, one teacher candidate admitted that using the blog was fun because he could just "rant" and tear his colleague's arguments apart:

I mean, I would just pick some…I would, I would just, it was the same kind of…I mean I didn't, I would find some person's entry and I would read it and then I would critique it and that was all I would do. I wouldn't comment, I wouldn't make up my own things. I would just kind of, kind of tear other people's arguments apart

His goal was to systematically critic the opinions he disagreed with. He admitted that he did not do the readings and often he would not know what people were talking about. However, he used the blog as a way to make his opinion known:

Some of it was obviously related to the textbook and I kind of didn't know what some of those people were talking about because if I hadn't read the textbook then you know… (Laughs). But, but the stuff that was brought up in the lectures, uh-m, the theory parts of it, if I disagreed than I would make my views known. It was good. It was a good idea to have that blog.

Such behavior was still very atypical on the blog. Once, the first author had an informal conversation in class with the teacher candidates regarding the blog, and they admitted that the reason why most of their postings and comments were so "cliché" was because they knew that the professor was going to read them. They knew that they were not going to be marked on the content but it did not matter. They admitted that it would have been better if it had been anonymous. It is true that for most teacher candidates the blog provided a safe and pleasant space to reflect but it was mostly because they could do it in an informal manner, at their own leisure and they did not have to the pressure of a live audience. The teacher candidates were also aware that their postings were part of the course requirements and it impacted the way that they managed their reflection. It was as if within the blog community the teacher candidates knew that there was a line that they could not to cross, like in the following blog entry:

Foot in Mouth Disease – Comparing ESL and Learning Disabilities I tend to be someone who likes to trigger controversial topics and discussions:) With that in mind, I suspect that this may be yet another example of me putting my foot in my mouth, but hopefully it will still provide some useful thoughts (or at least trigger someone else to say something useful). I alluded to this in class today trying to make it more concrete in my head before blurting it out, but I suspect in some ways we can make connections between how the ESL student and the IEP student are handled in the classroom...

This teacher candidate was aware of the fact that she was about to express an unpopular opinion about a controversial issue. She felt compelled to start her entry with a series of statements she thought would help the reader understand her behavior. As the title explains, it was not her fault she was ill: "Foot in mouth disease." Within the community of the blog she clearly identified as an outsider — someone who "likes to trigger controversial topics," which implied that the rest of the community did not like controversy. It is true that blogs have the potential to provide democratic spaces were bloggers can express their ideas and opinions freely, however, within the instructional context of an university program such potential is grounded within historical processes associated with the acts of teaching and learning; such processes do influence the way that one will integrate such medium within his/her learning and/or teaching practices. Within the institutional context of this case grading is one of the historical processes associated with teaching and learning

that impacted the way that the teacher candidates integrated the blog within their learning practice. As professors we never intervened on the blog but we were still very much part of it because the teacher candidates knew that we were going to read their postings and grade them. They knew that we could make them succeed or fail and it was quite an immense power considering everything that was at stakes for them. Whether we wanted it or not, as professors we were the leaders of this community both in class and on the blog.

SOLUTIONS AND RECOMMENDATIONS

In the previous section, we highlighted that fact although the blog did provide a space where student teachers could reflect in an informal way on the content of the course collectively and individually and at their own pace, it was not used to its full potential mostly because of managerial and institutional constraints. Most teacher candidates did not contribute to the blog on a regular basis and decided to post their comments and entries at the last minute. Moreover, it seemed that most of them did not feel safe to address any issue considered controversial or express contentious opinions. Some went so far as to state that it would have been better if the entries and messages were anonymous.

"It's funny because I feel like the blog was supposed to be this safe place so you could have that discussion; but I think without parameters on it, people don't..., it's a shame...because if you're not forced to do it, you don't do it right?"

We believe that this quote illustrates the paradox that we were confronted with as teacher educators. Originally, we thought that it would have been easier for the teacher candidates to make the blog their own if we did not participate in the discussions and if we kept the requirements to a minimum. However, it seems that within our institutional context it might not have been the best approach. The fact that we did not participate did not remove the power relations at work in this context..

Recommendation 1: All the expectations and instructions should be clearly written on the syllabus and consistently applied.

The essential information about the requirements was written in the syllabus. However, important information was also verbally provided in class and both were sometimes contradictory. For instance, it was noted in the written syllabus that they were expected to post one entry and one comment every week on the blog, but as the class progressed, we altered this by telling them verbally that they did not have to do it every week as long as at the end of the session the totality of the required messages were posted. In our institution the course syllabus is considered to be a contract between the professor and the students and it is the core document of reference. Since the teacher candidates were not willing to take any risk that might jeopardize their final grades, they relied mainly on what was written in the course syllabus. This is why we believe that it would have been more effective if all the instructions were clearly stated in the syllabus and consistently adhered to as the course progressed. For instance, it would have been best to also specify that being critically reflective in blog contributions was expected. By doing so, we might also have been able to avoid the confusion generated by the difference between our verbal and our written instructions.

Recommendation 2: Make it mandatory to post an entry and a comment every week.

As previously demonstrated in part because of the intensity of the program most of the student teachers posted their entries and their comments at the last minute. Consequently, it was very difficult for these teacher candidates to take full advantage of the discussions that were taking place on the blog. Moreover, we believe that the quality of the reflection would have been better if everybody posted a message on a regular basis. Then, the teacher candidates would have had more opportunity to feed their reflections with the ideas of all their peers and not just a few. Following on what a teacher candidate said earlier *"if you're not forced to do it, you don't do it right?"* within our institutional context it would have been best if the teacher candidates were required to post a message and an entry every week or if they were required to post at least one entry on a subject related to ESL that was not addressed in class.

Recommendation 3: Provide explicit guidance

At first we thought that on the blog teacher candidates could easily expand their reflection on what was addressed in class. However, because of the intensity of the program and the power relationship that were in place most of the teacher candidates did not feel comfortable addressing issues they felt might jeopardize their success. Within our institutional context, it would have been best if we had scaffolded the teacher candidates' reflective practices. For instance, to boost their reflection and encourage them to go beyond the context of the course we could have suggested every week topics for debates or asked questions that could be addressed on the blog.

Recommendation 4: Be a model

Teacher candidates would have felt more comfortable sharing their views if the postings were anonymous but in our institution we could not make the economy of a grade. Good leaders are the ones who can model the behaviors and attitudes that would lead the group to a collective goal. In our institutional context, another way to guide the teacher candidates could have been to participate in the blog discussions and model the behaviors and attitudes we expected from the teacher candidates. For instance, we could have modeled what it means to be critical and show that it was ok to talk about controversial issues in an un-politically correct manner. By doing so student teachers would have felt more comfortable to do the same and the one who did not know what "being critical" meant could have had a model to rely on.

REFERENCES

Almeida Soares, D. (2008). Understanding class blogs as a tool for language development. *Language Teaching Research, 12*(4), 517–533. doi:10.1177/1362168808097165

Bangou, F., & Waterhouse, M. (2008). On becoming technologically literate: A Multiple Literacies Theory perspective. *E-learning, 5*(4), 445–456. doi:10.2304/elea.2008.5.4.445

Campbell, A. P. (2003). Weblogs for use with ESL classes. *The Internet TESL Journal, 9*(2). Retrieved July, 5, 2009 from http://iteslj.org/Techniques/Campbell-Weblogs.html

Cutrim Schmid, E. (2006). Investigating the use of interactive whiteboards technology in the English language classroom through the lens of a critical theory of technology. *Computer Assisted Language Learning, 19*(1), 47–62. doi:10.1080/09588220600804012

Downes, S. (2004). Educational blogging. *EDUCAUSE Review, 29*(5), 14–26.

Feenberg, A. (1991). *Critical theory of technology.* New York: Oxford University Press.

Johnstone, B. (2008). *Discourse Analysis.* Blackwell Publishing.

Kerawalla, L., Minocha, S., Kirkup, G., & Conole, G. (2008). Characterising the different blogging behaviours of students on an online distance learning course. *Learning, Media and Technology, 33*(1), 31–33. doi:10.1080/17439880701868838

Kim, H. N. (2008). The phenomenon of blogs and theoretical model of blog use in educational contexts. *Computers & Education, 51,* 1342–1352. doi:10.1016/j.compedu.2007.12.005

Krause, S. D. (2005, June 24). Blogs as a tool for teaching. *The Chronicle of Higher Education,* B33.

Kuzu, A. (2007). Views of pre-service teachers on blog use for instruction and social interaction. *Turkish Online Journal of Distance Education, 8*(2), 34–51.

Lin, H.T., & Yuan S.M. (2006). Taking blogs as a platform of learning reflective journal. *ICWL,* 38-47.

Lipka, S. (2006, January 27). A blog gives professors space to vent about their students. *The Chronicle of Higher Education,* A37.

Luehmann, A. L. (2008). Using blogging in support of teacher professional identity development: A case study. *Journal of the Learning Sciences, 17*(3), 287–337. doi:10.1080/10508400802192706

Murray, L., & Hourigan, T. (2008). Blogs for specific purposes: Expressive or socio-cognitivist approach? *ReCALL, 1*(20), 82–07.

Nacherud, S., & Scaletta, K. (2008). Blogging in the academy. *New Directions for Student Services, 124,* Wiley Periodical Inc., 71-87.

Nakamura, L. (2000). Where do you want to go today? Cybernetic tourism, the Internet, and transnationality. In Kolko, B., Nakamura, L., & Rodman, G. (Eds.), *Race in Cyberspace* (pp. 15–27). New York: Routledge.

Rachaël, F. K. (2005). *An explanatory study on how weblog technologies fit virtual community members' social needs*. Paper presented at the Eleventh Americas Conference on Information Systems, Omaha, NE.

Scaletta, K. (2006). *To whom are these texts valuable? An inquiry into student blogging*. Retrieved from http://www.inms.umn.edu/events/past/newresearch_2006/papers/scaletta.pdf

Tognozzi, E. (2001). Italian Language Instruction: The Need for Teacher Development in Technology. *Italica, 78*(4), 487–498. doi:10.2307/3656077

Wang, K. T., Huang, Y. M., Jeng, Y. L., & Wang, T. I. (2008). A blog-based dynamic learning map. *Computers & Education, 51*, 262–278. doi:10.1016/j.compedu.2007.06.005

Wu, C. (2006). Blog in TEFL: A new promising vehicle. *US-China Education Review, 3*(5), 69–73.

ADDITIONAL READING

Bella, M. (2005). Weblogs in education. In Hoffman, B. (Ed.), *Encyclopedia of Educational Technology*. Retrieved July 5, 2009, from http://coe.sdsu.edu/eet/articles/blogsined/index.htm

Bloch, J., & Crosby, C. (2006). Creating a space for virtual democracy. *Essential Teacher, 3*(3), 38–41.

Blood, R. (2000). Weblogs: A History and Perspective. *Rebecca's Pocket*. Retrieved April 6, 2009, from, http://www.rebeccablood.net/essays/weblog_history.html

Blood, R. (2002). *Weblog Handbook: Practical Advice on Creating and Maintaining your Blog*. Cambridge, MA: Perseus Publishing.

Blood, R. (2002). *We've got blog: How weblogs are changing our culture*. Cambridge, MA: Perseus Press.

Bruns, A., & Jacobs, J. (2006). *Uses of Blogs*. New York: Peter Lang.

Camilleri, B., Ford, P., Leja, H., & Sollars, V. (2008). *Blogs: Web journals in language education*. Council of Europe.

Dickey, M. (2004). The impact of web-logs (blogs) on student perceptions of isolation and alienation in a web-based distance learning environment. *Open Learning, 19*, 279–291. doi:10.1080/0268051042000280138

Divitini, M., & Haugalokken, O. (2005). Blog to support learning in the field: Lessons learned from a fiasco. In Proceedings of the Fifth IEEE International Conference on Advanced Learning Technologies (pp. 219-221). Washington, DC: IEEE Computer Society.

Du, H. S., & Wagner, C. (2006). Weblog success: Exploring the role of technology. *International Journal of Human-Computer Studies, 64*, 789–798. doi:10.1016/j.ijhcs.2006.04.002

Ebenezer, J. V., Lugo, F., Beirnacka, D., & Puvirajah, A. (2003). Community building through electronic discussion boards: Pre-service teachers reflective dialogues. *Journal of Science Education and Technology, 12*, 397–411. doi:10.1023/B:JOST.0000006299.07433.eb

Efimova, L., & Fiedler, S. (2004, March). *Learning webs: Learning in weblogs networks*. Paper presented at the IADIS International Conference Web Based Communities 2004, Lisbon, Portugal.

Eteokleous, N. (2008). Evaluating computer technology integration in a centralized school system. *Computers & Education, 51*, 669–686. doi:10.1016/j.compedu.2007.07.004

Huann, T., John, O., & Yuen, J. (2005). Weblogs in education a literature review. *Edublog.net*. Retrieved July 1, 2009, from http://edublog.net/mt4/2005/09/weblogs-in-educ.html

Kerawalla, L., Minocha, S., Kirkup, G., & Conole, G. (2009). An empirically grounded framework to guide blogging in higher education. *Journal of Computer Assisted Learning, 25*(1), 31–42. doi:10.1111/j.1365-2729.2008.00286.x

Krause, S. D. (2004). When blogging goes bad: A cautionary tale about blogs, email lists, discussion, and interaction. *Kairos, 9*(1). Retrieved April 8, 2009, from http://english.ttu.edu/kairos/9.1/binder.html?praxis/krause/index.html

Martindale, T., & Wiley, D. (2005). Using weblogs in scholarship and teaching. *TechTrends, 49*(2), 55–61. doi:10.1007/BF02773972

Nardi, B. A., Schiano, D. J., Gumbrecht, M., & Swartz, L. (2004). Why we blog. *Communications of the ACM, 47*, 41–46. doi:10.1145/1035134.1035163

Richardson, W. (2009). *Blogs, wikis and podcast and other powerful web tools for classrooms* (2nd ed.). Thousand Oaks, CA: Corwin Press.

Rubin, V. L., & Luddy, E. D. (2006). Assessing credibility of weblogs. In *Proceedings of the AAAI* Spring Symposium on Computational Approaches to Analysing Weblogs. College Park, MD: University of Maryland.

Shoffner, M. (2006). We don't have the liberty of being brainless: Exploring preservice teachers' use of weblogs for informal reflection. *Dissertation Abstracts International* (UMI No. 3207340).

Stiler, G. (2003). Blogging and blogspots: An alternative format for encouraging reflective practice among preservice teacher. *Education, 123*(4), 789.

Stone, B. (2004). *Who let the Blogs out?* New York: St Martin's Press.

Warlick, D. (2007). Classroom Blogging (2nd ed.). Lulu.com.

Williams, J., & Jacobs, J. (2004). Exploring the use of blogs as learning spaces in the higher education sector. *Australasian Journal of Educational Technology, 20*, 232–247.

KEY TERMS AND DEFINITIONS

Blog Entry: A blog entry refers to the original posting of a person

Blog Comment: A blog comment is the response to an entry. It is usually attached to the entry and is written by another blogger.

Blogger: The word blogger refers to the individual who writes blogs.

English Language Learner: In our context an English language learner referred to a student whose first language was not English or was a variety of English that was different from the one spoken in the schools and needed additional support.

Teacher Candidate Knowledge Base: This concept refers to the fundamental knowledge acquired during a teacher education program that will serve as foundation for the knowledge that they will acquire later as teachers.

Technological Integration: This concept refers to the process of interpretation, utilization, construction and reconstruction of technology within an educational context.

Weblog: The word weblog aka blog refers to a web-based tool that enables individuals with basic technological skills to create interactive web pages (Rachael, 2005). Blogs provide a space where writers (e.g. bloggers) can share their ideas and readers can be co-authors by adding their comments to the blog content

Chapter 4

Adopting Synchronous Audiographic Web Conferencing:
A Tale from Two Regional Universities in Australia

Birgit Loch
Swinburne University of Technology, Australia

Shirley Reushle
University of Southern Queensland, Australia

Nicola Jayne
Southern Cross University, Australia

Stephen Rowe
Southern Cross University, Australia

ABSTRACT

This chapter provides a comparative study of two Australian regional universities with a similar student profile as they investigate the use of synchronous audiographic web conferencing as a learning and teaching tool. In both universities, the trials of the web conferencing tool, Elluminate Live! (Elluminate) were initially driven by individual academics with an interest in new technologies. While similar in some aspects at the beginning, the two universities then approached the software trials in different ways. As part of this comparison, issues and challenges relating to software trials in educational environments are highlighted, and recommendations provided for others who may be considering the adoption of similar technologies.

DOI: 10.4018/978-1-61520-751-0.ch004

INTRODUCTION

The two regional Universities under reference in this case currently have similar student and delivery profiles, with a high proportion of off-campus (distance) students. The two universities are similar in that they both have small on campus and large distance student populations, and have track records for exploring the use of emerging technologies to improve the student experience.

One regional university has more than three quarters of the 26,000 enrolled students studying at a distance in local, national and international locations, while in the case of the second regional university, distance proportion is just over half of their 15,000 enrolled students. For both universities, many students live in remote areas with no physical access to libraries or face-to-face study groups. Moreover, a large percentage of students are of mature age, working full-time and fitting part-time study into their busy schedules.

SETTING THE STAGE

This chapter adds to the emerging literature on the use of modern audiographic tools identified in a review by de Freitas and Neumann (2009). It brings together approaches adopted by two regional Australian universities – the University of Southern Queensland (USQ) and Southern Cross University (SCU) as they investigate the use of web conferencing as a learning and teaching tool. A comparison is made of the paths to, adoption of and lessons learned from the use of web conferencing to provide education and development opportunities at USQ and SCU. The web conferencing tool, Elluminate, was trialled at both universities, with the process in both institutions being initially driven by individual academics (teachers) with a desire to investigate the pedagogical benefits of new and emerging technologies. While the trials were in some aspects alike at the beginning, the two universities then continued along different

paths. Although the pedagogical considerations were comparable, the processes of evaluation, promotion of the technology to create a user base and the decision to adopt a web conferencing tool following the trials took quite different paths. For instance, at SCU the use of Elluminate has continued to expand while at USQ, despite the success of the trial, a different web conferencing tool has been adopted. Consistent with the aim of this book, these adaptations will be explored using the STEP dimensions, and the issues and challenges faced in each dimension will be highlighted.

The chapter is structured as follows. First, an overview of the organisational background of the two universities sets the stage by providing information on technology use for learning and teaching before the trials and then outlines the institutional moves to flexible modes of delivery. Information about the university contexts is provided as well as the motivations for using the web conferencing technology. Descriptions of the trials at institutional level are followed by more detailed case studies of two courses (one at each university) where the technology was implemented to support enhanced pedagogical outcomes. The chapter concludes with a discussion of issues and challenges identified by each institution along with a variety of recommendations.

USQ moved into distance education via dual mode teaching in 1977 as a viable alternative to the offerings at traditional universities (Reushle & McDonald, 2000). SCU entered this realm much later in the early 1990s but for similar reasons. This provision of distance education as well as classroom-based teaching has given both institutions a "multimodal" label. In traditional Australian distance education, a typical learning package consists of print-based materials sometimes supported by audio, video and computer-based resources. The package is designed to enable learners to interact independently with the materials. Frequently distance students were also supported by teletutorials and/or face-to-face workshops once or twice a semester. The emergence of learning management systems (LMS) around the turn of the century provided opportunities to address the traditional independence and isolation of distance learners largely through the use of asynchronous discussion features available within the LMS. This has generally led to a requirement for students to have reliable Internet access.

Focus on Learning Management Systems

In the early days of online deliberations at USQ and SCU, the tendency was to focus on learning management systems (LMS), with online material delivery and asynchronous and synchronous text-based discussions. While asynchronous discussion groups have been shown to be very successful in socio-constructivist learning paradigms, for example in the context of business courses (Birch & Volkov, 2005; Rowe, 2003) and those with primarily an education focus (Reushle & McDonald, 2004), they tend not to be utilised as much for symbol-based communication in disciplines such as sciences, mathematics or statistics. One of the reasons for this is that these disciplines require specialised tools for online communication not necessarily available through standard LMS, for instance the option to write or draw on a (synchronous) shared whiteboard while being able to talk about a topic through a text or voice-based channel.

The lack of such tools and frustration for instructors and students led to experimentation by individuals at USQ with a variety of web collaboration tools. A free synchronous chat client using text-based posts was tested in the disciplines of mathematics and statistics (Loch & McDonald, 2007). Other studies were conducted exploring innovative tools including the work by de Byl and Taylor (2007) who investigated the Web 2.0 ethos with respect to the pedagogical applications of 3D online virtual environments, and the research by Hafeez-Baig and Danaher (2007) into using mobile learning technologies. Web conferencing was seen

as promising technology to explore as it offers a variety of tools in one package, such as voice, video, text, shared screen and whiteboard.

At SCU, the use of LMS began in the late 1990s. Despite a slow uptake due to some less than promising initial trials (Hayden, Saenger & Parry, 1999), a good deal of experience and knowledge about online course delivery was learned (Statham, 2001) as well as the impact on assessment, especially for distance students (Morgan & O'Reilly, 1999). Once a stable LMS was in place, it was used, as at USQ, for online support, material delivery and asynchronous and synchronous text-based discussions (Newton & Ledgerwood, 2001). A range of uses of asynchronous text-based discussions in social sciences and business showed their value for flexible assessment and non-assessment activity encouraging student choices and improved time management (O'Reilly & Newton, 2002; Rowe, 2004; Vitartas & Rowe, 2003).

From Audiographics to Web Conferencing

Given the regional spread of students, reduction of the gap between services provided to on-campus and distance students has been a long term consideration at both universities. After early trials at USQ and SCU with audiographics in the 1990s, this technology was abandoned as it required student and teacher to attend sessions in dedicated physical spaces at agreed times and therefore lacked flexibility, did not reach all students and there was no provision to record and play back sessions which excluded those who could not attend.

Audiographics largely disappeared as the Web moved from institutional to private and commercial use and carried more educational content, allowing students to search and interact with resources and with each other. This change saw the standalone audiographic facility being replaced by web-based audiographics.

From the second half of the 1990s, many technology limitations evaporated as the use of the Internet grew and the technical capabilities of the Web evolved (Rowe, Ellis & Bao, 2006). Some of these technical improvements included cheaper, more reliable hardware and faster Internet connections for private use, allowing access to a broader range of participants from a wider range of physical locations. Emerging audiographic tools also worked across different platforms (Macs and PCs) allowing participation on computer equipment familiar to the participant. Very importantly, dramatic advances in storage capacity and compression techniques allowed the ability to record and playback sessions adding considerable learning opportunities for flexible review of the live session activity for those unable to participate.

Recent research has shown students have a strong appreciation for the flexibility and convenience offered by lecture recordings in an increasing variety of formats (Williams & Fardon, 2007). Current research reinforces what has been known (for example Dekkers & Cuskelly, 1990) about the reasons students give for their need and appreciation of the flexibility and convenience of recording of classes. These include a backup for when they are not able to attend classes due to illness, disability, work and family commitments, travel constraints, an additional study tool for revision of content and comprehension of complex concepts, ability to study at their own pace or to manage timetable clashes, and to minimise language barriers (McElroy & Blount, 2006; Phillips, Gosper, McNeill, Woo, Preston & Green, 2007).

Current web conferencing tools incorporate VoIP (Voice over Internet Protocol) for natural communication, a whiteboard and other integrated applications. The synchronous and asynchronous features of web-based audiographics when used in conjunction with a LMS enable a similar experience for all users without being constrained by access to institutional teaching and learning infrastructure. These technologies offer a fresh opportunity to explore richer, more student-centred learning environments and offer the potential to fulfil the purposes of the learning paradigm proposed by Barr and Tagg (1995, p. 16): " … produce learning, elicit student discovery and construction of knowledge, create powerful learning environments, improve the quality of learning and achieve success for diverse students".

Flexibility Agenda

Most of the technology explorations at USQ and SCU described above were conducted by individuals with interest in these tools, and have since moved into mainstream use. This is reflected at both universities by recent institutional efforts to move towards flexible study modes facilitated through technology, where the boundaries between on campus and distance students are increasingly

Table 1. timeline for USQ's trials of web conferencing

Period	Stage	Scope
Sept. 2006-Feb. 2007	Individual trials of Elluminate	Trial licences, in two courses (education and mathematics)
Feb. 2007	Report provided	
July-Nov. 2007	Institutional trial of Elluminate	All volunteering lecturers
Aug. & Oct. 2007	Reports provided	
Nov. 2007- Feb. 2008	Institutional trial of Wimba	All volunteering lecturers
Since Feb. 2008	Decision to adopt Wimba, roll out	Available to all lecturers

less rigid. Both universities have realised the importance of flexibility across all disciplines and included provision of "flexible learning experiences" as a direction in their strategic plans (USQ Strategic Plan 2009-2013; New Directions for Delivery at Southern Cross 2007). The use of web-based audiographics is mentioned in particular as offering a "virtual classroom" where synchronous communication is available in text, audio and shared media (USQ L&T Plan, 2009; Clark, 2009).

Further descriptions of the two university contexts follow including how the incorporation of web conferencing software and adaptation of the traditional distance delivery model has improved education and development opportunities for students and staff irrespective of their geographical location.

PEDAGOGICAL CONSIDERATIONS ADDRESSING THE STEP DIMENSIONS

Approaches to the Trials

The trials of the web conferencing tool described in this paper originated from a need by teachers to fulfil certain pedagogical and technical requirements. In the USQ context, the teachers initially experimented with the tool with postgraduate education and undergraduate mathematics students primarily studying at a distance. Results were reported to university management, who acknowledged that a more unified, university

supported trial was essential, open to every staff member and not only the technologically curious and proficient. This university-wide trial of the tool aimed to identify faculty-specific pedagogical requirements and the suitability of the tool in meeting those requirements. Preliminary findings from the trial were reported by Reushle and Loch (2008) and Loch and Reushle (2008) and initial recommendations were made to the university community. A second tool, Wimba, was then trialled over the short summer semester and consequently adopted across the institution from the following semester. Table 1 illustrates the timeline for the USQ trials.

Unlike USQ, the trial at SCU was very informal and moved through stages from individual interest, to School, to Faculty and finally University-wide in terms of both use and funding. Equally there was no requirement for any formal evaluation - rather the growth resulted from "word of mouth" and evidence of success and value directly from student and staff experience through informal channels. Table 2 summarises the expansion of the license and use at SCU.

During the first half of 2005, vendor demonstrations by Wimba and Elluminate resulted in the latter being chosen for a 6 month, 25 seat trial until the end of 2005 funded by the School of Commerce and Management at SCU. The success of this initial trial led to the license being extended to 50 seats for all of 2006, funded by the Faculty of Business. Rowe & Ellis (2006) reported the expanding range of uses and users during 2006 that underpinned the decision by the Vice-Chancellor to adopt and centrally fund an annual university-

Table 2. SCU elluminate live! license and usage growth 2005-2008

Period	License	Sessions Recorded	Recorded Sessions Downloaded
July-Dec. 2005	25 seats	19	3
Jan.-Dec.2006	50 seats	413	3,239
Jan.-Dec.2007	Unlimited seats	812	12,602
Jan.-May 2008	Unlimited seats	732	12,544

wide, unlimited seat license from 2007. Table 2 offers a glimpse of the continued growth in use resulting from that decision.

Social Accessibility

Initial evaluation findings from USQ reveal that distance students feel engaged and connected through web conferencing, which may lead to better student evaluations, higher university ranking and additional government funding (Reushle & Loch, 2008). Initial student feedback at SCU (Rowe, Ellis & Bao, 2006) mirrors these findings. The extension of the license outlined above has allowed SCU to successfully extend the use of web conferencing for on-campus as well as distance students. The change in pattern of contact with students from (phone) teletutorials to Elluminate sessions between 2005 and 2006 across approximately 50 courses offered in the Faculty of Business is evidence of this (Rowe & Ellis, 2007). The number of teletutorials conducted declined from 61 hours with 314 students to 26 hours for 135 students. The number of Elluminate sessions conducted increased from 31 (50 hours for 142 students) to 295 (446 hours for 1500 students) demonstrating that web conferencing has increased and resulted in more accessible communication between students and staff.

Some of the capabilities of the software extend what is possible in a physical classroom with far fewer resources, by providing students with access to virtual rooms for social activities, self-directed study groups, assessable group tasks or presentation practice, all without the need for direct staff involvement. The Elluminate breakout room feature caters for in-session small group activity that would normally only be available if students were in the same physical location. The rooms can also be used for formal and informal consultations and interviews between staff and students.

The following example serves to demonstrate the strength of web-based conferencing in terms of accessibility. In 2007, a SCU student moved to a remote property without running water and power 400 miles west of the main institutional campus. She and her family were living in a shed while their house was being constructed. She joined weekly web-based conferencing sessions with enthusiasm using her laptop, powered by the car battery, on the NextG (3G) mobile phone network.

Technological Adaptability

A significant development during 2007 that complemented the adoption of the university-wide Elluminate license at SCU was the decision to integrate web conferencing into the LMS. The creation and access of sessions (and recordings) became an easy process for staff and students within individual courses. The unlimited seat license could be used to run simultaneous sessions, thereby avoiding the constraints of a time-tabling process for booking virtual rooms at times when sessions were required. The continued expansion of use in the School of Commerce and Management has seen an informal calendar maintained by the course co-ordinator for course assessors to share their scheduled session times as a precaution to avoid clashes for students.

The usage data shown in Table 2 provides evidence of the successful integration of web-based conferencing into the LMS at SCU. The access of recordings by students for review of sessions and examination preparation offers strong evidence of the value of the asynchronous features of the tool. The number of recorded sessions downloaded follows the pattern of increase in the license shown in Table 2, with the number of downloads (12,544) nearly reaching the total for the previous year in the first five months of 2008 (Rowe & Ellis, 2008).

This high level of student activity supports the suggestion that staff are responding to challenges to explore new approaches to learning and teaching in order to offer greater autonomy and connectivity (McLouglin & Lee, 2008). This allows learners to interact with peers, experts, and the wider community leading to opportunities for reflective, self-directed learning. The ability to review a recording of session activity is indicative that even the divide between synchronous and asynchronous contact is converging (Rowe & Ellis, 2007a).

Economic Viability

Australian universities currently follow a business model, which places a value for money or return on investment figure on a technological tool. Rowe and Ellis (2007) provide an analysis of cost savings during the early period of web-based conferencing adoption at SCU, pointing out the impetus this provided for the expansion of the license in subsequent years shown in Table 2. During the initial trial, the very limited active use for teaching was supplemented by taking every opportunity to demonstrate the web-based conferencing features at staff meetings across other Schools and seminars through the Teaching and Learning Centre. This extended to delivery of classes and seminars live from the UK and France using dial-up and wireless broadband connections to demonstrate and emphasise the potential of the anywhere, anytime functionality of improvements in connectivity. The strategy proved successful in terms of the expanded usage shown in Table 2.

Using the change in contact with distance students from teletutorials (and face-to-face weekend workshops) to web-based conferencing between 2005 and 2006 in the Faculty of Business at SCU, Rowe and Ellis (2007) calculated savings of approximately $A50,000. This was powerful evidence to support the decision to continue to extend the license because these savings more than covered the annual cost of the 50 seat license for 2006. That these savings were for only one of several potential uses of web-based conferencing across a multi-campus university carried even more weight with management.

The availability of participation over the Web by students and staff, independent of geographi-cal location, allowed decisions to be made about limiting course offerings in individual locations to avoid low enrolments. Instead, the decision could be more appropriately made based on total course enrolments. The ability to take advantage of audiographic web conferencing to reduce the duplication of delivery across multiple locations allowed staff time to be liberated for scholarship and their own professional development. These are important elements that can then be explicitly explored in workload model variations.

On the other hand, at USQ at trial stage, it was found to be difficult to measure if web-based conferencing was a worthwhile innovation from institutional and economic points of view as all participants volunteered time and web conferencing was regarded as an "add-on". For instance, participation in online classes was sometimes lower than one would experience in face-to-face classes. However, since recordings can be made available, a measure of value should take into account live participants as well as those who accessed the recording afterwards. In addition to identifying value for money for the tool at the institutional level, each faculty needed to determine if the workload could be justified if only a handful of students attended the online sessions.

Political Agreeability

A very powerful indication of the political agreeability of the SCU adoption of web-based conferencing was the 2007 decision by the Vice-Chancellor to centralise the responsibility and funding for the annual license. Effective and innovative use of web-based conferencing was seen as contributing to the University's reputation and competitive edge in distance and online education and was also seen as supporting exploration of new ways of enhancing learning and teaching. The receipt of university, national and international recognition in the form of awards and citations of SCU staff involved in the integration of Elluminate provides additional evidence of this.

]The burgeoning use for cross-campus, regional, national and international meetings and staff collaborations for research are further evidence of enhanced visibility and support that web-based conferencing offers. Examples of these from an SCU perspective include establishing an online forum for Elluminate users at SCU and The Open University (UK), hosting Carrick Institute (now Australian Learning and Teaching Council) committee meetings and forums, enabling PhD and Masters candidate progress presentations online in addition to their regular support group meetings, the hosting of blended sessions for the national professional accounting body (CPA Australia) as part of their web-based conferencing trials in the delivery of professional development activities, sharing expertise with other non-university educators and presenting in the annual web-based Elluminate user group conferences. Combined with the economic viability factors discussed above, a picture of effective and viable flexible learning and teaching options using web-based conferencing begins to crystallise.

DISCUSSION

This section presents snap shots of two courses that have implemented web conferencing, one at each institution. While the use of web conferencing declined in the USQ course after the change to a different tool occurred and technical issues ensued, SCU shows a more structured approach through consecutive semesters and is able to report on the advantages of consistency and being able to plan ahead for future semesters.

Case 1: USQ - Foundation Course in Computing

Foundation Computing is a large first year service course offered by the Department of Mathematics and Computing. The course provides an introduction to computers, and covers applications such as word processing, spreadsheets, presentation software, but also operating systems, hardware, the internet, graphics and multimedia and basic web design. It is offered three semesters each year, to on-campus students at the main campus in Toowoomba and distance students.

Foundation computing attracts a wide spectrum of students: some are fairly computer literate while others, mainly mature age, have not used a computer before and face a steep but necessary learning curve to enable them to be successful with computer use throughout their studies and later professional life.

The course material is presented in multi-modal format produced in USQ's in-house Integrated Content Environment (http://ice.usq.edu.au/), i.e, printed study materials, on CD, as well as online, where the latter two include screencasts of concepts students find difficult to understand. The course uses USQ's LMS, Moodle, to provide access to this material and to recordings of lectures from a previous semester in Macromedia Breeze (now Adobe Connect) format. The Moodle site also hosts assignment instructions and an electronic submission system. It provides asynchronous discussion forums that have traditionally been used extensively in this course, with students encouraged to help each other rather than wait for a teacher's response. If not via the Moodle forum, student requests are responded to via email and phone. Since the lack of visual aids during a phone conversation made it difficult to explain, for instance, how to write code in HTML for the web design module, the need for a tool to share the screen with students outside a face-to-face situation was identified.

In semester 2 of 2007 with an enrolment of about 280 students (half in distance mode), it was decided to trial Elluminate tutorials for all students. In that semester, this was one of a number of changes made to the previous format of the course. No lectures were offered: mini-lectures in computer labs replaced the need for lecture theatre classes. The lectures were cancelled for strong pedagogical reasons as this course required more hands-on training than a standard lecture could provide. Web conferencing was trialled not with the aim to replace face-to-face classes, but to create an on-campus experience for distance students by offering additional regular tutorials, and to include these students in synchronous activities.

Weekly Elluminate tutorials were offered to all students, and an emphasis was placed on student-focused and peer-supported learning where the teacher became a facilitator or moderator, rather than delivering material. Students were encouraged to show other students how to perform tasks on the computer. For instance, a student sharing her screen and asking for help with a particular task in the word processor relinquished control over her computer to a fellow student, who then "walked" everyone through the required steps.

Students attended from as far as Hong Kong, but attendance at these tutorials was low, although it was offered to all students. However, recordings were made available for those who could not attend or wanted to view the session again. At the end of semester, students were asked to rank the learning tools most useful to them. Those who had attended Elluminate classes ranked these highly. Other students who had not attended but viewed the recordings asked for more sessions and recordings to be made available.

The mode of communication used most was audio, with quite a few students typing text messages to ask or answer questions so as not to interrupt the speaker. The student from Hong Kong appeared to be shy and was more comfortable typing answers, and microphone issues also prevented some students from using the audio capability.

Case 2: SCU - Core Course of Quantitative Analysis

Quantitative Analysis is a core first year course in the Bachelor of Business degree. The course is a mixture of business and financial mathematics and statistics with an Australian enrolment of 300 to 400. The course is offered on four campuses with approximately 40% distance students. All Australian students, and increasingly off-shore international students, have access to a common LMS site (Blackboard), which contains the curriculum for the course. The site includes links to the study guide, assessment items including online tests, sample assessment items and discussion boards.

Prior to 2006, on-campus students had face-to-face lectures and tutorials in addition to the LMS. Additional support for distance students consisted of teletutorials and/or face-to-face workshops once or twice a semester. These workshops were held in limited locations hence were not easily accessible to all distance students. Given that they did not have a visual component, teletutorials were of limited use in explaining the concepts required in the course and this support for distance students was far from ideal.

A sizable proportion of students entering the Bachelor of Business have extremely poor numeracy skills. These students require additional support to succeed in the course. In particular, many distance students require frequent real-time interaction with teaching staff to be successful. This was often provided on a one-to-one basis by either email or phone. Finally, an objective of the course is to "demonstrate the use of a spreadsheet package such as Excel in quantitative calculations". However, many students have poor Excel skills and/or are visual learners. They often found that the study guide and textbook instructions were not sufficient to acquire the necessary Excel skills.

In semester 2 of year 2005, it was decided to run an initial trial of web conferencing sessions to test the feasibility of replacing teletutorials and face-to-face workshops with Elluminate workshops for distance students and to test the effectiveness of Elluminate as a tool for showing and teaching Excel skills. However, rather than trialling Elluminate in this course, a second year statistics course, Statistical Analysis, was chosen for this trial. This course had the same issues as Quantitative Analysis but a more manageable enrolment of approximately 100 students.

During the trial, the weekly Elluminate sessions were accessed not only by distance students but also on-campus students who could not attend the weekly tutorials due to a timetable clash. These successful weekly sessions were a mixture of content, examples and Excel demonstration. One of the conclusions of the trial was that Elluminate sessions were superior to both teletutorials and face-to-face workshops for distance students by providing the opportunity for frequent real-time interaction with both peers (other students) and teaching staff. It was also concluded that Elluminate was an ideal method of demonstrating/teaching Excel skills, allowing students to see the steps, with the possibility of attempting them themselves at the same time.

At the conclusion of the trial, it was decided to use Elluminate sessions to support students in Quantitative Analysis from Semester 1 2006. During 2006 and 2007, Elluminate sessions provided supplementary support for all students enrolled in Quantitative Analysis. This was in addition to the usual lecture tutorial format for on-campus support.

These sessions included revision workshops on basic algebra and calculation skills at the beginning of the semester and exam revision sessions at the end. During the semester, several sessions, using application sharing, demonstrated the Excel skills required for the assessment tasks. In these sessions, students were encouraged to run Excel and follow the instructions. These sessions were recorded so students could review them if they could not attend. It was found that these sessions provided the additional support in revision and learning Excel required by students with poor numeracy and/or Excel skills.

Furthermore, primarily for distance students, weekly Elluminate sessions were held. These sessions introduced a topic, worked through several

examples, and allowed time for questions. They replaced the teletutorials and face-to-face workshops previously held for distance students, thus reducing staff travel time and expense. The Elluminate sessions also provided distance students with more frequent contact with staff and other students. On-campus students also could, and did, attend and from 2007 recordings were available for all sessions.

With supplementary support still provided, in 2008 Elluminate online lectures replaced face-to-face lectures for on-campus students and the weekly Elluminate sessions for distance students. That is, all students were expected to attend or review the weekly Elluminate lecture and on-campus students were also to attend a weekly 1.5 hour, increasing to 2 hours in 2009, tutorial each week.

The online lectures followed the same pattern as the previous weekly Elluminate sessions for distance students, introducing a topic, working through several examples, and allowing time for questions. This introduced consistency of delivery as all students had access to the same lectures and supplementary sessions, while on-campus students still had the face-to-face contact in the tutorials. Efficiencies for academic staff were also introduced as only one lecture needed to be prepared and delivered, with no travelling between campuses.

There was considerable resistance by on-campus, especially first year, students to the online lectures in 2008, leading to a decrease in the level of student satisfaction with the course. Student satisfaction increased in 2009, but not to the 2007 level. This increase was possibly due to increasing weekly tutorial sessions from 1.5 to 2 hours, and better communication about the advantages of online lectures, in particular the flexibility due to the ability to review recorded sessions and provision of recordings in several multimedia formats.

While a limited number of students attended the live sessions, many more students reviewed the recordings. From formal and informal feedback, students found the Elluminate sessions and recordings beneficial and supportive of their learning. In particular, students found reviewing a recording at their own pace, pausing, rewinding or fast forwarding as required extremely helpful. PowerPoint slides are provided before a session and a copy of the completed Elluminate whiteboard is provided after the session. Therefore, students know they can concentrate on the lecture or sessions and need not take notes during a live session or when watching a recording.

While many students are not comfortable with using the audio tools within the Elluminate session, they are comfortable using the text tool to ask questions of the presenter or each other. Use of the text tool enables the instructor to answer questions in a timely manner without disrupting a train of thought. Students are also comfortable using the text, polling or whiteboard tools to answer questions from the instructor. This enables the instructor to obtain feedback from all students in the session on their level of understanding of the material, which is difficult to do in a large lecture situation.

Summary of Student Outcomes

Important student outcomes from the adoption of web conferencing software at USQ and SCU include the establishment of social presence, particularly at the beginning of a semester, which means that students are more aware that they are part of a cohort of students who are experiencing the same challenges and can support each other. A reduction in student anxiety in statistics courses has been observed, and direct help in using software in computing courses has replaced long, imprecise written or verbal instructions. Visual explanations of symbol-based courses such as mathematics have been made possible and some students have experienced increased awareness of assessment methodology and teacher expectations.

CURRENT CHALLENGES AND RECOMMENDATIONS

This section outlines issues and challenges experienced during these web conferencing trials and provides recommendations for policy makers and educators embarking on trials of emerging tools to support learning and teaching.

Institutional Trial

A comparison of the SCU and USQ take up of web conferencing indicates the importance of carefully selecting a tool for a university-wide trial and continuing the use of this tool if the trial proves successful. While Elluminate is now used widely at SCU, its use was not continued at USQ. Technical issues with the adopted tool, Wimba, and the change from one tool to another meant that teaching staff had to become accustomed to another system.

Technology Adoption

As new technology moves from trial stage to mainstream use, student expectations need to be managed. At SCU, in the School of Commerce and Management, ten hours of Elluminate sessions are mandated per semester for each course. As some courses offer more sessions than others in the form of pre-recorded sessions, consultation or student support, there have been student complaints about the lack of online content if only the mandated ten hours are provided. This, of course, needs to be placed in context as this is more support than distance students received before the introduction of the new technology.

Mandating at least ten hours of Elluminate sessions for each course has meant that courses that may not have a pedagogical need for such sessions but would benefit from different technologies are not given the option to use an alternative. This leads to lecturers using web conferencing who do not see or have the need, and while this makes it easy to keep track of workload, it may not be a recommended pedagogical approach.

Change, particularly major change, often meets resistance. Negative responses from students are to be expected the first time new technology is used, particularly if it impacts on their comfort zone. In the SCU case, this was the removal of familiar face-to-face lectures for on-campus students. These responses need to be managed and monitored. At the same time, lecturers need to be open to changing formats and content in response to student needs and demands rather than using new technology in ways that were more appropriate before the technology was introduced. In the web conferencing context, the re-education of students and staff from traditional teaching-centred to student-centred pedagogy is an important task.

Faculty members have commented that synchronous sessions need to be built into the course from the outset, and not be treated as a last-minute add-on. Along the same lines, time commitment may be required to learn the pedagogical as well as the technical aspects of new technology. A well documented backup and support structure is essential when technical problems arise. While web conferencing has led to economic savings at SCU, the adoption of the tool should rather be seen as a way of using staff time more effectively and to improve student outcomes.

Since 2005, there has been only one recorded instance of misconduct in a web conferencing session at SCU which required intervention. This suggests respect for the process from participants, despite the opportunity of apparent anonymity. However, if accessed through an LMS, students are not anonymous and their use of the room and the tools can be tracked. Therefore, normal disciplinary procedures can be applied. It has been observed that attitude and ability of students of different cohorts varies significantly. Feedback about improvements of the use of technology obtained at the end of a semester may be taken on board and lead to modifications for the next

offer. However, the next cohort may have different needs and expectations. This factor is difficult to cater for but remains a challenge that all teachers experience, irrespective of the learning and teaching context.

The ongoing debate about the need to provide on-campus classes to international on-campus students offers a very real opportunity to demonstrate the benefits of the features outlined in this chapter and challenges the view that face-to-face is the "best". For example, video-conferencing is often accepted as equivalent to face-to-face. However, it offers little of the interactivity available with web-based audiographic conferencing. Therefore, why not demonstrate the equivalency, or superiority, of web-based audiographic conferencing as an alternative or supplement to face to face classes?

CONCLUSION

The chapter has presented how USQ and SCU have adapted a traditional distance delivery model to incorporate audiographic web conferencing to improve learning and teaching opportunities for students and staff, irrespective of their geographical location. The USQ trial was successful as it demonstrated the need for this particular type of technology to support teaching activities for distance students. It influenced the decision by Senior Management to include web conferencing technology in the suite of available tools to support flexible learning. Following a short trial of a second web conferencing package, USQ adopted the Wimba web conferencing tool and this is now available to all USQ staff and students, with no seat limitations.

The informal trials at SCU demonstrated that Elluminate sessions were a practical replacement for teletutorials and face-to-face workshops for distance students. This enabled savings in travel and teletutorial costs exceeding the cost of the license. Based on the demonstrated usefulness of Elluminate sessions and in particular, student use of recordings, SCU now has an unlimited seat licence and in the School of Commerce and Management a mandated minimum number of hours of Elluminate sessions per semester for each course.

Network-enhanced interaction can fulfil some pragmatic human needs at certain points in time by providing access, convenience, flexibility, utility, speed, and cost-effectiveness. Education is a powerful tool in the global educational environment and the Internet has enabled a new era in human collective activity.

REFERENCES

Barr, R. B., & Tagg, J. (1995). From teaching to learning – A new paradigm for undergraduate education. *Change*, (November/December): 13–25.

Birch, D., & Volkov, M. (2005, December). *Students' perceptions of compulsory asynchronous online discussion*. Australian and New Zealand Marketing Academy (ANZMAC) Conference 2005: Broadening the Boundaries, Fremantle, Western Australia.

Clark, P. (2009). *Vice-Chancellor's Progress Report: Becoming a truly multicampus institution – A Route Map*. Southern Cross University. Retrieved March 25, 2009, from http://staff.scu.edu.au/vc/index.php/dds?cat_id=76#cat76

de Byl, P., & Taylor, J. A. (2007). A web 2.0/web3D hybrid platform for engaging students in e-learning environments. *Turkish Online Journal of Distance Education*, 8(3), 108–127.

De Freitas, S., & Neumann, T. (2009). The use of 'exploratory learning' for supporting immersive learning in virtual environments. *British Journal of Educational Technology*, 40(6), 980–998. doi:10.1111/j.1467-8535.2008.00887.x

Dekkers, J., & Cuskelly, E. (1990). *The establishment and use of electronic mail for distance education*. University College of Central Queensland, Rockhampton.

Hafeez-Baig, A., & Danaher, P. A. (2007). Future possibilities for mobile learning technologies and applications at the University of Southern Queensland, Australia: Lessons from an academic focus group. In *1st International Conference on Mobile Learning Technologies and Applications*, 19 Feb., New Zealand: Auckland. Retrieved March 16, 2008, from http://eprints.usq.edu.au/2042/

Hayden, M., Saenger, H., & Parry, S. (1999). *An evaluation of the online units delivered in first semester 1999*. Southern Cross University, Teaching and Learning Centre.

Loch B., & McDonald C. (2007). Synchronous chat and electronic ink for distance support in mathematics. *Innovate, 3*(3).

Loch, B., & Reushle, S. E. (2008). The practice of web conferencing: Where are we now? In *Hello! Where are you in the landscape of educational technology? Proceedings of ASCILITE08*, Melbourne: Deakin University. Retrieved May 4, 2009, from http://www.ascilite.org.au/conferences/melbourne08/procs/loch.pdf

McElroy, J., & Blount, Y. (2006). You, me and iLecture. In *Who's learning? Who's technology? Proceedings of ASCILITE06* (pp. 549-558). Sydney: University of Sydney Conservatorium, Retrieved June 4, 2009, from http://www.ascilite.org.au/conferences/sydney06/proceeding/pdf_papers/p87.pdf

McLoughlin, C., & Lee, M. (2008). Future learning landscapes: Transforming pedagogy through social software. *Innovate, 4*(5). Retrieved June 4, 2009, from http://www.innovateonline.info/index.php?view=article&id=539

Morgan, C., & O'Reilly, M. (1999). *Assessing open and distance learners*. London: Kogan Page.

New Directions for Delivery at Southern Cross 2007. (n.d.). Unpublished SCU document.

Newton, D., & Ledgerwood, T. (2001). Evolving support for online learning: An action research model . In Wallace, M., Ellis, A., & Newton, D. (Eds.), *Proceedings of Moving online II: A conference to explore the challenges for workplaces, colleges and universities* (pp. 205–221). Gold Coast, Australia: Conrad Jupiters.

O'Reilly, M., & Newton, D. (2002). Interaction online: Above and beyond requirements of assessment. *Australian Journal of Educational Technology, 18*(1), 57–70.

Phillips, R., Gosper, M., McNeill, M., Woo, K., Preston, G., & Green, D. (2007). Staff and student perspectives on web-based lecture technologies: Insights into the great divide. In *ICT: Providing choices for learners and learning. Proceedings of ASCILITE07*, Singapore. Retrieved June 1, 2009, from http://www.ascilite.org.au/conferences/singapore07/procs/phillips.pdf

Reushle, S., & McDonald, J. (2004, November). *Online learning: Transcending the physical*. Effective Teaching and Learning Conference 2004, A Conference for University Teachers, Griffith University, Logan Campus, Brisbane.

Reushle, S. E., & Loch, B. (2008). Conducting a trial of web conferencing software: Why, how, and perceptions from the coalface. *Turkish Online Journal of Distance Education, 9*(3), 19-28. Retrieved May 4, 2009, from http://tojde.anadolu.edu.tr/tojde31/index.htm

Reushle, S. E., & McDonald, J. (2000). Moving an Australian dual mode university to the online environment: A case study. In [Canada: Montreal.]. *Proceedings of ED-MEDI, A2000*, 907–912.

Rowe, S. (2003). Working in a virtual classroom: What you CAN do to enrich the learning experience. In *Proceedings of NAWEB03*. November, Fredericton, Canada, University of New Brunswick. Retrieved March 13, 2009, from http://naweb.unb.ca/proceedings/2003/PaperRowe.html

Rowe, S. (2004). Reflections on adopting a Learning Management System to engage students in their learning. In *Proceedings of NAWEB04*, November, Fredericton, Canada: University of New Brunswick. Retrieved March 13, 2009, from http://naweb.unb.ca/04/papers/Rowe.html

Rowe, S., & Ellis, A. (2006). Audiographics moves to the web. In A. Treloar & A. Ellis (Eds.), *AusWeb06: Proceedings of the Twelfth Australasian World Wide Web Conference*, July 1-5, Noosa Lakes, Australia. Retrieved March 13, 2009, from http://ausweb.scu.edu.au/aw06/papers/refereed/rowe/paper.html

Rowe, S., & Ellis, A. (2007), The evolution of audiographic technologies. In C. Montgomerie & J. Seale (Eds.), *Proceedings of ED-MEDIA2007: World Conference on Educational Multimedia, Hypermedia & Telecommunications*, June 25-29, Vancouver, Canada.

Rowe, S., & Ellis, A. (2007a). How the web has changed lecturing: Going the full circle. In J. Richardson & A. Ellis (Eds.), *AusWeb07: Proceedings of the Thirteenth Australia World Wide Web Conference*, Novotel Pacific Bay Resort, Coffs Harbour, Australia. Retrieved March 13, 2009, from http://ausweb.scu.edu.au/aw07/papers/refereed/rowe/paper.html

Rowe, S., & Ellis, A. (2008). Enhancing the convenience and flexibility of student learning options: Using recorded audiographic web conferencing sessions. In C. Montgomerie & J. Seale (Eds.), *Proceedings (CD) for ED-MEDIA2008: World Conference on Educational Multimedia, Hypermedia & Telecommunications*, June 30-July 4, Vienna, Austria.

Rowe, S., Ellis, A., & Bao, T. Q. (2006). The evolution of audiographics: A case study of audiographics teaching in a business faculty. In *Who's learning? Who's technology? Proceedings of ASCILITE06*, December 3-6, Sydney: Sydney University. Retrieved March 23, 2009, from http://www.ascilite.org.au/conferences/sydney06/proceeding/pdf_papers/p194.pdf

Statham, A. (2001 January). *Virtual realities: A profile of online learning activity at Southern Cross University.* A report presented to the Online Review and Coordination Committee.

Strategic Plan, U. S. Q. *2009-2013.* (2009). Retrieved March 25, 2009, from http://www.usq.edu.au/planstats/quality/Docs/USQ_strategic_plan.pdf

USQ Learning and Teaching Plan 2009-2013: Summary. (2009). Retrieved March 25, 2009, from http://www.usq.edu.au/resources/usqtlplan0913.pdf

Vitartas, P., Jayne, N., Ellis, A., & Rowe, S. (2007). Student adoption of web based video conferencing software: A comparison of three student discipline groups. In *ICT: Providing choices for learners and learning. Proceedings of ASCILITE07*, December 2-5, Singapore: Nanyang Technological University. Retrieved March 23, 2009, from http://www.ascilite.org.au/conferences/singapore07/procs/vitartas.pdf

Vitartas, P., & Rowe, S. (2003). An assessment of contributions to an on-line discussion forum in Accounting Theory. In A. Treloar & A. Ellis (Eds.). *AusWeb03: Proceedings of the Ninth Australia World Wide Web Conference,* July 5-9, Gold Coast, Australia, Hyatt Regency Sanctuary Cove (pp. 412-419).

Williams, J., & Fardon, M. (2007). Perpetual connectivity: Lecture recordings and portable media players ICT: Providing choices for learners and learning. *Proceedings of ASCILITE07*, December 2-5, Singapore: Nanyang Technological University. Retrieved March 23, 2009, from http://www.ascilite.org.au/conferences/singapore07/procs/williams-jo.pdf

ADDITIONAL READING

Anderson, L., Fyvie, B., Koritko, B., McCarthy, K., Murillo Paz, S., Rizzuto, M., et al. (2006). Best practices in synchronous conferencing moderation. *The International Review of Research in Open and Distance Learning, 7*(1). Retrieved July 4, 2009, from http://www.irrodl.org/index.php/irrodl/article/view/308/511

Anderson, T. (Ed.). (2008). *The theory and practice of online learning* (2nd ed.). Edmonton, AB: AU Press.

Anderson, T., & Rourke, L. (2002). Using web-based group communication systems to support case study learning at a distance. *The International Review of Research in Open and Distance Learning, 3(2)*. Retrieved July 4, 2009, from http://www.irrodl.org/index.php/irrodl/article/view/107

Bonk, C. J., & Graham, C. R. (Eds.). (2006). *Handbook of blended learning: Global perspectives, local designs.* San Francisco, CA: Pfeiffer Publishing.

Bonk, C. J., & Zhang, K. (2008). *Empowering Online Learning: 100+ Activities For Reading, Reflecting, Displaying, & Doing.* San Francisco, CA: Jossey Bass.

Dalsgaard, C. (2006). Social software: E-learning beyond learning management systems. *European Journal of Open, Distance, and E-Learning*. Retrieved March 2, 2008, from http://www.eurodl.org/materials/contrib/2006/Christian_Dalsgaard.htm

Elluminate (2009). Elluminate application articles. Retrieved July 20, 2009, from http://www.elluminate.com/community/application_articles/

Elluminate (2009). Elluminate recorded demonstrations & events. Retrieved July 26, 2009, from https://sas.elluminate.com/site/external/event/playback

Elluminate (2009). Elluminate white papers. Retrieved July 20, 2009, from http://www.elluminate.com/whitepapers/

Finkelstein, J. (2006). *Learning in real time*. San Francisco, CA: Jossey Bass.

Harman, C., & Dorman, M. (1998). Enriching distance teaching and learning of undergraduate mathematics using videoconferencing and audiographics . *Distance Education, 19*(2), 299–318. doi:10.1080/0158791980190208

Kim, K.-J., & Bonk, C. J. (2002). *Cross-cultural comparisons of online collaboration. Journal of Computer-Mediated Communication, 8*(1). Retrieved July 20, 2009, from http://jcmc.indiana.edu/vol8/issue1/kimandbonk.html

NCVER. (2003). Flexibility through online learning: At a glance. SA: Leabrook. Retrieved 27 July, 2009 from http://www.ncver.edu.au/research/proj/nr1F12/nr1F12.pdf

Ng, K. C. (2007). Replacing face to face tutorials by synchronous online technologies: Challenges and pedagogical implications. *International Review of Research in Open and Distance Learning, 8*(1).

Porto, S. (2006). Synchronous online conferencing. *DE Oracle @ UMUC*. Retrieved July 20, 2009, from http://deoracle.org/online-pedagogy/synchronous-communication/synchronous-conferencing.html

Schullo, S., Hilbelink, A., Venable, A., & Barron, A. (2007) Selecting a Virtual Classroom System: Elluminate Live vs. Macromedia Breeze (Adobe Acrobat Connect Professional), *MERLOT Journal of Online Learning and Teaching, 3*(4), pp 331-345. Retrieved July 26, 2009 from http://jolt.merlot.org/Vol3_No4.htm

Selwyn, N., & Facer, K. (2007). Beyond the digital divide: Rethinking digital inclusion for the 21st century. Retrieved July 20, 2009, from http://www.futurelab.org.uk/resources/publications-reports-articles/opening-education-reports/Opening-Education-Report548

Shi, S., Bonk, C. J., Mishra, P., & Tan, S. (May 2008). Getting in syn with synchronous: The dynamics of synchronous facilitation in online discussions. *International Journal of Instructional Technology and Distance Learning, 5*(5). Retrieved July 20, 2009, from http://www.itdl.org/Journal/May_08/article01.htm

Shi, S., & Strause, K. D. (2007). Facilitating educational synchronous online discussions. In C. Crawford et al. (Eds.), *Proceedings of Society for Information Technology and Teacher Education International Conference 2007* (pp. 2462-2469). Chesapeake, VA: AACE. Retrieved July 20, 2009, from http://web.cortland.edu/shis/webfolio/SITE-SyncPaperWStrause.pdf

Sims, R. (2003). Promises of interactivity: Aligning learner perceptions and expectations with strategies for flexible and online learning . *Distance Education, 24*(1), 87–103. doi:10.1080/01587910303050

Southern Cross University. (2009). Retrieved 27 July, 2009 from http://www.scu.edu.au

University of Southern Queensland. (2009). Retrieved July 27, 2009 from http://www.usq. edu.au

KEY TERMS AND DEFINITIONS

Audiographics: Synchronous communication via audio and video or screen sharing. Not necessarily via the Web.

Elluminate, Wimba: Current all-in-one web conferencing tools.

Flexible Delivery: Enabling students to study anytime and anywhere, synchronously or asynchronously.

Technology Enhanced Learning: Technology-supported approaches to enable improved students' learning experience.

Teletutorial: Interactive tutorial activity conducted via telephone, usually led by the teacher.

Web Conferencing: Audio, video, and shared whiteboard conferencing via the Web.

Chapter 5
Marketing a Blended University Program:
An Action Research Case Study

Kathryn Ley
University of Houston Clear Lake, USA

Ruth Gannon-Cook
De Paul University, USA

ABSTRACT

This case study describes a successful marketing effort to recruit prospective graduate students for a blended program delivered to a culturally diverse urban and suburban adult nontraditional population. An effectiveness evaluation analyzed and measured program and per class enrollment from the marketing plan from inception through the first three years. The authors detail a plan grounded in simple marketing principles and revealed through analyses based on memoranda, documents, program enrollment data, and planning and meeting notes. A collaborative team developed, implemented and analyzed how the effort increased enrollments by over a third in less than two years.

INTRODUCTION

This marketing effort promoted a blended instructional technology program in culturally diverse, metropolitan area with 6 million residents within 580 square miles. Since its founding three decades earlier, the upper-division (junior-senior level) university had offered bachelor's, master's, and certificate programs housed within four curricular administrative units (science, business, education, and humanities) to the immediate community with the highest concentration of doctorates in the US,

and to the entire region in which 11 percent of the residents held bachelor's degrees.

The 7500-student public university within a larger regional, urban four-institution system, shared two system satellite site campuses with its three other system institutions; each site campus located within one of two different high-growth areas more than 30 miles from the primary campus was within the larger metropolitan region. The two site campuses enabled students in the high growth areas with an hour or more commute from the primary campus to attend in the institution's on-ground (courses limited to class sessions between instructor and students who are simultaneously physically present in the same

DOI: 10.4018/978-1-61520-751-0.ch005

classroom) courses a few minutes drive from their home or work. This mid-decade marketing effort began during period of strong regional economic and demographic growth to attract prospective students to one of the first two programs the upper division university offered online. The online courses evolved from an on-ground instructional technology program, initiated a few years earlier, to serve four burgeoning regional economic sectors: educational, biomedical, aerospace, and oil field services.

SETTING THE STAGE

The university, one of many embracing online education at the turn of this century, began offering faculty incentives, such as course releases, faculty honoraria, and development support personnel for every online course that faculty would design and develop to populate the institution's new commercial course management system (CMS). Faculty from two programs took advantage of the incentives and resources to develop online courses that comprised the first two university degree programs in which students could choose to complete course requirements online, on campus, or in any combination they chose. This case study describes marketing efforts for one of the two programs, a graduate education program.

During the initial design-development process to implement the online delivery option, a program coordinator with the Dean, who directed and managed the institution's education unit, scheduled courses for online development if the course was required for core curriculum or could fulfill the minimum elective course requirement. Between the two marketing phases described in this case study, the Dean chose a new program coordinator as part of a planned rotation agreed upon by faculty so that no one faculty member was burdened with program marketing and course scheduling responsibilities indefinitely; the position had no budget authority or responsibilities and

carried only a small stipend yet faculty still had to maintain research and teaching three courses per semester for two long semesters per year. The Dean appointed one of the two researchers as the new program coordinator from among the four tenure line positions; he continued to offer the faculty marketing agent, who was one of two full-time instructors and the other action researcher in this case study, a course release to market the online program because she brought several years experience as a successful sales and marketing representative for a major computer services corporation to the task. Several adjuncts completed the instructional technology program faculty ranks. The program coordinator during the second marketing phase implemented a team approach to build program enrollments with the eight full-time instructional technology program faculty, five of which held tenure line positions. The new program coordinator, who was one of the tenured faculty, and the instructor receiving a course release to market the program, co-authored this case study which documents how they collaboratively leveraged the blended delivery and degree and certificate curriculum options to increase enrollments.

The new program coordinator upon assuming responsibilities immediately prior to the fall semester established a faculty-team approach incorporating the eight full-time instructional technology program faculty. Program faculty had continued to develop online courses so that by the beginning of the second marketing phase, a student could complete course requirements for a Master's of Science degree in the program online although students still had to submit some forms and complete some capstone options in person at the instructional technology program campus. All online courses were either replaced during selected semesters with a web-enhanced delivery section or offered simultaneously since enrollments justified only one section of most courses per semester; students had a choice of delivery medium by choosing which semester to enroll in a course. Some electives were only offered on campus, but sufficient electives were offered online frequently enough to complete all degree course requirements online. All five core instructional technology courses and four core education courses in the graduate degree were offered every semester either online or on-ground.

CASE DESCRIPTION

Initiating the effort, university administration asked the instructional technology program coordinator how the graduate program could increase enrollments and gain greater market share in a large urban population and, eventually expand program recruitment efforts to rural, national, and international populations. Program faculty, collaborating with distance education support staff, effectively doubled program enrollment within two years. Data analyses revealed marketing elements and environmental conditions that contributed to program success and those which the plan and team had to ameliorate or overcome.

The marketing elements from which the plan was derived were based on marketing and change innovation theory (Berge & Muilenburg, 2001; Nootenberg, 2006; Robinson, 1995; Salmon, 2005). Research indicated there was a symbiotic relationship between organizational training-delivery capability and impediments, such as an organization's level of capability in electronic delivery and the barriers to detain its delivery. One of the biggest obstacles, ironically, is the entrenched culture of the organization itself, so the challenges to the implementation come from the establishment committed to its adoption (Berge & Muilenburg, 2001). One study related to implementation of new technologies and assessments (Bourner, Katz & Watson, 2000) focused on internal development frameworks, particularly with respect to professional training and professional collaborations (Bourner, Katz & Watson, 2000). The study seemed to report results that

reinforced the findings of the researcher in this study, and that is, there needs to be consistency and dependability of specific deliverables.

The marketing plan depended upon two educational groups adopting the innovative approach: first the faculty and university staff members implementing the marketing plan; and second, the targeted potential students. The program coordinator fostered innovation factors to promote adoption. Higher education administrators have promoted technological innovation, global education and eLearning through organizational collegiality, professional faculty training, and personal and professional collaborations (Barg, 2004; Berge & Muilenberg, 2001; Bourner, Katz & Watson, 2000; Ellsworth, 2000; Ely 1990; Gask, 2005; Havernik, Messerschmitt, Vandrick, 1997; Haverschmidt & Smith, 1998; Hergert, 2003; Nootenberg, 2006).

The two faculties who developed the phase two marketing plan selected an action research methodology to drive data collection for this case study. They documented every related meeting each attended and its results to chronicle the evolving marketing plan. They wrote memoranda, notes, and two reports assessing the marketing plan that became source documents for chronicling marketing plan activities and their results. The faculty marketing agent, one of the two action researchers on the marketing team and the one who shaped the direction of both phases, documented which aspects of the marketing plan worked best and succeeded and which aspects of the marketing plan failed in detailed journals and records.

ANTECEDENT PHASE:
A FALSE START

The antecedent to the phase one was a failed marketing effort which had transpired two years before the successful one documented here. This was collaborative effort between the program and the school district in which the program coordinator tried to establish school district cohorts with on-ground face-to-face courses. Without any history or formal evaluation of the early failed attempt to establish school based cohorts for the program, the faculty marketing agent met with ill-will for her phase one marketing attempt among prospective students and school administrators; many still recalled how teachers were promised on-ground cohort courses which never material-ized. A handful of teachers who had signed on for the ill-fated attempt to provide professional development had persisted by attending courses by commuting great distances to complete their Master's degrees or certificates at the program University campus.

The faculty marketing agent, unaware of the earlier false start, discovered this failure when she first visited the superintendent of a targeted school district. She encountered school district personnel whose trust had been breached by promises of on-ground face-to-face courses offered by the same program years before. She immediately began the delicate process of reestablishing dialogue and beginning to restore trust between herself as the new university representative and the offended district personnel. She offered assurances in the name of the university that this time promises would be kept if made; she and her university would not repeat past mistakes. Fortunately, in this case, her strong and clear assurances that the program would deliver, established her cred-ibility with the superintendent who was willing to work with the program one more time. She repeatedly asserted why this time the program would work and would have a positive outcome for the superintendent and for participating school district teachers.

Phase One: A Renewed Effort

The successful marketing process had two distinct phases. During phase one, the program coordinator convinced the Dean to capitalize on the market-ing experience of a recent addition to the faculty who had been a successful sales and marketing person in the computer services industry and to offer her a one-course release of a four course load in exchange for conducting recruitment and marketing activities for the same program in which she taught.

The phase one marketing team consisted of the phase one Instructional Technology program coordinator, and the faculty marketing agent drawn from the ranks of full-time program instructors, the remote-site campus director at one of two sites shared by the four-university system, and a university staff person who routinely staffed an office at the remote site and provided admis-sions and enrollment services. The program coordinator during phase one arranged for the full-time instructor now serving as a marketing agent to secure cohorts at key school districts. The faculty marketing agent, also one of two action researchers for this case study, began by identifying the potential for a renewed marketing effort to determine if there was sufficient interest among school district administrators and teachers to offer online courses which would be targeted to school district teachers instead of on-ground face-to-face cohort classes. The program coor-dinator was again attempting to build university system site enrollments, only this time through online courses while suggesting to school district personnel that with sufficient enrollments, the program might offer hybrid courses through one of two system sites conveniently located within the school districts and within 100 miles of the program university.

The program coordinator during phase one, at the university administration's directive, limited marketing to school districts within 60 miles from the university campus rather than the original 100-mile radius. Each of the four System universities were prohibited from direct marketing within the other three institutions' geographically-proscribed territory; on the other hand, students were able to enroll in any program at any of the four institutions or other State universities. Also each of the four system universities could recruit adjacent to the two system remote sites, each in its own building staffed by system personnel and offering courses selected by the four universities to promote their own programs. A geographic marketing constraint was also enforced for all public State universities; they were prohibited from direct recruiting activities for online programs outside their own State loosely proscribed region.

During the initial phase beginning with the fall semester, the faculty-researcher marketing agent identified key districts that met several criteria. Key districts had thousands of students and included hundreds of teachers; the final list included the two largest school districts and three smaller adjacent school districts within 60 miles of the university; all required periodic professional development courses for kindergarten through twelfth grade teachers; none of the districts had schools within a few miles of any of the other three system universities. After identifying the key districts, the marketing agent interviewed selected district teachers who were also currently enrolled in courses at the same university offering the to-be-marketed program. The interview data enabled the program coordinator and marketing agent responsible for marketing plan to identify the potential demand for program professional development certificates and advanced degrees among the five key district teachers. Her initial interview data from the district teachers yielded a potential student pool of a few hundred which was large enough to justify devoting university resources and personnel on additional recruitment efforts to market the Instructional Technology master's degrees and related certificate programs. The marketed program offered potential students two important advantages over the largest and flagship university among the four-institution system: Lower tuition and a soon-to-be 100% online degree program since sufficient courses were almost all offered either online or web-enhanced. Online courses offered attractive convenience but the promise of hybrid courses provided de-

sirable personalized faculty interaction valued by school district administrators and teachers. Web-enhanced courses were offered at either the program institution or one of two system remote sites shared among the four system universities.

Before fall mid-semester, the faculty-marketing agent proposed a plan based on the educational market data including school district names, school locations, State teacher certification renewal requirements and teacher population size. The faculty-marketing agent discussed the potential interest with the program coordinator who approved agent meetings with superintendents. The marketing agent began to cultivate cohorts that would matriculate in online courses to avoid promising on-ground courses that might again be cancelled without sufficient enrollments, about fifteen students. She made phone calls to all five key district superintendants and arranged meetings with each to discuss district professional development plans. During these fall semester individual meetings with each district superintendant, she carefully fostered each superintendant's interest in the university program and elicited their opinions about the barriers and drivers that might affect recruitment for professional development through program certificates and degrees among district teachers.

The faculty-marketing agent had to overcome a serious barrier – a lack of trust after a previous failed marketing effort by the university. The agent uncovered the problem after the superintendant of the largest targeted school district initially rebuffed her offer to provide educational services to district teachers. A few years earlier, the district had supported the program briefly and until the touted educational services were not implemented or maintained to meet the university's commitment. After discovering the problem, the faculty-marketing agent met repeatedly with the superintendant and district teachers; the meetings and her visits eventually established positive, trusting collegial relationships with district administrators and teachers. The marketing representative carefully built trust by committing only to services and course offerings that the university could accommodate; this time the university provided the product/service promised: online and hybrid courses sequenced to effectively and efficiently provide professional development certificates and degrees. The school district teachers and superintendant also met others involved in program delivery, e.g., the program coordinator, the university staff, and learned how the online program and delivery system could best meet student needs. By the end of the several weeks the agent thoroughly understood school district priorities and endeavored to include ways to address some of those priorities by emphasizing strong, positive relationships with new administrative staff who had been teachers and now were responsible for some aspect of teacher credentialing through university degree and certificate programs.

Eventually, three superintendents expressed strong interest in promoting the professional development opportunity described by the marketing agent. One of the districts included over 60 schools, 60,000 students and 9,000 full-time employees; the second, over 45 schools, 50,000 students, and 3,500 teachers; each district exceeded 160 square miles. Soon after her meeting with the three interested superintendants, the marketing agent asked each to host an information reception at their respective district offices so that teachers could meet program faculty, ask questions about the program, receive admission applications and program requirements brochures. All three agreed to host receptions early in the spring semester although one of them, approached by the system flagship university program soon after meeting with the instructional technology faculty marketing agent, arranged to provide professional development through the flagship program instead.

Fall marketing culminated in scheduling spring semester receptions for district teachers and attended by several assistant principals. After securing district administrative support for two district receptions, the marketing agent asked how each

would prefer to invite teachers to the receptions. At the beginning of the spring semester, she personally posted printed 8.5" x 11" announcement invitations in every elementary, middle, and high school teacher lounge and also posted them on the school bulletin boards in both districts where the principals gave permission. (This was a time consuming effort, but necessary since both district administrators demurred releasing teacher email addresses). About thirty teachers attended the first reception and forty, at a second reception in the same district. At another reception for the other district teachers another forty teachers learned about the professional development opportunities available through the program. Prospective students, the district teachers, spoke with faculty and a registrar's representative who answered their questions about fees, certificate options, degrees, and online courses.

The receptions, which personalized the program to potential students, served two additional purposes. First, the marketing agent assessed school district needs through conversations with attending faculty and administrators, usually assistant principals at these events; second, she would discuss with them how to parlay the school district commitment into a regional commitment from other school districts. The collaboration between school districts and the university program resulted in potential students applying for admissions or expressing intentions to apply and others requesting more application and program information. The program coordinator responded with a fall schedule offering online courses to meet district personnel's professional development needs through program certificates and degrees.

Administrative and political factors drove the coordinator's decision to list the online fall semester courses in the site schedule instead of exclusively listing them on the university schedule. The program coordinator chose the site located between the campus and the other site because it was the most convenient to the most prospective students from the interested districts and the site offered more extensive resources in an attractive new building adjacent to an expressway. Scheduling online courses through a site added value to an online course because the students would have access to site resources such as computer labs and library services. In addition, listing online program courses through the site established the program's right to offer the degree through the site and, there were other advantages. Also, listing online courses through a site schedule raised program visibility and aided future marketing to prospective students and supportive district administrators, both of which had many who lived or worked in the site's proximity. If enrollments eventually warranted, the program coordinator could schedule hybrid courses in the same site's classrooms and offering hybrid courses would be even more attractive than either online courses or campus hybrid courses for these prospective students. Online courses were for many students teaching in the districts much more convenient than driving to a program campus course at least 45 minutes and about 30 miles away. On the other hand, online courses were not as desirable as hybrid courses at a site half that distance and time or less because many students preferred instructor face-to-face, synchronous interaction to an online format with predominantly asynchronous written interactions. Furthermore, the program coordinator would have little trouble staffing hybrid courses with full-time faculty since at least two were eager to teach hybrid courses at either of the two systems sites because the sites were closer and more convenient to their homes than to the university campus.

Since certified teachers were eligible and interested in obtaining one of three State add-on teaching certificates, two different online courses each part of the State-approved certificate preparatory curriculum were scheduled and each was taught by one of the two full-time faculty members interested in teaching any future hybrid courses at the sites. Inexpensive brochures were created to disseminate to teachers throughout the school district. The university enrollment system was al-tered to easily identify and count new students who enrolled in the two online courses. Concurrently, the marketing agent secured the superintendent's program endorsement and this enhanced her marketing efforts of the program to the surrounding school district superintendents who, in turn, allowed the newly printed brochures to be disseminated among their schools. This marketing effort ultimately resulted in one of the adjacent districts endorsing the program. (Endorsement meant that the administrator would encourage the marketing of the program in that district too, and in doing so she would ask for special accommodations, such as periodic time offs and temporary teacher replacements for those teachers enrolled in the program. The superintendent had a vested interest in supporting the program because if more teachers in her district earned Master's degrees, there would be a much better chance of receiving more school district funding from the state). Throughout phase one the marketing agent repeatedly visited the district schools to ask teachers and administrators what courses, certificates, and delivery medium would best serve their needs. These visits with teachers and administrators established trust and built a personal and responsive relationship between prospective students and a program faculty member. The faculty marketing agent became the persuasive, accommodating spokesperson for a meaningful professional development opportunity. She relayed these prospective students' needs and preferences to the program coordinator continually until spring marketing and phase one drew to a close.

Phase Two: Measurable Success

After the first year and immediately prior to the fall semester, several personnel changes influenced phase two marketing. A new full-time distance education director assumed marketing responsibilities replacing the faculty marketing agent who returned to full-time teaching in the program; the program added a new full-time tenure-line faculty member; the Dean appointed a new program coordinator who revised the marketing plan for phase two aimed at increasing program site enrollments. The newly-appointed program coordinator convinced the Dean to fund a one-day faculty retreat at a local resort during which the eight-member graduate program faculty engaged in strategic planning activities and learned collaborative decision making; in short she set the ground rules for open, transparent, management style based on a consensus-building process to determine the program direction, procedures, and policies.

The program coordinator, guided by the faculty-generated marketing data, collaborated with the distance education director and former faculty marketing agent to identify when, where and how to best address the targeted educator's professional development needs. The three devised a program marketing plan designed to meet faculty, university, and school district personnel needs and appeal to program faculty. The plan scheduled courses in the sequence and with the delivery medium that accommodated prospective student needs and depended upon faculty strengths and preferences. Prospective students who enrolled in the program would be able to choose from among several certificates and two degrees to meet their professional development needs. Beginning in fall, the program delivered courses in the scheduled media and at the designated locations so that students could expect to complete certificate and degree curricula as efficiently and conveniently as possible.

Course delivery options appealed to a wide variety of students who demanded convenience but valued personal interactions with professors. Hybrid courses combined online activities for eight of the seven on-ground site classes during a fifteen-week semester. Online courses had no mandatory meetings. Instead faculty teaching these courses attended Saturday morning meetings offered to the students as optional office hours during which they met faculty. Because of State

requirements, faculty could not introduce any new material or penalize students not attending any of the optional meetings. The hybrid classes met one day a week, Monday to Thursday, every other week; site classes were purposely scheduled in one of two time slots, 4-7 p.m. and 7-10 p.m. Teachers working at nearby schools could take two courses in an evening if they chose and the times were the same as courses on the University campus and favored by faculty. On the other hand, when asked about when to schedule the group faculty optional office hours for two or three times a semester, online students almost unanimously requested Saturday morning; faculty agreed since the commitment was minimal and, in return for attending, the Dean agreed to cap their online enrollments at 23 instead of 30. This worked out particularly well because site directors wanted to build their site enrollments and community visibility. After the first few courses, however, the students felt comfortable enough and attendance at the optional office hour Saturday meetings decreased; student attendance at the last semester session was very low even the first semester the hybrid/online program was launched through the sites. Therefore faculty agreed to reduce scheduled, optional office hour meetings from three times to once or twice a semester.

Professional development and certificate preparation appealed to many of the potential students. A combination of online and web-enhanced courses that led to one of three institutional professional development certificates or one of three State teacher add-on certificate preparation programs became a cornerstone of the successful marketing plan. All instructional technology courses for the three institutional certificates could be applied to the instructional technology Master's degree. The one-course certificate required the only instructional technology course required for all graduate education degrees. The other two institutionally-granted professional development certificates, one in distance education and the other performance technology, required five and four courses respectively, all of which could be applied to the 39-hour Master's degree plan of studies. The three certificate preparatory plans enabled State-certified teachers to sit for one of three State examinations to earn either a grades EC-12, grades 8-12, or master technology teacher certificate; teachers perceived the State certifications as enhancing their own employability and professional desirability. Starting with three three-hour courses preparation for one certificate (grades 8-12), a student could add one more three-hour course for the second certificate preparation plan (grades EC-12), and for the third certificate, another three-hour course and two one-hour courses would prepare a certified teacher for a position as a district technology coordinator. The third certificate, entitled the teacher to additional pay in most schools.

Print flyers (Figure 1) that promoted these certificates were distributed every fall and spring semester at one to three optional meetings advertised as optional office hours were for program faculty, their current distance course students, and students' invited guests who might be interested in enrolling in the program. These one to three optional office hour meetings held at the system sites with the scheduled the online or hybrid course enabled students to meet their professors; the meetings afforded program faculty the opportunity to recruit potential students from the guest attendees. Meeting attendees were served refreshments while they listened to faculty briefly describe the program and answer their questions; faculty had time to hold individual office hours but avoided any additional or new instruction which would violate accreditation requirements for online courses. The promotional flyers listed which courses would be available online or at a system site the next semester and what certificates required the course. The institution's distance education director and her staff coordinated the room reservations, resources, refreshments, and provided admission information to and answered admission questions from potential students. Thus

the meetings were directed toward retaining current students and recruiting new students to the hybrid program.

MARKETING UNIVERSITY PROGRAMS: A DEARTH OF RESEARCH

Published research data on marketing university programs is somewhat limited due to the proprietary nature of most universities' data since data is used to make important management decisions for their universities (Daniel, 1996; Morgan & Hunt, 1994; Johnstone, Ewell, & Paulson, 2002; Jones, 2003; Hanna, 1998). However the research indicates that "a number of institutions are reacting to the changing market conditions by implementing mass marketing strategies to maintain and increase their market share of student recruitment and enrollments" (Shaik, 2005).

University Recruiting Becomes Marketing

One of the ways that universities may increase their market share is to offer unique programs that attract students who cannot, otherwise, attend a university; the program may be accessible either because it is independent of geographical constraints or may be more cost effective. The pressure to recruit has led university administrators to turn to marketing professionals, which some assume incorrectly and inappropriately assert student-university relationships are comparable to business-customer ones (Svenson & Wood, 2007). Yet, the university exists within a consumer culture that foments consumer values in any economic segment in which money is traded for educational services. Potential students, and their employers when they broker employee educational service access, choose from among many alternatives with whom to matriculate or to promote for employee educational services.

Figure 1. Marketing flyers indicating hybrid (web-enhanced) and online courses with relationship to degrees and certificates.

School of Education - Instructional Technology Program
Spring Course Offerings   *INST Web Courses*

Course No.	CIP#	Course Name	Classification
EDUC 5130.01	2490	Cognition & Instruction	INST Core
INST 5333.01	2472	Systematic Design	INST Core
INST 5333.02	2473	Systematic Design	INST Core
INST 5135.01	2507	Multimedia for Educators	Production Elective
INST 5535.01	2475	Internet for Instruction	Production Elective
INST 5931.01	2477	Research Topics: Trends & Issues	INST Core**
INST 6031.01	2478	Applications of Technology	Education Core
INST 6031.02	2481	Applications of Technology	Education Core
INST 6031.03	2482	Applications of Technology	Education Core
INST 6031.08	2484	Applications of Technology	Education Core
INST 6031.09	2486	Applications of Technology	Education Core
INST 6037.01	2487	Advanced Technology Applications	Advanced Topics Elective
INST 6537.01	2489	Managing Computer Resources	Advanced Topics Elective

INST MS - EDUCATION CORE WEB

Course No.	CIP#	Course Name	Classification
SILC 6030.04	2592	Foundations of Multicultural Education	Education Core
SILC 6030.05	2593	Foundations of Multicultural Education	Education Core
SILC 6030.06	2594	Foundations of Multicultural Education	Education Core
SILC 6030.07	2595	Foundations of Multicultural Education	Education Core
EDUC 6032.05	2553	Statistics and Measurement	Education Core
EDUC 6032.06	2554	Statistics and Measurement	Education Core
EDUC 6033.05	2559	Research Design and Analysis	Education Core

(a)

CLASSES BEGIN JANUARY 18TH

University
INSTRUCTIONAL TECHNOLOGY PROGRAM
CERTIFICATE COURSES
SPRING OFFERINGS

EARLY REGISTRATION: NOV 15TH – NOV 29TH
OPEN REGISTRATION: DEC 20TH – JAN 6TH
LATE REGISTRATION: JAN 18TH – JAN 24TH

Course Name	Instruction Mode	Applicable Certificates
INST 5130 Cognition & Instruction	WWW	Performance Tech EC-12 Tech Apps MTT
INST 5233 Performance Technology	Web Enhanced	Performance Tech
INST 5433 IT Project Mgt./Grant Writing	Web Enhanced	Performance Tech
INST 5535 Internet for Instruction	Web Enhanced	Online Distance Ed
INST 5635 Advanced Web Development	Web Enhanced	Online Distance Ed
INST 6031 Applications of Technology	WWW or Web Enhanced	8-12 Tech Apps EC-12 Tech Apps MTT
INST 6037 Advanced Technology Applications	WWW	8-12 Tech Apps EC-12 Tech Apps MTT
INST 5333 Systematic Design	WWW	Online Distance Ed Performance Tech MTT
INST 5931 Research Topics: Trends & Issues	WWW	Performance Tech

| 8-12 Tech Apps- EC-12 Tech Apps- MTT- | 8-12 Technology Applications Certificate EC-12 Technology Applications Certificate Master Technology Teacher Certificate | Online Distance Ed- Performance Tech- | Online Distance Educator Certificate Performance Technology |

(b)

Therefore, the decision process from among alternatives and subsequent exchange of money for services implicitly incorporates the salient features conducive to marketing methods.

Online instruction has fueled competition among programs simply because the number of programs and their accessibility to a much larger potential student population. On-line and blended programs offer these students viable learning opportunities, in some cases, many feasible alternatives where none existed before. While many universities have dramatically increased their online marketing efforts, money is not sufficient nor even necessary to build a program, as this case study evidences. Relationship marketing used in this case study required faculty time and effort but not a budgeted professional marketing firm. All program promotional materials were produced by faculty and with limited university staff hours. Hence faculty time and ability were maximized to foster trusting relationships and develop accessible educational services that were attractive, feasible, and desirable to potential student groups. This case study indicated the effective online-hybrid program marketing did not necessarily mean online marketing or external, costly marketing firms.

Relationship Marketing

Research through the last century has also pointed to the value of personal communications and establishing trust relationships (Hamel & Prahalad, 1994; Morgan& Hunt, 1994; Muson, 2005; Sheth & Parvatiyar, 2000; Van Doren & Corrigan, 2008). In a competitive global marketplace, there is value in helping a client identify problems, by employing strategic thinking and developing relationships with clients (Kaufman, 1998, 2000; Kaufman & Swart, 1995; Kaufman & Swart, 1995; Kaufman, Thigarajan, & MacGillis, 1997; Kaufman, Watkins, Triner, & Stith, 1998; Molebash, 2002). Helping clients address needs and provide possible solutions can lead to fiduciary relationships that can have long-term positive benefits and repercussions. The reverse can be true too, however, if there is a failure on the part of the marketing representative or the representative organization to keep the promises to the client and to breach that bond of trust. If that occurs, it may be a very long time before that trust can be restored, if ever. In this case the both the antecedent and the successful marketing effort respectively exemplify consequences of ignoring and of effectively using relationship marketing.

Marketing of educational services is about interactions between the institution and the students that form the basis of a process of relationship building. Management of educational services is the management of these relationship processes. It is more complex than managing products because products can be standardized whereas it is difficult to standardize (educational) services. (Shaik, 2005, Relationship Marketing, p. 2).

Educational services marketing differs somewhat from broader corporate marketing applications (Coates, 2005; Daniel, 1996; Ely, 1990; Hanna, 1998; Haworth & Conrad, 1997; Kaufman & Swart, 1995; Lepper & Whitmore, 1996; Lepper, Drake, & O'Donnell-Johnson, 1997: Nootenberg, 2006; Robinson, 1996; Salmon, 2005). Corporate marketing, driven by profit motives, seeks to increase sales and earnings, sell as much as possible to as many customers and to do so for the least cost. Likewise, educational marketing seeks to increase the sales of educational services, and costs to the educational institution are second to the quality, cost, and benefit to the service recipient the student. Educational services differ from other consumer services and products in that they necessarily help the client, and realize cost- savings only as it provides better service (Schmidt, 2001). Therefore, relationship marketing works so well because educational services implicitly serve the student and university program growth depends upon a student-university relationship built upon service. To that end, like in business, in education, meeting commitments, an essential feature of relationship marketing, promotes successful program building.

The essential ingredient in maintaining customer loyalty is follow-through. It is making sure that you deliver on what your value proposition promises; it means having regular personal contact with customers and listening closely to their needs; and it requires acting expeditiously to analyze and respond to complaints. (Muson, 2005, p.4)

Technology Components

Hybrid and online courses required students use Internet-accessible computers that could be their own, their district's/employer's, or even one of the two university site computer lab's. The latter option undesirably undercut program convenience since a student would have to commute to a site instead of home or work to participate in the course. The university delivered online and the distance component of hybrid courses through a commercial CMS administered by the university and delivered through client-side web browsers used by either of the two most common desk-top computer operating systems. Course delivery required only one client-side application, a web-browser. Online and hybrid course students usually completed course assignments in the dominant word processer, presentation, and spreadsheet applications which were available at the site and university campus labs and on most school district and employer's computers. faculty designed courses so that students could use free trial versions for other applications.

Technology Concerns

At first many students were novice online CMS users and some had difficulty using the password protected courses. Therefore to help novice students learn the system, the site-scheduled faculty optional office hour meeting at the beginning of the semester, usually the Saturday, during the first week of classes, included the opportunity to have site technical staff help any student having difficulty access the course. The marketing agent even demonstrated and confirmed course accessibility at a few key district schools

Computers with Internet access and web browsers were relatively ubiquitous but some were problematic for hybrid course student use. For example, students in a few selected courses or someone they could depend upon had to have administrative privileges and technical skill

sufficient to install and use downloadable trial software since course requirements stated that they were responsible for their technology. The site labs made every effort to install many of these applications if economically feasible given the software cost and student demand.

Employer firewalls presented another technical barrier for a handful of students behind firewalls that barred access to the CMS. In one strange instance work computers of the employees of another state university were barred from accessing the same course managements system that their own institution used and for which they were designing courses. Some students and even faculty occasionally used telephone modem access. Fortunately most course materials and assignments were not large enough to prohibit downloading or uploading. Generally access was rarely caused by modem speed or firewalls; more often, CMS instability did.

A few times a semester students or faculty might not be able to access the course for a few hours at most. In the rare event that it was the CMS server or University technology, the University technical staff provided logs to confirm the problem and faculty would not penalize students for late assignments due to university technology.

The program avoided using two-way interactive technology for course delivery because it could cost the student, the district or the university, and, far more importantly, undermine course convenience with additional scheduled events requiring students to attend at a specific time.

EVALUATION OF INITIAL PROGRAM AND CURRENT CHALLENGES FACING THE ORGANIZATION

The first marketing lesson learned was that over-promising and under-delivering poisons university-student relationships. The corollary is that, once damaged, re-establishing positive relationships is possible but only with patience, effort, time, skill, and by meticulously making and meeting every new commitment. These results, consistent with marketing research, indicated that adopting and maintaining educational innovations could be fatally flawed if not implemented as promised or remarkably effective if consistently supported and continually directed at the recipient's needs (Ellsworth, 2000; Ely, 2000; Gask, 2005; Robinson, 1995; Schott & Gannon-Cook, 2001).

The second lesson was to keep accurate records substantiating marketing effectiveness. During phase two the program coordinator assisted by the program secretary, created a data base to track graduate student participation since the enrollment services data base did not provide sufficient detailed information about who was enrolling, where they were located, and average course section size. The program database included student names for those admitted to the program, which followed university admission but was not recorded in any database. The program coordinator discovered discrepancies between the more accurate program database and the university database that did not list the students' originating campus locations, advisors, or admission dates. Only the department program database provided accurate marketing outcomes information.

Data revealed marketing successes by the end of phase two, year two, average per section enrollment for all courses and sections in the program was 21; thirteen online courses had an average per section enrollment of 20. Hybrid courses had an average section enrollment of 25 for five sections, which was an increase from 23 at the end of phase two, year one. Higher sustained and increasing hybrid enrollments indicated students preferred hybrid courses.

The program required sophisticated scheduling that gave priority to providing students courses in the format and sequence they required. For two years, the program coordinator during phase two had spent considerable time preparing marketing materials, attending site marketing events, and scheduling courses to meet the marketing priority:

provide courses when, how and where to meet student's needs. About the same time she asked to be relieved of the labor-intensive scheduling responsibilities, the time-consuming and skillful marketing efforts began by the faculty-marketing agent and sustained by a distance education director ceased. As a result, the program per section enrollments dropped and the faculty was reduced from eight full time faculty, to the current three tenure-line faculty, a visiting assistant professor, and an instructor supplemented by a handful of adjuncts.

Long-term budgetary shortages curtailed hybrid course offerings. Most courses are now offered online and the few remaining course offered each semester are all hybrid courses at the university in which enrollments rarely exceed ten. Hybrid courses are no longer offered at any sites but the online courses have eclipsed hybrid courses of which one or two a semester is cancelled, most have well below 10 students, and all are offered exclusively at the university campus.

Currently the University contracts with a national private marketing firm and faculty are prohibited from creating their own materials. The current program coordinator schedules courses according to faculty requests for new and innovative courses. No data on per section enrollments or cancelled courses is kept or reported to faculty or the program coordinator.

SOLUTIONS AND RECOMMENDATIONS

Results of this case study yield a multi-faceted cornerstone for effective educational services marketing and sustained program growth: Deliver a consistent message, establish trusting relationships between the providers and recipients, and meet commitments. Our findings support marketing literature imperatives to establish trusting relationships with clients or customers and consistently meet commitments (Hamel & Prahalad, 1994;

Morgan & Hunt, 1994; Muson, 2005; Sheth & Parvatiyar, 2000; Van Doren & Corrigan, 2008). University administrators would be for the need to have consistency in the long-term program growth proved to be perhaps the most important aspect of the study, because without the long-term university commitment to the program by the administration, the program would not have the ability to sustain itself (Wu, 1988).

The importance establishing a trust relationship cannot be overemphasized (Sergiovanni, 1994) especially in this case when the marketing agent discovered that a previous university representative had violated the trust with one of the largest and most important districts. The agent had to overcome well-earned mistrust of the superintendant for her program and university and then establish credibility for meeting commitments. Some of the marketing methods employed by the faculty agent to allay the superintendant's fears were to:

- determine why there was obviously an initial distrust; the faculty-marketing agent discretely investigated the history behind the mistrust in order to re-establish trust and assure those mistakes would not be repeated(Muson, 2005; Stribiak & Paul, 1998);
- ensure that the university delivered the promised educational services, so the representative needed to work with the program coordinator to set up a mechanism not only for implementation, but for follow up;
- identify a designated authoritative university representative take responsibility for closely monitoring implementation of promised services to assure their delivery and to quickly, effectively address and resolve problems; and
- "take advantage of every opportunity for

personal contact between company leaders (the university) and customers (the school district)" (Muson, 2005, p.4). The agent took every occasion for trust-building over an extended time to establish a trust relationship.

The second discovery, which could have more pervasive implications, was whether the university's long-term commitment was rhetoric or real. A program commitment should extend beyond two-years although that may not be possible if administrators have other priorities superseding the commitment. Although the expense of reimbursing faculty for a commute to a site to teach hybrid courses was only a few hundred dollars for each course, with pending budget constraints, other priorities could supplant the minimal cost marketing effort. Actuarial studies might be recommended to assess the value of developing programs that grow student population compared with the five year university budgets to be sure the program could comply with the budgetary requirements so that a sufficient bottom-line profit could be built into both the program's and university's plans.

This case study suggests a cost-effective approach to university marketing initiatives for hybrid courses and programs. If the target student population seeks face-to-face interaction with faculty but lacks online course experience, then hybrid courses offer benefits of both. Furthermore optional meetings to orient novice online students and introduce them to faculty help students and faculty transition to online learning environments. The case study outcomes offer evidence that hybrid courses can scaffold learning and assuage learner fears associated with online courses. At the same time, hybrid courses offer more time and place convenience than the traditional courses; they facilitate learners' transition to online courses.

We would also recommend including action research when conducting marketing. Action research, if included in the initial marketing campaign, can expand the body of knowledge in the research areas of innovation and diffusion of technology and benefit the learning environments in this millennium.

REFERENCES

Barg, R. (2004). Breaking down barriers: Collaborative education drives collective change. *Journal of Emergency Management, 2*(3). Retrieved on April 21, 2008 from http://www.ofm.gov.on.ca/english/FireService/announcements/2004/Breaking%20Down%20Barriers.asp

Berge, Z. L. (2002). Active, interactive, and reflective elearning. *Quarterly Review of Distance Education, 3*(2), 181–190.

Berge, Z. L., & Muilenburg, L. (2001). Obstacles faced at various stages of capability regarding DE in institutions of Higher Education: Survey results. *TechTrends, 45*(4), 40–44. doi:10.1007/BF02784824

Bourner, T., Katz, T., & Watson, D. (Eds.). (2000). *New directions in professional higher education*. London: The Open University Press.

Coates, H. (2005). Quality in higher education. *Quality in Higher Education, 11*(1), 25–36. doi:10.1080/13538320500074915

Daniel, J. S. (1996). *Megauniversities and knowledge media: Technology strategies for higher education*. London: Biddles Ltd.

Ellsworth, J. B. (2000). *Surviving change: A survey of educational change models*. Syracuse, NY: ERIC Clearinghouse on Information and Technology.

Ely, D. (1990). Conditions that facilitate the implementation of educational technology innovations. *Journal of Research on Computing in Education, 23*(2), 298–305.

Gask, L. (2005). *Overt and covert barriers to the integration of primary and specialist mental health care*. Manchester, UK: National Primary Care Research and Development Centre.

Hamel, G., & Prahalad, C. K. (1994). *Competing for the future: Breakthrough strategies for seizing control of your industry and creating the markets of tomorrow*. Cambridge, MA: Harvard Business School Press.

Hanna, D. E. (1998). Higher education in an era of digital competition: Emerging organizational models. *JALN, 2*(1), 67-95. Retrieved on May 3, 2009 from http://www.sloan-c.org/publications/jaln/v2n1/pdf/v2n1_hanna.pdf

Havernik, J., Messerschmitt, D., & Vandrick, S. (1997). Collaborative research: Why and how? *Educational Researcher, 26*(9), 31–35.

Haverschmidt, J., & Schmidt, D. (1998). The importance of the role of collaboration in higher education Instruction. *American Educational Research Journal, 35*, 10–16.

Haworth, J., & Conrad, C. (1997). *Emblems of quality: Developing and sustaining high quality programs*. Boston: Allyn and Bacon.

Hergert, M. (2003). Lessons from launching an online MBA program. *Online Journal of Distance Learning Administration, 6*(4). Retrieved March 18, 2009 from http://www.westga.edu/~distance/ojdla/winter64/hergert 64.htm

Johnstone, S. M., Ewell, P., & Paulson, K. (2002). Student learning as academic currency. *ACE Center 004 for Policy Analysis*. Retrieved February 25, 2005, from http://www.acenet.edu/bookstore/pdf/distributed-learning/distributed-learning-04.pdf

Jones, R. (2003). A recommendation for managing the predicted growth in college enrollment at a time of adverse economic conditions. *Online Journal of Distance Learning Administration, 6*(1). Retrieved February 25, 2005, from http://www.westga.edu/~distance/ojdla/spring61/jones61.htm

Kaufman, R. (1998). *Strategic thinking: A guide to identifying and solving problems (revised)*. Arlington, VA & Washington DC: American Society of Training & Development and International Society for Performance Improvement.

Kaufman, R. (2000). *Mega planning: Practical tools for organizational success*. Thousand Oaks, CA: Sage Publishing.

Kaufman, R., & Swart, W. (1995). Beyond conventional benchmarking: Integrating ideal visions, strategic planning, reengineering, and quality management. *Educational Technology, 35*(3), 11–14.

Kaufman, R., Thigarajan, S., & MacGillis, P. (Eds.). (1997). *The guidebook for performance improvement: Working with individuals and organizations*. San Francisco: Jossey-Bass/Pfeiffer.

Kaufman, R., Watkins, R., Triner, D., & Stith, M. (1998). The changing corporate mind: Organizations, visions, mission purposes, and indicators on the move toward societal payoff. *Performance Improvement, 37*(3), 32–44.

Lepper, M. R., Drake, M., & O'Donnell-Johnson, T. M. (1997). Scaffolding techniques of expert human tutors . In Hogan, K., & Pressley, M. (Eds.), *Scaffolding student learning: Instructional approaches and issues* (pp. 108–144). New York: Brookline Books.

Lepper, M. R., & Whitmore, P. (1996). Collaboration: A social–psychological perspective. *Cognitive Studies: The Bulletin of the Japanese Cognitive Science Society, 3*, 7–10.

Molebash, P. E. (2002). Phases of collaborative success: A response to Shoffner, Dias, and Thomas. *Contemporary Issues in Technology and Teacher Education*. Retrieved December 10, 2002, from http://www.citejournal.org/vol2/iss1/general/article1.cfm

Morgan, R., & Hunt, S. (1994). The commitment-trust theory of relationship marketing. *Journal of Marketing, 58*(4), 36–51.

Muson, H. (2005 August). How smaller companies earn customer loyalty. *The Conference Board, Executive Action Series*, (157).

Nootenberg, B. (2006). Organization, evolution, cognition and dynamic capabilities. *Center Discussion Paper Series No. 2006-41*. Nederlands: Tilburg University – Center and Faculty of Economics and Business Administration.

Robinson, B. (1995). The saber-tooth curriculum: Peddiwell and technology diffusion. Presentation made at Queens College, Cambridge, UK. Unpublished.

Salmon, G. (2005). Flying not flapping: A strategic framework for e-learning and pedagogical innovation in higher education institutions. *ALT-J, 13*(3), 201–218. doi:10.1080/09687760500376439

Schmidt, P. (2001, February 2). State budgets indicate lean times for public colleges. *The Chronicle of Higher Education*, ▪▪▪, A21–A22.

Schott, M., & Cook, R. (2002). *Distance education faculty compensation models at a southwestern university*. Paper presented at the Texas Distance Education Association, Houston, TX.

Sergiovanni, T. J. (1994). *Building community in schools*. San Francisco, CA: Jossey-Bass.

Shaik, N. (2005). Marketing distance learning programs and courses: A relationship marketing strategy. *Online Journal of Distance Learning Administration, 8*(2).

Sheth, J., & Parvatiyar, A. (2000). *Handbook of relationship marketing*. Thousand Oaks, CA: Sage Publications.

Stribiak, C. A., & Paul, J. (1998). *The team development fieldbook: A step-by-step approach for student teams*. New York: McGraw Hill.

Svenson, G., & Wood, G. (2007). Are university students really customers? When illusion may lead to delusion for all! *Journal of Marketing Education, 21*(1), 17–28.

Van Doren, D., & Corrigan, H. (2008). Designing a marketing course with field site visits. *Journal of Marketing Education, 30*(3), 189–206. doi:10.1177/0273475308318071

Vockell, E. L., & Asher, J. W. (1995). *Educational research* (2nd ed.). Englewood Cliffs, NJ: Prentice-Hall, Inc.

Wu, P. (1988). Why change is difficult? Lessons for staff development . *Journal of Staff Development, 9*(2), 10–14.

ADDITIONAL READING

Canterbury, R. M. (2000). Higher education marketing: A challenge. *Journal of Marketing for Higher Education, 9*(3), 15–24. doi:10.1300/J050v09n03_02

Chambers, D. P. (2004). From recruitment to graduation: A whole-of-institution approach to supporting online students. *Online Journal of Distance Learning Administration, 7*(4).

Cunningham, S., Ryan, Y., Stedman, L., Tapsall, S., Bagdon, K., Flew, T., et al. (2001). *The business of borderless education*. Canberra, Australia: Department of Education, Science, and Training. Retrieved from http://www.dest.gov.au/highered/eippubs/eip02_1/eip02_1. pdf.

Gibson, J. W., & Herrera, J. M. (1999). How to go from classroom based to online delivery in eighteen months or less: A case study in online program development. [Technological Horizons In Education]. *T.H.E. Journal, 26*(6), 57–58.

Goldgehn, L. A. (1991). Are US colleges and universities applying marketing techniques properly and within the context of an overall marketing plan? *Journal of Marketing for Higher Education, 3*(2), 39–62. doi:10.1300/J050v03n02_03

Goodyear, P., Salmon, G., Spector, J. M., Steeples, C., & Tickner, S. (2001). Competencies for online teaching: A special report. *Educational Technology Research and Development, 49*(1), 65–72. doi:10.1007/BF02504508

Hagel, J. III, & Armstrong, A. G. (1997). Net gain: Expanding markets through virtual communities. *Journal of Interactive Marketing, 13*(2), 55–65.

Kassop, M. (2003). Ten ways online education matches, or surpasses, face-to-face learning. *The Technology Source*. Retrieved from http://ts.mivu. org/default.asp?show=article&id=1034

King, D. W. (1982). Marketing secondary information products and services. *Journal of the American Society for Information Science American Society for Information Science, 33*(3). doi:10.1002/asi.4630330313

Kirp, D. L. (2003). *Shakespeare, Einstein, and the bottom line: The marketing of higher education*. Cambridge, MA: Harvard University Press.

Levy, S. (2003). Six factors to consider when planning online distance learning programs in higher education. *Online Journal of Distance Learning Administration, 6*(1).

Lockwood, F., & Gooley, A. (2001). *Innovation in open & distance learning: successful development of online and web-based learning*. New York: Routledge.

Mazzarol, T. (1998). Critical success factors for international education marketing. *International Journal of Educational Management, 12*(4), 163–175. doi:10.1108/09513549810220623

Merritt, S. (1991). Marketing ethics and education: Some empirical findings. *Journal of Business Ethics, 10*, 625–632. doi:10.1007/BF00382883

Pittinsky, M. S. (2003). The wired tower: Perspectives on the impact of the internet on higher education. Upper Saddle, NJ: Pearson Education, FT Press.

Rovai, A. P. (2002). Sense of community, perceived cognitive learning, and persistence in asynchronous learning networks. *The Internet and Higher Education, 5*, 319–332. doi:10.1016/S1096-7516(02)00130-6

Salmon, G. (2004). *E-moderating: The key to teaching and learning online*. New York: Routledge.

Schlager, M. S., Fusco, J., & Schank, P. (2002). Evolution of an online education community of practice . In Renninger, K. A., & Shumar, W. (Eds.), *Building virtual communities: Learning and change in cyberspace* (pp. 129–158).

Shoemaker, C. C. J. (1998). *Leadership in continuing and distance education in higher education*. Needham, MA: Allyn & Bacon.

KEY TERMS AND DEFINITIONS

Action Research: Action research is "the practical application of the scientific method or other forms of disciplined inquiry to the process of dealing with everyday problems" (Vockell & Asher, 1995, p. 445).

Certification: The process of completing the requirements to receive a certificate that may be issued by the granting institution, professional organization, or governmental entity.

Certificate Preparation: The process of providing training for any certificate which requires the applicant pass a test.

Face-to-Face: Interactions between instructor and students who are simultaneously physically present in the same classroom.

Hybrid: A course that substitutes online activities for one or more face-to-face classes.

Marketing: The systematic process of convincing people to exchange money for products or services.

On-Ground: Courses limited to class sessions between instructor and students who are simultaneously physically present in the same classroom.

Online: Courses or course interactions transpiring in virtual space and that may be asynchronous.

Outcomes: Any measurable results of systematically applied processes.

Relationship Marketing: The systematic process of convincing people to exchange money for products or services by establishing a personal, sustained interaction between the service/product provider and the service/product consumer

Web-Enhanced: Synonym for hybrid.

Chapter 6

Professional Development Programme in the Use of Educational Technology to Implement Technology– Enhanced Courses Successfully

Sibongile Simelane
Tshwane University of Technology, South Africa

ABSTRACT

Universities globally have realised that they need to educate instructors, lecturers and teachers in how to integrate technology into education. Some higher education institutions have already introduced professional development programmes in educational technology to ensure that technology will be effectively utilised, which in turn will enhance the quality of their educational practices. In this chapter, a case study of the implementation component of the e-TUTO programme will be discussed in depth with the findings from the participants who participated in the programme during June 2005 to June 2006. An overview of professional development programme in the use of educational technology to assist lecturers to implement technology-enhanced courses successfully is presented, as well as an overly demanding e-TUTO programme, which might hinder the successful implementation of a technology-

INTRODUCTION

Higher education institutions should take advantage of Internet technology to improve and supplement traditional courses. An advancement of the Internet is that it brings change in the process and organisational structure of teaching and learning (Ma & Runyon, 2004). The advantage of Internet technol-

ogy to improve and supplement traditional courses is explored in this chapter. In this regard, I explore in detail a professional development programme that utilises educational technology to assist lecturers to implement technology-enhanced courses successfully. This chapter illustrates the implementation component of the e-TUTO programme and also discusses the findings from the participants of the period, June 2005 to June 2006.

DOI: 10.4018/978-1-61520-751-0.ch006

The case study was conducted in 2007 at Tshwane University of Technology (TUT). The aim of the study was to examine the implementation component of the e-TUTO programme. This was accomplished in order to identify the success indicators and the challenges that prevent a successful implementation of the technology-enhanced courses. Qualitative data was collected by means of a case study that uses an interpretive approach and incorporates elements of ethnography. The participants in the study were fifteen staff members who participated in the e-TUTO programme from Tshwane University of Technology (TUT). E-TUTO is a development programme in educational technology for professionals that was devised and initiated in 2004 by the Directorate of Teaching and Learning with Technology at TUT. This programme was funded by the institution.

Professional development programmes should empower faculty members to utilise and integrate technology to enhance the quality of teaching and learning. The question is no longer about the value of the use of the Internet in higher education institutions but rather about the quality, influence and effectiveness of the online courses that are created. Based on this debate, I argue that, if higher education institutions are to implement technology-enhanced courses successfully, then they should consider empowering lecturers through professional development programmes. Further, institutions should ensure that success indicators are stipulated right at the beginning. Such a process will be helpful in monitoring progress throughout the implementation of the professional development programmes.

The chapter initially analyses and summarises literature relating to professional development programmes that use educational technology globally. This is followed by a review of research focusing on professional development programmes and the way these influence lecturers' teaching practices. Research methodology employed will be explained. A discussion of the case study of participants of the e-TUTO programme will follow. In this discussion, the focus will be on when implementing technology-enhanced courses, which include the e-TUTO programme, adequate funding, time management, lecturers' attitudes, capacity-building and computer skills. Finally, an argument on challenges that were encountered by the participants during the e-TUTO programme that hindered the successful implementation of technology-enhanced courses is advanced.

SETTING THE STAGE

What is a Professional Development Programme?

A professional development programme is a programme that teaches and empowers lecturers and non-academic staff members in both formal and informal ways to learn new skills, to develop new approaches to pedagogy and teaching practices, to discover and explore new technologies, and to understand both content and resources. According to Grant (nd), professional development is more than what is implied by the term training, with its implication of learning skills. The phrase professional development programme includes formal and informal means of helping lecturers not only to learn new skills but also to develop new insights into pedagogy and their own practice. It also implies helping lecturers to understand the content of their courses and the resources available to them. Grant(nd) notes that professional development also includes supporting lecturers as they grapple with the challenges that come from putting their evolving understanding of the uses of technology into practice. Current technologies offer resources to meet these challenges. They also help lecturers to grow in their professional skills, their understanding and their personal interests.

In this chapter, a "professional development programme" is defined as a programme that teaches and empowers lecturers and non-academic staff members in both formal and informal ways to learn new skills, develop new approaches to pedagogy and teaching practices, to discover and explore new technologies, and to understand both content and resources. In particular, the professional development programme described here is the e-TUTO programme.

Why Use of Educational Technology for Professional Development Programme?

Because the long-heralded information age has now become a reality in all spheres of life, universities have realised that they need to educate instructors, lecturers and teachers in how to integrate computer technology into education and other curricula (Poole, 1997, p. 10). Some higher education institutions have already introduced professional development programmes in educational technology to ensure that technology will be effectively utilised and that it will enhance the quality of their educational practices. It is necessary for institutions to make provision for well-planned, ongoing professional development programmes that are supported by both management and academic staff members so that lecturers can learn to use technology creatively and effectively in order for students to benefit from such initiatives. Researchers such as (Guri-Rosenblit, 2005; Quick & Lieb, 2000; Viel, Brantley, & Zulli, 2004) argue that a large number of international universities use professional development programmes to educate their staff in the use of technology in educational practice.

In recognising the importance of professional development programmes to educate their staff, Tshwane University of Technology embarked on developing e-TUTO. This programme was developed to support, engage and empower lectures to effectively use and take control of technology in their teaching and learning practices. The e-TUTO programme ran over a period of twelve months and contributed to the successful implementation of participants' technology-enhanced courses. The participants learned to appreciate the technologies that were available and to apply them in their teaching practice. They also valued the various components that were taught during the programme, which include capacity building, design and development, implementation and research components. They explored technology to a greater extent than they implemented it, and also experimented with individual research into the use of educational technologies.

Guri-Rosenblit (2005), Quick and Lieb (2000), and Viel, Brantley and Zulli (2004) maintain that educators have realised that computer technology has exerted a decisive influence on teaching and learning in the past decade or so in particular, and that information communication technologies in general have changed the face of education at all levels, including higher education. Online learning has grown exponentially in higher education over the past five years with the advent and implementation of course management platforms (Abel, 2005b). Twigg (2003) states that technology is utilised in most higher education institutions as a new way of making teaching and learning experiences more powerful and accessible. Professional development programmes in higher education such as *Course Redesign (Twigg, 2003), Programme for Educational Transformation through Technology (Bruce, Fugate, Kerr, & Wolf, 2004), Pioneers Online (Pete, Fregona, Allinson, & Cronje, 2002)* and *E-TUTO (Van Ryneveld & Van der Merwe, 2005)* were established. In addition, the study on *Alliance for Higher Education Competitiveness* and *Virtual Information Space* project at University of Stellenbosch (Ekermans, 2003) as well as *Centre for Technology Assisted Learning* unit at University of Johannesburg (Broere, Kruger, & Van Wyk, 2003), *Education Innovation* at University of Pretoria and *Teaching and Learning with Technology* at Tshwane University of Technology, and *Centre for Higher Education Development* at Durban University of Technology, were also introduced. These focus on how lecturers were empowered to integrate educational technology into their teaching and learning practices.

Influence of Educational Technology in Professional Development Programmes

Several research studies have been conducted in an attempt to determine the influence of technology in teaching and learning through professional development programmes in educational technology. Previous literature reveals some aspects affecting the success of online instructional program. Blignaut & Lillejord (2005) identified four lessons that have an influence on technology, project management, and online learning communities and cross-cultural issues. The study conducted by (Volery & Lord, 2000) also revealed the aspects influencing the effectiveness of online education. The fast growing trend of the Internet as a potential tool for course delivery in higher education institutions together with lifelong learning has constructed the important motivation for higher education institutions to develop online courses. Volery and Lord (2000) state that higher education institutions should embrace technology and its user friendliness or they will be left behind in the race for globalisation and technological development.

The debate on the growth of the Internet in education, the influence and the effectiveness of online courses or programmes to enhance teaching and learning and the implementation process of e-learning in higher education institutions is continuing. For the past decade, new information communication technologies, have had a massive influence or impact on the world economy. Higher education institutions have utilised the advantage of technologies on reorganising the teaching and learning practices and many of the higher education institutions failed to produce the results. In her study, Guri-Rosenblit (2005) attempted to highlight the inconsistency, impossibilities or illogicalities in implementing e-learning. She identifies eight paradoxes in the implementation process of e-learning in higher education that relates to:

1. The different infrastructures and readiness of different types of higher education institutions to utilise the technologies potential;
2. The extent to which the old distance education technologies and the new technologies replace teaching and learning practices in the classroom;
3. The role of real problems, barriers and obstacles in applying new technologies;
4. The impact of new technologies on different student clientele;
5. Information acquisition vs, knowledge construction in higher education
6. Cost consideration;
7. The human capacity to adapt new learning styles in the face of the rapid development of the technologies; and
8. The organizational cultures of academic and cooperative worlds

Guri–Rosenblit (2005) emphasises that it is important for higher education institutions to understand the above-mentioned paradoxes when implementing e-learning for the efficient and successful application of new technologies.

CASE DESCRIPTION

E-TUTO: The Professional Development Programme by the Use of Technology in Education

Because the long-heralded information age has now become a reality in all spheres of life, universities have realised that they need to educate instructors, lecturers and teachers in how to integrate computer technology into education and other curricula (Poole, 1997, p. 10). The e-TUTO programme constitutes a practical response to the needs of the information age. The participants in the e-TUTO programme are all permanent, full-time members of staff at Tshwane University of Technology. The university releases them from their normal duties so that they can participate in the programme between June in one year and June in the following year. The e-TUTO programme commenced in 2004 with thirteen participants, however, the intake differed from year to year. In both 2005 and 2006, there were fifteen participants. This programme empowered lecturers in utilising and integrating a variety of technologies to enhance their teaching and learning practice.

The e-TUTO programme invites a variety of stakeholders to actively support the participants as they engage in the activities of the programme. Stakeholders understand the kind of support that participants will need in the implementation phase. The stakeholders are the managers of the university, that is, deans, directors or heads of department (HOD), the participant himself/herself – (who is usually a lecturer in an academic department) and personnel from academic support departments such as Curriculum Design, Quality Promotions, Corporate Relations, Staff and Skills Development, Library and Information Services, Student Learning Academic Development, Research and Development, IT services as well as Teaching and Learning with Technology (Instructional Designers and Technical Staff).

According to the University of Florida (2005), a technology-enhanced module uses differing technologies to teach course materials. These technologies might include a website, video streaming, multimedia materials, and video conferencing. At TUT, technology-enhanced modules are developed with a variety of technologies such as virtual classrooms, videos, mobile learning, interactive multimedia material, video conferencing and electronic testing to enhance the traditional face-to-face method of teaching and learning (Van Ryneveld & Van der Merwe, 2005).

The Implementation Component of E-Tuto Programme

During the implementation component, participants schedule computer laboratories and compile timetables for their courses. They also check on the computer requirements for using learning management systems, videos and interactive multimedia, they test the reliability of the network, and teach their students how to access courses independently. The participants then integrate web-enabled course materials and other technology-enhanced teaching materials into their classroom teaching. During the implementation component, participants gather data for their research projects on technology-enhanced teaching and learning. They also help and guide their colleagues to integrate technology-enhancing materials with their subject content.

RESEARCH METHODOLOGY

Data was collected by means of a qualitative case study and an interpretivist paradigm in conjunction with a particular ethnographic approach. In this study the case study is defined by the implementation component of the e–TUTO programme and whether the e–TUTO programme assisted participants to implement their technology-enhanced courses successfully. The unit of analysis is the group of participants who participated in the e–TUTO programme between June 2005 and June 2006. A qualitative case study is not a methodological choice so much as a choice of the defined circumstances or situation that the researcher wishes to study (Stake, 2000, pp., p. 435). The researcher explores a single manifestation of reality bounded by time and activity and gathers data from it using various data collection techniques during the research period (White, 2005, pp., p. 105). The case study in this investigation also dictated the methodology required various data collection methods such as the focus group, individual reflections, a research diary, personal discussions and the analysis of documents and artefacts. The purpose of these data-collection methods was to investigate the case from an educational point of view.

Researchers use an interpretivist paradigm to understand phenomena through the medium of the meanings that people assign to them. The interpretivist paradigm seeks to explain individual consciousness and subjectivity by making use of the products, thoughts, actions, words, attitudes and artefacts that individuals produce (Burrell & Morgan, 2005, pp., p. 28). I will interpret the data collected from the participants' focus group, their project summaries and their individual reflections or blogs in order to understand the involvement of e–TUTO programme in the use of educational technology for participants to implement their technology-enhanced courses successfully and challenges. I will also support the participants' arguments and contentions by applying certain elements of ethnography and use the personal reflections of participants and Instructional Designers. Ethnography involves the study of a group of people in their own environment and in terms of their own worldviews. The ethnographer tries to gain a comprehensive understanding of situa-

tions of the subjects being studied by looking at a small number of variables in the context of a large number of subjects (Henning, Van Rensburg, & Smit, 2004, pp., p. 44).

Success Indicators in Implementing Technology-Enhanced Courses

Seven themes relating to the category of the e-TUTO programme as a professional development programme in the use of technology in education were identified. These seven themes were identified from text phrases that referred to funding, time, lecturer's attitude, capacity building, computer skills, the participant in an online environment, and e-moderation skills. In order to produce a clear understanding of the study, I have grouped these text phrases in terms of the following four clusters: adequate funding, time management, lecturer's attitude throughout the process and capacity building. Figure 1 illustrates the network that relates to the involvement of e-TUTO as the use of technology in education that contributed to the successful implementation of participants' projects.

Figure 1. The network that relates to the e-TUTO programme (© 2007 Tshwane University of Technology)

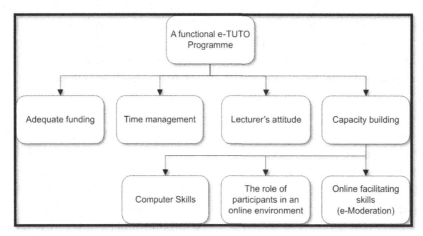

The Role of the e-TUTO Programme

A model similar to the RIPPLES model suggested by Ensminger and Surry (2002) for successful implementation, has been adopted at Tshwane University of Technology. This model focuses on resources, infrastructure, people, policy, learning, evaluation and support. The e-TUTO programme was originally introduced to train lecturers to integrate good pedagogical practice with technology-enhance courses by utilising various technologies.

Professional development programmes and face-to-face teacher education training are faced with the challenge of helping teachers to remain knowledgeable and up-to-date in the fast-changing domain of technology integration. Marra (2004) proposes five components for use in professional development programmes in educational technology when universities propose to integrate technology with teaching and learning. These components were duly implemented as a part of the e-TUTO programme. The five components include, firstly, engendering an awareness of the potential that technology offers. A participant said:

e-TUTO programme helped me as an educator to realise that computers can be used to enrich my subject. Another participant said that e-TUTO had assisted her to be able to expose learners to different technologies.

The second component proposed by Marra is the opportunity to explore the possibilities inherent in technology integration. A participant made the following observations:

e-TUTO provided me with the basics for becoming a knowledgeable educator in understanding the core foundation of learning and technology; integrating technology and media meaningfully into the curriculum.

The third component anticipated by Marra was having enough time to master the technology. A participant said the *e-TUTO programme is an excellent tool equipping lecturers with technology skills to enrich their teaching and learning.* Marra also proposed the application of the technology to teaching as the fourth component, and reflection on teaching by means of technology as the fifth component.

A participant indicated that *e-TUTO 2005 could be seen as a playground encompassing a lot of toys. In order to enjoy playing with these toys, one first has to know the rules of the play-ground and [know] what each toy [is] used for.* She also asserted that the Directorate of Teaching and Learning with Technology *provided the information (rules) and exposure to the various tools (and toys). The programme was filled with quality workshops, good presenters, a comfortable venue, good lunches, enough coffee and tea, and an informal, yet professional, setting.* One of the participants created formulas to describe the e-TUTO programme. She made the following observations: *About e-TUTO 2006, Albert Einstein said:*

If A equals success, then the formula for being a "participant" is: $A = X + Y + Z$, where X is "work", Y is "play", and Z is "keeping your mouth shut".

What this participant implied, was that if one wanted to succeed in integrating technology into teaching and learning, one needed to be a participant who worked hard, enjoyed using the various technologies, played with the various tools, and obeyed the rules of the game. Participants often observed that complaining about slow connections did not accomplish anything. The focus of the e-TUTO programme was therefore on a thorough needs analysis followed by thorough planning and an active management of the process. A participant referred to the e-TUTO programme as an incubator and stated that thanks to the Directorate of Teaching and Learning with Technology, she *could be taken from the library and placed in an "incubator" to participate in the technological adventure.* This participant referred to the e-TUTO programme as an "incubator" into which participants were placed after they had been taken out of their comfort zones of teaching and learning in order to spend six months in the programme. During this time, they were introduced to various technologies and were told how they could integrate these into their teaching and learning environment. They were also required to design their teaching and learning material by incorporating various technologies.

A participant mentioned that she considered herself to be *privileged to have been one of the partners in 2005.* Another participant indicated that *being part of this programme was a privilege* [in that she was able] *to reach out to learners in* [her] *large classes.* Participants appreciated the opportunity to be part of the participants' programme, and despite the work load that the accompanied the programme, they experienced *personal growth (technologically).* Participants also found that the e-TUTO programme gave them an environment within which they could work on improving their technological skills. A participant said that the programme gave her a place in which she *overcame* her *technophobia and got another opportunity to improve* her *software and computer literacy skills.*

The participants agreed that they had achieved a lot through the programme. A participant asserted that the *e-TUTO programme is a living proof that everything you conceive, you can achieve.* Even though participants had to persevere to keep up with the programme, they enjoyed the participation and mutual assistance that the format of the programme encouraged. Although the programme work load was enormous, all the participants recognised that it was a privilege to be part of the e-TUTO project. Although participants took programme work home in the evenings, this was

part of the programme. The participants were given laptops and Asymmetric Digital Subscriber Line (ADSL) Internet connections at home precisely so that they could continue with their work whenever they pleased. Some participants worked late in the evenings because they struggled with the content. Others worked late in the evenings because they preferred to do other things during the day, and so had to catch up at night.

Participants indicated that prior to their participation in the e-TUTO programme, they were faced with the challenge of trying to keep students interested in the work in a traditional teaching and learning environment. A participant indicated that she had *been offering these subjects for the past year and really needed to investigate alternative approaches to make it more exciting for herself and* her *students.* She *discussed this with* her *HOD and was then nominated to become a* participant *on the e-TUTO 2005 programme.* It is interesting and important to note that the e-TUTO programme was perceived as a solution to their problem by the head of her department. The participants also wanted to find out how the Directorate of Teaching and Learning with Technology could teach them about integrating technology into in their teaching and learning. They realised that it would be very difficult to integrate technology into their teaching and learning materials by themselves without any help from the Directorate of Teaching and Learning with Technology. The majority of the participants did not know much about the use of technology in teaching and learning prior to entering the programme. While most of them wanted to improve their teaching and learning practices, they could not do this without the intervention and assistance of the e-TUTO programme. A participant said that what had made her want to come to the Directorate of Teaching and Learning with Technology for help was the need *to explore something different in* [her] *teaching career, and to know what the Directorate of Teaching and Learning with Technology had to offer in terms of technology.*

Adequate Funding as a Success Indicator

It is important to note that the managers of successful professional development programmes in educational technology make certain that there projects are adequately funded. However, their projects are also successful because they take care to explain to their participants how they can spend their funding allocations legitimately and creatively.

The e-TUTO programme was funded by TUT (Tshwane University of Technology, 2005-2009). Funding is allocated for each participant in the programme. Each participant is funded by means of a "seed funding" that underwrites their projects. The funding in this case covers all costs relating to lecturer replacements for the duration of the programme, the production of videos, DVDs and CDs, the involvement of experts such as flash programmers and multimedia specialists, workshops conducted by external experts in their fields during the professional development programme in technology, research, conference attendance, software and hardware requirements, and access to resources (Van Ryneveld & Van der Merwe, 2005). The partners did not have to concern themselves with funding during the programme because the programme organisers took care of all funding details and also offered guidance and support about funding to any part that needed it.

The data shows that the participants regarded the e-TUTO programme as an opportunity to further their studies. One of the participants asserted that she had *received the Thuthuka Seed Funding Grant as a promising researcher to start the project by the National Research Foundation*. Funding and allocation of funds in the projects that are similar to e-TUTO can be successful when the project managers control and support the funding and use it according to the requirements of the project. Thus, for example, the participants received all the necessary forms of technology and all applications they needed to

participate meaningfully in the programme. Each of them was also given an ADSL line at home for continuous Internet access and connectivity. In addition, if the participants needed a particular piece of software, for example, they could ask the programme managers and the software would be bought out of their funds. This gave participants space and time to focus on their development and implementation work rather than to become bogged down in administrative details.

Time Management as a Success Indicator

The literature reviewed (Berge, 1998; Ensminger & Surry, 2002; Marra, 2004; Pete, et al., 2002; Twigg, 2003) indicates that, if one expects to be successful in implementing a professional development programme in educational technology, one should allocate *sufficient time* to train the participants to master the technology and to train them to perform their academic as well as their mentoring activities satisfactorily. Time allocated for training is one of the factors that influences the successful implementation of innovations (Ensminger & Surry, 2002). Berge (1998) agrees with Ensminger and Surry, and adds that online learning can only be successfully implemented if sufficient time is dedicated to training. Marra (2004) also argues that educational technologists should give participants enough time to master the technology itself and the methods and procedures that they will use when they incorporate it into teaching and learning.

According to the Tshwane University of Technology (2005-2009) document, time in the e-TUTO programme is utilised in various ways. Lecturers are released from their teaching duties to join the programme for six months. During that period, they develop technology-enhanced teaching and learning materials for their particular subject. However, time is also invested in training and professional development activities. The participants use the last six months of the programme to conduct and write up their research and to implement the learning materials that they have developed.

A participant revealed that she had *spent six months on the development of* [her course] *in a learning management system*. It was possible to implement the participants' technology-enhanced courses successfully during the implementation component because they were allocated a period of six months in which to design and develop their courses. Since one needs time in order to develop a truly successful course and adequate, the allocation of six months for the development process was a success indicator in this case. During their six-month period, the participants learned how to integrate technology with the curriculum – which is essentially what they would have been doing in teaching and learning anyway.

A participant said:

During my time as a participant I realised the importance of time management and planning in balancing my "life as a participant" and my "life as a wife and mother".

Lecturers' Attitude as a Success Indicator

The attitude of participants to the implementation of their technology-enhanced courses played a vital role during the implementation component. On the whole, participants were excited about the implementation of their technology-enhanced courses and indicated that they had gained skills and improved the quality of their teaching and learning during the capacity-building component of the programme. Above all, the participants enjoyed the new multimode method of teaching and learning. A participant asserted that she had been *armed with best methods, used worldwide and* [that she wanted] *to make a real difference in the teaching world!!!* They were positive and optimistic and ready to implement what they had learned because they felt that they had been

armed with all the equipment and approaches that they might need to make the implementation component a success.

Another participant mentioned that her *students found the use of animations to be extremely useful*. The other success indicator that was mentioned by participants was that their students understood the content better when it was presented in a multimodal manner. They noticed that the students enjoyed technology-enhanced learning because the concepts were explained visually, and that made it easier for students to understand, remember and apply the concepts in practice. A participant revealed that *all these programs – if not used properly and having student learning in mind – could be useless*. However, the students experienced the technology-enhanced teaching and learning activities and the multimodal approach as effective and helpful. This can partly be attributed to the fact that the participants had specifically designed their courses with their student end-users in mind.

Capacity-Building as a Success Indicator

The Directorate of Teaching and Learning with Technology involved the participants in an extensive capacity-building programme that included an initial block of face-to-face sessions followed by a later, more personal, phase in which they engaged in one contact day per week. These contact sessions were also supported by an online component (Van Ryneveld & Van der Merwe, 2005). During the block and weekly contact sessions, the participants networked, supported, and shared their progress through workshops and interactive teaching sessions. In addition to learning pedagogical and instructional design principles, the participants built up their capacity through designing an online course that enabled online collaboration and interaction. They were also tutored in course management and online facilitating. The participants therefore developed their technical skills through interacting with technology applications and systems such as Microsoft Office™, Blackboard™, Respondus™, Wimba™, Camtasia™, Impatica™, FrontPage™, Perception™, EndNote™, Turnitin™ and the Virtual Training Company™. Research capacity was one of the important elements in the capacity-building programme. In order to increase their research capacity, the participants were guided through a set of workshops on research publication. The participants stated that they had become familiar with various technologies and multimedia and the way to implement such technologies in their teaching and learning practice. A participant wrote:

In a very short time, you become familiar with PowerPoint, animation and graphics, digital photos, creating Web documents, Blackboard, PDA, software as Respondus, StudyMate, Camtasia, Front Page, [and] you start playing with DVD design and video scripting, tele- and video conferencing. [You also] attend courses on e-moderation, generic research methodology, needs assessments of peer courses, situational analysis, project plan and schedule, curriculum design and development, [and] you become comfortable in blogging, electronic database usage, recording sound, VTC, poster design and so much more. Even if not an expert yet, your horizon is much wider than ever before!

Computer Skills as a Success Indicator

In this section, I will discuss how the lecturers acquired computer skills, how they fulfilled the contracted e-TUTO requirements, and how they sharpened their online facilitating skills.

Volery and Lord (2000) argue that instructors who use technology in their teaching practices should be completely familiar with the technology and should in addition be able to perform troubleshooting exercises. The design and development component of this research as well as the capacity-building components of the e-TUTO

programme ensured that the participants were adequately familiar with the technology and that they were able to perform troubleshooting exercises. As one of the participants said: *I was nowhere technologically speaking, with no formal computer literacy training,* [and] *my skills were so much unreliable when I joined* e-TUTO *programme in June 2005.* Another participant stated that she *regarded computer skill as most sought skill that everyone must possess to acquire and secure jobs.* All of the participants had a strong desire to improve their technological skills.

One of the participants mentioned that she *overcame* her *technophobia and got another opportunity to improve* her *software and computer literacy skills* through the e-TUTO programme. The programme allowed participants to improve their technology-enhanced skills right from the beginning. A participant indicated that she *desired to update* her *technological skills, to be technological competent and to be able to build the entire Website from scratch, to reach to individual learners.* Because the programme empowered them with all these technological skills, the participants were in turn able to assist and empower their students to use the technology-enhanced courses and the various technologies integrated with the courses in an effective way – in some cases with the help of the instructional designer, but in other cases, by themselves.

Even though the e-TUTO programme did not provide a computer literacy course, the capacity-building component played a major role in assisting the participants to recognise and improve their level of technological and computer literacy skills. Most of the participants had to work very hard during this phase to improve their computer literacy skills and overcome their evident technophobia. However, when the time came for the participants to implement their courses, they were far more familiar with the various technologies and they were confident enough to present their technology-enhanced courses to their students and train their students in how to use the learning material. Because the participants' computer skills and their utilisation of these skills contributed to the successful implementation of the technology-enhanced courses, these skills can be regarded as a success indicator of the implementation component of a programme.

Contracted e-TUTO Requirements

Van Ryneveld and Van der Merwe (2005) state clearly in the e-TUTO manual what a participant commits to when he/she joins the programme. They mention that becoming a participant presupposes a great number of obligations as well as considerable intellectual and creative ability. Selected lecturers and academic support staff were released from their duties from between June 2005 and June 2006 so that they could become participants. The conditions that Van Ryneveld and Van der Merwe (2005) describe for becoming a participant will be described in the following paragraphs.

To become a participant, the lecturer/academic support staff member had to be permanently appointed at university and they needed to have a subject that will benefit from the integration of technology into its teaching method. Since the e-TUTO programme runs over a period of at least one year, participants have to commit themselves to the programme for at least one year. The participants then had to make themselves available, not only as mentors for the new intake of participants in the following year, but also for other lecturers in their faculties. They should be willing and able to arrange a replacement for themselves for the negotiated period between June 2005 and June 2006.

The funding for substituting participants is available to successful candidates in the form of seed funding. The participants in this case study had to be able to teach the course during the first semester of 2006 in order to implement their newly developed teaching and learning materials. They also had to be keen and willing to experiment with various technologies in order to improve their practice and the learning experience of their students. The participants also had to be able to prepare themselves to take an active part in a research programme, to present at least one national conference paper and to submit at least one academic journal article with the help of expert support and guidance as well as financial support. Finally, all participants had to be able to actively implement their new teaching and learning materials by using the online facilitating skills that they had mastered during the course of the year.

Online Facilitating Skills (e-Moderation)

The participants were also required to participate in an e-moderation online course that teaches the skills that are necessary for promoting online collaboration and interaction. This course taught facilitation skills and the management of online learning. The programme organisers arranged for participants to participate in the online facilitation course for a period of four weeks prior to the implementation of their technology-enhanced courses. Van Ryneveld and Van der Merwe (2005) state that this course teaches a variety of vital topics such as how to set up and access the system and how to increase motivation and interest among participants who engage in online socialisation, information exchange, and the construction and development of knowledge (Salmon, 2003). After the successful completion of the course, all participants received a certificate that indicated their specific achievements. One of the participants mentioned that she had *spent a month on an e-moderation* course *as a student which had introduced* her *to a virtual learning environment.* Another participant asserted that she had participated in *an online* [course] *by Gilly Salmon.* Participants enrolled for this course because it prepared them on how to implement their technology-enhanced courses and because it taught them the necessary skills needed by a facilitator in an online environment.

Participants applied the skills that they acquired from this course during the implementation component and also learned how to facilitate and manage online learning. The e-moderation course gave them the skills to approach the concept of e-learning and the virtual learning environment with confidence. It also taught them how to create features in their courses that were appropriate for distance teaching. It taught them how to evaluate, assess, and motivate learners online as part of a multimodal approach to traditional face-to-face teaching. A participant said:

I followed this strategy when I prepared my subject for the web. I exposed my learners to a variety of study materials. I made use of multimedia. I concentrated on creating e-tivities involving weaving and summarising. Attention was given to the integration of text and applications. I tried to assist students to take ownership of their studies and its content. I included challenges which were exciting, thus keeping the interest of the students.

The online facilitation course was a success because the participants used the skills that they had acquired in the course during the implementation component. It was noticeable that the participants had little difficulty in implementing their technology-enhanced course even when they had used a multimodal approach. Some of the activities they undertook were fully online, and they were able to check the activities of students from the campus as well as from home because the programme has given them ADSL access to the Internet.

CURRENT CHALLENGES

Professional Development Programme as a Challenge in Implementing Technology-Enhanced Courses

While this study revealed success indicator when implementing technology-enhanced courses. One might also look at the other side of the coin.

That is challenges that were encountered by the participants during the programme. Professional development programme might hinder the successful implementation of the technology-enhanced courses if not designed appropriately. Blignaut and Lillejord (2005) identified various challenges that were encountered by the Norwegian Council for Higher Education's programme for development research and education project management. These included issues relating to the perception of managerial issues, funding, technical support, laptops, expectations, misconceptions, the nature of the support being offered, the quality of leadership in online communications, and time management. The challenges that were encountered during the implementation component of the e-TUTO programme included contact session during the implementation of the technology-enhanced courses, interference of the programme with participants' social lives, too much work load and time management.

Contact Session as a Challenge

Attendance at scheduled contact sessions for the programme during the implementation component was an enormous obstacle to participants on the distance campuses because they had to travel about 300 km to attend workshops that lasted only half a day. A participant stated:

e-TUTO team might consider having more online contact sessions with the participants in place of face-to-face sessions. Due to some participants having to travel more than three hours per day to attend the formal sessions, their morale tends to decrease.

The participants raised questions about the wisdom of having to drive such long distances merely to attend contact sessions when they could just as well have learned what they needed to know by means of video conferencing on their own learning sites. These contact session during the implementation component were therefore regarded by the participants as challenges of the implementation.

E-TUTO Programme as a Challenge to Participant's Social Lives

Some of the participants felt that the e-TUTO programme made unwarranted demands on their social and family lives because they found that they were spending more time on the programme than with their families. A participant said: *Actually, the truth is that the majority of us felt like quitting the commitment as our personal lives were greatly interfered with.* Other participants regarded the participation in the e-TUTO programme as problematic but fulfilling. A participant described this in the following way: *This period in your life is unforgettable! (Blessing and hell at the same time ...) Sleepless working nights become your norm. You rediscover your infinite potential, your God nature, rediscover yourself!* The amount of time the participants were expected to devote to the e-TUTO programme interfered in most cases with their social and family lives, and so the load of the work they were expected to do could be seen as challenge to the successful implementation of the technology-enriched courses.

Too Much Work Load as a Challenge to Success

Some of the participants felt that the amount of work that they were required to do in the e-TUTO programme was simply too much. While some of the participants thrived under pressure and managed to produce three or four different technology-enhanced course, others battled to complete even the one that was required. Because participants had ADSL at home, they were expected to work at home as well. This requirement was regarded as a necessary component of the programme because all participants were relieved of their teaching loads. While it was obviously necessary to expect

such a commitment, it was also problematic because it meant the participants had to take personal responsibility for balancing the amount of time they spent on their work with the amount of time they allocated to their family and social lives. Those participants who were not able to manage their time effectively found that the time that they usually spend with their families was being spent on their programme projects.

However, even when some of the participants tried to ignore their work they would feel guilty because some of the other participants were frequently busy online even at midnight. Yahoo Messenger allowed participants to see one another working online. E-TUTO participants therefore felt as though they were falling behind in their work.

Time Management as Challenge to Success

Sandholtz *et al.* (1997, p. 154) state that most of the lecturers in their study who left the professional development centres to implement and integrate technology into teaching and learning encountered challenges such as *a lack of time*. The time factor was also an issue with participants in the research undertaken by Blignaut and Lillejord. The participants in that study also expressed the opinion that although they wished to participate in the online learning community, they simply did not have enough time to do so (Blignaut & Lillejord, 2005). Since the participants were obliged to participate in various activities in their departments, it was inevitable that they would fall behind in their implementation of the technology-enhanced course. One participant said: *I am a little behind with my schedule. Maybe it's the overload of my departmental work. Apart from lecturing two subjects, I am also committed to QIT and knowledge-sharing as I have also absorbed knowledge from e-TUTO which can help in my department.* Another participant mentioned that in the Library and Information Services Department, *various factors influence the current status of myTUTor work, of which TIME is obviously the main factor*

Another challenge in the way of successful implementation revolved around the time that was allocated to lecturers and students for the use of the computer laboratories. One participant revealed that the amount of time allocated for students in the computer laboratories was far too short for them to accomplish all the learning activities that were embedded in their technology-enhanced courses. This participant said: *Students only managed to calculate two things and give answers and then that's it. They come in at 4:00 and* [because] *some of the questions are very difficult, they need time to* [think about the process involved in solving the problem]. In this case implementation was further hindered because of inadequate bandwidth, poor network connections and slow access to the Internet.

RECOMMENDATIONS

It is recommended that for the implementation of technology-enhanced course to be successful, it is necessary to offer staff a comprehensive professional development programme on the use of technology for online teaching and learning. The professional development programme should empower faculty members to utilise and integrate technology to enhance the quality of teaching and learning. The question is no longer about the value of the use of the Internet in higher education institutions but rather about the quality, influence and the effectiveness of the online modules that are created.

It is crucial for every aspect of professional development programmes to be funded by institutions or by sponsors so that participants will not have to worry about the financial implications of what they are learning and trying to achieve during the process. It is up to the programme organisers to take control of the funding and to provide

whatever equipment the participating lecturers need for the programme.

It is also important for programme designers to design the programme in such a way that participants are given a reasonable and achievable amount of work so that they do not have to take too much home with them every evening.

Lecturers should also be prepared to change their role as teachers. In order to be successful as online facilitators, teachers and lecturers need to become guides and facilitators rather than dictatorial "talking heads".

Since students in the 21st century have grown up in a world where technological skills are taken for granted, it is necessary for lecturers to have the skills to keep up with them. It is essential to arrange for face-to-face contact sessions during capacity building so that lecturers can network with one another, support each other, and share their progress by means of workshops and other forms of interaction. An effective way of allowing for this is to create a capacity-building online course that enables online collaboration and interaction among lecturers and support staff.

It is essential that higher education institution that would like to implement technology-enhanced courses successfully also consider the challenges that were encountered by participants in this study and avoid the pitfall.

FUTURE RESEARCH

Recommended future research could serve to verify or modify the findings of this study with another professional development programme in the use of educational technology. In order to undertake this kind of research, a future researcher would have to keep records about the form of personal reflections during the implementation component and he/she should work closely with the participants. Future research is also needed to establish whether the success indicators and challenges that were encountered in this study will affect other groups of lecturers in other higher education institutions in the same way as they undertake the implementation of the technology-enhanced courses. Future research might also examine why some participants were motivated to implement their courses despite the challenges that they encountered with their first technology-enhanced material. Another fruitful area of research might be to examine student attitudes towards the subject matter and to correlate them with achievements and problems during online teaching and learning. It is also recommended that some future study take a careful look at lecturers' perceptions of the use and viability of online learning.

CONCLUSION

This chapter highlighted the success indicators and challenges during the implementation of technology-enhanced courses in the e-TUTO implementation component. It confirms the statement by Ma & Ruyon (2004) on how TUT took an initiative or advantage of Internet technology to improve and supplement traditional courses and the changes brought by Internet in teaching and learning. In this case study, this is indicated by the involvement of an e-TUTO professional development programme in the use of educational technology to prepare lecturers to integrate technology in their teaching and learning practices.

This chapter has identified, discussed and explained the success indicators of participants' technology-enhanced courses during the implementation component, such as e-TUTO programme, adequate funding, time management, lecturers' attitude, capacity building and computer skills. Some of these success indicators were also identified by various authors (Berge, 1998; Ensminger & Surry, 2002; Marra, 2004) during the implementation of technology-enhanced courses at various higher education institutions. It is crucial that other universities that would like to

implement technology-enhanced course consider these success indicators

We have seen in this chapter how an overly demanding professional development programme hindered the implementation component of technology-enhanced courses. Blignaut and Lillejord (2005) supports this view about the challenges encountered during the professional development programme. This chapter has also identified, discussed and explained the challenges that were encountered by participants during the implementation of technology-enhanced courses. These included, contact sessions during the implementation component, interference of the programme with participant's social lives, too much work load and time management.

REFERENCES

Abel, R. (2005b, November). *Implementing best practice in online learning: A recent study reveals common denominators for success in internet-supported learning* Retrieved December 14, 2005, from http://www.a-hec.org/e-learning_study.html

Berge, L. Z. (1998). Barriers to online teaching in post secondary institution: Can policy changes fix it? *Online Journal of Distance Learning Administration, 1*(2). Retrieved from http://www.westga.edu/~distance/ojdla/summer12/berge12.pdf.

Blignaut, A. S., & Lillejord, S. (2005). Lessons from a cross-cultural online learning community. *South African Journal of Higher Education, 19*(Special issue), 1350–1367.

Broere, I., Kruger, M., & Van Wyk, G. (2003 September). *A first @ RAU [First Innovative Reflective Strategic Touch at RAU].* Paper presented at the 5th Annual Conference on World Wide Web Application, Johannesburg.

Bruce, H., Fugate, C., Kerr, S., & Wolf, F. (2004). *The programme for educational transformation through technology*. London: University of Washington.

Burrell, G., & Morgan, G. (2005). *Sociological Paradigms and organisational analysis*. Aldershot, UK: Ashgate.

Ekermans, G. (2003). *An investigation into the usability of synchronous information technology for the virtual e-learning and information sharing at a university in South Africa*. Unpublished Dissertation, University of Stellenbosch, Cape Town.

Ensminger, C. D., & Surry, D. W. (2002). *Faculty perception of factors that facilitate the implementation of online programs* Retrieved March 3, 2007, from http://iphase.org/papers/msitc02.pdf

Grant, C. M. (n.d.). *Professional development in a technological age: New definitions, old challenges, new resources*. Retrieved 20 April, 2006, from http://www.ncrel.org/sdrs/areas/issues/educatrs/profdevl/pd2prof.htm

Guri-Rosenblit, S. (2005, March). *Eight paradoxes in the implementation process of e-learning in higher education*. Retrieved February 25, 2006, from http://www.palgrave-journals.com/hep/journal/v18/n1/fuu/8300069a.html

Henning, E., Van Rensburg, W., & Smit, B. (2004). *Finding your way in qualitative research*. Pretoria, South Africa: JL van Schaik.

Ma, Y., & Runyon, L. R. (2004, July/August). *Academic synergy in the age of technology-a new instructional paradigm*. Retrieved December 14, 2005, from http://proquest.umi.com/pdqweb?did=692351181&sid=1&Fmt=4&clientld=36149&RQT=309&VName=PQD

Marra, R. M. (2004). *An online course to help teachers use technology to enhance learning: Success and Limitations*. Retrieved 14 December, 2005, from http://proquest.umi.com/pdqweb?did=757578841&sid=12&Fmt=4&clientld=36149&RQT=309&VName=PQD

Pete, M., Fregona, C., Allinson, T., & Cronje, J. (2002). *Pioneers Online: Developing a community of online education practitioners at the Durban Institute of Technology*. Retrieved 11 April, 2006, from http://www.ukzn.ac.za/citte/papers/id1.pdf

Poole, B. J. (1997). *Education for an information age: Teaching in the computerized classroom*. New York: McGraw-Hill.

Quick, R., & Lieb, T. (2000). The heartfield project. *T.H.E. Journal, 28*(5), 40–46.

Salmon, G. (2003). E-moderating: The key to teaching and learning online (Second edition ed.). London: Taylor and Francis Books Ltd.

Sandholtz, J., Ringstaff, C., & Dwyer, D. (1997). *Teaching with technology: Creating student-centered classrooms*. London: Teacher College Press.

Stake, E. R. (2000). Case studies . In Denzin, N. K., & Lincoln, Y. S. (Eds.), *Handbook of qualitative research* (2nd ed.). London: SAGE.

Tshwane University of Technology. (2005-2009). *Institutional operating plan*. Pretoria, South Africa: Tshwane University of Technology.

Twigg, C. (2003). *Change. Improving quality and reducing cost; design for effective learning* Retrieved 19 July, 2005, from http://proquest.umi.com/pdweb?did=592388111&sid=10&Fmt=3&clientld=21888&RQT=309&VName=PQD

University of Florida. (2005). *Distance, off-campus and technology-enhanced courses*. Retrieved from http://www.distancelearning.ufl.edu/faculty/definedistance.asp

Van Ryneveld, L., & Van der Merwe, H. (2005). *Partners@Work Teaching and Learning with Technology 2005 Manual*. Pretoria, South Africa: Tshwane University of Technology.

Viel, W., Brantley, J., & Zulli, R. (2004). *Developing an online Geology course for preservice and inservice teachers: Enhancement for online learning*. Retrieved February 25, 2005, from http://www.citejournal.org/vol3/iss4/science/article1.cfm

Volery, T., & Lord, D. (2000). Critical success factors in online education. *International Journal of Educational Management*, *14*(5), 216–223. doi:10.1108/09513540010344731

White, C. J. (2005). *Research: A practical guide*. Pretoria, South Africa: Intuthuko Investments.

ADDITIONAL READING

Berge, L. Z., & Schrum, L. (1998). Linking strategic planning with program implementation for distance education. *Cause/Effect Journal*, *21*(3).

Brand, A. G. (1997). What research Says: Training Teachers for using Technology. *Journal of Staff Development*, *19*(1). Retrieved from http://www.wikieducator.org/images/0/04/Training_Teachers_to_Use_Computers.pdf.

Canadian Council on Learning. (2009, March 12). *Redefining how success is measured in First Nations, Inuit and Métis Learning*. Retrieved from http://www.ccl-cca.ca/CCL/Reports/RedefiningSuccessInAboriginalLearning/

E-Lead Leadership for Success. (n.d.). *Technology as a tool for professional development*. Retrieved March 12, 2009, from http://www.e-lead.org/resources/resources.asp?ResourceID=3

Freedman, V. A., Calkins, M., DeRosiers, M., & Van Haitsma, K. (2005). *Barriers to implementing technology in residential long-term care settings*. Washington, DC: Polisher Research.

Gagné, R. M. (1987). *Instructional technology: Foundations*. Retrieved from http://books.google.co.za/books?id=OndVwGgY3NsC

Garrison, D. R., & Anderson, T. (2004). [*st Century: A framework for research and Practice*. London: Taylor & Francis.]. *E-learning*, ▪▪▪, 21.

Harvey, B. (2003). *Technology professional development: Successful strategies for teacher change*. ERIC.

Laurillard, D., Oliver, M., Wasson, B., & Hoppe, U. (2009). Technology enhanced-learning: Principles and Product. In N. Balacheff, S. Ludvigsen, T. de Jong, A. Lazonder & S. Barnes (Eds.), *Implementing technology-enhanced learning*. Retrieved from http://www.springerlink.com/content/mvpj770012542395/

Lian, A. (2002). *Implementing Technology-Enhanced Language-Learning (TELL) in an increasingly globalised world*. University of Canberra.

McConnell, D. (2000). Implementing computer supported cooperative learning. Retrieved from http://books.google.co.za/books?id=M009AAAAIAAJ

McPherson, M., & Nunes, M. B. (2004). *Developing innovation in online learning: An action research framework*. London: Taylor & Francis.

Neir Tec. (n.d.). *Professional development*. Retrieved from http://www.neirtec.org/products/techbriefs/5.htm

Pajo, K., & Wallace, C. (2001). Barriers to the uptake of web-based technology by university teachers. *Journal of Distance Education*, *16*(1). Retrieved from http://www.jofde.ca/index.php/jde/article/viewArticle/171/127.

Rainsford, C., & Murphy, E. (2005). Technology-enhanced learning: An Irish industry perspective. *Journal of European Industrial Training, 29*(6), 457–471. Retrieved from http://www.emeraldinsight.com/Insight/view-ContentItem.do?contentType=Article&hdAction=lnkhtml&contentId=1513464&ini=xref. doi:10.1108/03090590510610254

Rogers, R. L. (2003). *Designing instruction for technology-enhanced learning.* Retrieved from http://books.google.co.za/books?id=QxB5IW4XKjUC

Salem, H. M. (2007). Critical success factors for e-learning acceptance: Confirmatory factor models. *Computers & Education, 49*(2), 396–413. Retrieved from http://www.sciencedirect.com/science?_ob=ArticleURL&_udi=B6VCJ-4HG69JW-2&_user=10&_rdoc=1&_fmt=&_orig=search&_sort=d&view=c&_acct=C000050221&_version=1&_urlVersion=0&_userid=10&md5=dc7a267107403414044a8ab8f04d19fe. doi:10.1016/j.compedu.2005.09.004

Schlager, M. S., & Fusco, J. (2003). Teacher professional development, and communities of practice: Are we putting the cart before the horse? *The Information Society, 19*(3), 203–220. doi:10.1080/01972240309464

Schrum, L. (2006). Technology professional development for teachers. *Educational Technology Research and Development, 47*(4), 83–90. Retrieved from http://www.springerlink.com/content/v71258403850650p/fulltext.pdf?page=1. doi:10.1007/BF02299599

Varma, K., Husic, F., & Linn, M. C. (2008). Targeted support for using technology-enhanced science inquiry modules. *Journal of Science Education and Technology, 17*(4), 341–356. Retrieved from http://www.springerlink.com/content/n73rm61414754267/. doi:10.1007/s10956-008-9104-8

Wedman, J., & Diggs, L. (2001). Identifying barriers to technology-enhanced learning environment in teacher education. *Computer in Human Behaviour, 17*(4), 421 - 430. Retrieved from http://www.sciencedirect.com/science?_ob=ArticleURL&_udi=B6VDC-43YY984-7&_user=4039543&_rdoc=1&_fmt=&_orig=search&_sort=d&view=c&_acct=C000057736&_version=1&_urlVersion=0&_userid=4039543&md5=0965ae58ae71f520c256da4ba7a081e0

Wedman, J. D. L. (2001). Identifying barriers to technology-enhanced learning environments in teacher education. *Computers in Human Behaviour, 17*(4), 421-430. Retrieved from http://www.sciencedirect.com/science?_ob=ArticleURL&_udi=B6VDC-43YY984-7&_user=4039543&_rdoc=1&_fmt=&_orig=search&_sort=d&view=c&_acct=C000057736&_version=1&_urlVersion=0&_userid=4039543&md5=0965ae58ae71f520c256da4ba7a081e0

WestEd with Edvance Research. (2008). *Evaluating online learning challenges and strategies for success: Innovations in education.* Washington, DC: U.S. Department of Education Office of Innovation and Improvement.

KEY TERMS AND DEFINITIONS

Professional Development Programme: Is a programme that teaches and empowers lecturers and non-academic staff members in both formal and informal ways to learn new skills, develop new approaches to pedagogy and teaching practices, to discover and explore new technologies, and to understand both content and resources. The professional development programme described in this study is the e-TUTO programme.

Educational Technology: Are the tools utilised in educational practice to broadcast, illustrate, communicate or submerge students and lecturers in activities objectively designed to encourage learning. It is also the theory and practice of design, development, utilisation, management and evaluation of processes and resources for learning.

e-TUTO: The e-TUTO programme is the professional development programme that train and empower lecturers to use and integrate technology in their teaching practices. It was set up by the Directorate of Teaching and Learning with Technology at Tshwane University of Technology in 2004. The first annual programme comprised thirteen partners. The aim of the programme is to empower lecturers to utilise various forms of technology and to improve their teaching and learning skills. Throughout the study, this programme is referred to as e-TUTO programme.

Implementation: Is to provide a practical means for accomplishing something. Is the realisation of an application or execution or carrying out of plan.

Technology-Enhanced Course: Is a teaching and learning course that is designed and developed utilising various technologies. This course is delivered in an online environment or in a virtual classroom. It is delivered through a learning management system. It includes various activities to engage student and promotes interaction among students and content, student and lecturer, lecturer and content as well as student and student. Technology-enhanced course utilises various tools such as course content, assessment, assignment, web links, communication tools, media library. It also provides tools for the designer, for the instructor and the student.

Higher Education: Refers to education that is offered to students who have obtained the National Senior Certificate, and it includes all education programmes at the post-school, pre-degree level, including certificates, diplomas and higher diplomas (Level 5 programmes), as well as all undergraduate degree and postgraduate degree programmes from bachelor degrees to doctorates (Level 6-8 programmes).

Success: Means the accomplishment or achievement of the results or outcomes specified by the e-TUTO programme.

Challenges: Means any condition that makes it difficult to make progress or to achieve an objective.

University of Technology: Comprises of interconnect, focus and interrelation between technology and the nature of university. The focus is on the study of technology from viewpoint of various field of study. University of technology means that all teaching or learning programmes and research projects are related to technology. Technology is therefore the qualifying factor fundamental to all academic activities.

Chapter 7
A Pilot Project to Teach Road Safety Using Desktop Virtual Reality

Emmanuel Fokides
University of the Aegean, Greece

Costas Tsolakidis
University of the Aegean, Greece

ABSTRACT

In this work the issue of road safety education is presented. Virtual Reality can be used for this purpose with very good results. An application was developed based on a 3D video game. This application was simulating the environment of a town with traffic and contained not only all of its elements (cars, traffic lights, pedestrian crossings) but also special conditions such as night and rain. It was developed to simulate the walk of a pedestrian and could accommodate many users simultaneously. It was tested by the students of the last three grades of a primary school in Athens. The acquired capabilities of the students/users were compared with the equivalent capabilities of students that had training in the class using printed material only and with the knowledge of another group that had no training at all.

INTRODUCTION

The University of the Aegean is a university network with departments in five islands and offices in Athens. It is a state university with 14, 000 students in all its 16 departments. It is a fast growing university with many postgraduate courses. The department of Education sensitive to the challenges of the area it operates, is developing know how that is not only to the benefit of education but also to the benefit of society. Therefore, all forms of distance education (synchronous, asynchronous, satellite, etc) are examined and researched, while applied extensively. Also nearly all forms of Virtual Reality are studied and applied not only in education in general but also to the remote schools of Greece, Europe and beyond.

SETTING THE STAGE

Road safety education can play an important role in the overall reduction of traffic related accidents, especially if it is introduced in early childhood

DOI: 10.4018/978-1-61520-751-0.ch007

(Thomson, Tolmie, Foot, & McLaren, 1996). This fact is identified by policy makers and relevant actions are introduced either in the school curricula and/or in the wider frame of a national policy for road safety. While the above holds true for many industrialized as well as developing countries (UK's Department for transport [DfT], 2003; New Zealand's Ministry of Transport, 2002; Road Safety Cambodia, 2008), in Greece, a country with a severe problem regarding road safety, very little is done. Whilst the government pledged that road safety education is going to be systematically taught in primary and secondary schools, the recent educational reform disproved all expectations.

Evidently, the lack of a specific teaching framework and didactic material is a fertile ground for any research group interested in developing and testing innovative techniques for teaching road safety to young students. We decided to address the subject using a 3D simulation, a Virtual Reality (VR) application, rather than a typical 2D application. The main reasons for this decision were the unique characteristics of VR applications, as they: i) allow training in a manner very close to real traffic conditions ii) permit the simulation of traffic situations that are very complicated to be presented in reality or extremely dangerous for students to be exposed to, iii) have a playful character similar to modern computer games and iv) provide the possibility to implement different teaching techniques (Fokides & Tsolakidis, 2008).

CASE DESCRIPTION

In our case, the task of creating a certain type of computer application was not that of converting the existing educational material in another form, since such material is non-existent. Consequently, we set the teaching objectives, determined the teaching methodology and we wrote, collected and modulated the teaching material. Furthermore,

we considered the following conditions of great importance:

- *Effectiveness:* Students should be able to learn a practical piece of knowledge and apply it in their everyday life;
- *Accessibility:* A large number of students should be able to access and work with it. Since schools are not equipped with high-end computers, the application should be lightweight enough in order to run smoothly in mid-range or even low-end computers:
- *Compliance:* The school life should not be disrupted with time consuming activities that will affect an already congested timetable and curriculum; and
- *Cost:* Not to have significant cost regarding its development.

To form the instructive framework, the necessary knowledge, dexterities and behaviors which would enable children to a safer conduct in the street environment were determined. These are: i) orientation in space and the detection of traffic, ii) detection and the evaluation of dangerous situations, iii) evaluation of the vehicles' distance and speed and iv) synchronization of perception and movement as well as the co-ordination of information from various directions (Fokides & Tsolakidis, 2008).

The decisive factors for the success of any road safety education program are the active participation of students in the educational process and the extensive practice of what they learned. The active attendance during the training process is very well documented by the learning theories that stress the importance of social interaction and interactive learning (Piaget, 1985; Vygotsky, 1978). Documentation on the value of practice in pedestrian skills is rich, since it provides children with a concrete and tangible frame in which they can apply concepts that orally or written are difficult to comprehend and follow (DfT, 2002; Sandels, 1975). The resulting teaching methodology that is appropriate for road safety education is a combination of adult guidance and students' collaboration, a "guided collaboration". The "guidance" part of this methodology is, in essence, the practice in the traffic environment and the "collaboration" part is teaching in the classroom using teaching practices and principles that derive from the learning theory of constructivism. For the specific project, and since use of computers by students was involved, the guidance part was constituted by having students work in a simulated traffic environment, each on his/her own computer, but also forming groups of three. The collaboration part was constituted by the activities that followed in the classroom.

In order to examine the feasibility of the application to be implemented without causing significant agitations in the school's timetable, it was decided to address it to students of the last three grades of the primary school, where the timetable is already full of lessons and activities. A realistic duration of the application was considered to be two months, with a frequency of a two consecutive didactic hours once a week, which meant that it could include 7-8 instructive units for each grade.

The analysis of the dexterities and behaviors that enable children to safely walk in the streets resulted in the following general instructive objectives:

- *Cognitive:* i) to know how to protect oneself in traffic environment, ii) to comprehend the role of the traffic signs, iii) to be aware of the problems that street users face (detachment of attention, weather conditions etc), iv) to understand when and how road accidents happen, and v) what to do in the event of an accident and how to ask for help.
- *Dexterities:* i) to orientate, ii) to detect the traffic, iii) to become aware of and evaluate dangerous situations, iv) to evaluate the distance and speed of the vehicles, v) to synchronize perception and movement,

and vi) to coordinate information from different sources and directions.

- *Behaviors:* i) to be able to give and follow directions to a destination, ii) to use the traffic lights and understand the basic traffic signs, iii) to apply the safety rules that administer the actions of pedestrians and drivers on various situations, iv) to comprehend the consequences of their actions to themselves and to others, and v) to resist acting impulsively and without prior thinking.

The above objectives were grouped and allocated in instructive units, the general content of which was:

- **Introductory unit.** Learning the handling of the application, acquaintance with the traffic environment of a city.
- **Unit 1.** Orientation, giving and taking directions to a destination.
- **Units 2 & 3.** Road and highway crossing, time that is required for the safe passing of a road, finding secure places for crossing a street.
- **Unit 4.** Traffic signs for pedestrians and drivers, complicated situations that a pedestrian might face (e.g. roads without pavement).
- **Unit 5.** Weather conditions, precautions, streets at night.
- **Unit 6.** Traffic accidents, actions in the event of an accident.
- **Unit 7.** Using the streets in a complex urban environment.

TECHNOLOGY CONCERNS

Selecting the Software for the Development of the Application

There are a number of different types of VR applications (desktop, immersed, augmented, etc), each having its advantages and disadvantages. Desktop VR, though considered by experts as the humble relative of the other types, causes none (or very low) additional hardware costs to users, in this case schools' computer labs. Hence, desktop VR applications can be accessible by almost all students, satisfying two of the above stated prerequisites (cost and accessibility) and -self-evidently- was the type chosen.

The software to be used had to comply with the same requirements as described earlier. VR development software packages offer the most satisfactory solution, since they provide an ergonomic and windowed environment. The main drawback is the acquisition cost which can -in some cases- be considerable. An unforeseen category of computer applications, capable of providing relatively easy-to-use and cost effective tools for the development of VR applications is the 3D computer games and specifically "first person shoot them up's". In these games, the user/player is placed in a 3D environment, eliminating "enemies", avoiding traps and solving puzzles. The characteristics that VR applications and 3D games share are so noteworthy, that the boundaries between the two are very difficult to discern.

These common characteristics are (Fokides & Tsolakidis, 2003):

1. Both types of applications are simulations of complex 3D environments, highly interactive and explorable.
2. Interactions and behavior of objects in general, are controlled through scripts or by triggers (programmable entities that control the flow of events in the virtual world).
3. Multi-channel sound and "3D sound" is supported.
4. The user can look up or down, turn left or right, move forward or backwards, walk, run, fly and can have first or third person view of the virtual environment. All these are the result of an imaginary camera placed in front or behind the user's avatar (the 3D model that represents the user).
5. Both provide network support, allowing a number of users/players (from few up to thousands) to use the application simultaneously. Network traffic is minimal by transmitting only the coordinates of each user/player while the actual 3D environment runs locally. Interestingly enough, games use this feature in order to record the course of the game not as a disk consuming video file but as a set of sequential coordinates that uses far less disk space. This feature can be very helpful either for research or for educational purposes.
6. VR applications utilize specialized -and expensive- equipment in order to increase the user's immersion. Games do not use these devices, but a joystick or a D-pad can totally replace the mouse and the keyboard. These devices function quite similar to that of VR navigation devices. Finally, glasses that are used for stereoscopic viewing are the same in both cases.

For the above reasons, it was decided to investigate towards this direction. One way to create a 3D game is to use game development software packages, the majority of them having a low or reasonable cost. Also, open source game development software packages, totally free of charge, are available. The other way is to use an in-game editor (the software tool that the game company used for the creation of the game). What is of interest is that most editors are included in the game packages, allowing users to create their own levels. Some in-game editors of older games are even distributed under the open source license.

The selection of a game editor has to carefully balance its cost on one hand and the features it provides on the other. What was realized, by studying and evaluating games, was that they take good advantage of the user's hardware and that the quality of the virtual environment, and of the 3D graphics in general, was high. It was also noted that the provided in-game editors are not -at first glance- easy to use and that external programs have to be used for content creation (e.g. 3D models, sounds, textures). The final conclusion was that almost all game editors could satisfy the needs of this application. Thus, the choice of one editor over another is subjective, depending on ones' personal preferences.

Development of the Application

The general idea was to create an application that simulates an urban environment. This environment would act as a platform for placing the cognitive elements of each instructive unit as well as to provide students with an area to practice and test these elements. The developing process included the following phases:

1. Familiarization with the game editor.
2. Construction and/or editing of 3D models, sounds and graphics.
3. Construction of the application's urban outline (e.g. roads, pavements, buildings).
4. Placement of the static and moving objects (e.g. trees, traffic signs and cars).
5. Placement of the basic interaction points (e.g. traffic lights).
6. Placement of the cognitive activities.

In each phase extensive tests were conducted, evaluating the application's performance and the validity of the pedagogic ideas incorporated within it.

For the construction of an urban setting, various 3D models were needed, mainly that of cars. Models of people, traffic signs, traffic lights and various other decorative elements (e.g. trees, street lights, trash cans and fences) were also needed. It was decided to use models that are freely available over the Internet in order to reduce the application's work load and cost. 3D models are constructed with the use of polygons (mainly triangles). The number of the polygons of each model was a point of concern. High polygon count models are very detailed but drain the computer's resources. For the buildings, pavements and streets we used simple parallelepipeds accordingly textured and that did not put strain on the application's performance since the number of polygons was extremely low. All the other models were edited in order to balance quality and polygon count. Also, three copies of each model were created, each having roughly half the polygons of the previous one. This was done in order to utilize the technique of "level of detail, LOD", which allows the replacement of a model with another less detailed when the distance from the user increases (Figure 1). By doing so, the number of models present at any given time was ample while the application functioned smoothly because of the reduced total number of polygons.

Figure 1. Level of detail and the final 3D model

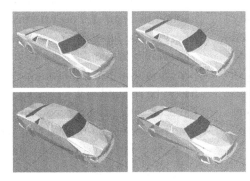

The placement of the building blocks, squares and roads was not simply the positioning of parallelepipeds of various sizes. Vital questions had to be answered regarding the density of the buildings, the distance between them and which street arrangement would be convenient for the movement of cars. Also, the placement of buildings and streets would have to create multiple routes to and fro a destination, while ensuring that all cognitive elements would be visited by students. Obviously, the streets were the central point of the application. Their width, in conjunction with the number and frequency of cars traveling in them, would determine the traffic "gaps" which would or would not allow users to cross them. Highways were also placed. In a number of places, the crossing of roads and of highways would be controlled by traffic lights introduced in a following stage. Finally, pedestrian crossings were regularly positioned in easy to find places.

The speed of cars and their flow in the streets was a matter of concern. To simulate real traffic conditions and at the same time to have a minimal number of moving 3D models, two techniques were used. The first was to circle the cars around building blocks. The second, applied when the cars were moving at a straight line, was to "teleport" them back when they reached the end of their path. The speed of each car was varied according to a predefined scheme. We have to mention that one-way or two-way roads had two lanes in each direction (three in highways). Cars in each lane had different speeds and distances than that of the other. The above resulted in having streets constantly filled with cars, which "seemed" to vary in numbers and speed. Therefore, in any given road, varying traffic "gaps" were created challenging the students to decide if and when to cross. At the same time, the traffic pattern was complex enough and seemingly random, making it not easily recognizable by students, discouraging them to try to resolve when the next safe "gap" would appear.

The next task was to regulate the motion and the turning speed of the head of the user's avatar. We determined that throughout the application the user should walk at a quick pace, since this is the speed with which one crosses a street. For a road 6-8 meters wide, 1.5 to 2 seconds for crossing were needed. Far more important was to settle on the rotation speed of the avatar's head. The speed should allow the user to thoroughly check the traffic. Two research studies (Whitebread & Neilson, 1999; Tolmie, Thomson & Foot, 2002) suggest that 4.68 (11 year old children) up to 5.45 (7 year old children) seconds are needed for checking (but not crossing). The second study also concludes that children check traffic for 3 up to 5 times before crossing. In a third study (Simpson, Johnston, & Richardson, 2003), traffic gaps of 6, 8 and 10 seconds were used. The findings suggest that for a one-way road, 6 meters wide, 8 seconds are needed for checking and safe crossing and 5.4 seconds allow checking but a marginally safe crossing. This study, even though it had a small research sample, is the only one in our knowledge that used an immersive VR application for establishing the way children perceive traffic gaps. We concluded that gaps of 8 to 10 seconds (depending on the type of the street) can be considered as "safe" for crossing, approximately 6 seconds gaps are marginally safe and below the threshold of 6 seconds gaps are unsafe. The rotation speed of the avatar's head was accordingly adjusted.

Programming the function of traffic lights was the most intricate interaction materialized in the application. Each crossroad has two pairs of traffic lights controlling the flow of cars and another two pairs for pedestrians. While one pair of car traffic lights is green, the other is red and vice-versa. While one pair is green, the pair of pedestrian traffic lights at this part of the crossroad has to be red and vice-versa. Car traffic lights in Greece change colors according to the following scheme: red-green-orange-red. When car traffic lights become red (or green), the corresponding

Figure 2. Triggers of traffic lights in a simple road

pedestrian traffic lights do not become green (or red) spontaneously, but after a few seconds, for safety reasons. Cars have to reduce their speed (in order to stop) when the traffic light is orange. Cars stop when the light is red, but in rare cases (not so rare in Greece) drivers violate this rule, forcing pedestrians to be more alert. In order to accomplish all the above, more than forty triggers were used in each and every crossroad and about twenty were placed in order to control the traffic lights placed of simple roads (Figure 2). It was also arranged for some traffic lights to be out of order and that -randomly- a car would violate the red traffic light.

While adding moving cars, trees, traffic sings and all the 3D models in general, the application became complex and its editing intricate. In addition, the large number of 3D models would cause the application to run with difficulty even in high-end computers. Therefore, the application was split in a number of levels equal to the number of the instructive units (Figure 3). Each level was also split in sub-levels. The user would be able to move from one to another sub-level using "'tele-portation", a concept widely used in 3D games. In this case, it was decided that it would be better for the users not to perceive teleportation, because the application might be mistakenly taken for a game. Exit and entry points in sub-levels were constructed in a manner that created the illusion of a single level. For instance, the architectural structure at the exit point of a sub-level was the same as the entry point of the next.

The cognitive elements were presented to the user when she/he pushed buttons or used levers. By doing so, the user could read or hear instructions on what to do in certain traffic situations, see an example using the 3D models present at the scene, or use these models to practice. For

Figure 3. Snapshots from the application

instance, on the instructive unit which dealt with weather conditions, students were able to push the brakes on cars that moved on dry or wet road surface (in low and high speeds) and measure the distance required for the cars to stop.

All levels were thoroughly tested, especially regarding the frame rate, which was constantly well above the threshold of 25fps (60 fps in average). Finally, to control the application's avatar, a PlayStation type of controller was used instead of the mouse and keyboard. The application was administered to a small number of students (with computer skills ranging from novice to good user) in order to have feedback concerning difficulties in using the application or difficulties in understanding certain cognitive parts.

As mentioned in a previous section, in-classroom activities followed the completion of each level. All these activities were printed and were given to students in the form of a booklet. The activities included but were not limited to presentations of the subjects of each level in theatrical sketches, in debates and drawings. Hence, the booklet acted as a quick reminder of what the students faced at a particular unit and as an area for taking notes or for doing their drawings. A booklet for the teacher was also written, which included the purpose and the general instructive objectives of road safety education, the specific instructive objectives of each unit and guidelines for the in-game and in-classroom activities. Finally, a manual for the installation and usage of the application was also written.

Implementation of the Application

To collect research data and evaluate the application, a public elementary school was selected, situated in central Athens. The selection criteria were: i) to be an urban school, ii) students of the last three grades never to have attended a road safety educational program of any kind, iii) teachers to be interested and available and iv) the availability of a computer lab. Students of a

neighboring school participated at a conventional road safety program. For this program, all the cognitive material and activities included at the virtual world were "transformed" in text, pictures and images and formed a printed students' handbook. Also, the in-classroom activities were the same. Students from a third nearby school were the control group, no road safety education lessons were taught to them.

A series of administrative-organizational and technical interventions were needed, essential for the uncomplicated implementation of the application. The school's computer laboratory was upgraded with the installation of new middle-range graphics cards. Earphones and joysticks were also fitted. The next step was to schedule the lessons. In conventional teaching, this task did not raise any problems since a unit could easily be taught to all students of a grade in two successive hours. In total, 21 two-hour lessons were planned (3 grades by 7 units, once a week). Altogether, 7 days were needed because teaching could take place in each grade's classroom and be conducted by each grade's teacher, hence a unit could be taught simultaneously in all three grades. The situation in the VR courses was far more complicated. Schools in Greece have one computer lab with 8 or 9 computers (9 in our case). This meant that in two successive hours, only three groups of three students of one grade could use the lab. During this time, no one else could use it; therefore, simultaneous teaching was not possible. In total, 7 groups of 3 teams of 3 students were formed, 49 two-hour lessons were planned (7 groups multiplied by 7 units, once a week) in a period of 49 days. Both VR and conventional courses started and ended together.

In order to collect research data, a complex system was established, combining questionnaires, interviews, observations during teaching, evaluation of the in-classroom activities, analyses of students' actions in the VR world and post-courses evaluation with the use of photographs and video clips. Data for the project were collected from multiple sources in order to have a more accurate and objective aspect of the entire procedure.

Prior to the beginning of the courses, two questionnaires were issued to all groups of students (to the ones that were going to use the VR application, to the ones of conventional teaching and to the ones of the control group). The purpose of the first one was to establish the degree of "traffic autonomy" of each student, i.e. to what extent she/he is exposed to traffic environment and how autonomously she/he functions in it. The second questionnaire's purpose was to establish the degree of infiltration of game consoles (e.g. Playstation, Nintendo, Gameboy, etc) and of computers in the children's daily life. Also, in collaboration with the schoolteachers, the psychological-intellectual profile of each student was outlined, in order to detect factors that influence their street behavior that might play an important role in the effectiveness of both types of teaching.

During the VR courses, attendance, interest expressed for the activities, "presence" in the VR world or detachment were recorded. Students were interviewed every two units. The duration of each interview was 15 minutes at the maximum. Students were not pressed to give answers and only the first spontaneous reaction-answer was recorded. The aim of the interviews was to collect data regarding technical and cognitive aspects of the application.

The students of the VR courses kept notes on the activities they performed. The answers they gave to various questions were also transferred to their handbooks. The same applied for the students of the conventional courses. Since the in-classroom activities that followed were common in both types of teaching, the evaluation of the handbooks and of the activities was the first method used to compare the effectiveness of the two forms of teaching. A month after the completion of both courses, a video was presented to students, consisting of twenty scenes, each having 20 to 25 seconds duration. Also, an album of 40 photographs was given to each student. Both the

video and the photo album presented groups of right and erroneous pedestrian actions-behaviors in no particular order. Students were asked to spot the right ones having limited time at their disposal (immediately after each video clip and ten minutes for all photographs). The same form of evaluation was also given to the control group.

The most comprehensive form of data collection was the build-in recording system of the virtual world. It was proven -by far- superior to a video camera recording each student. It allowed the exact timing of actions, repetition at will, simultaneous observations of the actions of the whole team and anybody could see what the student saw at the virtual world. For instance, it was possible -for each student- to monitor how many times she/he checked the road before crossing, how much time this action has taken and what types of mistakes were made.

Students in both forms of teaching were briefed that they will attend a series of courses regarding road safety, that they will work in a different way than usual and that they will not be examined or graded. During the introductory unit in the VR courses, instructions were given on the controls and the usage of the application. Students were informed that they were going to work in groups of three while inside the VR world as well as during the in-classroom activities. The majority of students, although used in playing computer games, proved to be unfamiliar with the first person view of the VR world (in contrast to the third person view of games, where the user sees his/her avatar). It took some time to come at ease with this way of viewing the VR world.

An interesting point was students' collaboration in VR world. It was observed that when a student crossed a road, she/he waited for the others to do the same. However, when a student had problems in crossing, the others told him when to do so. For this reason they were instructed that helping and collaboration holds for anything else but crossing. In general, the different way of working caused some difficulties to students, in

119

both forms of teaching, because they are used (or even depended) to the traditional model where "the teacher teaches and the students attend". In the conventional courses, that were more close to the traditional model, fewer problems occurred. In the VR courses, especially at the beginning, the teacher was literally bombarded with questions such as: "what do I have to do now?", "where should I go next?". Even though there were very few students in the computer lab, the teacher had to address each student or each group separately, because: i) students were wearing earphones and ii) all groups were not -most of the times- at the same section of the VR world, thus they were engaged in different activities.

At the introductory unit of the VR courses, a small portion of the urban environment was included. Almost all students crossed the streets from random spots, without checking and many "deaths" occurred. During the discussion that followed, students justified their actions by saying that this is what they do in reality. This is an indication that: i) they transferred their perceptions in street crossing from the real world to the virtual one, ii) the virtual world was considered "valid" and not a game and iii) their traffic culture

was very small if non-existent. Another clue that shows that students deemed the virtual world as "valid" was the way they walked on the pavement. Even though there were a lot of parks and open spaces with vegetation, students chose not to cross them diagonally in order to go from one point to the other. The explanation they gave was that "in parks it is not right to step on the grass".

Students welcomed both types of courses with joy and enthusiasm (Figure 4). In general, the positive attitude of students is a very powerful indication on how much and urgently a different philosophy in the way of teaching is needed.

DISCUSSION

The analysis of the quantitative and qualitative data collected by the system, eventually provides evidence for the application's value. It must be noted that there was a wealth of data to be analyzed (indicatively, for each student that participated in the VR courses, more than 750 variables were recorded), therefore in the following paragraphs only the most important findings will be presented.

Figure 4. Snapshots from the VR courses

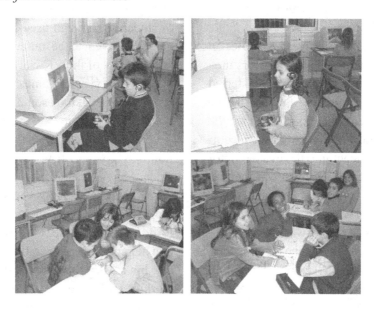

General Observations

In total, data were collected from 198 students (67 from the control group, 71 from the conventional teaching and 60 from the VR lessons). The initial number was higher, but we decided to exclude students that did not participate in all lessons (e.g. because of sickness). Their distribution by grade, gender and type of course is shown in table 1.

The analysis of the relevant questionnaires resulted in a grade that represented each student's traffic autonomy in a scale from 1 to 5 (the higher, the more autonomous). As expected, older students and boys are more autonomous (Table 2). In addition, the older the students are, the greater the difference between boys and girls becomes.

11% of students, do not own or use at home game consoles or computers. On the other hand, all use them either at school (ICT lessons) or at their friends' homes. Boys use game consoles far more than girls do (64% to 36%). On average, stu-dents spend around 3 hours every week (mainly at weekends) playing with game consoles, with boys spending an hour more than girls do. There are no significant differences regarding the students' age and the usage of game consoles. The situation with computers is different. Boys and girls use them equally (51.13% to 48.57%) and for the same amount of time. An interesting point is that students use game consoles twice the time they use computers. The most common use of computers is for games (86.4%). Other activities accumulate smaller percentages (e.g. 45.7% for writing and 28.6% for educational uses). The above provide the first clue that students to become accustomed with the application was not a problem, since they were already quite familiar with computer games or game consoles.

The second clue comes from analyzing how much time students needed to master the handling of the Play station's type of controller and how well it was used. Data were obtained through

Table 1. Distribution of students by grade, gender and type of course

Grade	Gender	Type of course	N
4th	Boy	Control group	16
		Conventional	16
		VR	8
	Girl	Control group	12
		Conventional	13
		VR	13
5th	Boy	Control group	9
		Conventional	9
		VR	11
	Girl	Control group	8
		Conventional	11
		VR	7
6th	Boy	Control group	12
		Conventional	12
		VR	13
	Girl	Control group	10
		Conventional	10
		VR	8

Table 2. Traffic Autonomy of students gender and type of course

Grade	Gender	N	Traffic autonomy			
			Min.	Max.	Mean	Std. dev.
4th	Boy	40	1	5	2.793	0.980
	Girl	38	1.25	4.5	2.447	0.872
5th	Boy	29	1.25	4.75	3.137	0.897
	Girl	26	1.25	4.5	2.644	0.778
6th	Boy	37	1.25	5	4.054	0.901
	Girl	28	2	4.75	3.330	0.729

observation (e.g. by taking notes of students' complains and recording how much time elapsed until a student could easily use the controller) and by analyzing the files created by the build-in recording system. Older students, boys and game console users needed less time. If a student was a computer user did not have an impact in how well she/he used the controller, a logical finding since the mouse and the keyboard are usually used in computer games. What is important is that from the third unit and thereafter, neither girls nor younger students had any problems (Figure 5). The students' interviews also confirmed the above. Only a student reported that it was very difficult to use the controller, while another one reported that she was confused by the position of the controller's levers.

More than half of the students (50%, 55% and 53.3% respectively in each interview) stated that they did not have any problems in understanding and performing the activities in the virtual world. The rest had minor complaints, while none had extreme problems. Observation remarks revealed that the most common cause of problems was that the students did not wait to hear all the audio instructions before performing an activity, which lead to misinterpretations and frustration because they had to repeat the whole process. When they were asked what was "the thing they liked most", the most common spontaneous answer was "everything" (53.3%, 31.7% and 38.3% respectively in each interview). When asked to be more spe-

cific, they gave a variety of answers that included almost all the elements of the virtual world. As to what they did not like, the most common answers regarded traffic in the streets (e.g. "cars are running fast", "I can get killed by a car", "there are too many cars and I cannot cross the street", "why some traffic lights are not working?").

The 6.77% of students had the opinion that the virtual world had no resemblance with the real one; a 16.67% considered the resemblance small and the rest (69.89%) characterized the resemblance as high or very high. Only two students had a very negative attitude towards the VR courses, stating that they already know enough about road safety. The rest stated that they learned quite a lot, that they were helped in feeling more secure in the streets and that they already apply some of the things they learned. It is worth mentioning that similar answers were given in the interviews by the conventional teaching students.

In total there were 86 "deaths" in the virtual world at all units, excluding the introductory one. As a variable it is not connected with how well the controller was handled. In addition, it does not correlate with gender with the exception of the last unit where the girls had a comparatively larger number of "deaths" than boys. Generally speaking, the number of "deaths" was small and no useful conclusions can be drawn. Consequently, we believe that the students' virtual accidents can be attributed to their carelessness while crossing the streets. A total of 2,968 street crossings were

Figure 5. Time needed for mastering the controller

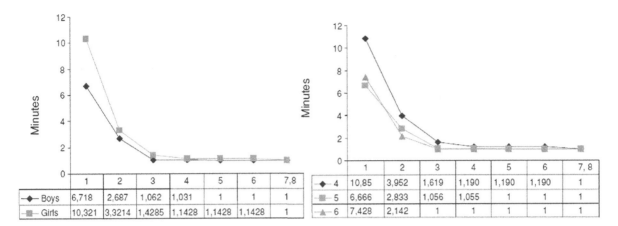

	1	2	3	4	5	6	7,8
Boys	6,718	2,687	1,062	1,031	1	1	1
Girls	10,321	3,3214	1,4285	1,1428	1,1428	1,1428	1

	1	2	3	4	5	6	7,8
4	10,85	3,952	1,619	1,190	1,190	1,190	1
5	6,666	2,833	1,056	1,055	1	1	1
6	7,428	2,142	1	1	1	1	1

made from the third to the last unit (the introductory unit and the second which had very few crossings were excluded from the analysis). From these crossings, 2,054 were right (69.2%). The most common mistake was partial checking before crossing (63.24% of wrong cases). All types of right and wrong actions in the virtual world are shown in table 3.

Regarding the right and erroneous actions of students per unit, a constant decrease of the percentage of wrong actions was observed that became more intense in the last unit, despite the fact that this was the most difficult and extensive. In fact, from a very high percentage in the introductory unit, errors drop to 31.79% in the 3rd and to 14.17% in the last unit.

In order to form an opinion on how well collaboration functioned, penalty points were given each time members of a team had problems in working together. Comparison of the final results shows that, in both types of courses, collaboration was smooth ($M_{conventional}$=4.24175, M_{VR}=4.3487, max.=5), and most problems were solved after the first two lessons. The same method was used in determining how interested students were. Again, it seems that the two teaching methods captured the students' interest ($M_{conventional}$=4.43806, M_{VR}=4,8028, max.=5).

The first indication that the two types of courses had different cognitive results came from the analysis of the in-classroom activities and of the students' handbooks. We have to stress out that all the oral, written, in-virtual world and in-classroom activities were not graded on the basis of how well they were done (e.g. how nice a drawing was, how well an essay was written or how well a sketch was presented). Instead, they were graded on the basis of if and to what extend basic road safety concepts were apprehended. Having that in mind, it seems that there are significant differences in the activities and exercises in the students' handbooks ($M_{conventional}$=3.68234, M_{VR}=4.24117, max.=5) and in the in-classroom activities ($M_{conventional}$=3.35387, M_{VR}=4.09792, max.=5).

Cognitive results were also evaluated using video clips and photographs as it was mentioned in the previous chapter. No bonus points were awarded for the right answers, while for the wrong 1, 2, 5 or 10 penalty points were given, depending on the error's seriousness. This kind of point system was applied because children often have the tendency to consider as erroneous a traffic situation, even if there is not really a problem (Lewis, Dunbar, & Hill, 1999). For instance, a number of students thought that pressing the button at a pelican crossing is wrong because by their

Table 3. Right and wrong actions at the virtual world

Action	N
Road crossing with/without traffic lights with no mistakes	2054
Passing of an obstacle in the pavement from the inside (from the side of the pavement)	227
Walking on a road without a pavement at the right side of the street	142
Rejection of a crossing point with limited visibility due to an obstacle	128
Selection of the right crossing point when two crossing points were available	64
Crossing a zebra crossing with incomplete check	578
Crossing a zebra crossing without checking at all	116
Crossing a road with traffic lights without checking if cars have stopped	74
Crossing a zebra crossing looking at the wrong direction	74
Selection of the wrong crossing point when two crossing points were available	48
Walking on a road without a pavement at the wrong side of the street	42
Usage of crossing point with limited visibility due to an obstacle	30
Crossing a street at a random point	29
Crossing a road with traffic lights while the pedestrian light was still red	13
Passing of an obstacle in the pavement from the outside (from the side of the road)	0

experience most of these systems do not function. A first glance at the results shows significant differences between the three groups of students ($M_{Control group}=60.10, M_{Conventional}=48.25, M_{VR}=19.03, M_{Total}=43.41$). An interesting finding is that for the same type of course boys and girls had the same amount of error points (Table 4).

Statistical Analysis

One way of interpreting the results is to examine one by one all the factors that influenced the

errors of students. Applying one-way ANOVA analysis, a common statistical procedure in the social sciences, it seems that there is a significant correlation between the number of errors made at the post-courses evaluation (the evaluation with video clips and a photo album) and the type of course (control group, conventional and VR) or between the number of errors and the students' age, while gender is not a factor. However, by comparing one factor each time with the results of the evaluation, it is not taken into consideration the impact of other factors. Therefore, a multiple

Table 4. Errors by gender and course type

Gender	Course type	N	Min.	Max.	Mean	Std. dev.
Boy	Control group	37	15	128	62.59	26.771
	Conventional	37	0	91	48.24	22.797
	VR	32	0	56	18.25	15.616
Girl	Control group	30	0	189	57.03	33.808
	Conventional	34	0	122	48.26	26.659
	VR	28	0	74	19.93	20.461

Table 5. R Square, Adjusted R Square and Durbin-Watson test of the post-courses evaluation model

R	R Square	Adjusted R Square	Durbin-Watson
0.811	0.658	0.638	1.984

regression model was formed to help to identify the relationship between several independent/predictor variables and the dependent variable (the results of the students' post-courses evaluation). The independent variables we used were: the student's age, gender, the degree of "traffic autonomy", elements of the psychological-intellectual profile (e.g. curiosity, self-confidence, eagerness, critical thinking) and finally the type of course. Stepwise regression analysis was used that lead to the factors that were significant.

The coefficient of determination (0.658) and the adjusted coefficient of determination (0.638) show that the model can explain around 65% of the dependent's variable (Table 5). This percentage is high, especially in the case where categorical variables are used as explanatory factors as in our case (Montgomery, 1976). The Durbin-Watson test used to detect the presence of autocorrelation in the residuals from the regression analysis, produces a value very close to 2 (1.984), therefore it is safe to use the model for drawing conclusions.

The independent variables that were included in the model are presented in Table 6. By far, the most important factor in reducing the number of errors made in post-courses evaluation is considered to be teaching using the VR application. There is also a reduction in the number of errors when

a student has good oral expression, is persistent and eager. At this point one has to make clear that characterizing a student's personality is a subjective matter and allows for various interpretations. A schoolteacher might judge a student not only by what he observes but also by his personal views and opinions. Thus, "eagerness" can be interpreted as willingness in helping others, but also as a zeal for learning. Respectively, "insistence" might be the tendency of a child not to be discouraged easily or an inclination to work with attention until difficulties are overcome.

Conventional teaching was not included as a statistically important factor. Therefore, it can be assumed that conventional teaching does not influence the evaluation of students, positively or negatively. The same applies for the control group. The students' age, gender and traffic autonomy were also absent from the model.

Various exercises in the students' handbooks, as well as in-classroom activities were used for evaluation purposes. Consequently, we examined whether the two types of courses had any statistically important impact in the evaluation outcomes of the handbooks and the in-classroom activities. The same method was used as in the post-courses evaluation, using the same independent variables. The coefficients of determination and the adjusted

Table 6. Factors that influenced the results in students' of the post-courses evaluation

	B	Std. Error	t	Sig.
VR courses	-24.712	3.736	-6.615	.000
Good oral expression	-7.416	2.457	-3.018	.003
Insistence	-4.208	1.888	-2.228	.029
Eagerness	-6.895	2.176	-3.169	.002
$M_{Control\ group}$=60,10, $M_{Conventional}$=48,25, M_{VR}= 19,03, M_{Total}=43,41				

coefficients of determination show that the models can explain pretty much (around 50-60%) the variability of the dependent variables (Table 7).

Handbook evaluation results were better when students had attended the VR courses. Boys and students with a good record in science subjects also had better results, while younger students (of 4th and 5th grade) had worst (Table 8). It seems that the various exercises in the handbooks needed to be better adjusted to these ages.

As for the in-classroom activities, once again the VR courses lead to better results. Students well adapted in school environment, with a good record in science and theoretical subjects, also had good results (Table 9). An interesting element is that students who are good in written expression did not produce equally well results. One has to keep in mind that these activities did not involve writing to a great extend, since they were theatrical sketches, presentation of subjects, debates and drawings. It is possible that students that are not so good in written expression had the chance to show virtues that are usually outshined by the importance teachers attribute to written expression.

Since the VR courses were the critical factor in having better results in both students' handbooks and in-classroom activities, we believe that they

also had an impact in meta-cognitive level. All the "exercises" were not like the standardized and somewhat mechanistic ones students are used to. They required comprehension and assimilation of the initial knowledge, critical thinking and application of this knowledge in a similar or in a totally different field. A characteristic example is an activity at the traffic signs unit. Students were asked to draw their own imaginary and humorous traffic sign. They had to understand the meaning and the rules that govern traffic signs (color and shape) and think of something original that follows these rules (without having been told to do so). This activity was executed much better by the students that attended the VR courses.

As mentioned in a previous chapter, students made in the VR world roughly 3,000 street crossings, most of them being two-way ones. For each crossing and for each student, the number of times traffic was checked and the type of "traffic gap" selected for crossing were recorded. Traffic gaps were placed in the following categories: i) below 6 seconds (unsafe crossing), ii) 6-8 seconds (marginally safe crossing), iii) 8-10 seconds (safe crossing) and iv) above 10 seconds (hesitant crossing). The above resulted in the following variables:

Table 7. R Square and Adjusted R Square of the handbooks and in-classroom activities evaluation models

Model	R	R Square	Adjusted R Square
Handbook evaluation	0.799	0.639	0.621
In-classroom activities evaluation	0.712	0.507	0.487

Table 8. Factors that influenced the results in students' handbooks evaluation

	B	Std. Error	t	Sig.
VR courses	0.553	0.053	10.417	0.000
4th grade	-0.564	0.063	-8.930	0.000
Gender (boys)	0.157	0.054	2.923	0.004
Good in science lessons	0.108	0.026	4.191	0.000
5th grade	-0.176	0.067	-2.619	0.010
$M_{conventional}$=3,68234, M_{VR}=4,24117, max.=5				

1. Times of checking before crossing a street
2. Ratio of <6" crossings to the total number of crossings
3. Ratio of 6-8" crossings to the total number of crossings
4. Ratio of 8-10" crossings to the total number of crossings
5. Ratio of >10" crossings to the total number of crossings

One can make the hypothesis that these variables are influenced by the knowledge and dexterities of children (e.g. traffic autonomy), the age and their sex. On the other hand, one might think that these variables depend on the students' experience in using game consoles and computers, since the application resembles a computer game. Tables 10, 11, 12, 13, and 14 present the variables.

In order to find out which factors play an important role, a generalized linear model was

Table 9. Factors that influenced the results in the in-classroom activities evaluation

	B	Std. Error	t	Sig.
VR courses	0.814	0.098	8.282	0.000
Well adapted in school environment	0.236	0.061	3.880	0.000
Good in theoretical subjects	0.265	0.082	3.231	0.002
Good in writing	-0.317	0.077	-4.106	0.000
Good in science subjects	0.189	0.079	2.382	0.019
$M_{conventional}$=3,35387, M_{VR}=4,09792, max.=5				

Table 10. Crossings in relation to age

Grade/Age		Times of checking before crossing	<6 sec	6-8 sec	8-10 sec	>10 sec
4th	Mean	2.76962	0.0729	0.1530	0.6255	0.1524
5th	Mean	2.10407	0.0881	0.1525	0.6409	0.1191
6th	Mean	1.58841	0.1145	0.2559	0.5529	0.0772

Table 11. Crossings in relation to gender

Gender		Times of checking before crossing	< 6 sec	6-8 sec	8-10 sec	>10 sec
Boy	Mean	1.87977	0.0817	0.2212	0.5951	0.1042
Girl	Mean	2.47283	0.1038	0.1519	0.6156	0.1297

Table 12. Crossings in relation to usage of game consoles

Game console		Times of checking before crossing	<6 sec	6-8 sec	8-10 sec	>10 sec
No	Mean	2.39133	0.0841	0.1958	0.6234	0.0977
Yes	Mean	1.98882	0.0976	0.1839	0.5913	0.1293

Table 13. Crossings in relation to usage of computers

Computer		Times of checking before crossing	< 6 sec	6-8 sec	8-10 sec	>10 sec
No	Mean	2.02779	0.0633	0.1864	0.6400	0.1112
Yes	Mean	2.21620	0.1053	0.1900	0.5883	0.1184

Table 14. Crossings in relation to instructive units

Instructive unit		Times of checking before crossing	< 6 sec	6-8 sec	8-10 sec	>10 sec
3	Mean	2.35050	0.1102	0.1852	0.4058	0.2988
4	Mean	2.24252	0.1025	0.184	0.4491	0.2644
5	Mean	2.11458	0.1031	0.1803	0.5012	0.2154
6	Mean	2.05460	0.1005	0.1932	0.5519	0.1545
7	Mean	2.17983	0.1123	0.2023	0.6002	0.0853
8	Mean	2.23517	0.0632	0.1685	0.6598	0.1085

Table 15. Factors that influence times of checking before crossing

	Type III Sum of squares	df	Mean square	F	Sig.
Grade/Age	34.037	2	17.019	12.363	0.000

Table 16. Factors that influence crossings <6"

	Type III Sum of squares	df	Mean square	F	Sig.
Computer	0.081	1	0.081	3.952	0.048

applied having as dependent variables the ones that measured crossing time and times of checking and as independent variables the grade/age, the gender, if students use game consoles, if they use computers, their traffic autonomy and the instructive units (3rd to 8th). Scatter plots revealed that traffic autonomy did not have any form of cross-correlation (linear or not-linear) with the under review dependent variables, therefore it was excluded from the analysis. Tables 15, 16, 17, 18, and 19 show the results of the generalized linear model for the statistically important factors.

The most important parameter was the crossings between 8-10 seconds that were the ideal. As it was observed, older students and the ones that use computers, made statistically fewer crossings within this time range. However, unit by unit, a statistically important increase in "right" time crossings was noted. Girls made fewer marginal crossings (6-8"), while older students made more. As for the unsafe crossings (<6"), computer users made more (although marginally). Hesitant crossings were influenced by the students' age and the instructive unit (decreasing while age and unit

Table 17. Factors that influence crossings 6-8"

	Type III Sum of squares	df	Mean square	F	Sig.
Grade/Age	0.382	2	0.191	7.864	0.001
Gender	0.198	1	0.198	8.139	0.005

Table 18. Factors that influence crossings 8-10"

	Type III Sum of squares	df	Mean square	F	Sig.
Grade/Age	0.411	2	0.206	5.223	0.006
Computer	0.190	1	0.190	4.816	0.030
Instructive unit	0.350	5	0.175	4.446	0.013

Table 19. Factors that influence crossings >10"

	Type III Sum of squares	df	Mean square	F	Sig.
Grade/Age	0.156	2	0.078	3.493	0.033
Instructive unit	0.149	5	0.074	3.321	0.038

increased). Finally, the students' age affected the times of checking before crossing (older students checked fewer times). The usage of game consoles did not affect any of the dependent variables, which is a positive finding, given the great resemblance of the application with computer games. On the other hand, computer usage seems to have a negative influence, leading to more unsafe crossings and less "right" ones.

A generalized linear model was also applied for checking whether errors made in the virtual world (expressed as the ratio of the number of errors to the total number of crossings) were affected by the independent variables used for analyzing crossings. As previously, traffic autonomy was not included in the analysis because once again scatter plots showed that it does not have any form of cross-correlation with the dependent variables. Table 20 presents the variables and Table 21 presents the results of the model.

All the under review factors played an important role in the errors that students made when crossing the streets of the virtual world. Computer users made fewer errors. However, those that play with game consoles made more. This result is not contradictory. Game consoles are used exclusively for games. It is possible that students considered street crossing as another form of game, despite the fact that game console usage did not seem to influence crossing times. Nevertheless, one has to remember that neither game consoles nor computers played an important role in all forms of students' evaluation. The same observations hold true for the students' gender and age. Girls made more errors and older students less.

By combining the results of the statistical analysis, various profiles of the students that used the application can be outlined. An older student is expected to check fewer times before crossing, will take less time in crossing a street, will not

Table 20. Errors in the virtual world in relation to age, gender, usage of game consoles-computers and instructive unit

Grade/Age	Mean	Std. dev.
4th	0.2393	0.14352
5th	0.2742	0.18574
6th	0.1903	0.12645

Game consoles	Mean	Std. dev.
No	0.2129	0.12845
Yes	0.2467	0.17100

Instructive unit	Mean	Std. dev.
3	0.3179	0.1578
4	0.2704	0.1626
5	0.2437	0.15389
6	0.2034	0.15871
7	0.1738	0.16307
8	0.1416	0.06927

Gender	Mean	Std. dev.
Boy	0.2082	0.14345
Girl	0.2606	0.16405

Computers	Mean	Std. dev.
No	0.2364	0.15830
Yes	0.2018	0.15435

hesitate, will make more marginal crossings and consequently will make less "right" time crossings, but eventually will make fewer mistakes. Precisely the opposite is expected from a younger student. Girls are more careful than boys regarding marginal crossings, but make more mistakes. Students that play with game consoles will make more errors and the ones that use computers will make less "right" time crossings, but will make fewer errors (in comparison to game console users). We cannot come to a definite conclusion whether the use of these electronic appliances affected negatively or positively. What is certain is that during the application's implementation there was a constant improvement of all the critical factors.

CONCLUSION

Greece is among the E.U. countries with a very high number of deaths and injuries due to traffic

Table 21. Factors that influence errors in the virtual world

	Type III Sum of Squares	df	Mean Square	F	Sig.
Grade/Age	0.249	2	0.125	7.025	0.001
Gender	0.258	1	0.258	14.547	0.000
Consoles	0.156	1	0.156	8.769	0.003
Computer	0.095	1	0.095	5.324	0.022
Instructive unit	1.029	5	0.343	19.325	0.000

accidents, in proportion to its population. Certainly there is the need for educational intervention. Conventional road safety programs well organized and with reasonable results do exist, but are inapplicable because of long duration, small numbers of pupils that can participate, or the requirement of special infrastructure. The luxury for the above is not affordable. The principal idea of the present work was to investigate for a solution that is fast, easy to apply and effective. Also, the basic assumption was that the use of virtual reality for teaching road safety can produce better cognitive results and develop the necessary skills better than conventional teaching. In favor to this assumption were findings the most important of which are listed below:

Technical Issues Concerning the VR Application

1. The application is compatible with the knowledge and dexterities students already have by using game consoles or computers.
2. The time taken for learning the controls of the application and becoming familiarized with it, sharply dropped from the first to the second session. Girls and students of the fourth grade had the greatest difficulties. From the third lesson and thereafter there were no problems.
3. More than half of the students reported that they had no problems in using the interactive system that provided the cognitive elements and guidelines and in comprehending the various activities. The rest reported minor problems at the first two units, because they did not listen to the entire audio instructions before proceeding.
4. The "presence" of students in the virtual world was active, meaning that they participated with enthusiasm in all activities.
5. Around 70% of students described the virtual world as having high or very high resemblance with the real one.

6. The application proved to be exceptionally stable and no crashes or problems were reported.
7. Replacement of the computers' graphics cards was needed for the application to run. The total cost of 1300€ (including the earphones and controllers) is considered well within the capacity of the school's budget.

General Issues Concerning the VR Application

1. The most common answer in the interviews (nearly 40%) was that students liked everything in the VR world. The elements that were not appealing were the difficulties students faced in the streets such as some traffic lights that were not functioning (on purpose), the high speed of a number of cars and those cars that could "kill". These were important teaching elements for the purpose of the application.
2. The errors in crossing the virtual streets from a very high percentage in the first unit, dropped to 30% in the third and to 14% in the last.
3. More than half of the errors in crossing were there partial/incomplete checking of the traffic. Only 5.32% of crossings were made without checking. At this point the present work differs considerably from the findings of previous studies that indicate that 25-50% of crossings are made without checking (Thomson, Tolmie, & McLaren, 1996; Tolmie, Thomson, & Foot, 2002).
4. Besides crossing streets, there were other situations a pedestrian might face. Students did not make errors in handling obstacles at the pavement (e.g. cars parked vertically). When students had to choose between two nearby crossing points where one of them had a problem, 57% made the right choice. On 80% of the situations that presented obstacles in visibility when crossing (e.g.

advertisement boards and parked cars) and streets with no pavements, the pupils behaved correctly.

5. The analysis of the errors made in the virtual world reveals that boys and the older students made fewer errors. There is no cross-correlation with the traffic autonomy of a child. This means that students with small autonomy (no rich experience in crossing real streets) were profited by the courses, together with students with enough autonomy, that probably knew how to use the streets but initially made mistakes.

6. Game consoles seem to have a negative influence. Students that use them often, made more mistakes and this is an indication that the application was considered a form of a game. What is puzzling is the fact that students who use computers often, made fewer crossing errors, but also made fewer "right" time crossings. In any case, it would be very difficult for a desktop VR application not to be affected by the perceptions game consoles and computer games impose to children.

7. Older students checked fewer times and were bolder in the virtual streets by making many marginal crossings. This fact was more or less expected, since they are more confident and experienced than the younger ones. This was verified by the hesitant crossings (e.g. checking many times or waiting for a large traffic gap), where the younger children made more. As expected, girls were more careful than boys, making less marginal crossings, but eventually made more mistakes. The above match the findings of studies regarding the behavior of children in real streets (Ampofo, & Thomson, 1990; Molen, 1981; Tolmie, & Thomson, 2002). This allows us to conclude that the students transferred in the virtual streets elements of their behavior in the real ones.

Comparison between the Two Types of Courses and Factors Influencing the Results

How well collaboration functioned during the in-classroom activities was not influenced by either type of courses. "Guided collaboration" is suitable for both course types. However, more time was needed in the VR courses for students to get accustomed to this form of teaching.

1. Almost all students in their interviews stated that they were considerably helped and that they already apply in the real streets what they have learned. Similar were the answers of the students that participated in conventional teaching.

2. The role of the schoolteacher was considerably different in the VR courses. He was able to provide individualized assistance, but on the other hand it was more difficult to get the attention of a student or a group of students because of the earphones they were wearing.

3. Students faced both courses with particular joy and enthusiasm. The students' interest was also very high.

4. Teaching with the use of the VR application resulted in significantly less errors in all forms of evaluation compared to conventional teaching.

5. Since conventional teaching was not included as a statistically important factor in any case, we can assume that this form of teaching had neither positive nor negative influence in the evaluation. This means that, students in conventional teaching are not expected to make either more nor fewer errors after the lessons.

6. The pupils' age, gender and traffic autonomy were not statistically important in the evaluation.

7. Factors of a student's idiosyncrasy/characteristics that played a statistically important

role in the reduction of errors or in having better results in the in-classroom activities and in the handbooks were insistence, eagerness, good record in science lessons and good oral expression. In any case, the weight of the positive influence these factors had was -by far- less than teaching with the VR application.

8. The answers of the exercises that were included in the students' handbooks were more "complete" and thorough in the VR courses. The same applied for the in-classroom activities. Taking into account that the exercises, as well as the activities, required comprehension and assimilation of the initial knowledge, it can be said that the VR courses had an impact in meta-cognitive level, something that the conventional teaching accomplished in a lesser degree.

Other Issues

1. The program was put into operation for the last three grades of primary school. The timetable of the last three grades had to be changed to schedule the VR lessons. The reason was the small number of computers in the school labs, which necessitated in splitting each grade in groups so that each person could work on one computer.

2. The research focused on students. Though data concerning teachers' reactions were not recorded, our sense is that teachers, as well as students, wish the general teaching framework to be changed. The effervescent interest of schoolteachers for the VR courses was the first indication. The fact that they accepted the upset in their program for two months was a second.

3. Cost-effectiveness. In terms of economic cost for the implementation of a project such as this, one can point out that it is well within the school's budget. In terms of cost for developing the application, one can use

freeware or open source software, but a lot working-hours are needed in order to produce a complete and versatile end-product, including the accompanying printed material.

REFERENCES

Ampofo-Boateng, K., & Thomson, J. A. (1990). Child pedestrian accidents: A case for preventative medicine. *Health Education Research: Theory and Practice, 5*, 265–274.

Fokides, E., & Tsolakidis, C. (2003). A theoretical and a technical framework for the development of Virtual Reality Educational Applications. In M. Auer (Ed.), *Proceedings of the Interactive Computer Aided Learning, ICL 2003* [CD-ROM]. Kassel, DE: Kassel University Press.

Fokides, E., & Tsolakidis, C. (2008). Virtual Reality in Education: A Theoretical Approach for Road Safety Training to Students. *European Journal of Open and Distance Learning (EU-RODL), 2008*(2). Retrieved May 13, 2009, from http://www.eurodl.org/materials/contrib/2008/Fokides_Tsolakidis.htm

Lewis, V., Dunbar, G., & Hill, R. (1999). *Children's knowledge of danger, attentional skills and child/parent communication: Relationships with behaviour on the road* (Road Safety Report No. 10). London, UK: Department for Transport. Retrieved May 13, 2009, from http://www.dft.gov.uk/pgr/roadsafety/research/ rsrr/theme1/childrensknowledgeofdangerno10?page=1

Montgomery, D. C. (1976). *Design and Analysis of Experiments*. New York: Wiley & Sons.

New Zealand's Ministry of Transport. (2002). *Road safety education Strategic Framework*. Wellington, NZ: National Road Safety Committee. Retrieved from http://www.transport.govt.nz/assets/NewPDFs/road-safety-web.pdf

Piaget, J. (1985). *The Equilibration of Cognitive Structures*. Chicago, IL: University of Chicago Press.

Road Safety Cambodia. (2008). *RS Education for Children*. Phnom Penh, Cambodia: Cambodia's National Road Safety Committee. Retrieved May 13, 2009 from http://www.roadsafetycambodia.info/action6

Sandels, S. (1975). *Children in Traffic*. London, UK: Elek Books.

Simpson, G., Johnston, L., & Richardson, M. (2003). An investigation of road crossing in a virtual environment. *Accident; Analysis and Prevention, 35*(5), 787–796. doi:10.1016/S0001-4575(02)00081-7

Thomson, J., Tolmie, A., Foot, H., & McLaren, B. (1996). *Child Development and the aims of road safety education: A review and analysis* (Road Safety Report No.1). London, UK: Department for Transport. Retrieved May 13, 2009 from http://www.dft.gov.uk/pgr/Roadsafety/research/rsrr/theme1/childdeve-lopmentandthe-aimsof4728

Tolmie, A., Thomson, J., & Foot, H. (2002). *Development and evaluation of a computer-based pedestrian training resource for children ages 5 to 11 years* (Road Safety Research Report No.27). London, UK: Department for Transport. c http://www.dft.gov.uk/pgr/roadsafety/research/rsrr/theme1/computerba-sedpedestriantrain4737

UK's Department for Transport. (2002). *Road Safety Research Compendium 2001 2002*. London, UK: Author. Retrieved from http://www.dft.gov.uk/pgr/roadsafety/research/rsrc/archive/roadsafetyresearchcompendium4721

UK's Department for Transport. (2003). *Road safety education in primary schools*. London, UK: Author. Retrieved from http://www.dft.gov.uk/pgr/roadsafety/child/education /roadsafety-educationinprimary4633

van der Molen, H. H. (1981). Child pedestrian's exposure, accidents and behaviour. *Accident; Analysis and Prevention, 13*, 193–224. doi:10.1016/0001-4575(81)90005-1

Vygotsky, L. S. (1978). *Mind in Society: The Development of Higher Psychological Processes*. Cambridge, MA: Harvard University Press.

Whitebread, D., & Neilson, K. (1999). *Cognitive And Metacognitive Processes Underlying the Development Of Children's Pedestrian Skills* (Road Safety Report No. 6). London, UK: Department for Transport. Retrieved May 13, 2009 from http://www.dft.gov.uk/pgr/ roadsafety/research/rsrr/theme1/cognitive-andmeta-cognitivepro4734

ADDITIONAL READING

Bowman, D., Kruijff, E., LaViola, J., & Poupyrev, I. (2004). *3D user interfaces: Theory and practice*. Boston, MA: Addison-Wesley Professional.

Brey, P. (1999). The ethics of representation and action in virtual reality. *Ethics and Information Technology, 1*, 5–14. doi:10.1023/A:1010069907461

Bruner, J. S. (1968). *Process of cognitive growth: Infancy*. Worcester, MA: Clark University Press.

Burdea, G., & Coiffet, P. (2008). *Virtual Reality technology*. New York: Wiley-IEEE Press.

Byrne, C. (1996). *Water on Tap: The use of Virtual Reality as an educational tool*. Unpublished doctoral dissertation, University of Washington, Washington.

Castronova, E. (2008). *Exodus to the virtual world: How online fun is changing reality*. New York: Palgrave Macmillan.

Chou, C., Hsu, H.-L., & Yao, Y.-S. (1997). Construction of a virtual reality learning environment for teaching structural analysis. *Computer Applications in Engineering Education, 5*(4), 223–230. doi:10.1002/(SICI)1099-0542(1997)5:4<223::AID-CAE1>3.0.CO;2-F

Delaney, D. (2002). *The market for visual simulation/virtual reality systems.* New York: CyberEdge Information Services Inc.

Demetre, J. D., Lee, D. N., Grieve, R., Pitcairn, T. K., Ampofo-Boateng, K., & Thomson, J. A. (1993). Young children's learning on road-crossing simulations. *The British Journal of Educational Psychology, 63,* 348–358.

Duffy, T. M., & Jonassen, D. H. (Eds.). (1992). *Constructivism and the technology of instruction: A conversation.* Hillsdale, NJ: Erlbaum.

Grady, S. (2003). *Virtual Reality: Simulating and enhancing the world with computers (Science and Technology in focus).* New York: Facts on File.

Gutiérrez, M., Vexo, F., & Thalmann, D. (2008). *Stepping into Virtual Reality.* New York: Springer. doi:10.1007/978-1-84800-117-6

Hedberg, J., & Alexander, S. (1994). Virtual Reality in education: Defining researchable issues. *Educational Media International, 31*(4), 214–220. doi:10.1080/0952398940310402

Johnson-Laird, P. N. (1988). *The computer and the mind.* Cambridge, MA: Harvard University Press.

Macpherson, C., & Keppell, M. (1998). Virtual Reality: What is the state of play in education? *Australian Journal of Educational Technology, 14*(1), 60–74.

Mikropoulos, T. A., Chalkidis, A., Katsikis, A., & Emvalotis, A. (1998). Students' attitudes towards educational virtual environments. *Education and Information Technologies, 3*(2), 137–148. doi:10.1023/A:1009687025419

Surwillo, W. W. (1977). Developmental changes in the speed of information processing. *The Journal of Psychology, 97,* 102.

Sutcliffe, A. (2003). *Multimedia and Virtual Reality: Designing multisensory user interfaces.* Hillsdale, NJ: Erlbaum.

Tesar, J. (2003). *Science on the edge-Virtual Reality.* Woodbridge, CT: Blackbirch Press.

Thalmann, D., & Feiner, S. (Eds.). (2000). IEEE Virtual Reality 2000: Proceedings 18-22 March 2000 New Brunswick, New Jersey. Los Alamitos, CA: IEEE Computer Society.

Valavuo, T. (1976). *Verkehrsverhalten der kinder und die schulische verkehrerziehung.* Unpublished doctoral dissertation, University of Innsbruck, Innsbruck.

Vince, J. (2004). *Introduction to Virtual Reality.* New York: Springer.

Wiederhold, B. (2005). *Virtual Reality resources.* San Diego, CA: Interactive Media Institute.

Wiederhold, B., & Wiederhold, M. (2004). *Virtual Reality therapy for anxiety disorders: Advances in evaluation and treatment.* Washington, DC: American Psychological Association.

Yoon, S. Y. (2007). Exploring usability of web-based Virtual Reality technology-An interdisciplinary approach. Saarbrücken, Germany: VDM Verlag Dr. Mueller e.K.

Young, D. S., & Lee, D. N. (1987). Training children in road crossing skills using a roadside simulation. *Accident; Analysis and Prevention, 19,* 327–341. doi:10.1016/0001-4575(87)90020-0

KEY TERMS AND DEFINITIONS

3D Game: An electronic game that simulates a three dimensional environment and involves interaction with a user interface to generate visual feedback on a video device. The electronic systems used to play 3D games and video games in general, are known as platforms (computers and video game consoles).

Constructivism: A psychological theory of knowledge which argues that humans generate knowledge and meaning from their experiences. Constructivism although not a specific pedagogy, is an underlying theme of many education reform movements

First/Third Person View: The viewpoint the user has of the virtual world. It involves the use of an imaginary camera. When this camera is placed in front of the user's representation (avatar) and at the height of his head, first person view is achieved. When the camera is placed behind and above the user's avatar, third person view is achieved.

Game Editor: A software tool used for the creation or modification of games. Can be either platform depended or not. It can also be game specific (allowing the alteration of a specific game, in-game editor), or not (allowing the creation of a variety of games).

Road Safety Education: An educational framework that provides an opportunity for achieving an improvement in behavior of pedestrians and drivers, change and reduction in road trauma (especially for children and young people).

Trigger: An entity in the virtual world, associated with entities, models or other triggers. By setting its attributes, the developer determines when it is triggered (i.e. by the collision of the user with an object). Its triggering allows the materialization of simple or complex events.

Virtual Reality: A technology which allows a user to interact with a computer-simulated environment, whether this environment is a simulation of the real world or an imaginary world.

Chapter 8
Blending Traditional and Technological Factors in Teacher Education in Jamaica

Aleric Joyce Josephs
University of the West Indies - Mona Campus, West Indies

ABSTRACT

This chapter highlights the challenges and opportunities in blending traditional and technological factors in teacher education. It examines the partnership between one Caribbean state and one campus of a regional institution to develop an ODL teacher upgrading program which has become the model for a regional Bachelor of Education distance program. The aim is to use the teaching of History to make the case for using a blended approach in transitioning to ODL and for careful consideration of the use of technology in the delivery of ODL programs. It discusses how a Bachelor of Education program articulates distance learning and face-to-face modalities and examines the skills needed and the challenges involved in developing a curriculum for teaching History to distant learners using a blended approach and incorporating available technology. It suggests that readiness of faculty and learner to adopt technology as well as careful consideration of the use of technology is crucial for the success of blended learning approach in traditional teaching environment.

INTRODUCTION

The formal education system in Jamaica has traditionally developed around teacher centered forms of delivery with students attending face-to-face classes. For teachers, this meant spending 3 to 4 years in an institution, often residential and away from home and family. From time to time, the state

DOI: 10.4018/978-1-61520-751-0.ch008

found it necessary to introduce programs employing open and distant learning strategies to keep the number of trained teachers in the classrooms at an appreciable rate or to upgrade their already trained and practicing teachers to meet new syllabi or new developments in the school system. In Jamaica, for example, there was a short-term measure introduced in the mid-1970s to provide training for persons employed as teachers before they were trained. The In-service Teacher Education Thrust

(ISTET) offered pre-trained teachers the chance to become trained teachers by attending classes on weekends or during the summer breaks at centers away from the teacher training colleges. In practice, ISTET was a face-to-face program though there were overlaps with elements of open and distance teaching modalities. Of this, Errol Miller concluded:

The ISTET model of teacher education mirrored the conventional face-to-face model used by colleges in all but two aspects. First, all the trainees were employed full-time as teachers and could be regarded as a type of part-time student. Second, the instruction was delivered on weekends and in school vacation periods. In it these two features overlap with the distance teaching modality in that the students were not conventional college students. (Miller, 2001, p.142)

Open and distance learning strategies are now being employed to upgrade trained teachers with an undergraduate diploma to the Bachelor of Education degree level. The state entered into partnership with a regional tertiary and degree granting institution to deliver a blended program combining distance modalities with face-to-face delivery with courses in the methodology of teaching as well as courses designed to improve and expand subject content for the teachers. A significance of this program rests in the fact that it was a short-term project, designed for a particular client, a national Ministry of Education, but worked as a pilot for an expanded distance regional education program offered by the training institution. It offers the opportunity to examine some key factors in using distance education to expand opportunities for study at the tertiary level in small states and at transnational scale.

SETTING THE STAGE

This chapter examines the partnership between one Caribbean state and one campus of a regional institution to develop an ODL teacher upgrading program which has become the model for a regional Bachelor of Education distance program. The aim is to use the teaching of History to make the case for using a blended approach in transitioning to ODL and for careful consideration of the use of technology in the delivery of ODL programs. It discusses how a Bachelor of Education program articulates distance learning and face-to-face modalities and examines the skills needed and the challenges involved in developing a curriculum for teaching History to distant learners using a blended approach and incorporating available technology. The responses of students to online instruction and assessment as against face-to-face sessions are explored using anecdotal and other qualitative material.

The study reveals that there are both challenges and opportunities in using ODL in in-service teacher education, and in engrafting distance programs on an established face-to-face institution. A major challenge is the adoption of online instruction in a country where internet connectivity is not pervasive or affordable even for the educated middle class professionals.

Literature Review

There is a preponderance of literature on open and distance education (ODL). Invariably the discourse focuses on one or more of the many issues related to broadening access to higher education. What is clear from the ongoing discussion is that ODL is not a solution for all that is ill with the traditional mode of education delivery, even while it offers flexible options to teaching and learning. The literature emphasizes that technology is not a panacea for all that is problematic in open and distance learning, but it is value added. (Spaeth & Cameron, 2000, p.325). The theoretical perspective and research findings suggest that other factors are equally important; the instructional design, flexibility in program and courses and of specific relevance to this case, the application of blended learning in ODL.

Blended learning (BL) is the current popular choice in ODL. According to the ongoing discourse, it is the wave of the future and is set to transform higher education. (Stacey & Gerbic, 2007; Garison and Vaughn, 2008). The popular perspective highlighted in the literature is that the application of blended learning gives access to digital resources and facilitates interactive communication or active and engaged learning. There is the value added of variation in the teaching/learning strategies, of enhanced communication which in turn enhances the learning process and the satisfaction of teachers and learners with the learning outcomes. (Stacey & Gerbic, 2007; Garison and Vaughn, 2008). Current discourse supports the claim that BL combines the best of face-to-face with online delivery, but the implementation is not without challenges. (Garison and Vaughn, 2008, p. 4; Spaeth & Cameron, 2000, p.325)

Competency in skills related to information technology is an important value added to both teaching and learning from the blended approach. In the teaching of History, it helps learners to develop new types of research skills specific to online research. (Dzuiban et al, 2004; Spaeth and Cameron, 2000). When BL is treated as a pedagogical approach, "not merely as a temporal construct, but rather as a fundamental redesign of the instructional mode" (Dzuiban et al, 2004, p.3) it facilitates greater learning outcomes and lower attrition rates. This was found for the University of Central Florida and Stanford University (Dzuiban et al, 2004; Singh, 2003). These outcomes are more than likely driven by the fact that a blended learning strategy forces university teachers to revisit the issue of pedagogy so as to create an effective teaching and learning environment that will keep the learner engaged. This need is emphasized as the teacher is removed from the learner.

It is in the context of the need to focus on pedagogy that an instructional design (ID) becomes a key element in developing material for the online learning component. Troha (2002) argues that the ID is as important as time and money, emphasizing the value. The instructional design recognizes the pedagogical factors; consideration is given to the learner, the learning objectives and the content and facilitates what Dzuiban and his colleagues suggest as important pedagogical features in their definition of blended learning: it "combines the effectiveness and socialization opportunities of the classroom with the technologically enhanced active learning possibilities of the online environment." (Dzuiban et al, 200, p.3). So the instructional design aids in building effective learning programs. The online component involves more than merely putting content on line; there is the mixing of various web-based activities to maximize active learning. Strategies and activities include 'a mix of traditional instructor-led training, synchronous online conferencing or training, asynchronous self-paced study, and structured on-the-job training." (Singh, 2003, p. 53)

The blended learning approach in of itself moves the learning experience from a teacher centered method to a learner centered approach. According to Ausburn (2004) adult learners, those more often than not making use of ODL, value the options, personalization, self-direction, variety and the provision of a learning community associated with online education. (Ausburn, 2004. p.327). The online environment allows for active learning linked with self-paced material (Singh, 2003, p. 53) and this is indeed provided in the blended approach. BL thus offers flexibility learning in the delivery mode and teaching/learning strategies. Flexibility is considered a vital component of distance education; it is not only advantageous but the most prominent attraction for distance learners. (Debating Distance, 2007) Yet it has its drawbacks. Fagerberg and Rikkelal (2004) in promoting flexibility through m-learning suggests that online delivery can in fact reduce flexibility; this happens when there is limited or no access to the internet or learners must visit a fixed place at fix times. (Fagerberg & Rikkelal, 2004, p.4). In this lies a challenge in implementing technology driven component; technology is constantly changing and although apparently widespread it is not pervasive. So an important question for course/program developers is "how pervasive is the technology to be used?

It is recognized however that technology, in this case computer enhanced course delivery is not a panacea. It does facilitate the shift from the traditional teacher-centered learning of face-to-face delivery and enable the development of independent learners. This is found by Spaeth and Cameron (2000) who furthered the discourse by looking at the value added of computers to the teaching of history. The case is made for custom research packs using online resources in developing skills in evaluation and critical analysis. For them the computer is invaluable in resource-based history teaching as it allows the learners the time to critically evaluate content and to be independent learners. (Spaeth & Cameron, 2000. p.325) No doubt the computer is a good tool for historical research as it gives access to a mass of potentially useful material, especially, primary material, as espoused by Spaeth and Cameron (2000). However, in the context of the case under review, the difficulty rests with the type of material that is readily accessible; Caribbean-specific material might not be so available online. So while the strategy of using custom packs may be pedagogically sound, technology driven resource packages can be counter-productive. What is sound practice is to consider the skill sets desired from the pack and create a suitable pact to fit the technology available and accessible.

The ongoing discourse brings the question of the real value of blended learning given the challenges. Both teachers and learners find it difficult to transition from face-to-face to distance learning and so blended learning is in fact a good model to manage the transition. As technologies, computers

in particular, are incorporated into ODL, it forces university and higher education institutions and providers to revisit the pedagogical issues of teaching and learning. This case of the Bachelor of Education (Secondary) Distance Program examines some of the issues raised in the ongoing discourse as highlighted above.

CASE DESCRIPTION

The Program

The case examined in this paper is the Bachelor of Education (Secondary) Distance Program developed for the Ministry of Education in Jamaica. It is a part-time program tailored to meet the needs of teachers in schools that were formerly designated as secondary schools, but were upgraded to high schools. The target community is trained teachers, holding a Diploma in Teacher Education, but whose earlier tertiary training did not provide the depth or breath of knowledge in their areas of specialization to prepare students for the syllabi offered at the high school level. The teachers already employed in the school system are given the chance to upgrade their qualifications, enhance their knowledge in their subjects and sharpen their teaching skills with exposures to new pedagogical approaches to teaching and learning while they continue to serve on the job. So the program offers both content related and pedagogical courses and is comparable to the face-to-face History Education degree program offered at the leading regional university. Modeling of the existing degree program is important as ODL programs are often seen as inferior to the traditional programs, "as the despised poor relation of face-to-face teaching" (Morgan, 2001, p.107) so parity had to be maintained. The History content component of the program comprised ten courses selected from existing course offerings in the face-to-face program and provides the participants with the knowledge needed to teach the Caribbean

Examination Certificate of Secondary Education (CSEC) syllabus for History or the Caribbean Advanced Proficiency Examination (CAPE).

The program was developed and implemented over a three year period as a collaborative effort of the Faculties of Humanities and Education and Pure and Applied Sciences. With the logistics of the program in place, one year was set aside for the writing of courses. In reality, courses continue to be written beyond the scheduled time. The speed with which it was conceived, developed and implemented was largely due to the fact that it piggy-backed on the existing face-to-face History Education degree program. Courses were drawn from the university pool of courses. The decision to use the blended approach meant that not all courses had to be written for delivery through distance learning modalities which can be a time consuming and costly process, especially when e-learning is incorporated.

Flexibility is desirable in ODL as it is recognised that open and distance learning modalities have a vital role to play in meeting the growing needs for tertiary education in unconventional settings and against a background of individuals needing lifelong learning (Chandra, 2001). Flexibility is desirable but the literature suggests that online delivery in fact may circumvent that flexibility as it is dependent on computer access (Fagerberg & Rekkedal, 2004). The program satisfied this demand for flexibility, allowing for changes in delivery methods and timetabling as the project unfolded but as will be seen, it also indicates that online delivery does in fact offer challenges to this flexibility; many students in fact have no internet access and can only access online course material from fixed sites and do not have 24/7 access to such sites. The first cohorts of students began a four-year degree program in the second semester of the academic year 2002/03. However, within two years the client asked for a change to a three-year program as a result of students' complaints about the time it took for them to graduate. This change called for flexibility in

the semester in which the courses were offered and signalled both an opportunity for and a challenge to those involved in the delivery. The demand for a reduction in the time for completion from the students could be facilitated because of the use of e-learning technology; once the course material was online, courses could be easily repeated within a given year without the cost to produce printed course material. The challenges came with the administration of such flexible delivery; registration for courses had to be strictly monitored and registration systems, usually online, had to be calibrated to accommodate the changes in any given year of course offerings.

Flexibility was built in the original design of the program. While the course offerings in this program were drawn from existing face-to-face programs, the timetables of the traditional face-to-face program and the ODL program were not integrated. The distance program began in the second semester of the academic year which at the time was a deviation from the norm. In addition, while the summer term continues to be optional for conventional students, it was not optional for students registered in this program. The two summer programs did not coincide as the ODL program's summer schedule was informed by the learners' working schedule; teachers are not released until the beginning of July to attend the classes on the university campus and the summer program for conventional students begins in late May/early June. With the new and full online regional program, this variation in time tabling becomes unnecessary.

The condensing of the History content component to three year meant that students had to do 10 courses over 9 instead of 12 semesters. With this new schedule, provision had to be made to do repeat offerings of second year courses in one year, a deviation from the norm then, to help students affected by the adjustment to complete in the new scheduled time. The students' request for a shorter time in which to complete the program emphasizes that ODL programs, needed to be flexible, responding to the needs of the client(s), but accommodation of flexibility thereafter was also linked to other factors. Flexibility aimed at ensuring that the students completed all courses to graduate in a timely way and before the project ended, and that when too few students registered for a course for the delivery to be cost effective, the course is offered at another time. The claim to the benefits of ODL in relation to economies of scale was not supported by this program (Chandra, 2001), but could be due to the project and client specific nature of the project. With the regional application this is likely to change. With the last cohorts of students registered and with some students from earlier cohorts still having out-standing courses, every attempt had to be made to ensure that such students complete the program within scheduled duration of the project.

It would appear that the four years traditionally needed to do a part-time degree could be effectively reduced to three years by using ODL strategies; it may be useful to revisit this reduction in time. Many of the participants met the three year requirement requested by the client but to date there are some students who are having difficulty graduating in three years. What are the factors involved in the delay? As will be seen later, the availability of technology is a likely factor.

The flexibility demanded by the clients was specific to the project nature of the program, but it points to the possibilities of an ODL program with fixed course options and e-learning components. The History courses offered were selected by the Department of History, guided by the syllabi requirements of the high schools. Pre-selection of courses by the department was no different for the full-time face-to-face History Education students. It is more cost effective and reduces the administrative challenge in delivering an ODL program with wide choices. With flexibility in delivery options, the project coordinator had to be proactive, being in constant discussion with the department's subject coordinator to ensure that department was ready to deliver courses in

the adjusted schedule and that the University Registry and Examination Section adjusted the course offerings and were prepared to carry out the examinations as needed. There was constant need for liaison with individual students facilitating their need for adjustment in their program and registration.

Without intranet, email and mobile technology, the dialogue among the stakeholders would have been difficult. A simple email reminder such as "we need to offer [a specific course in] September, since we did not offer it in summer" to the subject coordinator would set off a whole chain of communication to get the program continuing as smoothly as possible. Contacting a learner by mobile phone may have been the only ready way to get an adjustment to course registration. Such ready access was not only necessary in a flexible program but helped to reduce a sense of being far removed from the learner or vice-versa and helped to achieve a cardinal rule in the development of ODL programs - knowing the learner- not only in a general sense, but individually.

This ten year project was client specific and to some extent informed by the client's e-learning policy. While it was not conceived of as a pilot program, it operated as such; the last cohort of students was registered in 2007 but the program has been adapted to become a full fledged online program with a regional instead of national reach. This was facilitated because the training institution offering the program is in fact a regional one with trans-national reach and had for several decades been positioning itself to add an additional campus – an open campus.

The Learner

The Bachelor of Education (Secondary) Distance Program targeted a particular set of learners, diploma teachers trained to teach at the secondary level who were actually on the job in an upgraded high school. They were given the chance to upgrade their qualifications to a degree in the subject they were actually teaching. So although several teachers trained to teach at the primary school level and were actually teaching in the upgraded schools were interested in participating in the program, they were excluded. A 2007 report on the program stated:

A review of application received indicated that there are many teachers in the secondary school system who pursued the Primary diploma in college. These teachers are desirous of pursuing the program but did not meet the matriculation requirement. On the other hand there are diploma trained teachers who are not teaching the subject which they wish to pursue at the university (Project Office Report, 2007, p.5).

These particular concerns were not derived only from the matriculation requirement of the training institution. The Bachelor of Education (Secondary) Distance Program was designed to equip teachers to prepare students doing a Grade 11 examination after five years of high school. The university only taught certain types of subjects so there were limited course offerings for content subjects. Subject choices were limited to English, Spanish, Geography, Computer Science, English/Literature/Linguistics, Chemistry/Biology/Physics, Mathematics and History. This limitation rested in the fact that the training institution traditionally offered classical education and although it adjusted to the demand of the modern marketplace, it still maintained a program for graduates of traditional grammar type schools while the newly upgraded schools were comprehensive schools. The schools whose teachers were the targeted learners had a more diverse subject offering. So teachers of Food and Nutrition, for example, could not be accommodated in this program.

These limitations of the program suggest one difficulty in grafting a need-specific distance program onto the curriculum of an existing institution. While the university was on the path to become

a dual mode institution with an open campus, the offerings were not as 'open' as might have been desirable. Matriculation requirements had to be satisfied and the courses that could be offered had to satisfy the existing degree programs for parity with the degrees granted in the conventional program. The need to satisfy matriculation requirements should have been readily met as in principle holders of Teachers' Diploma are able to matriculate for the traditional programs. The targeting of a particular set of learners revealed that there was limited articulation of the content base of the college trained teachers with the content readiness for the degree courses offered by the university. This was not the case for the History content component; but it was especially true for some sciences.

The program offered was in fact on the job training; learners were expected to put into practice on the job what they were learning in terms of content and pedagogy. This informed the way the program was structured and even limited the extent to which certain types of technology could be used in program delivery. A blended approach in both content and pedagogical courses was used, facilitating distance modalities during the school term and face-to-face during the summer, but learner access to the technology needed could be impaired by their location – work and home.

Administering ODL Programs

At the center of the consideration in the development of the Bachelor of Education (Secondary) Distance program is the idea of 'blending', a concept usually applied to pedagogical issues. Yet pedagogy has to take place within a particular context which affects operational issues. With this national and group specific ODL program, the concept can also be applied to the administrative or operational factors in delivery of such a program. ODL is an old strategy of delivering learning opportunities which have evolved overtime – from correspondent courses to e-learning. Traditional face-to-face institutions are increasingly adopting the dual mode of delivery. However, except in the case of blended ODL programs, the two modes of delivery are treated as separate and distinct, parallel rather than complementary (Morgan, 2001). This is reflected in the way the Bachelor of Education (Secondary) Distance program is administered. The program is administered by a special project office. It liaises with the contributing departments which provide content specialists, specialists in pedagogy, specialists in information systems and educational technology as well as existing distance education centers and sites. Ultimately the project office is the administrative arm of the university and the work of this office is engrafted onto or 'blended' into the existing administrative process.

The university is a traditional face-to-face institution which over several decades pursued an experiment to offer education at a distance. By the twenty-first century, there was an operational distance education center and today the university boasts of an open campus which administers all the continuing education programs which were essentially a part of the university open education as well as its distance program but as cited earlier, course delivery was essentially through face-to-face modality. The question here is how does a traditional institution such as this university graft an ODL program onto its existing system?

The Bachelor of Education (Secondary) Distance program reveals the challenge in such engrafting. The way the university and particular departments do business, how they administer students' affairs had to be considered. A parallel administrative yet integrated system is the outcome and the engrafting is facilitated by technology; just as the computer and internet access facilitates blended learning. Online registration came on stream during the early years of this program and facilitated the registration of students although face-to-face orientation continued with student coming to the campus for this. Issues related to how medical certificate, for absence from exami-

nations or delay in submission of assignments, was obtained and submitted, had to be reviewed as the students were not campus based and so did not have access to the university health center.

The engrafting of the administration of the ODL program took place through the development of new offices/posts for liaison. For example, the subject coordinator of History acts as the liaison between the office of the project coordinator and the Department of History which administers History courses in the program and ensures quality control. The subject coordinator mobilizes faculty to become part of the transition from face-to-face to dual delivery. This development of this office emphasizes that this particular program is an engrafted one and needs careful monitoring to ensure that all administrative issues specific to each subject option are properly addressed. Will the need for this office/post continue to exist once the project is terminated? Can the new program exist without this office once it is fully developed and on line? It would appear from examination of other distance programs' administrative structure, that where the institution is a dual mode institution, these offices or comparable ones become necessary. For the program under study, the subject coordinator plays an important role in the smooth delivery of the project. As a dual mode institution in which the faculty is operating across modes and with a degree program having cross-faculty input, the offices of project and subject coordinator remains central to operation.

The evolution from single individual courses to full degree programs such as Bachelor of Education (Secondary) Distance Program has strategically positioned the Department of History which operated on the periphery of the distance center offering occasional courses in the past to contribute to the new thrust for ODL of the university. However, the distance program is still an adjunct program administered by the department. The taking on of this has resulted in the department having a core of resource persons prepared to do collaborative work, not usually required in the face-to-face delivery programs, in developing ODL courses.

The Bachelor of Education (Secondary) Distance Program also indicated that integrating an ODL program into an established face-to-face institution needed a transitional period for articulation or integration into the established program offerings. One lesson seems to be that an administrative unit devoted to oversee the program and liaison officers in each department are essential to the smooth operation of an ODL program. It highlighted the need for the Subject Coordinator who had responsibility to liaise with the Project Coordinator's office. These offices are retained by the new online program.

Teaching History at a Distance

Teaching history using the distance education mode appears to challenge the teacher centered approach found in traditional teaching. In fact, teaching history at a distance requires so much more of the practitioner than in the face-to-face modality; the teacher not only creates the learning environment but as course leader directs what happens in that environment. The course leader directs the student to learning materials, created or selected from published or unpublished sources by the leader. While learning is self-directed, the course leader as a teacher has the challenge of writing the learning material, as well as teaching in the virtual classroom.

The History option of the Bachelor of Education (Secondary) Distance Program, the general case for this study, had two components - content courses and courses in educational methodology. History as a content course is used as the specific focus of this section of the study. Six of the ten History content courses are offered in the distance mode while the other four employ face-to-face instruction in the summer. At the beginning of the project, the courses offered in the distance mode were print-driven with some teleconference sessions. The teleconference sessions allowed for

voice interaction among learners and with course leaders. Learners had to go to a university distance site to participate, but one site was on the university campus and so the learners assigned to that site sat in the room with the course leader. While these sessions made use of technology, and most students were removed from direct contact with teachers, it was essentially a teacher-centered delivery aimed at setting the parameters of the course or units and to give feedback at interval on tests. The challenge was timetabling the sessions; the teleconference facilities were in demand for use for other ODL programs and available times were mostly when teachers doing in-service training were still at school. This was cited as a problem by the learners. So the use of teleconference technology for mass delivery did not work very well, as the facilities available were limited. The learners also reported that the teleconference system sometimes failed.

So the challenge in having the interaction desired by students through teleconference sessions contributed to the change made to the project's method of delivery after the first year; the distance courses were offered online through the university's e-learning program.

While History content courses do not continue to access the option to use some teleconferencing it was still possible to do so once timetabling could be worked out. There is also the option to use face-to-face tutorial sessions, but this has not been used in the teaching of History content; the wide dispersal of and the number of students do not merit the cost that would be incurred.

Open and Distance Learning, especially with the use of e-learning, is widely embraced as facilitating wider access to education and reducing the centrality of the teachers' role. What is overlooked is the expanded role of the 'teacher' in the careful preparation of course material. How is the content of the courses to be provided when the teacher is not physically present and the learner does not have the access to the vast array of books to be researched? This latter consideration is vitally important in offering History content courses that incorporate some semi-independent research and historiographical analysis and where online resources are not available to facilitate the teaching of such components of a course. For the Caribbean, the challenge is even greater as more often than not texts on the Caribbean past are not currently available online in sufficient quantity. These considerations expand the 'new' role of the 'teacher' – as course writer. The teacher must provide course material for teaching History at a distance and this is sometimes a daunting task. The blended program approach reduces the pressure on any department to produce such material for several courses especially in a short space of time, but does not remove the need to consider a blended approach in course content delivery. For this program, the current strategy is to provide content online and printed supplemental reading material.

It is easier to have the blended approach combining face-to-face and online program delivery where the offer is for one nation – a small nation. It is difficult to duplicate such a program in a trans-national environment without increasing the cost exponentially since face-to-face instruction would have to be duplicated in each territory, either through movement of faculty or duplication of faculty. The new Bachelor of Education Distance program which was birthed from the case studied has replaced the face-to-face component with distance mode delivery since it is offered regionally.

The teacher as subject expert has to become a writer of learning material and with the peer reviewer has to provide content material in printed manuals or online. An important consideration is the readiness of the 'teachers' to become course writers. In the traditional university classroom, lecturers often have little more than a course outline and will talk for a hour or more from memory or a few jottings. In the virtual classroom, it is not a matter of merely putting notes on an intranet; the course leader has to consider the pedagogical

skills required and design the material to be given to the learner with that in mind. With the Bachelor of Education (Secondary) Distance Program, the participating lecturers had to consider what they actually wished to take place in the classroom, and especially as they had to model what the learners would be doing in the second component of the History program – the educational methodologies. The course writer must consider the technical issues of delivering at a distance by asking a number of questions - about the learner, instructional design, and the amount of content and specific reading material to be provided.

The 'teacher' may never actually interact with the students but 'teaches' through the material provided. The material is markedly different in format from what History teachers at the university level usually write for their peers and publication. The learners have to be the focus and the strategy has to be self-directed learning. With the learner at a distance without the opportunity to interact readily with the teacher as the course proceeds, or for the teacher to learn about the learner as the course unfolds, the 'teacher' as course writer has to decide on the key content areas, anticipate questions from the learner and invariably provide more in writing than he does in a face-to-face lecture. This is particularly true for History courses where there is no online library and so there is limited additional research material. In a program for teachers, the teacher as writer has to provide a model for the learner and this is facilitated when the course is developed from a carefully thought out instructional design (ID) (Figure 1).

This systematic approach is not usually followed in preparation for the traditional university classroom where the focus is a given topic with little reference to curriculum development which may or may not have been considered in the initial development of a course. The more recent trend however is the application of curriculum techniques in the quest for quality assurance. The use of an ID in course development ensures that the key content areas of a course are readily identified

Figure 1. Components for an instructional design

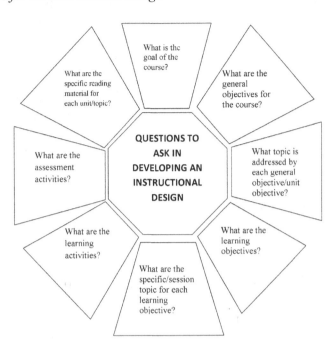

by the learner and likely areas of assessment are identified. Pedagogical issues such as the cognitive skills involved in teaching and learning must be considered in the process of preparing material to be used by the distance learner. Understanding the cognitive domain and the hierarchal classification levels of learning is important in the development of general objectives and measurable learning objectives (Huitt, Bloom et al., 2004; Atherton, 2005). Another emerging competency for teachers which is crucial for distance learning is what is referred to as 'instructor presence'. (Kinshuk et al, 2007, p.3). This is important for learners schooled in the traditional classroom. The participants in this program fall in this category of learners and indicate in their response to survey questionnaire and other media that this is desirable and accounts for their preference for the summer face-to-face component to the online component even when they admit that the online component brings a new dimension to the program.

While a technical approach to teaching is not unique to ODL, the systematic application of pedagogical skills becomes even more important as the teacher prepares to engage the learner at a distance. Consideration must be given to the strategies to be employed; what is the best way to present the intended messages? In the traditional classroom, this can be adjusted on an ongoing manner as the teacher gauges the response or lack of it of the learner. For the online environment, the writer/teacher must be ever aware that learning is self-directed and employs strategies that will engage the learner. If this is done then there will be correlation between content, learning objectives and assessment. The ODL student manual will demonstrate through this correlation how the students' achievement will be recognized.

In the traditional classroom, quality delivery is assumed but for ODL, this is not taken for granted as the peer review of the manual ensures not only accuracy of content but that there is in fact correlation between the stated objectives, content and the activities for learning and assessment, that is, there is validity and reliability of the content. It ensures that the depth and breadth of the content satisfies the course level.

One of the marked variations from the face-to-face delivery is the selection of specific reading material. It is not enough to provide a long list of books and articles to be accessed through the university library. The writer/teacher has to realize that although the distance learner in this particular program, Bachelor of Education (Secondary) Distance Program, could access books through a link on the university library's web page, that access can be time consuming and counterproductive for a semester based program. The available selections of references at the nearest distance centers also have challenges. So clearly stated learning objectives become crucial in the selection. Online links are not readily accessible since there are often restrictions for off campus access through academic search engines and subject portals. Yet even where access to online resources is not restricted, internet access is not always possible. Here technology does not necessarily facilitate ODL, or put differently 'low tech' may be better

than 'high tech'. Printed versions of carefully selected reading material are the solution. But even this poses problem of cost where copyright becomes a factor in reproduction.

For the teaching of History at a distance, the access to supplemental reading material is a major consideration in designing the courses. History teachers desire learners to develop their research, critical thinking and analytical skills by reading widely, especially in the final year. How then do writers/teachers provide for the development of these skills without using the traditional approach? How do you get learners to be aware of the debate among historians, to collate material from diverse sources and carry out some form of independent research? One solution is to develop course readers with contribution from multiple authors. This is one consideration for any distance learning institution where internet access is limited as it moves towards an open campus.

The popular argument is that education should incorporate technology in education because of its pervasive use in modern life (Kimble, 1999)

Figure 2. Blending high and low technology in ODL

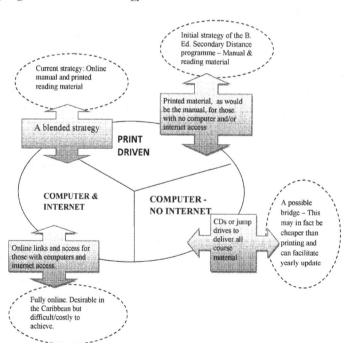

but many communities in developing countries do not have access to the technology needed to bring them into the information age. The difficulty of accessing supplemental reading material via the internet established that technology in the twenty-first century is still for many 'low tech'. Printed material is 'low tech' in a world where there is the information highway by way of computer technology, but in Caribbean islands the less than pervasive presence of computer use and internet access other forms of technology is necessary. A blended approach in providing supplemental reading material is a possible solution. What constitute a blended approach? Figure 2 illustrates the possibility of blending 'high tech' and 'low tech' in facilitating ODL where computer and internet access is fraught with difficulties.

This blend would be a direct outcome of knowledge about the learner and the social and geographical context from which he/she operates. The rural communities in which many schools are located, and where many teachers in the program work may not have this access. It is therefore imperative for the creators of ODL programs which target learners in these areas to consider flexibility in not only how courses are delivered but by extension in how supplemental reading material is presented – a hybrid of high and low tech strategies such as interactive CD's might prove more useful than a full web-based delivery.

So while teachers of the twenty first century must adjust to the recent developments in educational technology, it must be understood that there are areas of the world that are not served by these technology and may not be for a long time. There is already the suggestion in ODL circles that there should be diverse instructional material for online courses. (Moallem, 2007; Singh, 2003) We need to take it a step further. This may mean that the developers of course material for ODL programs have to consider using multiple instructional material – not just to have a blended program but blending in courses to cater to the learners' societal and geographical context.

Given the depth and breadth of preparation for teaching at a distance discussed above, it is not surprising that lecturers schooled in traditional face-to-face university education shy away from what is perceived as far too time consuming – teaching History at a distance. Anecdotal evidence and observation suggest that such lecturers do not usually write their lectures and so to be engaged in ODL delivery becomes a major shift in how they prepare for teaching and learning. However, collaboration among History lecturers can facilitate the writing of distance material. Collaboration for quality assurance is embedded in the writing of ODL material through the peer review process, so it can be taken further by team writing. This may be as simple as was done in the writing of one course for teaching Caribbean History online. The work of writing in that instance was divided among three history teachers as illustrated in Figure 3.

Figure 3. Collaboration in writing distance courses

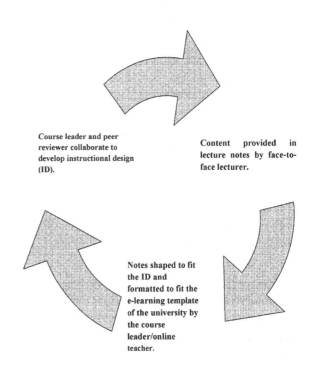

Course leader and peer reviewer collaborate to develop instructional design (ID).

Content provided in lecture notes by face-to-face lecturer.

Notes shaped to fit the ID and formatted to fit the e-learning template of the university by the course leader/online teacher.

The peer input is not only notable for the value of team work, but it plays an important role in ensuring the quality of university teaching. Traditionally the input of peers is twofold – at the course development stage when the outline is finalized and as second examiner. The input in ODL is more extensive; for the History courses there is contribution at the development of the instructional design, there is review of the course content and the type of activities as well as the usual vetting of scripts. The enriching by peer input is furthered with the ability to draw on subject experts from different campuses in a regional university to develop course content and to be online tutors. In this program one course was written and taught by a member of faculty from another campus located on another island.

Teaching at a distance for the case under study highlights the value of team work, especially for a trans–national and multi-campus university as the pre-packing of the course content allows for the use of the skills and expertise from a wider cross-section of the university and with some internet access allows for online tutoring transnationally. Such trans-national collaboration can in fact broaden and enrich the course offering of an ODL program.

In any case, for effective delivery of any distance program, the work has to be collaborative and teaching history at a distance is not different. Subject specialists have to work with curriculum development specialists and persons skilled in computer and educational technology. The technical specialists train course leaders in writing and the use of the online environment. The final product of any ODL course is the work of course writer, peer reviewer, curriculum development or the instructional design experts and the librarian.

Reference has been made to 'leading' as a component of ODL. It reflects an important digression from face-to-face in ODL - the focus on learning rather than teaching in the traditional sense. To emphasize this shift the term 'leading'

rather than 'teaching' is used to represent what the teacher does and highlights the student-centered nature of the program and self-directed learning expected. The difference is further emphasized as the course writer of the student manual/online material, may not in fact actually interact with the learner directly; he/she may not be the 'course leader' and if so may interact with online or face-to-face tutors, guiding them in the interaction with the learners.

While theoretically course leading suggests self-directed learning and so less input of the course leader than may be required in the traditional face-to-face delivery, in practice, the demands of the learner could require frequent interaction online and it may be necessary to be constantly online to keep learners actively involved in the learning process. Online delivery can be more time consuming than in a face-to-face tutorial and structured office hours as feedback is often for individual submissions. The diverse methods of assessment and activities in the online courses also add to the challenges for the course leader; learning and assessment activities in the form of forum discussions, short discussion responses uploaded as text files, quizzes, or online tests become necessary to maintain learner involvement.

An apparent contradiction to the claim that ODL is self-directed learning is begged by the observation that the course leader does more 'teaching" than in the face-to-face mode of delivery, as learners demand greater interaction than anticipated especially since they had already had post-secondary education. The fact that they have guidelines to help in the timely completion of tasks and to prepare them for the assessment activities is not enough. The job of the course leader when he/she interacts with students is to provide feedback on both learning and assessment activities. The course leader or online tutor soon finds that it is not enough to set up the activities, arranges for chat room activities and gives feedback to specific activities. There has to be constant interaction and monitoring of time devoted to the course, to check on the extent of supplemental reading and to discuss personal life challenges. This type of monitoring is possible because the platform used in the university's virtual learning environment records the learners' online activity.

A possible explanation for this unexpected and expanded need of adult learners is the fact that the educational experience of the learners was rooted in face-to-face delivery and teacher center pedagogy. This program therefore indicates that learners who have been shaped by this will need more time to adjust to ODL strategies and this may be compounded by the fact that the program used a blended delivery mode.

The literature supports a definition that sees blended delivery as internet integration in course delivery. In short, this meant using multiple media to deliver and enhance learning. This course varied in that it speaks of blended in relation to the components of the full program.

Computer and Educational Technology in Teaching at a Distance

With the growth and prevalence of the internet, when one thinks of technology in education, especially ODL, online learning is readily brought to mind. There is the claim that "the Web can free teaching and learning from the physical boundaries of classrooms and time restraints of class and schedules ..... can help us re-focus our institutions from teaching to learning, from teacher to student." (Owston, 2008, p.27) This at best is an ideal; in the case of the Bachelor of Education Distance Program, there is evidence that the claim is far too sweeping. The pervasive access to computers and the internet militates again this ideal.

In Jamaica, there is a bias towards online learning. While this may be the desirable path to take, there is the need to recognize that the delivery of open and distance learning within the context of the Caribbean with limited resources, there will be a need to take a blended approach in ODL.

An important area of concern in the transition to a dual mode institution is whether or not the teaching institution is ready to provide technical support for effective delivery of online courses. Equally important is the question of the computer literacy of the learners and the availability of the technology away from the center of learning. The real challenge in transitioning to online delivery, was not so much that the university was not ready, but because state was not and the students were not. The university had for years experimented with distance courses and had by the turn of the century an operational distance education center, an information technology unit and several sites away from the main university campus.

Online delivery became the preferred form of delivery for the client, but how was this to be done? What platform was to be used for course delivery? Selection of a template involved consideration of cost. For example, the university had made use of *WebCt* for a limited time and for a limited number of courses, but access was through a license. *Moodle* e-learning platform was chosen as the university platform – it was an open source and its potential for adaptability made it the preferred platform. The decision to locate the online delivery in the information technology center meant that the center had operators who were trained in educational technology and could train both writers and learners in the use of the system. However they did not have the experience of the distance education center where there were curriculum development specialists and experts in editing distance education material. This added to the work of the course writers who had to provide material ready to be uploaded.

Printed course material was abandoned, teleconference proved difficult to schedule and was possibly not as reliable for outlying areas as desirable, but could the internet adequately replace these forms of technology? This remains an important question for most subject specialists who were not competent in the manipulation of the online environment at the outset, even with user-friendly *Moodle* platform. Collaborative work, in the use of computer and educational technology, is vital to the delivery of the courses. Subject specialists depend on the information technology specialists to ensure that the course material uploaded is in a learner friendly format. The use of the same basic template for all online courses facilitates students moving around in the online environment with minimal difficulty from course to course; we are mindful that the students are mostly on their own and do not always have technical assistance.

Moodle e-learning platform proved a wise choice as it was not only user-friendly but it facilitated the social interaction needed, both synchronous and asynchronous interaction and a variety of evaluation approaches. Most importantly it worked well with the available bandwidth at the university and effectively interfaced with the Microsoft software used by most faculty and students

The *Moodle* platform was enhanced because it was adapted by university's information technology unit to provide a uniform template for all courses. The use of this template for all courses meant that the course material uploaded was presented in a familiar format that enhanced usability by students and reinforced their knowledge of the technology overtime. The end result was that even students who were not competent in Information Communication Technology (ICT) would have ended the program more computer literate than at the initiation of the program. This confirmed the finding at the University of Central Florida that blended learning was more than a program structure or delivery mode; it was pedagogical and had definite learning outcomes. (Dziuban, Charles et al, 2004)

Moodle, through the facility to set up chat rooms and forum discussions enhanced academic discourse and provided the opportunities for socialization and active learning. This level of interaction among students and between faculty and students from all reports suggests the potential for enhanced learning. The assessment tools of quiz, uploading of short responses or essays allowed for ongoing assessment and ready feedback. The ease with which faculty and students could interact through the messaging feature embedded in the adapted template was very useful for group notices or individual conversation...The ability to insert pop-up and the calendar feature on the home page of each course ensured that students could readily see what was new as the course unfolded.

The difficulties of internet access in this particular case meant that it was important that there was also asynchronous interaction. *Moodle* facilitates monitoring of asynchronous online activity, that is the length of time spent online independently by the students studying the material posted online, in chat room and forum discussions. Faculty is able to provide feedback to these activities at anytime because the students' online work is stored. Access for faculty and learners was theoretically 24/7 but students without personal computers and internet access at work or home did not have such access.

CHALLENGES AND LIMITATIONS

What of the learners' readiness towards adaptability for technology based learning? While the learners were given some orientation to the system, this was inadequate, especially for those who were not computer literate. Once the blended learning strategy employed meant online and face-to-face, students were required to ensure they had access to the internet. Many students did not have personal computers or if they had computers, they did not have internet access. Some were fortunate to teach at schools where there were computers and internet access. From a 2007 survey of the then registered learners in the Bachelor of (Secondary) Education program, 59% of the teachers did not use computers in the classroom. The same percentage did not have internet access at home. The alternative was to go to the distance education centers of the university around the island – after work. This could mean travelling over 20 miles by public transportation from home or work for some participants. Those with computer and internet access admitted to going to the assigned centers only to drop off assignments. 41% had to go to distance sites, use a friend's or other facility such as an internet cafe. These were not usually free and not widespread in rural areas. A few stations could be found at post offices. The university sites were at times many miles from work and home. Matters are compounded when we add the fact that only 73% of the students admitted to being competent in Microsoft office while the others had little or no knowledge of the software.

This ignorance of the basic tool needed for online courses affected their ability to register online and generated complaints such as inability to upload assignments. Synchronous online activity by the leader is decreased if learners lack access to computers for full 24 hours a day, which was the case with many in the Bachelor of Education (Secondary) Distance program. It was therefore difficult to schedule chat room activities and any synchronous online activity. Even asynchronous activities could not be left open indefinitely and learners found it difficult to meet extended deadlines. No doubt these technical difficulties also explain the number of students who have withdrawn from the program, have incomplete assignments and in some cases have underperformed.

What is instructive is the students' response to a questionnaire on preference to methods of delivery, format of assessment and activities. The preference in all three areas shows that students leanedd more to those methods, activities and assessment which had a greater correlation with traditional pedagogical methods. The response to an online questionnaire in itself indicate that learners either did not have ready access or shied away from any type of online activity. The feedback from the responses was revealing. For methods of course delivery, the preference was for printed manual and summer face-to-face sessions which

could also reflect the fact that they could focus more on the work at hand than during the term when their attention was divided. The response to online learning activities was varied with 50% of respondents giving chat room a high rating as against 75% for forum discussion and online quiz and 100% uploaded text pages. It would appear that those activities that were not synchronous had a more positive response. This conclusion is substantiated by the rating of assessments: the highest rating was for research essays submitted at the sites and tests done at the sites. For ongoing assessment, uploaded essays and online quiz were rated high as well.

Some participants are biased towards face-to-face delivery while the program has a bias towards ODL. They complain: "When the program started, a variety of methods were used to get the lessons across, such as teleconference, face-to-face and by the Internet. Now it is only being offered over the Internet." They want to be "called... in for a face-to-face session during the... semester" and seem to be less than pleased that they only see lecturers when they "go on campus for six week in the summer. (Thorney, 2008, p. 7)

These responses reflect the experience as a course leader and subject coordinator. There is no doubt that ODL experience is rewarding from the improvement in university teaching through improved instructional design (Conceição, 2006) but the students' response make the task especially challenging as engaging the students online proves difficult – they avoid chat rooms even when set up to be asynchronous and more often than not only do assessment activities, avoiding the learning activities. This may be a function of the difficulty of access which prevents the ability to participate in the online activities as expected. This is suggested in one student's response to query about incomplete tasks in forum discussion:

The time given to complete the various discussions is too close behind each other. I cannot get enough time to complete one discussion before another is asked for. Please remember we have other courses that we are engaged in and the internet is only available to me at work or at a site. (Forum Discussion, 2007)

Throughout the project there was experimentation as to best practices in testing and assessment online. Initially the established structure was applied with the print driven program; face-to-face at the distance centers. As the project unfolded and courses were delivered online, online assessment, using a variety of forms – from quizzes to forum discussions. Lack of 24 hour access to computers, students lack of computer literacy meant that forum discussions and any synchronous discussion had to be opened long after the relevant unit was completed to maximize input from participants. Tests had to be reformulated as students got locked out of tests before the time allowed was completed either because of they were technologically challenged or the system shut down for one reason or another. Blended assessment persisted as a result.

SOLUTIONS AND RECOMMENDATIONS

The use of ODL in tertiary and in particular teacher education is not new but it is now driven by government policy and the changing technology and has become the cutting edge mode of delivery in the aim to expand educational opportunities. It brings many challenges but suggests opportunities that should be embraced and instituted where possible. The Bachelor of Education (Secondary) Distance Program offers a model for teaching History at a distance. Some participants welcomed the chance to upgrade their qualification while on the job and found the experience worthwhile and were able to complete the program in the shortest possible time. Others struggled with completing the programs in the time required. The challenges which seemed to be derived mainly from internet

access but also from the learners' readiness to move from conventional pedagogy to transformational education must be considered in the way courses are prepared and in the nature of the instructional blend. The dual transformation in the program delivery and structure may have been counter-productive; a blend of print-driven ODL material and online delivery would have been more reflective of the learners' need. A careful study of the context in which the learner operates was needed before the change.

This study supports the view that there are both challenges and opportunities in offering an ODL program in a university built on face-to-face delivery. For effective delivery there is the need for collaboration at all levels. The blended approach as used in this program is not only a good template for the teaching of History at a distance, but may be a necessary transition to a full online program, but the components in the blend may need to be revisited if such a program is to have a greater reach for developing countries like Jamaica.

REFERENCES

Atherton, J. S. (2005). *Learning and teaching: Bloom's taxonomy.* Retrieved March 14, 2008, from Website: http://www.learningandteaching.info/learning/bloomtax.htm

Chandra, R. (2000). From dual-mode to multi-modal, flexible teaching and learning: Distance education at the University of the South Pacific. In *Distance Education in Small States, 2000 Conference proceedings. UWI/COL, 2001* (pp. 31-47). Retrieved from http://www.Col.org/colweb/site/pid3338

Debating Distance? (n.d.). Retrieved July 21, 2009 from http://www.instudy.com/articles/in-distance02.htm

Dzuiban, C. D., Hartman, J. L., & Moskal, P. D. (2004). Blended Learning. *Educause Center for Applier Research, Research Bulletin, 2004*(7). Retrieved July 20, 2009 from http://www.educause.edu/

Fagerberg, T., & Rekkedal, T. (2004). *Enhancing the flexibility of distance education – designing and trying out a learning environment for mobile distance learners*. Retrieved July 21, 2009, from http://www.ericsson.com/ericsson/corpinfo/.../eclo_nki_paper.pdf

Garrison, D. R., & Vaughan, N. D. (2008). *Blended learning in higher education: framework, principles, and guidelines*. San Francisco, CA: Jossey Bass.

Huitt, W. E. (2004). *Bloom 's Taxonomy of the Cognitive Domain*. Educational Psychology Interactive. Valdosta, GA: Valdosta State University. Retrieved March 14, 2008, from http://chiron.valdosta.edu/whuitt/col/cogsys/bloom.html

Kimble, C. (May 1999). The impact of technology on mearning: Making sense of the research. *Mid-Continent Regional Educational Laboratory*, 1-6.

Kinshuk. (2007). Special issue introduction: A critical view of technology-enhanced learning and instruction in the digital Age. *International Society for Technology in Education, 40*(1), 2-3.

Miller, E. (2000). Models in distance teaching in teacher education in Jamaica. In *Distance Education in Small States, 2000 Conference proceedings, UWI/COL, 2001* (pp. 141-147). Retrieved January 11, 2008, from http://www.Col.org/colweb/site/pid3338

Moallem, M. (2007). Accommodating individual differences in the design of online learning environments: A Comparative Study. *Journal of Research on Technology in Education, 40*(2), 219–247.

Morgan, P. (2000). Strengthening the stakes: Combing distance and face-to-face teaching strategies – Preliminary discussion issues. *Distance Education in Small States, 2000 Conference proceedings, UWI/COL, 2001* (pp. 106-112). Retrieved January 11, 2008, from http://www.Col.org/colweb/site/pid3338

Owston, R. D. (1997). The world wide web: Technology to enhance teaching and learning? [from http://www.edu.yorku.ca~rowston/article.html]. *Education Researcher, 26*(2), 27–33. Retrieved March 14, 2008.

Project Office. (2007). *Report of the B. Ed (Secondary) Distance Program*.

Simone, C. O. (2006). Faculty lived experiences in the online environment. *Adult Education Quarterly, 27*(1), 26–45.

Singh, H. (2003). Building Effective Learnign Programs. *Educational Technology, 43*(3), 51-54. Retrieved July 20, 2009 from http://asianvu.com/bookstoread/framework/blended-learning.pdf

Spaeth, D. A., & Cameron, S. (2000). Computers & Resource – Based History Teaching: A UK Perspective. *Computers and the Humanities, 34*(3), 325–343. .doi:10.1023/A:1002448312963

Stacey, E., & Gerbic, P. (2007). Teaching for learning – Research perspectives from on-campus and distance students. *Education and Information Technologies, 12*(3). .doi:10.1007/s10639-007-9037-5

Thorney, A. (2008, July 28). Teachers facing study problems. Letter to the Editor, *The Jamaica Gleaner.*

Troha, F. J. (2002). Bulletproof instructional design. A model for blended learnign. *USDLA Journal, 16*(5). Eric Document Number EJ654051. Retrieved from http://www.eric.ed.gov/

ADDITIONAL READING

Allan, B. (2007). *Blended Learning: Tools for Teaching and Training*. London: Facet Publishing.

Alvarez, S. (2005). Blended learning solutions. In B. Hoffman (Ed.), *Encyclopaedia of Educational Technology*. Retrieved July 20, 2009, from http://coe.sdsu.edu/eet/Articles/blendedlearning/start.htm

Amrein-Beardsley, A. (2007). Examining the development of a hybrid degree program: Using student and instructor data to inform decision-making. *Journal of Research on Technology in Education, 39*, 331–357.

Ausburn, L. J. (n.d.). *Course design elements most valued by adult learners in blended online education*. Educational Media international, 41*(4)*, 327-337. doi:10.1080/0952398042000314820

Bach, S., Haynes, P. P., & Smith, J. L. (2006). *Online learning and teaching in higher education*. Maidenhead, UK: Open University Press.

Bates, A. W., & Tony Bates, T. (2005). *Technology, e-learning and distance education*. New York: Routledge.

Bersin, J. (2004). *The Blended Learning Book: Best Practices, Proven Methodologies, and Lessons Learned*. New York: Wiley.

Bonk, C. J., & Graham, C. R. (Eds.). (2006). *The Handbook of Blended Learning: Global Perspectives, Local Designs*. San Francisco: Pfeiffer.

Bullen, M., & Janes, D. P. (2006). *Making the transition to E-learning: strategies and issues*. Hershey, PA: IGI Global.

Carliner, S. (2002). *Designing e-learning*. Alexandria, VA: American Society for Training and Development Press.

Cheung, Y. C. (2001). *New Teacher Education for the Future: International Perspectives*. New York: Springer.

DeZure, D. (1999). Learning from Change: Landmarks in Teaching. Sterling, VA: Stylus Publishing, LLC

Dye, A., & Rekkedal, T. (2008). *Enhancing the flexibility of distance education through mobile learning*. Retrieved July 21, 2009, from http://www.ericsson.com/ericsson/corpinfo/programs/resource_documents/eclo_nki_paper.pdf

Finekel, A. (1985). Teaching history at a distance. *Distance Education, 6*(1), 56–67. doi:10.1080/0158791850060103

French, D. (2003). *Blended Learning: An Ongoing Process for Internet Integration*. Bloomington, IN: Trafford Publishing.

French, D., Hale, C., & Johnson, C. (1998). Internet based learning: an introduction and framework for higher education. Sterling, VA: Stylus Publishing, LLC.

Gärdenfors, P., & Johansson, P. (2005). *Cognition, education, and communication technology*. New York: Routledge.

Hartley, P., Woods, A., & Pill, M. (2005). *Enhancing teaching in higher education: new approaches for improving student*. New York: Routledge.

Kovalchuk, A., & Dawson, K. (2004). Education and Technology [electronic resource]: an encyclopaedia. Santa Barbara, Calif. ABC-CLIO.

Lytras, M. D., Gasevic, D., De Pablos, P. O., & Huang, W. (2008). *Technology Enhanced Learning: Best Practices*. Hershey, PA: IGI Global.

MacDonald, J. (2008). *Blended Learning and Online Tutoring: Planning Learner Support and Activity*. Hampshire, UK: Gower Publishing Company.

Marrett, C. (1989). Interactive distance teaching in the Caribbean. *Journal of Distance Education, 4*(2), 89–92.

Marrett, C., & Marshall, S. (2006). *The Caribbean University Project for integrated distance education: Collaborating to overcome the difficulties faced by small island developing states.* Retrieved January 11, 2008, from http://pcf4.dec. uwi/viewpaper.php?id=450

Petrides, L. A. (2000). *Case Studies on Information Technology in Higher Education: Implications for Policy and Practice.* Hershey, PA: IGI Publishing.

Rosenberg, M. J. (2001). *E-Learning: Strategies for Delivering Knowledge in the Digital Age.* Columbus, OH: The McGraw Hill Companies, Inc.

Shank, P. (2007). *The online learning idea book: 95 proven ways to enhance technology-based and blended learning.* San Francisco: Pfeiffer.

Thorpe, K. (2003). *Blended learning: how to integrate online & traditional learning.* Sterling, VA: Kogan Page.

KEY TERMS AND DEFINITIONS

Active Learning: Classroom behavior and teaching/learning strategy which is student centered. It incorporates learning activities which are participatory.

Blended Approach: The use of mixed modalities, in particular face-to-face and distance mode delivery, in teaching. For this case, the concept is applied not just to the use of mixed mode delivery within a course, but is used to define the mixing of delivery modes within a program.

CAPE: Caribbean Advance Proficiency Examination, offered by the Caribbean Examination Council (CXC) is done by schools in the English-speaking Caribbean. The examination is done by students on the Grade 12 and 13 and allows them to matriculate for universities in the region.

CSEC: Caribbean Secondary Education examination done at the end of Grade 11. It is offered by the Caribbean Examination Council (CXC).

Flexible Learning: Often used interchangeably with 'flexibility' the concept refers to a range of options available in open and distance learning made possible through the online component of the blended approach. The options include the structure of the program, the teaching strategies and learning activities employed to facilitate the distance learners' access as well as learning.

Historiographical Analysis: The examination and discussion of history texts using a historical approach, that is, setting the work within the historical genre and evaluating the development of the thesis in relation to the evidence.

Instructional Design: An instrument used by a course developer to give structure to and focus in the course development. It includes goals, courses and learning objectives, learning and assessment activities as well as details as to which tools will be used for each activity, for example, forum discussion or journal entry.

ISTET: The In-Service Teacher Education Thrust was a teacher education upgrading program introduced by the Ministry of Education in Jamaica in the 1970s. It was used to provide on the job training for teachers already in the classroom but who were not formally trained as teachers. Structurally it was an open and distance education program only in so far that learners were on the job and were full-time students at any Teachers' College. The course delivery mode was face-to face.

Chapter 9

Person–Centered Learning:
An Investigation of Perceptions of Learners Utilizing the Person–Centered Model of Instruction

Christopher T. Miller
Morehead State University, USA

ABSTRACT

As the distance grows between the instructor and student within education it becomes necessary to explore new ways of addressing the instruction that goes into distance education. This chapter will describe a distance-based instructional model, the person-centered model of instruction, as well as a case study implementation of the person-centered model of instruction in a web-based course. The case study will focus on an investigation of whether differences in significant learning occurred between a group that used the person-centered model of instruction and a group participating in a constructivist learning experience.

INTRODUCTION

If you look at the history of distance learning there is a common thread running through it. That thread, from early mail-based correspondence courses to instructional television and now to web-based courses, is the constant changing nature of the technology that supports distance learning. Consider when web-based instruction was first used as a delivery system for distance learning. It was primarily asynchronous with support from e-mail, web pages, discussion boards, as well as support from other technologies like audiocassettes, vid-

eocassettes, and print materials. While there may have been instances of telnet-based chats it is likely that the primary synchronous technology to support early web-based instruction was the telephone. Now there are a variety of synchronous technologies that support web-based instruction such as audio/video web conferencing tools, and instant messaging.

As the technology changes, the issue of distance is still at the heart. The instructor is not typically close to the student to physically assist them. The issue of distance has not only required the use of various forms of both asynchronous and synchronous communication but has shifted the focus of education on the idea of person-centered instruction. Within this idea the learner needs to take on more

DOI: 10.4018/978-1-61520-751-0.ch009

personal responsibility for their activities while the instructor takes on a more facilitative role including providing resources to the learners. As learner control is increased the learners' responsibilities for learning affect the learner's feelings that learning success is a result of their own work (Altmann & Arambasich, 1982; Rotter, 1989).

It is with these considerations that instructors of distance learning experiences need to consider the use of new models of instruction as well as adaptations of current instructional models to best support learners at a distance. One model of instruction attempting to address this shift of control from instructor to learner in distance learning environments is the person-centered model of instruction based on the humanistic learning theory of Carl Rogers (1969).

The person-centered model of instruction developed by Miller and Mazur (2001) attempts to address the changing format of web-based learning where the learner takes on more responsibility for their educational activities. Three outcomes were theorized for the person-centered model of instruction: (1) the development of a creative product, which should be original and useful to the learner; (2) significant learning, which is an accumulation of knowledge and satisfaction with the learning experience, a desire to master the experience and greater understanding of the problem and potential solutions (Rogers & Freiberg, 1994); and (3) an increase in self-actualization or striving for individual perfection through learning and development of interests.

This case study explores the use of Miller and Mazur's (2001) person-centered model of instruction within an online graduate elementary reading course at a regional accredited university in the Midwestern U.S. A second online graduate elementary reading course taught by the same instructor using their typical constructivist teaching technique was used as a comparison to better understand the potential changes that occurred using the person-centered model of instruction. While three outcomes have been theorized for

the person-centered model of instruction this case study description focuses specifically on whether students experienced significant learning. While the other outcomes of self-actualization and development of creative products are not the central focus in this case study description they are discussed elsewhere (Miller, 2007).

The central question focused upon in this case study is whether there is a difference in significant learning between learners participating in a person-centered instructional experience and learners participating in a constructivist instructional experience. Differences will be based on results from a personal perception form given to participants of both instructional experiences as well as an analysis of course products. It should be understood that significant learning has many meanings and in this context should not be confused with statistical significance. When discussing the person-centered model of instruction, significant learning is the term used by Rogers and Freiberg (1994) that describes not only an accumulation of knowledge, but also a satisfaction in the learning, a desire to master the experience, and a greater understanding of the problem and potential solutions. While all three outcomes are desired when using the person-centered model of instruction it is believed that many instructors considering the use of this instructional model will be most interested in the outcome of significant learning within their own web-based learning environments. The outcomes explored in this case study are important to many instructors because the accumulation of knowledge, increased understanding of the problem or concepts, development of quality work, and satisfaction in the learning are typically the desired results of instruction.

THE PERSON-CENTERED MODEL OF INSTRUCTION

Since the twentieth century a wide variety of instructional design models based on behaviorism

Table 1. Comparison of aspects of instructional centering

Instructional Component	Teacher-centered	Learner-centered	Person-centered
Instruction	Content-driven	Learning-process driven	Personal enhancement driven
Learner Role	Passive recipient	Engaged learner	Initiates and self-directs learning (in consultation with instructor)
Instructor Role	Knowledge provider	Learning and co-evaluation with learner	Facilitator and resource among resources and co-evaluator
Assessment	Monitor learning	Promote and diagnosis learning	Self-evaluation of learning
Environment	Competitive and individualistic	Cooperative and collaborative	Cooperative, non-competitive, and positive
Accountability for learning	Teacher is accountable	Teacher and learner share accountability	Learner is accountable

that have been developed such as the Intrinsic Programming (Crowder, 1960), Systematic Design of Instruction (Dick, L. Carey, & J. O. Carey, 2008) as well as cognitive psychology-based instructional models like Component Display Theory (Merrill, 1983), Constructivist Design (Jonassen, 1999), Problem-Based Learning (Savery & Duffy, 1995), or Scaffolding (Wood, Bruner, & Ross, 1976) to name a few. Beyond these instructional design models based on behavioral and cognitive psychology another area of psychology, humanistic psychology, is focused on the development of the individual person (Snelbecker, 1974). The instructional model based on humanistic psychology used in this case study is the person-centered model of instruction (Miller & Mazur, 2001). There are several key differences between the behavioral and cognitive based models to the humanistic models.

The first difference is in the instructional centering of the person-centered model of instruction compared to instructional design models based on behaviorist and cognitive theory. Most instructional models are focused on being either instructor centered or learner centered, but a humanistic learning theory based model may be person-centered. There are some learner centered models such as Malcolm Knowles (1984) Andragogy model that may seem similar to the person-centered model of instruction, but they are not the same. It is important to note that there is a differ-

ence between teacher-centered, learner-centered and person-centered instruction. Teacher-centered instruction focuses on the content and delivering it to the learner. Learner centered instruction provides opportunities to engage the learner, but ultimately it is focused on the learning process. Person-centered instruction is different in that the instruction is focused on the enhancement of the person. Table 1 provides a comparison of aspects of the instructional centering.

The second difference is the focus on outcomes related to performance in behavioral-based models or problem solving in cognitive-based models, whereas humanistic models focus on a broader focus of education such as learning how to learn and instilling an interest in continuing to learn (Kolesnik, 1975). Table 2 provides a comparison of multiple instructional design models and outcomes. Not only does humanistic theory focus on development of the person, but also Rogers and Freiberg (1994) take it further by adding the concept of significant learning.

This concept of significant learning focuses on the learner becoming personally involved in the learning process by initiating, directing, and assessing the learning. It is this concept of significant learning that is at the heart of the person-centered model of instruction, which was designed for web-based learning experiences. There are three outcomes that were theorized by Miller and Mazur (2001) for using the person-centered model

Table 2. Comparison of instructional design models

Instructional Design Model	Citations	Type of Instructional Design	Instructional centering	Instructional Design Procedure Family	Instructional Outcomes
Intrinsic Programming	(Crowder, 1960)	Behavioral	Instructor centered	Programmed Instruction	Errorless performance
Systematic Design of Instruction	(Dick et al., 2008)	Behavioral	Instructor centered	Presentation Theory	Goal achievement
Component Display Theory	(Merrill, 1983)	Behavioral	Instructor centered	Presentation Theory	Goal performance
Constructivist Design	(Jonassen, 1999)	Cognitive	Learner centered	Constructivism	Solution of a problem and further inquiry
Problem Based Learning	(Savery & Duffy, 1995)	Cognitive	Learner centered	Constructivism	Solution of a problem and further inquiry
Scaffolding	(Wood et al., 1976)	Cognitive	Instructor centered	Constructivism	Mastery of task or concept
Person-centered Model of Instruction	(Miller & Mazur, 2001)	Humanistic	Person centered	Humanistic	Development of a creative product, Rogers and Freiberg's significant learning, and increased self-actualization

of instruction that include the learner learning to learn, a positive attitude towards the learning experience, the development of a creative product, and the development of the individual learner to become a more fully functioning and self-actualizing person. The following section describes the basic components of the person-centered model of instruction for web-based learning.

COMPONENTS OF THE PERSON-CENTERED MODEL OF INSTRUCTION

Like many of the other instructional design models utilized in designing learning experiences the person-centered model of instruction follows the criteria, particularly the detailed component methods, established by Reigeluth (1999). These components include learner, task, environmental, and goal analysis as well as the development and implementation of assessments, teaching strategies, resources, and evaluation. The following will provide a brief description of each of these components.

Learner Analysis and Task Formation

The purpose of the learner analysis in this instructional model is for the instructor to become a strong facilitator of the learning environment and help the learners direct their own learning. To best prepare the instructor, the learner analysis is conducted to examine the learners' interests, personal ability, and knowledge of the relevant topic (Miller & Mazur, 2001). Once the learner analysis is complete instructional tasks can be determined that meet the identified skills and interests of the learners. Additionally, these tasks need to be as realistic as possible to confront the learners with relevant issues and problems.

CREATING THE LEARNING ENVIRONMENT

First and foremost the environment needs to be designed in a way that allows the learners to cooperate and to take responsibility for what needs to be created. To accomplish this the instructor needs to determine which technologies are needed to support a cooperative web-based learning environment. Another aspect of the environmental design is for the establishment of a positive environmental setting that promotes genuineness, acceptance, and trust to support the imagination and creativity of the learners as they move towards significant learning.

DEVELOPING THE PERSONALIZED LEARNING EXPERIENCE

After establishing the facilitative virtual environment the instructor will need to establish a set of achievable objectives or options for self and/or peer assessment with each learner (Miller & Mazur, 2001). This allows the learner to take responsibility for establishing his or her own objectives and assessments within the context of the learning experience. Miller and Mazur (2001) recommend the use of a learning contract negotiated between the instructor and the learner to focus the personalized learning experience to establish the expectations and form of assessment. Rogers (1994) believed that through the use of a self-assessed contract learners would have a sense of control over their learning. Also, the contract allows the instructor to understand how the instruction is conducted and assessed so that instructional assistance can be provided.

SUPPORTING THE PERSONALIZED LEARNING EXPERIENCE

Once the learner contracts have been agreed upon, the instructor is able to identify and select additional resources to support the learning process as well as organize and sequence the areas of interest for learning (Miller & Mazur, 2001). While the instructor needs to assist in the sequencing of the learning experience, the control should be maintained by the learner allowing the instructor

to take on a primary role of guide and resource for the learning process. It is important to remember, particularly at this stage of the instructional experience, that the learners control the learning experience to support significant learning. While the learner should control the learning experience, the instructor should monitor the experience and help guide the learners if they appear to be stuck or off-track. If there is disagreement on the instructor intervention then it is possible that the contract can be renegotiated or the problem be addressed in the assessment. It is important to remember that facilitating the learning experience does not mean that anything goes. There is still the topical goal that the learner needs to focus upon and achieve within the context of their contracted learning experience.

EVALUATING THE PERSONALIZED LEARNING EXPERIENCE

As part of the learning contract, the learner establishes a creative product that can be assessed by both the learner, the instructor and/or others. This creative product should be individualized for each learner to demonstrate mastery of the content, which the learner wanted to focus upon based on his or her skills, needs, and understanding. Additionally, the learner will negotiate their own form of assessment as well as conducting a self-assessment upon completing the learning tasks. Beyond the various forms of assessing achievement, it is also important that the learner assesses their level of personal involvement, the level of involvement that was self-initiated, and the learner's pervasiveness. The reasoning for adding these additional aspects of assessment is so that not only does the learner evaluate their own learning, but it also allows the learner to reflect on the level of responsibility taken for their accomplishments and the level of achievement.

OUTCOMES OF THE PERSON-CENTERED MODEL OF INSTRUCTION

Miller and Mazur (2001) asserted three outcomes for the person-centered model of instruction. The first outcome was the development of a creative product, which should be original and useful to the learner. The second was significant learning as defined by Rogers and Freiberg (1994). The third outcome for the model was an increase in self-actualization within the learners, which is the striving for individual perfection through learning and development of interests. Each of the outcomes are directly linked to Roger's (1969) person-centered learning theory. It is within this case study that the second of the three outcomes, Rogers and Freiberg's (1994) significant learning is focused upon.

DESCRIPTION OF THE CASE STUDY

This case study was conducted as a first application of the person-centered model of instruction. While three outcomes are theorized for the person-centered model of instruction this case study description focuses on the outcomes of Rogers and Freiberg's (1994) significant learning. Specifically, this case addresses the question of whether learners experiencing the person-centered model of instruction demonstrate Rogers and Freiberg's (1994) significant learning. The aspects of significant learning focused upon in this case are an accumulation of knowledge and satisfaction with the learning experience, a desire to master the experience, and a greater understanding of the problem and its potential solutions.

SAMPLE DESCRIPTION

A convenience sample of student participants was gathered for the study from two online elementary school reading courses offered over two semesters. The courses were offered online through the BlackBoard course management system at an accredited regional university in the Midwestern U.S. and taught by the same instructor. While 50 students were anticipated to participate in the study only 32 students volunteered due to unforeseen complications in the course enrollment process and low course enrollment numbers, particularly during the semester 1. Table 3 describes sample enrollment of the groups used in this case study with the classes categorized as the person-centered instruction (PCI) and comparison instruction (CI) groups. The same instructor taught both of the classes.

DESCRIPTION OF INSTRUMENTS

Demographic Questionnaire

A demographic questionnaire was developed to gather general information about the sample groups to make inferences about the general group characteristics. The questionnaire includes items about age, gender, occupation, education, and web-based course experience.

Table 3. Sample group enrollments

Sample Group	Abbreviation	Education Course	Sample Group Enrollment
Intervention Group (Person-centered instruction)	PCI	Semester 2 Elementary School Reading	20
Comparison Group 1 (Constructivist instruction)	CI	Semester 1 Elementary School Reading	12

Participant Perception Form

The participant perception form (PPF) was developed by the investigator to measure the perceptions of individual control over learning, the instructor's facilitation of the learning experience, the provision of resources in the learning experience, and the overall learning experience. The survey form included three distinct dimensions of questions based on a content analysis of Rogers's (1969, 1961) person-centered learning theory. The content analysis revealed three dimensions of Rogers's humanistic learning theory. Table 4 provides a breakdown of the thirty-one questions related to the three distinct dimensions of Rogers's learning theory. Each of the questions in the survey form are based on a Likert scale of agreement with 0= no control to 4= total control. A validity study of the PPF was not conducted prior to this case study due to this case being the first time the person-centered model of instruction was implemented in a course and utilizing questions focused on Rogers's (1969, 1961) person-centered learning theory.

CREATIVE PRODUCTS

The students in both groups were required to develop a final project to demonstrate mastery of the topic scaffolded reading experiences. The CI group participants had specific requirements for their final project that included a 20-minute scaffolding lesson that was videotaped as the final project. The PCI group participants developed a final learning project based on a contract that was negotiated with the instructor and based on their knowledge, understanding, and interests on scaffolding topics.

MATERIALS USED FOR IMPLEMENTING THE PCI INSTRUCTION

Several materials were used to implement the person-centered instruction in the semester 2 Reading in the Elementary School course for the PCI group. Some of the materials were common between both courses such as the course syllabus and the instructional module descriptions. Other materials; such as the Learner Analysis Questionnaire (LAQ), learning contract, and instructor negotiation protocols were specifically used by the participants and the instructor for negotiating the learning experiences.

The Learner Analysis Questionnaire (LAQ) was developed in cooperation with the course instructor and based on a content analysis on scaffolded reading experiences from the course text. The format for the learning analysis questionnaire was based on the competency and diagnostic and planning guide developed by Malcolm Knowles (1986). A sample concept from the LAQ can be seen in Table 5. The learner would respond on a scale of none, low, medium, or high for each concept under three headings of prior knowledge of the topic, personal understanding of the topic, and interest in the topic. The learner then self-analyzes the LAQ results to determine the most appropriate instructional experience based on their knowledge, understanding, and interests related to

Table 4. Relation of participant perception form questions to Rogers's person-centered learning theory

PPF Question Numbers	Aspect of Rogers's Person-centered Learning Theory
1-8	Learner control over the learning
9-16	Instructor as a facilitator and provider of resources
17-31	Attitudes towards learning experience

Table 5. Sample question from the learning analysis questionnaire (LAQ)

	Prior Knowledge of the Topic (Check one)				Personal Understanding of the Topic (Check one)				Interest in the Topic (Check one)			
	None	Low	Med.	High	None	Low	Med.	High	None	Low	Med.	High
1.1.1: Defining a purpose for the reading.												

the instructional topic. The instructor also reviews the LAQ to help facilitate the instructional contract negotiations with the learner.

The investigator also created a learning contract used in the person-centered instructional intervention based on a modified lesson plan format commonly used by teachers in the state as well as being the required lesson plan format in the instructor's courses. The contract was used to assist learners in designing a project demonstrating their knowledge of their selected learning topic. The contract also included directions on how to create a self-assessment that the learners could use to assess their project. The instructor and each learner negotiated the terms of the learning contract once it was completed and was used as a binding agreement for the personalized learning experience.

Finally, a set of negotiation protocols was developed to assist the instructor. The investigator working with the course instructor developed the negotiation protocols based on the questions provided in the LAQ and the project contract. Examples of the negotiation questions were:

- What statements in the Planning Phase section of the LAQ did you find that you have the least amount of knowledge about?
- How do you feel your project will demonstrate your mastery of the chosen topic and answer the focus question?

CASE STUDY PROCEDURES

The procedures for this study occurred over a three-week period in each course, which were taught in two different academic semesters. Both groups focused upon the same topic of scaffolded reading experiences within their classes. The instructional treatments provided for the two groups were considerably different. The differences in the two instructional treatments can be seen in Table 6.

Semester 1: CI Group Procedures

The CI group participated in the instructional experience that was commonly used within the course using a constructivist instructional method commonly used by the instructor. This experience began with the participants in the CI group completing the demographic questionnaire, which was made available to them through the Black-Board course website used for the elementary school reading courses. The participants then critiqued the textbook reading on scaffolded reading experiences as well as critiqued three videos modeling scaffolded instruction. The culminating experience for the CI group was the development, implementation, and videotaping of a 20-minute scaffolding lesson the participants created. After submitting the project the CI group participants completed the participant perception form, which was provided on the BlackBoard course website used in the course.

Table 6. Differences between the CI and PCI instructional treatments

Group	Description of Instructional Treatment
CI	• Critique textbook reading on scaffolding. • Critique three model teaching videos. • Write 20-minute scaffolding lesson. • Videotape the lesson. • Submit lesson plan and videotape.
POI	• Participants read the scaffolding chapter in the textbook. • Learner Analysis Questionnaire (LAQ) provided to participants to self-evaluate knowledge, understanding and interests on scaffolding topics. • Participants develop learning contract. • Contract for learning project negotiated with the instructor. • Complete contracted project. • Submit the contract, project, and self-assessment. • LAQ provided to participants to self-evaluate changes in knowledge, understanding, and interests on scaffolding topics.

Semester 2: PCI Group Procedures

The instructional experience that the PCI group received was centered on the person-centered model of instruction. Semester 2 data collection started with the participants completing the demographic questionnaire located on the BlackBoard course website. Participants were then assigned to read the scaffolding chapter in the course textbook. After reading the text the participants completed the learner analysis questionnaire (LAQ) to self-evaluate their personal knowledge, understanding and interests on scaffolding topics covered in the chapter. This questionnaire was used to help focus the participants on the most appropriate area of focus for them in their learning experience. Upon completing the LAQ the participants complete a learning contract based on a modified lesson plan document to develop their personalized learning experience. The contract includes the description of a project to demonstrate level of mastery on a selected scaffolding instructional technique and a form of self-assessment of the project. Once completed, the contract was negotiated between the participant and the instructor via e-mail or the BlackBoard course website chat feature. The participants were also able to contact the instructor to negotiate modifications to the contract that were needed during the learning experience. Once the contract was agreed upon the participant began their personalized learning experience.

Participants developed and submitted a project to demonstrate their contracted learning and conducted their own self or peer assessment of the project. The participants also completed the LAQ for a second time to self-assess how their knowledge, understanding, and interests changed through the learning experience. After submitting the project the CI group participants also completed the participant perception form, which was provided on the BlackBoard course website used in the course.

DATA ANALYSIS

Due to low course enrollment resulting in smaller sample sizes a non-parametric statistical approach was used for the data analysis. A Mann-Whitney U statistic for independent samples was used to test whether the two independent samples come from the sample population. A content analysis (Merriam, 1998) of the qualitative data gathered from the creative products was used to detail connections to aspects of Rogers and Freiberg's (1994) significant learning.

Table 7. Type of graduate programs enrolled in by the participants

Graduate Program	CI Group	PCI Group
Masters	8	18
Special Education	0	1
Educational Specialist	3	0
Non-degree Program	1	1

CASE STUDY FINDINGS

Three sets of data were gathered for this case study. The first was demographic data to provide a description of the participants within the two groups. The second data set was gathered from results of the participant perception form, which was a survey used to measure aspects of significant learning. The third was the creative products developed by the PCI group participants, which were analyzed for evidence of significant learning.

DEMOGRAPHIC DATA FINDINGS

The two groups represented in this case study were comprised primarily of female participants with one male participant in each of the groups. The participants were primarily in the 25-40 year old range. The CI group (n=12) was comprised of education graduate students enrolled in the semester 1 elementary school reading course in which they received instruction using a constructivist instructional method employed by the instructor. The age range of the CI group was evenly split with six participants between the ages of 25-30 and 31-40. The intervention group (PCI group) was also made up of elementary education graduate students in the semester 2 elementary school reading course that experienced instruction using the person-centered model of instruction. The age range of the PCI group included nine participants

in the 25-30 age range, seven in the 31-40 age range, and four in the 41-50 age range.

The data also showed that the majority of the participants in both groups were enrolled in a master's degree. Eight of the CI group participants were taking the course for a Master's degree, three were taking the course for a specialist program, and one participant was using the course for a non-degree program. The PCI group included eighteen of the participants taking the online graduate course towards a Master's degree. One PCI group participant was using the course in a non-degree program and one participant was in a special education program, but did not specify at what graduate level. Table 7 details the graduate programs that participants were enrolled.

The majority of both sample groups were current teachers listing elementary teaching as their job. Half of the CI group was currently teaching at the elementary level and four of the CI group participants in the group taught in specialized areas such as special education or social studies. There was one participant that was not currently teaching and one participant that did not respond to the question related to the area of teaching. Thirteen of the PCI group participants were current elementary school teachers and six taught in specialized areas such as special education, social studies, and English. There was one participant in the PCI group that was not currently teaching. See Table 8 for a breakdown of teaching areas by sample group.

Another question of interest was related to the participant's experiences with online courses. It was found that over half of each sample group had some experience with web-based courses. Nine of the CI group participants had experienced a web-based course format in which all of the coursework was conducted online and two participants had some coursework completed online. One CI group participant did not respond to the question about online course format experienced. Nine of the PCI

Table 8. Teaching areas of participants

Teaching Areas	CI Group	PCI Group
Elementary	6	13
Special Education	3	4
Social Studies	1	0
English	0	1
Preschool	0	1
No response	2	1

group participants had experienced a web-based course format in which all of the coursework was conducted online, six had some coursework completed online, and one PCI group participant had experienced both formats web-based course formats. Four PCI group participants did not respond to the question about online course format experienced.

PARTICIPANT PERCEPTION FORM FINDINGS

The participant perception form (PPF) was developed as a survey of Likert scale questions with three distinct dimensions related to Rogers's (1969) person-centered learning theory. The three dimensions included learner control over the learning, instructor as a facilitator and provider of resources, and attitudes towards the learning experience. Both groups received the PPF at the end of the course module six, scaffolded reading experiences.

The survey results were analyzed using the Mann-Whitney U statistical procedure for independent samples with a significance level of .05 due to low sample sizes. The Mann-Whitney test is a non-parametric analog to the t-test that tests the differences between two populations using an independent measure and ranking the cases. The findings from the PPF are broken into two large categories focusing on significant learning

and how well the course fit Roger's theory of a humanistic educational experience.

SIGNIFICANT LEARNING

There are three groups of questions related to a component of significant learning. These three groups included satisfaction with learning, desire to master the experience, and a greater understanding of the instructional topic. Each aspect of significant learning was measured with several questions.

SATISFACTION WITH LEARNING

Three questions focused on the participants' satisfaction with the learning in the course, the project, and the overall learning experience. Participants responded on a scale of one to four with one being strongly disagree and four being strongly agree. While no statistical significant difference was found between the two groups on the satisfaction of learning questions there was a slightly higher response for the PCI group on the satisfaction of the project and satisfaction with the learning experience questions. Table 9 provides the mean differences between the two groups and the level of significance related to the satisfaction with learning questions.

DESIRE TO MASTER THE EXPERIENCE

There were two questions relating to the desire to master the experience including asking participants their interest in mastering the course topics through further study or by completing a similar course. Data results from these two questions can be seen in Table 10. A significant positive difference (.03) was found on the ques-

Table 9. Differences for PPF satisfaction of learning questions

PPF Question	CI Mean	PCI Mean	Level of Significant Difference*
Course was interesting	3.67	3.45	.65
Satisfied with the Project	3.17	3.70	.09
Satisfied with my learning experience	3.67	3.70	.85

* p≤.05

Table 10. Differences for PPF desire to master the course topics questions

PPF Question	CI Mean	PCI Mean	Level of Significant Difference*
Interested in further study on the course topics	3.42	3.05	.22
Like to take another similar course	3.58	2.80	.03

* p≤.05

tion related to taking a similar course with the CI group showing a mean response of agree (3.58) over the PCI group having a mean response of disagree (2.80). The data also showed that both groups agreed they were interested in further study of the course topics, but with a stronger interest from the CI group.

GREATER UNDERSTANDING OF THE INSTRUCTIONAL TOPIC

Four questions focused on the participants' understanding of the instructional topic of scaffolding. A significant difference of .04 was found on the question dealing with whether the course taught more about scaffolding with the PCI group having a higher mean response of agree (3.90) compared to the CI group with a mean response of agree (3.58). While there wasn't a significant difference on the other three questions the PCI group had a higher mean response on the questions focusing on the project helping to better understand the project topic and the project contributing to learning. Results for these questions can be seen in Table 11.

CONSISTENCY OF THE LEARNING EXPERIENCE WITH ROGERS'S THEORY OF A HUMANISTIC EDUCATIONAL EXPERIENCE

Three groups of questions focused on aspects of course consistency with Rogers's person-centered learning theory. The three groups included whether the learning experience was learner centered, learning experience provided instructor facilitation, and learning experience provided personal interaction.

LEARNING EXPERIENCE IS LEARNER CENTERED

Eight questions were designed to address the level of participants' control over the learning experience. A higher mean was found for the PCI group compared to the CI group on all of the control related questions with significant differences found on five of the questions. The questions with significant differences focused primarily on the areas of contract development and self-assessment. Not only were there higher mean responses for the PCI group, but also six of the questions had a mean response of great control. Two of the ques-

Table 11. Differences for PPF understanding of the instructional topic questions

PPF Question	CI Mean	PCI Mean	Level of Significant Difference*
Course taught more about scaffolding	3.58	3.90	.04
Project helped to better understand my project topic	3.25	3.70	.21
Project contributed to my learning	3.33	3.60	.34
BlackBoard web links helped with finding scaffolding information	3.42	2.65	.06

* p≤.05

Table 12. Differences for PPF control related questions

PPF Question	CI Mean	PCI Mean	Level of Significant Difference*
Control of project topic selection	2.92	3.50	.14
Control of project format	1.25	3.40	.00
Control of project negotiation	1.92	3.00	.00
Control of developing learning tasks	2.92	3.40	.05
Control of selecting resources	3.00	3.50	.09
Control of developing self-assessment	2.08	3.20	.00
Control of project assessment	2.08	2.80	.03
Control of learning direction	2.42	2.85	.204

* p≤.05

tions had a mean response of some control for the PCI group. The CI group had several levels of responses from great control to little control. Results for the control over the learning experience questions can be seen in Table 12.

LEARNING EXPERIENCE PROVIDES INSTRUCTOR FACILITATION

Eight specific questions were developed to measure the participants' attitudes regarding the facilitation of the course and course project by the instructor. The findings for each of the questions can be seen in Table 13. One question within this grouping, instructor helped in developing the contract, had a significant difference of .01. No significant difference was found on any of the other questions relating to instructor facilitation. While there was only a significant difference found on

one question, four of the questions had a higher mean score for the PCI over the CI group. All of the questions that had a higher mean score for the PCI group were related to aspects of the contract, self-assessment, and provision of resources.

LEARNING EXPERIENCE PROVIDES PERSONAL INTERACTION

A series of four questions were used to gauge the level of personal interaction the participants felt through their learning experience using the chat and discussion board features of the BlackBoard course website. A significant difference was found for the question chat feature helped me communicate with other students (within the course) with the PCI group having a mean response of agree (3.55) and the CI group having a mean response of strongly disagree (1.50). It was also found that

Table 13. Differences for PPF instructor facilitation questions

PPF Question	CI Mean	PCI Mean	Level of Significant Difference*
Instructor eased learning	3.42	3.20	.69
Instructor helped in project topic selection	2.08	2.00	.98
Instructor helped in contract development	1.75	2.85	.01
Instructor helped in project format selection	2.58	2.65	.537
Instructor helped in developing self-assessment	1.83	2.30	.51
Instructor provided resources	2.83	3.05	.49
Instructor provided tasks to support learning	3.50	3.25	.22
Instructor provided adequate appropriate feedback	3.33	3.25	.65

* $p \leq .05$

Table 14. Differences for PPF blackBoard communication questions

PPF Question	CI Mean	PCI Mean	Level of Significant Difference*
Chat feature helped with instructor communication	1.83	3.50	.059
Chat feature helped with student communication	1.50	3.55	.00
Discussion board helped with instructor communication	2.42	3.00	.76
Discussion board helped with student interaction	1.92	2.95	.058

$p \leq .05$

Table 15. Number of participants for primary project focus areas

Number of Participants	Primary Project Focus
7	Pre-reading activities
3	During reading activities
8	Post-Reading Activities
1	Other topics
1	No information

the PCI group had a higher mean response on all of the personal interaction questions. The results for each of the questions can be seen in Table 14.

COURSE PROJECT FINDINGS

The participants for both groups were required as part of their course to develop a final project. All of the participants in the CI group were required to submit a lesson plan for a 20-minute scaffolded lesson as well as a video of the teaching of the scaffolded lesson. The participants of the PCI group were able to contract with the instructor for the specific project that would be developed based on a scaffolding topic.

Project Focus

The PCI group projects were reviewed for aspects of significant learning. It was found that the participants had a primary focus on topics related to understanding one of the scaffolded reading experience phases (pre-reading, during reading, or post-reading). While the majority of the participants focused on the scaffolded reading experience phases, one participant determined they had a greater need to understand the differences between the effectiveness of reading recovery and

Table 16. Participants and products developed

PCI Participant	Products Developed						
	Research paper	Reflection paper	Video	Audio recording	Lesson plan	Digital photograph	PowerPoint
1	X						X
2		X	X		X		
3		X	X				
5		X			X	X	X
6	X						
8	X				X		X
9		X	X				
10	X				X	X	
11	X				X		
12					X		X
13					X		X
14		X	X		X		
16		X			X		
17	X				X		
18					X		X
19		X		X	X		
20	X				X		
7 and 15	X				X	X	
TOTALS	8	6	5	1	14	3	6

accelerated reader rather than scaffolding. After discussion with the instructor during the negotiation phase it was determined that this focus would be allowed. Additionally, two participants were granted a request to work on a project together. No data was available for one participant due to a computer error when transferring the data and the original data could not be recovered. Table 15 provides the number of participants that selected the various project focus areas.

Project Format

Another finding from the projects submitted by the PCI group participants was the wide variety of products developed such as research papers, reflection papers, video recordings, audio record-

ings, lesson plans, digital photographs, and PowerPoint presentations. Additionally, participants selected multiple formats to exhibit mastery. This demonstrated that when given the freedom of choice the participants not only utilized a variety of tools but were willing to use multiple tools for demonstrating their mastery of the selected topic. Table 16 provides the product formats for the PCI group participants. When discussing the differences between the CI and PCI groups the instructor stated there were differences. The instructor stated: "I think the thing that happened that really made it striking for me was that I felt my students (PCI group participants) were more precise in what they were doing. I got more specifics." Additionally, the instructor believed that the contract, making up your own mind, and templates helped them (the PCI group participants) become more focused, more strategic, and much more precise. This suggests that the participants gained a greater understanding of the problem and potential solutions, which is an aspect of significant learning.

There are several items to note based on the analysis of the course projects. First, participant 6 focused on researching a non-scaffolding topic related to reading recovery and accelerated reader and produced a research paper. Next, the project files for participant 4 were missing due to a computer error when transferring the data and the original data could not be recovered. Finally, participant 7 and 15 were granted permission to work together on their project.

Project Attitudes

During the review of the submitted projects multiple comments were found that demonstrated participants were learning about their own learning process from the project. Several comments were made regarding the project. Participant 12 stated in a reflection paper: "I learned as much from this unit as my students did. I now know how to build scaffolding tools from scratch and use them in the classroom to assure student success." Another statement was provided in the reflection paper by participant 17: It's not the easiest for me to admit this, but I can even use many of these strategies myself [e.g. context clues], when I had never really thought about it before…It just goes to show that a person is never too old to learn.

PCI group participants also showed a positive attitude regarding the learning experience. Some of the positive attitudes were related to satisfaction with the project and achieving personal goals. Other participants expressed positive attitudes regarding how the projects impacted the students. Table 17 provides a sampling of expressed positive attitudes from PCI group participants.

Finally, two participants described how the project has helped them with an accumulation of knowledge as well as a greater understanding of the problem and potential solutions. Participant 2

Table 17. Sampling of positive attitudes expressed by PCI group participants

PCI Participant	Expressed Positive Attitude
17	"I learned a lot from the research. I have had students come up to me while reading and ask me what a certain word means. I give them the definition of the word, or would tell them to go look it up in the dictionary, but to really gain meaning of the word, what they really needed was to see how it was used in context. This research gave me a lot of valuable tools to use in my classroom. By the end of the unit on teaching the use of context clues, I was amazed at how quickly they picked this up. Now when we do our daily oral language of a morning, they seldom come back to my desk and ask what a word means when they are asked to write down the word's meaning based on the words around. Before, few of them could usually figure out the meaning of the word."
11	"I feel that my students enjoyed the pre-reading activities They were much more involved with our lessons. I did pre-reading activities before, but I didn't get as involved… I will involve my students in more pre-reading activities in the future because of the success I observed this week."
19	"I gave the students storybook paper and they just began drawing some of the very best pictures that they have drawn all year. After they finished their drawings and began their writings, I was amazed at what some of them had written. Their responses were so creative and really showed that they were using their imaginations and what they knew about the characters in the stories. I do not know if the tape got all of this because it ran out during the end, but when the students read their responses, they read them very proudly. They knew that they had done a very good job and they wanted everyone else to hear their stories. I was very proud of them. I think a lot of this had to do with the techniques that I had used from the video clip. One thing that I had never done before was to just sit down in the floor with them. I had always used my rocking chair. Even such things as simple as this seem to make the children more alert to what is happening and even more into the story." "I can tell a huge difference in my students ability to comprehend material as well as in their artistic expression in their writing… Their work was so well constructed for first graders that I included it in their writing folders to go on with them to second grade. I feel that in completing this project, I gained knowledge that I will use from now on in my lessons."

described in their reflection that they had grown as an educator and that the students would reap the benefits. Participant 19 described that they felt more confident when teaching their lessons now because the students were more enthusiastic about their learning and eager to demonstrate it. They believed that the module had long-term effects on their teaching and hoped in the future to learn teaching techniques as helpful as this one (scaffolding) had been.

IMPLICATIONS OF THE CASE STUDY FINDINGS

This case study was focused on examining the use of the person-centered model of instruction for web-based instruction and whether the significant learning described by Rogers and Freiberg (1994) occurred. As a way of measuring whether significant learning occurred, the case study was conducted as a first application of the person-centered model compared to a constructivist instructional method over a three-week period in which graduate student participants worked on an instructional module topic related to scaffolded reading experiences, in an online elementary reading course.

The primary difference between the two groups was the development of the instructional module topic. The participants in the CI group were provided instruction on scaffolded reading experiences and then developed and video taped the teaching of a lesson using scaffolded reading techniques. The participants in the PCI group were provided the tools to construct their own learning and develop a project focused on scaffolded reading experiences. Both negative and positive implications from this particular case study were found.

POSITIVE IMPLICATIONS OF THE CASE STUDY

Implications of the Participant Perception Form

The majority of the findings from the Participant Perception Form (PPF) showed a higher mean response from the PCI group for the questions related to the learning experience. Eight questions with positive significant differences for the PCI group were found. Five of those significant differences were focused on the participant's instructional control, which is a key component to Rogers's person-centered learning theory. The overall positive trends that were found for the PCI group help provide support that significant learning did occur for the PCI group in that participants found the learning satisfying, was interested in further study of the instructional topic, and believed that the project helped to better understand the instructional topic selected. Additionally, the positive trends in the areas of project control, some aspects of instructor facilitation, and communication suggest that the learning experience met Roger's learning theory of person-centered learning.

Implications of the Course Projects

The findings from the course projects showed not only a variety of topics, but also a variety of project formats an interest by the students to demonstrate mastery over the chosen topics. The instructor also found that the quality level and detail produced by the participants in the PCI group exceeded those of the participants in the CI group. Another finding from the course projects was the positive attitude expressed by multiple students regarding the experience. While there were only a few participants that wrote reflection papers, these documents provided opportunities for the participants to share their satisfaction with the learning experience, how the learning experience impacted their own teaching, or how they better understood the topic and looked forward to other learning opportunities. One additional positive implication of the study was the instance of a PCI group participant, with support of the instructor, stepping outside the scaffolded reading experience topic to focus on answering a related reading question of interest to them. This suggests that the learner was focusing on what interested them, which is another aspect of the person-centered model of instruction.

NEGATIVE IMPLICATIONS OF THE CASE STUDY

While the majority of the questions showed a higher mean response from the PCI group there were nine of the 31 questions including one that had a significant difference, where the CI group had a higher mean response. Four of the responses in which the CI group had a higher mean response were focused around instructor facilitation questions such as easing learning, helping project topic selection, providing tasks to support learning, and providing adequate appropriate feedback. While these results could be connected to the improper implementation of the contract negotiations by the instructor it could also be connected to a level of discomfort by the PCI group participants with being given control over their learning.

The one question exhibiting a significant difference where the CI group had a higher mean difference was focused on whether the participants would like to take another similar course. There is no real way to determine why this occurred, but one reason might be related to the unexpected level of control that the PCI group participants received in the learning experience.

Another negative implication of the case study was that the instructor did not implement the self-evaluation component of the learning contract. The instructor as facilitator should have instructed and assisted the participants in constructing some form of self-assessment. This portion of the

project could have given greater insight into the participants' perception of the creative products created. The self-assessment could also have helped provide strength to the perceived outcomes for the person-centered model.

CHALLENGES FACED DURING THE IMPLEMENTATION OF THE PERSON-CENTERED MODEL OF INSTRUCTION

Two major problems occurred during the implementation of the person-centered learning experience that may have impacted results from the participants on the participant perception form. The first problem was that the instructor did not implement some aspects of the person-centered model even though training was provided before initiating the new instructional model. One component not implemented as described earlier was the self-assessment. As described in the instructional model, guidance should have been given to the participants to construct some form of assessment. It is important at the early stages of evaluating and refining the person-centered model of instruction that all of the components be implemented to their fullest.

Another problem encountered was the level of communication during the negotiations between the PCI participants and the instructor. A set of negotiation questions was provided to the instructor to facilitate the negotiation discussion about the project, but the instructor utilized them differently. Rather than having a virtual meeting the participants the instructor e-mailed the negotiation questions to each of the PCI participants and had them respond to the questions and send their responses back to the instructor. The instructor then reviewed the responses and sent back a confirmation response to the participants. While the negotiation questions were used, it is uncertain the level of support they provided in facilitating the negotiation of the project contract.

While these problems did not hinder the overall implementation of the person-centered model of instruction within the course module it is possible that they could have impacted the responses on the participant perception form.

CASE STUDY LIMITATIONS

Beyond the challenges that occurred during the case study there were also several limitations that need to be considered regarding the case study. These limitations included investigator bias, low course enrollment, limited time for training in the use of the person-centered model of instruction, and case study methodological limitations.

The first limitation was investigator bias due to the investigator being the co-developer of the instructional model. While distance was maintained from the classroom activities there were times when the investigator had to provide just-in-time training for the course instructor on the use of the person-centered model to ensure successful application. While a level of distance was maintained between the investigator and the case study participants there is always the potential for bias influencing the study due to personal interest in the successful application of the person-centered model of instruction. It will be necessary for additional testing of this instructional model by other investigators to decrease bias associated with testing of the model.

A second limitation was low enrollment in the case study. A sample enrollment of 25 students per course was expected, but due to course scheduling issues there was a lower than anticipated enrollment, particularly for the semester 1 elementary reading course that was used for the comparison group. The low enrollment created a need for using non-parametric statistics for small sample groups but there can be issues with power compared to using parametric statistics with a larger sample. Also the sample groups were not equal, which can cause issues with power.

The third limitation of this study was the limited time for instructor training. While the instructor was provided training on how to integrate the instructional model, there was a limited timeframe to provide the training on use of the model and person-centered learning concepts. Also, as this was the first application of the instructional model there were no previous examples of implementation to assist in training. It is believed that the limited time for training translated into some of the implementation challenges that occurred during the case study.

The last limitation was the case study method. While it is believed that the implementation of the person-centered model of instruction was generally successful the results cannot be generalized outside this particular case study. The only way to resolve this limitation is to repeat the study multiple times and analyze the results from each case study to identify trends that develop to make wider generalizations for implementation.

CONCLUSION AND RECOMMENDATIONS

Based on the findings of the case study, it appears that significant learning, as described by Rogers and Freiberg (1994) did occur. While significant learning and may have occurred, the findings also show that there may have been some discomfort with the change in instructional control. Making the transition to learner control of the learning experience is one refinement that is needed for the model to reach its fullest potential. This refinement can occur with additional testing of the model with web-based courses.

There are two major recommendations that can be made for additional case implementations of the person-centered model of instruction. The first recommendation is preparation of the instructor. For successful implementation of the person-centered model of instruction it is important to not only have appropriate training to implement all aspects of the instructional model, but also the instructor needs to fully understand the purpose of person centering and its benefits.

The second recommendation is to smooth the transition of control to the learners. One way to ease the transition of control might be for the instructor to help the learners understand why the change of control is beneficial to them. It is important that the instructor continually express genuineness in the understanding of the learners' fear regarding his or her concerns about the experience. This reassurance and encouragement from the instructor to the learners should help to ease the transition of control as well as letting the learners know that the instructor is with them in the learning experience.

The findings show that the person-centered model of instruction was successful within this case study, but further case study investigations need to be conducted. It is important that further cases be conducted to begin developing generalizations on the implementation of the model. Also, it would be beneficial for case studies with different instructors be utilized as well as different types of learners. It is possible that there may be other learning groups beyond the online college classroom that could put this model to use. Only through continual case studies of the use of the instructional model can a more definitive answer be provided to the question of whether the person-centered model of instruction works as well as what types of learning groups could benefit from it.

REFERENCES

Altmann, H., & Arambasich, L. (1982). A study of locus of control with adult students. *Canadian Counsellor*, *16*(2), 97–101.

Crowder, N. (1960). Automatic tutoring by intrinsic programming . In Lumsdaine, A., & Glaser, R. (Eds.), *Teaching machines and programmed learning: A source book* (pp. 286–298). Washington, D.C.: National Education Association of the United States.

Dick, W., Carey, L., & Carey, J. O. (2008). *The systematic design of instruction* (7th ed.). New York: Allyn and Bacon.

Jonassen, D. (1999). Designing constructivist learning environments . In *Instructional-design theories and models: A new paradigm of instructional theory* (*Vol. 2*, pp. 215–240). Mahwah, NJ: Lawrence Erlbaum Associates.

Knowles, M. (1984). *Andragogy in action*. San Francisco, CA: Jossey-Bass Publishers.

Knowles, M. (1986). *Using learning contracts*. San Francisco: Jossey-Bass Publishers.

Kolesnik, W. (1975). *Humanism and/or behaviorism in education*. Boston: Allyn and Bacon, Inc.

Merriam, S. (1998). *Qualitative research and case study applications in education*. San Francisco, CA: Jossey-Bass.

Merrill, M. (1983). Component display theory . In *Instructional-design theories and models: An overview of their current status*. Hillsdale, NJ: Lawrence Erlbaum Associates, Publishers.

Miller, C. T. (2007). Enhancing web-based instruction using a person-centered model of instruction. *Quarterly Review of Distance Education*, *8*(1), 25–34.

Miller, C. T., & Mazur, J. (2001). Towards a person-centered model of instruction: Can an emphasis on the personal enhance instruction in cyberspace? *Quarterly Review of Distance Education*, *2*(3), 193–207.

Reigeluth, C. (1999). What is Instructional-Design Theory and How Is It Changing? In *Instructional-Design Theories and Models: A New Paradigm of Instructional Theory*. Mahwah, NJ: Lawrence Erlbaum Associates, Publishers.

Rogers, C. R. (1961). *On Becoming a Person*. Boston: Houghton Mifflin Company.

Rogers, C. R. (1969). *Freedom to Learn*. Columbus, OH: Merrill Publishing.

Rogers, C. R., & Freiberg, H. (1994). *Freedom to learn* (*Vol. 3*). New York: Merrill.

Rotter, J. (1989). Internal versus external control of reinforcement. *The American Psychologist, 45*(4), 489–493. doi:10.1037/0003-066X.45.4.489

Savery, J., & Duffy, T. (1995). Problem based learning: An instructional model and its constructivist framework. *Educational Technology, 35*(5), 31–38.

Snelbecker, G. (1974). *Learning theory, instructional theory, and psychoeducational design*. New York: McGraw-Hill Book Company.

Wood, D., Bruner, J., & Ross, G. (1976). The role of tutoring in problem solving. *Journal of Child Psychology and Psychiatry, and Allied Disciplines, 17*(2), 89–100. doi:10.1111/j.1469-7610.1976.tb00381.x

FURTHER READING

Alam, D. (1983). Humanism: A theoretical perspective. *The Journal of Humanistic Education and Development, 21*(3), 101–106.

Aspy, D. (1977). An interpersonal approach to humanizing education. In Humanistic Education: Visions and Realities. Berkeley, CA: McCutchan Publishing.

Brockett, R. (1997). Humanism as an instructional paradigm . In *Instructional development paradigms*. Englewood Cliffs, NJ: Educational Technology Publications.

Gagne, R., Briggs, L., & Wager, W. (1988). *Principles of Instructional Design*. Chicago: Holt, Rinehart, and Winston, Inc.

Gibbs, G. (1999). Learning how to learn using a virtual learning environment for philosophy. *Journal of Computer Assisted Learning, 15*(3), 221–231. doi:10.1046/j.1365-2729.1999.153096.x

Gilliver, R., Randall, B., & Pok, Y. (1998). Learning in Cyberspace: Shaping the Future. *Journal of Computer Assisted Learning, 14*(3), 212–222. doi:10.1046/j.1365-2729.1998.143058.x

Jury, L., Willower, D., & DeLacy, W. (1975). Teacher self-actualization and pupil control ideology. *The Alberta Journal of Educational Research, 21*(4), 295–301.

Liaw, S., & Huang, H. (2000). Enhancing interactivity in web-based instruction: A review of the literature. *Educational Technology, 40*(3), 41–45.

Maslow, A. (1954). *Motivation and personality*. New York: Harper & Brothers.

Maslow, A. (1979). Humanistic Education: Two articles by Abraham Maslow. *Journal of Humanistic Psychology, 19*(3), 13–25. doi:10.1177/002216787901900305

Miller, C. T. (2001). The application of Carl Rogers' person-centered learning theory to web-based instruction. In *Proceedings of selected research and development presentations at the national convention of the Association for Educational Communications and Technlogy* (Vol. 24). Presented at the Association for Educational Communications and Technology, Atlanta, GA.

Miller, C. T. (2007). Enhancing web-based instruction using a person-centered model of instruction. *Quarterly Review of Distance Education, 8*(1), 25–34.

Pine, G., & Boy, A. (1979). The humanist as a teacher. *The Humanist Educator, 17*(4), 146–153.

Reigeluth, C. (1983). *Instructional-design theories and models: An overview of their current status.* Hillsdale, NJ: Lawrence Erlbaum Associates.

Reigeluth, C. (1999). *Instructional-design theories and models: A new paradigm of instructional theory.* Mahwah, NJ: Lawrence Erlbaum Associates.

Rogers, C. R. (1957). Personal thoughts on teaching and learning. *Merrill-Palmer Quarterly, 3,* 241–243.

Rogers, C. R. (1961). *On Becoming a Person.* Boston: Houghton Mifflin Company.

Rogers, C. R. (1969). *Freedom to Learn.* Columbus, OH: Merrill Publishing.

Rogers, C. R. (1974). Can learning encompass both ideas and feelings? *Education, 95*(2), 103–114.

Rogers, C. R. (1986). Carl Rogers on the development of the person-centered approach. *Person Centered Review, 1*(3), 257–259.

Saba, R. (1983). A basic proposition of humanistic psychology. *The Journal of Humanistic Education and Development, 21*(3), 107–114.

Schwier, R. (2001). Catalysts, emphases and elements of virtual learning communities: Implications for research and practice. *The Quarterly Review of Distance Education, 2*(1), 5–18.

KEY TERMS AND DEFINITIONS

Humanistic Learning Theory: A type of learning that emphasizes the development of the whole person within the learning experience.

Instructional Facilitator: An instructor that takes on a role of support and resource within the learning experience rather than maintaining the position of didactic teacher.

Instructional Model: A prescriptive process for designing, developing, implementing, and assessing the instruction.

Learner Analysis: An instructional task in which the instructor determines who will be participating within the learning experience so as to design the instruction to meet the overall needs of the learners.

Learner Analysis Questionnaire (LAQ): An instrument to self-evaluate the learner's knowledge, understanding and interests regarding a particular instructional topic.

Learner-Centered Instruction: A type of learning experience that is learning-process driven with experiences designed to engage the learner. This type of instruction is often used in constructivist-based instructional design models.

Participant Perception Form: a data collection instrument based on a content analysis of Carl Roger's person-centered learning theory to measure the perceptions of individual control over learning, the instructor's facilitation of the learning experience, the provision of resources in the learning experience, and the overall learning experience.

Person-Centered Learning: A type of learning experience in which learners are presented with realistic learning situations focused on their own interests and skills with the goal of enhancement of the person.

Personalized Learning Experience: This is a learning experience that is developed based on the interests, prior knowledge, and skills of the learners.

Significant Learning: A type of learning that requires the learners to become personally involved in the learning experience with outcomes of knowledge accumulation, learning satisfaction, interest in mastering the topic, and a stronger understanding of the instructional situation.

Teacher-Centered Learning: A content-driven type of instruction that is based on instructor control and delivery to the learner.

Chapter 10
Distance Education and ICT–Supported Learning in Lesotho:
Issues and Evidence

Angelina Khoro
Lesotho College of Education, Lesotho

ABSTRACT

Information and Communication Technologies (ICT) are regarded as a major contributor to the transforming of distance learning. The researcher assumed that education practitioners in developing countries like Lesotho, have limited, or no access at all to ICT for supporting instruction, since they still rely heavily on print and tutor/learner meetings as their distance mode of course delivery. The study assessed the feasibility of introducing ICT-mediated education for tutors and learners on a Distance Education Programme in Lesotho. The paper specifically focused on issues relating to the place of ICT in teaching and learning at a distance, ICT policy initiatives and challenges of infrastructure, human resource capacity, and cost as they affect provision of, and access to computer-mediated learning. Interventions critical to alleviating the situation are also discussed. Policy-makers and distance education practitioners require this type of feedback to be able to effect meaningful improvements in ODL programmes.

INTRODUCTION

This College of Education which is located in Lesotho, originated from the government's decision to amalgamate the three prominent denominational teacher education institutions owned by the Roman Catholic Church, the Lesotho Evangelical Church, and the Anglican Church of Lesotho. Since then, the college has been the only teacher training insti-

tution in the whole country. In 2002, it became an autonomous college. The institution offers diploma programmes to primary and secondary school teachers through full-and part-time (distance) modes of learning. Both forms of programme delivery are administered and monitored from within a conventional setting; by the college management team. Decision-making processes that is typical of a hierarchical decision-making structure. The distance education programme was introduced 2000 for unqualified and under-qualified primary

DOI: 10.4018/978-1-61520-751-0.ch010

school teachers who are already serving in Lesotho schools. Unqualified teachers neither have appropriate content nor teaching skills as many of them go into the classroom straight from the high school; while under-qualified teachers have long years of teaching experience but basically lack professional training to become academically qualified even for further education.

The distance education programme uses printed course materials (modules) that are backed-up by face-to-face learner meeting with their subject tutors, held twice every three months in a semester. Learners are allocated to a nearest tutorial centre comprising of a cluster of sites. Finances of the college come in the form of government subvention that is largely used for the payment of staff salaries. Other expenditures are met partly through payment of tuition fees and by donors.

SETTING THE STAGE

To-date, the College of Education, which is the sole provider in Lesotho of basic, pre-service teacher education to the diploma level, and the only provider of in-service, part-time distance teacher education to the diploma level too, still relies heavily on the use of print-based self-study materials; often backed-up by meetings with subject tutors in designated areas. Of course, this paper does not in any way, intend to discredit print as a mode of distance education delivery; but simply attempts to highlight the pace of technological advancement in the country. In essence, distance learners in Lesotho still have limited use of, and/or no access at all to ICT devices. The computer, not to mention internet, still remains a foreign machine for most learners. Of the varied ICT equipment available, internet is often regarded as one of the latest tools that can be used to support distance learners, streamline administration and enhance communication among distance education staff (Commonwealth of Learning, 2009).

Given that Lesotho is one of the countries whose telecommunications sector is typical of least developed countries (Moloisane, Tlebere, and O'Droma, 2007); surfing its educational system with computers and internet services might indeed, seem like a luxury for a country struggling with poverty, disease and other basic needs. This perception is however, argued by (Madamombe, 2007, p. 16) who reported that experts in a recent NEPAD-sponsored conference in Nairobi, Kenya, warned that "development will be seriously hindered if Africa fails to bridge the ICT gap that separates the continent from developed countries". In the same gathering, he further noted, experts highlighted alarming figures of only 2.5 percent of Africa's 800 million people to have internet access, compared with 17.8 per cent in the rest of the world.

These figures are worrying in this century of ICT centred earning. Advanced institutions have responded to this challenge by developing online programmes. We need to acknowledge though, that ICT is not limited to computers or satellites and internet technologies (Evoh, 2007); but that radio, cassette and television are also part of ICT because they all have to do with information and communication. Therefore, this paper will highlight issues and evidence relating to accessibility of ICT as a supportive mechanism for distance learning. Understanding the basic problems leading to limited use of, and/or unavailability of ICT and overcoming them will be critical to successful introduction of, and user-friendliness of ICT-enabled education in Lesotho.

This college has a relatively small Information and Communication Technology (ICT) unit which, although served by only three people; that is, two lectures and a technician, provides full-time students with computer literacy skills. The computer unit comprises of two computer laboratories, one used for students' lectures and the other used as a School of Technology Innovation Centre (STIC) whose objective is to serve as one of the centres for best practice and innovation in the use of ICT in teaching and learning. The centre was launched in partnership with Microsoft (South Africa) and the Lesotho Ministry of Education and Training. The STIC is mainly for the development of In-service teachers (other than those enrolled with the college) in relation to using ICT for instruction. Computer literacy in distance education was actually infused into the Study Skills course which, has, unfortunately not been introduced either during off-campus or on-campus sessions of the distance learning programme.

CASE DESCRIPTION

ICT in Teaching and Learning

According to the Ministry of Education and Training (MOET) (2006, p. 10), ICT in education can be understood as "the application of digital equipment to all aspects of teaching and learning." Information Technology (IT) has evolved for years. Initially it was associated with stand-alone computers. At some stage IT implied communicating through locally networked computers. But as time went on, IT represented a worldwide connection using the international network; sometimes referred to as the Internet, the World Wide Web or simply the Web or Net. Lately, the term 'IT' has evolved into ICT, as additional communications technologies are introduced (Fallows & Bhanot, 2002). More recently, "the development of computers and digital media has exploded, offering people previously unavailable opportunities to improve their craft as educators" (Moller, 2002, p.151).

The craft of teaching through ICT is becoming more popular and yet more challenging than ever before. A challenge for some teachers can mean many things. At some point, it can be seen as difficult or quite threatening; especially when teachers feel insecure with new technologies and their own use of them in the classroom. ICT is claimed to perform multi-functions in the learning process;

that of enhancing cognitive learning, developing problem-solving and higher-level thinking skills (Loveless, 1995). It is generally believed that to-day's student teachers will teach to-morrow as they are taught to-day. The most important question to ask is whether this cycle can ever be broken. Moller maintains that as technology moves to the centre in schools and classrooms, it should also by now form an integral part of all teacher education programmes. Teacher education should always be one step ahead, not only to cater for the changing needs in the schools, but also to prepare teacher learners in such a way that they become needed in the growing competitive world. Producing competitive teachers can be a difficult task because it is an endeavour that calls for many and varied resources to be fulfilled. If teacher education institutions are to establish the use of ICT, they need to provide access to on-line facilities so that individual tutors and learners can adapt the machine easily.

ICT and 'Distance' in Distance Education

The 'distance' aspect of distance learning takes away much of the social interactions that would be present in traditional environments. 'Distance' in distance learning can be caused by varied factors. This study will highlight three basic ones that often determine what services and facilities learners might be able to access. These relate to information and communication technology, the physical structure of the country, and other resources available to it. These do not only have influence on the overall management and administration of a distance education programme, but that they also create diverse, significant, and challenging role(s) for distance education tutors and learners.

The effective management of a programme will depend upon infrastructure for a distance learning activity which exists in the providing institution.

Learners, who join distance education, engage in a form of education and training that "is heavily dependent on support services." Unfortunately, the kinds of services that learners require are sometimes "constrained by technical and operational boundaries" (Black, 2000: p. 82). Technically, there are issues for which difficult and yet practicable decisions would have to be made to ensure successful integration of ICT into the programme. For example, in the case of using the computer to facilitate teaching and learning, LCE would have to decide whether to centralise hardware and operators, distribute operators or distribute both (Barta, Telem, & Gev, 1995). Other decisions might have to include refining roles and responsibilities for various users of the selected media. Understandably, there might be those who will find the changes threatening and this could cause some degree of resistance which in turn, will require practicable resolutions.

Thus, students' way of life can distance them from their academic work and sometimes deprive them of their right to be technologically literate as learners. Cultural conditions also influence the kinds of resources that may be available to students (Hauff et al., 1999; cited in Rossie' and Prummer, 2001). This directly relates to two more prominent forms of distance that LCE distance learners encounter, namely: the geographical separation and communicative conditions, for example the lapses in time taken for a distance learner to physically reach different subject tutors and get individual or group support of any kind. The priority needs of the greater proportions of students – those who live and work in rural areas are given minimal attention.

LCE teacher learners are sparsely scattered throughout Lesotho, especially in the remote rural areas where qualified teachers often fear to treat. The reason is simple. Most learners work as unpaid volunteer in schools for purposes of gaining teaching experience; which in turn, is a pre-requisite requirement for entry into a distance learning programme. Lesotho is a country whose features are divided into four major regions: the lowlands, foothills, Senqu River Valley, and highlands/ mountains. The highland region is largely occupied by a range of mountains with isolated places that can only be accessed on foot or on horseback, and has severe climatic conditions in winter. On the other hand, the lowland region is occupied by urban and industrial centres. The national infrastructure is generally concentrated in this area. The foothills lay between the highlands and the lowlands and are suitable for both crop cultivation and cattle rearing; while the Senqu River Valley is a zone that rests between the Lowland and the Foothills.

The learners' localities have greater influence on the nature and level of support that the providing institution can offer. Undoubtedly, the introduction of ICT-based instruction for distance learners in Lesotho would not only supplement print as a basic mode of their course delivery at the moment, but would also rescue learners from varying forms of distance they may be experiencing due to inadequacies of the support system in place. Although something is being done at the national level to improve access to ICT in different parts of the country, the college still has to work harder to ensure equitable distribution and use of its ICT resources; especially among students in the full and part time programmes of the college. Already there are obvious challenges that should be dealt with, if the introduction of ICT-supported learning in the distance education programme is to be made possible.

National Policy and Initiatives

In order to ensure telecommunications for all, the government of Lesotho wished to extend the benefits of telecommunications to the entire population, especially to the rural area where most of its people live (Mangoaela, 2003). In this respect, the Director of Telecommunications Authority, contemplated that, even though Lesotho ICT policy takes account of the fact that technology is developing at the pace which seems to be 'out of control,' in various schools, there are no Internet facilities even though some teachers have been trained on ICT (LENA 12/02/2009). At the same gathering, the Director further urged stakeholders dealing with ICT issues to bring value to it by sharing its importance to the society, adding that it is through ICT that the country and its people can liaise with the global and international world. The above views were echoed by a report on the views of the nation on ICT. The report revealed that Basotho (the nationals of Lesotho) have realised and stipulated the importance of ICT injection in the education system from the Early Childhood Development (ECD) programme into Adult and Non-Formal Education (ANFE) and indeed into Institutions of Higher Education.

In Lesotho, there are few primary and secondary schools that took the initiative to impart ICT skills and knowledge to young Basotho and also to use ICT for purposes of improving teaching and learning. Although schools are introducing ICT from their own initiatives, the numbers of schools are gradually increasing. According MOET, (2006) "the partnership that the government of Lesotho has entered with the New Partnership of Africa's Development (NEPAD), has further increased the number of secondary schools offering ICT." Despite these efforts, it is contested that "Lesotho is still far from other SADC countries in terms of using ICT" (LENA, 12/02/2009). This may be true in many respects. So far, no attempts have been made to use ICT as a support mechanism in delivering distance education. While one acknowledges the importance of ICT-based initiatives that are currently in place, it is worth arguing that if similar programmes had been introduced for the college teacher trainees, such initiatives would probably be more cost effective because learners who graduate from the college will have been introduced to ICT- enabled learning. This new approach to teaching and learning would spread faster into the education system – thus, tackling

the problem from within rather than from outside; as is the practice at the moment.

The Lesotho national ICT policy highlights ICTs as tools to enable the country achieve its development goals as articulated in the Lesotho Vision 2020 policy document and the Poverty Reduction Strategy Paper. The policy also provides a brief stakeholder analysis and the roles that are expected in realising the goal. These include "promoting electronic distance learning to maximise scarce resources and expand access to educational training and research" (Sefika, 2007). The education sector, for example, is charged with a number of responsibilities. These include: improving teaching and learning mechanisms that promote ICT, encouraging all educational institutions to invest in computers, and working with the private sector to create affordable packages and schemes under which students, teachers, and educational institutions can afford ICT products and services.

With regard ICT policy implementation, Lesotho has realised an increase of 91 percent of mobile subscribers and a total of 28 Internet cafe's in the country. Of the ten districts in Lesotho, Maseru, the capital city, appeared to be leading in terms of ICT coverage. Others districts followed with the exception of only two, one in the foothills and the other in the mountain regions of the country that still had no internet cafes. Reports indicate that approximately, 10 out of 1,477 primary schools have any form of basic access to ICT, and that, sometimes this is in the form of only one PC with no Internet access. It is further stated that, of the total number of about 1,700 schools in Lesotho, only 20 have electricity. On the basis of this data, many would agree with the citation that Lesotho has a severely underdeveloped infrastructure.

LCE Policy and Initiatives

In support of its mission of teaching, research and service, the college provides access to the computing and information resources, within institutional priorities and financial capabilities. As the main source of qualified teachers for schools in Lesotho, the college receives government subvention for the payment of staff salaries. Other expenditures are met partly through payment of tuition fees and by donors. This college offers diploma programmes to both primary and secondary school teacher trainees; through full-time and part-time modes of learning. Both forms of programme delivery are run, administered and monitored from within a conventional setting; which is answerable to an established management team.

The part-time course for in-service teachers is delivered through distance education, using a combination of residential sessions, text materials for self-study and meetings with subject tutors in designated areas around the country. The Distance Teacher Education Program (DTEP) was designed for unqualified and under-qualified primary school teachers who are already serving in Lesotho schools. Unqualified teachers neither have appropriate content nor teaching skills as many of them go into the classroom straight from the high school. On the other hand, the under-qualified teachers have long years of teaching experience but basically lack professional training to become academically qualified even for further education.

Education in computer literacy is provided to college staff through occasional computer literacy sessions. Such sessions are more regular for full time students. This is, however not the case with the distance education learners who seem to miss this kind of opportunity. Computer literacy in distance education was actually infused into the Study Skills course which, for one reason or another, never materialised. Although the ICT unit of the college is not adequately staffed to be able to manage instruction in all programmes of the college, it continues to experience some pockets of success.

In 2008, the college launched the School of Technology Innovation Centre (STIC) in partner-ship with Microsoft and the Lesotho Ministry of Education and Training; to serve as one of the centres for the best practice and innovation in the use of ICT in teaching and learning. The programme focuses on in-service teacher development. Though the STIC, the college has trained 75 school principals in ICT administration skills. A further 287, primary and secondary school teachers were trained on Microsoft ICT skills. In fact, the college would do well to strategise means through which the current full and part-time students could also benefit from the STIC. By the time learners graduate they will have been prepared to use ICT to enrich schooling for pupils in their places of work rather than having to come back to the college because the teaching demands require them to do so.

In the following sections, an attempt has been made to present the findings of the research study on assessing the feasibility of introducing and accessing ICT-mediated education for teachers and learners in a DTEP of the LCE. This study was conducted at the LCE.

Purpose of the Study

This study assessed the feasibility of introducing and accessing ICT-mediated education for tutors and learners in a DTEP of the Lesotho College of Education. Understanding factors affecting access to ICT mediated learning will be critical to the transformation of distance education programmes in the future. The paper therefore intends to:

- Determine learners' and tutors' awareness of ICT available for use in teaching and learning.
- Learners' and Tutors' Indications of ICT Tools Accessible for Use in Supporting Their Learning
- Assess learners' and tutors' perceptions of the role of ICT in their education.
- Highlight issues affecting learners' and tutors' access and use of ICT tools.

Rationale for the Study

The assumption was that, views of the ultimate practitioners of distance education, that is tutors and learners in this context, would provide constructive feedback on the assessment of their access to ICT as a form of support in teaching and/or learning at a distance. Data collected would be used for determining the possibility of introducing ICT- mediated education for learners on a DTEP.

There is a general consensus that modern ICT tools transform various aspects of human activity; in particular, the crafts of teaching and learning. Many countries have acknowledged the fact that an investment in ICT is an investment in human capital development. This understanding should be seen in the context that in low income countries, ICT resources are frequently limited in rural and impoverished areas; such that, it may not be possible for this strategy to be employed equitably. For ICT to meet its objectives, it requires a more structured distribution of ICT recourses at the institutional and national levels. The assessment is intended to highlight factors that affect tutor and learner access to ICT and thus, the feasibility of using ICT to support their learning.

The study would be particularly significant to various ODL practitioners; namely:

- The college management, as the immediate bodies to develop ICT policies and effect meaningful changes that provide for ICT access for distance learners;
- Tutors and learners, who would be the consumers of technologically enabled teaching and/or learning in distance education;

Methodology

This paper has a feature of a small scale 'case' study that employed mixed methodology approach. Bryman (2001) stated that a 'case' is a term that is commonly linked with a setting like a community or an organisation. The study which accessed the feasibility of introducing and accessing ICT-mediated education for tutors and learners on a DTEP of the Lesotho College of Education is therefore, typical of a case. It focused on a single programme that operates within a specific setting. Data was collected from primary and secondary sources using a triangulation of methods. Most of the information used in this research was sourced from policy documents, books and internet materials; particularly those that reflected on issues of ICT- mediated education in the African context. Quantitative data was obtained from tutors and learners on a distance education programme.

Participants

The sample for this study was derived from 520 second year distance teacher learners who are enrolled on DTEP of the Lesotho College of Education. The sample of 175 participants was purposefully selected. 30 tutors who served in the same programme were also included in the sample; bringing the total number of respondents to 200. The participants were representative of five clusters from five regions within which the programme operated. The clusters were randomly selected from the four geographical zones of Lesotho.

Instrument

A questionnaire comprising closed and open-ended items was administered by the researcher. Closed question items elicited factual information while open-ended items were meant to follow-up on responses for purposes of clarity of ideas. This was conducted during scheduled tutor/learner face-to-face tutorials in different DTEP clusters. Of the 175 questionnaire distributed among learners, only 140 were completed. On the other hand, 28 tutors filled and returned the questionnaire. Only two tutors had not attended the sessions when the activity was conducted. Questions were classified

Table 1. Learners' and tutors' indications of ICT tools accessible for use in supporting their learning

Variables (ICT Tools)	Learners' Responses in Frequency and Percentage N = 140		Tutors' Responses in Frequency and Percentage N = 26	
Landline phone	34	24%	03	12%
Cell phone	74	53%	10	38%
Public phone	22	16%	03	12%
Personal Computer	03	02%	05	19%
Laptop	00	00%	03	12%
Internet	07	05%	02	07%
TOTAL	140	100%	26	100%

into three categories; based on main objectives of the study.

Results

Table 1 shows that the ICT tool that learners (53%) and tutors (38%) access, and perhaps use most is the cell phone. However, there were claims made by learners with regard the use of cell phones. Some of the learners acknowledged that they had limited freedom in using their cell phones whenever and wherever they needed to do so; due to problems of network connectivity and/or electricity power for charging batteries when they run flat. The above table further indicate that the telephone ranked as second favoured tool among learners and tutors in terms of its accessibility and use. We also learn that a good number of tutors (19% and 12%) respectively, used both the computer and the laptop. On the contrary, none of the learners had access to computers. Many of them indicated that they have never, that is, (personally) used a computer; but that they access commercialised Internet services from the Internet café's. Only (02%) reported that even though their families owned computers, as learners, they never used them because they lacked skill. Interestingly, almost all the learners expressed desire to use a computer. Internet facilities seem to be minimally accessed by both learners and tutors since only (05%) of the learners and (07%) of the tutors claimed to use Internet.

On the whole, learners and tutors have access to cell phones more than to other ICT equipment. This confirms findings from other studies that, cell phone subscribers really sweep the ICT market in Lesotho.

On the basis of Table 2, distance learners and tutors mostly use or would like to use ICT for a non-verbal communication purposes; (sending and receiving messages) and also for seeking information. On the whole, the number of learners (27%) and tutors (19%) who access ICT for information search is encouraging. Findings further show that a substantial number of tutors (19%) intend using ICT for studying on-line, while a fewer percentage (06% of the learners, and 08% tutors) associated ICT as a news agency.

According to Table 3, unavailability of electricity as well as lack of ICT-related skills are the overriding causes for learners' inability to access ICT; (24% and 29%) respectively and tutors. On the other hand, tutors (31% and 19%) respectively, understood that a lack of both skills and finances were the main issues affecting their exposure to the use of ICT tools. Learners in particular identified inadequacy of training opportunities in ICT as another serious concern affecting access to ICT tools. A good number of the respondents, (13% of the learners) and (08% of the tutors) indicated that their use of ICT is to a large extent affected by their inability to manage the expenses related to the ICT services provided.

Table 2. Learners' and tutors' use of available ICT tools

Variables (Uses of ICT Tools)	Learners' Responses in Frequency and Percentage N = 140		Tutors' Responses in Frequency and Percentage N = 26	
Send messages	43	31%	08	31%
Receive messages	38	27%	06	23%
Find information	38	27%	05	19%
Do On-line courses	13	09%	05	19%
Read news	08	06%	02	08%
TOTAL	140	100%	26	100%

CURRENT CHALLENGES FACING THE ORGANISATION

A range of challenges impede access to ICT; hence the necessity to assess the practicalities of introducing it for distance teacher learners in Lesotho. These include insufficient ICT infrastructure, lack of funding, and lack of training opportunities and human resource capacity.

Infrastructure

Progress reports on the implementation of ICT policy made strong claims about infrastructure and access as some of the constraining features in the education system of Lesotho. The lack of national infrastructure is reported to seriously constrain the use of ICTs in Lesotho's education institutions. It is indicated that approximately, only ten (10) schools out of an estimated 1,477 primary schools have any form of basic access to ICT; and sometimes this is in the form of one PC with no internet access. There are concerns that Internet connection in Lesotho is still very low, basically due to high costs and low awareness of Internet's benefits (Moloisane, Tlebere, & O'Droma, 2007). We learn from the ICT policy document analysis that telecommunications coverage in the rural areas has always been a challenge for the Lesotho Telecommunications Authority (LTA). While there are documented improvements of late, in terms mobile penetration in the mountain areas (Mangoaela, 2003), the uneven distribution of access to the ICT is still worrying, especially

Table 3. Factors affecting learners' and tutors' access to ICT tools

Variables (Access to use of ICT Tools)	Learners' Responses in Frequency and Percentage N = 140		Tutors' Responses in Frequency and Percentage N = 26	
Lack of electricity	33	24%	04	15%
Lack of network for telephone services	07	05%	03	12%
Lack of computer skills	40	29%	08	31%
Lack of finances to pay fees charged by ICT service providers	18	13%	02	08%
Lack of finances to buy ICT equipment	16	11%	05	19%
Lack of training opportunities	26	18%	04	15%
TOTAL	140	100%	26	100%

between the rural and urban areas. The imbalances in the provision of ICT services as caused by the national infrastructure are obvious.

Results on the assessment of tutors' and learners' access to ICTs revealed that a majority of respondents owned cell phones despite the fact that the network coverage was not in their favour. Worse still, some of them had no electricity. So, for them to use their cell phones, two activities were eminent. In the first instance, they had to scout places from which they could access the signal before using their cell phones. It was also be impossible for them to receive calls if they were out of coverage. Another unique experience for these particular respondents was about having to search for electricity in order to charge their cell-phones. The important question therefore, to ask in this circumstance, is whether statistical results can be used to determine which ICT tool would be a viable option for use to facilitate learning in DTEP.

Funding

ICT-facilitated learning is a necessarily expensive but cost effective endeavour. One of the major constraints for the college to introduce ICT supported learning in the distance education programme relates to lack of fiscal resources. In many parts of Africa, initiatives similar to this one, whose fruits are meant to benefit almost the entire nation, normally succeed through a joined effort approach. Until such time the college identifies a suitable private partner among the ICT service providers, ICT-mediated education may remain a dream unfulfilled for the DTEP.

Students' enrolments increase dramatically with new programmes introduced to meet the ever-growing demands of trained teachers in Lesotho. The increase in numbers cut right from Early-Childhood to Secondary levels of education in Lesotho. But, it is sensible to attempt to discover what costs are associated with print as the current mode of DTEP delivery; and also with Internet

for example, as a tool for facilitating distance learning. The college needs to know about the budgetary implications of any particular mode. This could help the programme manager to make informed decisions of how best they could move along with technological changes and at the same time sustain the effectiveness in the delivery of the programme.

Training Opportunities

Earlier on, we noted that distance education learners mostly come from the remote rural areas. Given the environment from which they come, and the challenges related to it, it would be proper to provide them with basic computer literacy skills while they are still on the programme. It is true that distance learners follow tight academic schedules while they are at the college for on-campus sessions. Alternatively, the college might have to consider 'growing small.' It could begin by equipping each of the five administrative regions within which distance education operates, with a few computers as a means of decentralising its resources for the benefit of many. Of course, tutors would also have to be included in arrangements made for such trainings to be able to integrate ICT into teaching and learning. The fact remains that adequate training for human resource will be a long term encounter for an institution like LCE. Even at the level of the county, there remains a very limited layer of skilled personnel and champions within ministries to drive the national policy implementation (Isaacs, 2007).

Teachers constitute a single, most human resource input in the education system of Lesotho as may be the case elsewhere. Training teacher educators on how to facilitate learning at a distance through the use of ICT is an urgent but difficult task. What tutors need most would be skills — both theory and practice of integrating ICT into instruction. Many tutors and learners in the DTEP have little chance of accessing computers or using technology in education because of the low level of economic and technical conditions. This creates an unimaginably difficult situation for training. It is evident therefore that "the plight of the average citizen in many parts of the world seem little improved. Economic disparities between the rich and the poor widen with each passing year" (Todaro, 1992, p. 331); because upper income groups often have better opportunities to access and benefit from the use of these technological facilities. This situation creates a deep gap between the social groups and countries; the gap which unarguably leads to sharp social, economic and cultural differences. Quite often, gaps created by differences of this nature, tend to determine what developing countries can and cannot afford to do; given their economic status.

SOLUTIONS AND RECOMMENDATIONS

Distance learning institutions across the globe are experiencing rapid technological changes, continuous shifts in learning environments, and a generation of students exhibiting diverse ICT proficiency skills. Yet, this is not the case with similar institutions of learning in the developing countries (Keengwe, 2007). Therefore, this study provides a baseline data on the assessment of the feasibility of introducing ICT-mediated education for tutors and learners on a DTEP of the College of Education in Lesotho. The paper observes that since ICT resources are frequently limited in rural or impoverished areas, Lesotho, and perhaps, the college in particular, should consider the following suggestions as some of the possible strategies to be employed if ICT resources should be equitably distributed.

Technically, there are issues for which difficult and yet practicable decisions would have to be made by the college to ensure access of ICT into its distance education programme. For example, in the case of using the computer to facilitate teaching and learning, the college would have

to decide whether to centralise its hardware and operators, distribute operators or distribute both. Other decisions relate to roles. The college would have to refine roles and responsibilities for various users of the selected media; right from the site level, through the cluster and regional levels, and up to the distance education division at the college level. However, decisions about how and when to access ICT tool in use, should rest at with the region to begin with; and then later, with the cluster, provided resources allow for a more decentralised access to ICT for ICT-enabled education.

This leads us to the second option about improved access to ICT. The researcher recommends cluster approaches and full-service schools (decentralisation of services) as experienced by Kenya, (one of the developing countries like Lesotho). A collective support for schools can take a number of different forms. Kenya has experimented with an approach where strong schools support the development of weaker schools that are geographically located (clustered) nearby. Since the government of Lesotho, under the support of the New Partnership for Africa's Development (NEPAD) has piloted ICT-supported learning (e-school initiative project) in six secondary schools, these could be identified as 'big schools' by virtue of their being well equipped with ICT equipment. For a more sustained ICT- facilitated learning, the college should initiate partnership with these schools and develop a structure that with a centralised distance education centre that serves several distance learners from nearby schools. If resources are clustered in a way that serve multiple schools, or coordinate work across schools, these are two strategies that reduce duplication of services; by using resources for the advantage of more than one school.

Findings made on the assessment of the accessibility of ICT by tutors and learners in the distance education programme revealed that most learners have access to cell phones. It was made clear that cell phones were not used effectively among learners in particular; as some of them neither had reliable network coverage nor energy in the form of electricity energy to charge their cell-phone batteries. Problems about areas of the country that have no electricity and/or ICT network coverage are not new. To this end, the paper recommends localised research as one of the strategies to help contextualise barriers of access to ICT in particular locations and settings, as determined by the physical structure of the country. It is only then, that strategies planned for the introduction of, and sustained ICT-facilitated learning actually fit local realities.

With a localised research available, and barriers of access to ICT contextualised, the college would have a better platform to negotiate for partnership with the ICT private providers to establish open computer centres; at least one centre in each of the ten districts in the country.

Where does this now leave ICT-mediated education in Lesotho? Reference made to the discussions in this paper, the following recommendations become evident specifically for the college of education in Lesotho:

- Development of the organisation's policy that clearly stipulates how ICT would be introduced to practitioners in the DTEP of the college.
- Identification of strategies through which distance learners could be provided ICT skills in computer literacy.
- Expansion of college ICT unit in terms of facilities and staffing in order to access ICT to learners on distance education programme during on-campus sessions.

However, for the development of ICT-mediated education in Lesotho in general, the following aspects become evident:

- For distance and technology-based education to be a viable option, educational institutions like LCE need to have access to the forms of technology and equipment necessary for the transmission of the educational content. Since such resources are frequently limited in rural or impoverished areas, it may not be possible for this strategy to be employed equitably unless the providing institution makes concerted effort to participate in transforming the situation.
- Distance education institutions cannot introduce and sustain ICT- facilitate education alone, that is, as a separate entity from other ICT users and providers, due to high investment costs; hence the need to partner with the private sector and relevant government ministries in this endeavour. However, the college would have to handle the situation with care since it is likely to suffer undue pressures from the private sector as a strategy to ensure returns in their investment.
- Obviously, there are many intelligent students out there in rural Lesotho, who might not get the chance to demonstrate the best of their academic work; or who might even end up falling out of the DTEP, simply because they cannot access ICT to support their education as distance learners. But if the college introduces them to ICT- mediated learning through initiatives as already suggested, they will create not only their own livelihood, but also help their country develop.

REFERENCES

Barta, B., Telem, M., & Gev, Y. (1995). *Information Technology in Educational Management*. London: Chapman &Hall.

Commonwealth of Learning. (2009). Women and ICT in Open Schools. *Connections, 14*(1).

Evoh, C. J. (2007). Policy Networks and the Transformation of Secondary Education Through ICT in Africa: The Prospects and Challenges of NEPAD e-schools Initiative. *International Journal of Education and development Using ICT* [Online], *3*(1). Retrieved June 05, 2009, from http://www.ijedict.dec.uwi.edu/viewarticle.php?id=272

Ferreira, F. (2008). *Children and Young People.* A Paper Presented at the Fifth Pan-Commonwealth Forum on Open Learning. University of London: U.K.

Isman, A., Altinay, Z., & Altinay, F. (2004). Roles of the Students and Teachers in Distance Education. *Turkish Online Journal of Distance Education, 5*(4), 1302-6488. Retrieved December 2008, from http://tojde.anadolu.edu.tr

Keengwe, J. (2007). Faculty Integration of Technology into Instruction and Students' Perception of Computer Technology to Improve Student Learning. *Journal of Information Technology Education, 1*, 169–178.

Lesotho College of Education. (2001). *Diploma in Education (primary), Students' Handbook.* Maseru, Lesotho: Ministry of Education.

Lesotho College of Education. (2002). *Lesotho College of Education Strategic Plan: 2002/3 – 2006/7.* Maseru: Author.

Lesotho College of Education. (2008). *College Calendar 2008-2009.* Maseru, Lesotho: Morija Printing Works.

Lesotho Communications Authority (LCA) Chief Executive, Mr. Monehela Posholi. Source: *Lena 12/02/2009.*

Lesotho National Development Corporation. (2009). *Lesotho Review: An Overview of the Kingdom of Lesotho's Economy.* Maseru: LNDC.

Loveless, A. (1995). *The Role of IT: Practical Issues for the Primary Teacher.* London: Cassel.

Madamombe, I. (2007). Internet Enriches Learning in Rural Uganda: NEPAD e-schools connecting students to the world. *Africa Renewal - United Nations department of Public Information, 21*(1), 16-17.

Mangoaela, P. (2008). *Lesotho Telecommunication Authority.* Retrieved June 05, 2009, from http://www.connect.world.com/article/free-article.php?oid=AME-11-2003-08

Ministry of Education and Training. (2006). *Summary of the Views of Basotho on Education in the Districts.* Kingdom of Lesotho: MOET.

Moloisane, A., Tlebere, G., & O'Droma, M. (2007). *Lesotho Lays Foundation for Internet Access.* Retrieved June 05, from http://www.afrol.com/news2001/Les009-internet-foundation.htm

Passey, D., & Samways, B. (1997). *Information Technology: Supporting Change Through Teacher Education.* London: Chapman & Hall.

Peters, O. (2001). *Learning and Teaching in Distance Education: Analysis and Interpretation from an Interpersonal Perspective.* London: Kogan Page.

Potashnik, M., & Capper, J. (2004). Distance Education - Growth and Diversity. In LIBRARY Articles on Education, 2001-2004 World of Education. Retrieved January 2008, from http:/www.world bank.org/fandd/English/0398/articles/0110398.htm

Somekh, B. (2007). *Pedagogy and Learning with ICT – Reaching the Art of Innovation.* London: Routledge.

Torado, M. P. (1992). *Economic Development in the Third World.* New York: Longman.

UNESCO. (2003-04). *Gender and Education for All: The Leap to Quality.* Global Monitoring Report 2003-04. UNESCO Publishing.

UNICEF. (2007). Transition to Post-primary Education with Special Focus to Girls: Medium-Term Strategy for Developing Post-primary education. In *Eastern and Southern Africa*. Nairobi, Kenya: Author.

Van de Veer, A., Moloisane, A., Tlebere, G., & O'Droma, M. (2001). *Lesotho Lays Foundation for Internet Access*. Retrieved June 05, 2009, from http://www.afrol.com/news2001/ Les009-internet-foundation.htm

FURTHER READING

Bhalalusesa, E. (2001). Supporting Women Distance Learners in Tanzania. *Journal of Open Learning*, *16*(2), 155–167. doi:10.1080/02680510120050316

Black, M. (2000). Are we all managers. *Journal of Open and Distance Learning*, *15*(1), 82–83.

Burge, E. J., & Haughey, M. (2001). *Using Learning Technologies: International Perspectives on Practice*. New York: Routledge/ Falmer.

Calderhead, J., & Shorrock, S. B. (1997). *Understanding Teacher Education*. London: Falmer Press.

Chen, T. (2002). *Incorporating Web-Based Learning into a Mixed- Mode Distance Education Delivery format: Challenges and Possibilities*. A Paper Presented at the Pan-Commonwealth Forum on Open Learning. South Africa: International Convention Centre, Durban.

Corry, N., & Lelliot, T. (2003). Supporting the Masse? Learner Perception of a South African ODL Programme . In Mills, R., & Tait, A. (Eds.), *Re-Thinking learner Support in Distance Education* (pp. 28–38). London: Pitman.

Crosling, G., & Webb, G. (2002). *Supporting Student Learning. Case Studies, Experience and Practice from Higher Education*. University of Dunelm: Kogan Page.

Garvey, B. (2002). *Beyond Knowledge Management*. London: Pearson Education Ltd.

Guri, R. (1992). Teachers as a Special Target Population at the Open University of Israel. *Journal of Open Learning*, *7*(1), 40–45. doi:10.1080/0268051920070105

Hon-Chan, C., & Mukherjee, H. (2003). Policy, Planning and Management of Distance Education for Teacher Education . In Robinson, B., & Latchem, C. (Eds.), *Teacher Education Through Open and Distance Learning* (pp. 48–71). London: The Commonwealth of Learning.

Koble, M. A. (1996). Integrating Technologies in Distance Education. *Open Learning*, *11*(3), 41–44. doi:10.1080/0268051960110306

Marrett, C., & Harvey, C. (2003). Getting the System Right: Experience at the University of West Indies . In Mills, R., & Tait, A. (Eds.), *Re-Thinking learner Support in Distance Education* (pp. 38–47). London: Pitman.

Nicholson, J., & Nicholson, D. (2008). Examination of Effects of Technology Attributes on Learning: A Contingency Perspective. *Journal of Information Technology Education*, *7*, 192–199.

KEY TERMS AND DEFINITIONS

Access: Implies the possibilities for learners to avail and use ICT devices in support for their learning.

Distance Education: A form of education and training through which learners study the same course material as would be taught in a classroom setting through means other than the classroom so that they are not confined to a specific place or time in order for them to learn.

Education Practitioners: Refers to all those who are directly involved in the processes of teaching and/or learning.

ICT Policy: Implies a set of principles that guide action in the provision and use of ICT tools.

ICT-Supported Learning: Refers to the application of digital equipment to all aspects of teaching and learning.

Infrastructure: Refers to a network of communicative devices including ease of transportation to access such tools.

Under Qualified Teachers: Means teachers have long years of teaching experience but basically lack professional training to become academically qualified even for further education.

Unqualified Teachers: Means teachers who neither have appropriate content nor teaching skills as many of them go into the classroom straight from the high school.

Chapter 11
Management Training in Higher Education through DVD:
Looking for Charisma

Wolfram Laaser
FernUniversität in Hagen, Germany

ABSTRACT

In the following chapter the author will discuss and report on the production and use of DVD-technology in management distance education. The applications and developments refer to development at one of the university in Germany, however the technical and didactic considerations are widely independent of the institutional environment. After discussing some general characteristics of DVDs and qualification profiles necessary for production, the author will report more in detail on concrete productions in the area of business administration and management training, namely the DVD-production "Looking for Charisma." The underlying pedagogical concepts will be explained, especially how real business applications are related to the theoretical knowledge background concepts gained from textbooks. Special attention is given to the aspect of producing bilingual versions (German/English). Finally some preliminary results from questionnaires will be reported.

INTRODUCTION

Why Choosing DVD as a Medium?

Currently DVD players and DVDs themselves are sweeping the consumer market and prices are coming down continuously. However up to now the DVD seems to have not yet gained the same importance in educational applications at least not at tertiary level. DVDs with complex educational content are still a rare bird. Nevertheless in the commercial market for audiovisuals, the DVD has outperformed the traditional video cassette. The new optical data carrier offers greater storage capacity that can be used for better image quality and is actually sold with every new PC as a combined CD ROM/DVD drive. The price of separate DVD players came down to less than 40 Euros.

The University under reference in this case explored intensively the potential of DVD with

DOI: 10.4018/978-1-61520-751-0.ch011

respect to didactic concepts, design and technical production. The university is actually the biggest German university in terms of student numbers (43,000). It has special characteristics of beeing an autonomous distance teaching institution with a nationwide network of regional study centres. Universities teaching mainly at a distance have the special characteristic of being dependent on technical media to distribute their teaching content. A dominant role in the media spectre is played by printed course modules. However over the past 30 years step by step other media have been added.

From Table 1, it can be seen that today DVD is one medium in a large variety of educational media used. The first model productions on DVD had been launched in 2003 covering different academic areas such as education, sociology and business administration. The reasons for exploring DVD as a medium for distribution can be seen in the regular academic TV programs transmitted by a public TV channel which, since 1983, have been distributed to our students so far as VHS cassettes. Videotapes have been also sold to interested public and as part of special programs for continuous education. Compared to VHS cassettes, DVDs allow for much better image quality. Furthermore, video recorders were expected to be outphased in the market. On the other hand authoring systems for DVD allow for more selective access and interactivity compared to continuous flow of video and TV programs. Therefore, DVDs through the new media characteristics, offered new options for design which became relevant when cooperation with public TV had stopped in 2004. One of the pilot developments in this respect was the DVD "Looking for Charisma".

BACKGROUND

The University offers BA and MA degrees in education, economics and business administra-

tion, computer science and systems engineering, law and mathematics. The DVD "Looking for Charisma" was produced for the faculty of business administration, which offers among other subjects courses in the area of personnel management. The courses are distributed in printed modules accompanied by some CD ROMs with interactive exercises and animations. What was lacking in these materials were interesting visual material which demonstrates practical relevance and applications in business enterprises. To provide educational material for these objectives, a cooperation between the chair of personnel management and organization and the Centre for Distance Study Development (later integrated into the Centre for Media and IT) with specialized pedagogical and media production facilities was agreed upon.

CASE DESCRIPTION

Technical Characteristics of DVD

There are different types of DVDs. For our clientele the most relevant type is the DVD-video that can be played by DVD player or PC. However, if content of CD-ROM character is added it can be played on PC only. DVDs are composed of two halves. According to the number of writable sides and layers the storage capacity of a DVD varies, e.g. DVD-5 (4,7GB), 1 Side / 1 layer.

The basic formats of writable DVDs are Digital video (MPEG-2) and Digital audio (PCM, AC3, DTS, MPEG-1). The maximum playtime can exceed 1 hour, widescreen and surround-sound can be provided. Attention should be paid to regional code settings.

For learning, some important characteristics are the following:

- Seamless Switching Between Streams:
  - up to 9 videostreams ("multi camera angle")

Table 1. Media development at the German distance teaching university

1975: Printed self sufficient course units
1976: Audiocassettes as complementary teaching aid
1978: Supplementary videocassettes
1980: First application of electronic text processing
1983: Cooperation with public TV channel (WDR)
1986: Interactive videotext (BTX)
1988: Development of interactive courseware for personal computers
1990: TV by satellite (European programs)
1990: Computer conferencing
1991: Videoconferencing (multi-point)
1993: Multimedia teachware on CD-ROM
1995: First virtual seminars and online courses using a prototype platform for a virtual university environment
1997: Integrated web design for the virtual university, data bank development
2000: First version of a proprietary platform for a learning management system
2002: Online courses in PDF, HTML enriched by Java Applets
2003: Internet Real time Broadcasts of tutorials and lectures, TV programs and video on interactive DVD
2005: Partial integration of administrative services and individualization of some platform components
2006: Introduction of a complementary platform (Moodle)
2007: Virtual classroom lectures with Adobe Connect
2007: Start of a complete redesign of the present IT and media infrastructure including a single-sign-on campus management system

Source: updated from W. Laaser (2002)

- ○ 8 audiostream for every videostream (different languages, different audio formats)
- ○ up to 32 Subtitles (languages, Bitmaps)
- Weblinks Attached to Menu-buttons:
  - ○ Link to URLs
- Integration of DVD-Video-Content with html-Environment:
  - ○ Steering the DVD by scripts from a Website

Planning of the Production

The topic selected from the area of personnel management was "charismatic leadership", which is an issue frequently discussed today in management journals. The concept should be explained in the light of current theoretical approaches. Also, the historical roots should be communicated. Then as a practical showcase, a leading German manager should be evaluated in terms of his leadership style and how his leadership was perceived by his co-workers. It should be especially checked to what extent his leadership might be labelled charismatic. To make the DVD more interactive, two questionnaires have to be answered by students to analyze two in-depth interviews. Furthermore, the DVD "Looking for Charisma" was to be produced like the DVD "From Balanced Scorecard to Performance Measurement" in a bilingual mode German/English to train students in the use of specific english vocabulary used in management education.

From these objectives, we derived a structure of the DVD in different chapters or sequences (see Figure 1).

Figure 1. DVD-screenshot 1 (Weibler, J., Laaser, W. 2004)

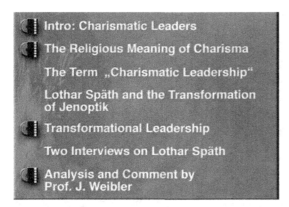

Figure 2. DVD-screenshot 2 (Weibler, J., Laaser, W., 2004)

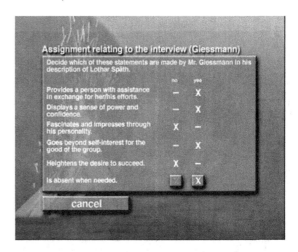

The structure of the production was planned to give first a motivating introduction to the topic. So we selected three statements of so considered charismatic leaders from business (CEO of Daimler Chrysler), military (Eisenhower) and politics (Martin Luther King). We took the necessary short clips from internet and in case of Daimler Chrysler, we used a VHS recording of a shareholders meeting. All these materials were freely available. For the religious background of the meaning of the word "charisma", we contacted a catholic priest who was performing also from time to time on religeous TV programs. We filmed his statement in the shopping area of Frankfurt, where a small niche was established especially for prayers.

As the core of our case, we selected the personality of Lothar Späth, former Prime Minister of the State of Baden-Württemberg. He was assigned the task to convert the huge socialist optical trust "Jenoptic" into a competitive modern capitalist enterprise. Luckily, we could use some documentary about his personality transmitted by a regional TV program. We bought the rights to use the material and re-edited a short version with the most important aspects relevant for our production. The portrait of Lothar Späth was introduced by a short history of milestones in the development of the enterprise.

To analyse, whether Lothar Späth was perceived by his co-workers as a charismatic leader, we carried out two in-depth interviews, one with the then CEO who worked many years under the leadership of Lothar Späth, and the second one with a young public relations officer of the enterprise. The interviews were accompanied by a short CV of the persons interviewed. As it was also our objective to relate the theoretical concept laid down in the course units with our case studies, we included two larger graphical presentations about the meaning of charisma and the elements of charismatic leadership. Finally we wanted to let students check wether they could detect attribute of charismatic leadership in the typical statements of interviews. For further information, some literature references were included at the end.

The didactic principle that guided the didactic structure was one of varying the presentation format from scene to scene to make the production attractive for the viewer. The graphics design had two features. The theoretical arguments were presented in schematic diagrams and stepwise developed according to the off commentary. The second element was a burning fire that symbolizes the power of a charismatic leader to motivate people. This graph was repeated various times with

Figure 3. DVD-screenshot 3 (Weibler, J., Laaser, W. 2004)

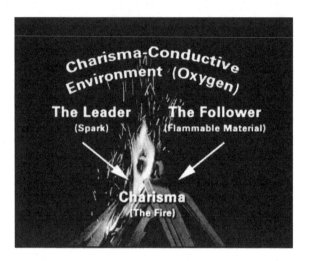

Figure 4. DVD-screenshot 4 (Weibler, J., Laaser, W. 2004)

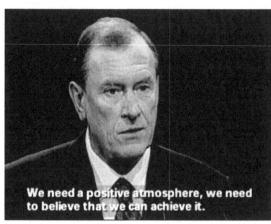

a short musical jingle to underline the structure of the production as they were offered the options to see the film without interruption or to access the different chapters directly.

Before we go to the technical aspects of the

DVD production, we would like to explain the work related to the preparation of the English version. Translation of the narrative and the graphics text was done by the linguistics department of Marburg University. To record the different voices (interviewer, interviewees, presenter and expert) with native speakers, we contacted the

Figure 5. Source: Berßelis

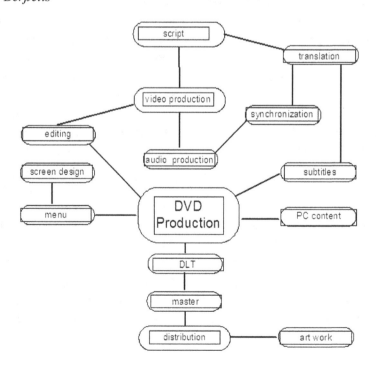

British BFBS radio station in Germany to provide the audio files, which we sent on a CD-ROM and implemented the voice at our studio. To make a relatively good match according to the German audio, we had set a time limit for spoken text of each paragraph, so we did not reach exact lip synchronous sound track but an acceptable fit. Some internet video clips in German language that we could not re-edit had been subtitled in English.

Technical Production of the DVD

The steps of DVD production are shown in Figure 5. It is quite similar to those for video productions, however due to the necessary modular structure some additional sequences are included such as linking to the different video streams.

The workflow in producing a DVD is called "mastering" and includes a series of different steps:

- Concept (target group, available funds, duration of video, design of user interactions),

- Media Preparation (e.g. video and audio recording, editing, graphics for menus, buttons, script for subtitles),
- Encoding (calculate bit-budget and then set coding parameters for audio and video)
- Asset Collection (import of source data (video, audio, graphics, subtitles etc.)
- Authoring
- Pre-mastering
- Mastering
- Distribution/sales

Composing the Tracks

- Videotracks (camera angles)
- Audiotracks (languages)
- Sub picture (subtitles, slides)
- Setting of labels for chapters

Graphics

- menu design
- background graphic or video

Figure 6. Screenshot, Sonic DVD Authoring Software (Timelines for video, audio, subpictures and actions)

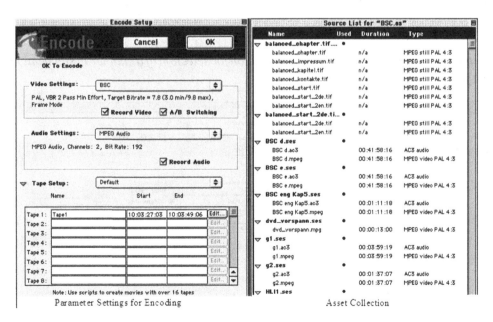

Figure 7. Screenshot of Sonic DVD Authoring Software (Timelines for video, audio, subpictures and actions)

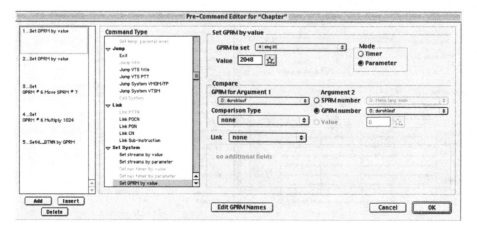

- highlight-Effects (Overlay)
- buttons

Programming

- Jump commands
- "set audio / subpicture / angle-commands"
- timer functions
- random functions
- if / then - Routines
- programming with variables

Qualifications Needed in DVD Production

There are many specific qualifications necessary in DVD production and these are:

Asset Collection

- know formats and specifications;
- video techniques;
- audio techniques; and
- editing

Figure 8. Setting of parameters for highlighting a button for selection of a chapter in submenu "English". (Screenshot from Sonic DVD Authoring Software

Design

- graphic and screen-design (Menu pages, background, overlay effects, buttons); and
- 3D-animation

Encoding

- MPEG-2 video compression techniques
- data rates, field/frame, CBR (Constant-Bit-Rate), VBR (Variable-Bit-Rate);
- bit budget calculation; and
- compression errors
- Audio compression
- Dolby Digital (AC3); and
- evtl. pre-processing
- quality control

Authoring

- creative programming; and
- knowledge of DVD-specification and syntax

Related Productions on Management Education

The DVD "Looking for Charisma" is just one example of our productions in the area of management education. Other related topics are "From Balanced Scorecard to Performance Measurement", European Personnel Management", "Conflict and Stress in Organizations" and "Quality Management of Services".

The structure of the DVD about the balanced scorecard is very similar to that of charismatic leadership. Graphical explanations about the theoretical concepts are mixed with an industrial case study "Continental Tyres" and with expert interviews. The DVD "Euro-Personnel Management" formed part of a joint European MBA program among the Netherlands, Ireland and Germany. The idea was to show students in an attractive way as how enterprises are adjusting towards the European Common Market. Video in this case is a convincing mean to show authentic documents of business cases.

The production starts showing a small handicraft firm that uses tax and wage advantages in a

Figure 9. DVD-screenshot (Weibler, J., Laaser, W., 2004)

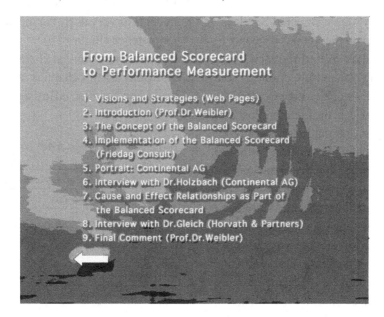

bordering zone between Luxembourg and Germany. It is followed by an interview about how the chamber of commerce is supporting SMEs by language training and marketing studies. Next, a frozen food company is presented to show how tasks and personnel recruitment are handled when national companies act internationally via regional substitutes. Then, the size of the enterprise under analysis is enlarged to show the merger of French-German helicopter production. Here, concepts of intercultural training and co-determination are exemplified. The final example given in the first part of the DVD is about a multinational company where personnel management issues of a large international company are discussed such as salary and taxing strategies. The didactic approach starts with a small ethno-centric enterprise, followed by a polycentric company and then by bi-national merger. It ends up finally with the multinational firm. At every stage, some typical adjustment strategies are discussed. After a short portrait of the company, high level representatives explain the strategic options. In the other two parts of the DVD additional issues are presented, e.g. How different institutions such as business schools, employment agencies, consultants and trainers are reacting on the requirements of Europeanization of business.

The DVD "Quality Management of Services" again tries to relate some theoretical concepts to practical examples taken from different service providers. Following the introduction by the chair professor, case studies are presented for the German Train Services, the German Post and the Ernst & Young, an international accounting and consulting company. Interviews with top managers responsible for quality management are supplemented by enterprise portraits, job descriptions, and organizational schemes embedded with quality management. Also, instruments for quality assessments such as the "mystery customer concept" are filmed in authentic environments. This source material delivers excellent teaching aids for management training both in distance education settings as well as in face to face teaching environments.

The most recent DVD production is about "Conflict and Stress in Organizations". In this DVD, we used some role playing exercises to demonstrate typical conflicts in business enterprises. For the performance, we used semi professional actors. Furthermore, we interviewed practioneers and researchers working in this field. We also had a chance to film a short sequence of stress reduction training.

EVALUATION RESULTS

The quality of the DVD has been evaluated through the questionnaire for the DVD "From Balanced Scorecard to Performance Measurement" which is very similar in the didactic and technical design to the DVD "Looking for Charisma". Therefore, evaluation results of the general patterns can be regarded as comparable. 34 students responded to the questionnaire with a response rate of 33%. In general, the DVD concept received a very positive feedback (see Table 2).

This holds true for the image quality, graphical design and presentation speed. An interesting aspect was that the DVD has been rated by many students as very useful in increasing professional competence (Figure 10).

From the technical characteristics, direct accessibility of the chapters was rated to be very important. As reflected in the previous evaluations,

Table 2. Data taken from Helms (2005)

	Overall Evaluation		Learning Efficiency	
	Responses	%	Responses	%
Very Good	6	17.6	2	5.9
Good	22	64.7	20	58.8
Satisfactory	5	14.7	10	29.4
Not Acceptable	1	2.9	2	5.9
Total	34	100	34	100

Figure 10. Usefulness to increase professional competence (Data taken from Helms (2005))

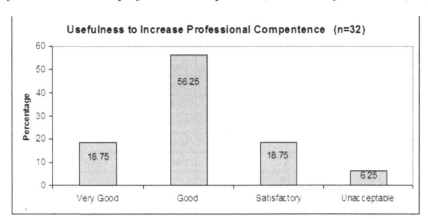

Figure 11. Usefulness of additional booklet (n=33) (Data taken from Helms (2005))

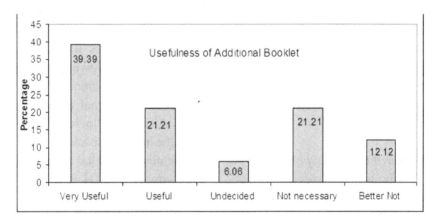

students ask for additional printed booklets with supplementary information (bibliographic references, exercises, summaries) (Figure 11).

Another important issue was how the English version of DVD (Table 3), which was offered in addition to the German version has been received by the students. It is important to mention here that the English version is a supplementary element and not directly linked to pass the exams. Here, we could confirm that there is a substantial interest amongst the students for English version, although the English version has been viewed only by a minority of them. With regard to the emerging European Educational Market for learning objects, bilingual productions will gain even more importance.

Finally, we would like to mention that some of the free comments although these are individual and do not form the representative statements.

"The English version significantly increases the use of the DVD. Personally, I live in an English speaking environment to which I could therefore show the DVD".

"Good DVD, however the price of 20 € is by far too high, therefore I would not order the DVD once again".

"Especially the real life applications shown in the interviews have been very interesting and a good complement to the course unit."

Table 3. English Version of DVD and its Importance

English version Viewed?			Importance of English Version		
	Responses	%		Responses	%
Not Interested	9	27.3	Very Important	2	6.3
Perhaps later	12	36.4	Important	11	34.4
Definitely later	2	6.1	Un decided	6	18.8
Yes, but just short	5	15.2	Un important	4	12.5
Yes, but most of the film	1	3.0	Very Unimportant	9	28.1
Yes, completely	4	12.1	Total	32	100.0
Total	33	100.0			

Data taken from Helms (2005)

"Important to me was that the author of the course led through the program and could be seen on the screen, in this case Prof. Weibler. I enjoyed that very much."

"Very good was that the experts from industry have been involved and talked about insights from their practical work experience."

"I would recommend that such type of DVDs should be produced for other courses as well so that the theoretical content can be enriched by examples and real applications".

"My chief asked me unexpected to make a presentation about the topic of the DVD. So I appreciated the possibility to use the DVD content form y preparation. I turned out to be an informed staff member. Thanks a lot!"

"I considered it even a disadvantage that there was also a version in German. I would have rather preferred a completely English version. It is a matter of fact, that in the Human Ressources area most of the relevant results come from the anglo-saxon countries and to keep up the knowledge reading of journals such as "The Journal of Human Resources" or the "Journal of Economic Behavior and Organization" is indispensable."

RECOMMENDATIONS FOR FURTHER DEVELOPMENT

The DVD provides the definite alternative to video cassettes. However technical production requires some additional and new qualifications as well as additional and different production tools. Also, didactic settings remain widely to be still explored especially when combined with supplementary digital files of CD-ROM type. Furthermore, DVDs still lack in some more standardization and need more storage capacity. The standard DVD (4.7 GB) is actually not conducive for a video of more than one hour and that too in good quality. As storage capacity will improve in the near future, the DVD will be the prime medium for further education packages including audiovisual information. However, with increasing speed of personal computers, the DVD might be replaced by online audiovisual material and integration with other web content will be achieved. With regard to the emerging European Educational Market for learning objects bilingual productions will gain importance. Presentation style and academic content have to be different compared to the "talking heads" known from many management training programs.

REFERENCES

Bass, B. M., & Avolio, B. J. (1995). The Multifactor Leadership Questionnaire – 5X Short Form. Redwood City, Canada

Berßelis, T. (n.d.). DVD-Video-Mastering, Version 0.9.5. *Handbook for Sonic DVD Creator and DVD Fusion*.

Fliess, S., & Lasshof, B. (2005). Qualitätsmanagement von Dienstleistungen . In Laaser, W. (Ed.), *DVD*. Hagen: FernUniversität.

Helms, F. P. (2005). *Evaluation der DVD. Von der Balanced Scorecard zum Performance Measurement*. Hagen: FernUniversität.

Klein, K. J., & House, R. J. (1995). On fire: Charismatic Leadership and levels of analysis. *The Leadership Quarterly*, *6*, 183–198. doi:10.1016/1048-9843(95)90034-9

Laaser, W. (2002). A Virtual University Environment, The German Experience . In *Advancing Virtual University Education No. 1* (pp. 47–57). Joensuu, Finland: University of Joensuu.

Wächter, H., Laaser, W., & Blettner, K. (1994). *Euro-Personnel Management* [DVD]. Hagen: FernUniversität

Weibler, J., & Laaser, W. (2003). *From Balanced Score Card to Performance Measurement* [DVD]. Hagen: FernUniversität

Weibler, J., & Laaser, W. (2004). *Looking for Charisma* [DVD]. Hagen: FernUniversität

Weibler, J., & Laaser, W. (2009) *Conflict and Stress in Organisations* [DVD]. Hagen: FernUniversität

Koumi, J. (2006). *Designing Video and Multimedia for Open and Flexible Learning*. London: Routledge.

Laaser, W. (2004). Multimedia Enrichment for Online Courses in Economics and Business Administration. *Malaysian Online Journal of Instructional Technology, 1*(2).

Laaser, W., & Stanford, J. (1984). The Use of Video in Distance Education As Applied to Economics . In Zuber-Skerrit, O. (Ed.), *Video in Higher Education*. London: Kogan Page.

KEY TERMS AND DEFINITIONS

Asset Collection: It means collection of source data (audio, video, graphics) and its import into the authoring software

Authoring: It is the process of creating a DVD video by using appropriate editing software

DVD: Digital Versatile Disc is an *optical disc storage* media format. Its main uses are video and data storage.

Encoding: It is the transformation from one format to the other, e.g. from AVI to MPEG2

Learning Management System: These are web based systems to support and enhance learning via networks

Mastering: It is the process data transfer to physical media such as DVD-Rs

Multimedia: Multimedia is the combination of text, audio and video information on a single data carrier

Virtual Classrooms: Virtual classrooms are web based conferencing system using joint viewing and editing

FURTHER READING

Howard, D., & Mabley, E. (1993). *The Tools of Screenwriting*. New York: St. Martin's Griffin.

Chapter 12
Global Education Greenhouse:
Constructing and Organizing Online Global Knowledge

Karen Kaun
Knowledge iTrust, USA

Payal Arora
Erasmus University, the Netherlands

ABSTRACT

Knowledge iTrust (KIT), a non-profit organization, through the co-operation of educational institutions, NGOs, and the private sector, launched the Peace Diaries[1] following September 11, 2001 to establish a forum where educators, students and their families of diverse cultural backgrounds and discourse groups could gather and submit multi-modal literary works (e.g. text, artwork, audio recordings, etc.) that address issues of personal, local and global significance. While this project was a successful demonstration model of what is possible in the way of global learning in collaboration with many stakeholders and actors, there is enormous potential to extend and transform this initiative into a more synthesized and sustainable online global education portal. This learning will be incorporated into Global Education Greenhouse, a corporation in formation, that will create a new class of products and services for students in primary and secondary schools/grades k-12 that address a void in the current educational system.

SETTING THE STAGE

Education, and the knowledge it generates, is seen as a means to effective participation in societies and economies that are affected by globalization (UNESCO). The United Nations Decade of Education for Sustainable Development (2005-2015) was declared by a Resolution of the General Assembly, in December 2002, with a goal to re-focus on educa-tion and learning as central to the common pursuit and achievement of the Millennium Development Goals. The United Nations General Assembly has stated that education for all is essential for achiev-ing the goals of eradicating poverty, reducing child mortality, curbing population growth, achieving gender equality, and ensuring sustainable develop-ment, peace and democracy[2]. Education is viewed as key to participation in the global economy as well as critical to local prosperity.

DOI: 10.4018/978-1-61520-751-0.ch012

What marks this debate as unique to the 21st century is its deep relationship to information technology. Intrinsically combining education and information technology is viewed as endemic in preparing the global youth to face the challenges of the knowledge economy (Monahan, 2005; Arora, 2005). The Internet promises a novel and cost effective means of transmitting knowledge, allowing for the rhetoric of global learning to become a genuine possibility. The hope is that education leverages on the current phenomena of transnational connectivity and cross-cultural sociality, leading to the birthing of new knowledge. In fact, much of this effort is structured to move away from the chronic center-periphery flow of information of prior decades, focusing on a more global diffusion model (Haywood, 1995).

In 2004 alone, governments of the world invested 1.97 trillion U.S. dollars or 4.4% of global GDP in PPP (purchasing power parities) on education (UNESCO). Further, the Information Technology in Education Study[3] revealed that developed countries had succeeded in establishing connectivity across its schools in the 70-90 percent range in 1999 with full connectivity by 2001. Amongst developing countries, there has been a strong financial and political commitment to bridge the digital divide in education with a goal to achieve 100% e-literacy (Norris, 2001).

Yet, despite the trillions of dollars spent on education and technological connectivity for global education, a 2005 article in ScienceDirect reports a rapid decline in worldwide innovation. Recent studies by bi-partisan panels have concluded that we cannot achieve change by "patching the system," but only "by changing the system itself." (National Center on Education and Economy, 2008). In other words, access to technologies and people alone does not shape global education. Much effort is needed to pioneer an international model of knowledge formation and sharing that does full justice to transnational social and technological participation amongst youth, teachers, administrators, curriculum ex-perts, policy makers and other actors in pursuit of a new global education.

CASE DESCRIPTION

Need for a New Approach

We live in an ever-changing society where world-wide issues affect our local communities (e.g. global climate change, energy and food production and consumption, monetary system upheavals, crime, war, poverty, etc.). The need for global understanding is not a luxury but a profound necessity; "we predict that global awareness will become the first new basic skill of the twenty-first century, as computer literacy has so rapidly become a basic skill in the final decades of the twentieth century" (Tye, 1992, p.7). The crisis in contemporary education persists as it struggles to transform its institutional, curricula and technical realms (Lewis, 2000).

In 1992, the Earth Summit at Rio brought together 172 countries, 108 heads of state, 2,400 representatives of non-governmental organizations and 17,000 people attending the parallel NGO forum to discuss the impact of economic development on the planet. The adoption of Agenda 21 placed emphasis on education for environmental concerns. Today, the vision has broadened to encompass socio-cultural and socio-political aspects of development, including "issues of equity, poverty, democracy, and quality of life" (UNESCO, 2005). The world has also witnessed an explosion in the development of new technological innovations in Information and Communication Technologies (ICT), which, as noted by UN Secretary-General Kofi Annan in his opening address to the third meeting of the UN Information and Communication Technologies Task Force (2002), is a "powerful instrument for speeding up the realization" of the Millennium Development Goals. Therefore, we are behooved to create innovative education curriculum, tools and technologies that will teach people how to interconnect across cultures and socio-economic strata to harness our vast, collective knowledge, collaborate, plan and agree upon possible solutions for the sustainable, ethical economies.

This effort has been gaining serious traction in the last decade (Mason, 1998; Arora, 2006a; 2006b; 2006c; 2007). Transformation is happening at an institutional level where some academic programs are moving beyond its domestic horizons through online distance learning. Curricula are getting reengineered for certain topics, incorporating multiple perspectives and novel teaching styles to suit this new cyber-environment. The focus here is more on developing critical and creative thinking and problem-solving skills than information accumulation and regurgitation. That said, global education continues to be deeply fragmented, asynchronized and mostly compartmentalized, viewed as supplemental to main public education (Gaudelli, 2003). The viewing of knowledge through the lens of the nation-state continues to dominate current educational practice.

Global Education Greenhouse

A networked content and software development community of schools, educators and technologists is envisioned to create curricular materials, tools and elearning products designed to prepare all students with information, new skills and talents for our 21st Century, global society (Drake & Burns, 2004; Tye & Tye, 1992; Gura & Percy, 2005). These products and services will address critical development needs articulated by international organizations (e.g. UN, UNESCO, UNICEF, etc.) and national governments. For example, the United Nations General Assembly has stated that basic education for all is essential for achieving the goals of eradicating poverty, reducing child mortality, curbing population growth, achieving gender equality, and ensuring sustainable development, peace and democracy[4] and former Secretary

General Kofi Annan has said that ICT can help to speed the realization of the goals.

The Partnership for 21st Century Skills, a bi-partisan study group commissioned by the federal government of the United States of America, has identified "global awareness" as one of the significant emerging content areas critical to success in communities and workplaces. Furthermore, the Research and Policy Committee for Economic Development (2006) stated, "It is increasingly important that America be better versed in the languages, cultures, and traditions of other world regions, particularly the Middle East (p. 2)." The group has also recommended federal incentives to design and create model schools with innovative approaches to teaching international content that can be replicated by other schools.

Global Education Greenhouse as an idea and institutional entity will have an innovative and unique market niche in the global education marketplace. Currently, there is a large and growing demand in the primary and secondary education consumer markets for books, curricular materials, tools and elearning products that are designed to prepare youth to comprehend the full scale of global social, economic, political, and scientific issues (e.g. worldwide monetary fluctuations, climate change, pandemic disease) and to interact, collaborate and problem-solve both locally and globally to develop ethical solutions that benefit the greatest numbers of people.

Product

In the first 3-5 years of operation, Global Education Greenhouse will serve as a global education provider that invites a worldwide community of academics/researchers/educators/software developers to research, incubate and develop a global education framework, products (e.g. curriculum, toolkits, software) and services (teacher professional development) that will be utilized by partner schools, ministries of education and other educational institutions, as well as parents in homes, around the globe to educate children ages 5-17.

Features

- Global Greenhouse Community Web Site with expert development panels
- Publishing and Development Forums
- Collaborative Development Tools
- Content Indexing, Search, Networking and Distribution System
- Ecommerce

Objectives

- Create a new class of products and services for students in primary and secondary schools/grades k-12 that address a void in the current educational system.
- Connect stakeholders from the international and national public and private sector to collaborate in forums and advise on the development of products and services that address global and local political, economic and development needs.
- Harness the intellectual capital of diverse groups of people and break down artificial and real boundaries that have impeded the kind of understanding and collaboration that is needed to move forward onto a more sustainable and systemic development path.

PILOT

Peace Diaries was launched in response to the events of September 11, 2001. Knowledge iTrust, the non-profit organization, worked with the New York City Department of Education (NYCDOE) to develop Web-based educational tools for teachers that can be integrated into classroom instruction. Through the co-operation of educational institu-

tions, NGOs, and the private sector, our non-profit organization, Knowledge iTrust (KIT), developed this model for the integration of ICT and classroom education for development, for consideration and further research. In January 2002, we launched the *Peace Diaries* to establish a forum where educators, students and their families of diverse cultural backgrounds and discourse groups could gather and submit multi-modal literary works (e.g. text, artwork, audio recordings, etc.) that address issues of personal, local and global significance.

According to Warschauer (2003) "the Web is an ideal writing medium for students' to explore and develop their evolving relationship to their community, culture and world" (p. 164). This contributes to "a sense of agency, as learners take public action through their writing" (Kramsch, Ness & Lam, 2000; Warschauer, 2000a cited in Warschauer, 2003, p. 164). The choice to integrate ICT with classroom practices was driven by the fact that this was a unique opportunity to connect diverse communities of learners together on global issues, post-September 11, when the awareness of and desire to participate in this kind of discourse was heightened by events and the media. *Peace Diaries* was driven by need and a sense of purpose:

High student engagement in writing for the Web depends on students' understanding the purpose of the activity, viewing the purpose as socially and/or culturally relevant, finding the electronic medium advantageous for fulfilling the purpose, and being encouraged and enabled to use medium-appropriate rhetorical features to fulfill the purpose. (Warschauer, 2003, pp. 164)

Open source technology provided by OpenVES[5] was customized as an online, password-protected learning environment with web-based writing, editing and annotation tools, semantic-map search engine, resource library and curriculum and learning units developed in consultancy with The Peace Education Center of Teachers College Columbia University. We reached out to schools' administrators and educators with the help of ePals Classroom Exchange[6] and recruited teachers in Argentina, Armenia, Azerbaijan, Canada, Chile, Ghana, Great Britain, Haiti, Peru, Sierra Leone, South Africa, Taiwan, Ukraine and the United States. Teachers were provided with a 28-page curriculum manual and illustrated technical user's guide and training was conducted onsite or through Internet technologies (email and Web). Throughout the program, teacher questions were answered usually within a day via help desk and email. Every teacher and student was assigned their own password-protected workspace to compose and edit essays, upload artwork and collect data. The community also collaborated and communicated via email or electronic bulletin board.

Development and Funding

The first iteration of *Peace Diaries* was built and launched on a shoestring with an initial $10,000 grant from the W.T. Grant Foundation and the pro bono contributions of the non-profit's founder's and board's supporters. The grant paid for a PHP/SQL programmer to build out the beta Web site's registration, password protection, journaling, editing and display functionality. A co-founder of Knowledge iTrust is also a Web designer and developer. She designed the user interfaces for the Web site and all the html pages, pro bono. Another team member of Knowledge iTrust wrote grants, developed partnerships with NGOs and other international education organizations and schools, and recruited professionally developed teachers in New York City to use the Web site, pro bono. Teachers in other countries and States in the United States were provided with virtual professional development and help desk through email. The beta Web site was hosted on a ViaVerio virtual server.

Following the beta launch and successful pilot of the *Peace Diaries*, the W.K. Kellogg Founda-

tion awarded Knowledge iTrust a larger grant ($125,000) to continue to build out the program. The New York State Department of Education also funded a portion of the *Peace Diaries* through a Learning Technology Grant to a NYCDOE regional education office. In addition, OpenVES provided Knowledge iTrust with a free license to utilize a multi-million dollar elearning/epublishing Web software that was initially developed for the Massachusetts Department of Education and then spun-off into a non-profit organization for proliferation amongst state's departments of education. It was the intention of OpenVES to showcase the Web software's capabilities through the *Peace Diaries* program, which was a live demonstration of how teachers and students could collaborate across far-flung boundaries in real-time.

Partners

The organizations that contributed to the success of *Peace Diaries* represented both the public and private sector, including: the New York City Department of Education, the New York State Education Department, the W.T. Grant Foundation, W.K. Kellogg Foundation, OpenVES, ePALs classroom exchange and Project Harmony. The W.T. Grant Foundation, the W.K. Kellogg Foundation and the New York State Education Department provided the funding. OpenVes, a non-profit organization, provided free access to a multi-million dollar elearning and epublishing environment.

The Director of Instructional Technology for the NYCDOE supported the program and promoted it via a Technology and Education conference entitled, "Tech to Go" at Fordham University. Teachers who attended the conference signed up for the initial pilot program. ePals Classroom Exchange, a for-profit global elearning community promoted the *Peace Diaries* to teachers in its network and helped Knowledge iTrust to recruit teachers from countries that included Argentina, Chile, France, Ghana, Israel and South Africa. Project Harmony, a non-governmental organization funded in part by the USAID, brought the countries of Azerbaijan and Armenia to the *Peace Diaries*. A *Peace Diaries* teacher in South Africa eventually evolved into a project manager for Knowledge iTrust and recruited teachers from Taiwan, Sierra Leone and Canada. Other teachers from Great Britain, Haiti, Peru, Ukraine and the United States (e.g. California, Colorado, Massachusetts, and Pennsylvania) learned of the program through the UN and other peace and education organizations and joined.

Online Curriculum

The challenge in developing and implementing a true global education framework range from securing agreements on what should be taught, and how (McKeown, 2002; Hernandez & Mayur, 1999), to those of access and digital divide (UNESCO, 2005; UN, 1998). Following, September 11, many NYCDOE teachers have been seeking resources that can support them in helping their students to understand the causes of September 11 and to express their feelings through journaling and other forms of creative expression. *Peace Diaries* as a pilot for Global Education Greenhouse serves as an online global initiative to help students to engage in inquiry about the salient issues of humanity and to question how human needs can be fulfilled through non-violent means. A password protected web-based environment was developed to enable teachers to access lessons and students to access online journaling tools to write about themselves and topics of "a local-global nature."

The first *Peace Diaries* activity asked students in classrooms in seven countries to introduce themselves to each other through illustrated totem drawings/representations of themselves and written essays explaining the artifacts that were embedded in the totems and their significance. This exercise gave students the opportunity to compare and contrast what was similar and different about each other. Another activity asked students to write about a favorite recipe and a

story, memory, folktale, holiday, etc. associated with it. Students were also asked to identify the source of the ingredients (e.g. whether they were grown locally or shipped; were they purchased in a farmers' market or a grocery store etc.). These seemingly simple exercises subtly introduced teachers and students to more complex issues of culture, sustainable development, food security, etc. This built upon each other in a two-year scope and sequence that gradually immersed students in critical thinking about global climate change, pandemic illness, quality of life and human rights, through local and international responses and implications. All the students completed essays have been archived on servers and is now shown on the Web site. The students' collective works have been published in three volumes of printed books.

By the end of this two year pilot study, the *Peace Diaries* community grew where teachers and students from classrooms in fourteen countries participated in the programs. This translated into creating curriculum that helped students to find their own explanations for larger global issues from the point of view of their every day lives. This approach is supported by the theory of Occam's Razor, which posits that "one should choose simpler explanations in preference to more complex ones" (Baum, 2004). Henceforth, *Peace Diaries* took very complex ideas about global issues and broke them down into their most simplistic meanings for each person at their level of knowledge and the scale of their own community (e.g., family, classroom, village and / or city). The challenge of sustainable development, for instance, then becomes less daunting, more feasible and empowers the individual to collaborate and contribute their talents and knowledge for the greater whole.

Three thematic topics comprised the learning units of *Peace Diaries*. The topics are "Recipes for Life," "Healing Planet," and "Quality of Life." Each of the topics has two Activity Layers that take students into deeper inquiry and learning. Layer 1: Cultural and Social; and Layer 2: Science and Economy. Teachers decide how many layers they would like to complete. A primary goal of *Peace Diaries* was to develop students' capacity to realize their potential for change through their relative point of view.

SAMPLE LEARNING UNIT

The learning unit introduces issues that are familiar to all people (e.g., access to food) in new contexts (e.g., Edith's chicken rearing story) and provides students with a background to identify and illustrate similar situations from their own, everyday points of view. For example, a Canadian, First Nations' student, who contributed to *Peace Diaries*, describes his family's practice of dip netting for and drying salmon each summer and how each part of the salmon is consumed. A Taiwanese student relates her story of the family harvest and the special meaning of the rice pudding that sustained them in hard times. Another student from Sierra Leone writes about cassava leaves or "sakii tomboi," which among the Mendes people means nourishment. He says, "The leaves are not only used to make a favorite sauce, but are credited with saving lives during the war when there was "no other food to be found." Many students in the United States described farm life and memories of grandparents who wasted nothing.

The ideas in these essays illustrate the least common denominators of what it means to be human from socio-cultural, economic, and environmental perspectives which are, according to UNESCO (2005), the three pillars of sustainable development that are described by international discourse and key to sustainable learning. Also important, the ideas in the essays demonstrate how the community is making linkages to these three pillars and ultimately to each other, through their culture. UNESCO (2005) notes that cultural "practices, identity, and values" help build common commitments.

Teachers and students who participated gathered research, wrote essays, produced artwork, shared best practices and gathered scientific information that was collected and stored in a database for access by the international community. Over a period of two years, KIT worked with students, teachers and administrators in sixteen countries that have contributed to the publication of *Peace Diaries* in the form of the World Wide Web, three books and broadcasts on radio.

ACTIVITY 1: "Recipes for Life"

- **Layer Two:** Science and Economy
- **Concepts:** Agriculture, Local Food Supplies (Indigenous vs. Planted) and Import / Export

Objectives

Students will learn about....

- Where the ingredients in foods come from
- Whether or not they can grow the ingredients in their community, school or family garden
- The relationship between food, natural resources, commerce, politics, history

Layer Two — Framing Discussion, (Preparatory)

In an effort to feed more people, farmers have experimented with ways to increase agricultural yields. Some large-scale farming techniques have proven harmful (i.e. use of DDT pesticide) to the environment, humans, and animals. Today groups of scientists, and agricultural and ecological organizations and educators are working together to develop sustainable agriculture methods – farming practices that will produce food for human or animal consumption without causing harm to the environment or animals or humans. One area of interest to these groups is local food gardening. Community gardens are springing up in urban lots, schoolyards and people's home yards around the world. These gardens produce not only nutritious foods, but in some cases, a small income for the growers.

Questions

1. Where do the ingredients in your recipe come from?
2. Are they grown locally or are they imported? What are the ingredients' histories?
3. Why do we import and export food?
4. What is the significance of local gardening versus importing and exporting?
5. What challenges do countries dependent on food exports face?
6. Do people all over the world have access to enough food? Do children in our own country have enough to eat?
7. What are some of the factors that contribute to food insecurity? (These can include poverty, lack of access to land, environmental degradation, war, lack of access to education.)
8. Why are women important to food security (access to enough food)?
9. Before your city/town/community was developed, was it originally farmland? What crops were grown there? If not, what was the land used for (e.g., grazing by animals, early industry)?

Listen: UN Radio: "Women are the pillars of food security throughout most of the world. According to the UN Food and Agriculture Organization (FAO), they produce between 60 and 80 percent of all food in developing countries" http://www.un.org/womenwatch/news/unradio/progs/2001Jul09.html.

Listen: *Peace Diaries* Radio[7]. Show 10 "Women and Gender Equality." Full transcripts of the show and the radio shows themselves, in wav format, are available on the *Peace Diaries*

Web site http://www.peacediaries.org/2_community/2_1_radio_sh10.html. An excerpt of Show 10 is below.

01:03 – 01:25 (Narr Intro)

According to a Ghanaian proverb, if you educate a man you educate an individual, but if you educate a woman you educate a nation. The center of family- and most community-life across the developing world, women still remain the most marginalized.

06:15 – 06:44 (Narr)

The Food Gardens Foundation in South Africa was founded 2-and-a-half decades ago by two women who wanted to train the unemployed and rural poor how to raise fresh vegetables on the smallest plot of land possible. Food Gardens volunteer, Betty Hanratty, says although the gardens help many women, they still face huge obstacles. Hanratty worked in Driftsands, a community outside Cape Town, and remembers how a young mother and resident, Edith, struggled to survive...

06:45 – 07:37 (Hanratty)

Her husband had abandoned her for another woman when her youngest child was born, and she struggled and then she managed to get one of the children through college. Then he reappeared in their old age, so she took him back in. In the meantime we had introduced the women to rearing chickens, so that they could have eggs to eat, eggs to sell and manure for their gardens. Edith's family in the Transkei had some problem and she had to go, so she left her husband, Wellington, in charge. When she came back there were only 11 hens. So she went to Wellington and said, "Where's my other hen?" And he said, "I ate it." Well, Edith was devastated, because that was part of her income gone.

END LEARNING UNIT

TECHNOLOGY CONCERNS

In the first *Peace Diaries* beta Web site, the PHP coding was not thoroughly debugged and tested. This resulted in Web site errors and crashes that often frustrated teachers and students. For example, a student might write an entire essay in her password protected journaling space and click on a save button only to receive an error message and lose all her work. In New York City, a Symantec filtering software often blocked access to the *Peace Diaries* Web site from teachers' classrooms. In addition, many schools in the United States and other participating countries had slow or unreliable Internet access. Some country teachers (e.g. Ghana and Sierra Leone) who had no computers or Internet access at all in their schools, literally took students' hand written essays to Internet cafes, typed the essays and submitted them via email to Knowledge iTrust. These essays were then uploaded to the Web site. While the students could not view their work online unless they went to an Internet café, they did receive printed books of their collective work.

In the preceding *Peace Diaries* version II, OpenVes provided additional functionality (e.g. bulletin boards, search, maps), but also was not without its challenges. Because the technology was licensed to Knowledge iTrust, the non-profit's programmers and producers did not have access to code or the back room administrative tools and thereby could not easily make modifications to the Web site as needed. In addition, while a great deal of funding went into the development of the site, there was still debugging to be done and crashes from time to time. In 2002 through 2004, integrating technology in classroom instruction was still a fairly new idea for many teachers and it was critical that the Web site was intuitive, easy to navigate, accessible and as error free as possible. Anything less would result in participation fallout.

Organizational Concerns: For Profit versus Non-Profit

While non-profit status often affords organizations the ability to apply for grants that are not available to for-profit entities, non-profits are often subject to the whims of donors and hard-pressed to develop sustainability models (beyond the next grant) for their programs. Case in point, when the W.K. Kellogg Foundation re-aligned its grant giving focus in 2004, there was no longer an interest in funding "a peace initiative." It was therefore necessary for our Knowledge iTrust to reconsider its development focus and priorities. Another drawback of the non-profit world is that often the "assets" that are developed with grant money are public domain property, making it difficult to generate the "income" that is the foundation of sustainability.

Outcomes from the Pilot Project

Peace Diaries combined ICT, education and best practices of UN agencies and local communities to address six of the eight Millennium Development Goals: poverty and hunger, primary education, gender equality, HIV/AIDS and other diseases, environmental sustainability and global partnerships. These projects promoted awareness and action through lesson plans that supported literacy, global studies, science, and the UN tenants of peace, etc., that build students academic skills within the context of practical exercises that are applicable to their daily lives. Teachers who participated in the project were continuously surveyed in-person and via email on their experiences using the technology and curriculum. Though technical glitches were sometimes reported as issues that slowed access to the Web site and contributions of materials by teachers and students, teachers generally reported positive outcomes, including: students were motivated to participate in a world forum and felt empowered by seeing their work online and in printed books. Students also achieved an elevated awareness of global issues, cultures and ways of living through the submissions. Below are selected quotes from students[8]:

The "Four Herbs Soup" is one of the Buddhist recipes used by the monks to cure their patients. "Satisfaction," "gratitude," "thoughtfulness," and "generosity" are the four types of spiritual medicine. - Taiwan

"We do drying of salmon every summer. We all go to the Fraser River, which runs through the fishing grounds of Lillooet. This is where I live. This summer we will go again to the river as a family to enjoy the gifts of the Fraser River as generations before me have done." – Canada

"I love Turshu Syiig very much, especially in winter when it is cold outside. Granny told me that when she was young they never got medicine; they used to eat turshu syiig when they were ill. It's better to use traditional medicine. It is useful and safe. I agree with my granny." - Azerbaijan

"Most people never come to realize what is important to them until their lives are ending, when it is too late to change. The best contribution they can give to their world is to teach their children what is important, and hope that they will remember and live fulfilling lives." - USA

CONCLUSION

Drawing from the *Peace Diaries* pilot project, Global Education Greenhouse can benefit tremendously from its institutional, curricula and technical issues. The *Peace Diaries* illustrated that a global knowledge exchange amongst classrooms around the world is possible and welcome by educators. The next step in the evolution of a true global education network is to take a page out of the open source community. Global Educa-

tion Greenhouse was conceptualized with these goals in mind:

1. Connect stakeholders from the international and national public and private sector to collaborate in forums and advise on the development of products and services that address global and local political, economic and development needs.
2. Harness the intellectual capital of diverse groups of people and break down artificial and real boundaries that have impeded the kind of understanding and collaboration that is needed to move forward onto a more sustainable and systemic development path.
3. Reward all participants in the development community.

As noted by UNESCO (2005), ICTs are not universally available, as they are limited by cost, infrastructure, energy supplies and telephone connections. To address this challenge, KIT collaborated with technologists, educators, UN agencies, NGOs, other non-profit organizations and educational institutions to envision the future of local to global collaborative learning. We have articulated a blueprint for an open, connected, locally customizable learning environment that would be available to schools and communities around the world. It is a modular system that is broken down into components that include an e-learning platform for students, family or professional or community development; hardware; power sources (e.g., solar power) and digital connectivity (e.g., satellite). Since we believe it is important to work with local resources such as regional leaders, groups and organizations, we did not propose to introduce ideas that would not integrate immediately or out of context to the existing society, culture or economy. Thus, the modules are designed to work independently to enable community leaders to choose appropriate tools for their level of knowledge and the scale of their respective community. This returns us to the premise of *Peace Diaries*, which is to approach development from the individual's point of view that will create more feasible and empowered outcomes and contribute to a larger whole.

The World Bank Development and Communication Division states that, among other purposes, development communication empowers grassroots organizations' participation in matters of public discourse. Information Communication Technology is a vehicle to connect the local to global for the greatest participation. As delineated in the UNESCO (2005) Draft International Implementation Scheme for the United Nations Decade of Education for Sustainable Development, sustainable development begins locally and then "radiates out to an ever-increasing number of stakeholders." A guiding principle of our work to date can be expressed by the words of Margaret Mead who said, "Never doubt that a small group of thoughtful, committed citizens can change the world. Indeed it is the only thing that ever has." We submit that for the achievement of sustainable development, government policy-makers, educational institutions, NGOs, and private sector corporations should look to the local citizens, acknowledge their ways of doing things, learn from them, and support them with technology and tools that make it possible for them to share their perspectives and ideas with others transnationally and cross-culturally.

As previously stated, the effectiveness of *Peace Diaries* was contingent on the careful integration of ICT with classroom curriculum to fulfill a discourse need driven by time, events, and media. Educators and students felt that their words had purpose; to unite the world in peace as expressed by this student "For me peace is simple. If each one took the time and had patience to know foreign people, the world would be better" (*Peace Diaries*, 2002). This project was deeply dependant on the sharing of a common goal amongst all participants.

The Way Forward

While this project is viewed as a successful demonstration model of what is possible in the way of global learning in collaboration with many stakeholders and actors, there is enormous potential to extend and transform this initiative into a more synthesized and sustainable online global education portal. This learning will be incorporated into Global Education Greenhouse, a corporation in formation. Global Education Greenhouse (GEG) will create a new class of products and services for students in primary and secondary schools/grades k-12 that address a void in the current educational system. It will connect stakeholders from the international and national public and private sector to advise on the development of products and services that address global and local political, economic and development needs. GEG will harness the intellectual capital of diverse groups of people and break down artificial and real boundaries that have impeded the kind of understanding and collaboration that is needed to move forward onto a more sustainable and systemic development path. Its partners will create critical thinking tools and building blocks through a k-12 global education curriculum spiral that deliver educational experiences that help learners to develop intellectual independence; to be able to use knowledge to continue to evolve as productive citizens and contributors to the nation and the world. GEG will ensure that teachers are trained to harness the power of emerging technologies and encourage students and their parents to participate and have a voice in the education process.

Finally, the mission of GEG is to prepare all students for the demands of the future world.

For example, working with more and a diverse range of educators and community leaders to gather and develop a critical mass of culturally relevant sub-text would serve as a highly effective launching pad of global education. Providing more starting points for students by activating their prior knowledge/schema, potentially produces richer output and data or indicators on how sustainable development works.

Also, at a technical level, the open source movement encourages collaborative development efforts amongst a variety of stakeholders and at the same time embraces new revenue generation models for the good of all participants. Fast forwarding to 2009, wiki, blog and open source elearning platform technology makes it possible to launch programs like *Peace Diaries* without a great deal of backend development. In addition, Web applications such as MediaWiki, WordPress and Moodle are relatively flexible, powerful, scalable and debugged. In addition, the next generation of Smartphones offer new ways to network, communicate and share knowledge amongst a larger global audience that was not possible in the early days of *Peace Diaries*.

REFERENCES

Annan, K. (2002). *Remarks at opening of the third meeting of the United Nations information and communication technologies task force.* New York. Retrieved October 30, 2002 from http://www.unictaskforce.org/thirdmeeting/sg_speech.html

Arora, P. (2005). Profiting from empowerment? Investigating dissemination avenues for educational technology content within an emerging market solutions project. *International Journal of Education and Development using Information and Communication Technology, 1*(4), 18-29.

Arora, P. (2006). The ICT laboratory: An analysis of computers in public high schools in rural India. *Association of Advancement in Computing in Education, 15*(1), 57–72.

Arora, P. (2006a). *E-karaoke for gender empowerment.* Paper presented at the Information and Communication Technologies for Development 2006, Berkeley, California.

Arora, P. (2006b). Karaoke for social and cultural change. *Information . Communication and Ethics in Society, 4*(3), 121–130.

Arora, P. (2007). Evaluating asynchronous online engagement on international security. *Electronic Journal of e-Learning, 6*(1), 1-10.

Baum, E. (2004). *What is thought?* Cambridge, MA: The MIT Press.

Benham Tye, B., & Tye, K. (1992). *Global education: A study of school change.* New York: SUNY Press.

Drake, S. M., & Burns, R. C. (2004). *Meeting standards through integrated curriculum.* Association for Supervision & Curriculum Deve Publications.

Food and Agriculture Organization of the United Nations. (1999). Agricultural trade and food security: FAO fact sheets. In *Third WTO Ministerial Conference, Seattle.* Retrieved June 15, 2002, from http://www.fao.org/documents/show_cdr.asp?url_file=/DOCREP/003/X6730E/X6730E00.HTM

Food and Agriculture Organization of the United Nations. (n.d.). *Women and food security.* Retrieved June 15, 2002, from:http://www.fao.org/FOCUS/E/Women/Sustin-e.htm

Gaudelli, W. (2003). *World class: Teaching and learning in global times.* New York: Erlbaum Associates.

Gura, M., & Percy, B. (2005). *Recapturing technology for education: Keeping tomorrow in today's classrooms.* Lanham, MD: Scarecrow Education.

Haywood, T. (1995). *Info rich/info poor: Access and exchange in the global information society.* London: Bowker-Saur.

Hernandez, C., & Nevin, J. (1999). Education for sustainable development: The ultimate value of life depends upon awareness and the power of contemplation rather than upon mere survival. In Hernandez, C., & Mayur, R. (Eds.), *Pedagogy of the earth: Education for a sustainable future* (pp. 15–28). Bloomfield, CT: Kumarian Press, Inc.

Kramsch, C. A., A'Ness, F., & Lam, E. (2000). Authenticity and authorship in the computer-mediated acquisition of L2 literacy. *Language Learning & Technology, 4*(2), 78–104.

Lewis, M. W. (2000). Global Ignorance. *Geographical Review, 90*(4), 603–628. doi:10.2307/3250786

McKeown, R. (2002). *ESD toolkit*. Retrieved March 1, 2005, from http://www.esdtoolkit.org

Monahan, T. (2005). *Globalization, technological change, and public education*. London: Routledge Pub.

Moshman, D. (1999). *Adolescent psychological development. Rationality, morality and identity*. Mahwah, NJ: Erlbaum.

Norris, P. (2001). *Digital divide: Civic engagement, information poverty, and the internet worldwide*. Cambridge, UK: Cambridge University Press.

Tye, B. B. (1999). *Global education: A study of school change*. New York: SUNY Press.

UNESCO. (2005). *Draft International Implementation Scheme for the United Nations Decade of Education for Sustainable Development 2005-2014*. Retrieved March 1, 2005, from http:www.isa.unu.edu/binaries2/IIS_2004.doc

Warschauer, M. (2000a). The changing global economy and the future of English teaching. *TESOL Quarterly, 34*, 511–535. doi:10.2307/3587741

Warschauer. (2003). Technology and second language writing: Researching a moving target. *Journal of Second Language Writing, 12*, 151-179.

World Bank. (1986). Poverty and hunger: Issues and options for food security in developing countries. Washington, DC.

World Commission on Sustainable Development. (1987). *Our common future*. New York: Oxford University Press.

FURTHER READING

Anderson-Levitt, K. M. (2003). *Local meanings, global schooling: Anthropology and world culture theory* (1st ed.). New York: Palgrave Macmillan. doi:10.1057/9781403980359

Arora, P. (2008). Perspectives of schooling through karaoke: A metaphorical analysis. *Educational Philosophy and Theory, 40*(3), 1–21.

Brown, J. S., & Duguid, P. (2002). *The social life of information*. Boston: Harvard Business School.

Castells, M. (1996). *The rise of the network society*. Cambridge, UK: Blackwell Publishers.

Fischer, F. (1990). *Technocracy and the politics of expertise*. Newbury Park, CA: Sage Publications.

Foucault, M. (1972). *The archaeology of knowledge* (1st American ed.). New York: Pantheon Books.

Freire, P., & Freire, P. (1973). *Education for critical consciousness* (1st American ed.). New York: Seabury Press.

Friedman, T. L. (2007). *The world is flat: A brief history of the twenty-first century*. New York: Farrar, Straus and Giroux.

Giddens, A. (2000). *Runaway world: How globalization is reshaping our lives*. New York: Routledge.

Hampson, T., & Whalen, L. (1991). *Tales of the heart: Affective approaches to global education*. New York: Friendship Press.

Hawkridge, D. G., Jaworski, J., & McMahon, H. (1990). *Computers in third-world schools: Examples, experience, and issues*. New York: Macmillan.

Leonard, E. (2005). *The onset of global governance*. Aldershot, UK: Ashgate.

Mason, R., & ebrary Inc. (1998). *Global education trends and applications*. Retrieved from http://www.columbia.edu/cgi-bin/cul/resolve?clio5562594

Meyer, J., W, Boli, J., Thomas, G. M., & Ramirez, F. O. (1997). World society and the nation-state. *American Journal of Sociology, 103*(1), 144–181. doi:10.1086/231174

Mohd. Tengku, S. (2003). *Digital libraries: Technology and management of indigenous knowledge for global access. In 6th international conference on Asian digital libraries, ICADL 2003, Kuala Lumpur, Malaysia, December 2003*. Berlin, New York: Springer.

Selfe, C. L. (1999). *Technology and literacy in the twenty-first century: The importance of paying attention*. Carbondale, IL: Southern Illinois University Press.

Servon, L. J. (2002). *Bridging the digital divide: Technology, community, and public policy*. Malden, UK: Blackwell Pub. doi:10.1002/9780470773529

Sillitoe, P. (2007). *Local science vs. Global science: Approaches to indigenous knowledge in international development*. New York: Berghahn Books.

Spring, J. H., & NetLibrary Inc. (1998). *Education and the rise of the global economy*. Retrieved from http://www.columbia.edu/cgi-bin/cul/resolve?clio4247973

Street, B. V. (1993). *Cross-cultural approaches to literacy*. Cambridge, UK: Cambridge University Press.

Tyner, K. R. (1998). *Literacy in a digital world: Teaching and learning in the age of information*. Mahwah, NJ: Erlbaum Associates.

UNESCO Institute for Statistics. (2008). *Global education digest 2008 comparing education statistics across the world*. Retrieved from http://www.columbia.edu/cgi-bin/cul/resolve?clio7191137

KEY TERMS AND DEFINITIONS

Global Education: Innovative education curriculum, tools and technologies that will teach people how to interconnect across cultures and socio-economic strata to harness vast, collective and diverse knowledge through collaboration for possible solutions for sustainable, ethical economies.

Peace Diaries: A global literacy project by Knowledge iTrust at www.peacediaries.org

E-Learning: Broadening and extending our understandings to the online arena

ICT: Information communication technology, both hardware and software.

Sustainable Development: Eschewing mass consumerism for small scale living.

Ethical Economies: Participants are compelled to learn about the needs of their local community, their nations and the world to be able to become contributors with solutions that will benefit the greatest numbers.

ENDNOTES

[1] www.peacediaries.org

[2] United Nations General Assembly Resolution A/C.3/52/L.II/Rev.1 / 29 October 1997

[3] SRI (2003). Second Information Technology in Education Study: Module 2 (SITES M2)

[4] United Nations General Assembly Resolution A/C.3/52/L.II/Rev.1 / 29 October 1997

[5] OpenVES (www.openves.org) is a non-profit organization dedicated to the research, development and global dissemination of an open architecture, standards based eLearning platform for pk12 education.

[6] Epals (www.epals.com) global network connects 101,506 classrooms in 191 countries through email and collaborative technology for education.

[7] As heard on the Peace Diaries radio programme, broadcast by Worldspace Satellite Network for the World Summit for Sustainable Development (WSSD), Johannesburg, South Africa, 2002.

[8] We refer to relative points of view as the students' subjective perspectives, which are their primary realities (Moshman, 1999).

Chapter 13

Employing Fuzzy Logic for a Real–Time Comprehensive Quality Assessment Model of Service Providers in E–Learning Environments

Hamed Fazlollahtabar
Mazandaran University of Science and Technology, Iran

ABSTRACT

Assessing quality is obviously a key concern in many aspects of learning, education and training, so why should it be especially crucial in relation to e-learning? The e-learners, as with other distance learners, are working in isolation with limited or sometimes non-existent human support. This means that the first impact of any failure in the providers' quality assessment regime falls directly on the e-learner. When an e-learner encounters errors caused by a failure in a providers' quality assessment regime the impact might be immediately evident or not become evident until the learner undertakes an assessed outcome. Since e-learning development is fundamentally a team-based activity, the effectiveness or quality of an e-learning program depends on the weakest link in the production chain. E-learning exists at a point of convergence between technology based disciplines and human-centered disciplines.

ORGANIZATION BACKGROUND

Mazandaran University of Science and Technology (MUST), situated in the city of Babol in the Province of Mazandaran (North of Iran) 15 km away from Caspian Sea, was founded in 1992. Blessed with a temperate climate, a plethora of colorful blossoms and removed from the turmoil and upheaval as-

sociated with big cities, Babol provides a suitable environment for academic activities. In recent years, MUST has scaled such enviable heights to become a conglomeration of different provinces and cultures. This university provides different fields of studies in and various programs. Industrial Engineering, Computer Engineering, Information Technology Engineering, Civil Engineering, and MBA are the programs offered by MUST.

DOI: 10.4018/978-1-61520-751-0.ch013

Figure 1. E-learning supports all aspects of education

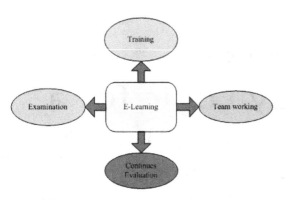

SETTING THE STAGE

Recently, an e-learning research center has been founded to investigate different aspects of optimization in e-learning environment. One of the objectives of this center is to analyze different aspects of quality in e-learning. As regards what respondents understand by quality in e-learning, the predominant view is that quality relates to obtaining the best learning achievements. Together with 'something that is excellent in performance,' this primarily pedagogical understanding was more widespread than options related to best value for money or marketing.

The issue of quality in e-learning is both topical and widely discussed. On the one hand, it provides material for political debate at national and European level, and on the other, it leaves those involved in e-learning scratching their heads. How can quality be best developed? And, even more important, what is in fact the right kind of quality? At first there was an attempt to find one concept that would be right for all, but we have now become more cautious. Various types of analytical description now head the list. These are intended to ascertain and describe how quality development functions in different sectors of education and in different countries.

The European Quality Observatory is one such observation platform for quality development in European e-learning. However, there is more to it than 'pure' data collection and description. A key aim is to analyze what actually makes successful approaches successful. In a way, the aim is to find a quality concept for quality concepts. Decision-making and implementation strategies also need to be designed. One thing is clear today: the main problem is not finding a quality approach, rather choosing the right one from among the huge number of quality strategies available.

One of the main purposes of this study on e-learning is to achieve the following objectives:

Design of complex educational systems, involves multiple disciplines and hence a diverse assembly of engineers and facilities that are not necessarily placed at the same geographical location. Furthermore, there has been a clear interest in the industry in harmonizing technological expertise amongst various societies, which further facilitates outsourcing resources. Consequently, the notion of global virtual design teams, as a disseminated collection of people and resources that are integrated through geographical, cultural and functional borders, should be applied. A multifaceted curriculum aims at training students who can work at multinational corporations in teams composed of a wide range of expertise and technical. Therefore, the formation of interdisciplinary, inter-university engineering programs that has changed course from wishful thinking to serious planning, usually labeled as e-learning.

An e-learning solution for designing pedagogy must therefore bridge the gap between the physical and virtual worlds with a comprehensive framework based on modular components, which provides students with remote access to software and hardware resources, and establishes a virtual collaborative community. A configuration of e-learning is represented in Figure 1.

(a) To ascertain the distribution of quality approaches: who uses what?

(b) To investigate the use of quality approaches: how are they used?

(c) To identify possible factors for success, on which the development of quality may depend.

As a theoretical yardstick, the concept of quality competence was developed by analogy with that of media competence (Baacke, 1996). This assumes that quality development is a competence that must be possessed by those involved in the learning process – in e-learning, for example, by tutors, media designers, authors and of course learners – if successful quality development is to be made possible. This competence can be broken down into four dimensions:

(a) Knowledge of what opportunities are available for quality development;

(b) Ability to act and experience of using existing quality strategies;

(c) Ability to adapt and further develop, or to design original quality strategies;

(d) Critical judgment and analytical ability to enhance quality in one's own field of operation.

This study arose out of the need to establish the usage and state of the art of quality in e-learning. In this endeavor, quality competence acted as a guiding concept for the analysis of the prevailing situation. In other words, this study aims to analyze the quality competence of those involved in e-learning and to make recommendations for research and support measures.

Our investigation for the observation and analysis of the development of quality in e-learning, shows clearly that although there are already a wide range of strategies and proposals for quality development, many of those involved in e-learning as decision-makers at an institutional or policy level, as teachers applying e-learning at the operational everyday level, or as media designers developing e-learning, as well as many users, demonstrate too little quality competence to meet the 'quality' challenge. This study therefore investigates primarily what quality concepts there are in e-learning, which of these are regarded as successful and on what grounds, and what degree of quality competence users, decision-makers and learners demonstrate in dealing with the issue of quality.

As a result individuals typically possess the knowledge and skills appropriate to their original role, overlaid with a veneer of knowledge and skills gathered on an informal basis from colleagues within an e-learning development team. Finding answers to questions regarding quality in e-learning is one of the central challenges for theory and practice if e-learning is to become as important as traditional qualification measures in the future. The question arises how such a complex concept as quality, can be conceptualized systematically. Three different dimensions can be distinguished here: different meanings of quality, different quality perspectives and different levels of the educational process to which quality can apply (Figure 2).

Therefore, e-learning without quality considerations fails to provide perfect services for the users. Taking into account this significance, MUST decided to conduct an investigation on quality assessment in the e-learning center.

CASE DESCRIPTION

The MUST Quality e-learning Standards (MQeLs) are based on best practices and research in distributed learning and learning technologies, developed through an international consultation process, and sponsored and endorsed by a number of national and international organizations. Project participants stipulated that the e-learning quality standards meet the following criteria:

Figure 2. Multiple dimensions of the quality concept in e-learning

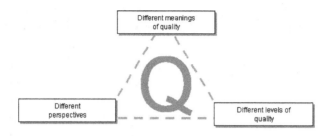

- Consumer oriented — developed with particular attention to return on investment in e-learning for learners;
- Consensus based — developed through consultation with a balance of provider and consumer groups;
- Comprehensive — inclusive of all elements of the learning system: outcomes and outputs, processes and practices, inputs and resources;
- Recommended only — using persuasion and market forces rather than legislation to ratchet up the quality of e-learning;
- Futuristic — describing a preferred future rather than the present circumstances for design and delivery; and
- Adaptable — best used for adult and post-secondary education and training, but adaptable to other levels of learning services. These are criteria that contribute to the unique nature of the OeQLs and the resulting quality assurance approach.

This work is an extension of the FuturEd research on Learn where quality (Barker, 1997, 1998), school effectiveness (ibid., 1998) and uses of Information and communication Technologies (ICT) in international education at Canada's postsecondary institutions (ibid., 2001, 2003), return on investment in e-learning (Barker, 2005) have been focussed. The FuturEd approach to e-learning quality — the same process of environmental scanning, drafting of inclusive and comprehensive

quality standards, consensus-based approval, and endorsement with subsequent consumers guide and quality assurance tools for informed choice — has been used in the context of national training standards (Barker, 1994), prior learning assessment standards (Barker, 1998, 2001), e-portfolio quality standards (Barker, 2004) and, most recently, learning objects (Barker, 2006).

Under FuturEd leadership, beginning in 1998 with funding from the Canadian federal government, e-learning experts in Canada began work on quality standards. To develop the consumer-based CanREGs, FuturEd undertook five steps. The first was to assemble an expert panel representing a balance of consumers and providers from seven national and international organizations, including Human Resources Development Canada (HRDC), SchoolNet (Industry Canada), and the Commonwealth of Learning. The second was an extensive literature search for both complete sets of guidelines and individual quality indicators for distance learning, education in general, and the use of learning technologies, resulting a background paper and draft standards for consultation purposes. The third step was a national consultation process, including workshops and an online workbook. The fourth step was refinement of the standards into the form of the Canadian Recommended E-learning Guidelines (CanREGs), based on consultation input, with experts from the field. The final step was the creation of a consumers guide to e-learning based on the CanREGs — providing potential purchasers with the questions to ask in order to identify quality e-learning and make informed choices. Comparing four different methods of e-learning quality assurance, Parker (2004) notes:

In Iran, the responsibility for providing education rests at the university level and not at the national level. Each university has its own quality assurance framework or approach to determining whether postsecondary programs are eligible for student funding or to receive public money. The degree to which a university might regulate or even provide subsidies to private or for-profit educational institutions varies widely. It is fitting, then, that the Iranian example of quality guidelines originates with a private corporation sponsored by community and government-funded agencies. It should be stated that the system has not been implemented yet. The system is proposed and being under control tests for diagnosing the possible defects.

Underlying Principles and Conceptual Basis

The project to create e-learning quality standards in MUST focused on the development of consumer-based quality guidelines that:

1. Described either minimum acceptability and/or excellence in the application of learning technologies;
2. Took the form of statements/principles of good practice or best practices, and included all elements of the learning system;
3. Were developed by MUST consumers to reflect Canadian values and concerns, but had potential applicability to the international environment;
4. Were created through a consensus-based process involving actual consumers;
5. Included a method of implementation that was neither cumbersome nor costly;
6. Incorporated the most current thinking on the effective use of learning technologies; and

7. Contributed to increasing the effectiveness and efficiency of learning technologies and MUST learning culture.

At that time of project inception, there were no commonly accepted standards of excellence in technology-based distance learning in MUST. There was, however, a great deal of useful advice in both literature and practice specific to quality assurance in education and training; applications of technology in education and training; quality assurance in Internet information sources and online practices in education and training; and excellence in distance education, distance learning, and distance delivery of education/training.

Quality Assurance in Education and Training

In the context of products and services such as education/training, quality had been defined as having the characteristics of being well thought out, prepared with care, and implemented with responsibility; having a firm direction but flexible enough to cope with contextual variation; and being positively responsive to comment and criticism (Lucent Technologies, 1999).

An example of the definition of a quality educational experience, arrived at through stakeholder consensus, included the following elements: the quality of learning materials, the availability of materials, support for students through well-trained staff, a well-managed system, monitoring, and feedback mechanisms to improve the system (Barker, 1994). For the MUST, quality education was seen as education that produces an independent learner.

The literature on quality assurance in education and training was vast, ranging over such topics as standards, national standards, quality assurance, accountability, effective schools, and so on. The focus had largely been on the provider's perspective; however, there were increasing demands from the public and from education/training consumers to be involved in describing and improving quality in learning systems.

Quality Assurance in the Uses of Educational Technologies

Quality in the use of educational technologies is viewed from many different perspectives: (1) what learning technologies are touted to achieve; (2) quality assurance in the appropriate uses of technologies; and (3) issues of quality and the Internet.

From the earliest uses of learning technologies, there have been claims or hopes about what educational technologies could achieve. For example, according to the BC Ministry of Education, Skills and Training (BC MEST, 1996), technology was used to assist with the attainment of such educational goals as individualization; increasing proficiency at accessing, evaluating, and communicating information; increasing quantity and quality of students' thinking and writing; improving students' ability to solve complex problems; nurturing artistic expression; increasing global awareness; creating opportunities for students to do meaningful work; providing access to high-level and high-interest courses; making students feel comfortable with tools of the information age; and increasing the productivity and efficiency of schools. Similarly, Frayer and West (1997) identified the following ways in which instructional technology should support learning: enabling active engagement in construction of knowledge; making available real-world situations; providing representations in multiple modalities; drilling students on basic concepts to reach mastery; facilitating collaborative activity among students; seeing interconnections among concepts through hypertext; learning to use the tools of scholarship; and simulating laboratory work. From yet another perspective, NCREL (North Central Regional Educational Laboratory) developed a "technology effectiveness framework" which theorized that the intersection of two continua — with learning on

one end of the axis and technology performance on the other — defines what a particular technology could achieve vis-à-vis student learning. One quality criterion, then, must relate to the use of appropriate technologies. These goals all contributed to a conceptualization of e-learning quality.

Technology has multiple uses in the context of education and learning, for example, information management (IT), learning management, and distance delivery. As well, technology has the capacity to deliver better forms of student assessment, that is, what the International Society for Technology in Education calls "authentic testing."

To ensure the best uses of technology, the Open University in the UK differentiated between different media according to ease of use, availability, access, questions, contacts, experts, opportunity to question experts, integration, status, and synergy. The categories for comparison used were learners' needs, usage, effectiveness, perceived value, and comparative value. For the University of California, the four key characteristics of effective software are presentability, accountability, customizability, and extensibility. A second type of quality criteria, then, is the appropriate use of technology.

As the Internet was increasingly used in distance delivery of education/training, both for information retrieval (distributed learning) and for online delivery of courses and programs (distance learning), there was a need for quality criteria for both Internet sources and use of the Internet. The criteria for evaluating Internet information range from the simplistic to the highly complex. At the simplistic end of the scale, according to the University of Citation, are Continuity, Censorship, Connectivity, Comparability, and Context. At the complex end of the scale, Wilkinson and others at the University of Georgia developed a list including 11 criteria and 125 indicators in Evaluating the Quality of Internet Information Sources: Consolidated Listing of Evaluation Criteria and Quality Indicators, including but not limited to: site access and usability (18 indicators), resource identification (13 indicators), author identification (9 indicators), authority of author (5 indicators), information structure and design (19 indicators), relevance and scope of content (6 indicators), validity of content (9 indicators), accuracy and balance of content (8 indicators), navigation within the document (12 indicators), quality of the links (13 indicators), and aesthetic and affective aspects (13 indicators). They concluded that the indicators of (1) information quality and (2) site quality were ranked in importance by experienced Internet users. Somewhere in the middle, the Internet Public Library has a selection policy for quality information sources, and resources that are selected / approved by the IPL receive the IPL Ready Reference Seal. In summation, it is a particular concern of educators that the sources they use on the Internet are reliable, accurate, authoritative, current, fair, adequate, and efficient. These were all factored into the understanding of quality e-learning.

Further considered were quality education practices on the Internet. Specific to education and training offered on the Internet, a variety of tools and standards were created. At the broadest level, the American Association for Higher Education produced a Bill of Rights and Responsibilities for the Electronic Community of Learners, which set out the rights and responsibilities of individuals together with the rights and responsibilities of educational institutions. Teachers considering web-based instruction were strongly encouraged to consider choice of pedagogy over choice of available technology, particularly when some research suggested that the use of technology to enable instruction conveys no significant difference in student achievement (Reeves, 1997).

As stated above, different classifications are presented for quality in e-learning. Here, we categorize the quality criteria and the corresponded sub-criteria. Some examples of detecting the parameters are associated with the sub-criteria. The configuration of this categorization is shown in Figure 3.

In the next sections we describe the solution process for the problem of quality in e-learning. Of course, quality is an elusive concept in analysis because of uncertainty. Therefore, the proposed mechanism considers the uncertainty to analyze the quality in e-learning.

CURRENT CHALLENGES FACING THE ORGANIZATION

The most important challenge was the consideration of uncertainty in the quality assessment of e-learning. Because of the uncertain nature of quality it was hard to control the parameters. The

Figure 3. Categorization of quality criteria, sub-criteria and detection examples

Outcomes and Outputs
Skills and knowledge acquired
Learning skills acquired
Credits and credentials awarded
Credits and credentials are:
Recognized by relevant professional bodies
Recognized by other education institutions
Of the same value as on-site delivery
Transferable within and between programs, institutions, and countries
Return on investment
Processes and Practices
Management of students
Delivery and management of learning
Approaches to learning
Appropriately used technologies
Communications
Build on learner's strengths
Inputs and Resources
Teaching/learning materials
Curriculum content
Intended learning outcomes
Intended learning outcomes are:
clearly stated
relevant
observable / demonstrable
measurable
achievable and realistic
appropriate to the degree
consistent with provider mandate
Product/service information
Appropriate learning technologies
Sound technical design
Personnel
Learning resources
Complete learning package
Comprehensive course package
Routine review and evaluation
Program plans and budget
Advertising and admissions information

remedy was considered through fuzzy approach. Fuzzy logic helped to control the quality factors via linguistic variables. Another challenge is the computation of the proposed mechanism. To solve this problem, a computer programming team is set up to prepare software for this approach.

SOLUTIONS AND RECOMMENDATIONS

Here, using the concept of quality in e-learning and applying fuzzy logic approach, we propose a comprehensive assessment model. Fuzzy logic is a useful decision aid tool in uncertainty which is thee nature of qualitative assessments. Initially, we categorize the aspects of quality in e-learning and then an uncertainty is considered in each category via fuzzy logic. After that a control mechanism is designed which helps diagnosing the defects and improving them by a feedback report to the real time learning management system.

Fuzzy Logic

Fuzzy Logic (FL) is a problem-solving control system methodology that lends itself to implementation in systems ranging from simple, small, embedded micro-controllers to large, networked, multi-channel PC or workstation-based data acquisition and control systems. It can be implemented in hardware, software, or a combination of both. FL provides a simple way to arrive at a definite conclusion based upon vague, ambiguous, imprecise, noisy, or missing input information. FL's approach to control problems mimics how a person would make decisions, only much faster.

FL incorporates a simple, rule-based IF X AND Y THEN Z approach to a solving control problem rather than attempting to model a system mathematically. The FL model is empirically-based, relying on an operator's experience rather than their technical understanding of the system.

FL requires some numerical parameters in order to operate such as what is considered significant error and significant rate-of-change-of-error, but exact values of these numbers are usually not critical unless very responsive performance is required in which case empirical tuning would determine them. For example, a simple temperature control system could use a single temperature feedback sensor whose data is subtracted from the command signal to compute "error" and then time-differentiated to yield the error slope or rate-of-change-of-error, hereafter called "error-dot". Error might have units of degs F and a small error considered to be 2F while a large error is 5F. The "error-dot" might then have units of degs/min with a small error-dot being 5F/min and a large one being 15F/min. These values don't have to be symmetrical and can be "tweaked" once the system is operating in order to optimize performance. Generally, FL is so forgiving that the system will probably work the first time without any tweaking.

FL works as follows:

1) Define the control objectives and criteria: What am I trying to control? What do I have to do to control the system? What kind of response do I need? What are the possible (probable) system failure modes?

2) Determine the input and output relationships and choose a minimum number of variables for input to the FL engine (typically error and rate-of-change-of-error).

3) Using the rule-based structure of FL, break the control problem down into a series of IF X AND Y THEN Z rules that define the desired system output response for given system input conditions. The number and complexity of rules depends on the number of input parameters that are to be processed and the number fuzzy variables associated with each parameter. If possible, use at least one variable and its time derivative. Although

it is possible to use a single, instantaneous error parameter without knowing its rate of change, this cripples the system's ability to minimize overshoot for a step inputs.

4) Create FL membership functions that define the meaning (values) of Input/Output terms used in the rules.

5) Create the necessary pre- and post-processing FL routines if implementing in S/W, otherwise program the rules into the FL H/W engine.

6) Test the system, evaluate the results, tune the rules and membership functions, and retest until satisfactory results are obtained.

In 1973, Professor Lotfi Zadeh proposed the concept of linguistic or "fuzzy" variables. Think of them as linguistic objects or words, rather than numbers. The sensor input is a noun, e.g. "temperature", "displacement", "velocity", "flow", "pressure", etc. Since error is just the difference, it can be thought of the same way. The fuzzy variables themselves are adjectives that modify the variable (e.g. "large positive" error, "small positive" error, "zero" error, "small negative" error, and "large negative" error). As a minimum, one could simply have "positive", "zero", and "negative" variables for each of the parameters. Additional ranges such as "very large" and "very small" could also be added to extend the responsiveness to exceptional or very nonlinear conditions, but aren't necessary in a basic system.

A fuzzy expert system is an expert system that uses a collection of fuzzy membership functions and rules, instead of Boolean logic, to reason about data. The rules in a fuzzy expert system are usually of a form similar to the following:

if x is low and y is high then z = medium

where x and y are input variables (names for know data values), z is an output variable (a name for a data value to be computed), low is a membership function (fuzzy subset) defined on x, high is a membership function defined on y, and medium is a membership function defined on z.

The antecedent (the rule's premise) describes to what degree the rule applies, while the conclusion (the rule's consequent) assigns a membership function to each of one or more output variables. Most tools for working with fuzzy expert systems allow more than one conclusion per rule. The set of rules in a fuzzy expert system is known as the rulebase or knowledge base.

The general inference process proceeds in three (or four) steps.

1. Under FUZZIFICATION, the membership functions defined on the input variables are applied to their actual values, to determine the degree of truth for each rule premise.

2. Under INFERENCE, the truth value for the premise of each rule is computed, and applied to the conclusion part of each rule. This results in one fuzzy subset to be assigned to each output variable for each rule. Usually only MIN or PRODUCT are used as inference rules. In MIN inferencing, the output membership function is clipped off at a height corresponding to the rule premise's computed degree of truth (fuzzy logic AND). In PRODUCT inferencing, the output membership function is scaled by the rule premise's computed degree of truth.

3. Under COMPOSITION, all of the fuzzy subsets assigned to each output variable are combined together to form a single fuzzy subset for each output variable. Again, usually MAX or SUM are used. In MAX composition, the combined output fuzzy subset is constructed by taking the point wise maximum over all of the fuzzy subsets assigned to variable by the inference rule (fuzzy logic OR). In SUM composition, the combined output fuzzy subset is constructed by taking the point wise sum over all of the fuzzy subsets assigned to the output variable by the inference rule.

4. Finally is the (optional) DEFUZZIFICATION, which is used when it is useful to convert the fuzzy output set to a crisp number. There are more defuzzification methods than you can shake a stick at (at least 30). Two of the more common techniques are the CENTROID and MAXIMUM methods. In the CENTROID method, the crisp value of the output variable is computed by finding the variable value of the center of gravity of the membership function for the fuzzy value. In the MAXIMUM method, one of the variable values at which the fuzzy subset has its maximum truth value is chosen as the crisp value for the output variable.

Determining the Rules

Initially, regarding to the parameters and their corresponded sub-criteria, some rules are defined. But before that, the linguistic variables should be clarified. Here, we apply the following linguistic variable for outcomes and outputs, process and practices, and inputs and resources:

```
Outcomes and outputs {weak, fair,
strong}; process and practices {weak,
fair, strong}; inputs and resources
{weak, fair, strong}.
```

The following rule is designed for analyzing the total quality of the e-learning system:

```
Rule₁: If outcomes and outputs =a, And
process and practices = g, And inputs and
resources = s, Then the Quality=U.
```

Note that the above rule can be expanded to twenty seven statuses (3*3*3), i.e. each of the main criteria of quality is accompanied by three types of linguistic variables. As we stated before, the above main criteria, which affect the quality directly, are corresponded with some sub-criteria. To imply this relationship we can configure the following hierarchy in Figure 4.

Figure 4. The effective criteria and their related sub-criteria

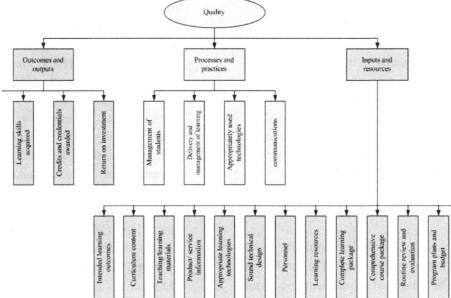

As shown in Figure 4, we can find three levels of hierarchy. The first level is the total quality, the second level consists of three direct effective parameters, and the third level presents twenty one sub-criteria that affect the quality indirectly. Furthermore, some of the depicted criteria are related to teachers and some to students. $Rule_1$ shows the direct parameters of quality. Now, we have to define the rules for indirect sub-criteria that affect the quality. Three sets of rules should be defined to analyze the criteria and their related sub-criteria. Therefore, the following linguistic variables and the related rules are defined:

```
Skills and knowledge acquired {Low, me-
dium, high}; learning skills acquired
{Low, medium, high}; credits and creden-
tials awarded {Low, medium, high}; return
on investment {Low, medium, high}.
```
Rule₂: If Skills and knowledge acquired = b, **And** Learning skills acquired = c , **And** Credits and credentials awarded = d , **And** Return on investment = e, **Then** the outcomes and outputs = a.

Note that the above rule can be expanded to eighty one statuses (3*3*3*3), i.e. each of the sub-criteria for the direct effective parameters of quality is accompanied by three types of linguistic variables.

```
Management of students {weak, fair,
strong}; Delivery and management of
learning {weak, fair, strong}; appro-
priately used technologies {weak, fair,
strong}; Communications {weak, fair,
strong}.
```
Rule₃: If Management of students = h, **And** Delivery and management of learning = i, **And** appropriately used technologies = j, **And** Communications = k, **Then** the process and practices = g.

Note that the above rule can be expanded to eighty one statuses (3*3*3*3), i.e. each of the

sub-criteria for the direct effective parameters of quality is accompanied by three types of linguistic variables.

```
Teaching/learning materials {bad, fair,
good}; Curriculum content {bad, fair,
good}; Intended learning outcomes {bad,
fair, good}; Product/service information
{bad, fair, good}; Appropriate learn-
ing technologies {bad, fair, good}; Sound
technical design {bad, fair, good};
Personnel {bad, fair, good}; Learning
resources {bad, fair, good}; Complete
learning package {bad, fair, good}; Com-
prehensive course package {bad, fair,
good}; Routine review and evaluation
{bad, fair, good}; Program plans and bud-
get {bad, fair, good}; Advertising and
admissions information {bad, fair, good}.
```
Rule₄: If Teaching/learning materials = l, **And** Curriculum content = m, **And** Intended learning outcomes = n, **And** Product/service information = o, **And** Appropriate learning technologies = p, **And** Sound technical design = q, **And** Personnel = r, **And** Learning resources = s, **And** Complete learning package = t, **And** Comprehensive course package = v, **And** Routine review and evaluation = w, **And** Program plans and budget = x, **And** Advertising and admissions information = y, **Then** the process and practices = g.

Note that the above rule can be expanded to 1594323 statuses (3*3*...*3 [thirteen times]), i.e. each of the sub-criteria for the direct effective parameters of quality is accompanied by three types of linguistic variables.

The total output of each of the above three group of rules will be a value for outcomes and outputs, process and practices, and inputs and resources, respectively. These values are inserted in the first rule and the total quality is gained. Next section gives the membership functions for each direct effective criteria and indirect sub-criteria.

Proposing the Membership Functions

Here, we show all the existed rules. The aim of the rules is to find the utility. The linguistic variables for quality are,

$$U = \begin{cases} \text{very low} & u \in [0,20] \\ \text{low} & u \in (20,40] \\ \text{medium} & u \in (40,60] \\ \text{high} & u \in (60,80] \\ \text{very high} & u \in (80,100] \end{cases}$$

where the quality of "very low" indicates that the numerical value of quality is zero to twenty and so on.

To gain the quality, we analyze three items of outcomes and outputs, process and practices, and inputs and resources and their sub-criteria. Each of the outcomes and outputs, process and practices, and inputs and resources is expressed by linguistic variables. The membership function for outcomes and outputs is,

$$\mu_{\text{outcomes and outputs}} = \begin{cases} \left[1 + \left(\frac{a-10}{3}\right)^{-2}\right]^{-1} & a \in [10,16] \to weak \\ \left[1 + \left(\frac{a-16}{3}\right)^{-2}\right]^{-1} & a \in (16,20] \to fair \\ \left[1 + \left(\frac{a-20}{3}\right)^{-2}\right]^{-1} & a \in (20,\infty] \to strong \end{cases}$$

where if the outcomes and outputs is seventeen, its related linguistic variable is fair and using the corresponded mathematical relation the numerical value of the membership function is applied.

The membership function for process and practices is:

$$\mu_{\text{process and practices}} = \begin{cases} 2.\left|\frac{g-12}{g-1}\right| & g \in [12,15] \to weak \\ 2.\left|\frac{g-15}{g-1}\right| & g \in (15,17] \to fair \\ 2.\left|\frac{g-17}{g-1}\right| & g \in (17,20] \to strong \end{cases}$$

where the process and practices of strong is for the category between seventeen and twenty. The membership function for inputs and resources is:

$$\mu_{\text{inputs and resources}} = \begin{cases} e^{\frac{s-0}{3}} & s \in [0,3] \to weak \\ e^{\frac{s-3}{3}} & s \in (3,6] \to fair \\ e^{\frac{s-6}{3}} & s \in (6,10] \to strong \end{cases}$$

where if the inputs and resources is low, regarding to an expert's decision, then the numerical value is from zero to three and the corresponded membership is computed.

After proposing the membership functions for the main effective criteria, the same process is repeated for sub-criteria. Each sub-criterion would have its own membership function. As stated before, each main criterion is associated with some sun-criteria. Therefore, the aggregation of the corresponded sub-criteria of a main criterion should be considered. Rules 2, 3, and 4 are proposed for this consideration. Using those rules we can include all of the aspects of a service provider to assess the quality of e-learning. The outputs of rules 2, 3, and 4 will be included in rule 1 and ensued to the linguistic variable for the quality of the system. To obtain the numerical value of quality we should defuzzify the variables.

For defuzification we use center of sum (COS) method as follows:

$$u^{\text{consqeuence}} = \frac{\int_{\upsilon} u.\sum_{n} \mu_{n.}(u)\,du}{\sum_{n} \mu_{n.}(u)\,du} \quad \Re = a,g,s.$$

The resulted u will be used as a control mechanism for the quality of the system. When this quality detection is achieved, then a feedback regarding to the status of the system should be considered. This feedback is given based on a real-time mechanism which will be described in the next section.

Real-Time Feedback Mechanism

To modify our proposed system of quality assessment we need to monitor the outputs and reform the required items included in the quality evaluations.

Typically we have got two kinds of student, local student and remote student. The local students are instructor of our knowledge expert bases system. The integrated e-learning environment model using real-time system is illustrated in Figure 5.

For the ability and performance of real time system to create real models, the real time system that can control our virtual environment in the best way and update it regularly, is used. Real time system should control the e-learning system during the execution of education from quality view point. The elements of the e-learning application that make it unique to a specific learning application are as follows:

1. User Interface (or web interface)
2. Knowledge Expert system
3. Real-time system (controller)

User Interface

The training environment helps a student to achieve the qualified theoretical and practical aspects of education, simultaneously. Frequently when the students try to use the learning system remotely, they confront some module like simulation learning, hypermedia learning, training and etc. In Figure 6 some elements of user interface are shown.

Our render model should apply practical and theoretical courses. Thereby, the student should have suitable understanding from the concept of this system to obtain quality assured contents and services from the service providers. The fundamental premise for training in this environment is: if the student can understand how the system operates from a theoretical point of view, he or she will better troubleshoot real life malfunctions or other unexpected behaviors in a more effective and efficient manner.

In a typical environment, a student considers system schematics which can be represented by simple block diagrams and/or detailed computer graphic drawings and images. The student can select and display schematics of specific systems

Figure 5. Integrated E-learning real-time system

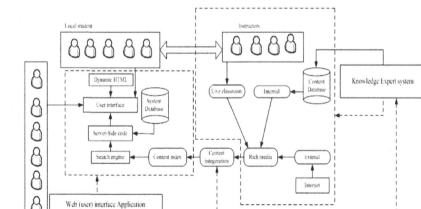

Figure 6. Elements of user interface

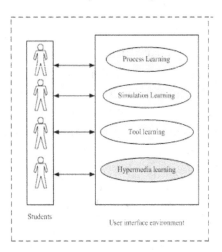

and subsystems along with a graphic display of diagnostic tools. Furthermore, they should pass the practical courses at their place via E-learning system because one of the important aspects of education is practical courses.

Knowledge Expert System

Expert system is a kind of information system which could execute the system like real expert person. For modeling expert system due to each condition that happen in real world like that in real system, we should do special react in front of each problem. The expert system can do this for us like real person (Teachers, university and etc). There are two kinds of expert systems: heuristic and model-based. The former which tries to mimic the reasoning of human expert, are usually implemented by sets of rules. In contrast, model-based expert systems are based on the explicit representation of cause-effect relations. Knowledge represented by knowledge expert systems which should be able to confront student training and their up growing problems. The knowledge expert system is the expert system that could decide and solve all problems of the students during their education under virtual environment (E-learning). For preparing knowledge expert system, information

from students and teachers in real life should be gathered. Our proposed knowledge expert system model is illustrated in Figure 7.

We use three parts (two Databases and one Inference engine) to configure our knowledge expert system which should be based on the student. Global Data Base consists of students and teachers information. Also the quality parameters of the students, their needs and their situations are gathered in the global database. After gathering the information from student and teacher using inference engine we analyze and investigate the teacher's explanation situation, database information and knowledge base rules and facts which are ensued from the effective criteria and their related sub-criteria have shown in Figure 3. By this model a suitable expert system that could provide the quality detection is prepared.

Real Time Process in the Proposed Knowledge Expert System

There are a number of characteristics that make real-time systems a powerful tool, considered as one of the most used techniques in modeling procedure. Firstly, its inherent ability to evaluate complex systems with a large number of variables and interactions for which there is no analytic solution. Secondly, real-time system can model the dynamic and stochastic aspects of systems, generating more precise results comparing with static and deterministic spreadsheet calculations. It is also considered as a tool to answer "What if" questions. In this case, real-time system could answer not only "What if" questions but also it answers "How to" questions, providing with the best set of input variables that optimize the performance of the system. Real-time systems can be classified into 3 categories regarding to the optimization of quantitative variables: the first category tends to use the "trial and error" method, varying the input variables in order to find which set gives the best performance. The second category tends to systematically vary the

Figure 7. Knowledge expert system

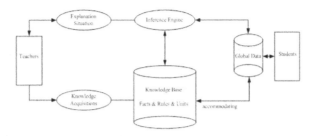

input variables, to see their effects on the output variables. The third category will apply an automated simulation optimization approach. In this study the concentration is on the first category.

One of the important elements of E-learning system is the real time assessment system, as their controller. The student quality condition might be changed within education periods. Our integrated system should support this concept. At the beginning, the students' performance is inferred via fuzzy logic and is deposited in the data base of the integrated system. Then, each variation in the quality of the learning process is detected by knowledge base system and reported to inference engine. Here, a feedback is given to global data to reform the rules and the procedure repeated regularly.

REFERENCES

Baacke, D. (1996). Gesamtkonzept Medienkompetenz [The concept of media literacy]. In agenda: Zeitschrift für Medien, Bildung, Kultur [Agenda: journal for media, education, culture], 19, 12-14.

Barker, K. C. (1994). *National training standards.* Ottawa, ON: Canadian Labour Force Development Board.

Barker, K. C. (1997). *Learnware quality background paper.* Vancouver, Canada: FuturEd for HRDC. Retrieved May 4, 2007, from http://www.futured.com/library_paper9710a.htm

Barker, K. C. (1998). *Achieving public policy goals with quality PLAR: Prior learning and assessment recognition.* Ottawa, ON: Canadian Labour Force Development Board. Retrieved December 4, 2006, from http://www.futured.com/pdf/PLAR%20quality%20and%20policy%20goals.pdf

Barker, K. C. (1999). *Linking the literature: School effectiveness and virtual schools.* Retrieved December 4, 2006, from http://www.futured.com/pdf/Virtual.pdf

Barker, K. C. (1999). Serving the learning needs of education consumers. *Education Canada, 38*(4), 25–27.

Barker, K. C. (1999, March). *Quality guidelines for technology-assisted distance education.* Retrieved December 4, 2006, from http://www.futured.com/pdf/distance.pdf

Barker, K. C. (2001). *The FuturEd PLA/PLAR quality audit.* Vancouver, Canada: FuturEd. Retrieved May 10, 2007, from http://www.futured.com/pdf/QualityAudit.pdf

Barker, K. C. (2001, February). *E-learning: Studying Canada's virtual secondary schools.* Kelowna, Canada: Society for Advancement of Excellence in Education.

Barker, K. C. (2001, October). *Information and communication technology in international education in Canada's public post-secondary education system: Literature review.* Canadian Bureau for International Education. Retrieved May 10, 2007, from http://www.cbie.ca/download/publications/Conf%20paper%20ICTs %20and%20IE%20final.pdf

Barker, K. C. (2002, February). *Consumer's guide to e-learning.* Vancouver, BC: FuturEd for the Canadian Association for Community Education and Office of Learning Technologies, HRDC. Retrieved December 4, 2006, from http://www.futured.com/pdf/ConGuide%20Eng%20CD.pdf

Barker, K. C. (2002, February). E-learning in three easy steps. *School Business Affairs, 68*(2), 4–8.

Barker, K. C. (2002, January). *Canadian recommended e-learning guidelines.* Vancouver, BC: FuturEd for Canadian Association for Community Education and Office of Learning Technologies, HRDC. Retrieved December 4, 2006, from http://www.futured.com/pdf/CanREGs%20Eng.pdf

Barker, K. C. (2003 November 4). E-learning in Canada: Who can you trust? *National Post Business.*

Barker, K. C. (2003, April). *Studying ICT use in international education: Comparing on-line and on-site delivery of international education.* Canadian Bureau for International Education. Retrieved May, 10, 2007 from http://www.cbie.ca/download/ict/Phase4final.pdf

Barker, K. C. (2003, July–September). Canadian e-learning guidelines protect consumers. *The Learning Citizen, 6*(13). Retrieved May 10, 2007, from http://www.learningcitizen.net/download/LCCN_Newsletter_N6.pdf

Barker, K. C. (2004, April). *Consumer's guide to ePortfolio products and services.* Vancouver, Canada: FuturEd. Retrieved December 4, 2006, from http://www.futured.com/documents/ePConsumersGuide.pdf

Barker, K. C. (2004, April). *ePortfolio quality standards.* Vancouver, BC: FuturEd. Retrieved December 4, 2006, from http://www.futured.com/pdf/ePortfolio%20Quality%20Discussion%20Paper.pdf

Barker, K. C. (2004, May). *Bridging program benchmarks, recommendations and evaluation framework.* FuturEd for the BC Ministry of Community, Aboriginal and Women's Issues. Retrieved April 28, 2007, from http://www.futured.com/documents/BridgingPrograms.pdf

Barker, K. C. (2005, November). *Return on investment in e-learning: Discussion and ROI tool.* Toronto, Canada: ABC CANADA Literacy Foundation. Retrieved December 4, 2006, from http://www.futured.com/documents/elearningandLiteracyROIGuide2005_000.pdf

Barker, K. C. (2006). Quality Standards for Consumer Protection . In Hope, A., & Guiton, P. (Eds.), *Strategies for sustainable open and distance learning.* London, New York: Routledge and Commonwealth of Learning.

Barker, K. C. (2006, September). *ePortfolio: A tool for quality assurance* [White Paper]. Vancouver, BC: FuturEd. Retrieved December 4, 2006, from http://www.futured.com/documents/ePortfolioforQuality Assurance_000.pdf

Barker, K. C. (2006, Spring). *Quality standards and quality assessment of learning objects.* Vancouver, Canada: FuturEd. Retrieved December 4, 2006, from http://www.futured.com/documents/LearningObjectsQualityStandardsandAssessment.pdf

Barker, K. C., et al. (1998). *Survey of perceptions and attitudes toward learnware quality in Canada*. Office of Learning Technologies. Retrieved December 4, 1998, from http://olt-bta.hrdc drhc. gc.ca/resources/Survey_e.pdf

BC MEST. (1996). *The status of technology in the education system: A literature review*. Community Learning Network of the BC Ministry of Education, Skills, and Training.

Candy, P. C., Crebert, G., & O'Leary, J. (1994). *Developing lifelong learners through undergraduate education*. Retrieved May 10, 2007, from http://www.dest.gov.au/sectors/training_skills / publications_resources/profiles/nbeet/hec/developing_lifelong_learners_through_undergraduate. htm

Frayer, D. A., & West, L. B. (1997). *Creating a new world of learning possibilities through instructional technology*. Retrieved May 10, 2007, from http://horizon.unc.edu/projects/monograph/ CD/Instructional_ Technology/Frayer.asp

GATE. (1996). *Notes from Transnational Education and the Quality Imperative*. Global Alliance for Transnational Education, Retrieved May 10, 2007, from http://www.adec.edu/international/ gate2.html

Parker, N. (2004). The quality dilemma in online education. In *Theory and practice of online learning*. Athabasca, Canada: Athabasca University Press. Retrieved December 4, 2006, from http:// cde.athabascau.ca/online_book/ch16.html

Reeves, T. C. (1997). *A model of the effective dimensions of interactive learning on the World Wide Web*. Retrieved May 10, 2007, from http://itech1. coe.uga.edu/Faculty/treeves/WebPaper.pdf

FURTHER READING

Bacsich, P. (2005). *Theory of benchmarking for e-learning: A top-level literature review*. Retrieved May 12, 2007, from http://www.cs.mdx.ac.uk/ news/Benchmark-theory.pdf

Call for Proposals: Preparatory and Innovative Actions elearning Action Plan (2001, June 9). *Official Journal of the European Communities*, C166/38.

CEN/ISSS/WS – LT Project Team Quality Assurance and Guidelines. *Version 1*. (2002, August 18). Retrieved from http://jtc1sc36.org/doc/36N0299. pdf

Chelimsky, E., & Shadish, W. R. (Eds.). (1997). *Evaluation for the 21st century: A handbook*. Thousand Oaks, CA: Sage Publications.

Collier, G., & Robson, R. (2002). *eLearning Interoperability Standards*. Sun MicroSystems White Paper. Retrieved from http://www.sun. com/

Connolly, M., Jones, N., & O'Shea, J. (2005). Quality assurance and e-learning: Reflections from the front line. *Quality in Higher Education*, *11*(1), 59–67. doi:10.1080/13538320500077660

Council Resolution of 13 July 2001 on e-Learning. (2001, July 20). Official Journal of the European Communities, C 204/3. Retrieved from http:// europa.eu.int/comm/education/programmes/ elearning/reso_en.pdf

Courtney, K. (2004). Developing and delivering a short distance learning certificate course in peace and reconciliation studies: A case study. In S. Banks, P. Goodyear, V. Hodgson, C. Jones, V. Lally, D. Mcconnell, & C. Steeples (Eds.), Networked Learning 2004. Lancaster: Lancaster University & University of Sheffield, 5–7 April 2004.

Cousin, G., Deepwell, F., Land, R., & Ponti, M. (2004). Theorising implementation: Variation and commonality in European approaches to e-learning. In S. Banks, P. Goodyear, V. Hodgson, C. Jones, V. Lally, D. McConnell, & C. Steeples, C. (Eds.), Proceedings of Networked Learning 2004. Lancaster, Lancaster University & University of Sheffield, 5–7 April 2004.

Davidson, A., & Orsini-Jones, M. (2002). Motivational factors in students' online learning . In Fallows, S., & Bhanot, R. (Eds.), *Educational development through information and communications technology* (pp. 73–85). London: Kogan Page.

Davies, W.J.K., Guilford Educational Services, & Caliber-net Consortium. (1998). *A guide for developers of Open and distance Learning.* Caliber-net Consortium.

Deepwell, F., & Beaty, L. (2005). Moving into uncertain terrain: Implementing online higher education . In Fallows, S., & Bhanot, R. (Eds.), *Quality issues in ICT-based higher education* (pp. 7–23). London: Routledge Falmer. doi:10.4324/9780203416198_chapter_2

Deepwell, F., & Syson, A. (1999). Online learning at Coventry University: You can lead a horse to water. *Educational Technology & Society, 2*(4), 122–124.

Ehlers, U., Goertz, L., Hildebrandt, B., & Pawlowski, J. M. (2004). Quality in e-learning: Use and dissemination of quality approaches in European e-learning. *European Centre for the Development of Vocational Training (Cedefop) Panorama series, 116.*

Embedding, L. T. I. *(ELTI) project.* (2003). Retrieved July 12, 2006, from http://www.jisc.ac.uk/index.cfm?name=project_elti

European University Association (EUA). (n.d.). *Survey on Master Degrees and Joint Degrees in Europe.* Retrieved from http://www.unige.ch/eua/En/Publications/Survey_Master_Joint_degrees.pdf

Fetterman, D. M. (2001). *Foundations of empowerment evaluation.* Thousand Oaks, CA: Sage Publications.

Hope, A. (2001). Quality Assurance. In Farrel, G. M. (Ed.),*The Changing faces of Virtual Education.* The Commonwealth of Learning. Retrieved from http://www.col.org/virtualed/

House, E. (2001). Responsive evaluation (and its influence on deliberative democratic evaluation) . In Greene, J., & Abma, T. (Eds.), *Responsive evaluation: New directions for evaluation.* San Francisco, CA: Jossey-Bass.

Institute for Higher Educational Policy. *Quality on Line.* (n.d.). Retrieved from http://www.ihep.com/Pubs/PDF/Quality.pdf

Kirkpatrick, D. L. (1998). *Evaluating training programs: The four levels* (2nd Ed.). San Francisco, CA: Berrett-Koehler Open and Distance Learning Quality Council. (n.d.). *Standards in Open and Distance Learning.* Retrieved from http://www.odlqc.org.uk/odlqc/standard.htm

Quality Assurance Agency. (1999) *Distance learning guidelines.* Retrieved July 12, 2006, from http://www.qaa.ac.uk/academicinfrastructure/codeofpractice/distancelearning/default.asp.

Quality Assurance Agency for Higher Education. (n.d.). *Guidelines on the Quality Assurance of Distance Learning.* Retrieved from http://www.qaa.ac.uk/public/dlg/dlg_textonly.htm

Quality Assurance Agency for Higher Education. (n.d.). *Guidelines on the Quality Assurance of Distance Learning.* Retrieved from http://www.qaa.ac.uk/aboutqaa/aboutQAA.htm

Review of Recommended Quality Assurance Standards for Distance Education. (1999, February). *Summary of Findings*. Retrieved from http://www.academic.com/academic_com/library/Distance_Ed.pdf

Rothman, J. (2003). Action evaluation. In G. Burgess & H. Burgess (Eds.), *Beyond Intractability*. Boulder, CO: Conflict Research Consortium, University of Colorado. Retrieved July 12, 2006, from http://www.beyondintractability.org/essay/action_evaluation/

Shadish, W. R., Cook, D., & Leviton, L. C. (1991). *Foundations of program evaluation: Theories of practice*. Newbury Park, CA: Sage.

Smith, M., & Deepwell, F. (2004). The impact of goal-setting on learner motivation. Paper presented at Learning and Teaching Conference 2004: Delivering Excellence, University of Hertfordshire, 29 June–1 July 2004.

Stake, R. (1967). The countenance of educational evaluation. *Teachers College Record, 68(7)*. Retrieved July 12, 2006, from http://www.ed.uiuc.edu/circe/Publications/Countenance.pdf

Stake, R. (2004). *Standards-based & responsive evaluation*. Thousand Oaks, CA: Sage.

Stake, R., & Schwandt, T. (2006). On discerning quality in evaluation. In I. F. Shaw, J. C. Greene, & M. M. Mark (Eds.), *Handbook of Evaluation*. London: Sage. Retrieved July 12, 2006, from http://www.ed.uiuc.edu/circe/Publications/Discerning_Qual_w_Schwandt.doc

Stronach, I., & MacLure, M. (1997). *Educational research undone: the postmodern embrace*. Maidenhead, UK: Open University Press.

Sturdy, A., & Grey, C. (2003). Beneath and beyond organisational change management: Exploring Alternatives. *Organization*, *10*(4), 651–662. doi:10.1177/13505084030104006

The European Higher Education Area. (1999). Joint Declaration of the European ministers of Education Convened in Bologna. Retrieved from http://www.esib.org/BPC/docs/Archives/CoP007_Bologna_Declaration.html

KEY TERMS AND DEFINITIONS

Assessment: One way of deciding about effectiveness of something.

E-Learning: A new method of distance learning implemented with web items.

Fuzzy Logic: An approach to present uncertainty in decision making.

Quality: A subjective criterion for evaluation.

Real-Time: A feedback based reaction to identify defects in a system.

Service Provider: A managerial system that prepare the substantial elements of a service.

Chapter 14

Learning without Boundaries:
Designing and Teaching an E-Learning Program in Horticulture and Environmental Science

Elena Verezub
Swinburne University of Technology, Australia

ABSTRACT

Technological innovations have transformed the boundaries of research priorities within the Vocational Education and Training (VET) sector. In line with research priorities set by NCVER, Swinburne University of Technology has made an ongoing commitment to the development of research that aims at improving the flexible delivery of program for students in the Training and Further Education (TAFE) sector. The present study showcases a research project conducted at Swinburne. The aim of the project was to design an e-learning program for students studying within the Department of Horticulture and Environmental Science, with an additional focus on improving students' reading comprehension of hypertexts in the subject-specific context. This case study also discusses social and educational, technological, economic as well as political/organizational issues the project had to deal with.

ORGANIZATION BACKGROUND

Swinburne University of Technology in Melbourne, Victoria, is a dual sector (Higher Education and Training and Further Education, i.e. TAFE) institution, well-known in Australia and overseas. Swinburne was established in the Melbourne's suburb of Hawthorn in 1908 and has earned its enviable reputation for the excellent quality in teaching and learning as well as constantly growing research.

The university was ranked the 4th best in Australia for its teaching and learning quality (Swinburne University of Technology, 2005b). Teaching and learning enhancement is one of the strategic priorities of the university. Student surveys conducted at Swinburne consistently demonstrate good results, and thus are indicators of quality educational outcomes (Young, 2008).

Swinburne University is one of the few universities in Australia that offers a range of programs and courses, from apprenticeships to PhDs. Swinburne has created a number of study pathways that allow

DOI: 10.4018/978-1-61520-751-0.ch014

students to move from TAFE to Higher Education, from TAFE based VCE courses into TAFE programs or from Higher Education to TAFE. The university is committed to providing students with great flexibility to complete their courses. They can choose different study options, including full-time, part-time or on-line. Swinburne was one of the first universities to develop and adopt Industry Based Learning (IBL), a program that places students directly in industry for vocational employment as an integral part of the course structure. Thus, the university maintains strong and important links with industry (Swinburne University of Technology, 2008). According to the University's Statement of Direction 2015 (Swinburne University of Technology, 2005a), 'Swinburne will be recognized for its flexible approaches to learning and teaching which will create an engaging, stimulating and modern environment in which students can learn in different ways and in different places to achieve their desired outcomes'.

According to the Vice-Chancellor of the University, Ian Young (2008), a sound Swinburne budget of 300M has been developed "…through a transparent and formula-driven revenue distribution process, strong student growth, growing commercial income and the achievement of significant efficiencies across administrative activities of the University."

SETTING THE STAGE

The rapid development of information and communication technology (ICT) has brought its changes to the education sector. In particular, the e-learning concept has been widely included in contemporary education, since it blurs the limitation of time, distance and space. In addition, it offers flexibility and convenience to both learners and educators by providing social and technological advantages. These changes also have implications for governments and their policies as well as education sectors which implement innovation programs to reflect changing needs and expectations.

The introduction of ICT has evolved and will continue to evolve, forcing people to keep up with these changes and the challenges that they bring. In the area of education, ICT has reshaped the meaning of "literacy", which is a complex concept that includes the ability to read and comprehend the various forms of conventional texts and internet-based texts or *hypertexts* (OECD, 2001).

The era of web literacy or technological revolution has not evolved without its critics and has been regarded by some as signaling the end of print-based materials and the skills associated with them. However Kellner (2002) has argued that this technological revolution brings the opportunity to reshape education to better serve democratic needs and to prepare citizens for a global multicultural world. Also Kellner (2002) stresses that the debate about the role of computers in education should be about how they are used in education not whether they are good or bad.

The use of ICT in learning and teaching will continue as new technological tools are made available for the purpose of education. Policies promote the development and use of these technological tools which are regarded as innovative and important in the area of education. By utilizing these tools people will develop skills needed for the workplace as well as life-long skills in general. Some ICTs such as the Internet, email and digital media are now used routinely in many schools across all sectors, primary, secondary and tertiary.

Since the early 1990s in the state of Victoria, Australia, it has been a government educational policy to introduce technology into the curriculum and equip students with computer knowledge (Snyder, 1997). The objectives of the Victorian government policy reflect a vision for the future that includes the use of IT in schools. For example, in tertiary institutions where independent learning is a feature of many courses, Web Course Tools

(WebCT) is a medium that allows such learning. In fact, it has become mandatory in many institutions to deliver a percentage of courses online.

Swinburne University staff have been encouraged to incorporate technology-assisted techniques (including WebCT) in both traditional classrooms and distance learning courses. For example, overall, in 2007 the University aimed at increasing the students' use and engagement in WebCT across all Departments by 25% (Strategic Development Group, 2007). Similar figures are given for 2008 and 2009.

Incorporating the national research priorities set by NCVER, Swinburne University of Technology has made an ongoing commitment to the development of research that focuses on enhancing the flexible delivery of Vocational Education and Training (VET) programs (Swinburne University of Technology, 2003). Recent national and international research conducted into adult literacy has been largely concerned with the effective reading and comprehension of conventional written texts (Block, Gambrell, & Pressley, 2002; Mastropieri & Scruggs, 1997; Munro, 1996; Pearson, 1985; Pressley, Brown, El-Dinary, & Afflerbach, 1995; Vaidya, 1999) although there has been some research into the use of e-based texts and on-line learning (Bissland & Cashion, 2002; Corio, 2003; Verezub, 2003; Verezub & Munro, 2002). However, little research has been done within the VET sector in relation to the effective reading and comprehension of *hypertexts*. Thus there is a current need for research that targets building e-based literacy for VET students.

The project "Building e-based literacy for VET students" was initiated by the author of this case study. The project was related to the Horticulture and Environmental Science course at Swinburne. A research proposal was successful and won funding from the Professional Development Unit. An interdepartmental project team of four people was established; it included, a project manager and a primary researcher (myself), two associate researchers and a web designer.

The first associate researcher, from the Access Department, was responsible for conducting a literature review and developing tasks as well as guidelines for assessment at the pre-test, post-test and training sessions. The second associate researcher, a content specialist from the Department of Horticulture and Environmental Science, was responsible for developing subject-related texts (in the area of Conservation Land and Management) and identifying a group of students for a pilot study. A primary role of the web designer was to design a web site for the program. My role as the project manager and primary researcher was to prepare an ethics application for approval to conduct this research. Also, I taught and evaluated the pilot program. Finally, I prepared a set of recommendations that have served as a base for the development of an e-learning program for students studying within the Department of Horticulture and Environmental Science.

It is important to notice that the development of the e-learning program itself was done after the completion of the major project and was funded by the Department of Horticulture and Environmental Science.

CASE DESCRIPTION

This study showcases a research based project "Building e-based literacy for VET students" that aimed at developing an interactive on-line program for students studying within the Department of Horticulture and Environmental Science at Swinburne. In turn, the purpose of this program was to teach subject-related content with an additional focus on improving students' comprehension skills when reading hypertexts. The program consisted of five sessions. Each session included instructions for reading hypertexts with the focus on: metacognitive strategies; three hypertexts with text and picture links; and assessment tasks.

In order to design the above mentioned program, research was conducted to investigate students' reading and learning bahaviour in the e-learning environment. Successful reading and understanding of hypertexs requires that students constantly monitor their reading process. While reading, they should be able to determine when comprehension fails and use appropriate strategies to repair it. Thus, in particular, the research investigated the influence of metacognitive reading strategies training and types of hyperlinks on overall comprehension as well as expressive and recognition comprehension of hypertexts with text, picture and audio links.

The four main issues related to the case are presented in Figure 1. They are: social and educational; technological; economical; and political and organisational issues. Each one is discussed in detail below.

Social and Educational Issues

One of the main challenges was to design an on-line program based on the research findings. There is no doubt that a research-based program would be the most effective and reliable. The project began with conducting a literature review, with the main focus on e-learning and teaching metacognitive reading comprehension strategies.

In designing a hypertext, it is very important to consider the learning outcomes expected as well as the nature of learners. Hypertext offers new forms of information access and provides students with a new type of interactive learning experience. However, a hypertext may also present a set of problems. One of these is the effective use of a hypertext system that puts too heavy cognitive demand on the users. Empirical findings show that some readers become lost in hyperspace because of their poor skills in using hypertext. Obviously, it is necessary to ensure that readers are able to navigate through hypertext in an efficient way.

It was found that hypertexts with linear structure are frequently used for reading and comprehending in the classroom. In such texts, information usually follows a planned sequence with links to other nodes and the whole structure of the sequence is provided by adherence to a main text. Texts with linear structure are simple in navigation. In this case students do not face the problem of being lost in hyperspace and they can easily concentrate on their learning task.

Another important issue in hypertext presentation is investigating the optimum conditions for presenting computer-displayed texts. It has

Figure 1. Project related issues

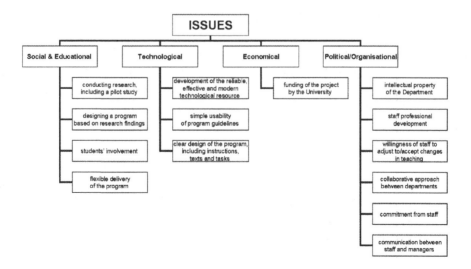

been found that the effective presentation of hypertexts incorporates some of the psychological principles obtained from investigations featuring a conventional written text. Due to the nature of hypertext, several differences such as methods of text justification, character density, and the optimum number of characters per line have also been found. Thus, in designing hypertexts, the right choice of visual presentation can increase comprehension.

Hyperlinks, and their wording, in particular, play an important role in hypertext browsing and navigation, as hyperlinks inform users what they will read in a new node, as well as attract their attention (Wei et al., 2005). Links could be text, picture, video, audio, or a combination of these. Text links could be used to introduce background information of a particular topic, or explain some new terminology. Pictures could be utilized to assist and strengthen learners' visualization. Video and audio links could be helpful in acquiring information from a multimedia prospective.

Research has shown that there exist internal and external factors that influence hypertext comprehension (Johnson-Glenberg, 2007; Murray & MacPherson, 2005; Snyder, 2002; Thurstun, 2004). The following factors can be related to the internal ones: familiarity with the navigation system; motivation; learners' characteristics; and purpose for reading. The external factors are content presentation, hypertext design and learning task. Integration of internal and external factors, and taking them into account while interacting with hypertext can provide an effective outcome in learning.

Some research has been done to investigate the comprehension processes for hypertexts (Corio, 2003; Thurstun, 2004). For example, Corio used the definition of comprehension set out by the 2002 RAND Reading Study Group Report (cited in Corio, 2003, p. 459) which defines reading comprehension as "the process of simultaneously extracting and constructing meaning through interaction and involvement with the written language". Thus, in order to fully capture the reading comprehension process of webtexts which have different characteristics, the definition of reading comprehension must be expanded. This definition should include the recognition that reading on the Internet requires new processes of thinking as well as metacognitive skills.

Metacognition is defined as the knowledge and understanding a reader has about their thinking process while reading (Gunning, 2003; Harvey & Goudvis, 2000). Metacognitive strategies are used by proficient readers when planning, monitoring and evaluating their learning of strategy performance. They include: activating relevant prior knowledge before, during, and after reading a text; determining the most important ideas in the text; asking questions of the text; creating visual and other sensory images from text during and after reading; drawing inferences from text; synthesizing what has been read; and using a variety of fix-up strategies to repair comprehension when it breaks down (Block et al., 2002).

Models for teaching metacognition in the conventional written text context that were developed, share some similarities. For example, the instructional model developed by Palinscar and Brown (1989), and the model of the direct explanation of comprehension strategies (DECS), by Duffy (2002), stress the importance of teaching strategies explicitly, by modeling and guiding students towards the independent use of the strategies. It is obvious that more research into metacognition and hypertext reading is needed (Johnson-Glenberg, 2007; Schneider, 2005). Thus, the present research aimed at addressing explicit teaching of metacognitive strategies in the hypertext context.

The next step was to develop fifteen hypertexts related to different aspects of River restoration management. These texts were spread over 5 sessions, three hypertexts in each one. The first session was a pre-test, followed by three training sessions and a post-test. This task of designing hypertexts was a collaborative work between a researcher from the Department of Horticulture and Environmental Science, who was a 'content specialist' and a web designer. Different types of links (text, picture or audio) were incorporated into these hypertexts. One of the challenges here was to find photos suitable for the content of hypertexts. Finally the pictures were found from different sources; they were provided by the web-designer, and other people who were not directly involved in the project as well as taken from public domain.

Furthermore, reading tasks were developed hypertexts which varied in length and the level of difficulty. The tasks were developed keeping in mind the skills the learners would be asked to practice. They included answering two types of questions, literal and inferential. Also, a cloze or sentence completion task was prepared. The tasks were edited and reworked according to feedback from the project manager. Guidelines for instructional and assessment procedures were also developed.

Table 1 shows the design of the training program, which was delivered to students over five 1.5 hour sessions on a weekly basis. To compare results of pre- and post-tests (sessions 1 and 5 respectively), the texts were of the same length and had the same number of links in each text. All hypertexts had the same readability level, as they were based on reading material used for this level of study.

Training was based on the principles of explicit or direct instructions (DECS) outlined by Duffy (2002). Each session was set up so the learners would receive instructions as to how to use a critical approach to reading hypertexts. In addition to training, reading and completing comprehension tasks, the learners were asked to complete self-evaluation reports during training sessions.

Once the ethics application to conduct research was approved by the University Ethics Committee, thirty-eight students who commenced their first year Diploma within the Department of Horticulture and Environmental Science (TAFE

Table 1. Design of a training e-learning program

Session	Text	Text length	Type of link	Number of links	Tasks	
					questions	cloze
1	1	500	Text	5	5	5 gaps
	2	500	Picture	5	5	5 gaps
	3	500	Audio	5	5	5 gaps
2	1	300	Text	3	2	2 gaps
	2	400	Text	4	3	3 gaps
	3	500	Text	5	4	5 gaps
3	1	300	Picture	3	2	2 gaps
	2	400	Picture	4	3	3 gaps
	3	500	Picture	5	4	5 gaps
4	1	300	Audio	3	2	2 gaps
	2	400	Audio	4	3	3 gaps
	3	500	Audio	5	4	5 gaps
5	1	500	Text	5	5	5 gaps
	2	500	Picture	5	5	5 gaps
	3	500	Audio	5	5	5 gaps

Division) were chosen to participate in the study. The sample was chosen on the basis that all the students signed the consent form and agreed to take part in the pilot study. Although all the students expressed their interest and willingness to participate, seven students withdrew from the project for various reasons and the final number of participants was 31 (14 male and 17 female students). We did not follow up with the students who decided not to participate as it was stated in the consent form that 'participation is voluntary and it is possible to withdraw from the project at any time'. Still, we consider that the retention rate was reasonably high, which is an indication that the students considered their participation in the study as a valuable and useful experience.

The full results of the pilot study were presented in the articles (Verezub, Grossi, Howard, & Watkins, 2008; Verezub & Wang, 2008). Highlights of these results are given below.

It was found that expressive comprehension of a hypertext, under the metacognitive training conditions, was enhanced (Figure 2). This demonstrated that while reading, students monitored their progress, discriminated between important

and less important ideas and asked questions of themselves, the reading and the authors. Also the students' improved recognition comprehension in the hypertext context (Figure 3) confirms the readers' ability to monitor their progress, search for connections, repair comprehension and synthesize information within and across hypertexts. This means that during the reading of hypertexts, students were able to keep the whole context in mind.

The findings represented in Figures 2 and 3 provide additional support for the use of instruction in metacognitive reading comprehension strategies in the hypertext environment. They also extend the findings of similar investigations conducted by numerous researchers on comprehension of a conventional written text while using these strategies (Gunning, 2003; Harvey & Goudvis, 2000; Pearson, Roehler, Dole, & Duffy, 1992).

The analysis of trends in comprehension after training (Table 2) shows that for both expressive and recognition comprehension, hypertext with text links dominated over hypertexts with picture and audio links. This is consistent with findings by Felder (1993) and Dunser and Jirasko (2005) that

Figure 2. Trends in expressive comprehension for hypertexts with different types of links

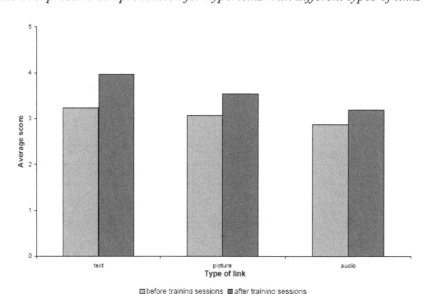

Figure 3. Trends in recognition comprehension for hypertexts with different types of links

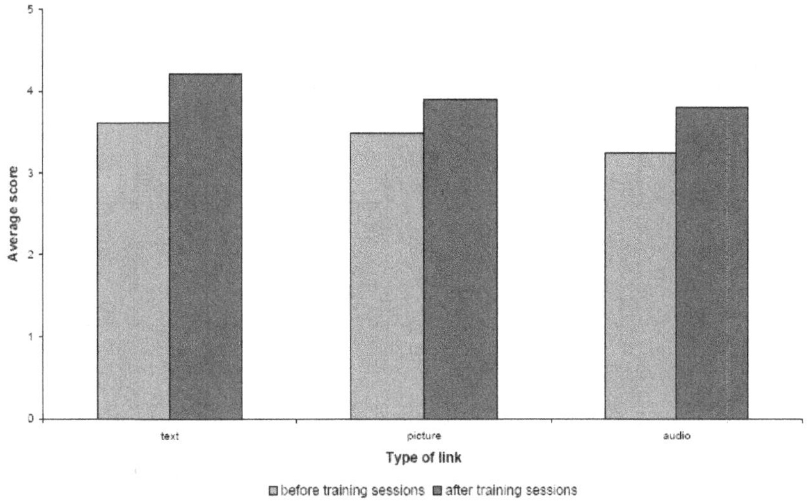

hypertext with text links represents "…a logical progression of small incremental steps" (Felder, 1993, p. 286), or sequential learning style. It is predicted that this learning style dominated in this cohort. Thus, by employing strategies appropriate for a particular situation, students monitored their comprehension when moving from one link to another.

In relation to hypertexts with picture and audio links, in expressive comprehension (Figure 4), students' understanding of hypertext with picture links was significantly better than of hypertext with audio links. Visualising from pictures allowed

Table 2. The influence of text, picture and audio hyperlinks on expressive and recognition comprehension after training sessions

	t
Session 5; text-1; task-1 - Session 5; text-2; task-1	2.493*
Session 5; text-1; task-1 - Session 5; text-3; task-1	4.246**
Session 5; text-2; task-1 - Session 5; text-3; task-1	2.079*
Session 5; text-1; task-2 - Session 5; text-2; task-2	2.061*
Session 5; text-1; task-2 - Session 5; text-3; task-2	2.693*
Session 5; text-2; task-2 - Session 5; text-3; task-2	0.692

** $p < 0.01$ level (2-tailed) * $p < 0.05$ level (2-tailed)

students to get more information than from spoken words (audio links). Students had to translate spoken words into mental images in order to understand them. It can be assumed that during the process of translating words into images, students tended to lose minor details presented in the sound links; however these details were required when answering the comprehension questions. Thus students were unable to present information in full details. This is in line with Felder's findings (1993) that sensory learners tend to obtain lower comprehension scores.

The results for recognition comprehension (Figure 5) did not demonstrate any significant difference between reading hypertext with picture links and hypertext with audio links. This can be explained by the fact that the cloze task, measuring recognition comprehension, involved recognition of key words (i.e. major details). In the case of hypertexts with picture and audio links, students showed the same level of ability to monitor their comprehension and identify as well as to remember the critical content of the text.

After the completion of the research and obtaining the results, our next step was to design an e-learning program which would be suitable for use in the classroom as well as for distance educa-

Figure 4. Trends in expressive comprehension after training sessions for hypertexts with different types of links

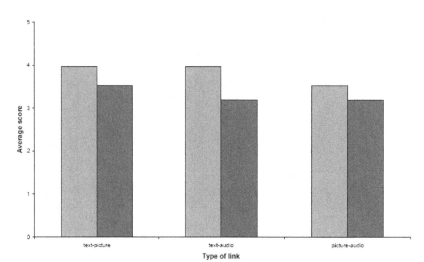

Figure 5. Trends in recognition comprehension after training sessions for hypertexts with different types of links

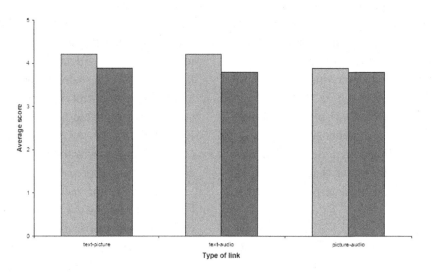

tion. The developed e-learning program included "Hints and Tips for Reading Hypertext" which provided an introduction to reading skills, and instructions how to comprehend hypertexts effectively. In the pilot study, the students were trained by the teacher who explained how to interact with hypertext and get the most of it. Students had an opportunity to ask questions and clarify informa-

tion immediately, in the classroom. In the case of the e-learning program, we aimed at writing these instructions in a simple and clear way in order to minimise the chance for students to misunderstand or misinterpret the information if they do not have immediate access to the teacher.

Hypertexts had to be modified taking into account the results of the pilot study. In some texts, where students experienced difficulties in comprehending audio links, we changed them to text links. Also, more pictures were added as we found that visualising helped students' effective comprehension. Thus, the e-learning program consisted of five sessions containing hypertexts with text, picture and audio links. Also, each hypertext was accompanied by a set of reading comprehension tasks that enabled assessment of students' understanding of material.

In summary, this study has addressed some social and educational issues. By conducting research which involved an interdepartmental team equipped with a broad range of skills as well as involving students from the Department of Horticulture and Environmental Science, we managed to design a flexible delivery resource which is suitable for classroom teaching, blended learning as well as distance education.

Technological Issues

As stated by McPherson and Nunes (2006), "...the success of e-learning cannot be attributed solely to the acquisition of leading edge technologies, but it far more dependent on what is done with these ICTs in terms of both design and delivery" (p. 553). In the case of our project, the challenges lay in developing a reliable, effective and modern technological resource which is clear in design and simple in usability.

A significant amount of research has investigated the optimal forms for screen images. On a computer display the main methods of text justification are the following:

a) fully-justified;
b) left-justified;
c) center-justified (Hooper & Hannafin, 1986).

Fully justified text features lines of equal length. The spacing between the words is varied and words are sometimes broken at line endings to achieve this goal. Left-justified (or right-ragged) text features varied line lengths, uniform spacing between words and complete, unbroken words at line endings. Center justified text is balanced with respect to an imaginary vertical line, which extends down the center of the page (Hartley, 1978).

Hartley (1982) found that reading left-justified texts causes less reading difficulties for both young and old readers. Inconsistent placement of the left margin serves only to confuse the reader unnecessarily. Also, left-justified text, for example, may be preferred to either center or fully justified text, although the benefits may be inconsequential with regard to actual learning.

Another aspect of hypertext displays is optimum line length. This aspect can be divided into two areas: character density and the number of characters per line (Hooper & Hannafin, 1986). With regard to a hypertext, 80 characters per line is often preferred to 40 characters per line (Duchnicky & Kolers, 1983; Hathaway, 1984; Heines, 1984). Duchnikey and Kolers (1983) determined that lines ranging from 2/3 to full screen width were read equally well, and were read significantly faster than text presented at 40 characters per line. Kolers, Duchnicky and Ferguson (1981) suggested that dense text presentation is often preferred since fewer fixations are required to read smaller characters.

In hypertext displays, it is also important to consider leading, that is, the insertion of space between lines. Reading efficiency has also been shown to improve when text presented on a computer display is double spaced as opposed to single spaced (Hathaway, 1984; Kolers et al., 1981; Kruk & Muter, 1984). With single spacing, more fixations per line are required. Each fixation contains fewer words and, consequently, reading time is increased. However, differences in reading speed were found to be of little practical importance (Kolers et al., 1981).

Instructional designers frequently use graphics and images to enhance the appearance of hypertexts. Visual-spatial perception has been a central issue in cognitive psychology for some time (Akins, 1996; Cornaldi & McDaniel, 1991; Johnson-Sheehan & Baehr, 2001; Kosslyn, 1994; Marks, 1990; Solso, 194).

Hypertexts require readers to think visually as they use them. The division between seeing and thinking has been discussed. With hypertexts, seeing and thinking need to be reunited for designers to understand how learners react visually and spatially. Visual thinking is the use of perception to navigate interactively, selectively, and even instinctively in three-dimensional spaces (Johnson-Sheehan & Baehr, 2001).

It is important to make decisions concerning the use and placement of images based on the needs of the learner. Often graphics and images that are employed solely for their aesthetic contributions can distract learners and reduce rather than enhance outcomes (Balajthy, 1990). The use of unnecessary elements in screen design extends to typography as well. The use of multiple colours, italics and various levels of headings does not appear to aid comprehension and readability and adds to the complexity of screen the design (Brooks, 1993).

Based on the above review, the characteristics for hypertext displays used in the present study were as follows: left-justified text; a character density of 80 characters per line; double spacing; proportionally spaced characters. In addition, each hypertext was accompanied with simple instructions as to how to navigate it depending on the types of links. Simple and clear design of the Home Page of the program (Figure 6) allowed students to avoid difficulties in accessing hypertexts, tasks and instructions.

Economic Issues

Within the economic issue which was identified, it is worth considering the point of funding the project. As mentioned earlier, the project included the research itself as well as the e-learning program development. In fact, one of the expected outcomes of the research was the professional development of the staff, and, in particular, training them how to conduct research. Thus, it was in line with the priorities set by the Swinburne TAFE Professional Development Unit. When the project was submitted to the Unit, it got a positive response and was funded.

However, at the end of the project, it was obvious that another source of funding was needed to develop the e-learning program itself. Another proposal was submitted to the Head of the Department of Horticulture Environmental Science. This proposal outlined the findings of the research; also a CD with the pilot e-learning program was attached. In the light of the results of this study it was proposed to develop an interactive on-line program for students studying within the Department of Horticulture and Environmental Science. This program aimed at teaching subject-related content with the additional focus on improving students' comprehension skills when reading hypertexts.

This initiative aligned the Departmental support with the University strategic directions. The Department aims at developing e-learning resources and teaching on-line. This, in turn, will allow the Department to target specific student population (e.g. students who work full time or live in the rural area) without investing additional resources in expanding Departmental facilities. It is believed that the attractiveness of this project also lay in bringing a reliable resource that could be utilised immediately and would not require much time as well as monetary investments to train teaching staff how to use it.

Thus, despite the fact that recently the issue of funding has been problematic, the issue can be solved if a project carries genuine benefits for the organisation.

Political and Organisational Issues

Political and organisational issues were part of the different stages of the project that have been

Figure 6. Home page of e-learning program. (© 2009, Swinburne University of Technology, Department of Horticulture and Environmental Science. Used with permission)

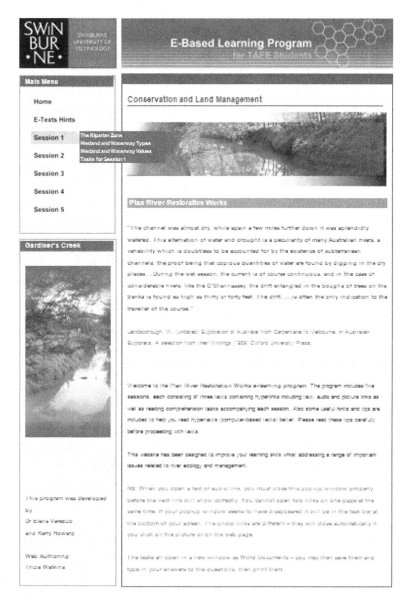

showcasing. Firstly, we had to take into account the policy on the issue of intellectual property. At present at the department, intellectual property of the materials developed in the hard copy format belongs to teachers as they take these materials with them when leaving the University. Thus, the departmental management was very keen on supporting this project as the development of online resources would allow shifting focus of the intellectual property from individual teacher to the Department.

Secondly, during the project, effective communication between staff and management played a critical role in the final success of the project. Frequent meetings as well as communication via phone and email were crucial to avoid misunderstanding, discuss any problems that arise along the way and obtain a second opinion on a controversial issue. As mentioned earlier, this project was the interdepartmental one involved collaboration between different people, such as the experts in education, subject matter specialist and a web designer. In the study of Lebow (1993), it was found that these people often speak different 'languages' and may not understand problems of the others. Thus, it was important for us to integrate and support the dialogue between these specialists. By means of regular communication, we managed to avoid these difficulties. We gave the staff every opportunity to be part in the decision making process and be actively involved in the project.

Furthermore, it was a great professional development opportunity for the staff involved. The staff learnt the principles of conducting different stages of research, working collaboratively as well as communicating effectively in the team. One the project researchers gave her feedback on her work which is provided below. It is worth mentioning that this staff member was so inspired by doing this research, she decided to do a PhD degree and is currently enrolled in the course in one of the Australian Universities.

"The opportunity to work on this project has been both valuable and satisfying from a professional point of view. It has given me much knowledge about a field I work within and given the chance to update on current thought on theoretical issues that relate to teaching practice. The experience I have gained whilst working with the team continues to reverberate in my teaching practice as well as other areas of my professional life. I would like to outline these as follows:

1. One of my tasks was to compile the Literature Review which was of particular interest to me. As a practicing teacher this provided me with the opportunity to read about current reading theories directly related to the modules I deliver.

It is particular relevant, if not mandatory, to be reading about new literacies at a time when the workplace is changing and our practice needs to be informed by these theories. One example of this the shifting definition of text and how technology shapes our working and learning environments.

2. Working in a team from different areas of TAFE as well as different areas of the Access Department was also invaluable. Often for pat-time teachers it is difficult to even know what other departments are doing.

3. Developing materials for testing and the moderation was extremely invaluable. Test design is a major part of ESL teaching area but to apply these skills to different areas provided added depth and insight.

4. As a direct result of this project I feel I have learnt research skills and become familiar with database searching. This has proven useful for other areas of my work.

5. For quite a while I have had an interest in Visual literacy and participation in this project has led me to follow up on other areas. Firstly the preparation of reading/listening materials for an interactive website for low proficiency ESL learners (in progress together with Multimedia Students). Secondly, it has led to an interest and work in resource development for WebCT delivery across ESL modules as part of my role of ILC co-ordinator. Lastly, his has also led further research in the visual literacy area and to the preparation of a workshop to be given at Valbec Conference on May 4th titled 'Using film-as-text in the ESL classroom.'"

In addition, staff members' exceptional commitment and time management skills were demonstrated throughout the project. Although at some stages more time was required to accomplish the task, none of the deadline was missed. The project was completed according to the timeline. Finally, we hope that the project team members' enthusiasm and willingness to accept changes brought by online delivery will be transferred to the departmental staff who will be involved in teaching this program.

CURRENT CHALLENGES FACING THE ORGANIZATION

Nowadays, every organization is facing many different challenges. The most common challenges for TAFE Divisions are:

- people and their skills; and
- availability of funds to conduct research activities.

In order to develop a portfolio of services and products (e.g. online learning resources) spread over many areas, the TAFE Division must encourage and support teachers to obtain higher level qualifications in Vocational Education and Training (VET) Practice. Achieving the goal outlined above, the highly focused and motivated staff are required. As it was outlined in Swinburne in 2015 document, it could be achieved by introducing a 'reward system for individuals and teams that relates directly to the profitability of their commercial activity' (Young, 2008).

Availability of funds is another challenge for TAFE Divisions. There are not so many external organizations that can support TAFE research activities. However in order to develop learning and teaching resources that determine the best mode, style and pathway for each student, research activities are required. The best people to do these tasks are people who are currently working in TAFE environments, or TAFE teachers. However, without proper funding and broader opportunities it will be hard to accomplish this task.

SOLUTIONS AND RECOMMENDATIONS

Funding is a major issue for any research project. However nowadays it is easier to get funds for projects that can deliver a 'product' that can be implemented or sold immediately after completion of the project. It means the benefits from the investment are obvious and can be guaranteed in a very near future.

Furthermore, designing subject-related e-learning materials proved to be effective. In the development of customized materials, it is possible to take into account a number of issues, such as hypertext design issues, especially if the development is in the area of education. Also, materials designed for a particular cohort, can cater different learning styles and, thus, incorporate hyperlinks which are the most suitable for the group.

Finally, staff professional development was a worthwhile investment. By supporting staff in their professional development activities, the university got teachers who are now capable to conduct research, do a web design, and prepare subject-related e-learning materials. There is no doubt that these staff members will transfer the skills gained during their participation in the project, into classroom teaching and preparation of learning resources. This, in turn, will increase the effectiveness of teaching and learning in the organisation.

From showcasing the work on the project "Building E-literacy for VET students", a number of possible avenues of recommendation for future work can be outlined. A first avenue is to further develop research based interactive online resources taking into account students' individual learning styles. Here, a predication could be made that online learning would depend on students' learning styles and the better learning outcomes would occur if online materials were tailored to the preferred learning styles. Also, before designing e-learning materials containing hypertexts, it can be important to find out the types of links preferred by a particular cohort as this can increase the level of comprehension of hypertexts. The main principle in designing online programs should be moving from the online environment which best serves logical and passive learners to a more interactive, with different types of links, personalised environment.

A second avenue is to verify experimentally whether reading strategies can be taught and be effective for comprehending hypertexts with hierarchical and referential structures. These investigations would first require running a training program, designed for teaching reading comprehension strategies as well as encouraging familiarity with hypertext interaction using different structures. Assisting learners to become familiar with these forms of hypertext could prevent difficulties in their navigation, since hypertext forms with hierarchical structure gives readers more freedom in choosing paths to information. Hypertext that contains referential links and a relatively unstructured learning environment where readers are free to move between nodes through referential links could be more accessible with training in use. In addition, more training on teaching strategies for hypertexts with hierarchical and referential structures than for hypertexts with linear structure is required. After students have been trained, a series of tests may be employed to establish the possibilities of reading strategies use for hypertexts with different structures.

A third avenue is to continue the development of online materials which are subject or course related. From the economic point of view, it is much cheaper to use materials that have already been developed. However they will not be necessarily tailored to the specific course taught. Despite the fact that it is cost effective, it may not be the most effective from the teaching point as well as the learning outcome. This study has proved that it is worth investing money into this kind of research based projects which have not only theoretical but also great practical benefits for teaching and learning.

REFERENCES

Akins, K. (1996). *Perception*. New York: Oxford University Press.

Balajthy, E. (1990). Hypertext, hypermedia and metacognition. Research and instructional implications for disabled readers. *Journal of Reading . Writing and Learning Disabilities*, *6*(2), 183–202.

Bissland, J., & Cashion, J. (2002). *Pedagogically Sound On-line Education - How to make this a reality for your organisation*. Paper presented at the 2nd World Congress of Colleges and Polytechnics, Melbourne.

Block, C. C., Gambrell, B. L., & Pressley, M. (2002). *Improving Comprehension Instruction: rethinking research, theory and classroom practice*. Jossey-Bass.

Brooks, R. (1993). Principles for effective hypermedia design. *Technical Communication*, *40*(3), 422–428.

Corio, J. (2003). Exploring Literacy on the Internet. Reading comprehension on the Internet: Expanding our understanding of reading comprehension to encompass new literacies. *The Reading Teacher*, *56*(5), 458–464.

Cornaldi, C., & McDaniel, M. (1991). *Imagery and cognition*. New York: Springer.

Duchnicky, R. L., & Kolers, P. A. (1983). Readability of text scrolled on visual display terminals as a function of window size. *Human Factors*, *25*(6), 683–692.

Duffy, G. (2002). The case for direct explanation of strategies . In Block, C. C., & Pressley, M. (Eds.), *Comprehension instruction: Research-based best practices* (pp. 28–41). New York: Guilford.

Dunser, A., & Jirasko, M. (2005). Interaction of Hypertext Forms and Global versus Sequential Learning Styles. *Journal of Educational Computing Research*, *32*(1), 79–91. doi:10.2190/1J25-LWQF-PQ3W-LABM

Felder, R. M. (1993). Reaching the second tier: Learning and Teaching Styles in College Science Education. *Journal of College Science Teaching*, *23*(5), 286–290.

Gunning, T. G. (2003). *Building Literacy in the Content Areas*. London: Oxford University Press.

Hartley, J. (1978). *Designing instructional text*. New York: Nichols Publishing Company.

Hartley, J. (1982). Designing instructional text . In Jonassen, D. H. (Ed.), *The technology of text: Principles for structuring, designing and displaying text*. Englewood Cliffs, NJ: Educational Technology Publications Inc.

Harvey, S., & Goudvis, A. (2000). *Strategies that Work: Teaching Comprehension to Enhance Understanding*. Stenhouse Publishers.

Hathaway, M. D. (1984). Variables of computer screen design and how hey affect learning. *Journal of Educational Technology*, *24*(1), 7–11.

Heines, J. M. (1984). *Screen design strategies for computer assisted instruction*. Bedford, MA: Digital Press.

Hooper, S., & Hannafin, M. (1986). Variables affecting the legibility of computer generated text. *Journal of Instructional Development*, *9*(5), 22–28. doi:10.1007/BF02908315

Johnson-Glenberg, M. C. (2007). Web-based reading comprehension instruction: Three studies of 3D-readers . In McNamara, D. (Ed.), *Reading comprehension strategies: Theories, interventions and education in the electronic age* (pp. 154–169). London: Routledge.

Johnson-Sheehan, R., & Baehr, C. (2001). Visual-spatial thinking in hypertexts. *Technical Communication*, *48*(1), 22–30.

Kellner, D. (2002). Technological Revolution, Multiple Literacies, and the Restructuring of Education . In Snyder, I. (Ed.), *Silicon Literacies: Communication, Innovation and Education in the Electronic Age* (pp. 154–169). London: Routledge.

Kolers, P. A., Duchnicky, R. L., & Ferguson, D. C. (1981). Eye movement measurement of readability of C.R.T. displays. *Human Factors*, *23*(5), 517–527.

Kosslyn, S. (1994). *Image and brain. The resolution of the imagery debate*. Cambridge, MA: MIT Press.

Kruk, R. S., & Muter, P. (1984). Reading of continuous text on video screens. *Human Factors*, *26*(3), 339–345.

Lebow, D. (1993). Constructivist values for instructional systems design: five principles toward a new mindset. *Educational Technology Research and Development*, *41*(3), 4–16. doi:10.1007/BF02297354

Marks, D. (1990). The relationship between imagery, body and mind . In Hampson, D., Marks, D., & Richardson, J. (Eds.), *Imagery: Current developments* (pp. 1–38). London: Routledge.

Mastropieri, M. A., & Scruggs, T. E. (1997). Best Practice in Promoting Reading Comprehension in Students with Learning Disabilities. *Remedial and Special Education*, *18*, 197–213. doi:10.1177/074193259701800402

McPherson, M., & Nunes, M. B. (2006). Organisational issues for e-learning: Critical success factors as identified by HE practitioners. *International Journal of Educational Management*, *20*(7), 542–558. doi:10.1108/09513540610704645

Munro, J. (1996). *Teaching Reading Strategies*. Melbourne: Hawthorn.

Murray, D., & MacPherson, P. (2005). *Navigating to read - reading to navigate*. Sydney, Australia: Sydney AMEP Research Centre.

OECD. (2001). *Literacy skills for the knowledge society*. Retrieved from http://www.oecd.org

Palincsar, A., Sullivan, A., & Brown, A. L. (1989). Instruction for Self-Regulated Reading . In Resnick, B. L., & Klopfer, L. E. (Eds.), *Toward the thinking Curriculum: Current Cognitive Research* (pp. 19–39). Alexandria, VA: ASCD.

Pearson, P. (1985). Changing the Face of Reading Comprehension Instruction. *The Reading Teacher*, *38*, 724–738.

Pearson, P., Roehler, L. R., Dole, J. A., & Duffy, G. (1992). Developing Expertise in Reading Comprehension . In Samuels, S. J., & Farstrup, A. E. (Eds.), *What Research Has to say About Reading Instruction* (2nd ed., pp. 145–199). Newark, DE: International Reading Association.

Pressley, M., Brown, R., El-Dinary, P. D., & Afflerbach, P. (1995). The Comprehension Instruction that Students Need: Instructions Fostering Constructively Responsive Reading. *Learning Disabilities Research & Practice*, *10*, 215–224.

Schneider, R. (2005). Hypertect narrative and the reader: A view from cognitive theory. *European Journal of English Studies*, *9*(2), 197–208. doi:10.1080/13825570500172067

Snyder, I. (1997). *Page to Screen: taking literacy into the electronic media*. Sydney, Australia: Allen & Unwin.

Snyder, I. (2002). *Silicon Literacies: Communication, Innovation and Education in the Electronic Age*. London: Routledge.

Solso, R. (194). *Cognition and the visual arts*. Cambridge, MA: MIT Press.

Strategic Development Group. (2007). *2007-2009 TAFE Division Plan: Swinburne University of Technology*.

Swinburne University of Technology. (2003). *Swinburne TAFE Division Research Strategy 2003-2005*. Melbourne: Author.

Swinburne University of Technology. (2005a). *Statement of Direction 2015: Building a sustainable future. Retrieved from* http://www.tafe. swinburne.edu.au/sdg/planning/statement_direction.htm.

Swinburne University of Technology. *(2005b)*. Swinburne ranked fourth in the nation for learning and teaching quality. Retrieved from http://www.swinburne.edu.au/corporate/marketing/mediacentre/core/vc_releases_article. php?releaseid=569.

Swinburne University of Technology. (2008). *Profile of Swinburne*. Retrieved from http://www. swinburne.edu.au/profile.htm

Thurstun, J. (2004). Teaching and learning the reading of homepages. *Prospect*, *19*(2), 56–80.

Vaidya, S. R. (1999). Metacognitive Learning Strategies for Students with Learning Disabilities. *Education*, *120*, 186–189.

Verezub, E. (2003). The Effect of the Teaching Conditions on Reading Comprehension of a Conventional Written Text versus Hypertext for Grade 6 Students. Collection of papers of National Technical University 'Kharkov Polytechnical Institute', 217-223.

Verezub, E., Grossi, V., Howard, K., & Watkins, P. (2008). Building E-based literacy for vocational education and training students. *Australasian Journal of Educational Technology*, *24*(3), 326–338.

Verezub, E., & Munro, J. (2002). Teaching and Learning with a Hypertext versus a Conventional Written Text. Collection of papers of National Technical University 'Kharkov Polytechnical Institute', 329-333.

Verezub, E., & Wang, H. (2008). *The role of metacognitive reading strategies instructions and various types of links in comprehending hypertexts.* Paper presented at the Hello! Where are you in the landscape of educational technology? Melbourne.

Wei, C. Y., Evans, M. B., Eliot, M., Barrick, J., Maust, B., & Spyridakis, J. H. (2005). Influencing web-browsing behavior with intriguing hyperlink wording. *Journal of Information Science, 31*(5), 433–445. doi:10.1177/0165551505055703

Young, I. (2008). *Swinburne in 2015.* Retrieved from http://www.swinburne.edu.au/chance/vc/documents/opinionpieces/Swinburne2015.pdf

ADDITIONAL READING

Arthur, L., Beecher, B., Elliott, R., & Newman, L. (2006a, 3 - 6 December). *E-learning: Do our students want it and do we care?* Paper presented at the The 23rd Annual Conference of the Australian Society for Computers in Learning in Tertiary Education, Sydney.

Arthur, L., Beecher, B., Elliott, R., & Newman, L. (2006b, 3 - 6 December 2006). *E-learning: Do our students want it or do we care?* Paper presented at The 23rd Annual Conference of the Australasian Society for Computers in Learning in Tertiary Education, Sydney.

Davies, J., & Graff, M. (2005). Performance in e-learning: online participation and student grades. *British Journal of Educational Technology, 36*(4), 657–663. doi:10.1111/j.1467-8535.2005.00542.x

Garrison, D. R., & Anderson, T. (2003). *E-learning in the 21st century: A framework for research and practice.* London: Routledge Falmer.

Holmes, B., & Gardner, J. (2006). *E-Learning: Concepts and Practice.* London: SAGE Publications.

Hrastinski, S. (2008). What is online learner participation? A literature review. *Computers & Education, 51*, 1755–1765. doi:10.1016/j.compedu.2008.05.005

Marques, C. G., Niovo, J., & Verissimo, M. (2007). e-QUAL: e-Learning with Quality. Proposal of an evaluation model on the quality of e-learning courses. In A. Mendes, M. Percira & R. Costa (Eds.), Computers and Education: Towards Educational Change and Innovation (pp. 83 - 90). Dordrecht: Springer.

McPherson, M. A., & Nunes, B. (2006a, 3 May). *Flying High or Crash Landing? Technological Critical Success Factors for e-Learning.* Paper presented at the The First Conference on Supported Online Learning for Students Using Technology for Information and Communication in Their Education (SOLSTICE), Lancashire.

McPherson, M. A., & Nunes, B. (2006b). Organisational issues for e-learning: Critical success factors as identified by HE practitioners. *International Journal of Educational Management, 20*(7), 542–558. doi:10.1108/09513540610704645

McPherson, M. A., & Nunes, B. (2007a, 25 - 29 June). *Kindling a Passion for Acquiring New Knowledge: Critical Success Factors for Creating Appropriate Curricula for e-Learning.* Paper presented at the ED-MEDIA 2007: World Conference on Educational Multimedia, Hypermedia and Telecommunications, Vancouver, Canada.

McPherson, M. A., & Nunes, B. (2007b, 27 - 20 September). *Negotiating the Path from Curriculum Design to E-Learning Course Delivery: A Study of Critical Success Factors for Instructional System Design.* Paper presented at the 2nd European Conference on Technology Enhanced Learning: Creating New Learning Experience on a Global Scale, Crete, Greece.

McPherson, M. A., & Nunes, B. (2008). Critical issues for e-learning delivery: what may seem obvious is not always put into practice. *Journal of Computer Assisted Learning, 24,* 433–445. doi:10.1111/j.1365-2729.2008.00281.x

Rosenberg, M. J. (2001). *E-Learning: Strategies for Delivering Knowledge in the Digital Age.* New York: McGraw-Hill.

Rovai, A. (2002). Building sense of community at a distance. *International Review of Research in Open and Distance Learning, 3*(1), 1–16.

Shank, P. (2008). Thinking Critically to Move e-Learning Forward . In Carliner, S., & Shank, P. (Eds.), *E-Learning Handbook: Past Promises, Present Challenges* (pp. 15–25). Hoboken, NJ: Pfeiffer.

Stufflebeam, D. L. (1983). The CIPP Model for Program Evaluation . In Madaus, G. F., Scriven, M., & Stufflebeam, D. L. (Eds.), *Evaluation Models: Viewpoints on educational and human services evaluation* (pp. 117–141). Boston: Kluwer-Nijhoff Publishing.

Vonderwell, S., & Zachariah, S. (2005). Factors that influence participation in online learning. *Journal of Research on Technology in Education, 38*(2), 213–230.

KEY TERMS AND DEFINITIONS

Explicit Instructions: Explicit instructions are the type of direct instructions given to students.

Hypertext: Hypertext is a semantic structure of nodes of information linked either linearly, or hierarchically, or referentially.

Linearly Structured Hypertext: Linearly structured hypertext is a hypertext that follows a planned sequence with links to other sites and nodes.

Metacognitive Strategies: Metacognitive strategies are reading strategies used by proficient readers when planning, monitoring and evaluating learning of strategy performance.

Reading Comprehension: Reading comprehension is the process of constructing the writer's intended meaning of a text during or after reading it, using readers' existing knowledge.

Chapter 15
Technology Enhanced Learning in China

Victor C. X. Wang
California State University, Long Beach, USA

ABSTRACT

This case shall reveal technology enhanced learning in China in light of technology enhanced learning in the United States of America. As China has depended on radio and TV to deliver its educational programs to the masses, web technologies have not been used like its counterparts in North America (e.g., the United States of America). As a result of this dependence upon radio and TV, unique issues and challenges have emerged in the Chinese educational settings. Although this chapter focuses on one case related to a typical university of foreign languages in northern China, this case can be considered as a generic one as the issues and challenges of this case are similar to those as revealed in all other universities across China's educational settings.

ORGANIZATION BACKGROUND

As soon as Chinese communists came to power in 1949, China began to model after the Russian educational model (Wang, 2004-2005) in terms all levels of education including its distance education. The main characteristics of China's education—national, scientific, and popular—according to Kaplan, Sobin and Andors (1979), derived from a major essay by Mao Tse-tung published in January 1940, called "On New Democracy" (p. 217). It is worth noting

that Mao followed the Soviet's leadership even in directing the future of China's education. Towards this end, the future course was set as follows:

The culture and education of the People's Republic of China are new democratic, that is, national, scientific, and popular. The main tasks for raising the cultural level of the people are: training of personnel for national construction work; liquidating of feudal, comprador, fascist ideology; and developing of the ideology of serving the people. (Kaplan, Sobin, & Andors, 1979, p. 217)

DOI: 10.4018/978-1-61520-751-0.ch015

This future course or national policy has affected the establishment of various kinds of universities and colleges in China. At the very beginning, a few universities of foreign languages were set up in China's major cities such as Beijing, Shanghai and Tianjin. These universities were built in order for China's youths to learn from advanced science and technology from especially industrialized nations such as the United States. At the same time, China's leaders at the time were so afraid of the West's so-called "democratic individualism" which was considered a key threat to the Chinese people and one that had to be rooted out through education (Wang, 2008, p. 68). Between 1949 and even 1975, education in China had to strike a forthrightly nationalistic policy (specifically with respect to China's enemies), emphasizing not only the inherent attributes of the country, its people, and its leaders, but also China's commitment to revolution and its Marxist-Leninist ideals, especially the Soviet's ideals as paraphrased in Mao's essays. To ensure that China could follow the Soviet's ideals, political study was thus placed at the focal point of curriculum development for all levels of schooling, including distance education with technology.

As China was tasked to educate and train people to hold aloft the red banner of Marxist-Leninist ideals and Mao-Tse-tung thought for its seemingly national construction, its limited universities and colleges could not provide an open door policy to all students who wished to receive a college education. Prior to its infamous Great Cultural Revolution launched by Mao in 1966, more universities and colleges were established.

One of the eight universities of foreign languages was set up in Northern China. For the sake of this case study, I would like to call it XX University of foreign languages in Northern China. XX University was established in 1964 under the leadership of the late premier, Zhou enlai who passed away in 1976. The very first departments of this university were the department of Russian, department of Japanese and department of English. As the Russian educational model was modeled after at the time, the department of Russian became one of the key departments at the XX University from the very beginning. Although the university has a physical campus in a major city in China, its students, faculty and staff members were sent to "learn from the peasants" in the countryside. Students were engaged in heavy farm work in order to learn to appreciate physical labor. To the outsiders from China, this was considered a movement towards alleviating China's unemployment for urban youths. But the leaders at the time would not admit this. XX University was first sponsored by the central government in Beijing and later the central Beijing government (Ministry of Education) delegated its authority to a provincial ministry of education. The university has been under the jurisdiction of that provincial ministry of education for years. In other words, it can be considered a state funded university in Western terms.

In its present form, the XX University seems to be comprehensive as Curriculum encompasses English, Russian, French, Korean, German, Spanish, Arabic, Italian, Chinese, Chinese Literature, Teaching Chinese as a Second language, Art Design, Tourism Management, International Economics & Trade, Computer Science & Technology, Information Management and Information Systems, Computer Software Engineering, Journalism and Music Studies. Still compared with a large comprehensive university by the standards in the United States, XX University can be considered a small liberal arts college although the university is tasked to educate and train over 10,000 full time and part time students. Noteworthy is the fact that its adult and continuing school is rather like a university as the school has thousands of learners from inside the province and outside the province. The school has its own president and vice presidents and other administrative leaders.

As its curriculum indicates the XX University engages in producing scholars/teachers who will serve primarily as foreign language workers who can work as officials, translators, interpreters in Chinese embassies in foreign countries, teachers of foreign languages in all levels of schools, business professionals in all types of foreign trade companies, joint ventures, and the like. While the University is funded through state dollars, all its faculty and staff including administrators are under paid compared with their Western counterparts. In order to increase their salaries, the University makes a lot of money from collecting tuition fees from those so-called special students or distance learning students via technology. Its management structure is similar to the management structure in other countries except that their Ministry of Education places a party secretary through all levels of management. The most powerful party of secretary is tasked to ensure the implementation of any party lines from the central government. The party secretaries at the department levels respond to the most powerful party secretary.

Prior to the 1980s, the most powerful party secretary had more power than a university president. Now, all university presidents seem to focus more on administrative work, including allocating money to different schools or departments. Naturally, it is obvious that party secretaries seem to focus more on political study. To some extent, their power has been lessened. Although any university would argue that decisions regarding educational policies are made collectively with wide consultation with other leaders and faculty at all levels, in actuality, most decisions are made by a few most powerful individuals based on their own perceptions. Regardless who makes the decisions, their decisions cannot deviate from the absolute leadership of the Chinese communist party with its headquarters in Beijing. The leadership of the Chinese communist party in Beijing prescribes overall directions and educational policies for all universities located in other provinces and regions throughout China. This is what we call centralization versus decentralization in Western terms.

In the West, especially in the United States, education is characterized by decentralization,

which means different universities make their own policies. The federal government does not closely scrutinize universities' educational activities because this task has been given to different accreditation agencies. For thirty years, China's economic growth has been at around 10% (GDP) (Goodman, 2006). It goes without saying that XX University together with other universities have substantially contributed to this remarkable economic growth. By sending qualified foreign language workers to the country's workforce, the university's unique contributions have been recognized both at the national and international levels. In terms of promoting and marketing China's "soft-power", China has launched its initiative to set up Confucius Institutes worldwide. In response to this call, XX University has set up this type of institutes to promote Chinese culture in countries such as Russia, South Korea, Japan and North America including the United States. To get an overall view, the following chart (See Figure 1) illustrates this university's management structure which is the norm for all universities in China.

SETTING THE STAGE

Prior to the advent of Web Technologies, XX University depended on Radio, TV and correspondence education to deliver its educational programs especially to working adults who cannot come to their face to face meetings on their physical campus. Towards this end, a night school was established. Those high school students, including working adults, are required to take some entrance exams to be admitted in this night school. The exams are administered at different times other than the three days designated for the entrance exams for universities. Even though XX University is titled a university of foreign languages, its curriculum includes Chinese language and English/American literature, Marxist-Leninist philosophy, economics, and CCP history; mathematics; foreign

Figure 1. Organization Chart of XX University

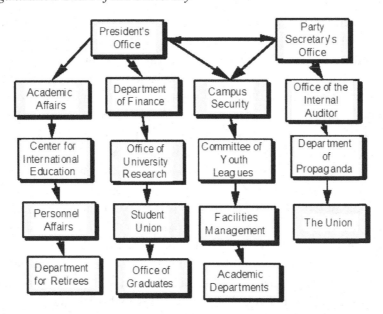

languages (most commonly English, followed by Russian and other Western languages); geography; history and physical culture. Art and music are often integrated into extracurricular activities. In other universities, physics and chemistry are often grouped together as "common knowledge of industry and agriculture.

In 1978, China held its national science conference. The meeting's outline report indicated that China was 15-20 years behind advanced world levels, a gap that it planned to cut in half by 1985. One of the goals of this conference was to popularize science and technology among the masses by means of a huge educational effort involving film, radio, television, journals, correspondence, evening courses, science competitions and exhibitions. XX University seized this opportunity and began to offer its educational programs through radio, television, correspondence education and evening classes to students and working adults. Its management philosophy was to generate enough funds to offer salary increases for its low paid faculty, staff and administrators. Additionally, the money generated by distance education has been used to fund instruction and research related projects.

As Web technologies were widely adopted in the developed countries in the early 1990s, only the elite in China began to use emails for communication. The leading universities such as Beijing and Qinghua Universities began to use emails and other web related technologies. Beijing University was also engaged in developing certain software for instructional/research and also business purposes. XX University's faculty may have involved in creating email accounts by using Yahoo or Hotmail, but the university has never created its own email account ending with edu. It was not until the early 2000s the university created its own email system for its faculty, staffers and administrators. However, most people in this university prefer free email accounts such as accounts from Google. The management philosophy prior to initiation of the Web-Technologies at XX University was no different from that in all other universities all across China. Even to this day, XX University has the same philosophy, that is, to reach a large number of students in the least possible time (Wang & Redhead, 2008, p. 101). The philosophy is the so-called Russian teaching philosophy popularized in 1876 in North America by Victor Della Voss (Wang,

2008). China's universities have never deviated from this teaching philosophy as China has the largest number of college students given the fact that its population has exceeded 1.5 billion. This is the estimated number, not its official reported number. With such a large number of students, China found the Russian teaching philosophy "helpful and effective" by reaching students via Radio and Television.

To date, XX University has been competitive by sending its faculty to teach English, or Japanese in the Beijing or Liaoning (provincial) radio stations and their teaching has reached thousands of learners who are not enrolled in their degree programs at the university. Although distance education learners in China are mostly adult learners, China's faculty are never familiar with the Western style of helping adult learners learn. According to the Western andragogy (as defined by Knowles (1975, 1984, 1986) as the art and science of helping adults learn), we cannot teach another individual directly; we have to facilitate their learning. Teachers/or adult educators talk with adult learners instead of talking to them. Teachers teach little by linking students to learning resources especially with We-Technologies. However, the Chinese faculty are used to one teaching approach, which is lecture. They lecture heavily even through Radio and Television. They believe in one philosophy, that is, to teach is to teach books and educate students (Paine, 1992; Wang, 2007, p. 115). Therefore, they must be excellent performers in front of their students. Their performance is judged by how eloquently they can talk before their students. They like to be considered authority figures by their students. Their role as teachers is something between a god and a parent. Those students who talk back to their teachers are considered as students with no manners. Truly, Chinese teachers strive to be sages on the stage. Western teaching methods such as discussion, simulation are less explored or used. With the advent of Web-Technologies in the early 2000s in China, Chinese universities including

XX University have been very cautious in using these technologies to reach their students. One primary reason is that Chinese people have been highly skeptical about the use of technology. In other words, they don't have a great deal of faith in online teaching or learning. Any student returning from overseas who has obtained the degrees from online universities abroad is frowned upon. When it comes to finding employment in China, these students are considered graduates with second hand degrees. Another primary reason is that Chinese government supervises all of the Internet activities (Wang, 2006, p. 46).

Teachers do not seem to have absolute freedom to teach whatever they wish to teach via technologies. Is there any Internet education other than Radio, TV or correspondence education in China? Have Web-Technologies such as the wide use of WebCT and Blackboard programs in North America reached China at all? Knowles (1975) predicted that education in the 21st century would be delivered electronically and his prediction came true (Wang, 2005). Has his prediction affected China's largest number of adult learners? The answer is definitely a yes, but only on a small scale. To this day, there have been four major networks in China and they were established by returning Chinese graduates from American universities. They are China Network, the China Golden Bridge Network, the China Education and Research Network, and the China Science and Technology Network (Tang, 2000). These networks do shoulder the responsibility of providing educational programs to approximately 10 million students at all educational levels (Mau, 2003). According to Yang (2005), some colleges and universities have used a campus network to carry out online education. However, online education has not been pursued actively. Compared with the large number of Chinese students, 10 million is such a small number to say the least. Also for any university in North America, at least one third of their courses are delivered via WebCT or Blackboard. Teaching courses via Web-Technologies has become more and more popular especially during times of economic recession when brutal budget cuts have been the norm in order to save money.

Another primary reason why online education cannot be popularized is that Chinese universities do not have as many computer labs as their Western counterparts. Students in rural areas are without computers, making online education impossible. Most university libraries are not open especially after 9:00PM at night to students. According to Yang (2005, p. 18), "online education is still immature and limited in number." The same thing can be said about XX University in Northern China. Online education virtually does not exist. Students choose to access Voice of America, British Broad Cast on their own. These agencies sponsor some educational programs, but they are not closely related to Chinese students' prescribed curriculum. However, they do serve to enhance their learning experience.

The major players in XX University are of course their university president, vice presidents and party secretaries at all levels. Faculty are hardly involved in any decision making process. There may be some committees regarding faculty governance, but they are unlike Western committees; these people just obey any decisions or policies implemented by the school's administrators or party secretaries. It must be pointed out that XX University leaders may not even know how to use Web-Technologies as their office secretaries handle email communications on their behalf and none of these leaders has been educated, in using WebCT or Blackboard. Some of them may have received a foreign education, but they did so when Web 2.0 technologies were not even popular at that time. Money should not be an issue for XX University as the University's enrollment has been on the increase.

The more China remains open to the outside world, the more foreign language workers Chinese society will need. China has been determined to remain open for centuries to come. China's remaining open to the outside world says a lot about XX University's skyrocketing enrollment. Even though more and more students from northern China request to receive an education from XX University, the leaders in this University have failed to accommodate their learning needs as they are reluctant to use Web-Technologies to reach those potential learners. With money invested in foreign travels for its leaders, in promoting its soft-power such as establishing more Confucius institutes abroad, virtually no money has been spent on developing Web-Technologies for XX University students. Although those returning from abroad make recommendations regarding the use of technology for teaching and learning, these recommendations have been largely ignored. No further discussions have been pursued.

CASE DESCRIPTION

The author of this case study (Victor C. X. Wang) graduated from XX University with a bachelor's degree and was asked to teach for this university for 8 years prior to coming to work and study in the United States. In furthering his studies in the United States, he obtained an additional graduate level degree in educational technology in order to enhance his teaching and learning for online students. As a result, he pioneered online teaching and learning for his current department where he has been a full time faculty. Recently he developed hybrid classes for his students in California in the United States. Those students who are closer to campus are required to come to his face to face meetings; those who cannot make it to campus because of distance are allowed to take his classes entirely online. Although he was well educated, he found little use of Chinese teacher-centered, information-based and test-driven instructional approaches (Wang & Kreysa, 2006, p. 1) in the Western teaching and learning context, especially for online education. Instead, his classes via Blackboard are characterized by syllabus-based projects, learning activities, and teaching tools that are designed to create collaborative learning environments and relevant experience for students. In addition, his teaching via technology is driven by the Western problem-based learning models that differ from lecture-based and is usually predicted on a great deal of self-directed learning and collaboration (Wang & Kreysa, 2006). These Western teaching approaches are in striking contrast with Chinese teaching methods, which focus heavily on lecture. It has been the author's dream and desire to help XX University with the use of prevalent Web-Technologies to reach more learners for China's universities and even the current university he works for in the United States. It has been his hope to create a win-win situation for both Chinese universities and American universities.

As his current university began to market and promote its graduate programs to leading universities in China, Western Europe and the Middle East countries in early 2004, the author served as an MC, explaining the university's programs in both English and Chinese. All these activities were delivered via Web-Technologies. Although interest in teaching and learning was aroused among Chinese students, little interest was shown on the part of Chinese university's administrators. One delegation composed of university presidents, party secretary and faculty told the author in person, "If we can do this to reach a large number of learners via Radio and Television, why bother to spend millions of dollars on developing Western technology to reach them?" "If our students can take our online courses with only 600 RMB per course, why ask them to pay $600 for American universities' course per course?" The then exchange rate between Chinese currency and U.S. dollars was $1 equaled 8.30 Chinese RMB. In a nutshell, Chinese universities' administrators have no desire to explore the teaching and learning tools that WebCT or Blackboard can offer. Although a small number of leading universities in China rely on technology to educate and train their students, online education has been provided actually by universities from the United States, UK, Australia,

New Zealand or Canada. Chinese students take advantage of technologies from Western universities if they fail to get visas to go to these countries to study or if they do not have the financial means to travel to these countries to study.

In 2008, the author of this case study approached XX University's middle level administrators again with the hope that the university would invest financial resources in technology, especially WebCT or Blackboard. The author proposed to take American students via a study abroad program to XX University's campus to demonstrate teaching and learning via technology. XX University showed little interest in this new proposal. Therefore, the proposed teaching activity was cancelled. Without completely giving up hope, the author contacted yet another university administrator at XX University. This administrator showed some interest and promised to come to visit the author's campus between late February and early March, 2009 when most Chinese universities have their winter vacations. The author of this chapter may eventually persuade XX University to adopt technology for its teaching and learning in China. However, the following technology concerns may explain the strong resistance towards adopting technology for Chinese students.

Technology Concerns

Since Radio and Television and correspondence education have successfully reached China's millions of learners, Chinese universities' administrators including administrators from XX University are reluctant to invest any financial resources in exploring the use of Western Web-Technologies. It was the late Chinese leader Deng Xiaoping who launched what we now call an anti-Western spiritual pollution campaign as early as in 1983. As a result, various Chinese leaders including XX University leaders still believe that the West's so-called "democratic individualism" is a key threat to the Chinese students and one that has to be rooted out through face to face education. If Western theories or concepts have eroded Chinese students' belief in looking up to their instructors/ leaders as authority figures, XX University's leaders do not wish this erosion to happen. In addition, spending millions of dollars on Web 2.0 technologies will dilute their money used for their international travel and salary increase as discussed earlier in this chapter. Teaching and learning via technology is simply not their priority. Without mastering technology themselves, they are afraid to lose any control of their students because XX University leaders do not want to delegate any power to followers including students. Their teaching philosophies do not match those that should be used when using technology to teach and learn. Lack of personal computers on the part of students is another excuse why XX University would not pursue the use of technology in their teaching and learning. Using Web-Technologies would involve hiring computer professionals to work for this university. Again, this is not their priority at this point. Those who are most qualified must be those who have returned from abroad after years of graduate studies. However, it is these people who may make XX University's leaders feel threatened, let alone hire them to implement technology in teaching and learning.

Technology Components

XX University does have a small team of technicians or technologists. While technicians graduate from two year colleges, technologists graduate from four year universities. These technicians or technologists engage primarily in rudimentary technology, such as maintaining their satellite dishes to receive foreign languages programs, maintaining their Websites in Chinese and providing basic computer training classes. Seminars on educational statistics using statistical soft-wares are never heard of on XX University campus. Seminars on how to teach well via WebCT or Blackboard are still a rarity. They may have

advanced computers, but their these technicians or technologists are not engaged in advancing teaching and learning via Web-technologies. Whenever XX University needs new software, they may purchase one from Beijing University as Beijing University takes the lead in developing new software. XX University, like most other universities in China, does not have the capacity to develop its own software for teaching and learning. Because of such a situation, grading or taking exams online is not possible at XX University. As a result, a large of number of trees is still being cut to fulfill China's educational goals and objectives. In most universities in Japan, computers are changed every three years. This is not the case with XX University and other universities in China. Although most universities have adopted broad band for their internet connection, because of limited numbers of computers, this has not made students' life a lot easier. Not every book at the XX University library has been catalogued by computers or linked to World Cat, a search engine to show how many universities libraries have catalogued books or articles.

Management and Organizational Concerns

Its management has been pretty much top-down, which means technologists or technicians have to report to the university presidents and party secretaries at XX University. These technologists or technicians have to act on any directives or instructions coming from top level officials at the university. Their tasks have been pretty much prescribed and they are not encouraged to go beyond their prescribed activities. With limited resources, these technicians or technologists find it hard to be innovative in developing technology for the sake of teaching and learning. The rigid management has taken away their incentives to be innovative. XX University can be considered a typical static organization that is first of all rigid (Knowles, 1978). In this university, much energy is given to maintaining permanent departments, committees. Respect is given to tradition, constitution, and by laws. This university is hierarchical. In other words, they adhere to a chain of command. Employees' roles are defined rather narrowly. Both organizational leaders and employees focus on tasks (Hersey & Blanchard, 1969). The organizational atmosphere is impersonal, cold, formal, reserved and suspicious with personnel managed through coercive power. Employees, especially technicians or technologists are cautious and low risk-taking. They tend to avoid errors. It is not an open system (McGregor, 1960). Instead, XX University features closed systems regarding sharing resources and there is little tolerance for ambiguity. In XX University, there is high participation at top level, but low participation at bottom echelons. Employees are reserved and do not work wholeheartedly for organizational goals. There is a clear distinction between policy-making and policy-execution. It is worth noting that decisions are made by legal mechanisms and that any decision is considered final. While natural flow of communication is restricted, it is one-way or only downward. Feelings are rather repressed or hidden.

As shown in the organizational chart (Figure 1), it is unclear whether XX University has a technology enhanced learning center. Or this technology center is managed by Facilities Management or Department of Finance? Another feature of this organizational chart reveals the fact that the Party Secretary's Office seems to have a considerable amount of power over other departments in the organization. The chief function of this office is to make certain that Party Lines are carried out to the letter.

CURRENT CHALLENGES FACING THE ORGANIZATION

The project that the author has started to implement is still in its early stages or infancy. As a result of XX University's management philosophy, various challenges and problems have emerged at different levels. These challenges and problems will prevent this project of implementing teaching and learning via Western WebCT or Blackboard from its fruition for the large number of Chinese students. While China's XX University has so far missed using cutting edge technology to reach its learners, the adverse effect can be devastating. Technology provides multiple accesses to knowledge and knowledge management. Technology reinforces the concept that it will facilitate learning and eventually make learners self-directed in learning. It is obvious that self-directed learners can maximize learning themselves. Without the wide adoption of cutting edge technologies (Web 2.0), XX University's students will lag behind in terms of mastering knowledge to serve their own country in the four areas of agriculture, industry, military and science and technology.

Without the use of Web-Technologies, Chinese teaching is limited. Radio or television can only offer synchronous learning and no interaction between instructors and students can be expected as instructors and students are separated. Web-Technologies can connect instructors with students via other enhancing software such as Elluminate.com. Students can ask questions and talk to not only their instructors, but also their fellow students. The asynchronous nature of online education can not be underestimated. Web-Technologies make learning occur 24/7, which means learning occurs anywhere any time. The convenience and flexibility that Web-Technologies can offer cannot occur with teaching via Radio or Television.

One of the serious challenges facing XX University is its philosophy. If its leaders have prejudice against using technology to reach students, technicians or technologists won't get financial support to develop online classes for their students. If the Chinese government still supervises teaching and learning activities on the Internet, faculty is afraid to teach there in cyberspace. If leaders have never learned to use technology themselves, they are reluctant to try out any novel learning experience with technology. XX University's leaders and faculty like all other leaders and faculty in China enjoy being considered as authority figures before their students. And they like to serve as role models. If role models don't know how to use technology, there is no way they can demonstrate the use of technology before their students. Also note worthy is the fact that XX University is just another static organization characterized with rigidity and inflexibility. Since it is not a learning organization, implementing any novel technologies would be hard. XX University's rigid management style is indicative of the aforementioned challenges and problems. This is not to say that these problems cannot be resolved. Chinese society is a typical society that reforms can be carried out successfully if they are initiated from top down (Wang, 2004-2005). Just like its curriculum described by Ministry of Education, buying of technology would be possible if top officials are convinced that it will serve the learning needs of students throughout China. Then central directives will be followed through by universities at the provincial level and all other levels.

SOLUTIONS AND RECOMMENDATIONS

Given the societal differences, XX University seems to have justified their unsupportive role in the wide adoption of cutting edge technology to enhance learning. Web-Technologies have the power to enhance learning. Research (King & Griggs, 2006) shows that technology can not only increase higher education opportunities, but also increase access and completion. All educators need to do is to harness the power of innovative technology to enhance learning for all levels of education. Since the whole society in China has prejudice against technology enhanced learning, it is extremely hard for XX University to adopt

cutting edge technology for its instructional purposes. Their administrators do not have the slightest inclination to invest money on innovative technology. Teaching and learning through technology simply is not on their priority list. Teaching in China still revolves around conventional ideas and a passive orientation to knowledge, and the educational system produces teachers who continue these practices (Wang, 2007, p. 115). For thousands of years, Chinese educators have maintained that all education encompasses twin goals: teaching books (Chen, 1981) and teaching learners (Price, 1992). From these teaching or management philosophies, it seems hard for anyone to find a place in the use of innovative technology in teaching. XX University administrators and all other university administrators would not want technology to replace their faculty. Of course, technology can by no means replace teachers/instructors. At least, without exploring the benefits of using technology, these Chinese administrators have such a fear. Little have they realized that Web 2.0 technologies can produce the following benefits for learners:

- The working mother in rural Nebraska completing her bachelor's degree online through her local state university while her children sleep at night.
- The mid-career business woman executive pursuing her doctorate in education via a hybrid online and residency program in order to change careers.
- The retired bus driver engaged in a collaborative webinar for his class through a University of Beijing class on the Eastern perspective of global issues. (King, 2006, p. 16)

As we have entered the Information Age, Radio or Television cannot be the leader in technology enhanced learning as it can only offer synchronous learning. It is Web-Technologies that can offer not only asynchronous learning but also synchronous learning. In addition live interaction can be offered via other supporting software. When addressing blended learning, virtual education, instructional technology, flexible learning, distance education, and collaborative learning, Radio or Television is not in a position to do all of the above. It is Web 2.0 technologies that are capable of all the afore-mentioned learning. In addition, in this informa-tion age, when talking about all the buzz terms such as IT education, mobile/wireless computing, networking/telecommunication, multimedia, so-cial computing and other web technologies, we know for sure we are not talking about radio or television or correspondence education; we are raving about Web-2.0 technologies.

Change your philosophy and you change your world. XX University administrators prob-ably need to change their views on learning via technology. Just because you have not done it, it does not mean what others have done is not valid. Online universities have emerged as a result of cutting technology, especially web technologies. Web technologies have made online teaching and learning possible. How many CEOs have got their degree via online teaching and learn-ing? In 2002, the University of Phoenix, part of the Apollo Group, saw its enrollment surpass 100,000 students—making it the largest institu-tion of higher learning in the United States (Bash, 2003). University of Phoenix could be the largest university of virtual learning via technology on earth.

Chinese graduates from American institu-tions of higher learning should never stop trying to persuade current XX University leaders and other university leaders to adopt technology to enhance teaching and learning. Those Chinese faculty who work in other industrialize nations should continue to take students to Chinese campuses to illustrate teaching and learning via technology. XX University administrators will not believe in the benefits of technology enhanced learning until they see demonstration with their own eyes. Send them statistics and demographics

to indicate how many CEOs have obtained their degrees from online universities. Facts always speak louder than words. XX University leaders should start to enroll some of their students in online courses sponsored by foreign universities. Then, comparison should be made between the student learning outcomes by traditional teaching and the student learning outcomes by technology enhanced learning. If no discrepancy can be found, then start to adopt Web Technologies to enhance learning. When XX University leaders are ready to adopt technology, it is always wise to follow Gibson's (2006, p. 148) suggestions:

- Support for the technological infrastructure;
- Inclusive instructional designs that are not only culturally appropriate, but also ac-cessible for differently-abled or those for whom English is not their first language;
- Learner support including preparatory ed-ucational experiences to help learners learn at a distance, learn with technology, and learn in adulthood;
- Technology support to ensure both facul-ty and learners are able to function in the environment and have ready help when needed;
- Faculty support for teaching with technol-ogy and the design of instruction.

Teaching and learning with technology is ex-pensive and it is no easy task. It can be achieved through partnerships. If XX University is willing to partner with the current university the author of this case study is working for, the process could be a lot easier. According to Gibson (2006), partnerships take time, energy, communications, willingness to work across boundaries, and the ability to discard past territorialism towards providing access to and success in education for all (p. 149). As XX University is engaged in increasing its soft-power by establishing more Confucius institutes through-out the globe, technology enhanced learning will empower even its Confucius institutes. As China imports more advanced technology to enhance its agriculture, industry, military and science, teaching and learning should be enhanced by advanced technology as well. It is technology enhanced teaching and learning that will provide a more skillful workforce to meet the manpower needs of the Chinese society. In this information age, it is unwise to shy away from the wide adoption of Web-Technologies.

REFERENCES

Bash, L. (2003). *Adult learners in the academy*. Bolton, MA: Anker Publishing Company.

Chen, T. H. (1981). *Chinese education since 1949: Academic and revolutionary models*. New York: Pergamon Press.

Gibson, C. C. (2006). Increasing equity: Seeking mainstream advantages for all. In King, K. P., & Griggs, J. K. (Eds.), *Harnessing innovative technology in higher education: Access, policy, & instruction* (pp. 133–150). Madison, WI: Atwood Publishing.

Goodman, P. S. (2006). *Foreign currency piles up in China: Reserve fund soared to record in 2005*. Retrieved March 3, 2009, from http://www.washingtonpost.com/wp-dyn/content/article/2006/01/16/AR2006011600450.html

Hersey, P., & Blanchard, K. (1969). *Management of organizational behavior: Utilizing human resources*. Englewood Cliffs, NJ: Prentice-Hall.

Kaplan, F. M., Sobin, J. M., & Andors, S. (1979). *Encyclopedia of china today*. New York: Harper & Row, Publishers.

King, K. P. (2006). Introduction. In King, K. P., & Griggs, K. J. (Eds.), *Harnessing innovative technology in higher education: Access, equity, polity, & instruction* (pp. 15–28). Madison, WI: Atwood Publishing.

King, K. P., & Griggs, J. K. (Eds.). (2006). *Harnessing innovative technology in higher education: Access, equity, polity, & instruction*. Madison, WI: Atwood Publishing.

Knowles, M. S. (1975). *Self-directed learning: A guide for learners and teachers*. New York: Association Press.

Knowles, M. S. (1978). *The adult learner: A neglected species* (2nd ed.). Houston, TX: Gulf.

Knowles, M. S. (1984). *Andragogy in action*. San Francisco: Jossey-Bass.

Knowles, M. S. (1986). *Using learning contracts*. San Francisco: Jossey-Bass.

McGregor, D. (1960). *The human side of enterprise*. New York: McGraw Hill.

Paine, L. (1992). Teaching and modernization in contemporary China. In Hayhoe, R. (Ed.), *Education and modernization: The Chinese experience* (pp. 183–209). New York: Pergamon Press.

Price, R. (1992). Moral-political education and modernization. In Hayhoe, R. (Ed.), *Education and modernization: The Chinese experience* (pp. 211–237). New York: Pergamon Press.

Tang, J. (2000). Recent Internet developments in the People's Republic of China. *Online Information Review, 24*(4), 316–321. doi:10.1108/14684520010350669

Wang, V. (2004-2005). Adult education reality: three generations, different transformation the impact of social context: three generations of Chinese adult learners. *The New York Journal of Adult Learning, 3*(1), 17–32.

Wang, V. (2005). Perceptions of Teaching Preferences of Online Instructors. *Journal on Excellence in College Teaching, 16*(3), 33–54.

Wang, V. (2006). The instructional patterns of Chinese online educators in China. *Asian Journal of Distance Education, 4*(1), 43–55.

Wang, V. (2008). Enhancing the right to education through distance education in China. *Asian Journal of Distance Education, 6*(2), 66–76.

Wang, V., & Redhead, C. K. (2008). Comparing the Russian, the Sloyd, and the Arts and Crafts movement training system. In Wang, V., & King, K. P. (Eds.), *Innovations in career and technical education: Strategic approaches towards workforce competencies around the globe* (pp. 99–116). Charlotte, NC: Information Age Publishing.

Wang, V. C. X. (2007). Chinese knowledge transmitters or western learning facilitators adult teaching methods compared. In King, K. P., & Wang, V. C. X. (Eds.), *Comparative adult education around the globe* (pp. 113–137). Hangzhou, China: Zhejiang University Press.

Wang, V. C. X., & Kreysa, P. (2006). Instructional strategies of distance education instructors in China. *The Journal of Educators Online, 3*(1), 1–25.

Yang, D. P. (2005). China's education in 2003: From growth to reform. (J. Eagleton, Trans). [Original work published in 2003]. *Chinese Education & Society, 38*(4), 11–45.

ADDITIONAL READING

Brown, G. (2006). New perspectives on instructional effectiveness through distance education. In King, K. P., & Griggs, J. K. (Eds.), *Harnessing innovative technology in higher education: Access, policy, & instruction* (pp. 97–109). Madison, WI: ATWOOD PUBLISHING.

Conceicao, S. C. O. (2006). Faculty lived experiences in the online environment. *Adult Education Quarterly, 57*(1), 26–45. doi:10.1177/1059601106292247

Gagne, R. M., Wager, W. W., Golas, K. C., & Keller, J. M. (2005). *Principles of instructional design* (5th ed.). USA: Thomson Learning Inc.

Heinich, R., Molenda, M., Russell, J. D., & Smaldino, S. E. (2002). *Instructional media and technologies for learning* (7th ed.). Columbus, OH: Merrill Prentice Hall.

King, K. P. (1999). Unleashing technology in the classroom: What adult basic education teachers and organizations need to know. *Adult Basic Education, 9*(3), 162–175.

Palloff, R. M., & Pratt, K. (1999). *Building learning communities in cyberspace*. San Francisco: Jossey-Bass.

Rhoda, K. I. (2005). The role of distance education in enhancing accessibility for adult learners. In Bash, L. (Ed.), *Best practices in adult learning* (pp. 149–172). Bolton, MA: Anker Publishing Company, Inc.

Schrum, L. (2000). Online teaching and learning: Essential conditions for success! In Lau, L. (Ed.), *Distance Learning technologies: Issues, trends and opportunities* (pp. 91–106). Hershey, PA: Idea Group Publishing.

Sproull, L., & Kiesler, S. (1991). *Connections: New ways of working in the networked organization*. Cambridge, MA: MIT Press.

(TEFL) in China. *International Forum of Teaching and Studies, 2*(2), 61-77.

Torres, I. T., & Arias, M. (Eds.), *Encyclopedia of human resources information systems: Challenges in e-HRM* (pp. 752–757). Hershey, PA: IGI Global.

Wang, V. (2006). Implementing andragogy in teaching English as a foreign language

Wang, V. (2006). From pedagogues to andragogues: How changing social contexts can lead to changing educational practices. *International Forum of Teaching and Studies, 2*(3), 5–22.

Wang, V. (2008). Learning organizations versus static organizations in the context of e-HRM. In Torres, T., & Arias, M. (Eds.), *Encyclopedia of human resources information systems: Challenges in e-HRM* (pp. 617–622). Hershey, PA: IGI Global.

Wang, V. (2008). Andragogy and pedagogy in learning theories. In Torres, T., & Arias, M. (Eds.), *Encyclopedia of human resources information systems: Challenges in e-HRM* (pp. 42–47). Hershey, PA: IGI Global.

Wang, V. (2008). Knowledge facilitator versus knowledge dictator in today's organizations. In Torres, T., & Arias, M. (Eds.), *Encyclopedia of human resources information systems: Challenges in e-HRM* (pp. 592–597). Hershey, PA: IGI Global.

Wang, V. (2008). The Right Work Ethic for Human Resource Managers.

Wang, V. (2008). Traditional leadership in light of e-HRMS. In Torres, T., & Arias, M. (Eds.), *Encyclopedia of human resources information systems: Challenges in e-HRM* (pp. 849–854). Hershey, PA: IGI Global.

Wang, V. (2008). Distance learning specialists. In Tomei, L. (Ed.), *Encyclopedia of information technology curriculum integration (EITCI)* (pp. 254–258). Hershey, PA: IGI Global.

Wang, V. (2008). Discussion groups in distance education. In Tomei, L. (Ed.), *Encyclopedia of information technology curriculum integration (EITCI)* (pp. 238–242). Hershey, PA: IGI Global.

Wang, V. (2008). Distance education and learning style. In Tomei, L. (Ed.), *Encyclopedia of information technology curriculum integration (EITCI)* (pp. 243–247). Hershey, PA: IGI Global.

Wang, V. (2008). Learning theories fundamentals. In Tomei, L. (Ed.), *Encyclopedia of information technology curriculum integration (EITCI)* (pp. 347–352). Hershey, PA: IGI Global.

Wang, V. (2008). Transformative learning. In Tomei, L. (Ed.), *Encyclopedia of information technology curriculum integration (EITCI)* (pp. 913–917). Hershey, PA: IGI Global.

Wang, V. (2008). Distance learning essentials. In Tomei, L. (Ed.), *Encyclopedia of information technology curriculum integration (EITCI)* (pp. 248–253). Hershey, PA: IGI Global.

Wang, V. (2008). Classroom without borders. In Tomei, L. (Ed.), *Encyclopedia of information technology curriculum integration (EITCI)* (pp. 99–103). Hershey, PA: IGI Global.

Wang, V. (2008). Active learning online. In Tomei, L. (Ed.), *Encyclopedia of information technology curriculum integration (EITCI)* (pp. 9–13). Hershey, PA: IGI Global.

Wang, V. (2008). Adult education philosophies in post modern China. *International Forum of Teaching and Studies, 4*(1), 21–38.

(2008). In Wang, V. (Ed.). Curriculum development for adult learners in the global community: *Vol. I. Strategic approaches*. Malabar, FL: Krieger.

(2009). In Wang, V. (Ed.). Curriculum development for adult learners in the global community: *Vol. II. Teaching and learning*. Malabar, FL: Krieger.

Wang, V. (Ed.). (2009). *Handbook of research on E-learning applications for career and technical education: Technologies for vocational training*. Hershey, PA: Information Science Reference.

Wang, V., & King, K. P. (2009). *Building workforce competencies in career and technical education.* Charlotte, NC: Information Age Publishing.

Wang, V., & King, K. P. (Eds.). (2009). *Fundamentals of human performance and training.* Charlotte, NC: Information Age Publishing.

Wang, V., & King, K. P. (Eds.). (2009). *Human performance models revealed in the global context.* Charlotte, NC: Information Age Publishing.

KEY TERMS AND DEFINITIONS

IT Education: This refers to Information Technology education.

Multimedia Technology: Multimedia technology includes a combination of text, audio, still images, animation, video, and interactivity content forms.

Social Computing: It is a general term for an area of computer science that is concerned with the intersection of social behavior and computational systems. Blogs, email, instant messaging, social network services, wikis, social bookmarking are elements of social computing.

telecommunication: It refers to the assisted transmission of signals over a distance for the purpose of communication.

Web 2.0 Technologies: This term is used interchangeably with web technologies.

Web Technologies: This refers to a perceived second generation of web development and design, that aims to facilitate communication, secure information sharing, interoperability, and collaboration on the World Wide Web.

Wireless Computing: It refers to today's workers use portable computing devices and have constant access to the Internet and data on other computers.

Chapter 16
Extending Educational Opportunities in Rural Areas:
Application of Distance Education in Rural Schools

Wallace Hannum
University of North Carolina at Chapel Hill, USA

Matthew Irvin
University of North Carolina at Chapel Hill, USA

Claire de la Varre
University of North Carolina at Chapel Hill, USA

ABSTRACT

Rural schools in many countries face problems in providing educational opportunities to children and youth for a variety of reasons. There has been the tendency in many countries to migrate to urban areas, often in search of better economic opportunities. The resulting shift from rural areas to urban/suburban areas has placed increased pressures on schools in rural communities. Schools often form the hub of social and civic activity in rural communities. Although they are an important component to rural communities, many rural schools are struggling under the weight of declining populations, declining budgets, staffing difficulties, and increased pressures to better prepare students for the workforce or further education. Rural schools face particular difficulties in attracting and retaining qualified teachers. Faced with problems of providing a comprehensive curriculum and qualified teachers, many rural schools in the United States have turned to distance education. This case explores the use of distance education in the United States through a national survey of distance education use, analysis of barriers to distance education and an experimental study of enhancing distance education through more appropriate training of local facilitators to support students.

DOI: 10.4018/978-1-61520-751-0.ch016

ORGANIZATIONAL BACKGROUND

The National Research Center on Rural Education Support (NRCRES) was established in 2004 with funding from the Institute for Educational Sciences of the U.S. Department of Education. This center was based at the University of North Carolina at Chapel Hill. NRCRES conducts a focused program of research that addresses significant problems in rural education. More than 40% of all American schools are in rural areas and 30% of all students attend rural schools. The research and development work of NRCRES seeks solutions that will improve the quality of rural education. A number of issues limit the ability to make progress in rural education. The programs conducted by NRCRES address the following issues in rural education:

- retention of qualified teachers
- student achievement and dropout
- availability of and access to opportunities for advanced placement courses
- improvement in teacher quality through professional development

The approach taken by NRCRES is based on principles derived from empirical evidence. Through a series of research studies NRCRES addressed these issues that face rural education. A team of 20 researchers at NRCRES conducted research studies and implements training for teachers in participating rural schools. The purpose was to work toward improved teaching, learning and student achievement in rural schools nationwide. This, in turn, helps strengthen rural communities throughout the United States. The work involved collaboration among faculty and researchers at the School of Education, the Center for Developmental Science, and The Frank Porter Graham Child Development Institute. The center housed multidisciplinary research on all aspects of human development by faculty from several colleges and universities. The Distance Education Program within the National Research Center on Rural Education Support was investigating the use of distance education in rural schools and the feasibility of offering advanced and upper-level courses though distance education. Distance education technology has changed a great deal over the last decades as communications technologies continue to evolve. These changes have resulted in a greater diversity in the type of delivery systems as well as possible differences in the effectiveness of types of delivery systems for differing courses.

SETTING THE STAGE

As in many countries, during the past several decades the population in the United States has tended to migrate from rural areas to the cities. While the cities have grown, a considerable segment of the population remains in rural communities despite the decline in the number of people engaged in farming and other economic pursuits associated with rural life. One impact of this shift from rural areas to urban/suburban areas has been increasing pressures on schools in rural communities. Schools often form the hub of social and civic activity in rural communities serving as the community center. They are an important component to rural communities, but many rural schools are struggling under the weight of declining populations, declining budgets, staffing difficulties, and increased pressures to better prepare students for the workforce or postsecondary education. While there may be some benefits from attending small rural schools (Huang & Howley, 1993; Howley, Strange, & Bickel, 2000; Nye, Hedges, & Konstantopoulos, 2000; Johnson & Strange, 2007), many rural communities in the United States are losing population and losing jobs, which further impact rural schools. National assessment programs in the United States do not make distinctions between rural and urban/suburban schools in terms of expectations. The same standards that apply to larger and better-funded suburban schools apply equally to smaller, more remote and less well funded rural schools. Yet the level of funding, availability of qualified teachers, access to well-equipped facilities for teaching such as labs, and comprehensive course offerings, especially advanced upper-level courses, are often lacking in rural schools. As a result, students in rural schools do not have access to the same educational opportunities they would find in urban/suburban schools. In fact, one reason given by some families for moving away from rural areas is to find better educational opportunities for their children.

While there have been and continue to be shifts in population from rural areas to cities in the United States, approximately one third of the public schools and 10 million students in the United States are rural (Johnson & Strange, 2007; Provasnik, KewalRamani, Coleman, Gilbertson, Herring, & Xie, 2007). Rural schools represent a sizable segment of the overall public education in the United States. Yet for all their importance and size in the overall educational system, rural schools are facing some significant challenges. One of the most pressing challenges for small, remote, and low-income rural schools is attracting and retaining certified and highly qualified teachers (Barley & Brigham, 2008; Beeson & Strange, 2000; Herzog & Pittman, 1995; Hobbs, 2004; Holloway, 2002; Lowe, 2006; Monk 2007). As a direct result of difficulties attracting and retaining teachers, rural schools are often not able to offer a comprehensive curriculum necessary to prepare students for postsecondary education or the workforce.

Rural schools have sought different options for dealing with the situations they face. As staffing difficulties combine with community population losses and resultant economic decline, some rural school districts have elected to close or to consolidate with other districts (Hobbs, 2004; Jimerson, 2006; Schafft, Alter, & Bridger, 2006; Seal & Harmon, 1995). When consolidating, two or more small rural school districts combine to form one larger district. Closure or consolidation not only lessens the benefits of attending rural schools

for students, but also takes away the community social center and a primary employment source (D'Amico, Matthes, Sankar, Merchant, & Zurita, 1996; Jennings, Swidler, & Koliba, 2005; Lyson, 2002; Schafft, Alter, & Bridger, 2006). When rural schools close the whole community suffers as jobs are lost, the social center of the community disappears, residents with school-age children often move out, and students who remain often have to be transported longer distances to attend a school. Thus, many rural communities want to avoid school closure or consolidation as they seek to maintain social and economic viability. These problems of rural schools are not unique to the United States. Indeed, many countries experience similar issues in their rural areas. In developing countries, the issues of providing education to rural communities are especially profound due to a more acute lack of resources. Thus, the gap between urban and rural schools in terms of providing adequate educational opportunities can be even greater in these countries. Similarly, there has been and continues to be population migration from rural areas to urban areas in many developing nations. This has been driven by the perception and reality of greater educational and economic opportunities elsewhere. Strengthening the social and economic fabric in rural communities depends in large part on strengthening their schools through offering more a comprehensive curriculum and more advanced courses to better prepare their students, especially at the secondary level. In short, the educational opportunities available to a student in a rural community should be similar to that opportunity available to students in urban/suburban communities.

CASE DESCRIPTION

The purpose of this chapter is to explore the use of technology, in the form of distance education, to expand educational opportunities in rural communities. This allows students to have access to courses which rural secondary schools would otherwise be unable to provide. Three aspects of distance education in rural schools are examined by the work reported in this chapter. The first aspect was to document though a national survey the extent of distance education use by rural schools in the United States and their experiences with distance education. The second aspect was to identify barriers rural schools face when considering and using distance education. The third aspect was to conduct a large-scale experiment that attempted to improve the results rural schools achieve through distance education by exploring how to best prepare local facilitators to support students taking advanced online courses.

DISTANCE EDUCATION BACKGROUND

The common defining feature of distance education is the separation of the teacher and learner. This is primarily what sets distance education apart from face-to-face instruction. Most definitions of distance education have several common elements some of which were identified by Keegan (1988):

- physical separation of teacher and learner
- influence of an educational organization
- use of technical media to convey educational content
- provision of two-way communication
- possibility of occasional face-to-face meetings

Other definitions of distance education specify that it is a planned and systematic activity that includes presentation of teaching materials, supervision, and support of student learning (Schlosser & Anderson, 1994). Several definitions of distance education include specific reference to information and computing technologies (ICTs) that enable teachers and learners to interact over distance. Garrison and Shale (1987) indicated that the majority of communications between and among teacher and students is mediated through two-way communications media done continuously. Many definitions of distance education indicate that it should occur under the auspices of an educational institution, and that it should be a planned educational experience. This distinguishes distance education from the types of informal learning that might occur every day as people interact with each other, read books, view videos, and use the Internet to access information. Undoubtedly people learn through these processes, however, this is not considered distance education by most observers, since it is not planned or sponsored by an educational organization nor is it for the express purpose of learning.

While distance education predates ICTs by well over a century, many recent definitions of distance education often include reference to use of these technologies. There is a tendency to define distance education as instruction delivered over the Internet, but the concept of distance education is much broader and much older. Examples of distance education would include students who were participating in formal courses offered through television both by cable or satellite, correspondence courses offered through mail or e-mail, one-way video conferencing, two-way videoconferencing, self-instructional computer-based tutorials, as well as web-based or online courses. Undoubtedly over the next decade, new ICTs will emerge and will be used to bring learners into contact with teachers and other learners, as well as with educational materials. Despite the fact that we don't know now what these technologies might be, their use will likely fit within current definitions of distance education. Although the technologies have evolved and will continue to evolve, the concept of distance education has remained reasonably stable. We consider distance education to be formal instruction offered by an educational organization for the express purpose of teaching in which the teacher and students are separated by physical distance and interact through the use of some media that can include print or electronic media such as videoconferencing, e-mail, chat rooms, and discussion forums. This definition follows from prior work on distance education, and is broadly representative of other definitions of distance education.

ROLE OF DISTANCE EDUCATION IN RURAL SCHOOLS

Distance education, principally in the form of online courses, has been proposed as an alternative to school closure or consolidation as well as a way for rural schools to provide access to a comprehensive curriculum and advanced courses that better prepare their students for postsecondary education or entering the workforce (Barbour & Mulcahy, 2006; Burney & Cross, 2006; Hobbs, 2004; Jimerson, 2006). Effective distance education could bring enhanced educational opportunities to students in rural schools that they would not otherwise have. Small rural schools often cannot justify hiring a teacher and offering an advanced course in their school when few students are interested in or prepared for such a course. Even if numbers were sufficient, many rural schools would not have a suitably-qualified teacher and would struggle to recruit one. However, regardless of school size or location, distance education offers a solution. Thus, a student in a rural school wishing to take a foreign language course or an advanced science or mathematics course that was not available locally, could most likely find and take the course via distance education. This would allow the student to remain in the community and receive a comprehensive education and adequate preparation for the workforce or further education. Without this option, the student either would have to move to a larger school with more courses or not take these courses at all. In the first instance, the student becomes part of the general trend of declining population in rural areas; in the second,

the rural community would retain the student, but that student would not have the essential skills to be competitive in a 21st century workforce. Undoubtedly this is why our survey of rural school districts found that a large majority of rural school districts had offered distance education courses (Hannum, et al., 2009). Clearly, rural schools see distance education as a way to expand the educational opportunities they provide rural youth in the United States.

Survey of Distance Education Use

Studies have consistently shown that distance education is as effective as traditional classroom instruction in terms of promoting learning outcomes (Bernard et al., 2004; Cavanaugh, Gillan, Kromrey, Hess, & Blomeyer, 2004; Hobbs, 2004; Waxman, Lin, & Georgette, 2003). Recent improvements in rural infrastructure and affordability in the United States have made Internet availability more comparable to non-rural areas. This has also made distance education viable in rural areas (Hobbs, 2004; Jimerson, 2006; Malecki, 2003). Accordingly, rural districts in the United States are increasingly using distance education as a way to deal with some of the social and economic challenges they face at the local level. Setzer and Lewis (2005) reported that the proportion of rural districts with students taking distance education (46 percent) is nearly twice that of urban (23 percent) and suburban (28 percent) districts. In a national survey of distance education use in rural schools conducted by NRCRES, Hannum et al. (2009) found that 85.0% of small and low-income rural schools were currently using or previously had used distance education as a way to offer courses they needed. 92.1% of these schools indicated they were either somewhat satisfied or very satisfied with the distance education they were using or had used. Furthermore, 81.3% reported that they needed distance education in order to provide advanced or enrichment courses for students. Without distance education, students in these rural schools would not be able to take advanced placement courses that are often essential for university acceptance. Without distance education most of these schools would be unable to offer the courses their students need either because there would be too few students interested in and prepared for an advanced course to justify hiring a teacher for this course, or these schools would be unable to find and recruit a qualified teachers for the advanced course. Because of the more limited salaries and lack of social and cultural opportunities available in many rural areas, recent college graduates are less willing to locate in rural areas and teach school. Thus technology in the form of distance education has to be employed to extend greater educational opportunities to students in rural areas. Our recent national survey of rural schools in the United States documents that this is happening, and that the acceptance of distance education in rural schools is high.

Barriers to Distance Education in Rural Schools

While there has been a rise in use of distance education at all education levels and across various geographic areas, several types of barriers to distance education are evident. If not overcome, these barriers may prevent and limit the use of distance education to solve some challenges rural schools face. Berge and colleagues (e.g., Berge, 1998; Berge & Mrozowski, 1999) identified several types of barriers common to distance education in organizations and various postsecondary settings: academic barriers (e.g., lack of student time, large class size, lack of teacher support for student learning to use technology), cultural barriers (e.g., lack leadership support for, faculty expertise to use, and understanding of distance education), and technical barriers (e.g., inadequate connectivity/access, availability computers and necessary programs). While they report financial issues are less of a barrier, organizational support

(e.g., strategic planning), technical expertise, and faculty support are often barriers in Berge's research (Berge et al., 2002; Cho & Berge, 2002). A national study of postsecondary academic institutions found that distance education program development costs were frequently a barrier (U.S. Department of Education and National Center for Education Statistics, 1997). Technological factors (e.g., infrastructure, equipment problems and maintenance) were likewise often cited as barriers but were not considered major problems (U.S. Department of Education and National Center for Education Statistics, 1997).

Zirkle (2002) examined barriers among college students enrolled in a trade and industrial teacher education program at a Midwestern university. This work differentiated several types of distance education barriers including institutional barriers (e.g., availability of courses, student support services, required materials, cost), student barriers (e.g., computer skills, contact with and feedback from instructor, isolation from other students), and instructional barriers (e.g., faculty training, time commitment, and technical expertise) (Zirkle (2001, 2002, 2004). Similar to many rural secondary schools, the university was offering numerous distance education courses in part because of geographic isolation (Zirkle, 2002). Results indicated that course availability and scheduling were ranked highly as institutional barriers. Problems with technical assistance and support were also barriers. The availability of computers, Internet connectivity, and students' computer skills were among the lowest barriers. Zirkle (2004) then examined the perceptions of teacher educators regarding the barriers to distance education at their institution. All of the career and technical teacher educators across a Midwestern state participated. In terms of institutional barriers, costs and funding issues ranked highly. A lack of strategic planning and common vision were also a barrier. Technical support and technology-enhanced classrooms were less of a barrier in this study. Instructor training, teaching skills, and technical expertise for distance education were higher ranked barriers. For students, their ability to learn and the isolation or limited interaction with instructors were considered barriers, but students' technical expertise was not.

Picciano and Seaman (2007) completed one of the few studies of distance education in K-12 schools by conducting a national survey with school district administrators. This research was the first to focus on and compare specific forms of distance education in K-12 schools, online learning and blended learning (i.e., a course where one- to two-thirds of the content is delivered online and remaining content is delivered face-to-face). A follow-up survey of online and blended learning in K-12 schools conducted two years later was recently published (Picciano & Seaman, 2009). The initial and follow-up surveys found similar results concerning the barriers and issues reported by participating schools. In general, the major barriers involved concerns about course quality, course development and/or costs, receiving funding based on student attendance, and needs for teacher training (Picciano & Seaman, 2007, 2009).

While distance education barriers have been well documented and are widely recognized (Zirkle, 2001, 2004), most research has examined distance education barriers in postsecondary settings (for exceptions see Picciano & Seaman, 2007, 2009; Sezter & Lewis, 2005). These results may or may not be applicable to secondary schools. A factor that questions the applicability of postsecondary research in distance education to secondary schools is the different distance education models that are often used in each of these settings. Distance education in secondary schools often features students working on their distance education courses during an assigned period in the school day, often under the supervision of a facilitator who is in the room with them. In postsecondary institutions, students complete distance education courses in a more independent fashion working on their own whenever and from wherever they choose. It is likely that different barriers may be at play in these two scenarios. Thus, extrapolating from the postsecondary research on barriers to distance education use and applying this directly to secondary schools is questionable at best.

In a study of barriers we conducted in a national sample of rural secondary schools selected at random in the United States, the five most common barriers were not having a need for distance education (i.e., not needed for curriculum requirements), funding, scheduling, not being a district priority, and personnel not trained. The least mentioned barriers related to technology including maintenance and connectivity (Irvin, Hannum & de la Varre, 2009). Distance education not being needed for curriculum requirements, not having sufficient funding, and not being a district priority were three of the most common barriers reported. This was similar to prior research demonstrating that barriers in postsecondary settings include organizational support (e.g., Berge et al., 2002; Cho & Berge, 2002), a lack of strategic planning and a common vision (Zirkle, 2004), funding (U.S. Department of Education and National Center for Education Statistics, 1997; Zirkle, 2004), and administrative support (Murphy & Terry, 1998). In addition, Picciano and Seaman (2007, 2009) found that issues related to costs (e.g., course purchasing) and funding were major barriers in K-12 schools.

Our results found that logistical barriers were the next most frequent type of barriers in rural schools. In particular, scheduling problems was the third most often cited barrier. Most likely scheduling problems arise when using synchronous distance education delivery. School systems that are on a slightly different time schedule are not able to participate in the same synchronous course because the class time would start at different times in the different schools. Scheduling is likely less of a problem with asynchronous delivery. Personnel barriers were, as a group, the next type of barriers most apparent in rural schools. Furthermore, not having personnel trained to use distance education was among the five barriers reported most often. Others have found similar barriers in postsecondary agricultural education (e.g., Miller & Miller, 2000; Murphy & Terry, 1998) and K-12 schools (Picciano & Seaman, 2007, 2009). It also seems worth notice that over 30% of participating rural districts reportedly did not have personnel to support distance education. Few rural districts reported lacking the technical expertise needed, but this has been a barrier in postsecondary settings (e.g., Berge et al., 2002; Zirkle, 2002, 2004). Finally, technology barriers (e.g., lack technology enhanced classrooms, maintenance, or sufficient connectivity) were rarely barriers for small and low-income rural schools, which was also consistent with prior research (Murphy & Terry, 1998).

Any attempt to implement distance education in rural schools should consider these barriers to distance education use. Successful distance education programs will have to moderate the potential negative effects these barriers can have on distance education programs. Toward that end, an important first step at the local level entails an assessment of barriers that also considers distance education capabilities and learners' needs (Cho & Berge, 2002). Once barriers and related factors have been identified, the next step would involve developing plans for addressing these barriers. Rural schools may find it useful to consult several sources including other rural schools implementing distance education, universities that may have distance experts, and appropriate government agencies that may be available. Policymakers may also help rural schools overcome these barriers by enacting policies and providing funds intended to support and stimulate the use of distance education in rural districts.

EXPERIMENTAL STUDY OF DISTANCE EDUCATION IN RURAL SCHOOLS

While the extent of distance education use and acceptance in rural secondary schools is high, there are significant opportunities to improve the effectiveness of distance education in these schools. Although the achievement outcomes from distance education seem equivalent to the outcomes from traditional classroom instruction, we see a need to improve the results from distance education use in rural secondary schools by paying more attention to factors that have been shown to affect learning and motivation. First, being equivalent to the outcomes in traditional instruction, while encouraging, is not sufficient. The typical pattern of achievement in schools approximates the familiar bell-shaped curve. For all the students towards the upper levels of the curve who are achieving at high levels, there is an equal number of students at the lower levels who are achieving at much lower levels. Faced with the economic challenges in rural communities today and with limited employment opportunities when compared with prior years, lower levels of achievement are not acceptable. Second, while achievement outcomes between distance education and traditional classrooms may be the same, students often fail to complete distance education courses at rates much greater than in traditional classroom courses. If distance education is to provide assistance to overcome some of the social and economic factors in rural communities, we need to keep students engaged in distance education courses and completing them at rates at least as great as in traditional courses. Without such support distance education will fail to reach its potential.

Emphasis on Pedagogy

When seeking to improve the quality of distance education, we would do well to look beyond the technology itself, as the mere presence of technology has very small, often negligible, effects on learning outcomes. We believe that any learning gains resulting from technology-based instruction, including distance education, will result from attention to the design of the learning environment, not the fact that technology was used (Clark, 1994; Hannum, 2007). An element of effective pedagogy often missing in distance education courses is support for learning (Bonk & Dennen, 1999; McCombs & Vakili, 2005). To be effective, students require more than just delivery of content, regardless of the form in which the content is delivered. This concept of supporting learners is fundamental to an adequate pedagogy for distance education. It recognizes the complexity of the learning environment as requiring more than simply supporting the acquisition of knowledge. Learning in any context requires us to balance a consideration of the learner, the learning process and the learning context. This is especially true in distance education. If we are to provide support for learning, which is essential, then we must go beyond transmission of information via ICTs and attend not only to the learning process and all its complexity, but also to the individual learners, the social nature of learning, and the learning context. Many distance education courses "push" content to learners via the Internet or ICTs, but fail to provide students with the necessary support for learning that is essential for success. We believe that when used appropriately ICTs can help us provide support for learners in distance education courses. However, distance education courses often fail to do this because by their very nature teacher and student are separated. An alternative to many distance education courses would be to have someone who knows the learner and fully understands the local context of the learning to be physically present with the learner. This person does not have to be a teacher and would not have responsibility for providing instructional content to students. Unfortunately many distance education courses ignore this piece that is essential for learning: direct human contact. Students recognize

when this is missing and undoubtedly this is why so many drop out of distance education courses and often rate these poorly. We believe that having someone physically present with the learner who knows the learner and fully understands the local context of the learning can be beneficial in supporting learners taking distance education courses, especially in rural schools.

The limitations of traditional education can be exacerbated in distance education courses that follow a traditional approach to instruction as many distance education courses do. When the familiar environment of the classroom and the physical presence of a teacher and classmates are absent as they are in distance education classes, some students struggle to be successful. Many students fail to complete distance education courses, likely as a result of the lack of support from teachers and classmates. It is easier to fall behind in a distance education course, especially when the pedagogy of the course involves little more than distributing online content to students who then work independently and individually to complete their assignments. Students working independently in distance education courses can find themselves too far behind to catch up, and consequently may drop the course.

The concept of education as transmission of content to students has been criticized as limiting the learning that takes place in traditional schools. This view of education as transmission of content to students is particularly ineffective in distance education because one-way transmission of content in distance education courses reduces the possibility of engagement, interaction with peers and instructors, social construction of knowledge, feedback, and many other factors that serve to influence learning (Marzano, 2005). While this teacher-center view of instruction is a problem in schools and undoubtedly contributes to the uneven learning outcomes commonly found in traditional education, students experience greater problems when interaction and collaboration are missing in distance education courses.

We believe that many distance education courses suffer for reasons of weak or inappropriate pedagogy. Among these problems is a lack of sufficient and appropriate interactivity. It is not unusual to find that a "modern" distance education course uses the latest ICTs to do little more than pass papers back and forth from teacher to student. That is, the teacher creates a website or uses a content management system to post content for the student to read, view or listen to. The student, in turn, goes through this content and then may have to complete and send in send some assignment, perhaps a paper or a presentation, to the teacher to be graded. The technology may be thoroughly modern, but the underlying pedagogy is the simple correspondence instruction model of the World War II era. There is little interaction or engagement between teacher and learner and even less engagement and interaction among students. The frequency of feedback to learners, and often the quality as well, was poor in the correspondence courses of the 1940s and 1950s. While today's ICTs provide us with means to dramatically change this, our conception of education and the underlying pedagogical model we build upon keeps us from providing learners with truly interactive courses that provide the support they require to be successful. For example, students often cite the lack of feedback in distance education courses as a major criticism. Students in distance education courses also report heightened feelings of isolation when compared to traditional courses.

Learner-Centered Principles

In 1997, the American Psychological Association (APA) developed a set of 14 learner-centered principles (LCPs) intended to guide educational reform at all levels and informed by a number of different research perspectives (APA Work Group of the Board of Education Affairs, 1997). The evidence on the effectiveness of these LCPs in classrooms has been widely documented (McCombs & Miller, 2007). This theoretical framework has recently

been applied to distance education approaches to learning (McCombs & Vakili, 2005). LCPs indicate that learning is social in nature and that social interactions are a key element in learning. LCPs also outline other factors critical for learning, focusing on four research-validated domains, which can be summarized as follows:

- The cognitive and metacognitive domain refers to thought processes involved in learning, including self-reflection.
- The motivational and affective domain refers to effort and engagement while learning, affective and emotional factors, and the beliefs and interests that directly influence learning.
- The developmental and social domain refers to the previous experiences of students and their learning readiness (i.e., developmental factors) as well as interpersonal relations between and among students and teachers (i.e., social factors) that affect current learning.
- The individual differences domain refers to the differences between and within students that influence learning. Students have different strategies and skills for learning based on their backgrounds and prior learning experiences.

Study Design

We recently conducted a randomized controlled trial with a national sample of small, rural secondary schools geographically dispersed across the United States to explore the effectiveness of training local facilitators in these learner-centered principles and having them support learners in a distance education course. High school students took a year-long online class in AP English Composition and Literature (Hannum et al., 2008). The study was conducted to ascertain whether having an adult facilitator trained in applying empirically-validated LCPs to support secondary school students as they completed an online distance education course was an effective way to enhance the engagement of students and increase their rate of completion of an online course. The goal of the study was to determine if preparing local facilitators in using LCPs would increase students' progress in and completion of online distance education courses more than was possible if facilitators did not have this training (Hannum & McCombs, 2008). Our intervention was designed to train on-site facilitators to become learner-centered in their perspectives and the practices they used to support their students. We designed an online training module that emphasized community building. This element was intended to allow facilitators to become familiar with the online environment and the technology that their students would be using, and to enable them to interact with, and hence get to know, other facilitators in rural schools around the country. This ideally would counteract any feelings of isolation on the part of the facilitators, as well as giving them a resource for the exchange of advice, strategies and information. The intent of this online training in LCPs was to raise the facilitators' awareness of the social supports that are necessary for student success in online distance education. The training modules exposed facilitators to LCPs, presented them with a set of scenarios in which the LCPs could be applied to solve problems that students would potentially encounter and included a discussion forum in which they posted their responses to these scenarios.

Role of Facilitators

The primary role of the distance education facilitators was supporting and guiding students. The distance education teachers provided all the instruction from their remote locations. The local facilitators who were with the students dealt with various issues such as troubleshooting computer problems, coordinating efforts with instructors and course administrators, monitoring student at-

tendance, collecting some homework assignments, proctoring exams, and helping students with any problems students felt they could not discuss with the instructors. The role of the facilitator differed from that of the distance education instructor in several respects. Facilitators were physically present in the room with students when students were online during the schools scheduled daily period for their students to be in the distance education class. The course instructors were not physically present and may or may not have been available online or directly accessible during that time since the course was asynchronous. Instructors and students communicated through mediated means such as posting assignments, comments, and reflections through threaded discussion boards, and by email. An additional difference was that facilitators, unlike the course instructors, did not teach content. Indeed, facilitators were not expected to have the requisite knowledge or skills to do so. The instructors alone were responsible for course design and delivery of all content. Facilitators who participated in the project were teachers, principals, secretaries, librarians, teachers of other subjects, or coaches.

Facilitator Training Intervention

Half the facilitators were selected at random to receive only basic training in the mechanics of using the distance education software as their standard training. This included how to register students, how to assign/change passwords, how students can access the courses on the Web, how students handle the mechanics of uploading and downloading files, how to send postings in the discussion forum, and how to check student grades. The other half of the facilitators received this same standard training but were also provided training regarding the LCPs and how to apply these to deal with common issues students encounter in distance education.

Following the overview of the LCPs, this training provided facilitators in the intervention group with scenarios depicting common issues and problems that arise for students in distance education. These scenarios were derived from our findings and experiences in a pilot study with rural students and schools. These were intended to provide facilitators a better idea of what to expect and how the LCPs may help them deal with these situations. The scenarios were provided over a period of several weeks starting before the course began and continued over the first few weeks of the class. The scenarios were delivered in a multimedia format that included text, audio clips, and images. Each scenario featured one or more students with a problem to which a model facilitator responded. These included the following issues and topics:

- **First day of school**. This scenario presented strategies for introductions and ice-breakers. The goal was to model the creation of an atmosphere that allows students to collaborate, problem-solve and openly discuss anything course-related.
- **Discussing assignments**. This scenario modeled a facilitator setting aside a class period in the first week of the year to go over course logistics. Facilitators were asked to encourage students to brainstorm strategies for solving specific problems relating to technology, grades, feeling overwhelmed, or confusion over an assignment.
- **Student fears**. This scenario depicted a reluctant student having a conversation with the facilitator concerning the student's fears about the course. The facilitator modeled some strategies that might be used for dealing with such issues.
- **Time management**. This scenario featured a student who tended to procrastinate and is discussing this with the facilitator. The facilitator covered a number of strategies for effectively organizing the workload.
- **Helping students help themselves**. This scenario was designed to encourage

students to interact with their online peers.
- **Too much work**. In this scenario, a student was overwhelmed by the workload and is far less confident than the student initially appeared and believed. The facilitator modeled several strategies that address these.
- **Disengaged**. A student who was at the top of the class during the first weeks of the course but later had failing grades and seemed increasingly disengaged was portrayed in this scenario. The facilitator discussed this with the student to find out more about where the student was having difficulties and what may have been the source.
- **Worries about grades**. This scenario had a student who was considering dropping the course because of concerns about the grade in the online course being lower than grades received in other courses and this adversely affecting their Grade Point Average (GPA). The student was also having difficulties managing the workload. The facilitator attempted to allay the student's anxieties by discussing college expectations and the benefits of taking challenging courses.

Facilitators in this intervention group were provided an online discussion board related to each scenario and were asked to post their comments about the scenario, which LCPs they believed were evident, what they think the LCPs suggested could be done in the situation, and any comments about other facilitator's postings. The intervention was also designed to form a community of support among intervention facilitators. Intervention facilitators were informed that the discussion board was where they could post questions to other facilitators and use this to support each other.

The attempt to form a community among the facilitators in the intervention group was intended to provide the professional support and collegial interaction they may be accustomed to from their experience in small rural schools. Given that being a facilitator in a distance education course was for many a new role and a new context, having this support and awareness among facilitators may have been reassuring. In addition, it is possible that other intervention facilitators may collectively have the knowledge, experience, and expertise in dealing with some of the particular issues that a facilitator might face, and thus the group of facilitators could represent a resource any facilitator can access if needed. Control facilitators also had access to a discussion board that they could use as needed. However, control facilitators were not provided the overview of the LCPs, scenarios, or directed to discussion boards to discuss the scenarios and to form a community with other facilitators.

Another key feature of the intervention was the use of data to provide feedback to and professional development for facilitators in the intervention condition during the semester. Specifically, students and facilitators completed rating scales assessing relevant LCPs and related factors including beliefs about learning, motivation, class experiences, and facilitator support. The results of this survey were aggregated at the classroom level and provided to intervention facilitators. Members of the project staff then conducted brief feedback sessions over the telephone with intervention facilitators to discuss and interpret the results. A main focus of the survey and feedback session was how students perceived their distance education setting in terms of several LCPs and related factors. In addition, the implications from these results and suggested steps facilitators in the intervention condition might have taken were provided.

RESULTS

The facilitator discussion forums clearly illustrated the different experiences of the control and intervention facilitators. Our control group facilitators were provided with a single, online discussion forum, but were not provided with any scenarios or information about LCPs. The discussion in the control group was initially promising, with facilitators introducing themselves and discussing technical issues. However, facilitators were somewhat unclear about what their responsibilities were or how to support struggling students. Without LCP training or the online training module used in the intervention group, control facilitators did not have access to effective strategies to help their students manage their workload and cope with the rigors of the course, and even commented on the issues that distance education is prone to regarding the lack of social interaction. After some talk about student frustration with the course, the discussion dropped to nothing before the end of the first semester.

The experiences of the intervention facilitators were different. While similar frustrations were expressed on the discussion board, the LCP materials provided both strategies and language for developing a classroom climate that supported the online course. Facilitators reported that they used some of the communication strategies detailed in the training modules and were aware that this was within their scope of responsibility in this role. The total response to these challenges was broader than just the context of the online course or the physical classroom. Other facilitators gave examples in which the wider community – including parents, other teachers, principals and school counselors – was involved. They described their interactions with students in ways that clearly indicated both the use of learner-centered strategies and the understanding that the facilitator role is to foster students' intrinsic motivation. The content of the discussion boards indicated that the facilitators in the intervention group had an expanded view of themselves in the facilitator role as active participants in their students' learning experiences.

We found that the dropout rate for students in the control condition (57%) in which their facilitators were not trained in using a learner-centered approach was within the range other researchers have reported (Carr, 2000; Roblyer, 2006; Rovai & Wighting, 2005; Simpson, 2004). However the dropout rates of students in the intervention condition (34%) whose facilitators were trained in using a learner-centered approach was considerably less (Hannum, et al., 2008). This difference was statistically significant. This finding of a significantly lower drop out rate when students taking distance education courses have local facilitators who are trained in using the learner-centered principles affirms that use of these principles could help students complete distance education courses.

CHALLENGES FACING THE ORGANIZATION

As an organization with the mission of doing research to improve education in rural schools, the National Research Center on Rural Education Support was challenged to design and conduct research that is relevant to rural schools. An aspect of this was ensuring the cooperation of rural schools in the various research programs and projects. Obviously this required that NRCRES design research studies that took into account the perspectives and realities of rural schools. Unless rural schools see potential value in a research study, they are not likely to participate. Thus, we sought a partnership with rural schools that would have benefits in both directions. When designing research studies we had to be careful about any costs that may accrue to rural schools and plan budgets so that they offset costs to schools allowing their participation to be at least revenue neutral, even better if some funding can flow to schools as a result of their participation. The goals of a research project need to map onto goals of the schools that participate so that participation helps the schools move in directions they seek. In the distance education research this meant helping

schools offer a course through distance education that they would not otherwise be able to offer and that otherwise their students would not be able to take. It also meant compensating the school for any staff time that was required by these projects and purchase of necessary textbooks that would not have been a part of the regular school budget. Another aspect to this was finding the appropriate technology to use for distance education. This is where having the national survey of distance education in rural schools was important, for it allowed us to determine what technologies were available and the extent of connectivity in rural schools.

SOLUTIONS AND RECOMMENDATIONS

In addition to the challenges faced by an organization doing research in rural schools, rural schools in the United States themselves face a variety of challenges including being able to offer a comprehensive curriculum to its students. We believe that distance education using ICTs has a demonstrated potential to enhance the educational opportunities available in rural communities and thus improve the social and economic circumstances in these communities. Doing this successfully requires more than simply delivering courses via ICTs to rural schools. Rural school districts must overcome barriers to distance education use. Those designing distance education courses must employ a more appropriate pedagogy in these courses to ensure success. Simply taking existing content whether in the form of printed materials or books, recorded lectures or other presentations in audio or video formats and delivering these through ICTs as a distance education course will be less than successful. Effective education requires a pedagogy that extends beyond the idea of education as presentation of content. This was recognized years ago by Freire (2000) and remains important today. This is especially true for distance education. We must design distance education courses that actively engage students in interacting with the content and collaborating with other students and teachers to make meaning from the lessons. We believe an important part of this is having a local facilitator who is trained in using learner-centered principles available to students as they complete distance education courses. The role of the facilitator is to provide necessary support to students as well as serve as the eyes and ears of the remote teacher to help them understand what the students need to be successful in their learning. With distance education being a worldwide phenomenon and rural communities in many countries facing some of the same problems of having a sufficient number of adequately trained teachers to offer a comprehensive curriculum of a high quality, we believe that distance education will continue to grow and be an important part of how countries can extend educational opportunities throughout their borders, especially in rural areas. ICTs can help us extend our reach, but it is only through attention to appropriate pedagogy that we can ensure these courses are successful. In doing so, we believe that social and economic aspects of rural communities can be improved. As a minimum we want to create circumstances where students and their families living in rural areas do not have to move in order to find the educational opportunities they desire. We also want to contribute to the research base of effective practices for distance education so that rural schools will have access to better distance education courses that produce greater learning outcomes, enhanced student satisfaction and fewer dropouts.

REFERENCES

Barbour, M., & Mulcahy, D. (2006). An inquiry into retention and achievement differences in campus based and web based AP Courses. *Rural Educator, 27*, 8–12.

Barley, Z. A., & Brigham, N. (2008). *Preparing teachers to teach in rural schools*. Washington, DC: Institute for Educational Sciences.

Beeson, E., & Strange, M. (2000). *Why rural matters: The need for every state to take action on rural education*. Washington, DC: Rural School and Community Trust.

Berge, Z. L. (1998). Overcoming obstacles to distance education in the k-12 classroom. In J. Baggaley, T. Anderson, & M. Haughey (Eds.), *Partners in learning: Proceedings of the 14th Annual Conference of the Canadian Association for Distance Education* (Vol. 1, pp. 31-32).

Berge, Z. L., & Mrozowski, S. (1999). Barriers to online teaching in elementary, secondary, and teacher education. *Canadian Journal of Educational Communication, 27*(2), 125–138.

Berge, Z. L., Muilenberg, L. Y., & Van Haneghan, J. (2002). Barriers to distance education and training: Survey results. *The Quarterly Review of Distance Education, 3*, 409–418.

Bernard, R. M., Abrami, P. C., Lou, Y., Borokhovski, E., Wade, A., & Wozney, L. (2004). How does distance education compare with classroom instruction? A meta-analysis of the empirical literature. *Review of Educational Research, 74*, 379–439. doi:10.3102/00346543074003379

Bonk, C. J., & Dennen, V. P. (1999). Teaching on the Web: With a little help from my pedagogical friends. *Journal of Computing in Higher Education, 11*(1), 3–28. doi:10.1007/BF02940840

Burney, V. H., & Cross, T. L. (2006). Impoverished students with academic promise in rural settings: 10 lessons from Project Aspire. *Gifted Child Today, 29*, 14–21.

Carr, S. (2000). As distance education comes of age, the challenge is keeping the students. *The Chronicle of Higher Education, 47*(8), A39–A41.

Cavanaugh, C., Gillan, K. J., Kromrey, J., Hess, M., & Blomeyer, R. (2004). *The effects of distance education on K-12 student outcomes: A meta-analysis*. Naperville, IL: Learning Point Associates.

Cho, S. K., & Berge, Z. L. (2002). Overcoming barriers to distance training and education. *Education at a Distance, 16*(1). Retrieved February 27, 2009 from http://www.usdla.org/html/journal/JAN02_Issue/article01.html

Clark, R. E. (1994). Media will never influence learning. *Educational Technology Research and Development, 42*(2), 21–29. doi:10.1007/BF02299088

D'Amico, J. J., Matthes, W., Sankar, A., Merchant, B., & Zurita, M. (1996). Young voices from the rural Midwest. *Journal of Research in Rural Education, 12*(3). Retrieved January 21, 2008 from http://www.jrre.psu.edu/articles/v12,n3,p142-149,DAmico.pdf

Freire, P. (2000). *Pedagogy of the oppressed*. New York: Continuum.

Garrison, D., & Shale, D. (1987). Mapping the boundaries of distance education: Problems in defining the field. *American Journal of Distance Education, 1*, 4–13. doi:10.1080/08923648709526567

Hannum, W., Irvin, M. J., Lei, P.-W., & Farmer, T. W. (2008). Effectiveness of using learner-centered principles on student retention in distance education courses in rural schools. *Distance Education, 29*, 211–229. doi:10.1080/01587910802395763

Hannum, W. H. (2007). When computers teach: A review of the instructional effectiveness of computers. *Educational Technology, 47*(2), 5–13.

Hannum, W. H., Irvin, M. J., Banks, J. B., & Farmer, T. W. (2009). Distance Education Use in Rural Schools. *Journal of Research in Rural Education, 24*(3), 1–15.

Hannum, W. H., & McCombs, B. L. (2008). Enhancing distance learning with Learner-Centered Principles. *Educational Technology, 48*(4), 11–12.

Herzog, M. J., & Pittman, R. B. (1995). Home, family, and community: Ingredients in the rural education equation. *Phi Delta Kappan, 77*, 113–118.

Hobbs, V. (2004). *The promise and the power of online learning in rural education*. Arlington, VA: Rural School and Community Trust.

Holloway, D. L. (2002). Using research to ensure quality teaching in rural schools. *Journal of Research in Rural Education, 17*(3). Retrieved January 20, 2008 from http://www.jrre.psu.edu/articles/v17,n3,p138-153,Holloway.pdf

Howley, C., Strange, M., & Bickel, R. (2000). Research about school size and school performance in impoverished communities. ERIC Digest. Charleston, WV: ERIC Clearinghouse on Rural Education and Small Schools (ERIC Document Reproduction Service No. ED448968).

Huang, G., & Howley, C. (1993). Mitigating disadvantage: Effects of small-scale schooling on student achievement in Alaska. *Journal of Research in Rural Education, 9*(3). Retrieved June 2, 2008 from http://www.jrre.psu.edu/articles/v9,n3,p137-149,Huang.pdf

Irvin, M. J., Hannum, W. H., & de la Varre, C. (2009). Barriers to distance education in rural schools. Paper presented at the annual meeting of the American Educational Research Association, Rural Special Interest Group, San Diego, CA.

Jennings, N., Swidler, S., & Koliba, C. (2005). Place-based education in the standards-based reform era: Conflict or complement? *American Journal of Education, 122*, 44–65. doi:10.1086/444522

Jimerson, L. (2006). *Breaking the fall: Cushioning the impact of rural declining enrollment.* Arlington, VA: The Rural School and Community Trust.

Johnson, J., & Strange, M. (2007). *Why rural matters 2007: The realities of rural education growth.* Arlington, VA: Rural School and Community Trust.

Keegan, D. J. (1988). Problems in defining the field of distance education. *American Journal of Distance Education, 2*(2), 4–11. doi:10.1080/08923648809526619

Lewis, L., Alexander, D., & Farris, E. (1997). *Distance Education in Higher Education Institutions. National Center for Education Statistics, NCES 98-062.* Washington, DC: US Department of Education.

Lowe, J. M. (2006). Rural Education: Attracting and retaining teachers in small schools. *Rural Educator, 27*(2), 28–32.

Lyson, T. A. (2002). What does a school mean to a community? Assessing the social and economic benefits of schools to rural villages in New York. *Journal of Research in Rural Education, 17*(3). Retrieved February 2, 2008 from http://www.jrre.psu.edu/articles/v17,n3,p131-137,Lyson.pdf

Malecki, E. J. (2003). Digital development in rural areas: Potentials and pitfalls. *Journal of Rural Studies, 19*, 201–214. doi:10.1016/S0743-0167(02)00068-2

McCombs, B., & Vakili, D. (2005). A learner-centered framework for e-learning. *Teachers College Record, 107*(8), 1582–1609. doi:10.1111/j.1467-9620.2005.00534.x

McCombs, B. L., & Miller, L. (2006). *Learner-centered classroom practices and assessments: Maximizing student motivation, learning, and achievement.* Thousand Oaks, CA: Corwin Press.

Miller, G., & Miller, W. (2000). A telecommunication network for distance learning: If it's built, will agriculture teachers use it? *Journal of Agricultural Education, 41*(1), 79–87.

Monk, D. (2007). Recruiting and retaining high-quality teachers in rural areas. *The Future of Children, 17*(1), 155–174. doi:10.1353/foc.2007.0009

Murphy, T. H., & Terry, H. R. (1998). Opportunities and obstacles for distance education in agricultural education. *Journal of Agricultural Education, 39*(1), 28–36.

Nye, B., Hedges, L. V., & Konstantopoulos, S. (2000). Do minorities experience larger lasting benefits from small classes? *The Journal of Educational Research, 98*, 94–100. doi:10.3200/JOER.98.2.94-114

Piacciano, A. G., & Seaman, J. (2007). *K-12 online learning: A survey of U.S. school district administrators.* Needham, MA: Sloan Consortium. Retrieved March 19, 2009 from http://www.sloan-c.org/publications/survey/pdf/K-12_Online_Learning.pdf

Piacciano, A. G., & Seaman, J. (2009). *K-12 online learning: A 2008 follow-up survey of U.S. school district administrators.* Needham, MA: Sloan Consortium. Retrieved March 11, 2009 from http://www.sloan-c.org/publications/survey/pdf/k-12_online_learning_2008.pdf

Provasnik, S., Ramani, A. K., Coleman, M. M., Gilbertson, L., Herring, W., & Xie, Q. (2007). Status of education in rural America (NCES 2007-040). Washington, DC: National Center for Education Statistics, Institute of Education Sciences, U.S. Department of Education.

Roblyer, M. D. (2006). Virtually successful: Defeating the dropout problem through online school programs. *Phi Delta Kappan, 88*(1), 31–36.

Rovai, A.P., & Wighting. (2005). Feelings of alienation and community among higher education students in a virtual community. *The Internet and Higher Education, 8*, 97–110. doi:10.1016/j.iheduc.2005.03.001

Schafft, K. A., Alter, T. R., & Bridger, J. C. (2006, July 17). Bringing the community along: A case study of a school district's information technology rural development initiative. *Journal of Research in Rural Education, 21*(8). Retrieved January 20, 2008 from http://www.umaine.edu/jrre/21-8.pdf

Schlosser, C., & Anderson, A. (1994). *Distance Education: Review of the Literature. Monograph prepared for the Iowa Distance Education Alliance*. Washington, DC: AECT Publications.

Seal, K. R., & Harmon, H. L. (1995). Realities of rural school reform. *Phi Delta Kappan, 77*(2), 119–125.

Setzer, C. J., & Lewis, L. (2005). *Distance education courses for public elementary and secondary school students: 2002–2003 (No. NCES 2005-010)*. Washington, DC: National Center for Education Statistics.

Simpson, O. (2004). The impact on retention of interventions to support distance learning. *Open Learning, 19*(1), 79–96. doi:10.1080/0268051042000177863

Waxman, H. C., Lin, M.-F., & Georgette, M. M. (2003). *A meta-analysis of the effectiveness of teaching and learning with technology on student outcomes*. Naperville, IL: North Central Regional Educational Laboratory.

APA Work Group of the Board of Educational Affairs (1997, November). *Learner-centered psychological principles: A framework for school reform and redesign*. Washington, DC: American Psychological Association.

Zirkle, C. (2001). Access barriers in distance education. *Contemporary Education, 72*(2), 39–42.

Zirkle, C. (2002). Identification of distance education barriers for trade and industrial teacher education. *Journal of Industrial Teacher Education, 40*(1), 20-44. Retrieved July 30, 2008 from http://scholar.lib.vt.edu/ejournals/JITE/v40n1/zirkle.html

Zirkle, C. (2004). Distance education programming barriers in career and technical teacher education in Ohio. *Journal of Vocational Education Research, 29*(1). Retrieved July 30, 2008 from http://scholar.lib.vt.edu/ejournals/JVER/v29n3/zirkle.html#zirkle2001

ADDITIONAL READING

Beldarrain, Y. (2006). Distance education trends: Integrating new technologies to foster student interaction and collaboration. *Distance Education, 27*(2), 139–153. doi:10.1080/01587910600789498

Bernard, R. M., Abrami, P. C., Borokhovski, E., Wade, A., Wozney, L., & Wallet, P. A. (2004). How does distance education compare with classroom instruction: A meta-analysis of the empirical literature. *Review of Educational Research, 74*(3), 379–439. doi:10.3102/00346543074003379

Hannum, W., Irvin, M. J., Lei, P.-W., & Farmer, T. W. (2008). Effectiveness of using learner-centered principles on student retention in distance education courses in rural schools. *Distance Education, 29*, 211–229. doi:10.1080/01587910802395763

Hannum, W. H., Irvin, M. J., Banks, J. B., & Farmer, T. W. (2009). Distance Education Use in Rural Schools. *Journal of Research in Rural Education, 24*(3), 1–15.

Hannum, W. H., & McCombs, B. L. (2008). Enhancing distance learning with Learner-Centered Principles. *Educational Technology, 48*(4), 11–12.

Larreamendy-Joerns, J., & Leinhardt, G. (2006). Going the distance with online education. *Review of Educational Research, 76*(4), 567–605. doi:10.3102/00346543076004567

Talent-Runnels, M. K., Thomas, J. A., Lan, W. Y., Cooper, S., Ahern, T. C., Shaw, S. M., & Liu, X. (2006). Teaching Courses Online: A Review of the Research. *Review of Educational Research, 76*(1), 93–136. doi:10.3102/00346543076001093

Zhao, Y., Lei, J., Yan, B., Lai, C., & Tan, H. (2005). What makes the difference? A practical analysis of research on the effectiveness of distance education. *Teachers College Record, 107*(8), 1836–1884. doi:10.1111/j.1467-9620.2005.00544.x

KEY TERMS AND DEFINITIONS

Distance Education: Formal instruction offered by an educational organization for the express purpose of teaching in which the teacher and students are separated by physical distance and interact through the use of some media that can include print or electronic media such as videoconferencing, e-mail, chat rooms, and discussion forums.

Facilitator: An adult employee of a school who may or may not be a teacher and who has responsibility for supporting and guiding students who are taking a distance education course. The facilitator does not have responsibility for any teaching of the course; the course instructor who is located remotely from the students does all the instruction. However, the facilitator is present in the room with students during a regular class period as they complete course assignments to assist them with any technical matters as well as with issues of time management, study skills, scheduling, personal concerns and the like.

Learner-Centered Principles (LCPs): A set of 14 empirically-validated principles that have been shown to influence learning.

National Research Center on Rural Education Support (NRCRES): A research center located at the University of North Carolina at Chapel Hill in the United States that conducted research on rural education.

Chapter 17
Technological Adaptability in the Ethiopian Education System

Getnet Bitew
Goshen College, USA

ABSTRACT

Ethiopia has been using live "plasma" TV as a major mode of instructional delivery in the government secondary schools since 2004/2005 academic year. Since then, some improvements have been observed in terms of students' listening skill. However, many students, teachers and parents argued that students are becoming mere listeners of the TV. They were not active in the learning process due to the large amount of instructional time taken by the live transmission. The "plasma" TV was also too fast to understand, pre-programmed, non-rewindable, and non-repeatable in character. This mode of instructional delivery should be assessed in terms of, among other criteria, its appropriateness (benefit for students' learning); level of sophistication for the students (with respect to their language skill, etc); cost effectiveness; and availability and technical quality. Unfortunately, the current "plasma" TV was not effective in light of the above criteria. This study indicates that the "plasma" TV lessons shall be distributed on CDs to every school and teacher, and used as a supplementary instructional aid. The current "plasma" mode of instruction shall not continue in the way it is if we are genuinely intending to help our students develop their creativity, problem solving and critical skills. Teachers and students should get enough instructional time in the classrooms for discussion.

INTRODUCTION

Ethiopia is a developing country located in the Northeast part of Africa, commonly known as the Horn of Africa. It has an area of 1.13 million sq km and its population is about 83 million (2008 estimate). It is Africa's oldest independent country.

It has never been colonized except a five-year occupation by Italy during the World War II. Ethiopian economy is highly dependent on agriculture which is sometimes affected by drought and poor administration. The country's per capita income using Atlas method is $220 where $574 is regarded as low income and $37,572 is high income. The World's average per capita income is $7,995. Ethiopia is

DOI: 10.4018/978-1-61520-751-0.ch017

ranked as the 205th country (out of 209 countries in descending order) in its per capita income (The World Bank, 2008).

Modern education in Ethiopia has started just a century ago. The structure of the current Ethiopian education system is 4 + 4 + 2 + 2 +. Kindergarten education is from four to six years of age which is not a necessary condition to enter elementary school for most children of the rural areas. The 4 + 4 indicates eight years of elementary education which is subdivided into four years of basic education (grade 1 to grade 4) and four years of general education (grade 5 to grade 8). 2 + 2 represents a four years of secondary education which is subdivided into two years of general secondary education (grades 9 and 10) and two years of preparatory senior secondary education (grades 11 and 12) that prepares students for tertiary level or higher education (Transitional Government of Ethiopia /TGE/, 1994). Despite the recent introduction of the modern education, Ethiopian students and parents give high value to education. This is because the students and the society in general considered education as the only means for a better life in the future. This helped students to develop high motivation for learning (Bitew, 2008). Despite the students' motivation for learning, recent research findings (ibid.) showed that the students, parents and teachers are highly concerned about the methods of teaching currently being used in all the government secondary schools of the country.

As in other countries, several technological media (e.g. radio, television) have been used to support the formal and informal education system of Ethiopia (Tilson & Bekele, 2000). In addition, the country introduced the use of a new "plasma" TV since 2004/2005 academic year as a major means of transmission of the lessons in the Government secondary schools (grade nine and above). These transmissions were prepared in the Republic of South Africa and sent to the Ethiopian Educational Media Agency where they were transmitted to all government secondary schools via satellite connections. A Satellite

Educational Project located in Johannesburg was responsible for the production of the "plasma" TV instructional programs. Most of the subject experts who have been preparing the programs were South Africans. The project was also called "*Memar* TV" which the Ethiopian government signed a contract agreement with a joint venture between two South African companies - Kagiso Educational TV (KET) and Sasani Ltd. The companies claimed of producing "the equivalent of 45 hours of quality television, accompanied by educationally sound teacher and student guides" per week (Kagiso TV, 2007: 1). They added "due to the time constraints and extensive educational material required, we had to deliver at an average rate of seventy half hour programs" per week. One of the major problems, according to one of the companies, was related to the difficulty of building "long distance relationships with counterparts in Ethiopia" (ibid). The project was financed by a loan obtained from The World Bank.

For most of the subjects of the secondary school curriculum (e.g. Biology, Chemistry, Physics, Mathematics, English, Civics), thirty-five of the forty-five minutes of each lesson was spent by these "plasma" transmissions, leaving just ten minutes for class transition, student-student and student-teacher interactions, note-taking and other relevant classroom activities. Hence, the aim of this article is to discuss about the adaptability of the different technological media, and especially the "plasma" TV, in the Ethiopian classroom situation.

BACKGROUND

This article is primarily based on a comparative research which I conducted on "Using 'Plasma TV' Broadcasts in Ethiopian Secondary Schools" (Bitew, 2008). The comparison was made between the school experiences of students who have been attending the government and the Catholic schools. The government schools have been using the "plasma" TV mode of instruction. The Catholic schools have continued to use the traditional face-to-face mode of instruction and did not introduce the new "plasma" TV programs. The data were mainly obtained from interviews made with students, their parents and teachers; documents; and classroom observations of one selected Catholic and two government secondary schools. Additional data were also obtained from interviews with other students, teachers and parents about other government and Catholic secondary schools. Moreover, most of the student, teacher and parent participants of the three selected schools have given information about the common experiences of students in many of the government and Catholic secondary schools.

The findings of the research showed that the majority of students in both the government and Catholic schools had high interest to learn; gave high value to education; their school behavior was assessed generally as good; had relatively limited time for socialization in school but were generally good in their peer relationships; and had complained about the amount of content of most subjects (ibid.). On the other hand, it was found that the students' classroom activities in the government and Catholic schools were quite different. Their major differences were in their relationship with teachers and the teaching methodologies used where students of the Catholic schools were viewed as the better option in both of these instances. For example, students in the government schools were found spending the majority of their instructional time only by listening to the "plasma" TV transmission without opportunity for any live interaction. They were passive and dissatisfied with the "plasma" TV mode of instruction. The major factors associated with their dissatisfaction were the language incompatibility of the students vis-à-vis the "plasma" teacher; the speed of the transmissions, which made them unable to catch the concepts, and a shortage of instructional time for the students to discuss with their teachers and peers (ibid.).

On the other hand, students of the Catholic school were observed as more approving of their school's mode of instruction. In the Catholic school, students had enough time in the classroom to discuss what they have already learned. They were encouraged by the teachers to ask and answer questions, and to participate in class discussions. They also received regular feedback from their teachers. The implication of such diverse school experiences is clear. Students of the Catholic school had a more positive attitude towards their learning than the other students. Developing the skills of interaction in the classroom has also a potentially positive effect on their future life including university studies. There is also a greater potential for the students of the government schools to carry on the shy, obedient, submissive and passive character of the past, the attributes they shared with their parents as a result of the traditional education systems, that is, the earlier church and Islamic education. The possibility for maintaining these characteristics for students in the government schools was high because the students were existing only as passive listeners of the "plasma" TV in the classrooms (ibid.).

In addition to the above critical research which I (Bitew, 2008) conducted using interviews, documents and classroom observations, I used my recent informal school observations and discussions with teachers and students to write this article. I also used similar research studies to support my interviews and observations. The use of "plasma" TV is discussed here in relation to the socio-cultural, historical, pedagogical, economic, technological and political contexts.

SETTING THE STAGE

Relevance of the "Plasma" TV vis-à-vis the Historical and Socio-Cultural Environment of Ethiopia

The traditional system of Ethiopian education is a history of Church (Orthodox) and Islamic education for thousands of years. What does that contribute to the social values of its current citizens and to the use of technology in the class-rooms? As the traditional education system of Ethiopia was religious oriented (Chaillot, 2002), the major objective of the then education was to produce elites who can serve the Church, the Mosque and the state. Since there was no other source of trained personnel, church education was also expected to produce civil servants, such as judges, governors, scribes, treasurers and general administrators (Teshome, 1979). Children, in that system, were trained to be very loyal and obedient to their elders and the government. They were allowed to follow the strict rules of their elders. Although the education contributed a lot in serving the government and the society, it expanded a shy, docile, passive and excessively obedient common culture. In line with this, Kapuściński (1984), based on his interviews with the Ethiopian noblemen of the past, wrote that:

...we had a docile, resigned, God-fearing people not at all inclined to rebellion... To us humility is uppermost and even His Majesty (Emperor Haile Selassie), as a young lad, kissed his father's shoes. When the elders were eating, children had to stand with their faces to the wall to avoid any ungodly temptation of considering themselves equal to their parents. (Kapuściński, 1984, p. 95)

This kind of tradition has existed in the rural parts of the country though it might not be as strong as the way the tradition was practiced thirty five years ago. It influenced mainly the norms, values and culture of the existing society and it has been dominantly applicable from many years ago till now. It also affected the modern education system in many ways. The effect of this culture, which was undergoing transformation, was reflected in schools in many young men and women who had little exposure, as children, to the modern world. It also partly contributed to a very traditional teacher's method of teaching where the teacher is the only actor in the classroom of the modern schools. Supporting this, my previous study

(Bitew, 2008) showed that the majority of the students in government schools were labeled as *"shy and passive"*.

The objective of the "New Education and Training Policy" (TGE, 1994) was aimed at alleviating this problem and implementing a learner-centered approach in the classroom. However, research findings are showing that the introduction of the "plasma" TV in the classrooms exacerbated the traditional shy and passive character of the students by forcing them to listen thirty five of the forty five minutes of each lesson. Students' had no chance of interacting with each other or with the teacher during the live "plasma" transmission (Bitew, 2008; Hussein, 2006). Lemma (2006) confirmed the same in his classroom observations. He highlighted that both the students and the classroom teacher were completely passive throughout the "plasma" TV lesson except a five minutes introduction and summary made by the teacher without any participation, question or answer from the students. The research findings of Hussein (2006, p. 9) clearly indicated that the "plasma" TV mode if instruction "is an imposition of the old teacher-centered approaches on students as there is no any opportunity for the students to ask and get clarification from the plasma teacher." Hence, the effect of the "plasma" TV was contrary to the objective of the government. Tessema (2006, p. 7) also noted that "plasma" TV "positions students only in the role of passive listening - obedience and taking orders rather than negotiating meaning." Similarly, Dahlström (2007, p. 14) wrote his observation of the "plasma" TV mode of instruction as "the general impression is one of passivity and uni-directional lectures, contrary to the officially proclaimed student-centered policy, unless you define student-centered education as a practice where the teacher is seen as an obstacle in the classroom".

Historically, as mentioned above, Ethiopia, unlike other African countries, was never colonized, except a five year war with Italy during World War II. It also effectively closed its borders for thousands of years resulting in little exposure to the outside world. Besides, it lags behind many countries in introducing the modern technology to its citizens. This would have a negative effect on the technological adaptability in the country's current system of education. In line with this, although resistance to the use of technology in the classroom was predicted on the part of both the students and teachers, their complaint was not on the relevance of the "plasma" TV but more on the way it was being administered and on the allocated amount of time for it (Bitew, 2008; Lopez, 2009). The intended beneficiaries of the "plasma" TV transmission, the students, and their teachers did strongly agree on the importance of such kind of educational technology in helping them facilitate the learning-teaching process. However, they were urging a change in the system, flexibility in the transmission and reduction in the length of broadcasting. They also requested the use of the technology to be responsive towards the students' learning needs.

CASE DESCRIPTION

Adaptability of the "Plasma" TV to the Current Classrooms Situation of Ethiopia

How is the technological adaptability in a classroom where there is an average of ninety-five students per class? How the policy makers, curriculum developers and implementers, particularly teachers, cater for the needs of students and assist their learning with proper technology? Large classroom size is one of the major setbacks in implementing a learner-centered approach in the classroom. The majority of the Ethiopian classrooms in cities and towns have an average of ninety-five students per class. Although this by itself was a major problem for most of the students to interact with other students and teachers and overcome their passive character in the classroom,

there were possibilities for few students to ask questions in the classroom and the rest students had time to internalize the classroom discussion before the introduction of the "plasma" TV.

As a high school teacher and University lecturer for more than eleven years in Ethiopia, I have the experience of teaching up to one hundred and fifty students in one classroom. Although it was a very big challenge to make the lessons more learner-centered, there were several ways in which many students have participated in the class discussions. In fact, it was difficult to reach every student in the classroom in a single period but I had many opportunities, with the whole instructional time in hand, to motivate most of the students to participate in the discussions, ask and answer questions. I had also the opportunity to use any available educational technology depending on its need for the specific lessons and its potential to attract the students' interests. However, when the live "plasma" TV took around 80% of the instructional time, students were left just to be passive listeners and the chance for some students to ask questions in the classroom was no more a possibility. In fact, there were some questions and exercises provided by the "plasma" teachers during the live transmissions in some subjects with the aim of initiating students to practice the lessons delivered. However, the answers were given by the same "plasma" teachers within few seconds before the students understood the questions, let alone working on the exercises. There was no means of checking whether the students understood the lessons or not. The classroom teachers had also no chance of helping or checking the students' understanding within the given, very small, instructional time.

The "plasma" TV program had several pitfalls in terms of its adaptability to the Ethiopian students' situation, one of which was the medium of instruction. As mentioned elsewhere in this article, the majority of the students' English language skill (the medium of instruction of the "plasma" lessons) was far below the expected standard to understand the lessons. When I observed the classrooms, many students were seen as helpless and had lost their attention in despair during the "plasma" transmissions due to their lack of the necessary language skill to comprehend the content. These students were beginners not only in listening English but also in watching TV. Besides, the lessons were too fast to follow for these beginner students. Similar observations were also made by Lemma (2006, p. 81) who indicated that "each time more and more students regress towards sitting and watching what happens". He continued:

From my own experience as a student in a lecture-based system, even with the cruelest teacher, we had managed to ask questions or even win his/her sympathy to repeat some discussions in class. A human being and citizen speaking the regional language could be persuaded to become engaged in some form of discussion, I feel, unlike an inanimate TV system. (ibid.)

Other educators (e.g. Dahlström, 2007, p. 14) also commented about the "plasma" TV mode of delivery that "students try to follow the speedy lesson tempo at the beginning of each lesson but many eventually loose interests and turn into passive spectators of the plasma teacher as the TV lectures progress". A similar study conducted in six secondary schools indicated that "the majority of students, 364 out of 567 (64%), have difficulty to understand the lessons offered by the plasma TV" (Meless & Teshome, 2006, p. 95). According to their study, these 364 students also rated their level of understanding on a rating scale, and 216 of them (38% of the total sample) responded that they "sometimes" understood the lessons offered by the "plasma" TV teachers while 148 students (26%) said that they "rarely" or "not at all" understood the "plasma" instruction. Among the reasons mentioned by the students and teachers for the difficulty of the "plasma" TV lessons were the "TV lessons were too fast to follow" [51.8% of students and 47 out of 49 teachers (96%)] and language problem (40.5% of the students and 49%

of the teachers) (ibid.). The study also reported that when the participants were requested to write their overall comments, the majority of the students and teachers agreed on the presence of many problems on the part of the "plasma" TV mode of delivery such as communication problem (57.3%), too fast to listen (70.3%), short time to do class works (72.7%), no time to get support from the teacher (73%), too fast to take notes (80%), cannot replay back once missed (89.3%), etc. (ibid., p. 96). Again, students would prefer to have more time with their classroom teachers and get more academic help from them than spending most of their instructional time with the "plasma" TV teachers.

Since the program was prepared in South Africa, the accent of the teachers was also far different from what the students were used to hear from their Ethiopian classroom teachers. This exacerbated the students' problem of understanding the "plasma" TV lessons. In connection to this, Dahlström (2007) wrote his observation as "the plasma teachers are not Ethiopians but South Africans, the lessons are carried out in perfect English, but with a South African accent alien to students in Ethiopian secondary classrooms" (ibid., p. 14). Needless to mention, some of the contents and particularly the examples provided by the "plasma" TV teachers were alien to the culture and experience of the Ethiopian students (Bitew, 2008; Dahlström, 2007; Hussien, 2006; Lemma, 2006; Tessema, 2006; 2008) which worsen the students' problem of grasping the "plasma" lessons. For many decades in the past, the Ethiopian curriculum was criticized for just reflecting the Anglo-American tradition. The recent attempt for improving the country's curriculum was aimed at alleviating this problem as well. However, the "plasma" TV content and the examples provided were related to a reversion to the traditional fashion of importing the curriculum content from the Western countries.

As noted above, classroom teachers had little means of assessing students' understanding of the "plasma" lessons, though students' stress, which was explicitly observed from their faces during their attempt to listen and watch the broadcasting, clearly showed their struggle. Since the teachers were not participating in preparing the "plasma" instruction and their role was limited by a five minutes introduction and another five minutes summary, they were regarded as TV operators (Bitew, 2008; Hussiem, 2006; Tessema, 2006; 2008). Dahlström (2007) described this situation as:

The role of the ordinary teacher in the classroom is to unlock the cage where the screen is placed and to slide the screen in front of the class and eventually to introduce 'the topic' by writing it on the board. The teacher has five minutes for this work before the transmission starts following a nationally directed time schedule. During the entire lesson the teacher is then reduced to a spectator just like the students until the plasma television program ends. (Dahlström, 2007, p. 14)

This situation denied teachers the chance of considering and addressing their students' needs and problems in the classroom. The "plasma" mode of instruction also "dehumanized" and "deskilled" (Dahlström, 2007; Tessema, 2006; 2008) the teachers. The teachers were not able to use their training and experience for helping their students and facilitate the learning process when they were given only ten minutes, out of forty five, with the duty of just opening the TV, and introducing and summarizing the "plasma" lessons.

ADAPTABILITY OF THE CURRENT USE OF "PLASMA" TV TO THE BASIC PRINCIPLES OF LEARNING AND THE ECONOMIC SITUATION OF THE COUNTRY

The benefit of using technology in the classroom is indisputable when it is used appropriately. Many research findings (e.g. Chapman, Garrett & Mählck, 2004; Gabric et al, 2005; Hardman, 2005; Okojie & Olinzock, 2006; Schmid, 2007) reported the benefits of using different types of technology in the classroom in facilitating learning, catering for various learning styles, engaging the students and enhancing their motivation. Educational technology is also recognized for its benefit in reaching students and teachers in remote locations. Especially educational TV plays an important role in demonstrating expensive experiments in ordinary classrooms and compensates the shortage of qualified teachers and lab equipment which are usually unavailable in remote schools (Chapman, Garrett & Mählck, 2004; Evans, Stacey & Tregenza, 2001). Chapman, Garrett & Mählck (2004) also highlighted the advantage of using educational TV in locating maps and offsetting weak teacher preparation. Some of these benefits were also mentioned by the Federal Democratic Republic of Ethiopia (FDRE, 2004) as the driving force for introducing the "plasma" TV transmission. In the words of the FDRE document, the "plasma" TV "enables students to have access to model and competent teachers; and demonstrate laboratory equipment found in one place (classroom) to other learning classrooms" (FDRE, 2004, pp. 8-9). Like other developing countries, lack of qualified teachers and inaccessibility of lab equipment are burning issues in most rural schools of Ethiopia. Hence, the introduction of "plasma" TV instruction has a sound justification and it is an appropriate step towards a better education from its inception.

However, it is also mentioned in the introduction that Ethiopia is one of the poorest nations in the world where the majority of its citizens are living below the poverty line. Its per capita income using Atlas method is $220 (The World Bank, 2008). Lack of and limited access to the basic necessities of life such as pure water, food and health care are the major problems affecting the lives of the vast majority of the people of the nation. Even in this 21st Century, electricity, transportation, telecommunication and other services are undreamed of and beyond the reach of the majority of the people who are especially living in the rural areas (despite a recent attempt by the government to improve these services which should be appreciated).

With this dire economic situation of the country, the state spends 10% of its total budget for the "plasma" transmission. It installed state-of-the-art "plasma" TV in each classroom and a Satellite receiver in each government secondary school. An international journalist who observed the installation commented it as "the shock of the new" (Heavens, 2005, p. 1) and illustrated it as:

Students were all taking their lessons from a professor speaking through a state-of-the-art Samsung Plasma video screen that would be way beyond the budget of many schools in the UK. The lesson was being beamed in... via a huge satellite dish outside through a rack of Digital Video Broadcasting (DVB) receivers. (ibid.)

Taking all the current socio-economic conditions of the country into serious consideration, there were many educators, students, teachers and parents [in my interview sessions, Bitew (2008)] who shared the view that if the state spent this money to train more qualified teachers, reduce the class size, purchase books and essential equipment for labs, the quality of education would be much better than its current status. Heyneman and Haynes (2004, pp. 65 – 66) also question that "in a poor country with many people who are illiterate, low skilled and unemployed, should scarce foreign exchange money be spent on ICT rather than on addressing other priorities?" In connection to this, Castro (2004) suggested developing countries to focus on those educational technologies which bring the imagination and creativity of best teachers to students at low costs.

The customer case study of the main contractor involved in building the network, Cisco Systems (2006), indicated that the Ethiopian government worked closely with Cisco and the Internet Business Solutions Group (IBSGO) to use ICT in education. The report continued "one of the poorest nations on Earth is committing scarce economic resources... to a bold investment program that uses IP-based networking as a long-term solution to poverty... through wider access to education" (Cisco, 2006, pp. 1-3). Even the contractor, the main beneficiary of this project, did not deny the challenge ahead in the implementation of the ICT in the country's education system. The main problem lies on the basic question that 'does access to education alone guarantee quality education and that of poverty reduction?' What about those adults who completed their secondary education but stayed unemployed for many years? Are we promoting the development of critical thinking, creativity and problem solving skills in the process of students' learning by using the "plasma" TV?

When we see the current "plasma" TV instructional delivery with respect to the pedagogical principles of learning, as it is mentioned elsewhere in this article, it was an imposition from the top officials. It did not cater the needs of the students nor aimed at the development of the critical thinking, creativeness and problem solving skills of the students. It is difficult to think of students to develop creativity and critical thinking skills by listening and watching a pre-programmed TV lesson for about three hours of their four hours instructional time per day. Learning is also social in character in the sense that it involves classroom interaction and discussion where students must play an active role in the process. However, both students and teachers were denied of this essential part of the learning process due to the large amount of time being taken by the "plasma" TV lesson delivery.

The instructional delivery would be more productive and helpful for students' learning if it was using an interactive TV in which students got the access to watch while other students interact in the classroom on the same topic as well as if they were provided with additional time to discuss with their teachers and their fellow students. Research findings showed that using interactive TV in teaching was as effective as face-to-face instruction with regard to acquisition of critical thinking skills which included reasoning, problem solving, creating and evaluating knowledge (Huff, 2000). Interactive TV was favored for its potential in initiating students' discussion with each other. In connection to this, Friere (1993) strongly argued the necessity of a dialogue between students and students as well as students and teachers for a better and just learning to occur. Depriving them of this necessary dialogical relation is in turn an illegitimate exercise of the "banking" concept of education (ibid.).

As mentioned above, teachers' role in the preparation and implementation of the classroom lessons was very minimal. In line with this, Okojie & Olinzock (2006, p. 33) noted that "efforts to incorporate technology into the process of teaching/ learning has primarily emphasized teachers' ability to operate computers ('plasma' TV in this case) without taking into consideration pedagogical issues involved in teaching and learning." The current "plasma" TV mode of delivery not only suggests a mechanistic use of the educational technology without due consideration to pedagogical principles but also assumes teachers as mechanical beings. This may also diminish the possible development of the students' and teachers' "positive mind-set toward the use of technology" (ibid.) in the future.

It was also evident from my classroom observations (Bitew, 2008) that the government did not consider the already available educational infrastructure in the schools when it introduced the "plasma" TV transmission. In many classrooms of the country, there were laboratories, though impoverished, which were used to provide practical experiences to the students. I asked the teachers whether they used those laboratories after the "plasma" TV transmission came into effect. The participants of the different schools confirmed that they never used those laboratories after the

introduction of the "plasma" TV due to lack of time. Lemma's classroom observation also indicated the same. Lemma (2006, p. 73) observed that "today students do not use them (the laboratory facilities) as a result of the plasma TV lessons, which consume the time needed for laboratory work". Students were, therefore, restricted to watch laboratory experiments carried out by others from the "plasma" TV transmission. They did not practice it by themselves. However, conducting experiments or learning by doing is one of the best strategies of learning in several subjects.

THE CURRENT USE OF THE "PLASMA" TV AND ITS ESSENCE IN A TECHNOLOGICALLY LESS DEVELOPED COUNTRY

Another major problem of relying on the Plasma TV as the sole method of teaching in Ethiopian government secondary schools is its incompatibility with the technological development of the country. As I have witnessed and many participants also confirmed, there were many instances of electric power failure which blocked the live "plasma" lesson transmission. I observed this incident several times in my classroom observations of three schools in nine weeks (Bitew, 2008). Students and teachers were not surprised in the power interruption and they told me that "it is a common problem". This problem got worse as I was writing this article, in May 2009, where I was listening to the VOA Amharic radio which indicated that many towns faced an electric power cut for two or three days every week this season due to the decline of the amount of water in the water-dam. One of the commentators in Ethiopia said "it is depressing. The crisis is affecting the schools, hotels, government offices and factories. We do not know the specific time and date when the light would be cut off. It seems that there is a lack of preparation from the Ethiopian Electric Power Corporation in managing the problem"

(VOA Amharic Radio, Tuesday, 05/19/2009). Another classroom observation in one region conducted by Tessema (2008, p. 350) indicated that the "teacher has come to the class with a hope of the TV lesson. Soon he realizes the TV is not running from the server or because of some local technical problem." Similar observations were reported by Hussien (2006), and Meless and Teshome (2006).

In such occasions where there was technical problem or no electric power and thereby no "plasma" transmission, some teachers were observed trying to discuss with students about any content they expected as important for the students. But, I heard a grade nine Chemistry teacher saying to his students that "I do not know what the plasma teacher would explain next but ask me any question until the power is restored". This indicated me that the classroom teachers did not have the specific topics and detailed contents which were discussed by the "plasma" teacher. My discussion with the teachers confirmed that classroom teachers only knew what was written in the textbook and the major topics which were going to be explained by the "plasma" teacher but had no clue about the particular content until the lessons were broadcasted. That is, classroom teachers did not get the content of the lessons in advance. It is also reported by Tessema (2008, p. 350) that "teachers don't know exactly all the details about plasma lessons in advance". In a similar classroom observation at another school, Lemma (2006, p. 75) asked a Biology teacher what was going to be taught by the "plasma" teacher on that day by saying: "do you know what it is going to be about?" The Biology teacher responded "no". The teacher added "for the last two days we did not have satellite connection". Lemma (2006) also observed an electric power failure and thereby a similar interruption of the "plasma" transmission within twenty minutes after the lesson was started. Lemma described this scenario in his words as "the class was immediately plunged into silence followed by some murmuring. The class had not

attended TV lessons for the past two days and (the students and the teacher) were surprised that this phenomenon was repeated for the third day in a row" (Lemma, 2006, p. 76).

The most outstanding problem was that there was no means of retrieving the lessons that were already transmitted nationally and missed at the time of power failure in any school or town. Because power interruptions occur in some areas today and in other areas some other day, it created inequality and discrepancy in the lessons reached to each school, which was contrary to one of the objectives of introducing the "plasma" TV lessons. One of the aims of the government in using the "plasma" TV was to "transmit uniform education to many students found in different places at the same time" (FDRE, 2004, p. 8) and ensure equity in education. The shortcoming of the "plasma" TV was, hence, severe when it is assessed in terms of its pre-programmed, non-rewindable, and non-repeatable character (Tessema, 2006; 2008). Absence of spare parts and technicians in repairing the "plasma" TV on time was also another devastating problem at least in remote schools in that technologically underdeveloped country. The argument here is how can one take the "plasma" TV transmission as the sole, mandatory and guaranteed means of instructional delivery before making sure the sustainability of the basic installations such as electricity?

Another point of argument which many students and teachers raised was that the "plasma" TV mode of instruction favors the rich rather than the poor. The majority of the students were from very poor families who had no experience of watching and listening TV at home for they could not afford it to buy. However, few students who were from the well-to-do families had experience of watching and listing TV and films in English. The English language skill of the students from the rich families was far better than the students from the poor families. When the students from the rich families were attending the "plasma" TV from a fluent English speaker, they understand the lessons better than the students from the poor families. The two groups of students also take the same national examination which determined whether a student should attend higher education or not. The universities are always admitting the first few top students based on their results in the national examination. With no doubt, the students of the poor were lagging behind the others. This situation, according the participants, continued to widen the gab between the poor and the rich, and was not targeted to realize equity in education as promised. Mählck & Chapman (2004) also noted the potential of educational technology in exacerbating inequalities in education.

THE ROLE OF THE ETHIOPIAN POLITICS IN THE USE OF "PLASMA" TV IN EDUCATION

Most students, teachers and parents whom I contacted in my study and informal discussions were hesitant about the objective of the state in introducing the "plasma" TV. They were questioning whether the state has introduced the "plasma" TV transmission with a genuine intention of improving the quality and equity of education for the people (which is practically leading to the opposite) or with the political intention of maintaining its power by dehumanizing the students' thinking skills that hinder them from exchanging ideas in classrooms. Tessema (2006, p. 7) described this situation as "the implicit ideology of dominant groups to perpetuate the culture of silence is apparently at work." He continued that "the national televised education program is an attempt to centralize knowledge and curriculum, and by doing so, to control the hearts and minds of students. It is to make the teacher powerless as a political and liberating agent." (ibid.)

I met students and teachers who described this situation with anger by saying the govern-ment was trying to block our potential to discuss in the classroom by keeping us listen and watch the "plasma" TV. These participants of my study believed that the government was using a politically motivated technique to spend the students' school time just by forcing them to listen which hinders the possibilities of the students to raise political questions in the classroom (Bitew, 2008). At most, since the "plasma" TV was introduced without assessing the needs and experiences of the students, the students and teachers felt it as an imposition from the top and gave a lukewarm reception.

There were also several educators (e.g. Tessema, 2006) who believe that the introduction of the "plasma" TV mode of delivery was, at best, helpful to expand a marketization agenda aimed at producing consumers of the global movie industry. Such type of marketization agenda was also described by Giroux (2000, p. 85) as a means of transforming "public education from a public good, benefiting all students, to a private good designed to expand the profits of investors, educate students as consumers..." Similar assertions were made by Callewaert (2006) as

Educational reforms have been presented in Ethiopia as necessary breaks with a pre-modern and modern conservative tradition, in the name of late modern progressive educational ideas and practices like learner-centered education. However, in fact, what may come about looks very much like technocratic submission to a globalizing market economy and not like emancipation of people, be they students or teachers... One example of such a technocratic change is the introduction without any professional or democratic discussion of teacher-centered South-African lessons in key secondary education subjects with the help of satellite broadcasts to plasma TV screens all over the country. (Callewaert, 2006, p. 128)

THE IMPACT OF A CENTRALLY DETERMINED, NATIONAL CURRICULUM TO THE PROPER USE OF ANY EDUCATIONAL TECHNOLOGY IN THE CLASSROOMS

The aim of a national curriculum is to ensure that the same content is taught in all schools, so that students throughout the nation receive the same program of education. It is primarily intended to keep the standard of education across the schools of the nation. It specifies what students should learn while they're at school and the standards they should achieve. Its aim is to standardize the content taught across schools in order to enable uniform assessment. Although some countries use a national curriculum framework than a detailed common curriculum to be implemented in schools, Ethiopia is implementing a highly centralized national curriculum in the secondary schools where the textbook of each subject specifies in detail what to be strictly followed and taught in all schools. This undoubtedly restricts the type of educational technology to be used in the classroom. Since classroom teachers and students have no role in curriculum development at any level, the strict top-down type of curriculum development is a "one size-fits-all" approach that does not take the students' specific backgrounds into consideration.

ACHIEVEMENTS SO FAR AS A RESULT OF THE TECHNOLOGICAL ADAPTABILITY IN THE ETHIOPIAN EDUCATION SYSTEM

Classroom teachers' informal observations (though not substantiated by a critical research) showed that many students were starting to come to school on time after the introduction of the "plasma" TV instruction. Lemma (2006, p. 81) also mentioned this point as "I could see that most students have started to become punctual because

of the TV lessons. It looks like they are aware of the risk that once they miss the TV lessons they miss them forever".

One of the best achievements of the introduction of the "plasma" TV so far was the development of the students' listening skill. Students and teachers observed improvement in the students' listening skill of the English language. In several regions of the country, the government enforces the students to learn by their regional language until grade eight. For these regions, English was a medium of instruction beginning from grade nine. However, there were also few regions who were allowed to use English as a medium of instruction starting from grade seven. I travelled to two regions (Amhara and Oromia) where the medium of instruction until grade eight was their respective regional languages. However, the students would like to learn all subjects in English starting from grade seven. These students had severe difficulty of understanding the "plasma" TV teacher when they started their grade nine lessons in English. After several months, the teachers and students confirmed that they saw improvement in the listening skill of these students. However, they were also in the opinion that if they were allowed to learn their lessons in English starting from grade seven, they would have had limited problem of understanding the "plasma" TV lessons which were broadcasted in English. According to these participants, since all the students of the nation were taking a national examination, the introduction of the "plasma" TV again contributed to another challenge for the promised equity in education.

THE HURDLES FACED AND STRATEGIES USED TO IMPROVE THE SYSTEM

The major hurdle in the adaptability of the "plasma" TV to the current Ethiopian classroom situation was its inflexibility and the time it takes compared to the available instructional time for each subject. A recent study on this issue at one of the regions of the country, Mekelle, showed that "teachers complain that 35 minutes of every 45 minute classroom period is devoted to plasma TV instruction, leaving only 10 minutes for any other activities" (Lopez, 2009, p. 10). Although my study and other recent studies supported the students' and teachers' preference that "the plasma instruction be used as a supplemental tool rather than the primary source of curriculum and instruction" (ibid.), no strategy has been implemented to improve the education system yet.

SOLUTIONS AND RECOMMENDATIONS

It has been seen that the current "plasma" TV teachers cannot replace the classroom teachers. Students' instructional needs confirmed this phenomenon. Effective learning and success in the development of students' critical thinking and problems solving skills cannot be achieved by the current "plasma" TV lessons alone. Hence, sufficient instructional time should be provided for student – student and student – teacher interactions and discussions. In fact, the "plasma" TV lessons can contribute a lot for a better learning if they are distributed on CDs to every school and teacher and used as a supplementary instructional aid. The current "plasma" mode of instruction shall not continue if we are genuinely intending to help our students. Above all, an educational technology based on students' needs, which is identified by a thorough needs analysis, is more productive and practical than the one which was imposed from top authorities. Hence, I recommend a bottom – up initiative of using educational technology that can be supported and adopted by central-level authorities, as it has been used in Jamaica. It is believed that when an effective educational technology is used, "teacher-centered lectures are moved to more student-centered,

constructivist learning strategies in which students are expected to research information, analyze data, and draw their own conclusions" (Mählck & Chapman, 2004, p. 298) unlike the one which we saw in the Ethiopian "plasma" TV mode of instructional delivery.

REFERENCES

Bitew, G. (2008). Using Plasma TV Broadcasts in Ethiopian Secondary Schools: A Brief Survey. *Australasian Journal of Educational Technology, 24*(2), 150–167.

Callewaert, S. (2006). Looking Back, But Not in Anger . In Dahlström, L., & Mannberg, J. (Eds.), *Critical Educational Visions and Practices in Neo-Liberal Times, 127 – 132. Umeå University: Global South Network Publisher.*

Castro, C. M. (2004). Are New Technologies Better Technologies? For Whom? In Chapman, D. W., & Mählck, L. O. (Eds.), *Adapting Technology for School Improvement: A Global Perspective, 39 – 54*. Paris: International Institute for Educational Planning.

Chaillot, C. (2002). *The Ethiopian Orthodox Tewahedo Church Tradition - a Brief Introduction to its Life and Spirituality*. Paris: Inter-Orthodox Dialogue.

Chapman, D. W., Garrett, A., & Mählck, L. O. (2004). The Role of Technology in School Improvement . In Chapman, D. W., & Mählck, L. O. (Eds.), *Adapting Technology for School Improvement: A Global Perspective* (pp. 19–38). Paris: International Institute for Educational Planning.

Cisco Systems. (2006). *Ethiopia Accelerates National Development Through Information and Communications Technology: A Customer Case Study*. San Jose, CA: Cisco Systems, Inc.

Evans, T., Stacey, E., & Tregenza, K. (2001). Interactive Television in Schools: An Australian Study of the Tensions of Educational Technology and Change. *International Review of Research in Open and Distance Learning, 2*(1).

FDRE (The Federal Democratic Republic of Ethiopia). (2004). *Development of Education in Ethiopia*. A Report to the UNESCO Forty-Seventh Session of the International Conference on Education, 8-11 September 2004, Geneva, Switzerland.

Freire, P. (1993). *Pedagogy of the Oppressed*. New York: The Continuum Publishing Company.

Giroux, H. A. (2000). *Stealing Innocence: Youth, Corporate Power, and the Politics of Culture*. New York: St. Martin's Press.

Hardman, J. (2005). An Exploratory Case Study of Computer Use in a Primary School Mathematics Classroom: New Technology, New Pedagogy? *Perspectives in Education, 23*(4), 99–111.

Heavens, A. (2005). *The Shock of the New*. Retrieved May 12, 2009, from http://www.meskelsquare.com/archives/2005/01/the_shock_of_th.html

Heyneman, S. P., & Haynes, K. T. (2004). International Uses of Education Technology: Threats and Opportunities . In Chapman, D. W., & Mählck, L. O. (Eds.), *Adapting Technology for School Improvement: A Global Perspective* (pp. 55–80). Paris: International Institute for Educational Planning.

Huff, M. (2000). A Comparison Study of Live Instruction Versus Interactive Television for Teaching MSW Students Critical Thinking Skills. *Research on Social Work Practice, 10*(4).

Hussien, J. (2006). Locating the Value Conflicts Between the Rhetoric and Practices of the Public and Teacher Education in Ethiopia within the Hegemony of the Global Neo-Liberalism and Seeking the Alternative in Critical Pedagogy. *Journal for Critical Education Policy Studies, 4*(2).

Kagiso, T. V. (2007). *Ethiopian Ministry of Education*. Retrieved July 10, 2009, from http://www.kagisotv.co.za/ClientPortfolio/Casestudies/MemarEthiopianEducationProject/tabid/944/language/en-US/Default.aspx

Kapuściński, R. (1984). *The Emperor*. London: Pan Books Ltd.

Lemma, B. (2006). Plasma Television Teachers - When a Different Reality Takes Over African Education. In L. Dahlström & J. Mannberg (Eds.), Critical Educational Visions and Practices in Neo-Liberal Times, 71-88. Umeå University: Global South Network Publisher.

Lopez, J. (2009). *Educational Access and Quality in Ethiopia: Successes and Challenges in the City of Mekelle*. Student Symposium on African Education – Interrogating Quality in the African Context, Teachers' College, Columbia University.

Mählck, L. O., & Chapman, D. W. (2004). Effective Use of Technology to Improve Education: Lessons for Planners . In Chapman, D. W., & Mählck, L. O. (Eds.), *Adapting Technology for School Improvement: A Global Perspective* (pp. 297–305). Paris: International Institute for Educational Planning.

Meless, K., & Teshome, Z. (2006). Assessment on the Impact of Plasma Television Implementation on the Teaching Learning Process of Mathematics Class: The Case on Selected Practicum Sites (High Schools) for Education Faculty of Jimma University. *Ethiopian Journal of Education and Science, 2*(1), 85–127.

Okojie, M. C., & Olinzock, A. (2006). Developing a Positive Mind-Set Toward the Use of Technology for Classroom Instruction. *International Journal of Instructional Media, 33*(1), 33–41.

Teshome, W. (1979). *Education in Ethiopia: Prospect and retrospect.* Rendale: Wiley Canada.

Tessema, K. (2006). Contradictions, Challenges, and Chaos in Ethiopian Teacher Education. *Journal for Critical Education Policy Studies, 4*(1).

Tessema, K. (2008). An Exploration for a Critical Practicum Pedagogy: Dialogical Relationships and Reflections among a Group of Student Teachers. *Educational Action Research, 16*(3), 345–360. doi:10.1080/09650790802260299

TGE /Transitional Government of Ethiopia/ (MOE). (1994). *Education and Training Policy.* Addis Ababa, Ethiopia: EMPDA.

The World Bank. (2008). *Gross National Income Per Capita 2007, Atlas Method and PPP.* World Development Indicators Database, The World Bank Group. Retrieved May 12, 2009, from http://siteresources.worldbank.org/DATASTATISTICS/Resources/GNIPC.pdf

Tilson, T., & Bekele, D. (2000). Ethiopia: Educational Radio and Television. *TeckKnowLogia, 2*(3). Retrieved May 12, 2009, from http://www.techknowlogia.org/TKL_active_pages2/ Currentarticles/main.asp?IssueNumber=5&FileType=HTML&ArticleID=121

VOA (Voice of America). (2009, May 19). *The Problem of Electricity in Ethiopia.* Voice of America, Amharic Program.

ADDITIONAL READING

Akyurek, F. (2005). A Model Proposal for Educational Television Programs. *Turkish Online Journal of Distance Education, 6*(2).

Bacon, S. F., & Jakovich, J. A. (2001). Instructional Television versus Traditional Teaching of an Introductory Psychology Course. *Teaching of Psychology, 28*(2), 88–92. doi:10.1207/S15328023TOP2802_02

Bitter, G. G., & Legacy, J. M. (2007). *Using Technology in the Classroom* (7th ed.). Boston: Allyn & Bacon, Inc.

Cruickshank, B. J. (2002). *College-Level General Chemistry Taught via Interactive Instructional Television (IITV) to Students at HOPI High School.* A Paper Presented to The American Chemical Society.

Donlevy, J. (2001). Instructional Media Initiatives: Focusing on the Educational Resources Center at Thirteen/WNET. *International Journal of Instructional Media, 28*(4), 333–336.

Fisch, S. M. (2004). *Children's Learning from Educational Television.* Mahwah, NJ: Lawrence Erlbaum Associates.

Freddolino, P. P. (2000). Assessing the Comparability of Classroom Environments in Graduate Social Work Education Delivered via Interactive Instructional Television. *Journal of Social Work Education, 36*(1), 115–129.

Gabric, K. M. (2005). Scientists in Their Own Classroom: The Use of Type II Technology in the Science Classroom. *Computers in the Schools, 22*(3/4), 77–91.

Greig, A., & Hedberg, J. G. (1988). A National Educational Television Network for Australia: Why, How and When. In J. Steel & J. G. Hedberg (Eds.), *Belconnen ACT: Australian Society for Educational Technology, Proceedings of the 1988 Conference of the Australian Society for Educational Technology,* Canberra College of Advanced Education (pp. 9 – 12).

Hadded, W. D., & Jurich, S. (2002). ICT for Education: Prerequisites and Constraints . In Haddad, W. D., & Draxler, A. (Eds.), *Technologies for Education – Potentials, Parameters and Prospects*. Paris: UNESCO.

Harris, J., Mishra, P., & Koehler, M. (2009). Teachers' technological pedagogical content knowledge and learning activity types: curriculum-based technology integration reframed. *Journal of Research on Technology in Education, 41*(4), 393–416.

Jansen, M. S. H. (1987). *An Investigation into the Use of Educational Television*. Ph.D. Dissertation, Murdoch University.

Januszewski, A., Molenda, M., & Harris, P. (2007). *Educational Technology: A Definition with Commentary* (2nd ed.). Portland, OR: Lawrence Erlbaum Associates, Inc.

Jonassen, D. H. (2007). *Meaningful Learning with Technology* (3rd ed.). New Jersey: Prentice Hall, Inc.

King, K. P. (2000). Educational Television:Let's Explore Science. *Journal of Science Education and Technology, 9*(3), 227–246. doi:10.1023/A:1009443617295

McCombs, B. L. (2000). Assessing the Role of Educational Technology in the Teaching and Learning Process: A Learner-Centered Perspective. In *Proceedings of The Secretary's Conference on Educational Technology, 2000: Measuring Impacts and Shaping the Future*, Alexandria, VA.

Pelgrum, W. J., & Law, N. (2003). *The Introduction of Information and Communication Technologies in Education*. Paris: IIEP – UNESCO.

Pitler, H. (2007). *Using Technology with Classroom Instruction That Works*. Alexandria, VA: Association for Supervision and Curriculum Development.

Reed, P., & Doviak, P. (2001). *Speaking with Interactive Educational Television Directors in Secondary Schools: Is IETV Making the Grade?* Paper presented at the Annual Meeting of the Mid-South Educational Research Association (30th, Little Rock, AR, November 14-16, 2001).

Reed, P., & Doviak, P. (2003). Effectiveness of a Technology Mediated Classroom: Adult Learners' Perceptions of an Interactive Instructional Television Class. *International Journal of Learning, 10*, 3089–3096.

Roblyer, M. D., & Doering, A. H. (2009). *Integrating Educational Technology into Teaching (with MyEducationLab)* (5th ed.). Boston: Allyn Bacon, Inc.

Schiller, S. S. (1991). Educational Applications of Instructional Television and Cable Programming. *Media and Methods, 27*(4), 20–21.

Schmid, E. C. (2008). Potential Pedagogical Benefits and Drawbacks of Multimedia Use in the English Language Classroom Equipped with Interactive Whiteboard Technology. *Computers & Education, 51*, 1553–1568. doi:10.1016/j.compedu.2008.02.005

Shomaker, D. (1993). A Statewide Instructional Television Program via Satellite for RN-to-BSN Students. *Journal of Professional Nursing, 9*(3), 153–158. doi:10.1016/8755-7223(93)90067-M

Weatherholt, T. N. (2007). Integrative Review of Educational Television for Young Children: Implications for Children from Low-Income Families. *NHSA Dialog: A Research-to-Practice Journal for the Early Intervention Field, 10*(3-4), 171 – 188.

Wellburn, E. (1996). *The Status of Technology in the Education System: A Literature Review*. British Columbia: Ministry of Education, Skills and Training, Technology and Distance Education Branch.

Williams, M. E., & Hall, E. R. (1994). Creating Educational Television Programs That Are Relevant to the Lives of Children. *Youth & Society*, *26*(2), 243–255. doi:10.1177/0044118X94026002005

KEY TERMS AND DEFINITIONS

Classroom Interaction: The communication, relationship and instructional collaboration between teacher and students as well as students and students in a classroom.

Educational TV: Television programs that transmit formal classroom instructional materials.

Ethiopia: A country located in the Northeast part of Africa.

Instructional Methods: Educational approach used for learning. It is the "how to" in the delivery of instruction. Methods are used by teachers to create learning environments and to specify the nature of the activity in which the teacher and learner will be involved during the lesson.

National Curriculum: The curriculum of subjects taught in all schools of the country. It is usually prepared by the Ministry of Education at the top.

Plasma TV: A flat-panel display or a Samsung video screen where students listen and watch an instructional program via a satellite dish receiver.

Secondary School: A formal school for students from grade 9 to 12, both inclusive.

Students' Learning: The knowledge, skills and attitudes students received through a formal schooling.

Chapter 18
Building an Interactive Fully–Online Degree Program

Jennie Mitchell
Saint Mary-of-the-Woods College, USA

Daesang Kim
Saint Mary-of-the-Woods College, USA

ABSTRACT

Saint Mary-of-the-Woods College (SMWC) expects to launch an interactive fully-online undergraduate degree program in 2010. This program will fill a market need not currently met at SMWC. The program is designed for an online community of learners with a format and focus that appeals to net generation (millennial), neo-millennial, and computer savvy non-traditional students, including military personnel. The General Studies in the new program will focus on seven themes of Leadership for Environmental and Social Justice and will build upon a subset of the existing General Studies. This new program will complement the Woods External Degree (WED), an existing distance education program, established in 1973, that was built on the "correspondence model." In the new program, students will not be required to come to campus, but will become a vibrant part of the SMWC community by being empowered to explore, discover, and interact through innovative technologies.

ORGANIZATION BACKGROUND

Saint Mary-of-the-Woods College (SMWC), the oldest Catholic liberal arts college for women in the United States is located on a 67-acre campus five miles northwest of Terre Haute, Indiana. Sponsored by the Sisters of Providence, the College was founded in 1840 by Saint Mother Theodore Guerin, who was canonized by the Roman Catholic Church on October 15, 2006. The College provides three distinct academic opportunities: 1) traditional campus-based undergraduate degree programs for women, 2) distance education undergraduate degree and teacher licensure programs (Woods External Degree) for women and men, and 3) distance education graduate degree and certificate programs for women and men.

The College serves a diverse community of learners in undergraduate and graduate programs. As of Fall 2008, 271 students were enrolled on campus

DOI: 10.4018/978-1-61520-751-0.ch018

Table 1. Current SMWC distance program formats

Woods External Degree (WED)	Master of Leadership Development (MLD) & Master of Education (M.Ed.)	Other graduate programs (Art Therapy, Earth Literacy, Music Therapy, and Pastoral Theology)
• Flexible schedule • Individual • Undergraduate (4yr, maximum 12 yr) • 20 weeks class time • One-day residency recommended at the beginning of each required course • Desire2Learn (course management system) course format recommended • Many courses use email, some still use mail • Individual assignments, very little if any team assignments • Accept ACE Guidelines • Assessment of prior learning (APL) for college credit	• Fixed schedule • Cohort • Graduate (1yr) • 8 weeks class time • Hybrid: Weekend residency every two months, online activities between residency • Desire2Learn course format required using required template • Webinar (seminar held over the Web) activity required • Many group assignments and projects	• Fixed schedule • Intensive format • Graduate (2 or 3 yr) • Five-day residencies at the beginning of each semester • Desire2Learn course format recommended • Individual assignments

and 1097 men and women (89% of whom were over the age of 26) were enrolled in the Woods External Degree (WED) program. Students can earn degrees in 39 major areas. The College is best known for its undergraduate programs in Equine Studies, Education, Business, and Pre-professional Studies. The WED program has a 35-year history of serving non-traditional adult students, and was one of the first independent-study degree programs in the nation. Today, students can earn degrees in 27 major areas through the WED program. Four of the graduate programs, Art Therapy, Earth Literacy, Music Therapy, and Pastoral Theology, enroll 116 students. The Master of Leadership Development (MLD) program enrolled its third cohort of 23 students in February 2009, and 9 additional students in a special cohort. The Master of Education (M.Ed.) program enrolled its first two cohorts totaling 20 students in 2008, with expectations of exceeding 25 students in 2009.

In addition to regional accreditation by the North Central Association of Colleges and Schools, specific programs are accredited or approved by the National Association of Schools of Music, the American Music Therapy Association, the National Council for Accreditation of Teacher Education, and the Institute for the Certification of Computer Professionals. U. S. News and Woods Online Report ranks Saint Mary-of-the-Woods College among the top 25 comprehensive colleges in the Midwest in 2009.

Setting the Stage

The College started a correspondence distance program in 1973 and delivered its first online course in 1996. SMWC currently provides different distance formats (see Table 1) available to both women and men. There are more than 2,500 distance students that have graduated or completed their programs at the College through these programs.

The MLD and M.Ed. programs were designed to be completed in one year using a hybrid-course format, with on-site-face-to-face cohort group seminars at the beginning and end of each course, an interactive webinar experience in the middle of the course, and web-based assignments/ discussions throughout the course. The term, *webinar*, is a combination of the terms "seminar" and "web". In effect, a webinar describes holding a synchronous seminar over the Web. It is often used to deliver a workshop, lecture, group discussion, question/ answer, and presentations.

Saint Mary-of-the-Woods College is cognizant of the fact that degree programs that are offered electronically (via the Internet) support and broaden the functions of educational institutions. Thus the College desires to respond, in a proactive manner, to such trends in higher education by (a) developing and implementing a new totally-online interactive program, and (b) incorporating online components into the existing WED program. Since there will be no residency requirement for students in the new program, SMWC strongly believes that the program will attract students that our existing programs cannot - geographically distant adult learners and computer savvy non-traditional students, and people serving in the US Military.

According to a Spring 2008 survey of approximately 400 people, conducted by the College's Program Development Team, there is strong interest among adult learners for such a program. Focus groups, conducted by Williams Randall, Inc. on behalf of the College, also indicate that there is strong interest among targeted groups in an interactive totally-online program. The focus group that expressed the most interest in a fully-online degree program was comprised of military personnel. According to the Department of Defense (DoD), as of October 31, 2007, the United States Military had 1,419,212 active members. Of that figure, 220,908 are officers and 1,143,399 are enlisted members. As of September 30, 2006, approximately 201,575 of those military members were female. Each service member is a potential student for WED and Woods Online. Throughout the years, the need for highly educated military service members has grown immensely as technology, both military technology and non-military technology has also grown at a very rapid rate. In addition, military service members are seeking college degrees as a means of earning promotions. For example, in August 2006, the Navy implemented a new rule that as of the year 2011, all sailors must have earned at least an associate degree in order to qualify for promotion in to senior enlisted ranks. Therefore, further need is constantly created for postsecondary education programs that are well-suited to the needs of military service members (Blumenstyk, 2006). The United States Military strongly desires service members who have either a knowledge base to build upon, or the ability to learn and educate themselves. It is a win-win situation for both the military and the service member (American Council on Education, 2007).

In addition, the College is confident that the proposed program will bring about a significant increase in enrollment, especially because the program will attract new student groups. The College emphasizes that the proposed online program and the current WED program are two distinct distance education models that complement, rather than compete, with one another. However, this should not cause any significant decrease in WED enrollment, because the individualized and flexible nature of the WED program is highly suitable for a majority of adult learners who prefer to complete their education part-time. The proposed inclusion of totally online and electronic components and the removal of the on-campus residency requirement in the WED program will appeal to a larger student market. The College expects students to take advantage of both programs.

The College strongly believes that the implementation of the proposed online program will have a significantly positive impact on our existing campus and WED programs. Many of the technology-components that the proposed program will feature will gradually percolate into and strengthen the existing programs as well.

Over eighty-five percent of WED students come from Indiana and Illinois. Based on the successful foundation of serving distance students through the WED program and graduate programs, the College intends to expand its reach *geographically* through a new fully-online program to untapped markets, such as millennial and neo-millennial students, computer savvy non-traditional students, and those serving in the US Military.

The College formed various task forces to get us ready for the new delivery formats in both the graduate programs and the anticipated launch of Woods Online. The authors, Dr. Jennie Mitchell (Professor & Director of the Woods Online Program) and Dr. Daesang Kim (Assistant Professor & Instructional Design Specialist) were part of every task force.

Case Description

In August, 2004, President Joan Lescinski, CSJ appointed a four-member faculty team which Dr. Mitchell chaired. This team was directed to "think outside the box" in helping the College to develop *new programs, new markets, and new delivery systems* that would generate *new sources of revenue*. During the fall of 2004, the team (now called the Program Development Team) visited other colleges, did lots of research, and lots of brainstorming. In 2005, the team met with the president with a list of "top ten ideas" for increasing revenue streams. One idea was to admit men into the Women's External Degree program This idea was fairly controversial for the College and was debated by faculty, staff, students, the Sisters of Providence, and alumnae. Later that year, the College did approve admitting men into the WED program, and by 2009, men made up about 10% of this program in the renamed "Woods External Degree" program. The campus remains all female.

A second idea supported by Lescinski was the development of a graduate degree program. According to the SMWC Institutional Plan (2005), New Product Development, the College should "implement at least one new academic program (degree, certification, delivery model) at least every two to three years" (p.8). Once given the authority to move forward, the Program Development Team (PDT) developed the Master of Leadership Development program (MLD) in 2007 and Master of Education (M.Ed.) in 2008. The development of the proposal considered a) initial

market research to assess demand; b) analysis of survey results from students, alumnae, and external participants; c) formal and informal meetings with SMWC faculty d) formal and informal meetings with Graduate Council; e) research of distance education technologies; f) feedback from an external Advisory Committee; g) focus groups; and h) consultations with the Chief Academic Officer and President of the College. The MLD was approved by Graduate Council on October 18, 2005, received approval from the Board of Trustees and the Higher Learning Commission in 2006. The first full cohort was admitted in February 2007, and the program was profitable the first year, something rare in the first year of new programs.

One of the most significant contributions of President Lescinski was to embrace the entrepreneurial approach taken by the PDT to develop the program. Every member of the PDT took ownership; in fact, PDT faculty members were so committed to the development of the MLD, that they worked without compensation for hundreds of hours in its development. The PDT identified their service on the PDT as a way to leave a legacy to The College. The entrepreneurial approach used a business plan with seven chapters to outline new programs: 1) description and rationale; 2) the planning process; 3) human resource requirements; 4) market potential and finances; 5) physical resource requirements; 6) instructional resource requirements; and 7) appendix of evidence. The same group used this business plan model to develop the Master of Education (M.Ed.) in 2007.

Now, the College expects to a launch new interactive fully-online undergraduate degree program, Woods Online, in 2010 that empower students to explore, discover, and interact (see Figure 1). SMWC adopted a constructivist model for teaching in the Woods Online program. As adopted, the faculty anticipate to "sets up problems and monitors student exploration, guides the direction of student inquiry and promotes new patterns of thinking" through innovative online

Figure 1. Process of SMWC online program development

learning environments (Southwest Educational Development Laboratory, 1995).

Woods Online is an online Bachelor's degree program that can attract a community of online learners that we currently do not serve. It is different from both the on-campus and WED undergraduate degree programs in that it:

- is a distance mode of delivery that is entirely online
- involves a specified General Studies (GS) curriculum, consistent with the existing GS objectives and learning outcomes, that is focused on Leadership for Environmental and Social Justice
- classes are accelerated, lasting only 8-weeks
- could provide an option for accelerated degree completion

The general studies in the new program focuses on seven themes of *Leadership for Environmental and Social Justice*. The themes were adapted from The Earth Charter, the Universal Declaration of Human Rights, and the Themes of Catholic Social Teaching. Originally, the Program Development Team reviewed the potential for a new major, social entrepreneurship for the new program. However, after meeting with the new President, Dr. David Behrs, the PDT investigated the possibility of using existing majors to start this program. According to Behrs, "The most benefit will be where majors share a common set of core courses" (personal communication, September 25, 2007). Since the College planned to use existing majors, President Behrs asked the PDT to move the launch date to January, 2010, instead of the proposed August, 2010.

The format of the new program's academic year includes five sessions that are eight weeks in length. This allows for a total of twelve weeks off throughout the year. Students will generally take six hours per session with an occasional eight hours to complete the program in four years. Because of a specified General Studies and pre-established electives, students will be given a clear picture of their academic journey from start to finish. Students in this program will be eligible for full-time financial aid. Transfer students will be accepted as early as August, 2010. Any major compatible with this format could be offered in the Woods Online program.

In March, 2009, preliminary conversations from a focus visit from the Higher Leaning Commission of North Central Association for Colleges and Schools (the accrediting body) indicated that the College had a thorough planning process and an excellent quality assurance process; however, a few challenges remained. Some of the challenges include: technologies that support an online learn-

Table 2. Characteristics by generations

	Matures	**Baby Boomers**	**Generation X**	**Net Generation**	**Current Generation Predictions**
Description	Greatest generation	Me generation	Latchkey generation	Millennials	Neo-millennials
Attributes	Command and control, self-sacrifice	Optimistic Workaholic	Independent Skeptical	Hopeful Determined	Connected Group problem solvers
Likes	Respect for authority, Family, Community involvement	Responsibility Work ethic, Can-do attitude	Freedom, MultitaskingWork-life balance	Public activism, Latest technology, Parents	Earth Public activism Ubiquitous computing immersion in virtual environment (community) Multitasking Personal customization
Dislikes	Waste Technology	Laziness Turning 50	Red tape Hype	Anything slow, Negativity	Impersonalized experiences One-size fits all

Note. Modified from by Oblinger, D. & Oblinger, J. (2005). Is it age or IT: first steps toward understanding the net generation. In D. Oblinger and J. Oblinger (Ed.), *Educating the Net Generation* (p. 20).

ing environment; academic-driven technologies (e.g. Web 2.0); professional development of faculty; and resources.

Technology Concerns

According to Oblinger & Oblinger (2005), each generation has unique characteristics as shown in Table 2.

The program is designed for an online community of learners with a format and focus that appeals to net generation (millennial), neo-millennial, and computer savvy non-traditional students, including military personnel. Because the program targeted a new market for SMWC, research was conducted to determine the type of I.T. support needed to support the academic and service infrastructure for a totally online degree. The PDT compiled some of the requirements for this new format from faculty. Faculty wanted to emphasize *personal touch* and *social connection* through technology (Woods Interactive Online Degree Proposal, p7) and suggested the following components:

- four-day response times from faculty for graded assignments (later reduced to three days)
- combination of independent and group assignments so students are socially connected
- opportunities for online chat rooms, lectures, and synchronous meeting online experiences
- opportunities to conduct research with faculty members
- opportunities to participate in virtual poster shows, virtual art shows, campus publications, traditional ceremonies (e.g. ring ceremony, graduation)
- opportunities for participation in specific social interactive groups using an Avatar, Second Life, or other online social engagement activities
- opportunities to participate in campus and professional organizations (perhaps through a portal)
- use of SMWC email, not other accounts (e.g. Yahoo, Gmail)

In summary, the Woods Online, was developed for technology savvy students, and unreliability of technology will be a critical concern. For example, if technology is down for one week, it's like losing one eighth of the course.

Management and Organizational Concerns

Palloff and Pratt (2001) suggested that "Not all faculty are suited for the online environment" (p.21). Teaching in a fully-online environment is more than uploading a syllabus and creating assignments on online. It requires a new teaching paradigm and recognition that the millennium student or net generation students are different. Inexperience in structuring "the way" millennials and neo-millennials think, learn and communicate will be a major concern for the new program.

In 2007, a total of twenty-nine faculty (counting the PDT and Dr. Chris Bahr, Interim VPAA) attended a faculty meeting to gain input on a launch of a new program. Twenty-two faculty provided input on the 8-week format and it represented a fairly positive response. Not all courses would need to be adapted to an online 8-week format, only those chosen for Woods Online. Eleven faculty addressed concerns related to faculty development and time issues and included:

- Need faculty time. Training is one thing, but time is critical.
- Faculty resources – design, design, design
- Inexperience in structuring "the way" millennials and neo-millennials think, learn and communicate.

As mentioned in the previous session, the college hired a marketing firm to conduct three focus groups. One of the major points made by the participants of focus groups was the quality of online courses. Dr. Mitchell observed one of the focus group sessions, without the knowledge of the group members, and was very surprised that no one in the focus group knew that SMWC had an existing distance program. Clearly, much needed to be done to prepare for the new program as well as repackage the existing WED program.

Since the College intends to increase online course offerings for its existing WED program, a student seeking a distance program could be served *concurrently* by both WED and Woods Online if registration calendars were coordinated. Research by Palloff & Pratt (2003) state: "Issues such as ease of registration, integration of admission functions, access to library services, and access to advising all must be addressed by the institution in order to effectively retain online students in courses and programs. When their needs are not addressed, online students can become disgruntled and withdraw" (p. 60). This is especially important if WED students perceive that Woods Online students receive preferential treatment. The College removed the WED residency requirement for most majors in September, 2008 and 45% of the students chose a non-residency registration. For such students, inclusion of the online (non-residency) registration option in the WED program provided a convenient alternative to the face-to-face on-campus residencies. The College realized that there were challenges beyond just having a solid academic technology. With the online option for WED and the launch of Woods Online, the College made a concerted effort to develop the institutional infrastructure, resources and culture required of online degree programs.

CURRENT CHALLENGES FACING THE ORGANIZATION

According to (Brown, 2005), it is possible to align net generation characteristics with learning principles, learning spaces and IT applications. However, the College has several hurdles to make this new program possible. For instance, when the WED program was established in 1973, it was classified as "independent study" by the accrediting body of the College. According to the Assurance Section of the Higher Learning Commission report conducted in 2004, "15% of all WED courses were online, 15% were offered in alternative format (weekend classes) and 68% were considered independent study" (Hanson, Clauson, Knowlton, & Gilliland, 2005). In 2004, the College used WebCT (course management system), for the online classes, but conducted most of the coursework using email one-on-one with each student.

The College appointed a task force to review a potential replacement for online learning environment including a course management system led by Dr. Joanne Golding, SP. WebCT had been bought out by Blackboard and a change was inevitable. The task force, comprised of several faculty (including authors, Dr. Mitchell with Dr. Kim joining later) and a member of IT, reviewed several content management systems including Moodle, Angel, Blackboard, Sakai, and Desire2Learn. Golding used EduTools for preliminary research to compare: a) communication tools; b) productivity tools; c) administrative tools; d) course delivery tools; e) curriculum design; f) hardware/software; and g) pricing. Edutools is a tool developed by WCET, "a membership cooperative of institutions and organizations dedicated to advancing access and excellence in higher education through the innovate use of technology" (WCET, 2006). After several months of review, the task force selected Desire2Learn. It was the most expensive of the products reviewed but it had several features that impressed the task force.

- First, Desire2Learn was the only product (at the time) that had a competency component. This component would allow the College to conduct assessment at the major level, the department level, and college-wide. In addition, it appeared that Desire2Learn might be able to replace LiveText (accreditation management system). Education faculty used LiveText as the assessment management system but

discovered that it did not work well for WED students (WED students can take up to twelve years to complete their degree).

- Second, Desire2Learn personnel had an excellent track record in responding to questions, issues, and update support.
- Third, Desire2Learn had many products in development that the task force hoped to utilize including LiveRoom, Learning Object Repository, and e-Portfolio.

The College appointed Golding to serve as the Desire2Learn faculty administrator and a member of the I.T. staff was responsible for the technical administration and server requirements (updates, issue resolution, etc.). Golding was also responsible for teaching faculty how to use Desire2Learn and took on additional duties of adding students to the Desire2Learn database. Although Desire2Learn uses IMS enterprise specification for student data, the registration integration would not work with the College's system, CampusAnyware™ (online registration and student information services). To this day, faculty enroll students *manually* in any Desire2Learn course.

SMWC faculty signed up for 2007 workshops and training as the College moved from WebCT to Desire2Learn. The first year was difficult for faculty as they migrated their courses from one environment to another. Although Desire2Learn indicated this would be easy, it was not. Faculty spent more time editing existing courses, than if they had started with a blank course. Basic workshops did not include technologies that would enhance content (e.g. multimedia) or promote interactive learning experiences. One of the authors, Dr. Daesang Kim, an instructional design specialist, was hired specifically to help launch the MLD program. He provided training for the MLD faculty, templates in Desire2Learn, and an introduction to technologies that supported online instruction. This contributed to the success of the MLD program; unfortunately, it only included faculty involved in the graduate program.

In 2007, SMWC hosted its first webinar for the new graduate program, Master of Leadership Development, using Convenos (web-based conferencing tool) and Gizmo5 (peer-to-peer Internet telephony and instant messaging software application). Although Convenos worked fairly well, Gizmo was often unreliable. The College kept Convenos and an 800 number using a conference call bridge. Although current graduates programs have a "webinar" as a requirement, many of the Woods Online instructors wanted to use this technology to connect to their students in a way that is more robust than just chat. In fact, additional I.T. support staff is necessary, specifically someone that understand online program requirements. The task force and the Program Development Team supported the hiring of an additional I.T. person. Additionally, the PDT suggested a late-afternoon to night shift to stretch the hours for helpdesk, and if they had the skills, to help with a portal, run backups, system updates, and monitor the infrastructures that support all programs.

Since there will be no residency requirement for students in this program (unlike the WED program in which students are *encouraged* to come to the SMWC campus for short residencies), the program requires building all resources online for all students from any part of the globe including those who serve in the US Military. First, online services and services must be supported by robust software that is integrated with the existing infrastructure. For example, the College has several legacy systems that do not integrate well. The College uses CampusAnyware™ (online registration and student information services), PowerFAIDS® (financial aid software system), Desire2Learn (course management system), and Sage MIP (fund accounting software). None of the software packages work seamlessly with the other. Second, there is a need for some semblance of a portal to support a community of learners. A web portal was suggested to support the Master of Leadership Development program (MLD), using SharePoint Services. The portal system

was never successfully implemented by I.T. As an alternative, the MLD program set up a "411" course that connected all students in the cohort to announcements, discussions, etc. This was a fix, but not an optimal solution. A portal system is an essential service for online students. And, third, web pages should be designed to appeal to various markets without confusing students looking for distance education. Students will have the option of only WED or only Woods Online, or some combination of both products.

Since the College has not pursued military markets, understanding this market was a huge undertaking for SMWC. Specifically, Coltharp and others, suggested that "military pages be created for each branch of the service" (Coltharp, 2008). Creating different web pages is not an issue, but developing content for these pages requires an understanding of this audience. Did SMWC understand the needs of military students? The Military Family Research Institute in The Higher Education Landscape identified issues relevant to challenges faced by Indiana colleges. Research conducted by the Military Research Institute asked a series of questions geared to determine an organizations' *military friendliness*. SMWC's plan to make degrees more accessible to service members and veterans through the development of the Woods Online program is a worthy goal, but is SMWC really *military friendly*? SMWC has no staff dedicated to military student support and few institutional resources to support the critical needs of veterans and service members. Furthermore, many staff and faculty in key areas were not aware of current policies that benefit military personnel or, when aware, offered conflicting information.

SOLUTIONS AND RECOMMENDATIONS

Because the Woods Online students never meet, interaction between students is a key component to developing a community of learners. The selection of the course management system, Desire2Learn was the foundation needed to build a fully-online program. It supports interaction as well as all the necessary features you would expect in a course management system. Woods Online faculty plan to use discussion forums for individual and groups, the paging function (somewhat like instant chat), chat break-out rooms, group drop-box folders, and group lockers (space to share files). The College expects to use the competency feature to assess programs by 2012. Furthermore, Woods Online faculty plan to empower students to explore, discover, and interact through the use of (or improvement) of innovative technology, professional development, the quality review process, and resources.

Acceptance to the Woods Online program will require students to take an online education readiness course, meet established college admissions standards, and have access to technologies to complete the program.

Innovative Technology

The College kept a task force to review existing technology to support the MLD, M.Ed., and the new Woods Online program. In 2009, the College adopted Adobe® Acrobat Connect Pro (web conferencing tool) to replace Convenos

to support webinar activity in all programs. Adobe® Acrobat Connect Pro web conferencing tool allows SMWC to captivate students with interactive web meetings and virtual classroom experiences. For instance, this tool allows participants to share presentations including their desktops with their web browsers and Adobe® Flash Player. In particular, Adobe® technology enables the use of rich multimedia presentations and interactivity to create a *personal touch* and *social connection* through our existing technology including Desire2Learn. The Webinar actively will be used to deliver a workshop, lecture, group discussion, question/answer, and presentations for students-to-students and students-to-instructor. In anticipation of online community of learners, the College adopted Atomic Learning™ that provides web-based software training for more than 110 of the most commonly used applications.

Course development contracts were awarded for the first ten courses in May of 2008, a year before delivery. The College required Woods Online faculty to adopt or use interactive technologies that would appeal to the net generation (millennial), neo-millennial, and computer savvy non-traditional students, including military personnel. A list of suggested technologies was included (see Figure 2), but soon faculty expressed interest in additional Web 2.0 technologies. In May 2008, the task force presented a series of workshops,

Figure 2. Change of innovative technology.

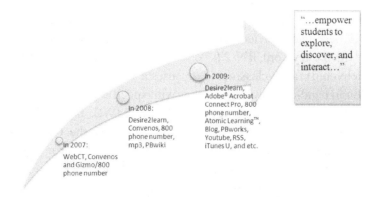

Discover the Possibilities, that incorporated many Web 2.0 technologies. This is covered in more depth in the next section.

Professional Development

Faculty who plan to teach in the Woods Online program were asked to attend training that included technology and instructional design strategies that would appeal to an online learner. In May of 2008, the College provided a ten-topic training session, entitled *Discover the Possibilities* that was led by experienced Desire2Learn instructors. There were Desire2Learn (an online course management system), Captivate and Camtasia (interactive presentation software), Webinars, and Podcasting. More that 50% of the faculty attended these sessions. Through this discovery of what is possible, faculty looked for ways to combine multimedia and active learning techniques. Faculty were energized by this process and looked forward to the next training sessions. Some of the key issues discussed how the role of the teacher changes when moving from a traditional campus class to hybrid courses or fully-online courses. For example, faculty often transition from an "expert" role to "guide on the side" and sometimes even a "co-learner." After the training session, the College developed an online resource site for all faculty including adjuncts. The site is to foster and support excellence in teaching and learning at the College, to promote the sharing of resources and ideas, to provide remote access of forms and documents, and to establish a dynamic and engaged learning community among all faculties.

In May of 2009, the College again provided ten-topic training sessions with the keyword, *Web 2.0*. The presentation was delivered in a lab-classroom to promote participation in hand-on activities by experienced Desire2Learn instructors. The key benefit of the training was to share real examples of how faculty can combine multimedia and active learning techniques to stimulate learning, and then practice through hands-on activities. These multi-

media components get and hold learners' interest, which many researchers believe is important when teaching the new generation (Jonassen, 2000, p. 208). Providing a rich multimedia instruction will help students to "select relevant information, organize it into coherent representations, and integrate it with other knowledge" (Mayer & Moreno, 2002, p. 111) as meaningful learning (Kim & Gilman, 2008). Furthermore, distance learning courses can benefit by enriching the student's experience with relevant multimedia and opportunities to interact with their peers. In fact, these components can create "bridges between the students' previous knowledge actively moving them towards more complex understanding…bringing alive the theory…" (Wiesenberg & Stacey, 2005, p. 393).

The Quality Review Process

In the fall of 2008, the process for quality review of online courses was established and ten courses from the fully-online undergraduate degree program were reviewed by the Quality Review Committee. The Quality Review Process used at SMWC is two-phased, and is modeled on many of the lessons learned in the Quality Matters™ program (Wells, 2007). The Quality Matters™ program was funded by the U.S. Department of Education. In the Quality Matters™ project, courses were assessed in forty specific rubric items in the following "categories: 1) course overview and introduction; 2) learning objectives; 3) assessment and measurement; 4) resources and materials; 5) learning engagement; 6) course technology; 7) learner support; and 8) accessibility" (MarylandOnline, 2006). The Quality Matters™ process uses a scoring rubric and a minimum total score with specific requirements.

At SMWC, the quality review process was researched by the Quality Review Committee consisting of the Program Development Team, the Instructional Design Specialist, and the Assistant Dean. Although, the Quality Matters™

process was reviewed and considered, the group felt that a scored approach would send the wrong signal to faculty members that were developing online courses for the new program. In addition, the committee wanted to promote interaction, a rich use of multimedia, collaboration, eight-week model content, and various other components that related to a general studies theme. Both authors are members of the Quality Review Committee and believe that by combining multimedia and active learning techniques, students are empowered to discover, explore, and interact.

Consistent with the Saint Mary-of-the-Woods College Institutional Assessment Plan, the Woods Online program will have an assessment system that incorporates ongoing, performance-based assessment of student learning based on the mission and learning outcomes of the programs. In fact, Desire2Learn is particularly helpful in collecting competency data and rubric data by student, by instructor, by course, by program, and campus-wide. All courses in the new interactive online degree program will be housed in the College content management system, Desire2Learn, and will take advantage of the robust assessment component. Specifically, assignments used for assessment must be scored with applicable rubrics and competencies. This is one of the requirements listed in the course design contracts. The Measures of Academic Proficiency and Progress standardized exam will also give information about the general studies learning of the online degree program. This exam allows comparison of freshmen and senior scores and also between peer institutions.

Resources

There have been many changes in the I.T. Department over the spring and summer of 2008, partially as a result of a technology audit that was completed by an outside firm in 2008. The firm conducted extensive interviews, reviewed materials and processes, and made several recommendations. In the summer of 2008, Michael Sims was hired as the Executive Director of the Information Technology Department. Mr. Sims brings years of experience in the I.T. industry and has made several changes. He conducted extensive meetings with the I.T. Department and various groups on campus. Within the first six weeks, he requested and received approval to purchase a 24/7 helpdesk software system. Additionally, he requested and received approval to hire a full-time Technical Support Specialist to support the 24/7 helpdesk initiative. Under his leadership, a User's Group made up of technology power users was for M.Ed. and the first meeting was held September 10, 2008. It is the purpose of this group to see that all constituents of the College are considered when technology decisions are made. This same group will work together to streamline all technology processes to minimize software conflicts and incompatibilities. The additional I.T. support provided to the MLD and M.Ed. programs (orientation, trouble-shooting, follow-up, etc) has been of tremendous value to both students and instructions. Although staffing can be eased by using student workers, they often require supervision. In anticipation of Woods Online, an additional I.T. person was hired July 1, 2009.

The College joined the Servicemembers Opportunities Colleges (SOC) consortium in August, 2008, and completed the paperwork to become a member of Concurrent Admissions Program (ConAP) in anticipation of understanding the needs of a military market. Since the military market is new for the College, representatives from financial aid, admission, and other offices attended the Servicemembers Opportunity Colleges (SOC) Consortium Workshop in November, 2008, or attended online webinars. In May, 2009, the College joined the Yellow Ribbon GI Education Enhancement Program (Yellow Ribbon program) which allows the VA to fund tuition expenses at the highest public in-state undergraduate tuition rate and match 50% of the difference (U.S. Department of Veterans Affairs, 2009). In May

2009, SMWC received the Ball Venture Grant to develop a Virtual Academic Support Team (V.A.S.T.) to support both WED students and Woods Online students. In addition, the College has written several grants that will help SMWC develop *military friendly* policies.

SMWC strongly believes that to attract as well as provide excellent educational opportunities to net generation (millennial), neo-millennial, and computer savvy non-traditional students, including military personnel, it has to develop and sustain a totally different program model that is completely online, structured, and interactive. With the advent of new computer technologies and electronic tools vis-à-vis rapid rise in computer literacy of the society, learning styles of students have changed substantially. Classical instructional methods that were once effective and relevant are quickly becoming ineffective and unsuitable to the present generation of students; these students learn better by visualization and interactive/hands-on activities rather than by listening and passive comprehension of concepts. The Internet and e-mail have revolutionized how we obtain and communicate information. The College has realized that a degree program that is fully interactive and online will be the most suitable solution to attract the student groups mentioned above.

Any institution that wants to develop an online program, should adopt the entrepreneurial model and require a business plan model to include all functions of the institution. This model supports faculty and staff buy-in. Faculty and staff must invest in the program and believe in its success. Most institutions do not have seed money to start a new program that will tap new markets. Understanding the needs of students in a new market is essential for the success of the program. Competition in the online market is intense, so the College needs to spend marketing dollars wisely. SMWC has built a quality product, now it needs to attract students to it. As you can see in Figure

Figure 3. SMWC's solutions for empowering students to explore, discover, and interact in their learning. (note: logo undergoing approval)

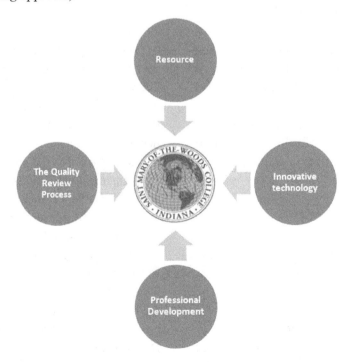

3, SMWC has built a foundation for this program on innovative technology, professional development, quality review, and resources. For this case, resources range from I.T. resources to scholarship resources for military students. SMWC continues to learn about the military market, and has written various grants in the last month to support students in a totally online environment and continues to look for resources to support faculty development including adjunct faculty.

REFERENCES

American Council on Education. (2007). *Military Installation Voluntary Education Review (MIVER) Orientation and Guidelines*. PDF File / Report, Center for Lifelong Learning.

Blumenstyk, G. (2006, July 7). The Military Market. *The Chronicle of Higher Education Money & Management*. Retrieved December 31, 2007, from http://www.chronicle.com//colloquy/2006/07/military

Brown, M. (2005). Learning Spaces . In Oblinger, D. G., & Oblinger, J. L. (Eds.), *Educating the Net Generation* (p. 267). Washington, DC, USA: Educause.

Coltharp, B. (2008). *OL 599: Organization leadership project - Woods interactive onLine degree (WILD), Target Audience Military Service Member Students*. Saint Mary-of-the-Woods, In Saint Mary-of-the-Woods College, Master of Leadership Development program.

Hanson, R. A., Clauson, K. M., Knowlton, D. D., & Gilliland, T. A. (2005). *Assurance Section: Report of a Comprehensive Evaluation Visit*. Chicago: The Higher Learning Commission.

Jonassen, D. (2000). *Computers as mindtools for schools engaging critical thinking* (2nd ed.). Upper Saddle River, NJ: Prentice-Hall.

Kim, D., & Gilman, D. (2008). Effects of Text, Audio, and Graphic Aids in Multimedia Instruction for Vocabulary Learning. *Educational Technology & Society*, *11*(3), 114–126.

MarylandOnline. (2006). *Quality Matters: Inter-Institutional Quality Assurance in OnlineLearning*. Retrieved March 18, 2009, from http://qualitymatters.org

Mayer, R., & Moreno, R. (2002). Aids to computer-based multimedia learning. *Learning and Instruction*, *12*, 107–119. doi:10.1016/S0959-4752(01)00018-4

Oblinger, D., & Oblinger, J. (2005). Is it age or IT: first steps toward understanding the net generation . In Oblinger, D., & Oblinger, J. (Eds.), *Educating the Net Generation* (p. 20). Boulder, CO: EDUCAUSE.

Palloff, R. M., & Pratt, K. (2001). *Lessons from the cyberspace classroom: The realities of online teaching*. San Francisco: Jossey-Bass.

Palloff, R. M., & Pratt, K. (2003). *The virtual student: A profile and guide to working with online learners*. San Francisco: Jossey-Bass.

Program Development Team. (2007). *Woods Interactive onLine Degree (WILD) Proposal for New Program & Format*. Saint Mary-of-the-Woods, In Saint Mary-of-the-Woods College.

Saint Mary-of-the-Woods College. (2005). *SMWC Institutional Plan*. Saint Mary-of-the-Woods, In Author.

Southwest Educational Development Laboratory. (1995) Constructing knowledge in the classroom. Retrieved on 5/31/2009 from http://www.sedl.org/scimath/compass/v01n03/1.html

U.S. Department of Veterans Affairs. (2009). *Yellow Ribbon Program*. Retrieved May 30, 2009, from https://www.gibill.va.gov/School_Info/Yellow_Ribbon/index.htm

WCET. (2006, May 20). *EduTools*. WCET: Partners for Change, Technologies in practice, Advances in education. Retrieved May 28, 2009, from http://www.wcet.info/2.0/

Wells, M. (2007, September 18). Quality Matters: Does Your Online Course Meet the Standards. *Magna Publications*. Madison WI, USA: Magna Publications. Retrieved from http://www.magnapubs.com/aboutus/history.html

Wiesenberg, F., & Stacey, E. (2005). Reflections on Teaching and Learning Online: Quality program design, delivery and support issues from a cross-global perspective. *Distance Education, 26*(3), 385–404. doi:10.1080/01587910500291496

FURTHER READING

Abel, R. (2005). *Achieving Success in Internet-Supported Learning in Higher Education: Case Studies Illuminate Success Factors, Challenges, and Future Directions*. Lake Mary, FL: Alliance for Higher Education Competitiveness.

Artino, A. R. (2008). Promoting Academic Motivation and Self-Regulation: Practical Guidelines for Online Instructors. *Tech Trends: Linking Research and Practice to Improve Learning, 52*(3), 37–45.

Badge, J., Dawson, E., Cann, A., & Scott, J. (2008, May 1). Assessing the Accessibility of Online Learning. *Innovations in Education and Teaching International, 45*(2), 103–113. doi:10.1080/14703290801948959

Beldarrain, Y. (2006). Distance education trends: Integrating new technologies to foster student interaction and collaboration. *Distance Education, 27*(2), 139–153. doi:10.1080/01587910600789498

Bolliger, D., & Wasilik, O. (2009, May). Factors influencing faculty satisfaction with online teaching and learning in higher education. *Distance Education, 30*(1), 103–116. doi:10.1080/01587910902845949

Chaney, B. H., Eddy, J. M., Dorman, S. M., Glessner, L., Green, B. L., & Lara-Alecio, R. (2007). Development of an instrument to assess student opinions of the quality of distance education courses. *American Journal of Distance Education, 21*(3), 145–164. doi:10.1080/08923640701341679

Chao, T., Saj, T., & Tessier, F. (2006). *Establishing a Quality Review for Online Courses*. Educause Quarterly: THE IT Practioner's Journal. EDUCAUSE. Retrieved November 8, 2008 from http://connect.educause.edu/

Churchill, D. (2009, January). Educational applications of Web 2.0: Using blogs to support teaching and learning. *British Journal of Educational Technology, 40*(1), 179–183. doi:10.1111/j.1467-8535.2008.00865.x

Collis, B., & Moonen, J. (2008, June 1). Web 2.0 Tools and Processes in Higher Education: Quality Perspectives. *Educational Media International, 45*(2), 93–106. doi:10.1080/09523980802107179

Commissions, C. (2001, March). *Best Practices for Electronicaly Offered Degree and Certificte Programs*. The Higher Learning Commission. Retrieved June 15, 2008, from http://www.ncahlc.org/download/Best_Pract_DEd.pdf

Donavant, B. (2009, May). The New, Modern Practice of Adult Education: Online Instruction in a Continuing Professional Education Setting. *Adult Education Quarterly, 59*(3), 227–245. doi:10.1177/0741713609331546

Dykman, C., & Davis, C. (2008, January 1). Online Education Forum--Part Three: A Quality Online Educational Experience. *Journal of Information Systems Education, 19*(3), 281–290.

Engstrom, M., Santo, S., & Yost, R. (2008, Summer). Knowledge Building In An Online Cohort. *Quarterly Review of Distance Education, 9*(2), 151–167.

Higdon, J., & Topaz, C. (2009, March 1). Blogs and Wikis as Instructional Tools: A Social Software Adaptation of Just-in-Time Teaching. *College Teaching, 57*(2), 105-110. (ERIC Document Reproduction Service No. EJ832458). Retrieved June 1, 2009, from ERIC database.

Huett, J., Moller, L., Foshay, W., & Coleman, C. (2008, September). The Evolution of Distance Education: Implications for Instructional Design on the Potential of the Web. *TechTrends: Linking Research & Practice to Improve Learning, 52*(5), 63–67.

Hussar, W., & Bailey, T. M. (2007). *Projection of Education Statistics to 2016 (NCES 2008-060).* National Center for Education Statistics, U. S. Department of Education. Washington, DC: Institute of Education Sciences.

Lee, M., McLoughlin, C., & Chan, A. (2008, May 1). Talk the Talk: Learner-Generated Podcasts as Catalysts for Knowledge Creation. *British Journal of Educational Technology, 39*(3), 501–521. doi:10.1111/j.1467-8535.2007.00746.x

Merrill, M. D., & Gilbert, C. C. (2008). Effective peer interaction in a problem-centered instruction strategy. *Distance Education, 29*(2), 199–207. doi:10.1080/01587910802154996

Milani, M. (2008). Cultural Impact on Online Education Quality Perception. (K. E. Curtis Farm, Ed.). Electronic Journal of e-Learning, 6(2).

Mitchell, J., Carlyle, B., Cunningham, E., & Ramachandran, B. R. (2008, February). *What features of a fully-online degee program appeal to you?* Retrieved from Survey - Saint Mary-of-the-Woods College.

Moller, L., Wellesley, R. F., & Huett, J. (2008). The Evolution of Distance Education: Implications for Instructional Design on the Potential of the Web. *TechTrends, 52*(3), 70–75. doi:10.1007/s11528-008-0158-5

Novak, R. J. (2002). Benchmarking Distance Education. *New Directions for Higher Education,* (118): 79–92. doi:10.1002/he.57

Rappa, N., Yip, D., & Baey, S. (2009, January 1). The Role of Teacher, Student and ICT in Enhancing Student Engagement in Multiuser Virtual Environments. *British Journal of Educational Technology, 40*(1), 61–69. doi:10.1111/j.1467-8535.2007.00798.x

Robinson, C., & Hullinger, H. (2008, January 1). New Benchmarks in Higher Education: Student Engagement in Online Learning. *Journal of Education for Business, 84,* 101–109. doi:10.3200/JOEB.84.2.101-109

Rughooputh, S., & Santally, M. (2009, February). Integrating text-to-speech software into pedagogically sound teaching and learning scenarios. *Educational Technology Research and Development, 57*(1), 131–145. doi:10.1007/s11423-008-9101-x

Smith, D., & Mitry, D. J. (2008). Investigation of Higher Education: The Real Costs and Quality of Online Programs. *Journal of Education for Business, 83*(3), 147–152. doi:10.3200/JOEB.83.3.147-152

Zembylas, M. (2008). Adult learners' emotions in online learning. *Distance Education, 29*(1), 71–87. doi:10.1080/01587910802004852

Zevenbergen, R., & Lerman, S. (2008, January 1). Learning Environments Using Interactive Whiteboards: New Learning Spaces or Reproduction of Old Technologies? *Mathematics Education Research Journal, 20*(1), 108–126.

KEY TERMS AND DEFINITIONS

Constructivist Model: The model of learning that concentrates on what happens during the process of learning. It identifies the central role of concepts and understandings that learners bring to new and learning and the way in which new and old ideas interact. It begins with learners using their existing frameworks of understanding to interpret what is being taught, and that these existing ideas influence the speed and effectiveness with which new ideas are learned i.e. generating knowledge and meaning from experience.

Entrepreneurial Approach: This refers to an organization being business like, forward thinking, well organized and responsive to change.

Millennial Students: These students are the largest and most diverse generation in the college or university and they are not like those students of earlier years. They have unique collective personality, thought processes, and educational tendencies. They are characterized by having lack of professional boundaries which is influenced by socialization, want to have immediate feedback, lack of critical thinking skills, unrealistic expectations, and an expected "how to" guide to succeed in and out of the classroom. They spend less time on work and have a desire for success with little effort.

Neo-Millennial Students: These are the new generation students who are online automatically and use a web that is an even more interactive, social place where they talk using programs. For example, they are familiar with Skype, software that gives them free calls around the world; with Wikis, server software that allows them to edit a web page; with Web 2.0 which is all about social interaction. They will also want to control their teaching agenda to whatever extent possible and create knowledge clusters without interacting with anyone.

Web 2.0 Technologies: These technologies refer to web development and web design that facilitates interaction information sharing, interoperability, user centered design and collaboration on the World Wide Web. Examples include web-based communities, hosted services, web applications, social networking, wikis, blog, etc.

Webinar: It is a combination of the terms "seminar" and "web" that describes holding a synchronous seminar over the Web and is often used to deliver a workshop, lecture, group discussion, question/answer, and presentations.

Chapter 19

Building Relationships in an International Blended Learning Program:
Opportunities and Challenges in a Central American Country

Ravisha Mathur
San José State University, USA

Lisa Oliver
San José State University, USA

ABSTRACT

Several challenges that were encountered in establishing a joint international Masters program in Instructional Technology in a Central American country were explored. These challenges involved aspects of program development, delivering effective course content, using appropriate learning strategies, operating in a cross-cultural context, and working in an organization that had limited technological capacities. The foundation for working with these challenges involved establishing strong, mutually beneficial relationships with the Central American country, the Central American University (CAU), and the students. In addition, the overriding theme in developing this blended learning program was to allow for capacity-building since one goal for creating this program was so that the North American University (NAU) would build the program and relationships to the point that the CAU would be able to take over and manage the Instructional Technology program on its own.

ORGANIZATION BACKGROUND

In the summer of 2002, the CAU contacted the NAU in order to begin negotiations to create an international Instructional Technology Master's program. There was a strong need for a program of this type because there was no other educational technology or project of this nature available in the Central American country. Since the Central American country had no total quality management which is necessary for international certification, it could not sell products internationally. Thus, Instructional Technology was critical for standardized

DOI: 10.4018/978-1-61520-751-0.ch019

training and technological literacy was vitally needed to assist the country in moving from a rural economy to an international economy. By combining technology with teaching, individuals from various social economic backgrounds would have access to and be able to play leadership roles in their communities. Faculty from both CAU and NAU were also interested in building capacity to integrate technology into teaching and learning in its public school programs.

Currently, the population of the Central American country is comprised of approximately 7 million people with a wide variety of mixed biological heritage who follow several customs and habits that constitute Spanish-American cultural patterns (Index Mundi, 2006). The land has limited productive territory (primarily agricultural) and a very high population density. Within this country, there are marked imbalances in income distribution that create sharp contrasts in standards of living and general quality of life between the powerful and wealthy elite and the poverty-stricken masses. These contrasting lifestyles have created serious rifts in society that have effectively divided the population into distinctive subcultural groups.

After emerging from years of civil war, several projects were created to enhance social reconstruction of the country (DeLugan, 2005). The new leadership wanted to strengthen the economy to further emphasize free market strategies and international trade. Thus, the Central American country's Ministry of Education established educational initiatives that were focused on transforming education to promote technical careers at higher levels and to extend commerce (DeLugan, 2005; Moncada-Davidson, 1995). One such initiative was to enhance the use of technology within the country and to improve the technological skills of educators and school children. The collaboration between the NAU and the CAU was a part of this technological initiative.

In November 2002, a Memorandum of Agreement preceding a formal Memorandum of Understanding was drafted between the two universities.

From both universities' perspectives, the goal of the collaboration was for the CAU faculty to eventually offer the Instructional Technology degree solely from their own university in their own country. In addition, it was planned that all course materials would be ultimately turned over to CAU faculty for management and project continuance. As yet, the effectiveness of the initiatives promoted by the Ministry of Education is still to be determined.

SETTING THE STAGE

Universities are increasing their international collaborations and as a result the number of distance education programs and students involved in these programs has subsequently also increased. However, the success of these programs is largely dependent on two factors: 1) appropriate access and use of technology, and 2) establishing good relationships with the countries, institutions, and students involved in program development and delivery. As several studies have documented, barriers within these two factors can prevent students from effectively learning in both an online and a multicultural context (Cegles, 1998; Leggett & Persichitte, 1998; Muilenburg & Berge, 2001).

In distance education courses, it is often the case that much of the relationship-building or collaboration between institutions takes place through an online format. For this collaborative program, it was an asynchronous learning environment in that there was a combination of face-to-face meetings as well as communication through technological means at different times throughout a single course delivery. Consequently, both faculty planning the degree and the students earning it used a variety of technology throughout the entire process. While planning the program, faculty used email and teleconferencing to supplement telephone and written communication. Through email communication, faculty quickly resolved issues as they developed. Teleconferencing was utilized when a dialogue was needed to resolve the issue. NAU faculty delivered course content through a learning management system (i.e., WebCT) and some portions of the courses were televised. In addition, course materials were burned to compact disc to resolve problems with bandwidth encountered by students. Students most often utilized email to resolve any issues that arose.

Building a cross-institutional program provided for institutional sharing of resources and expertise that could, at the very least, increase opportunities available for both faculty and students (Wang, Dannenhoffer, Davidson, & Spector, 2005). In essence, effective access to these opportunities necessitates a strong working relationship at both institutions. Several steps can be taken to ensure a good working relationship (see Gatliff & Wendel, 1998 for review). For example, including both institutions in the program planning process and formative evaluation stage contributes to a strong working relationship. Moreover, establishing an effective mode of communication with strong leaders at both institutions is vital for program success.

The first step in creating effective institutional relationships is to identify necessary departments and contacts equipped to direct the collaboration. So, at the NAU, it was decided that the Provost's office would manage the formal contracts between the two organizations and the international services would initially manage the coordination of courses being delivered in the Central American country. At the CAU, the Central American Academic Programs office served as the liaison between the two institutions and the office of graduate studies managed the direct contacts with faculty at the NAU.

The second step is to spend a considerable portion of time working on the predelivery planning phase of the blended program. Caffarella (2002) suggested that there are several components to developing successful programs through institutional and faculty commitment in this phase of program development. For example, some components included researching the other institution, investigating the wider environmental and cultural context of the program, and negotiating the needs of the different stakeholders. Wiesenberg (2004) also points out the need for effective communication and developing problem-solving strategies in this predelivery phase, particularly if faculty are co-teaching in the program. These components, if implemented, would also help to build stronger relationships between institutions and their faculty. In other words, communication and strategies to resolve conflict should be established early on, prior to program implementation, so that stronger and perhaps longer lasting relationships can be forged.

The NAU, prior to program implementation, developed a matrix of issues that were of concern when discussing how the two institutions were going to establish an effective partnership (see Figure 1). These concerns centered around describing similarities and differences in viewpoints of the project, publicity, funding, pedagogical focus of the institutions, collegiality, language, and conflict resolution from both institutional and faculty perspectives. As Figure 1 shows, there were many significant differences that needed to be resolved prior to program delivery.

For example, initially the CAU faculty were participating in the project because it was mandated by the Ministry of Education technological initiative whereas NAU faculty were participating because faculty were motivated to increase access to technology in the Central American country and establish their own program as a leading distance education program. These differences were discussed and communicated to both faculties and were resolved in a variety of ways (e.g., through increased face-to-face meetings, by providing technology training to faculty, and through increased email contact).

It was also important to note the similarities across institutions and faculty. One big similarity at the institutional level was the importance of public relations or publicity. Both institutional

Figure 1. Table of institutions and faculty perspectives

Area of Concern	CAU Ministry of Education	NAU Provost and International Services	CAU Faculty	NAU Faculty
Pedagogical Model	Use lecture and homework as prescribed by Ministry	Follow model practices of CAU	Interested in trying to change, not sure it could work	Constructivist viewpoint on teaching and learning
Publicity	PR very important	PR very important	Unconcerned	Unconcerned
Viewpoints on the Project	Participate project because it is negotiated. International community requires that the country have and use more technology in schools.	Participate project because it is negotiated. University desires a high profile international collaboration.	Initially participate in the project because it is mandated by the university.	Want to help provide access to technology (and help prominence of department)
Decision making and Conflict Resolution	Governance and interaction by a linear top down model	Coordinate and follow practices of CAU	Governance and interaction by a linear top down model	Faculty governance and consensus building
Collegiality Model	Not concerned	Follow practices of CAU	Want shared responsibility for teaching with NAU faculty	Want shared responsibility for teaching with CAU faculty
Instructional Language	All Spanish	All Spanish	Understand need for some English for degree in some courses	Mostly Spanish and capstone course in English to fulfill NAU graduate school requirements
Developmental Funds	Provide adequate funding throughout project	Costs will be recovered in future, no guaranteed commitment	Funding from CAU resources to support faculty network	Concerned about accumulated debt, will hold off working if funds are not available

organizations were excited to use the program as an opportunity to showcase their educational programs and participated in joint efforts to publicize the program (e.g., press conferences, placement in promotional material). In addition, both sets of faculty were motivated and interested in sharing responsibility for teaching the courses. This shared perspective helped in developing an effective co-teaching partnership throughout the program implementation and contributed to capacity-building.

A third step towards launching such partnerships is the importance in establishing effective communication among the partners. In an international program in which content may be delivered from a distant location, communication amongst co-teaching faculty is not only an advantage but a necessity. Most of the communication between NAU and CAU institutions and faculty was done online through electronic communications.

The final area of collaboration that is vital to building institutional and particularly faculty partnerships is through training and technical assistance. Although often mentioned as a barrier to distance education (Cegles, 1998; Muilenburg & Berge, 2001), training and providing technical assistance can be an additional opportunity towards building strong relationships (especially if done in the predelivery phase). Some faculty at the CAU did not only lack content area expertise, they lacked knowledge on how to use and access technology themselves. By participating in two face-to-face training sessions (as well as sustained contact through email), CAU faculty were able to get the training that was needed and they also had the opportunity to establish personal contact with one another and strengthen connections that were initially made, and later developed, online.

CASE DESCRIPTION

Technology Concerns

Relationships were disrupted due to challenges related to technology, particularly web accessibility. The internet bandwidth of this Central American country was very limited and could barely support 3,000-4,000 users. As a result, few people within the country have access to the internet not only because of a lack of internet bandwidth but also due to a lack of monetary funds; internet access is very expensive. In addition, many of the students did not own their own computers and so they had to travel to the CAU itself for access or go to one of the twenty satellite labs set up by the NAU.

Access to computers was, in fact, the biggest obstacle that faculty at both institutions had to face. At first, CAU and NAU faculty designed the courses so that students would download assignments, participate in online discussions, and email assignments when they were due. Once the courses began, it became evident that students were often traveling far distances to one of the satellite labs or to the CAU campus to participate in online discussions and to email assignments and questions to instructors. Also, downloading assignments took a long time due to the lack of computer capabilities and bandwidth. Beyond the demands of the class, the physical infrastructure in the Central American country was problematic. For example, electrical power to the labs and even at the CAU was unreliable (often power would go out and class would have to be stopped). As a consequence, the NAU purchased backup generators so that students could continue working despite interruptions in power. Another example involved the equipment at the satellite labs. As there were no lab monitors at the satellites and

these labs consisted of NAU donated (but older) technology, often equipment was broken (e.g., no ink, jammed paper) or outdated.

Once the NAU and CAU faculty became aware of these issues the courses were restructured, assignments were made available to the students on CD, and a budget to fund upgrades at the 20 satellite labs scattered throughout the country was allocated. However, until the telecommunications network of this Central American country can upgrade its hardware, access to technology will be a continuing challenge to developing web-based relationships within the country.

Another issue was the use of emails as it was the main form of contact between both universities and, between faculty and students. There are both benefits and drawbacks to using email communication. Email is quick, easy, and accessible to many individuals in terms of resolving issues that arise in developing relationships and materials. Information can be exchanged and shared quite expediently and concerns can be discussed and resolved in a timely fashion. However, possible drawbacks include incorrect translation across languages (leading to misinterpretation of messages), constraints in self-expression (since there are cultural differences in how people express feelings and misgivings in email and on paper), and style differences in written communication across languages that may make it difficult to communicate possible apprehensions.

A final technological concern was not with the technology itself, but instead with the users. One of the biggest challenges faced in developing this blended learning program was that the level of students' technological skills varied from complete novice to expert. Some students in the classes had never seen a computer before (much less turned one on) while others were frequent users. As students in this program were carefully selected by the Ministry of Education, faculty wanted to ensure that novice students would be able to access course content and materials along with other more expert students. Over time, with additional classes, and as students gained more technological skills, this concern was ameliorated.

Technology Components

There were several essential technological components to the establishment of this joint blended learning program such as the use of email communication, online classes, and physical infrastructure (e.g., hardware, networking).

Since the bulk of communication was through email, faculty were able to send email to multiple sources so that online discussions could take place. In addition, this type of communication also allowed faculty to develop relationships with one another and with time some email communication became more personal (e.g., referring to children and families of faculty members involved in the project). In general though, the email communication sent between the NAU and CAU focused on administrative issues: logistical (how and when to meet with other faculty), clarification (general questions and answers regarding different policies and procedures), financial (how money should be spent), and admissions (how to coordinate different academic calendars and different grading practices). Email communication was an essential component to the success of this program as it allowed faculty to problem-solve (from their home campuses) and also to communicate student needs and issues as they arose.

A second critical component was the blended learning environment itself. That is, the classes in this Instructional Technology program had a mix of both online and offline contact with instructors. However, the bulk of the course content was taught through a learning management system which, at times, included televised instruction. Televised instruction usually consisted of NAU faculty teaching the CAU students remotely from the NAU site where CAU students were able to call-in with any questions and interact with the instructor via video conferencing. So, students had to quickly

learn to navigate these learning environments and actively used them to establish relationships with instructors and other students.

A final component of this program involved the physical infrastructure and telecommunications network of the CAU and the country. In the process of developing the joint program, the NAU built an intranet, set-up satellite labs (to increase access to the online environment), added servers, and built networks so that faculty could more easily communicate with each other and to ease course delivery.

Management and Organizational Concerns

Several organizational concerns emerged through building this partnership. A major concern was linked to the student-teacher relationships in this program. In effect, one relationship that might be considered the prerequisite for student success in blended learning programs is the relationship that is established between the instructor and student during program implementation and then developed throughout coursework delivery. In fact, there have been several studies that have examined the effects of instructor-student interactions in these settings. For example, Swan, Shea, Fredricksen, Pickett, Pelz, and Maher (2000) found that students who reported the highest levels of instructor interaction in their asynchronous web-based classes also reported greater levels of perceived learning. Alternatively, less satisfaction and lower levels of learning were reported by students who had fewer opportunities or poorer access to interact with the instructor. Further, Hong (2002) found that students who viewed their interactions and relationships with instructors more positively (i.e., had greater satisfaction with their level of interaction with instructor) reported higher achievement and were more satisfied with the course overall.

The findings of these studies highlight the need for instructor involvement and commitment to the blended learning environment, and quality interactions between the instructor and students. Moreover, the interactions that these instructors have with students, especially in the online components of the course, are crucial to students' perceptions and their academic success. As a result, all CAU students were given email accounts to enable easy accessibility to faculty. In addition, there were weekly meetings with students so that NAU faculty could provide additional course information to students.

Another aspect of developing these relationships and fostering interaction is to ensure that students feel connected to the blended learning environment. When students in a blended learning course perceive high levels of collaborative learning, they tend to be more satisfied with their distance course than those who perceive low levels of collaborative learning (So & Brush, 2008). Collaborative learning can be encouraged via assignments and other technologically influenced exercises. Though the bulk of the current program was administered online, there was some face-to-face instructions as prescribed in blended learning programs. Earlier online learning research has shown that interaction among students, and between instructor and students, is vitally important for not only student satisfaction with the online course, but also achievement of course learning goals since these types of interactions encouraged the students to focus on learning (Berge, 1999; Moore, 1989). However, other researchers have highlighted the risk for isolation rather than the forging of connected relationships due to online learning, particularly online programs that are at a geographical distance (Berge, 1999; Northrup, 2002). That is, some students may be less likely to collaborate and have conversations with their fellow students and instructor unless there are active aspects of the course that are designed to increase communication. Consequently, in addition to the discussion boards that were part of all the courses, the NAU faculty set up a blog for students to communicate with one another. As a result, students were able to begin to use

one another as additional course resources. NAU faculty also facilitated the development of peer-tutoring groups that met weekly. With these types of activities, students have the opportunity to feel more connected to a blended learning program, in general.

Several factors can influence or enhance relationship development and community building in a blended environment. One factor is face-to-face meetings (especially early on in course delivery) to allow students to begin the community building process (Garrison, 1997). This face-to-face introduction allows for students to physically meet prior to attempting the more challenging establishment of online relationships. Another factor is instructor modeling. After students' discussions have started online, instructors can continue the threaded discussion with some levels of humor and self-disclosure (Wiesenberg & Stacey, 2005). In addition, instructors can initiate email contact between students or they can set-up specific instructions on effective communication strategies and actively monitor student discussions (e.g., organizing discussion threads, commenting on student responses). The NAU and CAU faculty members set up regular meetings to build their community. There was an effort made to increase collegial collaboration that included email distribution, weekly updates of project activities, and a master calendar that included milestones and tasks. As this example illustrates, the faculty were modeling the exact behavior they were seeking from, and trying to foster within, students while building group cohesion.

Without the benefit of relationship development and cross-cultural support in all contexts of this international blended learning program, the end result would not have been successful. In a thematic analysis of email messages between program development participants in the first year of program planning, 53% of the themes observed revolved around building relationships (Mathur & Oliver, 2008). Cross-cultural support or how support was offered between the Universities also emerged as an underlying cultural theme within the email messages (Oliver & Mathur, 2009). Though there were cultural differences in how support was offered, it was clear that all involved had the best intentions for all students and the future of the program. Ultimately, relationship development and cross-cultural support were crucial in overcoming any concerns.

CHALLENGES FACING THE ORGANIZATION

Although technology is making it easier to build relationships within blended learning programs, there are still several obstacles that can detract from the success of these types of international distance education programs. Two frameworks that are useful in describing possible barriers include Garland's (1993) categorization of barriers to distance education enrollment and Larrson, Boud, Dahlgren, Walters, and Sork's (2005) analysis of structural obstacles in establishing a transnational collaboration. Garland (1993) noted four barriers to distance education. Situational barriers are a result of aspects of the environment that provide obstacles such as transportation or time constraints. Institutional barriers emerge from different programs, policies or programs such as problems with admissions, course scheduling, and financial aid. Dispositional barriers are a result of conflicts involving attitude, motivation, and learning style. Epistemological barriers include aspects such as students: 1) not having the prerequisite knowledge for a course, 2) lacking personal interest in the content of the course, 3) failing to realize the relevance of the content of the course, or 4) believing the course is too technical. Larrson et al. (2005) found four other areas of obstacles when establishing a collaborative relationship: local decision-making processes, systems of examinations and grading, financial considerations, and informational technology (e.g., web accessibility).

The challenges that were encountered in building the relationships between the CAU and NAU fit into aspects of both of these frameworks. For example, there were several situational barriers to program participation by students. Several students did not have access to computers in their homes and as discussed earlier they would have to travel to the satellite labs or to the CAU campus. In addition, even though NAU instructors would spend time at the CAU campus delivering 2-3 day workshops, often due to time or difficulty with translation some material had to be placed online, instead of being discussed and clearly understood during the face-to-face meetings.

Institutional barriers included aspects of the policy environment and differences in how courses were scheduled and managed at both institutions. The CAU's Ministry of Education paid the course fees for the CAU students. However, CAU students who did not receive a passing grade would be required to repay the tuition fees (a considerable monetary hardship for these students). Thus, there was pressure on the students and subsequently the instructors to avoid poor final grades at all costs. It was also clear after program development that there were infrastructure issues within the CAU and educational hierarchy. Thus, the NAU took on additional costs that included building an intranet, adding servers, and building networks as well as providing continued funding for software, hardware, and equipment upgrades.

Several dispositional barriers also existed in the program. CAU students had some difficulty orienting to NAU-based student standards. CAU students were used to a system in which assignments were completed in class therefore class work completed outside of class time was not a culturally syntonic experience. Consequently, students would attend the face-to-face meetings and bring uncompleted work with the expectation that there would be class time set aside so that they could complete their assignments. Initially, students were also unaware of the importance of course attendance and participation in the online community. When the program was first implemented, some students would thus not come to all of the face-to-face meetings and did not participate in the online aspects of the course. Therefore, delivery of coursework was delayed at the beginning of the program.

In terms of epistemological barriers, there was an expectation that the CAU students had some English proficiency prior to program implementation. The program was set-up so that individuals who were able to pass the TOEFL would be granted a degree from the NAU, in addition to the CAU. However, after the program began it was quickly noticed that additional translation was needed. Although websites were translated with side-by-side translation, some course textbooks were not translated. Furthermore, there were additional difficulties as some technology words were new to the culture. To resolve these issues, some one-time fees were paid to translate some textbooks and instructors began to use alternative reading materials (that could be translated more inexpensively or that were already available in Spanish).

Finding faculty who were well trained at both sites was another barrier. The NAU needed instructors who had content area expertise in educational technology; this was a challenge in a country that offered no technology training. The CAU needed instructors who had some fluency in Spanish. Thus, the faculty at both institutions participated in email discussions and training sessions to resolve these issues. An additional benefit due to both of these opportunities was an enhancement of faculty relationships. That is, because faculty were being trained by one another, these discussions and trainings provided for additional time to build and foster stronger relationships as well as enhancing perceptions of equal contributions by faculty from both institutions.

Another set of barriers to building effective partnerships was linked to local decision-making processes at the institutional level. Initially, the bulk of communication and decision-making was completed by administrators at the institutional level or between the Ministry of Education and the NAU faculty. As a result, at times there was a communication lag between NAU and CAU faculty. For example, materials that were sent by NAU faculty through the administration to CAU faculty never reached them. To overcome this issue, all faculty met at the onset of the program and many of the issues with materials and resources were resolved.

SOLUTIONS AND RECOMMENDATIONS

Woods and Ebersole (2003) found that the use of discussion boards, particularly discussion boards that allow for personal (non-subject-matter-specific) comments greatly contributed to developing a more positive instructor-student relationship and also a stronger sense of community in the online environment. So, to foster a better sense of community and allow students to develop relationships with one another, instructors can set-up discussion folders that are not directly linked to course content. In this way, students can chat with one another as they would in a traditional learning classroom. Furthermore, for students who may be more reticent about joining these discussions (as they would be in a traditional learning classroom), these types of online discussion boards allow for them to observe and experience the community through their own observations that in turn helps them become part of the community (LaRose & Whitten, 2000).

Distance education courses with a blended learning format are an innovative approach to disseminate coursework to populations and countries who are trying to move from a rural economy to a technologically literate country. However, developing a blended learning program is not as straightforward as it may seem at first glance. Various unanticipated and underlying issues did emerge. For example, after considerable discussion of cultural perspectives amongst faculty coordinators of both NAU and CAU, NAU faculty recognized that many of the students were struggling to meet the demands of online learning within the context of their everyday lives. It was a challenge for some students to even access the technology within their homes (they could not personally afford the equipment nor costs to connect to the Internet from home). Consequently, it was difficult for the students to complete some of the assignments (e.g., downloading documents was extremely time consuming). As a result, compact discs were given to each CAU student that contained all the information available online so that CAU students did not have to spend valuable resources trying to download information. In addition, NAU faculty gained a more comprehensive awareness of the lives of their CAU students and realized that grades did not necessarily reflect a lack of motivation. Thus, NAU faculty had a shift in their perspective and adjusted some of their teaching techniques (e.g., allowing incompletes in classes until coursework was complete) as a result of better consciousness of students' needs and an expansion of their own cultural understanding and awareness.

The success of the collaboration to build effective relationships is dependent on a mutual commitment of all parties involved to plan accordingly and communicate effectively. All parties and individuals involved within the collaboration must make an effort to get to know one another and to understand each others' strengths and weaknesses. In addition, program designers need to be aware of the background and learning styles of their learners. It is important to anticipate the difficulties associated with different communication styles and possible language differences that may arise during translations. A common terminology may need to be developed so that all individuals involved are "on the same page" and as a result there are no misunderstandings. Also, geographic distance adds an additional challenge to the development of blended programs. Time can be saved

with email communication. However, face-to-face meetings are still essential to the success of the program. Relationships that include some type of personal contact are formed more easily and appear to be more personal.

Overall, various types of support are essential to the success of a blended learning program. After meeting the CAU students and learning about their resources and circumstances, changes were made by the NAU faculty so that expectations were more culturally appropriate yet still met the rigor of the NAU program. Translated materials were made more readily available to the CAU students which did not utilize significant NAU resources but were a tremendous support for the CAU students. Teaching support in the form of professional development should be made available to all faculty involved (i.e., to build their technological skills). Including a component that addresses the cultural needs of the students and instructor awareness of the culturally diverse online learner is essential. Particulars regarding administrative and technological support and the commitment of all institutions involved should not be assumed. Details need to be documented and decided upon prior to implementing this type of blended learning program.

With each new relationship and collaboration, there will be challenges and issues that arise. Knowing some of the possible hurdles that can arise can only facilitate the process and contribute to the future implementation and success of the program. Blended learning programs should be encouraged and supported, and these relationships should be developed so that future generations are given the opportunity to thrive and develop towards a global economy.

REFERENCES

Berge, Z. L. (1999). Interaction in post-secondary, web-based learning and teaching. *Educational Technology, 39*(1), 5–11.

Caffarella, R. S. (2002). *Planning programs for adult learners: A practical guide for educators, trainers, and staff developers* (2nd ed.). San Francisco: Jossey-Bass.

Cegles, K. A. (1998). *Emerging issues affecting distance education research and practice in higher education: A global futures perspective.* Ann Arbor, Michigan: UMI Publications.

DeLugan, R. M. (2005). Peace, culture, and governance in post-civil war El Salvador (1992-2000). *Journal of Human Rights*, *4*, 233–249. doi:10.1080/14754830590952161

Garland, M. (1993). Students' perceptions of the situational, institutional, dispositional and epistemological barriers to persistence. *Distance Education*, *14*(2), 181–198. doi:10.1080/0158791930140203

Garrison, D. R. (1997). Computer conferencing: The post-industrial age of distance education. *Open Learning*, *12*(2), 3–11. doi:10.1080/0268051970120202

Garrison, D. R., & Anderson, T. (2003). *E-learning in the 21st century*. London: Routledge. doi:10.4324/9780203166093

Gatliff, B., & Wendel, F. C. (1998). Inter-institutional collaboration and team teaching. *American Journal of Distance Education*, *12*(1), 26–37. doi:10.1080/08923649809526981

Graham, C. R. (2005). Blended learning systems: Definitions, current trends, and future directions. In Bonk, C. J., & Graham, C. R. (Eds.), *Handbook of blended learning: Global perspectives, local designs* (pp. 3–21). San Francisco: Pfeiffer.

Hong, K. S. (2002). Relationships between students' and instructional variables with satisfaction and learning from a web-based course. *The Internet and Higher Education*, *5*, 267–281. doi:10.1016/S1096-7516(02)00105-7

Index Mundi. (2006). *El Salvador's demographics profile 2006*. Retrieved August 3, 2006, from http://www.indexmundi.com/El Salvador/demographics _profile.html

LaRose, R., & Whitten, P. (2000). Re-thinking instructional immediacy for web courses: A social cognitive exploration. *Communication Education*, *49*(4), 320–388. doi:10.1080/03634520009379221

Larrson, S., Boud, D., Dahlgren, M. A., Walters, S., & Sork, T. (2005). Confronting globalization: Learning from intercontinental collaboration. *Innovations in Education and Teaching International*, *42*(1), 61–71. doi:10.1080/14703290500048960

Leggett, W. P., & Persichitte, K. A. (1998). Blood, sweat, and tears: 50 years of technology implementations obstacles. *TechTrends*, *43*(3), 33–36. doi:10.1007/BF02824053

Mathur, R., & Oliver, L. (2008, January). *Developing cultural partnerships through electronic communication: A thematic analysis.* Paper presented at the annual meeting of the Hawaii International Conference on Education, Honolulu, HI.

Moncada-Davidson, L. (1995). Education and its limitations in the maintenance of peace in El Salvador. *Comparative Education Review*, *39*(1), 54–75. doi:10.1086/447289

Moore, M. G. (1989). Editorial: Three types of interaction. *American Journal of Distance Education*, *3*, 1–6. doi:10.1080/08923648909526659

Moore, M. G., & Kearsley, G. (2005). *Distance education: A systems view*. Belmont, CA: Wadsworth.

Muilenberg, L., & Berge, Z. L. (2001). Barriers to distance education: A factor-analytic study. *American Journal of Distance Education*, *15*(2), 7–22. doi:10.1080/08923640109527081

Northrup, P. T. (2002). Online learner's preferences for interaction. *The Quarterly Review of Distance Education, 3*(2), 219–226.

Oliver, L., & Mathur, R. (2009, June). *Developing an international blended learning program: Cultural lessons learned.* Paper presented at the annual meeting of the ED-MEDIA World Conference on Educational Multimedia, Hypermedia, & Telecommunications, Honolulu, HI.

So, H., & Brush, T. (2008). Student perceptions of collaborative learning, social presence and satisfaction in a blended learning environment: Relationships and critical factors. *Computers & Education, 51*(1), 318–336. doi:10.1016/j.compedu.2007.05.009

Swan, K., Shea, P., Fredricksen, E., Pickett, A., Pelz, W., & Maher, G. (2000). Building knowledge building communities: Consistencies, contact and communication in the virtual classroom. *Journal of Educational Computing Research, 23*(4), 359–383.

Wang, X., Dannenhoffer, J. F., Davidson, B. D., & Spector, J. M. (2005). Design issues in a cross-institutional collaboration on a distance education course. *Distance Education, 26*(3), 405–423. doi:10.1080/01587910500291546

Wiesenberg, F., & Stacey, E. (2005). Reflections on teaching and learning online: Quality program design, delivery, and support issues from a cross-global perspective. *Distance Education, 26*(3), 385–404. doi:10.1080/01587910500291496

Wiesenberg, F. P. (2004). Designing and co-facilitating online graduate classes: Reflections and recommendations. *Canadian Journal of University of Continuing Education, 30*(2), 41–59.

Woods, R., & Ebersole, S. (2003). Using non-subject-matter-specific discussion boards to build connectedness in online learning. *American Journal of Distance Education, 17*(2), 99–118. doi:10.1207/S15389286AJDE1702_3

ADDITIONAL READING

Bishop, P., Cox, B., Fothergill, R., Kyle, J., Lawson, D., & Mitchell, M. (2001). Inter-institutional collaboration on easing the transition to university. *LTSN Maths and Stats Newsletter, 1*(1), 5–8.

Kupetz, R., & Ziegenmeyer, B. (2005). Blended learning in a teacher training course: Integrated interactive e-learning and contact learning. *ReCALL: Journal of Eurocall, 17*(2), 179–196. doi:10.1017/S0958344005000327

Mackey, T., & Ho, J. (2008). Exploring the relationships between Web usability and students' perceived learning in Web-based multimedia (WBMM) tutorials. *Computers & Education, 50*(1), 386–409. doi:10.1016/j.compedu.2006.08.006

Moore, M. G., & Kearsley, G. (2005). *Distance education: A systems view* (2nd ed.). Belmont, CA: Wadsworth.

Paton, R., & McCarthy, P. (2008). How transferable are management learning systems? Reflections on 15 years of large-scale transnational partnerships. *Management Learning, 39*(1), 93–111. doi:10.1177/1350507607085174

Woods, R. (2002). How much communication is enough in online courses? Exploring the relationship between frequency of instructor-initiated personal email and learners' perceptions of and participation in online learning. *International Journal of Instructional Media, 29*(4), 377–394.

KEY TERMS AND DEFINITIONS

Blended Learning: An "approach to blend different learning methods, techniques and resources and apply and deliver them in an interactive meaningful learning environment. Learners should have easy access to different learning resources to apply the knowledge and skills they learn under the supervision and support of the teacher inside and /or outside the classroom. Such approaches may apply face-to-face instruction with computer-mediated instruction"(Graham, 2005, p. 3).

Capacity-Building: The creation of a supportive environment with necessary policy and legal frameworks, and institutional development. The process includes community participation and the development of human resources and strengthening of managerial systems. In some cases, it refers to assistance that is provided to organizations, usually developing societies, which have a need to develop certain areas of competence, or for general upgrading of performance ability. Most capacity is built by societies themselves, at times in the government or in the private sector (Urban Capacity Building Network, 2009).

Distance Education: A type of pedagogy in which teachers and learners communicate at times of their own choosing through technology (or other electronic media) that allows them to communicate in real time and through other online ways (Moore & Kearsley, 2005)

Instructional Technology: "The theory and practice of design, development, utilization, management, and evaluation of processes and resources for learning," according to the Association for Educational Communications and Technology (AECT) Definitions and Terminology Committee (Garrison & Anderson, 2003).

Total Quality Management: A business management strategy focused on improving awareness of quality (maintaining high standards in manufacturing and eliminating defects and problems from work operations) in all organizational processes. It is a concept that has been used in manufacturing, government, and service industries.

Chapter 20
Curriculum Development, Implementation and Evaluation of Project Integrated Online Training

Peter Haber
Salzburg University of Applied Sciences, Austria

Erich Herber
Badegruber & Partner GmbH, Austria

Manfred Mayr
Salzburg University of Applied Sciences, Austria

ABSTRACT

New project management skills and processes are prerequisites to meet the challenges of the globalization. Enterprises, companies and institutions that are operating in transnational and distributed ICT projects on global market need highly qualified project-managers for virtual collaboration. Most training organizations and certification programs focus only on classical soft and technical skills. Participants and most important managers of distributed projects however need training and practice in virtual collaboration and intercultural aspects to be able to consider international socio-cultural issues encountered in business. Therefore, the target of Pool2Business (P2B) was to establish on the one hand a modular online course to address certain specific requirements and qualifications of a company as well language and culture specific differences between participants and on the other hand to ensure with Project Integrated Training parts that the learning outcomes can be immediately used in practical application. By following an adapted and extended ADDIE Model, the P2B-Consortium was able to establish the whole Curriculum more effectively by having the same strategies, following the same procedures and knowing the next steps to fulfill the target of P2B.

DOI: 10.4018/978-1-61520-751-0.ch020

ORGANIZATION BACKGROUND

The POOL2Business project consortium, a cluster of European industries and universities (realised by a European funded Lifelong Learning Programme project), has been established to put Project Organisation Online (POOL) processes into practice. It aims to enhance existing project management practices combining technical skills with soft skills in a virtual environment. The project assumes ICT systems to establish project collaboration merely virtually through the use of online communication and collaboration technology. By connecting projects virtually, the consortium ensures more secure, consistent and economical collaboration in project transactions.

The P2B Consortium (http://www.pool2business.eu) consists of five universities: FH Salzburg- University of Applied Science (Austria), University of Alicante (Spain), Galway Mayo Institute of Technology (Ireland), Kaunas College (Lithuania), Technical University of Cluj-Napoca (Romania) three small enterprises: Cockpit Consulting (Austria), Badegruber & Partner GmbH (Austria), IREAS Institute for structural policy (Czech Republic) with research focus and several promoting international companies as Hewlett Packard and Skidata from the engineering sector. The consortium ensures the innovative, international approach and the quality of the outcomes. The focus of the university partners was to develop the training program and the assessment as well the certification processes. The three enterprises have taken a key role in the analyzing phase of the target group and also in the transformation of the innovative approach to the companies and organizations. To get close to the target-group, four companies from engineering sector have supported the project-team. To guarantee the international acceptance chambers of commerce of each country provided their facilities to the project.

SETTING THE STAGE

The P2B Curriculum design followed a skills-based approach to accommodate the special focuses on work-orientation. Therefore, firstly competency profiles have been developed based on real-life tasks reflecting current work practices. The consultation and involvement of practitioners (industry partners) at early stage of the needs analysis as well as in the final evaluation phase was then a major guarantor for the appropriateness of the training units.

The approach reflects the findings and standardized procedures as provided in the ADDIE Model (Molenda,M.. & Pershing, J., 2004; Bichelmeyer, B. A., 2005) which consists of 5 phases, namely

- Analysis
- Design
- Development
- Implementation
- Evaluation,

and the work of the IEEE Learning Technology Standards Committee (LTSC). The operational execution of the curriculum design phases has been embedded in a project management and quality assurance procedure. The content and tasks of the 5 phases, which have to be fullfilled, are as below:

Needs Analysis

In the first phase the actual needs are determined and a set of job-related tasks are defined, which the training should refer to. It is crucial in this phase to get feedback from the labor market through questionnaires, surveys, and focus group interviews so that the curriculum is oriented towards and reflects the actual real-life workplace situation. So the industry partners, one of the main target groups, are already involved at this early stage.

Curriculum Design

This stage focuses on the training approach, the definition of learning objectives and performance measures, and finally the design of a training plan. Here both the pedagogical-didactic framework and the specific potential as well as constraints of the online medium have to be carefully considered.

Instructional Development

A competency profile is defined, which then directs the creation of learning modules/units and the selection of supportive media and materials. Special attention is given to using an approach to competency definition that is in line with the efforts of the IEEE Learning Technology Standards Committee (LTSC) and their Reusable Competency Definitions standard (IEEE WG20: Learning Technology Standards Committee, 2004).

It is not primarily intended to produce any materials but rather to select from existing materials which are suited for the specifics of the Online Training Model. Important is to provide quality criteria for materials to be included into curricula in line with the objective of creating a handbook to identify critical success factors for online training based on the overall pedagogical-didactic framework.

Principles for the Pedagogic Didactic Approach

The pedagogic-didactic approach in the curriculum modules is based on and quality-assured for the following principles:

- **Active Learner Involvement**: in adopting a moderate constructivist approach it is important to integrate acknowledge learner responsibility and learner self-organization as main principles for the acceptance and success of e-learning scenarios.
- **Provision of stimulating learning situations**: to follow the principles of problem-

based and project-based learning which logically follows from the nature of the intended training modules. An overall pragmatic view of what is really feasible in concrete project environments should facilitate the choice of actual instructional design and materials. This is particularly relevant for group assignments and group collaboration. An aspect that has to be considered is the variety of media and approaches to cater for multiple intelligences and different learner styles, some of which may even have gender-specific relevance. It is essential that specific potentials and constrains of the online medium have to be taken into consideration.

- **Selecting a learner-centered organizational and communicative framework**: that enhances motivation and provides the possibility for group interaction, community building peer-learning but also reflective learning possibilities such as web-logs and diaries.
- **Blended learning approach**: that utilizes both online and offline scenarios to their full potentials. It has now widely been accepted that a well-defined combination of online and off-line activities yields best results. This requires, however, careful planning and definition of interfaces.

Curriculum Implementation

A pilot training is used for formative evaluation of trainees and instructor performance as well as trainees feedback. It provides basis for necessary information and modifications. In this phase, the trainees as the main beneficiaries as well as the instructors as both curriculum designers and curriculum executors are centrally involved so that any necessary adjustments in the practical delivery can be made. Therefore, also a handbook should be created which documents all the experiences made throughout the implementation. Again here, the work of the IEEE (LTSC) on the Computer

Managed Instruction (IEEE WG11: Learning Technology Standards Committee, 2004) standard focusing on reusability of learning units and evaluation of trainee performance across different platforms is taken into account.

Curriculum Evaluation

Within the defined pilot training, the curriculum modules can be tested by a summative evaluation. The framework for the summative evaluation includes both quantitative and qualitative data. In addition, in a final evaluation phase, the curriculum modules and handbook chapters can be reviewed by a number of related experts.

Design Steps Evaluation and Quality Assurance Framework

The Evaluation and Quality Assurance Framework can be delivered by going through 6 phases:

- Research on existing frameworks and practices
- Comparison between parameters for offline and online training
- Specification of evaluation and quality assurance framework to be used and tested within pilot training
- Specification of feedback mechanisms and interaction with trainees
- Adaptation of evaluation and quality assurance framework based on formative and summative feedback
- Final validation testing of selected curriculum modules with selected experts

THE ADDIE-MODEL AND P2B

As the P2B Consortium has been a Lifelong Learning Program Project of the European Union and all members working on P2B have to collaborate for distributed - a common system to establish the curriculum was necessary. For that purpose,

the well and clear structured ADDIE model provided the best basis. At the Kick-Off Meeting of P2B, the ADDIE-model has been adapted and extended in respect to support the different work packages of the P2B, which have been defined by the project management. As a consequence, the ADDIE-model has been embedded into the project management procedure. The 5 phases of the model have been structured into different tasks leading to important milestones of the P2B project itself.

CASE DESCRIPTION

P2B (P2B – a Leonardo da Vinci Life Long Learning Program Project, 2009) - a 2-year Leonardo da Vinci project - aims to enhance existing training standards and practices, combining technical skills with project management training in online learning environments. The objective of the project is to assess the requirements that result from current virtual collaboration practice in transnational business projects, and to develop a curriculum and training methodologies that transfer practical knowledge and experience to existing business and university training, strongly involving online concepts and technology.

To respond to this objective, P2B has designed a new model curriculum after a one year phase of research and analysis as per the ADDIE model, During this period a set of relevant competencies for Online Project Management (OPM) was defined, which were further broken down into learning outcomes and incorporated into a training plan for OPM training. Each of these competencies was described at an abstract level using a set of predefined descriptors and parameters.

Environmental Requirements

For the purpose of adjusting the model curriculum with the needs of real life projects in business environments, P2B has cooperated with international

Table 1. Excerpt questionnaire qualitative research

Core questions	Supporting questions
How does operative project communication work within the team?	• How does communication within the project work? On fixed dates, variable dates, both? • Which topics are communicated in which way? • How does communication with the mother company look like? • Which role does the online platform play?
Which conflict do you face in international/national projects and how do you deal with them?	• What are the most common conflicts? *Distribution conflicts, evaluation conflicts, conflicts of goals, perception conflicts, relationship conflicts, role conflicts, ethnically/culturally base conflicts.* • Which solutions have been most successful? *Autonomous solution within the team, moderated conflict solution, external moderator, mediation* • How does the Steering-Team act in a conflict situation? • When does the Steering-Team intervene? • Which role does the online platform play in evolution, recognition and solution of conflicts?
Where do you see the weak points in your company's international and virtual project management?	• Do you document the weak points? • Where do you document them?

companies to spot weaknesses and to figure out needed competencies of these companies, as well as to develop a training approach that develops these competencies. A strong focus has been put on the requirements and shortcomings detected by an in-depth qualitative (Table 1) and quantitative research that had been undertaken by the P2B project team.

In the analysis phase, which included small and mid-sized organizations of various European countries, the following shortcomings and/or lessons learned were identified:

- Unstructured, bad communication is the biggest weakness in international project management.
- Virtual project organization leads to goal conflicts between different locations.
- Simple collaboration technology (e-Mails, file repository, intranet and project portals) is pre-dominant in practice. Usability, safety and technical availability are most important.
- Know-how is the key aspect for staffing decisions; cost arguments are secondary.
- Rough planning (on a milestone level)

is preferred to detailed work break down structures.

- Project Management (PM) practices applies existing standards (e.g. IPMA, PMI) and individual company principles (30%).
- Controlling is limited to oral or written reports, containing key facts and figures only.
- English is the pre-dominant language in international projects (75%).
- Insufficient language skills and inconsistent terminology are typical obstacles in communication.
- Face to face kick-offs, clear agreements, and clean communication are crucial to prevent failure.
- Basic PM Principles also apply to Online Project Management. Differences appear across branches and cultures.

Based on these results of the analysis and previous assumptions, P2B defined the target group of beneficiaries of the training programme. It was decided that P2B primarily focuses on adult learners who

Table 2. Target groups and the characteristics

Target Group	Characteristics
OPM Learners	Main Objective: Developing Basic OPM skills PM Proficiency: formal PM education or management experience in projects (1 year)
OPM Practitioners	Main Objective: Improving Practical OPM Skills PM Proficiency: management experience (at least 1 year) in online projects (OP)
OPM Experts	Main Objective: Sharing Expert Knowledge on OPM PM Proficiency: OPM and/or research experience (at least 3 years)

- require know-how about specific concepts and practices of OPM,
- need practical training and expert knowledge in project collaboration through online processes
- have a minimum knowledge or experience in managing projects (in theory and practice)
- are strongly self-directed, open to online learning, and accumulated project life experiences

As a secondary group, P2B decided to involve international experts and professionals also in OPM who want to share their knowledge, gain new knowledge, and contribute to sustain the future P2B network of OPM professionals and started therefore an online platform.

A classification, which checks the previous qualification of P2B beneficiaries, has been determined to associate them to the following target groups (Table 2).

Examples of the kinds of settings in which relevant experience is likely to be applied include: work as a project manager (PM), project assistant (PA), project team member (PT), project planner (PP), project evaluator (PE), project consultant (PC), package and/or task leader (PL/TL) in distributed project teams, OP's and/or international project environments as well as PM trainers and researchers in the field of OPM.

Technology Concerns

The rapid development and change of technology over the last decade has had a resounding impact on project management. As more and more project managers begin moving online for much of their work, project managers require new technical and organizational skills in online projects. Although project management practice in business requests for such skills and technologies, recent project environments and related training programmes yet involve merely traditional training technologies and methods. As a consequence, project management demands for new technology and training facilities around the issue of Project Management (PM).

Online technology (coupled with the explosion of knowledge transfer in the global business) has led to the emergence of new project management and training facilities, including virtual collaboration, online and collaborative learning, as well as blended learning.

The P2B training approach intends to exploit such modalities. While assuming learners to know the traditional tools and concepts, P2B exploits the advantages and concepts of ICT based facilities and online collaboration to develop the more sophisticated skills of Online Project Management (OPM). The P2B approach is undertaking a major effort to provide the best blend of conventional project practices with the power of online technologies. It creates online environments in which learners maintain contact with other participants and trainers throughout project collaboration and study periods by means of online collaboration systems (e.g. Learning Management System, Online Collaboration Systems, etc.).

- Learning Management System (to deliver the training material and feedback channels)
- Online Collaboration Systems (to enable the collaboration of learners throughout self-study periods and/or in their practical projects, e.g. Online PM Platform, Content Sharing, Video Conferencing, WIKI, etc.)

Networking is also a key component of the training programme. Learners develop a common understanding of concepts and improve their skills through collaboration with others in projects as well as through learning from each other throughout the training (collaborative learning). If learners identify problems in understanding important concepts of OPM (deriving from self-study periods or practical work), P2B provides assistance and advice in a variety of ways, including:

- Online Collaboration (online discussions through means of a Learning Management System, Virtual Classroom Training etc.)
- Online coaching (expert feedback to open questions through online meetings, forums, etc.)
- Online Repositories (sharing knowledge and lessons learned through WIKIs, open educational resources, etc.)

P2B puts a strong emphasis on developing such online communities among practitioners and experts in the field of online project management (Network of Excellence). Learners are encouraged to make use of the knowledge provided by this network. Here they meet people from a diverse range cultures and professional backgrounds,

and they have opportunities to learn from expert colleagues through online discussion, debate and collaborative study.

Technology Components

The P2B training program enhances online collaboration, provides the possibility for group interaction and community building, and supports self-directed and reflective learning possibilities.

A) Learning and Collaboration Technology

P2B applies a collaborative and communicative technology framework for the implementation of the training programme. The intention of the approach is to provide OPM training in online environments as flexible as possible so as to stimulate differences in learning styles and work attitudes while simulating settings of real online projects. The framework mainly combines the following technologies:

- **Learning Management System** - The P2B Learning Management System provides the technical environment especially for the independent learning periods. It delivers the e-Learning modules and other training materials, and additional services that support the training process, including feedback channels for group discussions (e.g. forums) and tracking methods (e.g. log statistics and study progress reports).
- **Online / PM Collaboration System** - The aim of P2B is to collaborate on joint results in simulated projects (study projects). This process needs to be supported by a virtual collaboration and communication environment (e.g. Online PM software, Social Software, WIKI Systems) that enables learners to collaborate on the projects in a

virtual setting (practical training). It serves as a collaboration environment to share knowledge and to sustain networks.

- **Online Communication System** - Online Communication Systems such as Virtual Classrooms or Audio/Video Conferencing systems are applied to provide the necessary instructional (online) training.
- **Content Authoring Tools** - Content authoring tools are used to create core e-learning modules to be published in the P2B training environment.

B) Repositories

In the training, a set of e-Learning repositories is used. The collection of training material for the POOL2Business training programme is stored at various repositories. The following repositories are exploited for the purpose of the training:

- POOL2Business Content Repository – A content repository was developed for the purpose of the P2B training programme; it facilitates the establishment of an OPM knowledge community with web based learning materials produced for the purpose of POOL2Business trainings, e.g. e-Learning modules, POOL2Business handbook, recording of online trainings, etc. In the core OPM e-Learning modules, learners are required to complete quizzes, assignments and/or assessments associated with the processes of the project management life cycle to enable them to assess their learning progress. They can be used by learners to test their understanding of the concepts and their ability to evaluate and adapt those to various project situations.
- Open Educational Resources - Instead of producing all content from anew, P2B exploits existing online communities and training materials which are suited for the training (according to a set of quality

criteria). Especially open educational resources where materials are free of charge, well-elaborated and sufficient in quality, are involved in the training programme. This includes teaching and learning materials of third party providers, e.g. full web based courses, course materials, content modules, link collections, lectures, homework assignments, quizzes, and e-journals, for both basic and advanced training programmes).

- WIKI Systems – P2B makes use of existing WIKI systems to create collaborative communities around the issue of Online Project Management, serving as a common knowledge sharepoint for OPM experts and learners (e.g. defining glossaries, documentation, learning material etc.)

MANAGEMENT AND ORGANIZATIONAL CONCERNS

Various management and organizational concerns have been related to the implementation of the program. It included three major steps: (a) the Instructional Development with the instructional design, the organizational requirements, and the selection of the course materials, (b) the Organizational Framework of the training, including training modules, training sessions and methodologies, (c) the Implementation of the Curriculum, considering training, trainer support and feedback mechanisms, as well as (d) the Evaluation of the training, including reflection and conclusions.

A) Instructional Development

Contrary to traditional (merely classroom based) training models, P2B trainings need to provide the highest flexibility in developing an understanding of the basic concepts of OPM. The difference to traditional learning lies in the diversity and interactivity of instruction and media. Considering this, some assumptions had to be made related to the prerequisites and objectives of the different target groups as well as the appropriate selection of instructional concepts and media.

Instructional Design Assumptions

Considering the different target groups and previous knowledge of the three B2B target groups (OPM learners, practitioners, experts), P2B assumes that:

- **It should also support learners with lack of experience** who wish to acquire knowledge in Online Project Management but whose previous education and/or experience does not qualify them. Mechanisms had to be found to assess and leverage the knowledge and skills of these learners so as to assure a consistent level of prequalification in the P2B training program. The overall objective is to harmonize the knowledge and experience of a heterogeneous group of P2B learners. To meet these requirements, a conversion course has been developed.
- **It should consider the target group of OPM learners** because there is a demand for knowledge and skills that can be easily associated with previous (traditional) PM knowledge and processes (task centered approach), as this is where the educational and practical background of most of the learners roots. In building the course modules for this target group we related to traditional PM structures and processes and explain the differences and characteristics of OPM. In practical examples and case reviews new concepts are demonstrated and understood more easily. The training program comprises periods of independent learning, instructional teaching, practical training (based on exercises and case studies) and networking, where trainees receive

expert guidance and feedback channels. In concludes with a case study assessment, where learners work under supervision and assess their practical skills.

- **It should target the group of OPM practitioners** (advanced learners) as there is a great demand for knowledge and skills that can be easily related to practical work and which is not primarily based on theory (problem centered approach). In building the course modules for this group of learners we provided practical examples and case studies that can be applied to a specific situation of the study project and/or to the learners' day-to-day work. Based on the experience, such 'put-into-practice' approaches help learners adopt new techniques and develop skills more easily. The training program puts a strong focus on the practical training (based on a study project) and networking, where trainees receive guidance and sufficient feedback from experts. It also provides e-Learning modules and online sessions to deepen the learners' knowledge through independent learning and instructional teaching. The program concludes with the assessment and presentation of the project that had been elaborated, where learners work under supervision and assess their practical skills.

Related to the selection of appropriate instructional concepts and media that can be used in online learning environments, both for individual and collaborative learning, the following represents some of the methods, media and materials that were supposed to be most useful.

- **Web Based Trainings** – a (summary) demonstration of the main issues to create a better understanding of the key concepts of the subject and demonstrate those on practical examples

Figure 1. Table of the training plan

	Pool2Business Conversion Course	Pool2Business Basic Course	Pool2Business Advanced Course
Blended Approach: *	▪ ▬	▬ ▬ ▬ ▪	▪ ▪ ▪ ▬ ▬ ▪ ▪
Module Level:	CONVERSION	BASIC	ADVANCED
Course Type:	Preparatory Course	Fundamental Training	Practical Training
Target Group:	Learners with lack of prequalification	OPM Learners	OPM Practitioners
Language:	English	English	English
Prerequisites (recommended):	Formal PM education	PM experience (1 year) or Conversion course	OPM experience (1 year) or Basic course
Course Material:	Preparatory	Task oriented	Problem oriented
Total Effort Hours:	15 hours	50 hours	100 hours
Credit Value (ECTS/PMI):	-	2 ECTS	4 ECTS
Duration (in months):	1 month	4 - 5 months	6 months
Entry:	anytime	anytime	per semester / per year
Pass Requirements:	100% Attendance 80% Success Rate	80% Attendance 80% Success Rate	80% Attendance 80% Success Rate

(▪ periods of learning & reflection (acquiring knowledge)/▬ periods of practical training (developing skills))

- **Case Studies / Best Practices** – approaches and practices that have proved very successful in realistic situations to generate additional information that typically cannot be generated by presentations and/or study texts
- **Interactive Study Materials** – e.g. study texts, check lists, videos, quizzes, etc. that support the process of learning through interaction and collaboration
- **Assignments / Exercises** – the application of knowledge based on practical examples (preparation for assessments)
- **Assessments** - various assessment methods will be used to evaluate the learning progress of the learner, such as individual questions (tests), individual feedback or monitoring of study activities.

Organizational Requirements

To describe the organizational requirements and indicators that provide the framework for this instructional approach, P2B developed a training plan that describes all activities, methods, learning objectives and related competencies. The specific setting and context of the training program depends on the competencies that need to be developed in the training. The individual training course considered the individual learning requirements and instructional assumptions that had been made related to every target group. The following Figure 1 describes the basic characteristics of the P2B training plan.

Selection of Course Material

P2B applies a set of online learning materials (e-Learning modules) for instruction. Appropriate se-

Figure 2. P2B e-Learning modules

lection of learning material, effective instructional design, powerful multi-media components, and appropriate use of learning materials are important aspects. The process of selecting these materials was based on a set of quality indicators:

- **educational** - the training material is an educational resource that corresponds to pedagogical standards of the curriculum, e. g. definition of learning time, target group, learning objectives.
- **thematic impact** - the training material addresses specific learning objectives of the curriculum
- **user generated / professionally produced** - the training material must have been created by the P2B consortium and/or other providers who are experts in the field
- **conformity with standards** - The training material needs to corresponds with common e-Learning and PM standards
- **target group** – the training material needs to have relevance to either of the target groups

The collection of learning material for the P2B training programme has been specifically tailored to the instructional requirements of the curriculum (competencies). For this purpose, the P2B consortium developed a set of core e-Learning modules, a glimpse of which has been given here in Figure 2.

P2B also exploits existing materials which are suited for the training (according to a set of quality criteria). Especially open educational resources where materials are free of charge, well-elaborated and sufficient in quality, are involved.

Organizational Framework of the Training

All three courses of the training plan have been developed and required organizational and structural aspects. This section describes the principles of these, explained for the POOL2Business Advanced Course.

Structure of the Course

The **POOL2Business Advanced Course** strongly focuses on the development of practical skills that are required in online projects. It explains best practices, tools and techniques that learners can apply in their own project management activities. In practical (simulation) projects, learners collaborate in group projects and develop practical skills of managing projects online.

The course is organized in three stages:

- **Stage 1 (Self-study Period)** – During this stage, learners elaborate a project assignment (in a self-study period) to prepare for their study project and to develop an understanding of the project. They also work through an introductory e-Learning module which explains critical aspects and provides practical tips for the study project. To deepen their understanding, the learners can make use of the existing P2B training network and the P2B e-Learning modules of the basic level.

- **Stage 2 (Practical Training, Independent Learning, Instructional Training, Networking)** – In the second stage of the program, learners start work in simulated online projects (practical training) where they are part of an online team. In a kick-off meeting (residential) learners meet the other team members (learners) of their study project. This meeting is important to develop the team, start with the planning, as well as to discuss important aspects of the project. A trainer / tutor provides additional guidance. The kick-off meeting should, if possible, be combined with the annual P2B Conference so that learners can also attend the conference and receive additional input regarding important aspects and current issues on Online Project Management (instructional training). After this meeting, learners work on their study projects, strongly collaborating with the distributed team. At this stage, learners learn how to use the whole collaborative

and communicative technology framework to manage their projects. Specific e-Learning modules (mainly based on open educational resources) are available throughout the practical training to deepen their knowledge on important practical aspects of Online Project Management (independent learning) to prevent or overcome problems in real projects. They refer to typical problems and shortcomings of Online Project Management (e.g. problems that had been identified by industries) and present possible solutions to these problems. In regular intervals, learners can additionally attend online coaching sessions in which they receive practical tips from experts and guidance in case of difficulties. Throughout the whole training process, learners have various opportunities to discuss their study projects with a trainer or tutor. The tutor supports the learner through expert knowledge or through self-control questions and exercises (e.g. every learner has to solve a planning task and has to submit the solution for feedback).

- **Stage 3 (Assessment)** – In a final project presentation, learners present their project and reflect on the lessons learned throughout their practical training. The results are evaluated by the tutors / trainers who have

Table 3. Training modules

Stage	Course Units	Training Concept	Study Time
STAGE-01	Online Project Management from a Practical Perspective	Self-Study Period	4 hrs
STAGE-01	Project Assignment / Case	Practical Training	5 hrs
STAGE-02	POOL2Business Conference / Project Kick-Off	Event / Conference	2 days
STAGE-02	Study Project	Practical Training	40 hrs
STAGE-02	Networking	Networking	5 hrs
STAGE-02	Specific Aspects of OPM (various e-Learning modules)	Self-Study Period	15 hrs
STAGE-02	Project Coaching	Instructional Training	10 hrs
STAGE-03	Final Project Presentation	Assessment	5 hrs

been playing the role of the online coaching in the online sessions.

Outline of the Training Modules

The module structure of the course is composed of the following units and topics (Table 3).

Deriving from the findings of the qualitative research as well as the results of the quantitative research, the most relevant training needs have been identified (competencies) for the defined target group, focusing on the following key areas summarized in the Table 4.

Methodologies Applied to Instruction

The program puts a strong focus on the practical training (based on a study project) and network-

ing, where trainees receive expert guidance and feedback channels. It also provides a collection of e-Learning modules to deepen the learners' knowledge through independent learning and instructional teaching. The program concludes with the assessment and presentation of the project that had been elaborated, where learners work under supervision and assess their practical skills.

The following blend of learning methods is applied to instruction (see Figure 3).

B) Implementation of the Curriculum

The whole training stages have been tested in a pilot training sessions with trainees from companies confronted to collaborate within real-life training case studies. For testing the curriculum

Table 4. Key areas and training needs

Key Area	Training needs
Fundamental Information related to OPM	• characteristics of international projects • managing projects in dynamic environments • domestic vs. international project management • tasks, role types & characteristics in online projects • typical life cycles of online / distributed project • the excellent "international" project manager • the excellent "online" project manager • online project success factors • applicability of PM standards
Virtual Communication & Collaboration in OP	• online collaboration techniques • effective communication strategies & technologies • collaborative information engineering • basics of online project management & collaboration • knowledge management and the use of KM systems in distributed teams • aspects of online knowledge transfer, project communications, and e-learning • software solutions for online communication, collaboration and project management
Soft Skills, Intercultural Communication, and Documentation Standards in OP	• effective communication online • Intercultural aspects in international projects • communicating with different cultural backgrounds • negotiating and co-operating in different cultures • differences of organizational cultures and work attitudes • managing foreign work structures and multinational teams
Project Planning, Time Management and Risk Management in OP	• planning and scheduling techniques for distributed work • setting up international calendars & scheduling approaches • collection of online data in online collaboration environments' • creating activities & relationships between teams in online environment • international risks & risk analysis in international settings • troubleshooting in transnational teams

Figure 3. Blended learning methods for instruction

Self Study Assignm.   Conference   Kick-Off / Study Project / Networking   Self-Study   Coaching / Present.

continuous feedback mechanism and assessment & evaluation methods are being adopted.

Continuous Feedback Mechanisms

The continuous feedback process has been integrated in the virtual environment to assure a better harmonization of practical activities and the theoretical background in the curriculum as well to strengthen the awareness of the learning outcomes and benefits, both to the learners and lecturers. The assessment framework has been tested completely on one of the training course units to see if it met the needs of the curriculum in which not only technical skills have to be assessed but also competences to fulfill the certification needs.

At the end of the whole pilot training an evaluation through all training packages has been done both from the trainees' and the trainers' side to evaluate course, teaching and competence quality. The evaluation shows that the evaluation and quality assurance framework worked very well as a quality life cycle instrument. The results have been incorporated as refinements and adaptations to the final curriculum.

Guidelines for Trainers and Instructors

Relevant experiences collected throughout the pilot training have been collected in a Course Handbook that is provided to PM trainers and OPM experts. All lessons learned throughout the trainings can be involved in future training processes or OPM research in the form of storyboards, case studies or best practice examples.

C) Assessment and Curriculum Evaluation

Based on the needs of the P2B certification process an assessment for the trainees and an evaluation for training quality has been designed.

Assessment Framework

An Assessment Framework has been established which describes the whole process of how to establish assessment (Table 5):

- **Learning Outcomes** - As a first important issue for the process for each training stage, six to nine learning outcomes have to be defined clearly and unambiguously without using academic language. These learning outcomes were divided into three categories: skills, competencies and knowledge. If course content is changing learning outcomes should be flexible enough to be changed as well, without changing the whole assessment. Learning outcomes therefore can be used as the main instruments how to perform the assessment.
- **Assessment Criteria** - As second step the definition of assessment criteria takes place to create valid and reliable assessments. The purpose is to judge the acquired skills, competencies and knowledge through the course by the criteria. With these criteria the assessment should be more measurable and comparable. In that intention the criteria has to be clearly defined to be open and understandable to all! Using learning outcome and assessment criteria helps trainees

Table 5. Learning outcomes and assessment criteria

Learning Outcomes	Assessment Criteria
• Be familiar with the process of online project planning and the efficiencies derived from planning. • Be able to define a complete project scope and break this scope into manageable virtual packages and activities • Know how to sequence the activities for a logical • Virtual project flow in a project plan as well as be able to schedule project activities and assign reasonable durations to the activities. • Be able to prepare a project plan and schedule and use as well as communicate it properly in the virtual environment. • Understand what resources are required and how they can be virtually coordinated in a well synchronized manner. • Be familiar with online project team role structures and processes the limitations and advantages. • Understand how to use communication and collaboration tools to communicate the project information properly and in time.	• Defines a project scope and the virtual objectives in a clear and unambiguous way • Writes a project plan including every important virtual aspect • Sequences activities fitting virtual roles and processes in a project • Assigns virtual tasks to activities with realistic duration • Communicates the project and problems to team members by using collaboration tools effectively in appropriate manner • Uses reasonable virtual resources in the project • Uses the communication tools in the correct way to be able to recognize and reacts in time if problems arise • Uses the project plan and time schedule for documentation purpose of changes and disputes

to understand what they are supposed to learn. Another advantage of assessment criteria is that trainees know what to expect and that the course efficiency / assessment efficacy is able to be compared and evaluated in a predefined way, which giving better reliability.

- **Assessment Implementation**: In a third step an online assessment should be established where the first distinction to traditional assessments can be seen. For an online assessment more time is required first: to develop the assessment for a virtual learning environment and second: to define the questions and answers. But by using standards like SCORM or QTI the whole assessment can be easily transferred and imported to other virtual learning environments and different kinds of question types (e.g. multiple choice questions) could be used to build up an assessment to assess the specific criteria. If an own assessment server system or in general an electronic assessment is used it is very important and necessary to test the system with a trainee account to avoid problems in advance.

- **Grading/Judging** – virtual learning environments or assessment server systems

often promote automatic grading and feedback features for the assessment process, but to develop a valid and reliable assessment - it has to be assumed that there is always a necessity to use open ended questions, which need to be corrected manually - external or internal from the virtual learning environments depending if it provides a user-friendly correction and feedback area.

- **Feedback** – for trainers as well for the institutions is necessary to get feedback from the trainees about the assessment process to improve in case the assessment. The Feedback should be given immediately after the whole assessment process. Otherwise the statements and complains will lose strength and the importance of giving feedback decreases. Furthermore the person that is giving the feedback should know the purpose; otherwise the consciousness is decreasing which results in non serious answers.

- **Assessment Outcome** – the last step in creating an assessment is to compare the achieved assessment outcome with the previously defined learning outcome, to verify that the defined learning outcome has actually been achieved. To make an assessment valid and especially reliable a comparison with results from other/same trainees, but taken at different times, is necessary. Questions which achieve on average the same results are reliable, because the date and the trainees were different but the result was nearly the same.

Quality Assurance Framework

Based on Research on existing frameworks and practices like Student Evaluation of Education Quality (SEEQ) instrument (Marsh, 1982, Coffey & Gibbs, 2001) and Course Experience Questionnaire (CEQ) (McInnis, Griffin, James & Coates, 2001) the Quality Assurance Framework (QAF) of the project consists of a set of evaluation processes, tools and guidelines within an institution/company/department for evaluation and improvement of the content. Therefore a list of 20 core areas and course delivery evaluation criterias has been defined for the whole curriculum. The main aims of Quality Assurance Framework are:

- To encourage reflective teaching practice through trainee, instructor and certification institute feedback;
- To maximize the involvement of trainees, trainers, certification institute in the evaluation of courses or curriculum;
- To ensure that feedback mechanisms are relevant to certified institution, department, staff, trainee needs;
- To ensure that feedback is analyzed, and that proposals for action are discussed and implemented at the appropriate level.

The defined core areas and criteria are used in three key areas of the evaluation to guarantee the Certification Process under this Quality Assurance Framework:

Evaluation of Course Quality is designed to obtain trainee feedback on course and course teaching. It is a web-based survey form with a questionnaire consisting of questions from core areas (e.g. Virtual Learning Environment, Generic Skills and Learning Community) concerning the quality of the course. Three open ended questions are added to ask for some feedback about good and bad aspects of the course, and on-line learning. This questionnaire is designed for use in any teaching mode. It primarily focused on the flexible approach of blended learning. The questionnaire is integrated into Virtual Learning Environment (VLE) and activated by an administrator at the end of a course when the trainees have an overview of the training and learning experiences. The criteria and related questions of this questionnaire are summarized in Table 6.

- **Evaluation of Teaching Quality** is separated in a Trainer self rating and a trainee evaluation of teaching. A key aspect of this evaluation is trainer self-evaluation which can be compared with the results of the trainee feedback on his/her teaching quality. Both evaluations are an instrument for the certificated institute and the teacher himself to ensure teaching quality and therefore learning outcomes.
- **Evaluation of Competences Quality** is the third and last part of P2B-QAF for evaluation and improvement of competences in the P2B curriculum: "How do they fit the needs of companies?" and "How are certified trainees prepared to demonstrate this in real work settings?". Evaluation of Competences in this framework is based on Employer Evaluation of Competences. A Web-based questionnaire with a list of P2B competences is used. The results are important for curriculum designers in future analysis, action planning and curriculum improvement.

Table 6. Criteria and core questions of a course evaluation questionnaire

3 Core Areas (Criteria)	Questions
Virtual Learning Environment	1. Access to my unit in VLE was easy 2. The design of the site aided my learning in this unit 3. The online learning activities in this unit were unaffected by technical problems 4. The instructions for using the online resources in VLE were clear 5. Submitting assessments online was successful 6. The facility to choose when and where trainee learned in this unit was valuable 7. Having access to online resource material assisted trainees learning in this unit 8. The online resources available through the VLE site aided trainees learning in this unit 9. The online quizzes were valuable learning exercises 10. The use of regular online quizzes helped keep trainee on track in this unit 11. Online quizzes provided trainee with important feedback about my understanding in this unit
Generic Skills	1. Trainees have learned to think more critically as a result of this course 2. The course helped to develop trainees problem solving skills 3. Trainees have learned to work more independently 4. Trainees were given the opportunity to choose some of their own learning experiences in this course 5. The course improved trainees skills in interpersonal communication 6. The course improved trainees skills in intercultural communication 7. The course improved trainees skills in collaboration 8. The trainees learned better different languages 9. The course improved trainees skills in team building
Online Learning Community	1. Group activities online were well designed 2. Group activities shared multicultural experience 3. Asynchronous online communication activities (e.g. Discussion Board) enhanced learning 4. Synchronous (real time) online communication enhanced learning 5. Each individual trainee felt part of a learning community while studying in this unit 6. The online discussion site aided trainee learning

Curriculum Coordination and Compilation

The whole curriculum design of the P2B curriculum has been based on a project management procedure in which the key steps has been structured in different tasks and milestones, which have been tested by a quality assurance circle.

CURRENT CHALLENGES FACING THE ORGANIZATION

Considering the target groups and nature of OPM training, P2B had to design and manage a training program that is based on self-directed knowledge and skills acquisition rather than enforced learning which adjusts to the needs of industries. This has implications on various aspects: training organization, integration into the work environment, and the accreditation (certification) of such programs.

Overcoming Traditional Training Methods

A key objective in the training is to provide opportunities for learners to encourage different learning styles and motives of learners (who have different cultural, educational and professional backgrounds and varying learning preferences) which usually is not the case in many traditional organizations and training programs.

P2B therefore follows an approach that provides a blend of conventional and online training methods. It presents an opportunity for organizations to harness the flexibility of the training, tailoring it to learners' needs, styles, and preferences, which usually is not the case in many traditional programs. A majority of the training takes place online, highly participative and interactively, encouraging learners to collaborate. It enables the highest flexibility in developing an understanding of the basic concepts of OPM. Learners acquire important OPM knowledge and concepts and they will develop their self-directed work abilities by working through web based training materials, such as e-Learning modules, online tutorials, exercises, case studies and assignments by themselves.

Breaking the Barriers of Training 'Off-the-Job'

Skills cannot be acquired through theoretical learning; they also need practical work experience. These practical aspects are difficult to achieve in many training programs that merely separate theoretical and practical training. Training and practical work are not synchronized (e.g. external seminars scheduled long time before or after skills are actually needed in real projects). This usually has organizational barriers (e.g. restricted no. of trainings in a year / other tasks I conflict with the training).

The P2B training program follows an interdisciplinary approach of theory and practice, which uses merely online learning to provide a thorough understanding of important online concepts in distributed work and learning situations. It uses collaborative project scenarios (simulations or real projects) to enable practical training and skills acquisition embedded in the work environment. The intention is to ensure that knowledge is acquired 'on-the-job' and applied in real projects rather than to explain them in theory.

Establishing Certification Programmes

To continuously ensure and guarantee the quality of the P2B training program on different locations, the quality life cycle, which has been set up within the Quality Assurance and the Assessment Framework of P2B, should now be embedded in certification programmes. Therfore, not only the P2B benificiaries - the learners - should be certified but also the trainers and institutions providing P2B Training Courses. The target is to establish an accredited International OPM Training Program.

SOLUTIONS AND RECOMMENDATIONS

The P2B Curriculum aims to enhance existing project management standards and practices through advanced skills development and training. The P2B Consortium therefore followed an approach that accommodates a special focus on work-orientation and practical relevance already in the design of the curriculum. By involving practitioners (from industry partners) at an early stage to analyze the business needs and applying an adapted form of the ADDIE Model, the P2B Consortium succeeded in establishing a curriculum that adjusts effectively to the needs of the targeted users and to the organizational requirements of the training organization.

This has had implications not only on the development and implementation of the curriculum; it also required and created new ways of how trainers, trainees and institutional bodies develop their trainings and/or skills in practice. Concepts of blended learning and project integrated learning were applied to implement the curriculum and effectively exploit the advantages of these in the training, and a pilot training had been realized to assess and evaluate the impact of the training sessions. Some effects that the training could achieve were strong practical relevance, flexibility of learning preferences, increased sustainability of knowledge acquisition, and an increased collaborative nature of skills development. It also created a new technical, organizational and didactic framework that leads to an increased quality of skills training and practical performance in Online Project Management.

Furthermore general conclusions in the following four areas can be drawn from the case below.

Curriculum Development Based on the ADDIE Model

With the adapted and extended ADDIE Model, the whole Curriculum has been developed very effectively. The additional expenditure of time to establish and follow such a model guarantees a successfully design output - furthermore a high quality is reached by accomplishing the evaluation phase which can be used as a touchstone for the training units as well for the assessment and quality assurance framework. Both frameworks maintain the quality life cycle which is important for trainee, trainer and institutional certification.

Harmonisation of Theory and Practice

The P2B model measures training activities on practical aspects and therefore sets realistic targets in the development of training programs. A continuous process of feedback also allows for a better harmonization of practical activities and the theoretical background in the curriculum. Training activities and outcomes are based on practical aspects and requirements of a real and concrete project. This strengthens the awareness of the learning outcomes and benefits, both to the learners and lecturers.

Knowledge Acquisition through Blended Learning

A blend of learning methods enables the highest flexibility in developing an understanding of the basic concepts of OPM. It encourages different learning styles and motives of heterogeneous groups of learners (who have different cultural, educational and professional values and believes and varying learning preferences). The difference to traditional learning lies in the diversity and interactivity of media: the exploitation of online technology and multi media in the learning process enables learners to learn independently from others, strongly self-directed, and in a flexible way. Appropriate selection of learning material, effective instructional design, powerful multi media components and appropriate use of e-Learning materials in the learning process therefore have important implications on the training.

Skills Development through Practical Training

Project integrated learning, that is the embedding of learning processes in simulated or real (online) projects, increases the practical character and practical outcomes of the training. Learners participate in projects and practice in an interdisciplinary array of competencies, reaching from intercultural and interpersonal skills, project management and technology related skills, to organisational skills. The collaborative nature of these processes and the realistic project scenarios ensure highest business relevance of the training and, most important, increase practical learning outcomes and sustainability.

REFERENCES

P2B – a Leonardo da Vinci Life Long Learning Program Project. (2009). *P2B – Pool to Business*. Retrieved July 30, 2009, from http://www.pool2business.eu

Bichelmeyer, B. A. (2005). *The ADDIE Model – A Metaphor for the Lack of Clarity in the field of IDT. IDT Futures Group Presentations*. IDT Record.

Coffey, M. G., & Gibbs, G. (2001). The Evaluation of the Student Evaluation of Educational Quality Questionnaire (SEEQ) in UK Higher Education, Assessment and Evaluation in Higher Education. Research note. *Assessment & Evaluation in Higher Education, 26*(1), 89–93.

Cronenbroeck, W. (2004). Internationales Projektmanagement – Handbuch. Berlin: Cornelsen Verlag Scriptor gmbh & Co KG.

Dittler, U. (2002). *E-Learning: Erfolgsfaktoren und Einsatzkonzepte mit interaktiven Medien*. Auflage, Oldenbourg Verlag.

IEEE. WG11: Learning Technology Standards Committee (2004). *IEEE Computing Managed Instructions*. Retrieved July 30, 2009, from http://ltsc.ieee.org/wg11

IEEE. WG20: Learning Technology Standards Committee (2004). *IEEE Reusable Competency Definitions*. Retrieved July 30, 2009, from http://ltsc.ieee.org/wg20

March, H. W. (1982). SEEQ: a reliable, valid and useful instrument for collecting students' evaluations of university teaching. *The British Journal of Educational Psychology, 52*, 77–95.

McInnis, C., Griffin, P., James, R., & Coates, H. (2001). *Development of the Course Experience Questionnaire*. Retrieved July 8, 2006, from http://www.dest.gov.au/archive/highered/ eippubs/ eip01_1/01_1.pdf

Molenda, M. (2003). Performance Improvement. In Search of the Elusive ADDIE Model. International Society for Performance Improvement, 42(5), 34-36.

Molenda, M., Pershing, J., & Reigeluth, C. (1996). Designing Instructional Systems. In Craig, R. R. (Ed.), *The ASTD Training and Development Handbook* (pp. 266–293). New York: McGraw-Hill.

Molenda, M., & Pershing, J. A. (2004). *The strategic impact model: An integrative approach to performance improvement and instructional systems design. Tech Trends Journal*. Springer Boston.

Strickland, A. W. (2006). *ADDIE*. Idaho State University College of Education Science, Math & Technology Education. Retrieved June 29, 2006, from http://ed.isu.edu/addie/index.html

ADDITIONAL READING

Abermann, G., Benimeli-Bofarull, E., & Haber, P. (2005). *A Multidimensional Approach towards Project Management Training in a Distributed Setting*. Paper presented at EDEN Annual Conference, Helsinki, Finland.

Benimeli-Bofarull, E., & Haber, P. (2006). *Establishing an interactive E-Learning Program by using Project based Computer Supported Collaborative Learning*. Paper presented at EDEN Annual Conference, Vienna, Austria.

Benimeli-Bofarull, E., Mündler, A., & Haber, P. (2006). *Transnational Online Project Management Curriculum Model for Engineering Students*. Paper presented at ICDE World Conference, Rio de Janeiro Brazil.

Cowell, C., Hopkins, P. C., McWhorter, R., & Jorden, D. L. (2006). Alternative Training Models. *Advances in Developing Human Resources, 8*, 460–475. doi:10.1177/1523422306292945

Gupta, K. (2007). *A Practical Guide to Needs Assessment*. Indianapolis, IN: Pfeiffer.

Gustafson, K., & Branch, R. (2002). *Survey of Instructional Development Models* (4th ed.). Syracuse, NY: ERIC Clearinghouse on Information and Technology.

Haber, P., Benimeli-Bofarull, E., Abermann, G., & Mayr, M. (2005). *Integrated Curriculum for Distributed, Transnational Project Management Training.* Paper presented at SEFI Annual Conference, Ankara, Turkey.

Haber, P., & Mayr, M. (Eds.). (2007). *POOL - Project Organisation Online: HANDBOOK.* Salzburg, Austria: Fachhochschule Salzburg GmbH - Studiengang ITS.

Haber, P., & Mayr, M. (Eds.). (2007). *POOL - Project Organisation Online: CURRICULUM.* Salzburg, Austria: Fachhochschule Salzburg GmbH - Studiengang ITS.

Haber, P., Mayr, M., & Weiss, T. (2008). *Pool - Project Organisation Online: A Practice and Feedback Oriented Curriculum Design for a Virtual Project Management Course.* Paper presented at INTED Conference, Valencia, Spain.

Harris, P., & Moran, R. (2007). *Managing Cultural Differences: Global Leadership Strategies for the 21st Century* (7th ed.). Amsterdam, Boston: Elsevier/Butterworth-Heinemann.

Herber, E., Benimeli-Bofarull, E., & Haber, P. (2006). *Modern curriculum design and knowledge transfer in a virtual collaborative environment.* Paper presented at SEFI Annual Conference, Uppsala, Sweden.

Herber, E., Haber, P., & Mayr, M. (2009). *Pool - Project Integrated Learning in Higher Education and Business.* Paper presented at IHEPI 2009 Conference Budapest, Hungary.

Hofstede, G. (2003). *Culture's Consequences: Comparing Values, Behaviors, Institutions, and Organizations Across Nations* (2nd ed.). London: Sage.

Hofstede, G. (2005). *Cultures and Organizations: Software of the Mind.* New York: McGraw-Hill.

Hogan-Garcia, M. (2007). *The Four Skills of Cultural Diversity Competence: A Process for Understanding and Practice* (3rd ed.). Belmont, CA: Thomson Brooks/Cole.

Hovland, K. (2006). *Shared Future: Global Learning and Liberal Education.* Washington, DC: Association of American Colleges and Universities.

LeBaron, M., & Pillay, V. (2006). *Conflict Across Cultures: A Unique Experience Bridging Differences.* Boston, MA: Nicholas Brealey.

Lederach, J. (1995). *Preparing for Peace: Conflict Transformation Across Cultures.* Syracuse, NY: Syracuse University Press.

Liu, G. Z. (2008). Innovating research topics in learning technology: Where are the new blue oceans? *British Journal of Educational Technology, 39*(4), 738–747. doi:10.1111/j.1467-8535.2008.00851.x

Marquardt, M., & Horvath, L. (2001). *Global Teams: How Top Multinationals Span Boundaries and Cultures With High-Speed Teamwork.* Palo Alto, CA: Davies-Black Publishing.

McKeachie, W., & Svinicki, M. (2006). *McKeachie's Teaching Tips: Strategies, Research, and Theory for College and University Teachers* (12th ed.). Boston, MA: Houghton Mifflin.

Mündler, A., Haber, P., & McCurry, F. (2006). *Online Assessment Methods for Virtual Project Management Training.* Paper presented at EDEN Annual Conference, Vienna, Austria.

Mündler, A., McCurry, F., Haber, P., & Benimeli-Bofarull, E. (2006). An Approach for Online Assessment in the Multinational EU Project: POOL Project Organization OnLine. In Neidl, W., & Tochtermann, K. (Eds.), *Lecture Notes in Computer Science 4227* (pp. 673–678). Berlin: Springer-Verlag.

Oetzel, J., & Ting-Toomey, S. (Eds.). (2006). *The SAGE Handbook of Conflict Communication: Integrating Theory, Research, and Practice*. Thousand Oaks, CA: Sage.

Olofsson, G. (2004). *When in Rome or Rio or Riyadh: Cultural Q&A's for Successful Business Behavior Around the World*. Yarmouth, ME: Intercultural Press.

Pauleen, D. (Ed.). (2004). *Virtual Teams: Projects, Protocols and Processes*. Hershey, PA: Idea Group.

Rothwell, W. (2007). *Instructor Excellence: Mastering the Delivery of Training* (2nd ed.). San Francisco, CA: Wiley/Pfeiffer.

Rothwell, W., & Kazanas, H. (2008). *Mastering the Instructional Design Process: A Systematic Approach* (4th ed.). San Francisco, CA: Jossey-Bass.

Scarborough, J. (2001). *The Origins of Cultural Differences and Their Impact on Management*. Westport, CT: Quorum Books.

Taylor, E. W. (Ed.). (2006). *Teaching for Change: Fostering Transformative Learning in the Classroom. New Directions for Adult and Continuing Education*. San Francisco, CA: Jossey-Bass.

Verma, G., Bagley, C., & Jha, M. (Eds.). (2007). *International Perspectives on Diversity and Inclusive Education*. New York, NY: Routledge.

Walker, D. M., Walker, T., & Schmitz, J. (2003). *Doing Business Internationally: The Guide to Cross-cultural Success* (2nd ed.). New York: McGraw-Hill.

Weisbord, M. (2004). Productive Workplaces Revisited: Dignity, Meaning, and Community in the 21st Century (2nd Ed.). San Francisco, CA: Jossey-Bass (Wiley).

Wlodkowski, R. (2008). *Enhancing Adult Motivation to Learn: A Comprehensive Guide for Teaching All Adults* (3rd ed.). San Francisco, CA: Jossey-Bass.

KEY TERMS AND DEFINITIONS

Blended Learning: Blended learning applies a mix of (traditional and/or new) learning methods and media to instruction in order to encourage different learning styles and motives of learners. It enables the highest flexibility in developing an understanding and enables learners to learn independently from others, strongly self-directed, and in a flexible way.

e-Learning: Electronic learning is a type of technology supported education/learning where the medium of instruction is solely through computer technology, particularly involving digital technologies and new media.

Online Project: A project is a set of similar, coordinated activities designed to achieve pre-defined, shared aims and objectives. It is designed to take place within a defined period of time, scope and budget. An online project is a project that strongly exploits online media for project planning, implementation, controlling and implementation. Online project typically involved teams in distributed environments.

Project Integrated Learning: Project Integrated learning is the embedding of learning processes in simulated or real (online) projects. Learners participate in projects and practice in an interdisciplinary array of skills from intercultural and interpersonal skills, project management and technology. The collaborative nature of these processes and the realistic project scenarios ensure highest business relevance of the training and, most important, increase practical learning outcomes.

Compilation of References

Abel, R. (2005, November). *Implementing best practice in online learning: A recent study reveals common denominators for success in internet-supported learning* Retrieved December 14, 2005, from http://www.a-hec.org/e-learning_study.html

Abermann, G., Benimeli-Bofarull, E., & Haber, P. (2005). *A Multidimensional Approach towards Project Management Training in a Distributed Setting*. Paper presented at EDEN Annual Conference, Helsinki, Finland.

Akins, K. (1996). *Perception*. New York: Oxford University Press.

Alfaro, J. Delrio, C., Dima, G., Dondi, C., Fischer, T., Kastis, N., Koskinen, T., Kretschmer, T., Kugemann, W.F., Lassnigg, L., Rotger, J.M., Szûcs, A., Unger, M., Vasiloglou, A., Vogtenhuber, S., Wermundsen, T., Zarka, D., and Zuheros, A. (2005). Understanding Change, Adapting to Change, Shaping the Future, Change Drivers, Trends & Core Tensions for European Learning Systems & Educational Policies. In *Learning in Europe; Observatory on National and International Evolution, LEONIE Project, MENON Network EEIG*. Retrieved August 7, from http://www.education-observatories.net/leonie/outputs/LEONIE_Executive_Summary_2006.pdf

Almeida Soares, D. (2008). Understanding class blogs as a tool for language development. *Language Teaching Research, 12*(4), 517–533. doi:10.1177/1362168808097165

Altmann, H., & Arambasich, L. (1982). A study of locus of control with adult students. *Canadian Counsellor, 16*(2), 97–101.

American Council on Education. (2007). *Military Installation Voluntary Education Review (MIVER) Orientation and Guidelines*. PDF File / Report, Center for Lifelong Learning.

Ampofo-Boateng, K., & Thomson, J. A. (1990). Child pedestrian accidents: A case for preventative medicine. *Health Education Research: Theory and Practice, 5*, 265–274.

Annan, K. (2002). *Remarks at opening of the third meeting of the United Nations information and communication technologies task force*. New York. Retrieved October 30, 2002 from http://www.unictaskforce.org/thirdmeeting/sg_speech.html

APA Work Group of the Board of Educational Affairs (1997, November). *Learner-centered psychological principles: A framework for school reform and redesign*. Washington, DC: American Psychological Association.

Ardichvili, A., Page, V., & Wentling, T. (2003). Motivation and barriers to participation in virtual knowledge-sharing communities of practice. *Journal of Knowledge Management, 70*(1), 64–77. doi:10.1108/13673270310463626

Arora, P. (2005). Profiting from empowerment? Investigating dissemination avenues for educational technology content within an emerging market solutions project. *International Journal of Education and Development using Information and Communication Technology, 1*(4), 18-29.

Arora, P. (2006). *E-karaoke for gender empowerment*. Paper presented at the Information and Communication Technologies for Development 2006, Berkeley, California.

Arora, P. (2006). Karaoke for social and cultural change. *Information. Communication and Ethics in Society, 4*(3), 121–130.

Arora, P. (2006). The ICT laboratory: An analysis of computers in public high schools in rural India. *Association of Advancement in Computing in Education, 15*(1), 57–72.

Arora, P. (2007). Evaluating asynchronous online engagement on international security. *Electronic Journal of e-Learning, 6*(1), 1-10.

Association for Learning Technology (ALT). (2009). *ALT Strategy: February 2008 to January 2011 (revised May 2009).* Retrieved 14 June 09, from http://www.alt.ac.uk/docs/ALT_2008-2011_Strategy.pdf

Atherton, J. S. (2005). *Learning and teaching: Bloom's taxonomy.* Retrieved March 14, 2008, from Website: http://www.learningandteaching.info/learning/bloomtax.htm

Baacke, D. (1996). Gesamtkonzept Medienkompetenz [The concept of media literacy]. In agenda: Zeitschrift für Medien, Bildung, Kultur [Agenda: journal for media, education, culture], 19, 12-14.

Balajthy, E. (1990). Hypertext, hypermedia and meta-cognition. Research and instructional implications for disabled readers. *Journal of Reading. Writing and Learning Disabilities, 6*(2), 183–202.

Bangou, F., & Waterhouse, M. (2008). On becoming technologically literate: A Multiple Literacies Theory perspective. *E-learning, 5*(4), 445–456. doi:10.2304/elea.2008.5.4.445

Barbour, M., & Mulcahy, D. (2006). An inquiry into retention and achievement differences in campus based and web based AP Courses. *Rural Educator, 27*, 8–12.

Barg, R. (2004). Breaking down barriers: Collaborative education drives collective change. *Journal of Emergency Management, 2*(3). Retrieved on April 21, 2008 from http://www.ofm.gov.on.ca/english/FireService/announcements/2004/Breaking%20Down%20Barriers.asp

Barker, K. C. (1994). *National training standards.* Ottawa, ON: Canadian Labour Force Development Board.

Barker, K. C. (1997). *Learnware quality background paper.* Vancouver, Canada: FuturEd for HRDC. Retrieved May 4, 2007, from http://www.futured.com/library_paper9710a.htm

Barker, K. C. (1998). *Achieving public policy goals with quality PLAR: Prior learning and assessment recognition.* Ottawa, ON: Canadian Labour Force Development Board. Retrieved December 4, 2006, from http://www.futured.com/pdf/PLAR%20quality%20and%20policy%20goals.pdf

Barker, K. C. (1999). *Linking the literature: School effectiveness and virtual schools.* Retrieved December 4, 2006, from http://www.futured.com/pdf/Virtual.pdf

Barker, K. C. (1999). Serving the learning needs of education consumers. *Education Canada, 38*(4), 25–27.

Barker, K. C. (1999, March). *Quality guidelines for technology-assisted distance education.* Retrieved December 4, 2006, from http://www.futured.com/pdf/distance.pdf

Barker, K. C. (2001). *The FuturEd PLA/PLAR quality audit.* Vancouver, Canada: FuturEd. Retrieved May 10, 2007, from http://www.futured.com/pdf/QualityAudit.pdf

Barker, K. C. (2001, February). *E-learning: Studying Canada's virtual secondary schools.* Kelowna, Canada: Society for Advancement of Excellence in Education.

Barker, K. C. (2001, October). *Information and communication technology in international education in Canada's public post-secondary education system: Literature review.* Canadian Bureau for International Education. Retrieved May 10, 2007, from http://www.cbie.ca/download/publications/Conf%20paper%20ICTs%20and%20IE%20final.pdf

Barker, K. C. (2002, February). *Consumer's guide to e-learning.* Vancouver, BC: FuturEd for the Canadian Association for Community Education and Office of Learning Technologies, HRDC. Retrieved December 4,

2006, from http://www.futured.com/pdf/ConGuide%20 Eng%20CD.pdf

Barker, K. C. (2002, February). E-learning in three easy steps. *School Business Affairs*, *68*(2), 4–8.

Barker, K. C. (2002, January). *Canadian recommended e-learning guidelines.* Vancouver, BC: FuturEd for Canadian Association for Community Education and Office of Learning Technologies, HRDC. Retrieved December 4, 2006, from http://www.futured.com/pdf/ CanREGs%20Eng.pdf

Barker, K. C. (2003 November 4). E-learning in Canada: Who can you trust? *National Post Business.*

Barker, K. C. (2003, April). *Studying ICT use in international education: Comparing on-line and on-site delivery of international education.* Canadian Bureau for International Education. Retrieved May, 10, 2007 from http://www.cbie.ca/download/ict/Phase4final.pdf

Barker, K. C. (2003, July–September). Canadian e-learning guidelines protect consumers. *The Learning Citizen, 6*(13). Retrieved May 10, 2007, from http:// www.learningcitizen.net/download/LCCN_Newsletter_N6.pdf

Barker, K. C. (2004, April). *Consumer's guide to ePortfolio products and services.* Vancouver, Canada: FuturEd. Retrieved December 4, 2006, from http://www.futured. com/documents/ePConsumersGuide.pdf

Barker, K. C. (2004, April). *ePortfolio quality standards.* Vancouver, BC: FuturEd. Retrieved December 4, 2006, from http://www.futured.com/pdf/ePortfolio%20Quality%20Discussion%20Paper.pdf

Barker, K. C. (2004, May). *Bridging program benchmarks, recommendations and evaluation framework.* FuturEd for the BC Ministry of Community, Aboriginal and Women's Issues. Retrieved April 28, 2007, from http:// www.futured.com/documents/BridgingPrograms.pdf

Barker, K. C. (2005, November). *Return on investment in e-learning: Discussion and ROI tool.* Toronto, Canada: ABC CANADA Literacy Foundation. Retrieved December 4, 2006, from http://www.futured.com/documents/ elearningandLiteracyROIGuide2005_ 000.pdf

Barker, K. C. (2006). Quality Standards for Consumer Protection. In Hope, A., & Guiton, P. (Eds.), *Strategies for sustainable open and distance learning.* London, New York: Routledge and Commonwealth of Learning.

Barker, K. C. (2006, September). *ePortfolio: A tool for quality assurance* [White Paper]. Vancouver, BC: FuturEd. Retrieved December 4, 2006, from http://www. futured.com/documents/ePortfolioforQuality Assurance_000.pdf

Barker, K. C. (2006, Spring). *Quality standards and quality assessment of learning objects.* Vancouver, Canada: FuturEd. Retrieved December 4, 2006, from http://www. futured.com/documents/LearningObjectsQualityStandardsandAssessment.pdf

Barker, K. C., et al. (1998). *Survey of perceptions and attitudes toward learnware quality in Canada.* Office of Learning Technologies. Retrieved December 4, 1998, from http://olt-bta.hrdc drhc.gc.ca/resources/Survey_e. pdf

Barley, Z. A., & Brigham, N. (2008). *Preparing teachers to teach in rural schools.* Washington, DC: Institute for Educational Sciences.

Barr, R. B., & Tagg, J. (1995). From teaching to learning – A new paradigm for undergraduate education. *Change*, (November/December): 13–25.

Barta, B., Telem, M., & Gev, Y. (1995). *Information Technology in Educational Management.* London: Chapman &Hall.

Bash, L. (2003). *Adult learners in the academy.* Bolton, MA: Anker Publishing Company.

Bass, B. M., & Avolio, B. J. (1995). The Multifactor Leadership Questionnaire – 5X Short Form. Redwood City, Canada

Baum, E. (2004). *What is thought?* Cambridge, MA: The MIT Press.

BC MEST. (1996). *The status of technology in the education system: A literature review.* Community Learning Network of the BC Ministry of Education, Skills, and Training.

Beeson, E., & Strange, M. (2000). *Why rural matters: The need for every state to take action on rural education.* Washington, DC: Rural School and Community Trust.

Benham Tye, B., & Tye, K. (1992). *Global education: A study of school change.* New York: SUNY Press.

Benimeli-Bofarull, E., & Haber, P. (2006). *Establishing an interactive E-Learning Program by using Project based Computer Supported Collaborative Learning.* Paper presented at EDEN Annual Conference, Vienna, Austria.

Benimeli-Bofarull, E., Mündler, A., & Haber, P. (2006). *Transnational Online Project Management Curriculum Model for Engineering Students.* Paper presented at ICDE World Conference, Rio de Janeiro Brazil.

Benyon, D., Turner, P., & Turner, S. (2005). *Designing for Interactive Systems.* Reading, MA: Addison Wesley.

Berge, L. Z. (1998). Barriers to online teaching in post secondary institution: Can policy changes fix it? *Online Journal of Distance Learning Administration, 1*(2). Retrieved from http://www.westga.edu/~distance/ojdla/summer12/berge12.pdf.

Berge, Z. L. (1998). Overcoming obstacles to distance education in the k-12 classroom. In J. Baggaley, T. Anderson, & M. Haughey (Eds.), *Partners in learning: Proceedings of the 14th Annual Conference of the Canadian Association for Distance Education* (Vol. 1, pp. 31-32).

Berge, Z. L. (1999). Interaction in post-secondary, web-based learning and teaching. *Educational Technology, 39*(1), 5–11.

Berge, Z. L. (2002). Active, interactive, and reflective elearning. *Quarterly Review of Distance Education, 3*(2), 181–190.

Berge, Z. L., & Mrozowski, S. (1999). Barriers to online teaching in elementary, secondary, and teacher education. *Canadian Journal of Educational Communication, 27*(2), 125–138.

Berge, Z. L., & Muilenburg, L. (2001). Obstacles faced at various stages of capability regarding DE in institutions of Higher Education: Survey results. *TechTrends, 45*(4), 40–44. doi:10.1007/BF02784824

Berge, Z. L., Muilenberg, L. Y., & Van Haneghan, J. (2002). Barriers to distance education and training: Survey results. *The Quarterly Review of Distance Education, 3*, 409–418.

Bernard, R. M., Abrami, P. C., Lou, Y., Borokhovski, E., Wade, A., & Wozney, L. (2004). How does distance education compare with classroom instruction? A meta-analysis of the empirical literature. *Review of Educational Research, 74*, 379–439. doi:10.3102/00346543074003379

Berßelis, T. (n.d.). DVD-Video-Mastering, Version 0.9.5. *Handbook for Sonic DVD Creator and DVD Fusion.*

Bichelmeyer, B. A. (2005). *The ADDIE Model – A Metaphor for the Lack of Clarity in the field of IDT. IDT Futures Group Presentations.* IDT Record.

Birch, D., & Volkov, M. (2005, December). *Students' perceptions of compulsory asynchronous online discussion.* Australian and New Zealand Marketing Academy (ANZMAC) Conference 2005: Broadening the Boundaries, Fremantle, Western Australia.

Bissland, J., & Cashion, J. (2002). *Pedagogically Sound On-line Education - How to make this a reality for your organisation.* Paper presented at the 2nd World Congress of Colleges and Polytechnics, Melbourne.

Bitew, G. (2008). Using Plasma TV Broadcasts in Ethiopian Secondary Schools: A Brief Survey. *Australasian Journal of Educational Technology, 24*(2), 150–167.

Blignaut, A. S., & Lillejord, S. (2005). Lessons from a cross-cultural online learning community. *South African Journal of Higher Education, 19*(Special issue), 1350–1367.

Bliss, J., Monk, M., & Ogborn, J. (1983). *Qualitative Data Analysis for Educational Research.* London: Croon Helm.

Block, C. C., Gambrell, B. L., & Pressley, M. (2002). *Improving Comprehension Instruction: rethinking research, theory and classroom practice.* Jossey-Bass.

Blumenstyk, G. (2006, July 7). The Military Market. *The Chronicle of Higher Education Money & Management*. Retrieved December 31, 2007, from http://www.chronicle.com//colloquy/2006/07/military

Bonk, C. J., & Dennen, V. P. (1999). Teaching on the Web: With a little help from my pedagogical friends. *Journal of Computing in Higher Education, 11*(1), 3–28. doi:10.1007/BF02940840

Bourner, T., Katz, T., & Watson, D. (Eds.). (2000). *New directions in professional higher education*. London: The Open University Press.

BRIDGES-LAC. (2009). *BRIDGES-LAC Project website*. Retrieved August 7, 2009, from http://www.bridges-lac.org/

Broere, I., Kruger, M., & Van Wyk, G. (2003 September). *A first @ RAU [First Innovative Reflective Strategic Touch at RAU]*. Paper presented at the 5th Annual Conference on World Wide Web Application, Johannesburg.

Brooks, R. (1993). Principles for effective hypermedia design. *Technical Communication, 40*(3), 422–428.

Brown, J. S., & Duguid, P. (1991). Organizational learning and communities of practice: toward a unified view of working, learning and innovation. *Organization Science, 2*(1), 40–57. doi:10.1287/orsc.2.1.40

Brown, J. S., & Duguid, P. (2000). Balancing act: how to capture knowledge without killing it. *Harvard Business Review, 78*(3), 73–78.

Brown, M. (2005). Learning Spaces. In Oblinger, D. G., & Oblinger, J. L. (Eds.), *Educating the Net Generation* (p. 267). Washington, DC, USA: Educause.

Bruce, H., Fugate, C., Kerr, S., & Wolf, F. (2004). *The programme for educational transformation through technology*. London: University of Washington.

Burney, V. H., & Cross, T. L. (2006). Impoverished students with academic promise in rural settings: 10 lessons from Project Aspire. *Gifted Child Today, 29*, 14–21.

Burrell, G., & Morgan, G. (2005). *Sociological Paradigms and organisational analysis*. Aldershot, UK: Ashgate.

Caffarella, R. S. (2002). *Planning programs for adult learners: A practical guide for educators, trainers, and staff developers* (2nd ed.). San Francisco: Jossey-Bass.

Callewaert, S. (2006). Looking Back, But Not in Anger. In Dahlström, L., & Mannberg, J. (Eds.), *Critical Educational Visions and Practices in Neo-Liberal Times, 127 - 132. Umeå University: Global South Network Publisher*.

Campbell, A. P. (2003). Weblogs for use with ESL classes. *The Internet TESL Journal, 9*(2). Retrieved July, 5, 2009 from http://iteslj.org/Techniques/Campbell-Weblogs.html

Candy, P. C., Crebert, G., & O'Leary, J. (1994). *Developing lifelong learners through undergraduate education*. Retrieved May 10, 2007, from http://www.dest.gov.au/sectors/training_skills/publications_resources/profiles/nbeet/hec/developing_lifelong_learners_through_undergraduate.htm

Carr, S. (2000). As distance education comes of age, the challenge is keeping the students. *The Chronicle of Higher Education, 47*(8), A39–A41.

Castro, C. M. (2004). Are New Technologies Better Technologies? For Whom? In Chapman, D. W., & Mählck, L. O. (Eds.), *Adapting Technology for School Improvement: A Global Perspective, 39 – 54*. Paris: International Institute for Educational Planning.

Cavanaugh, C., Gillan, K. J., Kromrey, J., Hess, M., & Blomeyer, R. (2004). *The effects of distance education on K-12 student outcomes: A meta-analysis*. Naperville, IL: Learning Point Associates.

Cegles, K. A. (1998). *Emerging issues affecting distance education research and practice in higher education: A global futures perspective*. Ann Arbor, Michigan: UMI Publications.

Chaillot, C. (2002). *The Ethiopian Orthodox Tewahedo Church Tradition - a Brief Introduction to its Life and Spirituality*. Paris: Inter-Orthodox Dialogue.

Chakravorti, B. (2004). The role of adoption networks in the success of innovations: a strategic perspective.

Technology in Society, 26(2-3), 469–482. doi:10.1016/j. techsoc.2004.01.007

Chandra, R. (2000). From dual-mode to multimodal, flexible teaching and learning: Distance education at the University of the South Pacific. In *Distance Education in Small States, 2000 Conference proceedings. UWI/ COL, 2001* (pp. 31-47). Retrieved from http://www.Col. org/colweb/site/pid3338

Chapman, D. W., Garrett, A., & Mählck, L. O. (2004). The Role of Technology in School Improvement. In Chapman, D. W., & Mählck, L. O. (Eds.), *Adapting Technology for School Improvement: A Global Perspective* (pp. 19–38). Paris: International Institute for Educational Planning.

Chen, T. H. (1981). *Chinese education since 1949: Academic and revolutionary models*. New York: Pergamon Press.

Cho, S. K., & Berge, Z. L. (2002). Overcoming barriers to distance training and education. *Education at a Distance, 16*(1). Retrieved February 27, 2009 from http://www. usdla.org/html/journal/JAN02_Issue/article01.html

Chua, A. Y. K. (2006). The Rise and Fall of a Community of practice: A Descriptive Case Study. *Knowledge and Process Management, 13*(2), 120–128. doi:10.1002/ kpm.239

Cisco Systems. (2006). *Ethiopia Accelerates National Development Through Information and Communications Technology: A Customer Case Study*. San Jose, CA: Cisco Systems, Inc.

Clark, P. (2009). *Vice-Chancellor's Progress Report: Becoming a truly multicampus institution – A Route Map*. Southern Cross University. Retrieved March 25, 2009, from http://staff.scu.edu.au/vc/index.php/ dds?cat_id=76#cat76

Clark, R. E. (1994). Media will never influence learning. *Educational Technology Research and Development, 42*(2), 21–29. doi:10.1007/BF02299088

Coates, H. (2005). Quality in higher education. *Quality in Higher Education, 11*(1), 25–36. doi:10.1080/13538320500074915

Coffey, M. G., & Gibbs, G. (2001). The Evaluation of the Student Evaluation of Educational Quality Questionnaire (SEEQ) in UK Higher Education, Assessment and Evaluation in Higher Education. Research note. *Assessment & Evaluation in Higher Education, 26*(1), 89–93.

Coltharp, B. (2008). *OL 599: Organization leadership project - Woods interactive onLine degree (WILD), Target Audience Military Service Member Students*. Saint Mary-of-the-Woods, In Saint Mary-of-the-Woods College, Master of Leadership Development program.

Commonwealth of Learning. (2009). Women and ICT in Open Schools. *Connections, 14*(1).

Cook, S. D. N., & Yanow, D. (1993). Culture and organizational learning. *Journal of Management Inquiry, 2*, 373–390. doi:10.1177/105649269324010

Corio, J. (2003). Exploring Literacy on the Internet. Reading comprehension on the Internet: Expanding our understanding of reading comprehension to encompass new literacies. *The Reading Teacher, 56*(5), 458–464.

Cornaldi, C., & McDaniel, M. (1991). *Imagery and cognition*. New York: Springer.

Cowell, C., Hopkins, P. C., McWhorter, R., & Jorden, D. L. (2006). Alternative Training Models. *Advances in Developing Human Resources, 8*, 460–475. doi:10.1177/1523422306292945

Cronenbroeck, W. (2004). Internationales Projektmanagement – Handbuch. Berlin: Cornelsen Verlag Scriptor gmbh & Co KG.

Crowder, N. (1960). Automatic tutoring by intrinsic programming. In Lumsdaine, A., & Glaser, R. (Eds.), *Teaching machines and programmed learning: A source book* (pp. 286–298). Washington, D.C.: National Education Association of the United States.

Cutrim Schmid, E. (2006). Investigating the use of interactive whiteboards technology in the English language classroom through the lens of a critical theory of technology. *Computer Assisted Language Learning, 19*(1), 47–62. doi:10.1080/09588220600804012

D'Amico, J. J., Matthes, W., Sankar, A., Merchant, B., & Zurita, M. (1996). Young voices from the rural Midwest. *Journal of Research in Rural Education, 12*(3). Retrieved January 21, 2008 from http://www.jrre.psu.edu/articles/v12,n3,p142-149,DAmico.pdf

Daley, B. J. (2001). Metaphors for Professional Learning. *Advances in Developing Human Resources, 3*(3), 322–332. doi:10.1177/15234220122238346

Daniel, J. S. (1996). *Megauniversities and knowledge media: Technology strategies for higher education.* London: Biddles Ltd.

Davenport, T. H., & Prusak, L. (1999). *Working Knowledge.* Boston, MA: Harvard Business School Press.

de Byl, P., & Taylor, J. A. (2007). A web 2.0/web3D hybrid platform for engaging students in e-learning environments. *Turkish Online Journal of Distance Education, 8*(3), 108–127.

De Freitas, S., & Neumann, T. (2009). The use of 'exploratory learning' for supporting immersive learning in virtual environments. *British Journal of Educational Technology, 40*(6), 980–998. doi:10.1111/j.1467-8535.2008.00887.x

Debating Distance? (n.d.). Retrieved July 21, 2009 from http://www.instudy.com/articles/indistance02.htm

Dekkers, J., & Cuskelly, E. (1990). *The establishment and use of electronic mail for distance education.* University College of Central Queensland, Rockhampton.

DeLugan, R. M. (2005). Peace, culture, and governance in post-civil war El Salvador (1992-2000). *Journal of Human Rights, 4,* 233–249. doi:10.1080/14754830590952161

Dick, W., Carey, L., & Carey, J. O. (2008). *The systematic design of instruction* (7th ed.). New York: Allyn and Bacon.

Dittler, U. (2002). *E-Learning: Erfolgsfaktoren und Einsatzkonzepte mit interaktiven Medien.* Auflage, Oldenbourg Verlag.

Downes, S. (2004). Educational blogging. *EDUCAUSE Review, 29*(5), 14–26.

Drake, S. M., & Burns, R. C. (2004). *Meeting standards through integrated curriculum.* Association for Supervision & Curriculum Deve Publications.

Dubé, L., Bourhis, A., & Jacob, R. (2004). "Structuring Spontaneity": the Impact of Management Practices on the Success of Intentionally Formed Virtual Communities of Practice. [online] *Cahiers du GReSI no. 04-20,* Retrieved on 19 March 2009, from gresi.hec.ca/cahier.asp

Duchnicky, R. L., & Kolers, P. A. (1983). Readability of text scrolled on visual display terminals as a function of window size. *Human Factors, 25*(6), 683–692.

Duffy, G. (2002). The case for direct explanation of strategies. In Block, C. C., & Pressley, M. (Eds.), *Comprehension instruction: Research-based best practices* (pp. 28–41). New York: Guilford.

Dunser, A., & Jirasko, M. (2005). Interaction of Hypertext Forms and Global versus Sequential Learning Styles. *Journal of Educational Computing Research, 32*(1), 79–91. doi:10.2190/1J25-LWQF-PQ3W-LABM

Dzuiban, C. D., Hartman, J. L., & Moskal, P. D. (2004). Blended Learning. *Educause Center for Applier Research, Research Bulletin, 2004*(7). Retrieved July 20, 2009 from http://www.educause.edu/

Eisenhardt, K. M. (1989). Building theories from case study research. *Academy of Management Review, 14,* 532–550. doi:10.2307/258557

Ekermans, G. (2003). *An investigation into the usability of synchronous information technology for the virtual e-learning and information sharing at a university in South Africa.* Unpublished Dissertation, University of Stellenbosch, Cape Town.

Ellsworth, J. B. (2000). *Surviving change: A survey of educational change models.* Syracuse, NY: ERIC Clearinghouse on Information and Technology.

Ely, D. (1990). Conditions that facilitate the implementation of educational technology innovations. *Journal of Research on Computing in Education, 23*(2), 298–305.

EMERGE. (2009). *JISC Users and Innovations EMERGE project.* Retrieved August 6, 2009, from http://elgg.jiscemerge.org.uk/

Ensminger, C. D., & Surry, D. W. (2002). *Faculty perception of factors that facilitate the implementation of online programs* Retrieved March 3, 2007, from http://iphase.org/papers/msitc02.pdf

Evans, T., Stacey, E., & Tregenza, K. (2001). Interactive Television in Schools: An Australian Study of the Tensions of Educational Technology and Change. *International Review of Research in Open and Distance Learning, 2*(1).

Evoh, C. J. (2007). Policy Networks and the Transformation of Secondary Education Through ICT in Africa: The Prospects and Challenges of NEPAD e-schools Initiative. *International Journal of Education and development Using ICT* [Online], *3*(1). Retrieved June 05, 2009, from http://www.ijedict.dec.uwi.edu/viewarticle.php?id=272

Fagerberg, T., & Rekkedal, T. (2004). *Enhancing the flexibility of distance education – designing and trying out a learning environment for mobile distance learners.* Retrieved July 21, 2009, from http://www.ericsson.com/ericsson/corpinfo/.../eclo_nki_paper.pdf

FDRE (The Federal Democratic Republic of Ethiopia). (2004). *Development of Education in Ethiopia.* A Report to the UNESCO Forty-Seventh Session of the International Conference on Education, 8-11 September 2004, Geneva, Switzerland.

Feenberg, A. (1991). *Critical theory of technology.* New York: Oxford University Press.

Felder, R. M. (1993). Reaching the second tier: Learning and Teaching Styles in College Science Education. *Journal of College Science Teaching, 23*(5), 286–290.

Ferreira, F. (2008). *Children and Young People.* A Paper Presented at the Fifth Pan-Commonwealth Forum on Open Learning. University of London: U.K.

Ferrell, G., & Kelly, J. (2006). Collaborative Approaches to the Management of e-Learning (CAMEL). In *European Universities Information Systems 12th International Conference Proceedings* (pp. 333-337).

Ferrell, G., & Kelly, J. (2006). Collaborative Approaches to the Management of e-Learning (CAMEL). In *European Universities Information Systems 12th International Conference Proceedings* (pp. 333-337).

Fliess, S., & Lasshof, B. (2005). Qualitätsmanagement von Dienstleistungen. In Laaser, W. (Ed.), *DVD*. Hagen: FernUniversität.

Fokides, E., & Tsolakidis, C. (2003). A theoretical and a technical framework for the development of Virtual Reality Educational Applications. In M. Auer (Ed.), *Proceedings of the Interactive Computer Aided Learning, ICL 2003* [CD-ROM]. Kassel, DE: Kassel University Press.

Fokides, E., & Tsolakidis, C. (2008). Virtual Reality in Education: A Theoretical Approach for Road Safety Training to Students. *European Journal of Open and Distance Learning (EURODL), 2008*(2). Retrieved May 13, 2009, from http://www.eurodl.org/materials/contrib/2008/Fokides_Tsolakidis.htm

Food and Agriculture Organization of the United Nations. (1999). Agricultural trade and food security: FAO fact sheets. In *Third WTO Ministerial Conference, Seattle.* Retrieved June 15, 2002, from http://www.fao.org/documents/show_cdr.asp?url_file=/DOCREP/003/X6730E/X6730E00.HTM

Food and Agriculture Organization of the United Nations. (n.d.). *Women and food security.* Retrieved June 15, 2002, from:http://www.fao.org/FOCUS/E/Women/Sustin-e.htm

Frayer, D. A., & West, L. B. (1997). *Creating a new world of learning possibilities through instructional technology.* Retrieved May 10, 2007, from http://horizon.unc.edu/projects/monograph/CD/Instructional_Technology/Frayer.asp

Freire, P. (1993). *Pedagogy of the Oppressed.* New York: The Continuum Publishing Company.

Gannon-Leary, P., & Fontainha, E. (2007) *Communities of Practice and virtual learning communities: benefits, barriers and success factors.*

Garland, M. (1993). Students' perceptions of the situational, institutional, dispositional and epistemological barriers to persistence. *Distance Education, 14*(2), 181–198. doi:10.1080/0158791930140203

Garrison, D. R. (1997). Computer conferencing: The post-industrial age of distance education. *Open Learning, 12*(2), 3–11. doi:10.1080/0268051970120202

Garrison, D. R., & Anderson, T. (2003). *E-learning in the 21st century*. London: Routledge. doi:10.4324/9780203166093

Garrison, D. R., & Vaughan, N. D. (2008). *Blended learning in higher education: framework, principles, and guidelines*. San Francisco, CA: Jossey Bass.

Garrison, D., & Shale, D. (1987). Mapping the boundaries of distance education: Problems in defining the field. *American Journal of Distance Education, 1*, 4–13. doi:10.1080/08923648709526567

Gask, L. (2005). *Overt and covert barriers to the integration of primary and specialist mental health care*. Manchester, UK: National Primary Care Research and Development Centre.

GATE. (1996). *Notes from Transnational Education and the Quality Imperative*. Global Alliance for Transnational Education, Retrieved May 10, 2007, from http://www.adec.edu/international/gate2.html

Gatliff, B., & Wendel, F. C. (1998). Inter-institutional collaboration and team teaching. *American Journal of Distance Education, 12*(1), 26–37. doi:10.1080/08923649809526981

Gaudelli, W. (2003). *World class: Teaching and learning in global times*. New York: Erlbaum Associates.

Gibson, C. C. (2006). Increasing equity: Seeking mainstream advantages for all. In King, K. P., & Griggs, J. K. (Eds.), *Harnessing innovative technology in higher education: Access, policy, & instruction* (pp. 133–150). Madison, WI: Atwood Publishing.

Gillham, W. E. C. (2000). *Case study research methods*. London: Continuum.

Giroux, H. A. (2000). *Stealing Innocence: Youth, Corporate Power, and the Politics of Culture*. New York: St. Martin's Press.

Glennie, W. P., & Hickok, J. (2003). Meeting critical defense needs with CoPs. *KM Review, 6*(3), 16–19.

GLOBE. (2009). *The Global Learning Objects Brokered Exchange (GLOBE) alliance*. Retrieved August 7, 2009, from http://www.globe-info.org/en/aboutglobe

Goodman, P. S. (2006). *Foreign currency piles up in China: Reserve fund soared to record in 2005*. Retrieved March 3, 2009, from http://www.washingtonpost.com/wp-dyn/content/article/2006/01/16/AR2006011600450.html

Graham, C. R. (2005). Blended learning systems: Definitions, current trends, and future directions. In Bonk, C. J., & Graham, C. R. (Eds.), *Handbook of blended learning: Global perspectives, local designs* (pp. 3–21). San Francisco: Pfeiffer.

Graham, D. (1990). *Knowledge Acquisition: A Case Study in Computer Fault Diagnosis and Repair*. Unpublished PhD thesis, Brunel University.

Graham, D., & Barrett, A. (1997). *Knowledge-Based Image Processing Systems*. Berlin: Springer-Verlag.

Graham, D., Benest, I., & Nicholl, P. (2007). Cognitive Issues in Information Visualisation Design for Interaction for the Visually Impaired. In *Proc. of the 11th International Conference on Information Visualisation IV07, IEEE Computer Society*, ETH Zurich, Switzerland, 4-6 July 2007 (pp. 917-920).

Graham, D., Benest, I., & Nicholl, P. (2007). Interaction Design for Visually Impaired Students: Initial Findings. In *Proc. of the 8th Annual Higher Education Academy Information Sciences HEA-ICS Conference*, University of Southampton, England, 28-30 August 2007 (pp. 116-12).

Graham, D., Benest, I., & Nicholl, P. (2007). Interaction Design for Teaching Visually Impaired Students. In *Proc. of the International Association for the Scientific Knowledge, IASK E-ALT 2007 International Conference*, Porto, Spain, 3-6 December 2007 (pp. 80-89).

Granovetter, M. S. (1973). The Strength of Weak Ties. *American Journal of Sociology, 78*(6), 1360–1380. doi:10.1086/225469

Grant, C. M. (n.d.). *Professional development in a technological age: New definitions, old challenges, new resources.* Retrieved 20 April, 2006, from http://www.ncrel. org/sdrs/areas/issues/educatrs/profdevl/pd2prof.htm

Grey, W. (2000). Metaphor and Meaning. *Minerva – An Internet Journal of Philosophy, 4*(4). Retrieved on March 30, 2009, from http://www.ul.ie/~philos/vol4/metaphor.html

Gunning, T. G. (2003). *Building Literacy in the Content Areas.* London: Oxford University Press.

Gupta, K. (2007). *A Practical Guide to Needs Assessment.* Indianapolis, IN: Pfeiffer.

Gura, M., & Percy, B. (2005). *Recapturing technology for education: Keeping tomorrow in today's classrooms.* Lanham, MD: Scarecrow Education.

Guri-Rosenblit, S. (2005, March). *Eight paradoxes in the implementation process of e-learning in higher education.* Retrieved February 25, 2006, from http://www.palgrave-journals.com/hep/journal/v18/n1/fuu/8300069a.html

Gustafson, K., & Branch, R. (2002). *Survey of Instructional Development Models* (4th ed.). Syracuse, NY: ERIC Clearinghouse on Information and Technology.

Haber, P., & Mayr, M. (Eds.). (2007). *POOL - Project Organisation Online: HANDBOOK.* Salzburg, Austria: Fachhochschule Salzburg GmbH - Studiengang ITS.

Haber, P., & Mayr, M. (Eds.). (2007). *POOL - Project Organisation Online: CURRICULUM.* Salzburg, Austria: Fachhochschule Salzburg GmbH - Studiengang ITS.

Haber, P., Benimeli-Bofarull, E., Abermann, G., & Mayr, M. (2005). *Integrated Curriculum for Distributed, Transnational Project Management Training.* Paper presented at SEFI Annual Conference, Ankara, Turkey.

Haber, P., Mayr, M., & Weiss, T. (2008). *POOL - Project Organisation Online: A Practice and Feedback Oriented Curriculum Design for a Virtual Project Management Course.* Paper presented at INTED Conference, Valencia, Spain.

Hafeez-Baig, A., & Danaher, P. A. (2007). Future possibilities for mobile learning technologies and applications at the University of Southern Queensland, Australia: Lessons from an academic focus group. In *1st International Conference on Mobile Learning Technologies and Applications,* 19 Feb., New Zealand: Auckland. Retrieved March 16, 2008, from http://eprints.usq.edu.au/2042/

Hamel, G., & Prahalad, C. K. (1994). *Competing for the future: Breakthrough strategies for seizing control of your industry and creating the markets of tomorrow.* Cambridge, MA: Harvard Business School Press.

Hanna, D. E. (1998). Higher education in an era of digital competition: Emerging organizational models. *JALN, 2*(1), 67-95. Retrieved on May 3, 2009 from http://www.sloan-c.org/publications/jaln/v2n1/pdf/v2n1_hanna.pdf

Hannum, W. H. (2007). When computers teach: A review of the instructional effectiveness of computers. *Educational Technology, 47*(2), 5–13.

Hannum, W. H., & McCombs, B. L. (2008). Enhancing distance learning with Learner-Centered Principles. *Educational Technology, 48*(4), 11–12.

Hannum, W. H., Irvin, M. J., Banks, J. B., & Farmer, T. W. (2009). Distance Education Use in Rural Schools. *Journal of Research in Rural Education, 24*(3), 1–15.

Hannum, W., Irvin, M. J., Lei, P.-W., & Farmer, T. W. (2008). Effectiveness of using learner-centered principles on student retention in distance education courses in rural schools. *Distance Education, 29,* 211–229. doi:10.1080/01587910802395763

Hanson, R. A., Clauson, K. M., Knowlton, D. D., & Gilliland, T. A. (2005). *Assurance Section: Report of a Comprehensive Evaluation Visit.* Chicago: The Higher Learning Commission.

Hardman, J. (2005). An Exploratory Case Study of Computer Use in a Primary School Mathematics Classroom: New Technology, New Pedagogy? *Perspectives in Education, 23*(4), 99–111.

Harris, P., & Moran, R. (2007). *Managing Cultural Differences: Global Leadership Strategies for the 21st Century* (7th ed.). Amsterdam, Boston: Elsevier/Butterworth-Heinemann.

Hartley, J. (1978). *Designing instructional text*. New York: Nichols Publishing Company.

Hartley, J. (1982). Designing instructional text. In Jonassen, D. H. (Ed.), *The technology of text: Principles for structuring, designing and displaying text*. Englewood Cliffs, NJ: Educational Technology Publications Inc.

Harvey, S., & Goudvis, A. (2000). *Strategies that Work: Teaching Comprehension to Enhance Understanding*. Stenhouse Publishers.

Hathaway, M. D. (1984). Variables of computer screen design and how hey affect learning. *Journal of Educational Technology, 24*(1), 7–11.

Havernik, J., Messerschmitt, D., & Vandrick, S. (1997). Collaborative research: Why and how? *Educational Researcher, 26*(9), 31–35.

Haverschmidt, J., & Schmidt, D. (1998). The importance of the role of collaboration in higher education Instruction. *American Educational Research Journal, 35*, 10–16.

Haworth, J., & Conrad, C. (1997). *Emblems of quality: Developing and sustaining high quality programs*. Boston: Allyn and Bacon.

Hayden, M., Saenger, H., & Parry, S. (1999). *An evaluation of the online units delivered in first semester 1999*. Southern Cross University, Teaching and Learning Centre.

Haywood, T. (1995). *Info rich/info poor: Access and exchange in the global information society*. London: Bowker-Saur.

Heavens, A. (2005). *The Shock of the New*. Retrieved May 12, 2009, from http://www.meskelsquare.com/archives/2005/01/the_shock_of_th.html

Heines, J. M. (1984). *Screen design strategies for computer assisted instruction*. Bedford, MA: Digital Press.

HELIOS. (2009). *HELIOS Project website*. Retrieved on August 6, 2009, from http://www.education-observatories.net/helios

Helms, F. P. (2005). *Evaluation der DVD. Von der Balanced Scorecard zum Performance Measurement*. Hagen: FernUniversität.

Henning, E., Van Rensburg, W., & Smit, B. (2004). *Finding your way in qualitative research*. Pretoria, South Africa: JL van Schaik.

Herber, E., Benimeli-Bofarull, E., & Haber, P. (2006). *Modern curriculum design and knowledge transfer in a virtual collaborative environment*. Paper presented at SEFI Annual Conference, Uppsala, Sweden.

Herber, E., Haber, P., & Mayr, M. (2009). *Pool - Project Integrated Learning in Higher Education and Business*. Paper presented at IHEPI 2009 Conference Budapest, Hungary.

Hergert, M. (2003). Lessons from launching an online MBA program. *Online Journal of Distance Learning Administration, 6*(4). Retrieved March 18, 2009 from http://www.westga.edu/~distance/ojdla/winter64/hergert64.htm

Hernandez, C., & Nevin, J. (1999). Education for sustainable development: The ultimate value of life depends upon awareness and the power of contemplation rather than upon mere survival. In Hernandez, C., & Mayur, R. (Eds.), *Pedagogy of the earth: Education for a sustainable future* (pp. 15–28). Bloomfield, CT: Kumarian Press, Inc.

Hersey, P., & Blanchard, K. (1969). *Management of organizational behavior: Utilizing human resources*. Englewood Cliffs, NJ: Prentice-Hall.

Herzog, M. J., & Pittman, R. B. (1995). Home, family, and community: Ingredients in the rural education equation. *Phi Delta Kappan, 77*, 113–118.

Heyneman, S. P., & Haynes, K. T. (2004). International Uses of Education Technology: Threats and Opportunities. In Chapman, D. W., & Mählck, L. O. (Eds.), *Adapting Technology for School Improvement: A Global Perspective* (pp. 55–80). Paris: International Institute for Educational Planning.

Hildreth, P., Kimble, C., & Wright, P. (2000). Communities of practice in the distributed international environment. *Journal of Knowledge Management, 4*(1), 27–37. doi:10.1108/13673270010315920

Hiltz, S. R., & Goldman, R. (2005). *Learning together online: Research on asynchronous learning.* Mahwah, NJ: Erlbaum.

Hobbs, V. (2004). *The promise and the power of online learning in rural education.* Arlington, VA: Rural School and Community Trust.

Hofstede, G. (2003). *Culture's Consequences: Comparing Values, Behaviors, Institutions, and Organizations Across Nations* (2nd ed.). London: Sage.

Hofstede, G. (2005). *Cultures and Organizations: Software of the Mind.* New York: McGraw-Hill.

Hogan-Garcia, M. (2007). *The Four Skills of Cultural Diversity Competence: A Process for Understanding and Practice* (3rd ed.). Belmont, CA: Thomson Brooks/Cole.

Holloway, D. L. (2002). Using research to ensure quality teaching in rural schools. *Journal of Research in Rural Education, 17*(3). Retrieved January 20, 2008 from http://www.jrre.psu.edu/articles/v17,n3,p138-153,Holloway.pdf

Hong, K. S. (2002). Relationships between students' and instructional variables with satisfaction and learning from a web-based course. *The Internet and Higher Education, 5,* 267–281. doi:10.1016/S1096-7516(02)00105-7

Hooper, S., & Hannafin, M. (1986). Variables affecting the legibility of computer generated text. *Journal of Instructional Development, 9*(5), 22–28. doi:10.1007/BF02908315

Hovland, K. (2006). *Shared Future: Global Learning and Liberal Education.* Washington, DC: Association of American Colleges and Universities.

Howley, C., Strange, M., & Bickel, R. (2000). Research about school size and school performance in impoverished communities. ERIC Digest. Charleston, WV: ERIC Clearinghouse on Rural Education and Small Schools (ERIC Document Reproduction Service No. ED448968).

Huang, G., & Howley, C. (1993). Mitigating disadvantage: Effects of small-scale schooling on student achievement in Alaska. *Journal of Research in Rural Education, 9*(3).

Retrieved June 2, 2008 from http://www.jrre.psu.edu/articles/v9,n3,p137-149,Huang.pdf

Huff, M. (2000). A Comparison Study of Live Instruction Versus Interactive Television for Teaching MSW Students Critical Thinking Skills. *Research on Social Work Practice, 10*(4).

Huitt, W. E. (2004). *Bloom's Taxonomy of the Cognitive Domain.* Educational Psychology Interactive. Valdosta, GA: Valdosta State University. Retrieved March 14, 2008, from http://chiron.valdosta.edu/whuitt/col/cogsys/bloom.html

Hussien, J. (2006). Locating the Value Conflicts Between the Rhetoric and Practices of the Public and Teacher Education in Ethiopia within the Hegemony of the Global Neo-Liberalism and Seeking the Alternative in Critical Pedagogy. *Journal for Critical Education Policy Studies, 4*(2).

IEEE. WG11: Learning Technology Standards Committee (2004). *IEEE Computing Managed Instructions.* Retrieved July 30, 2009, from http://ltsc.ieee.org/wg11

IEEE. WG20: Learning Technology Standards Committee (2004). *IEEE Reusable Competency Definitions.* Retrieved July 30, 2009, from http://ltsc.ieee.org/wg20

Index Mundi. (2006). *El Salvador's demographics profile 2006.* Retrieved August 3, 2006, from http://www.indexmundi.com/El Salvador/demographics _profile.html

Irvin, M. J., Hannum, W. H., & de la Varre, C. (2009). Barriers to distance education in rural schools. Paper presented at the annual meeting of the American Educational Research Association, Rural Special Interest Group, San Diego, CA.

Isman, A., Altinay, Z., & Altinay, F. (2004). Roles of the Students and Teachers in Distance Education. *Turkish Online Journal of Distance Education, 5*(4), 1302-6488. Retrieved December 2008, from http://tojde.anadolu.edu.tr

Jameson, J. (2007). *Investigating Collaborative Leadership for Communities of Practice in Learning and Skills.* Research Report funded and published by Lancaster

University Management School: Centre for Excellence in Leadership. Retrieved June 14, 2009, from http://www.centreforexcellence.org.uk/UsersDoc/Collab-Leadership.pdf

Jameson, J. (2008, May 6). The eLIDA CAMEL: Designed for Learning by Community. *ALT-N Newsletter Article: Featured Case Study, 12.* Retrieved June 14, 2009, from http://newsletter.alt.ac.uk/e_article001068464.cfm

Jameson, J., Ferrell, G., Kelly, J., Walker, S., & Ryan, M. (2006). Building trust & shared knowledge in communities of e-learning practice: collaborative leadership in the JISC eLISA and CAMEL lifelong learning projects. *British Journal of Educational Technology, 37*(6), 949–968. doi:10.1111/j.1467-8535.2006.00669.x

Jennings, N., Swidler, S., & Koliba, C. (2005). Place-based education in the standards-based reform era: Conflict or complement? *American Journal of Education, 122,* 44–65. doi:10.1086/444522

Jimerson, L. (2006). *Breaking the fall: Cushioning the impact of rural declining enrollment.* Arlington, VA: The Rural School and Community Trust.

JISC infoNet. (2006). *The CAMEL Project: Collaborative Approaches to the Management of E-Learning.* Northumbria University printed and on-line project report. Retrieved on March 21, 2009, from http://www.jiscinfonet.ac.uk/camel

JISC infoNet. (2006). *Using the CAMEL Model to Build a Community of Practice: Resources: Where did the idea come from?* Retrieved on June 14, 2009, from www.jiscinfonet.ac.uk/camel/camel-model/idea.mov

JISC infoNet. (2007). *Minutes of the final eLIDA CAMEL project meeting.* Unpublished notes in the eLIDA CAMEL project Moodle.

Johnson, J., & Strange, M. (2007). *Why rural matters 2007: The realities of rural education growth.* Arlington, VA: Rural School and Community Trust.

Johnson, L., & Johnson, N. (1987). Knowledge Elicitation Involving Teachback Interviewing. In Kidd, A. L. (Ed.), *Knowledge Acquisition for Expert Systems: a practical handbook* (pp. 91–108). New York: Plennum.

Johnson-Glenberg, M. C. (2007). Web-based reading comprehension instruction: Three studies of 3D-readers. In McNamara, D. (Ed.), *Reading comprehension strategies: Theories, interventions and education in the electronic age* (pp. 154–169). London: Routledge.

Johnson-Sheehan, R., & Baehr, C. (2001). Visual-spatial thinking in hypertexts. *Technical Communication, 48*(1), 22–30.

Johnstone, B. (2008). *Discourse Analysis.* Blackwell Publishing.

Johnstone, S. M., Ewell, P., & Paulson, K. (2002). Student learning as academic currency. *ACE Center 004 for Policy Analysis.* Retrieved February 25, 2005, from http://www.acenet.edu/bookstore/pdf/distributed-learning/distributed-learning-04.pdf

Joint Information Systems Committee (JISC). (2009). *JISC CETIS Design for Learning Projects Wiki, Shared Resources 2: Case Studies.* Retrieved August 7, 2009, from http://DfL.cetis.ac.uk/wiki/index.php/Shared_Resources2

Joint Information Systems Committee (JISC). (2009). *What we Do: Programmes: e-Learning Pedagogy.* e-Learning Independent Design Activities for Collaborative Approaches to the Management of e-Learning (eLIDA CAMEL) Project. Retrieved June 14, 2009, from http://www.jisc.ac.uk/whatwedo/programmes/elearningpedagogy/elidacamel.aspx

Jonassen, D. (1999). Designing constructivist learning environments. In *Instructional-design theories and models: A new paradigm of instructional theory* (*Vol. 2*, pp. 215–240). Mahwah, NJ: Lawrence Erlbaum Associates.

Jonassen, D. (2000). *Computers as mindtools for schools engaging critical thinking* (2nd ed.). Upper Saddle River, NJ: Prentice-Hall.

Jones, R. (2003). A recommendation for managing the predicted growth in college enrollment at a time of adverse economic conditions. *Online Journal of Distance Learning Administration, 6*(1). Retrieved February 25,

2005, from http://www.westga.edu/~distance/ojdla/spring61/jones61.htm

Kagiso, T. V. (2007). *Ethiopian Ministry of Education.* Retrieved July 10, 2009, from http://www.kagisotv.co.za/ClientPortfolio/Casestudies/MemarEthiopianEducation-Project/tabid/944/language/en-US/Default.aspx

Kaplan, F. M., Sobin, J. M., & Andors, S. (1979). *Encyclopedia of china today.* New York: Harper & Row, Publishers.

Kapuściński, R. (1984). *The Emperor.* London: Pan Books Ltd.

Kaufman, R. (1998). *Strategic thinking: A guide to identifying and solving problems (revised).* Arlington, VA & Washington DC: American Society of Training & Development and International Society for Performance Improvement.

Kaufman, R. (2000). *Mega planning: Practical tools for organizational success.* Thousand Oaks, CA: Sage Publishing.

Kaufman, R., & Swart, W. (1995). Beyond conventional benchmarking: Integrating ideal visions, strategic planning, reengineering, and quality management. *Educational Technology, 35*(3), 11–14.

Kaufman, R., Thigarajan, S., & MacGillis, P. (Eds.). (1997). *The guidebook for performance improvement: Working with individuals and organizations.* San Francisco: Jossey-Bass/Pfeiffer.

Kaufman, R., Watkins, R., Triner, D., & Stith, M. (1998). The changing corporate mind: Organizations, visions, mission purposes, and indicators on the move toward societal payoff. *Performance Improvement, 37*(3), 32–44.

Keegan, D. J. (1988). Problems in defining the field of distance education. *American Journal of Distance Education, 2*(2), 4–11. doi:10.1080/08923648809526619

Keengwe, J. (2007). Faculty Integration of Technology into Instruction and Students' Perception of Computer Technology to Improve Student Learning. *Journal of Information Technology Education, 1,* 169–178.

Kellner, D. (2002). Technological Revolution, Multiple Literacies, and the Restructuring of Education. In Snyder, I. (Ed.), *Silicon Literacies: Communication, Innovation and Education in the Electronic Age* (pp. 154–169). London: Routledge.

Kelly, J., & Riachi, R. (2006 July). CAMEL train heads for oasis. *ALT-N, 5.* Retrieved March 21, 2009, from http://newsletter.alt.ac.uk/e_article000615315.cfm?x=b11,0,w

Kerawalla, L., Minocha, S., Kirkup, G., & Conole, G. (2008). Characterising the different blogging behaviours of students on an online distance learning course. *Learning, Media and Technology, 33*(1), 31–33. doi:10.1080/17439880701868838

Kim, D., & Gilman, D. (2008). Effects of Text, Audio, and Graphic Aids in Multimedia Instruction for Vocabulary Learning. *Educational Technology & Society, 11*(3), 114–126.

Kim, H. N. (2008). The phenomenon of blogs and theoretical model of blog use in educational contexts. *Computers & Education, 51,* 1342–1352. doi:10.1016/j.compedu.2007.12.005

Kimble, C. (May 1999). The impact of technology on mearning: Making sense of the research. *Mid-Continent Regional Educational Laboratory,* 1-6.

King, K. P. (2006). Introduction. In King, K. P., & Griggs, K. J. (Eds.), *Harnessing innovative technology in higher education: Access, equity, polity, & instruction* (pp. 15–28). Madison, WI: Atwood Publishing.

King, K. P., & Griggs, J. K. (Eds.). (2006). *Harnessing innovative technology in higher education: Access, equity, polity, & instruction.* Madison, WI: Atwood Publishing.

Kinshuk. (2007). Special issue introduction: A critical view of technology-enhanced learning and instruction in the digital Age. *International Society for Technology in Education, 40*(1), 2-3.

Klein, K. J., & House, R. J. (1995). On fire: Charismatic Leadership and levels of analysis. *The Leadership Quarterly, 6,* 183–198. doi:10.1016/1048-9843(95)90034-9

Knowles, M. S. (1975). *Self-directed learning: A guide for learners and teachers*. New York: Association Press.

Knowles, M. S. (1978). *The adult learner: A neglected species* (2nd ed.). Houston, TX: Gulf.

Knowles, M. S. (1984). *Andragogy in action*. San Francisco: Jossey-Bass.

Knowles, M. S. (1986). *Using learning contracts*. San Francisco: Jossey-Bass.

Kolers, P. A., Duchnicky, R. L., & Ferguson, D. C. (1981). Eye movement measurement of readability of C.R.T. displays. *Human Factors, 23*(5), 517–527.

Kolesnik, W. (1975). *Humanism and/or behaviorism in education*. Boston: Allyn and Bacon, Inc.

Kosslyn, S. (1994). *Image and brain. The resolution of the imagery debate*. Cambridge, MA: MIT Press.

Kramsch, C. A., A'Ness, F., & Lam, E. (2000). Authenticity and authorship in the computer-mediated acquisition of L2 literacy. *Language Learning & Technology, 4*(2), 78–104.

Krause, S. D. (2005, June 24). Blogs as a tool for teaching. *The Chronicle of Higher Education*, B33.

Kruk, R. S., & Muter, P. (1984). Reading of continuous text on video screens. *Human Factors, 26*(3), 339–345.

Kuzu, A. (2007). Views of pre-service teachers on blog use for instruction and social interaction. *Turkish Online Journal of Distance Education, 8*(2), 34–51.

Laaser, W. (2002). A Virtual University Environment, The German Experience. In *Advancing Virtual University Education No. 1* (pp. 47–57). Joensuu, Finland: University of Joensuu.

LaRose, R., & Whitten, P. (2000). Re-thinking instructional immediacy for web courses: A social cognitive exploration. *Communication Education, 49*(4), 320–388. doi:10.1080/03634520009379221

Larrson, S., Boud, D., Dahlgren, M. A., Walters, S., & Sork, T. (2005). Confronting globalization: Learning from intercontinental collaboration. *Innovations in*

Education and Teaching International, 42(1), 61–71. doi:10.1080/14703290500048960

Lave, J., & Wenger, E. (1991). *Situated learning: Legitimate peripheral participation*. Cambridge, UK: Cambridge University Press.

Leadership Governance and Management Fund. (2009). *Collaborative Approaches to the Management of e-Learning, Leadership, Governance and Management Fund A-Z of Funded Projects*. Higher Education Council for England (HEFCE). Retrieved June 7, 2009, from http://www.hefce.ac.uk/lgm/build/lgmfund/projects/show.asp?id=14&cat=9

LeBaron, M., & Pillay, V. (2006). *Conflict Across Cultures: A Unique Experience Bridging Differences*. Boston, MA: Nicholas Brealey.

Lebow, D. (1993). Constructivist values for instructional systems design: five principles toward a new mindset. *Educational Technology Research and Development, 41*(3), 4–16. doi:10.1007/BF02297354

Lederach, J. (1995). *Preparing for Peace: Conflict Transformation Across Cultures*. Syracuse, NY: Syracuse University Press.

Leggett, W. P., & Persichitte, K. A. (1998). Blood, sweat, and tears: 50 years of technology implementations obstacles. *TechTrends, 43*(3), 33–36. doi:10.1007/BF02824053

Lemma, B. (2006). Plasma Television Teachers - When a Different Reality Takes Over African Education. In L. Dahlström & J. Mannberg (Eds.), Critical Educational Visions and Practices in Neo-Liberal Times, 71-88. Umeå University: Global South Network Publisher.

LEONIE. (2003). *Trends and drivers of change in learning system*. LEONIE Project Report. Retrieved August 7, 2009 from http://www.education-observatories.net/leonie/outputs/LEONIE__final_trends_of_change.pdf

LEONIE. (2009). *Leonie Project website*. Retrieved August 7, 2009, from http://www.education-observatories.net/leonie

Lepper, M. R., & Whitmore, P. (1996). Collaboration: A social–psychological perspective. *Cognitive Studies: The Bulletin of the Japanese Cognitive Science Society, 3*, 7–10.

Lepper, M. R., Drake, M., & O'Donnell-Johnson, T. M. (1997). Scaffolding techniques of expert human tutors. In Hogan, K., & Pressley, M. (Eds.), *Scaffolding student learning: Instructional approaches and issues* (pp. 108–144). New York: Brookline Books.

Lesotho College of Education. (2001). *Diploma in Education (primary), Students' Handbook*. Maseru, Lesotho: Ministry of Education.

Lesotho College of Education. (2002). *Lesotho College of Education Strategic Plan: 2002/3 – 2006/7*. Maseru: Author.

Lesotho College of Education. (2008). *College Calendar 2008-2009*. Maseru, Lesotho: Morija Printing Works.

Lesotho Communications Authority (LCA) Chief Executive, Mr. Monehela Posholi. Source: *Lena 12/02/2009*.

Lesotho National Development Corporation. (2009). *Lesotho Review: An Overview of the Kingdom of Lesotho's Economy*. Maseru: LNDC.

Lewis, L., Alexander, D., & Farris, E. (1997). *Distance Education in Higher Education Institutions. National Center for Education Statistics, NCES 98-062*. Washington, DC: US Department of Education.

Lewis, M. W. (2000). Global Ignorance. *Geographical Review, 90*(4), 603–628. doi:10.2307/3250786

Lewis, V., Dunbar, G., & Hill, R. (1999). *Children's knowledge of danger, attentional skills and child/parent communication: Relationships with behaviour on the road* (Road Safety Report No. 10). London, UK: Department for Transport. Retrieved May 13, 2009, from http://www.dft.gov.uk/pgr/roadsafety/research/ rsrr/theme1/childrensknowledgeofdangerno10?page=1

Lin, H.T., & Yuan S.M. (2006). Taking blogs as a platform of learning reflective journal. *ICWL*, 38-47.

Lipka, S. (2006, January 27). A blog gives professors space to vent about their students. *The Chronicle of Higher Education*, A37.

Liu, G. Z. (2008). Innovating research topics in learning technology: Where are the new blue oceans? *British Journal of Educational Technology, 39*(4), 738–747. doi:10.1111/j.1467-8535.2008.00851.x

Loch B., & McDonald C. (2007). Synchronous chat and electronic ink for distance support in mathematics. *Innovate, 3*(3).

Loch, B., & Reushle, S. E. (2008). The practice of web conferencing: Where are we now? In *Hello! Where are you in the landscape of educational technology? Proceedings of ASCILITE08*, Melbourne: Deakin University. Retrieved May 4, 2009, from http://www.ascilite.org.au/conferences/melbourne08/procs/loch.pdf

Longman. (1978). *Longman Dictionary of Contemporary English*. Harlow, UK: Longman Group Ltd.

Lopez, J. (2009). *Educational Access and Quality in Ethiopia: Successes and Challenges in the City of Mekelle*. Student Symposium on African Education – Interrogating Quality in the African Context, Teachers' College, Columbia University.

Loveless, A. (1995). *The Role of IT: Practical Issues for the Primary Teacher*. London: Cassel.

Lowe, J. M. (2006). Rural Education: Attracting and retaining teachers in small schools. *Rural Educator, 27*(2), 28–32.

Luehmann, A. L. (2008). Using blogging in support of teacher professional identity development: A case study. *Journal of the Learning Sciences, 17*(3), 287–337. doi:10.1080/10508400802192706

Lyson, T. A. (2002). What does a school mean to a community? Assessing the social and economic benefits of schools to rural villages in New York. *Journal of Research in Rural Education, 17*(3). Retrieved February 2, 2008 from http://www.jrre.psu.edu/articles/v17,n3,p131-137,Lyson.pdf

Ma, Y., & Runyon, L. R. (2004, July/August). *Academic synergy in the age of technology-a new instructional paradigm.* Retrieved December 14, 2005, from http://proquest.umi.com/pdqweb?did=692351181&sid=1&Fmt=4&clientld=36149&RQT=309&VName=PQD

Madamombe, I. (2007). Internet Enriches Learning in Rural Uganda: NEPAD e-schools connecting students to the world. *Africa Renewal - United Nations department of Public Information, 21*(1), 16-17.

Mählck, L. O., & Chapman, D. W. (2004). Effective Use of Technology to Improve Education: Lessons for Planners. In Chapman, D. W., & Mählck, L. O. (Eds.), *Adapting Technology for School Improvement: A Global Perspective* (pp. 297–305). Paris: International Institute for Educational Planning.

Malecki, E. J. (2003). Digital development in rural areas: Potentials and pitfalls. *Journal of Rural Studies, 19,* 201–214. doi:10.1016/S0743-0167(02)00068-2

MAN. (2009). *MERLOT Africa Network (MAN) project website.* Retrieved August 7, 2009, from http://man.merlot.org/

Mangoaela, P. (2008). *Lesotho Telecommunication Authority.* Retrieved June 05, 2009, from http://www.connect.world.com/article/free-article.php?oid=AME-11-2003-08

March, H. W. (1982). SEEQ: a reliable, valid and useful instrument for collecting students' evaluations of university teaching. *The British Journal of Educational Psychology, 52,* 77–95.

Marks, D. (1990). The relationship between imagery, body and mind. In Hampson, D., Marks, D., & Richardson, J. (Eds.), *Imagery: Current developments* (pp. 1–38). London: Routledge.

Marquardt, M., & Horvath, L. (2001). *Global Teams: How Top Multinationals Span Boundaries and Cultures With High-Speed Teamwork.* Palo Alto, CA: Davies-Black Publishing.

Marra, R. M. (2004). *An online course to help teachers use technology to enhance learning: Success and Limita-tions.* Retrieved 14 December, 2005, from http://proquest.umi.com/pdqweb?did=757578841&sid=12&Fmt=4&clientld=36149&RQT=309&VName=PQD

MarylandOnline. (2006). *Quality Matters: Inter-Institutional Quality Assurance in Online Learning.* Retrieved March 18, 2009, from http://qualitymatters.org

Masterman, E. (2008). *Evaluation Report for the eLIDA CAMEL Project.* Unpublished report contributing to the final report of the project to JISC, University of Greenwich.

Masterman, E., Jameson, J., & Walker, S. (2009). Capturing Teachers' Experience Of Learning Design Through Case Studies. *Distance Education Special Issue: Researching Learning Design.* In *Open.* Distance And Flexible Learning.

Mastropieri, M. A., & Scruggs, T. E. (1997). Best Practice in Promoting Reading Comprehension in Students with Learning Disabilities. *Remedial and Special Education, 18,* 197–213. doi:10.1177/074193259701800402

Mathur, R., & Oliver, L. (2008, January). *Developing cultural partnerships through electronic communication: A thematic analysis.* Paper presented at the annual meeting of the Hawaii International Conference on Education, Honolulu, HI.

Mayer, R., & Moreno, R. (2002). Aids to computer-based multimedia learning. *Learning and Instruction, 12,* 107–119. doi:10.1016/S0959-4752(01)00018-4

McCombs, B. L., & Miller, L. (2006). *Learner-centered classroom practices and assessments: Maximizing student motivation, learning, and achievement.* Thousand Oaks, CA: Corwin Press.

McCombs, B., & Vakili, D. (2005). A learner-centered framework for e-learning. *Teachers College Record, 107*(8), 1582–1609. doi:10.1111/j.1467-9620.2005.00534.x

McDermott, R. (2001) *Knowing in Community: 10 Critical Success Factors in Building Communities of Practice.* Community Intelligence Labs. Retrieved March 20, 2009, from www.co-i-l.com/coil/knowledge-garden/cop/knowing.shtml

McElroy, J., & Blount, Y. (2006). You, me and iLecture. In *Who's learning? Who's technology? Proceedings of ASCILITE06* (pp. 549-558). Sydney: University of Sydney Conservatorium, Retrieved June 4, 2009, from http://www.ascilite.org.au/conferences/sydney06/proceeding/pdf_papers/p87.pdf

McGregor, D. (1960). *The human side of enterprise.* New York: McGraw Hill.

McInnis, C., Griffin, P., James, R., & Coates, H. (2001). *Development of the Course Experience Questionnaire.* Retrieved July 8, 2006, from http://www.dest.gov.au/archive/highered/ eippubs/eip01_1/01_1.pdf

McKeachie, W., & Svinicki, M. (2006). *McKeachie's Teaching Tips: Strategies, Research, and Theory for College and University Teachers* (12th ed.). Boston, MA: Houghton Mifflin.

McKeown, R. (2002). *ESD toolkit.* Retrieved March 1, 2005, from http://www.esdtoolkit.org

McLoughlin, C., & Lee, M. (2008). Future learning landscapes: Transforming pedagogy through social software. *Innovate, 4*(5). Retrieved June 4, 2009, from http://www.innovateonline.info/index.php?view=article&id=539

McPherson, M., & Nunes, M. B. (2006). Organisational issues for e-learning: Critical success factors as identified by HE practitioners. *International Journal of Educational Management, 20*(7), 542–558. doi:10.1108/09513540610704645

Meless, K., & Teshome, Z. (2006). Assessment on the Impact of Plasma Television Implementation on the Teaching Learning Process of Mathematics Class: The Case on Selected Practicum Sites (High Schools) for Education Faculty of Jimma University. *Ethiopian Journal of Education and Science, 2*(1), 85–127.

MENON. (2009). *Menon project website*, retrieved 6 August, 2009, from http://www.menon.org/

MERLOT. (2009). *MERLOT Project.* Retrieved August 7, 2009, from http://www.merlot.org/merlot/index.htm

Merriam, S. (1998). *Qualitative research and case study applications in education.* San Francisco, CA: Jossey-Bass.

Merrill, M. (1983). Component display theory. In *Instructional-design theories and models: An overview of their current status.* Hillsdale, NJ: Lawrence Erlbaum Associates, Publishers.

Miller, C. T. (2007). Enhancing web-based instruction using a person-centered model of instruction. *Quarterly Review of Distance Education, 8*(1), 25–34.

Miller, C. T., & Mazur, J. (2001). Towards a person-centered model of instruction: Can an emphasis on the personal enhance instruction in cyberspace? *Quarterly Review of Distance Education, 2*(3), 193–207.

Miller, E. (2000). Models in distance teaching in teacher education in Jamaica. In *Distance Education in Small States, 2000 Conference proceedings, UWI/COL, 2001* (pp. 141-147). Retrieved January 11, 2008, from http://www.Col.org/colweb/site/pid3338

Miller, G., & Miller, W. (2000). A telecommunication network for distance learning: If it's built, will agriculture teachers use it? *Journal of Agricultural Education, 41*(1), 79–87.

Ministry of Education and Training. (2006). *Summary of the Views of Basotho on Education in the Districts.* Kingdom of Lesotho: MOET.

Moallem, M. (2007). Accommodating individual differences in the design of online learning environments: A Comparative Study. *Journal of Research on Technology in Education, 40*(2), 219–247.

Molebash, P. E. (2002). Phases of collaborative success: A response to Shoffner, Dias, and Thomas. *Contemporary Issues in Technology and Teacher Education.* Retrieved December 10, 2002, from http://www.citejournal.org/vol2/iss1/general/article1.cfm

Molenda, M. (2003). Performance Improvement. In Search of the Elusive ADDIE Model. International Society for Performance Improvement, 42(5), 34-36.

Molenda, M., & Pershing, J. A. (2004). *The strategic impact model: An integrative approach to performance improvement and instructional systems design. Tech Trends Journal.* Springer Boston.

Molenda, M., Pershing, J., & Reigeluth, C. (1996). Designing Instructional Systems. In Craig, R. (Ed.), *The ASTD Training and Development Handbook* (pp. 266–293). New York: McGraw-Hill.

Moloisane, A., Tlebere, G., & O'Droma, M. (2007). *Lesotho Lays Foundation for Internet Access.* Retrieved June 05, from http://www.afrol.com/news2001/Les009-internet-foundation.htm

Monahan, T. (2005). *Globalization, technological change, and public education.* London: Routledge Pub.

Moncada-Davidson, L. (1995). Education and its limitations in the maintenance of peace in El Salvador. *Comparative Education Review, 39*(1), 54–75. doi:10.1086/447289

Monk, D. (2007). Recruiting and retaining high-quality teachers in rural areas. *The Future of Children, 17*(1), 155–174. doi:10.1353/foc.2007.0009

Montgomery, D. C. (1976). *Design and Analysis of Experiments.* New York: Wiley & Sons.

Moore, M. G. (1989). Editorial: Three types of interaction. *American Journal of Distance Education, 3*, 1–6. doi:10.1080/08923648909526659

Moore, M. G., & Kearsley, G. (2005). *Distance education: A systems view.* Belmont, CA: Wadsworth.

Morgan, C., & O'Reilly, M. (1999). *Assessing open and distance learners.* London: Kogan Page.

Morgan, P. (2000). Strengthening the stakes: Combing distance and face-to-face teaching strategies – Preliminary discussion issues. *Distance Education in Small States, 2000 Conference proceedings, UWI/COL, 2001* (pp. 106-112). Retrieved January 11, 2008, from http://www.Col.org/colweb/site/pid3338

Morgan, R., & Hunt, S. (1994). The commitment-trust theory of relationship marketing. *Journal of Marketing, 58*(4), 36–51.

Moshman, D. (1999). *Adolescent psychological development. Rationality, morality and identity.* Mahwah, NJ: Erlbaum.

MOVEnation. (2000). *MOVEnation project website.* Retrieved August 6, 2009, from http://muvenation.org/about/

Mündler, A., Haber, P., & McCurry, F. (2006). *Online Assessment Methods for Virtual Project Management Training.* Paper presented at EDEN Annual Conference, Vienna, Austria.

Mündler, A., McCurry, F., Haber, P., & Benimeli-Bofarull, E. (2006). An Approach for Online Assessment in the Multinational EU Project: POOL Project Organization OnLine. In Neidl, W., & Tochtermann, K. (Eds.), *Lecture Notes in Computer Science 4227* (pp. 673–678). Berlin: Springer-Verlag.

Muilenberg, L., & Berge, Z. L. (2001). Barriers to distance education: A factor-analytic study. *American Journal of Distance Education, 15*(2), 7–22. doi:10.1080/08923640109527081

Munro, J. (1996). *Teaching Reading Strategies.* Melbourne: Hawthorn.

Murphy, T. H., & Terry, H. R. (1998). Opportunities and obstacles for distance education in agricultural education. *Journal of Agricultural Education, 39*(1), 28–36.

Murray, D., & MacPherson, P. (2005). *Navigating to read - reading to navigate.* Sydney, Australia: Sydney AMEP Research Centre.

Murray, L., & Hourigan, T. (2008). Blogs for specific purposes: Expressive or socio-cognitivist approach? *ReCALL, 1*(20), 82–07.

Muson, H. (2005 August). How smaller companies earn customer loyalty. *The Conference Board, Executive Action Series,* (157).

Nacherud, S., & Scaletta, K. (2008). Blogging in the academy. *New Directions for Student Services,* 124, Wiley Periodical Inc., 71-87.

Nahapiet, J., & Ghoshal, S. (1998). Social capital, intellectual capital, and the organizational advantage. *Academy of Management Review, 23*(2), 242–267. doi:10.2307/259373

Nakamura, L. (2000). Where do you want to go today? Cybernetic tourism, the Internet, and transnationality. In Kolko, B., Nakamura, L., & Rodman, G. (Eds.), *Race in Cyberspace* (pp. 15–27). New York: Routledge.

NCTD. (2006). *RNIB National Centre for Tactile Diagrams (NCTD) Web Site*. Retrieved December 9, 2006, from http://www.nctd.org.uk

NDA. (2006). Guidelines for Application Software Accessibility. *Irish National Disability Authority Guidelines Web Site*. Retrieved December 9, 2006, from http://www.acessit.nda.ie

New Directions for Delivery at Southern Cross 2007. (n.d.). Unpublished SCU document.

New Zealand's Ministry of Transport. (2002). *Road safety education Strategic Framework*. Wellington, NZ: National Road Safety Committee. Retrieved from http://www.transport.govt.nz/assets/NewPDFs/road-safety-web.pdf

Newton, D., & Ledgerwood, T. (2001). Evolving support for online learning: An action research model. In Wallace, M., Ellis, A., & Newton, D. (Eds.), *Proceedings of Moving online II: A conference to explore the challenges for workplaces, colleges and universities* (pp. 205–221). Gold Coast, Australia: Conrad Jupiters.

Nootenberg, B. (2006). Organization, evolution, cognition and dynamic capabilities. *Center Discussion Paper Series No. 2006-41*. Nederlands: Tilburg University – Center and Faculty of Economics and Business Administration.

Norris, P. (2001). *Digital divide: Civic engagement, information poverty, and the internet worldwide*. Cambridge, UK: Cambridge University Press.

Northrup, P. T. (2002). Online learner's preferences for interaction. *The Quarterly Review of Distance Education, 3*(2), 219–226.

Nye, B., Hedges, L. V., & Konstantopoulos, S. (2000). Do minorities experience larger lasting benefits from small classes? *The Journal of Educational Research, 98*, 94–100. doi:10.3200/JOER.98.2.94-114

O'Reilly, M., & Newton, D. (2002). Interaction online: Above and beyond requirements of assessment. *Australian Journal of Educational Technology, 18*(1), 57–70.

Oblinger, D., & Oblinger, J. (2005). Is it age or IT: first steps toward understanding the net generation. In Oblinger, D., & Oblinger, J. (Eds.), *Educating the Net Generation* (p. 20). Boulder, CO: EDUCAUSE.

OECD. (2001). *Literacy skills for the knowledge society.* Retrieved from http://www.oecd.org

Oetzel, J., & Ting-Toomey, S. (Eds.). (2006). *The SAGE Handbook of Conflict Communication: Integrating Theory, Research, and Practice*. Thousand Oaks, CA: Sage.

Okojie, M. C., & Olinzock, A. (2006). Developing a Positive Mind-Set Toward the Use of Technology for Classroom Instruction. *International Journal of Instructional Media, 33*(1), 33–41.

Oliver, L., & Mathur, R. (2009, June). *Developing an international blended learning program: Cultural lessons learned.* Paper presented at the annual meeting of the ED-MEDIA World Conference on Educational Multimedia, Hypermedia, & Telecommunications, Honolulu, HI.

Olofsson, G. (2004). *When in Rome or Rio or Riyadh: Cultural Q&A's for Successful Business Behavior Around the World*. Yarmouth, ME: Intercultural Press.

Orr, J. E. (1996). *Talking About Machines: An Ethnography of a Modern Job*. Ithaca, NY: ILR Press.

Owston, R. D. (1997). The world wide web: Technology to enhance teaching and learning? [from http://www.edu.yorku.ca~rowston/article.html]. *Education Researcher, 26*(2), 27–33. Retrieved March 14, 2008.

P2B – a Leonardo da Vinci Life Long Learning Program Project. (2009). *P2B – Pool to Business*. Retrieved July 30, 2009, from http://www.pool2business.eu

Paine, L. (1992). Teaching and modernization in contemporary China. In Hayhoe, R. (Ed.), *Education and modernization: The Chinese experience* (pp. 183–209). New York: Pergamon Press.

Palincsar, A., Sullivan, A., & Brown, A. L. (1989). Instruction for Self-Regulated Reading. In Resnick, B. L., & Klopfer, L. E. (Eds.), *Toward the thinking Curriculum: Current Cognitive Research* (pp. 19–39). Alexandria, VA: ASCD.

Palloff, R. M., & Pratt, K. (2001). *Lessons from the cyberspace classroom: The realities of online teaching.* San Francisco: Jossey-Bass.

Palloff, R. M., & Pratt, K. (2003). *The virtual student: A profile and guide to working with online learners.* San Francisco: Jossey-Bass.

Parker, N. (2004). The quality dilemma in online education. In *Theory and practice of online learning.* Athabasca, Canada: Athabasca University Press. Retrieved December 4, 2006, from http://cde.athabascau.ca/online_book/ch16.html

Passey, D., & Samways, B. (1997). *Information Technology: Supporting Change Through Teacher Education.* London: Chapman & Hall.

Pauleen, D. (Ed.). (2004). *Virtual Teams: Projects, Protocols and Processes.* Hershey, PA: Idea Group.

Pearson, P. (1985). Changing the Face of Reading Comprehension Instruction. *The Reading Teacher, 38,* 724–738.

Pearson, P., Roehler, L. R., Dole, J. A., & Duffy, G. (1992). Developing Expertise in Reading Comprehension. In Samuels, S. J., & Farstrup, A. E. (Eds.), *What Research Has to say About Reading Instruction* (2nd ed., pp. 145–199). Newark, DE: International Reading Association.

Pete, M., Fregona, C., Allinson, T., & Cronje, J. (2002). *Pioneers Online: Developing a community of online education practitioners at the Durban Institute of Technology.* Retrieved 11 April, 2006, from http://www.ukzn.ac.za/citte/papers/id1.pdf

Peters, O. (2001). *Learning and Teaching in Distance Education: Analysis and Interpretation from an Interpersonal Perspective.* London: Kogan Page.

Phillips, R., Gosper, M., McNeill, M., Woo, K., Preston, G., & Green, D. (2007). Staff and student perspectives on web-based lecture technologies: Insights into the great divide. In *ICT: Providing choices for learners and learning. Proceedings of ASCILITE07,* Singapore. Retrieved June 1, 2009, from http://www.ascilite.org.au/conferences/singapore07/procs/phillips.pdf

Piacciano, A. G., & Seaman, J. (2007). *K-12 online learning: A survey of U.S. school district administrators.* Needham, MA: Sloan Consortium. Retrieved March 19, 2009 from http://www.sloan-c.org/publications/survey/pdf/K-12_Online_Learning.pdf

Piacciano, A. G., & Seaman, J. (2009). *K-12 online learning: A 2008 follow-up survey of U.S. school district administrators.* Needham, MA: Sloan Consortium. Retrieved March 11, 2009 from http://www.sloan-c.org/publications/survey/pdf/k-12_online_learning_2008.pdf

Piaget, J. (1985). *The Equilibration of Cognitive Structures.* Chicago, IL: University of Chicago Press.

Polanyi, M. (1967). *The Tacit Dimension.* New York: Anchor Books.

POLE. (2009). *POLE: Policy Observatory for Lifelong Learning and Employability project website.* Retrieved August 6, 2009, from http://www.education-observatories.net/pole/reports_html

Poole, B. J. (1997). *Education for an information age: Teaching in the computerized classroom.* New York: McGraw-Hill.

Potashnik, M., & Capper, J. (2004). Distance Education - Growth and Diversity. In LIBRARY Articles on Education, 2001-2004 World of Education. Retrieved January 2008, from http:/www.world bank.org/fandd/English/0398/articles/0110398.htm

Preece, J., Rogers, Y., & Sharpe, H. (2002). *Interaction Design beyond human-computer interaction.* New York: Wiley.

Pressley, M., Brown, R., El-Dinary, P. D., & Afflerbach, P. (1995). The Comprehension Instruction that Students

Need: Instructions Fostering Constructively Responsive Reading. *Learning Disabilities Research & Practice, 10,* 215–224.

Price, R. (1992). Moral-political education and modernization. In Hayhoe, R. (Ed.), *Education and modernization: The Chinese experience* (pp. 211–237). New York: Pergamon Press.

Program Development Team. (2007). *Woods Interactive onLine Degree (WILD) Proposal for New Program & Format.* Saint Mary-of-the-Woods, In Saint Mary-of-the-Woods College.

Project Office. (2007). *Report of the B. Ed (Secondary) Distance Program.*

Provasnik, S., Ramani, A. K., Coleman, M. M., Gilbertson, L., Herring, W., & Xie, Q. (2007). Status of education in rural America (NCES 2007-040). Washington, DC: National Center for Education Statistics, Institute of Education Sciences, U.S. Department of Education.

Quick, R., & Lieb, T. (2000). The heartfield project. *T.H.E. Journal, 28*(5), 40–46.

Rachaël, F. K. (2005). *An explanatory study on how weblog technologies fit virtual community members' social needs.* Paper presented at the Eleventh Americas Conference on Information Systems, Omaha, NE.

Reeves, T. C. (1997). *A model of the effective dimensions of interactive learning on the World Wide Web.* Retrieved May 10, 2007, from http://itech1.coe.uga.edu/Faculty/treeves/WebPaper.pdf

Reigeluth, C. (1999). What is Instructional-Design Theory and How Is It Changing? In *Instructional-Design Theories and Models: A New Paradigm of Instructional Theory.* Mahwah, NJ: Lawrence Erlbaum Associates, Publishers.

Reushle, S. E., & Loch, B. (2008). Conducting a trial of web conferencing software: Why, how, and perceptions from the coalface. *Turkish Online Journal of Distance Education, 9*(3), 19-28. Retrieved May 4, 2009, from http://tojde.anadolu.edu.tr/tojde31/index.htm

Reushle, S. E., & McDonald, J. (2000). Moving an Australian dual mode university to the online environment: A case study. In [Canada: Montreal.]. *Proceedings of ED-MEDI, A2000, 907–912.

Reushle, S., & McDonald, J. (2004, November). *Online learning: Transcending the physical.* Effective Teaching and Learning Conference 2004, A Conference for University Teachers, Griffith University, Logan Campus, Brisbane.

RNIB. (2006). Using a Computer without Vision and Notetaking. *RNIB Web Site.* Retrieved December 9, 2006, from http://www.rnib.org.uk

Road Safety Cambodia. (2008). *RS Education for Children.* Phnom Penh, Cambodia: Cambodia's National Road Safety Committee. Retrieved May 13, 2009 from http://www.roadsafetycambodia.info/action6

Robinson, B. (1995). The saber-tooth curriculum: Peddiwell and technology diffusion. Presentation made at Queens College, Cambridge, UK. Unpublished.

Roblyer, M. D. (2006). Virtually successful: Defeating the dropout problem through online school programs. *Phi Delta Kappan, 88*(1), 31–36.

Rogers, C. R. (1961). *On Becoming a Person.* Boston: Houghton Mifflin Company.

Rogers, C. R. (1969). *Freedom to Learn.* Columbus, OH: Merrill Publishing.

Rogers, C. R., & Freiberg, H. (1994). *Freedom to learn* (*Vol. 3*). New York: Merrill.

Rothwell, W. (2007). *Instructor Excellence: Mastering the Delivery of Training* (2nd ed.). San Francisco, CA: Wiley/Pfeiffer.

Rothwell, W., & Kazanas, H. (2008). *Mastering the Instructional Design Process: A Systematic Approach* (4th ed.). San Francisco, CA: Jossey-Bass.

Rotter, J. (1989). Internal versus external control of reinforcement. *The American Psychologist, 45*(4), 489–493. doi:10.1037/0003-066X.45.4.489

Rovai, A.P., & Wighting. (2005). Feelings of alienation and community among higher education students in a virtual community. *The Internet and Higher Education, 8,* 97–110. doi:10.1016/j.iheduc.2005.03.001

Rowe, S. (2003). Working in a virtual classroom: What you CAN do to enrich the learning experience. In *Proceedings of NAWEB03.* November, Fredericton, Canada, University of New Brunswick. Retrieved March 13, 2009, from http://naweb.unb.ca/proceedings/2003/PaperRowe.html

Rowe, S. (2004). Reflections on adopting a Learning Management System to engage students in their learning. In *Proceedings of NAWEB04,* November, Fredericton, Canada: University of New Brunswick. Retrieved March 13, 2009, from http://naweb.unb.ca/04/papers/Rowe.html

Rowe, S., & Ellis, A. (2006). Audiographics moves to the web. In A. Treloar & A. Ellis (Eds.), *AusWeb06: Proceedings of the Twelfth Australasian World Wide Web Conference,* July 1-5, Noosa Lakes, Australia. Retrieved March 13, 2009, from http://ausweb.scu.edu.au/aw06/papers/refereed/rowe/paper.html

Rowe, S., & Ellis, A. (2007), The evolution of audiographic technologies. In C. Montgomerie & J. Seale (Eds.), *Proceedings of ED-MEDIA2007: World Conference on Educational Multimedia, Hypermedia & Telecommunications,* June 25-29, Vancouver, Canada.

Rowe, S., & Ellis, A. (2007). How the web has changed lecturing: Going the full circle. In J. Richardson & A.Ellis (Eds.), *AusWeb07: Proceedings of the Thirteenth Australia World Wide Web Conference,* Novotel Pacific Bay Resort, Coffs Harbour, Australia. Retrieved March 13, 2009, from http://ausweb.scu.edu.au/aw07/papers/refereed/rowe/paper.html

Rowe, S., & Ellis, A. (2008). Enhancing the convenience and flexibility of student learning options: Using recorded audiographic web conferencing sessions. In C. Montgomerie & J. Seale (Eds.), *Proceedings (CD) for ED-MEDIA2008: World Conference on Educational Multimedia, Hypermedia & Telecommunications,* June 30-July 4, Vienna, Austria.

Rowe, S., Ellis, A., & Bao, T. Q. (2006). The evolution of audiographics: A case study of audiographics teaching in a business faculty. In *Who's learning? Who's technology? Proceedings of ASCILITE06,* December 3-6, Sydney: Sydney University. Retrieved March 23, 2009, from http://www.ascilite.org.au/conferences/sydney06/proceeding/pdf_papers/p194.pdf

Ryberg, T., & Larsen, M. C. (2008). Networked identities: understanding relationships between strong and weak ties in networked environments. *Journal of Computer Assisted Learning, 24*(2), 103–115. doi:10.1111/j.1365-2729.2007.00272.x

Saint Mary-of-the-Woods College. (2005). *SMWC Institutional Plan.* Saint Mary-of-the-Woods, In Author.

Salmon, G. (2003). E-moderating: The key to teaching and learning online (Second edition ed.). London: Taylor and Francis Books Ltd.

Salmon, G. (2005). Flying not flapping: A strategic framework for e-learning and pedagogical innovation in higher education institutions. *ALT-J, 13*(3), 201–218. doi:10.1080/09687760500376439

Sandels, S. (1975). *Children in Traffic.* London, UK: Elek Books.

Sandholtz, J., Ringstaff, C., & Dwyer, D. (1997). *Teaching with technology: Creating student-centered classrooms.* London: Teacher College Press.

Savery, J., & Duffy, T. (1995). Problem based learning: An instructional model and its constructivist framework. *Educational Technology, 35*(5), 31–38.

Scaletta, K. (2006). *To whom are these texts valuable? An inquiry into student blogging.* Retrieved from http://www.inms.umn.edu/events/past/newresearch_2006/papers/scaletta.pdf

Scarborough, J. (2001). *The Origins of Cultural Differences and Their Impact on Management.* Westport, CT: Quorum Books.

Schafft, K. A., Alter, T. R., & Bridger, J. C. (2006, July 17). Bringing the community along: A case study of a school district's information technology rural development initiative. *Journal of Research in Rural Education, 21*(8). Retrieved January 20, 2008 from http://www.umaine.edu/jrre/21-8.pdf

Schlosser, C., & Anderson, A. (1994). *Distance Education: Review of the Literature. Monograph prepared for the Iowa Distance Education Alliance.* Washington, DC: AECT Publications.

Schmidt, P. (2001, February 2). State budgets indicate lean times for public colleges. *The Chronicle of Higher Education,* A21–A22.

Schneider, R. (2005). Hypertect narrative and the reader: A view from cognitive theory. *European Journal of English Studies, 9*(2), 197–208. doi:10.1080/13825570500172067

Schott, M., & Cook, R. (2002). *Distance education faculty compensation models at a southwestern university.* Paper presented at the Texas Distance Education Association, Houston, TX.

Seal, K. R., & Harmon, H. L. (1995). Realities of rural school reform. *Phi Delta Kappan, 77*(2), 119–125.

Sergiovanni, T. J. (1994). *Building community in schools.* San Francisco, CA: Jossey-Bass.

Setzer, C. J., & Lewis, L. (2005). *Distance education courses for public elementary and secondary school students: 2002–2003 (No. NCES 2005-010).* Washington, DC: National Center for Education Statistics.

Shaik, N. (2005). Marketing distance learning programs and courses: A relationship marketing strategy. *Online Journal of Distance Learning Administration, 8*(2).

Sheth, J., & Parvatiyar, A. (2000). *Handbook of relationship marketing.* Thousand Oaks, CA: Sage Publications.

Simone, C. O. (2006). Faculty lived experiences in the online environment. *Adult Education Quarterly, 27*(1), 26–45.

Simpson, G., Johnston, L., & Richardson, M. (2003). An investigation of road crossing in a virtual environment. *Accident; Analysis and Prevention, 35*(5), 787–796. doi:10.1016/S0001-4575(02)00081-7

Simpson, O. (2004). The impact on retention of interventions to support distance learning. *Open Learning, 19*(1), 79–96. doi:10.1080/0268051042000177863

Singh, H. (2003). Building Effective Learnign Programs. *Educational Technology, 43*(3), 51-54. Retrieved July 20, 2009 from http://asianvu.com/bookstoread/framework/blended-learning.pdf

Snelbecker, G. (1974). *Learning theory, instructional theory, and psychoeducational design.* New York: McGraw-Hill Book Company.

Snyder, I. (1997). *Page to Screen: taking literacy into the electronic media.* Sydney, Australia: Allen & Unwin.

Snyder, I. (2002). *Silicon Literacies: Communication, Innovation and Education in the Electronic Age.* London: Routledge.

So, H., & Brush, T. (2008). Student perceptions of collaborative learning, social presence and satisfaction in a blended learning environment: Relationships and critical factors. *Computers & Education, 51*(1), 318–336. doi:10.1016/j.compedu.2007.05.009

Solso, R. (194). *Cognition and the visual arts.* Cambridge, MA: MIT Press.

Somekh, B. (2007). *Pedagogy and Learning with ICT – Reaching the Art of Innovation.* London: Routledge.

Southwest Educational Development Laboratory. (1995) Constructing knowledge in the classroom. Retrieved on 5/31/2009 from http://www.sedl.org/scimath/compass/v01n03/1.html

Spaeth, D. A., & Cameron, S. (2000). Computers & Resource – Based History Teaching: A UK Perspective. *Computers and the Humanities, 34*(3), 325–343.. doi:10.1023/A:1002448312963

Stacey, E., & Gerbic, P. (2007). Teaching for learning – Research perspectives from on-campus and distance students. *Education and Information Technologies, 12*(3).. doi:10.1007/s10639-007-9037-5

Stake, E. R. (2000). Case studies. In Denzin, N. K., & Lincoln, Y. S. (Eds.), *Handbook of qualitative research* (2nd ed.). London: SAGE.

Statham, A. (2001 January). *Virtual realities: A profile of online learning activity at Southern Cross University.* A report presented to the Online Review and Coordination Committee.

Storey, J., & Barnett, E. (2000). Knowledge management initiatives: learning from failure. *Journal of Knowledge Management, 4*(2), 145–156. doi:10.1108/13673270010372279

Strategic Development Group. (2007). *2007-2009 TAFE Division Plan: Swinburne University of Technology.*

Strategic Plan, U. S. Q. *2009-2013.* (2009). Retrieved March 25, 2009, from http://www.usq.edu.au/planstats/quality/Docs/USQ_strategic_plan.pdf

Stribiak, C. A., & Paul, J. (1998). *The team development fieldbook: A step-by-step approach for student teams.* New York: McGraw Hill.

Strickland, A. W. (2006). *ADDIE.* Idaho State University College of Education Science, Math & Technology Education. Retrieved June 29, 2006, from http://ed.isu.edu/addie/index.html

Surowiecki, J. (2004). *The wisdom of crowds: why the many are smarter than the few and how collective wisdom shapes business, economics, society and nations.* London: Little, Brown.

Surowieki, J. (2005). Independent Individuals and Wise Crowds. *The New Yorker:* Audio log Retrieved 21 March 2009, from http://itc.conversationsnetwork.org/shows/detail468.html

Svenson, G., & Wood, G. (2007). Are university students really customers? When illusion may lead to delusion for all! *Journal of Marketing Education, 21*(1), 17–28.

Swan, K., Shea, P., Fredricksen, E., Pickett, A., Pelz, W., & Maher, G. (2000). Building knowledge building communities: Consistencies, contact and communication in the virtual classroom. *Journal of Educational Computing Research, 23*(4), 359–383.

Swinburne University of Technology. (2003). *Swinburne TAFE Division Research Strategy 2003-2005.* Melbourne: Author.

Swinburne University of Technology. (2005). *Statement of Direction 2015: Building a sustainable future. Retrieved from* http://www.tafe.swinburne.edu.au/sdg/planning/statement_direction.htm.

Swinburne University of Technology. *(2005).* Swinburne ranked fourth in the nation for learning and teaching quality. Retrieved from http://www.swinburne.edu.au/corporate/marketing/mediacentre/core/vc_releases_article.php?releaseid=569.

Swinburne University of Technology. (2008). *Profile of Swinburne.* Retrieved from http://www.swinburne.edu.au/profile.htm

T3. (2006). *T3, RNIB Web Site.* Retrieved December 9, 2006, from http://www.rncb.ac.uk/t3/index.html

Taiwan Culture Portal. (2009). *Taiwan Cultural Portal.* Retrieved August 8, 2009, from http://www.culture.tw/

Tang, J. (2000). Recent Internet developments in the People's Republic of China. *Online Information Review, 24*(4), 316–321. doi:10.1108/14684520010350669

Taylor, E. W. (Ed.). (2006). *Teaching for Change: Fostering Transformative Learning in the Classroom. New Directions for Adult and Continuing Education.* San Francisco, CA: Jossey-Bass.

TeDub. (2007). The TeDub System (Technical Drawings Understanding for the Blind). *TeDub Web Site.* Retrieved April 23, 2007, from www.tedug.org/tedub-system_en.html

TELDAP. (2009). *Taiwan e-Learning Digital Archives Project (TELDAP) website and collaboration portal.* Retrieved August 8, 2009, from http://teldap.tw/en/ http://collab.teldap.tw/index.php/archives/category/news_en

Teshome, W. (1979). *Education in Ethiopia: Prospect and retrospect.* Rendale: Wiley Canada.

Tessema, K. (2006). Contradictions, Challenges, and Chaos in Ethiopian Teacher Education. *Journal for Critical Education Policy Studies, 4*(1).

Tessema, K. (2008). An Exploration for a Critical Practicum Pedagogy: Dialogical Relationships and Reflections among a Group of Student Teachers. *Educational Action Research, 16*(3), 345–360. doi:10.1080/09650790802260299

TGE /Transitional Government of Ethiopia/ (MOE). (1994). *Education and Training Policy.* Addis Ababa, Ethiopia: EMPDA.

The World Bank. (2008). *Gross National Income Per Capita 2007, Atlas Method and PPP.* World Development Indicators Database, The World Bank Group. Retrieved May 12, 2009, from http://siteresources.worldbank.org/DATASTATISTICS/Resources/GNIPC.pdf

Thomson, J., Tolmie, A., Foot, H., & McLaren, B. (1996). *Child Development and the aims of road safety education: A review and analysis* (Road Safety Report No.1). London, UK: Department for Transport. Retrieved May 13, 2009 from http://www.dft.gov.uk/pgr/Roadsafety/research/rsrr/theme1/childdeve-lopmentandthe-aimsof4728

Thorney, A. (2008, July 28). Teachers facing study problems. Letter to the Editor, *The Jamaica Gleaner.*

Thurstun, J. (2004). Teaching and learning the reading of homepages. *Prospect, 19*(2), 56–80.

Tilson, T., & Bekele, D. (2000). Ethiopia: Educational Radio and Television. *TeckKnowLogia, 2*(3). Retrieved May 12, 2009, from http://www.techknowlogia.org/TKL_active_pages2/ Currentarticles/main.asp?IssueNumber=5&FileType=HTML&ArticleID=121

Tiresias (2006). User Needs Summary. *Tiresias Web Site.* Retrieved December 9, 2006, from http://www.tiresias.org

Tognozzi, E. (2001). Italian Language Instruction: The Need for Teacher Development in Technology. *Italica, 78*(4), 487–498. doi:10.2307/3656077

Tolmie, A., Thomson, J., & Foot, H. (2002). *Development and evaluation of a computer-based pedestrian training resource for children ages 5 to 11 years* (Road Safety Research Report No.27). London, UK: Department for Transport. c http://www.dft.gov.uk/pgr/roadsafety/research/rsrr/ theme1/computerba-sedpedestriantrain4737

Torado, M. P. (1992). *Economic Development in the Third World.* New York: Longman.

Totterdell, P., Holman, D., & Hukin, A. (2008). Social networkers: Measuring and examining individual differences in propensity to connect with others. *Social Networks, 30*(4), 283–296. doi:10.1016/j.socnet.2008.04.003

Troha, F. J. (2002). Bulletproof instructional design. A model for blended learnign. *USDLA Journal, 16*(5). Eric Document Number EJ654051. Retrieved from http://www.eric.ed.gov/

Trussler, S. (1998). The rules of the game. *The Journal of Business Strategy, 19*(1), 16–19. doi:10.1108/eb039904

Tshwane University of Technology. (2005-2009). *Institutional operating plan.* Pretoria, South Africa: Tshwane University of Technology.

Twigg, C. (2003). *Change. Improving quality and reducing cost; design for effective learning* Retrieved 19 July, 2005, from http://proquest.umi.com/pdweb?did=592388111&sid=10&Fmt=3&clientId=21888&RQT=309&VName=PQD

Tye, B. B. (1999). *Global education: A study of school change.* New York: SUNY Press.

U.S. Department of Veterans Affairs. (2009). *Yellow Ribbon Program.* Retrieved May 30, 2009, from https://www.gibill.va.gov/School_Info/Yellow_Ribbon/index.htm

UCEL. (2009). *Universities' Collaboration in e-Learning (UCEL) professional health community of e-learning practice website.* Retrieved August 7, 2009, from http://www.ucel.ac.uk

UK's Department for Transport. (2002). *Road Safety Research Compendium 2001 2002.* London, UK: Author. Retrieved from http://www.dft.gov.uk/pgr/roadsafety/research/rsrc/archive/ roadsafetyresearch-compendium4721

UK's Department for Transport. (2003). *Road safety education in primary schools.* London, UK: Author. Retrieved from http://www.dft.gov.uk/pgr/roadsafety/child/education /roadsafetyeducationinprimary4633

UNESCO. (2003-04). *Gender and Education for All: The Leap to Quality.* Global Monitoring Report 2003-04. UNESCO Publishing.

UNESCO. (2005). *Draft International Implementation Scheme for the United Nations Decade of Education for Sustainable Development 2005-2014.* Retrieved March 1, 2005, from http:www.isa.unu.edu/binaries2/IIS_2004.doc

UNICEF. (2007). Transition to Post-primary Education with Special Focus to Girls: Medium-Term Strategy for Developing Post-primary education. In *Eastern and Southern Africa.* Nairobi, Kenya: Author.

University of Florida. (2005). *Distance, off-campus and technology-enhanced courses.* Retrieved from http://www.distancelearning.ufl.edu/faculty/definedistance.asp

Usorol, A., Sharratt, M.W., Tsui, E., & Shekhar, S. (2007). Trust as an antecedent to knowledge sharing in virtual communities of practice. *Knowledge Management Research & Practice, 5,* 199–212.

USQ Learning and Teaching Plan 2009-2013: Summary. (2009). Retrieved March 25, 2009, from http://www.usq.edu.au/resources/usqtlplan0913.pdf

Vaidya, S. R. (1999). Metacognitive Learning Strategies for Students with Learning Disabilities. *Education, 120,* 186–189.

Van de Veer, A., Moloisane, A., Tlebere, G., & O'Droma, M. (2001). *Lesotho Lays Foundation for Internet Access.* Retrieved June 05, 2009, from http://www.afrol.com/news2001/ Les009-internet-foundation.htm

van der Molen, H. H. (1981). Child pedestrian's exposure, accidents and behaviour. *Accident; Analysis and Prevention, 13,* 193–224. doi:10.1016/0001-4575(81)90005-1

Van Doren, D., & Corrigan, H. (2008). Designing a marketing course with field site visits. *Journal of Marketing Education, 30*(3), 189–206. doi:10.1177/0273475308318071

Van Ryneveld, L., & Van der Merwe, H. (2005). *Partners@Work Teaching and Learning with Technology*

2005 Manual. Pretoria, South Africa: Tshwane University of Technology.

Verenikina, I. (2003). Understanding Scaffolding and the ZPD in Educational Research, Australian Association for Research in Education (AARE) and New Zealand Association for Research in Education (NZARE): *Joint AARE/NZARE Conference,* Auckland 2003, Conference Papers Paper Code: VER03682. Retrieved June 7, 2009 from: http://www.aare.edu.au/03pap/ver03682.pdf

Verezub, E. (2003). The Effect of the Teaching Conditions on Reading Comprehension of a Conventional Written Text versus Hypertext for Grade 6 Students. Collection of papers of National Technical University 'Kharkov Polytechnical Institute', 217-223.

Verezub, E., & Munro, J. (2002). Teaching and Learning with a Hypertext versus a Conventional Written Text. Collection of papers of National Technical University 'Kharkov Polytechnical Institute', 329-333.

Verezub, E., & Wang, H. (2008). *The role of metacognitive reading strategies instructions and various types of links in comprehending hypertexts.* Paper presented at the Hello! Where are you in the landscape of educational technology? Melbourne.

Verezub, E., Grossi, V., Howard, K., & Watkins, P. (2008). Building E-based literacy for vocational education and training students. *Australasian Journal of Educational Technology, 24*(3), 326–338.

Verma, G., Bagley, C., & Jha, M. (Eds.). (2007). *International Perspectives on Diversity and Inclusive Education.* New York, NY: Routledge.

Vestal, W. (2003). Ten traits for a successful community of practice. *KM Review, 5*(6), 6.

Viel, W., Brantley, J., & Zulli, R. (2004). *Developing an online Geology course for preservice and inservice teachers: Enhancement for online learning.* Retrieved February 25, 2005, from http://www.citejournal.org/vol3/iss4/science/article1.cfm

Vitartas, P., & Rowe, S. (2003). An assessment of contributions to an on-line discussion forum in Accounting

Theory. In A. Treloar & A. Ellis (Eds.). *AusWeb03: Proceedings of the Ninth Australia World Wide Web Conference,* July 5-9, Gold Coast, Australia, Hyatt Regency Sanctuary Cove (pp. 412-419).

Vitartas, P., Jayne, N., Ellis, A., & Rowe, S. (2007). Student adoption of web based video conferencing software: A comparison of three student discipline groups. In *ICT: Providing choices for learners and learning. Proceedings of ASCILITE07,* December 2-5, Singapore: Nanyang Technological University. Retrieved March 23, 2009, from http://www.ascilite.org.au/conferences/singapore07/procs/vitartas.pdf

VOA (Voice of America). (2009, May 19). *The Problem of Electricity in Ethiopia.* Voice of America, Amharic Program.

Vockell, E. L., & Asher, J. W. (1995). *Educational research* (2nd ed.). Englewood Cliffs, NJ: Prentice-Hall, Inc.

Volery, T., & Lord, D. (2000). Critical success factors in online education. *International Journal of Educational Management, 14*(5), 216–223. doi:10.1108/09513540010344731

Vygotsky, L. S. (1962). *Thought and Language.* Cambridge, MA: MIT Press. doi:10.1037/11193-000

Vygotsky, L. S. (1978). *Mind in society: The development of higher psychological processes.* Cambridge, MA: Harvard University Press.

Wächter, H., Laaser, W., & Blettner, K. (1994). *Euro-Personnel Management* [DVD]. Hagen: FernUniversität

Wai, Y., Kangas, K., & Brewster, S. (2003). Web-based Haptic Applications for Blind People to Create Virtual Graphs. In *Procs. of the 11th Symposium on Haptic Interfaces for Virtual Environment and Teleoperator Systems, 2003. HAPTICS 2003* (pp. 318-325). Retrieved April 23, 2007, from http://ieeexplore.ieee.org/Xplore/login.jsp?url=/iel5/8472/2296/01191310.pdf

Walker, D. M., Walker, T., & Schmitz, J. (2003). *Doing Business Internationally: The Guide to Cross-cultural Success* (2nd ed.). New York: McGraw-Hill.

Wang, K. T., Huang, Y. M., Jeng, Y. L., & Wang, T. I. (2008). A blog-based dynamic learning map. *Computers & Education, 51,* 262–278. doi:10.1016/j.compedu.2007.06.005

Wang, V. (2004-2005). Adult education reality: three generations, different transformation the impact of social context: three generations of Chinese adult learners. *The New York Journal of Adult Learning, 3*(1), 17–32.

Wang, V. (2005). Perceptions of Teaching Preferences of Online Instructors. *Journal on Excellence in College Teaching, 16*(3), 33–54.

Wang, V. (2006). The instructional patterns of Chinese online educators in China. *Asian Journal of Distance Education, 4*(1), 43–55.

Wang, V. (2008). Enhancing the right to education through distance education in China. *Asian Journal of Distance Education, 6*(2), 66–76.

Wang, V. C. X. (2007). Chinese knowledge transmitters or western learning facilitators adult teaching methods compared. In King, K. P., & Wang, V. C. X. (Eds.), *Comparative adult education around the globe* (pp. 113–137). Hangzhou, China: Zhejiang University Press.

Wang, V. C. X., & Kreysa, P. (2006). Instructional strategies of distance education instructors in China. *The Journal of Educators Online, 3*(1), 1–25.

Wang, V., & Redhead, C. K. (2008). Comparing the Russian, the Sloyd, and the Arts and Crafts movement training system. In Wang, V., & King, K. P. (Eds.), *Innovations in career and technical education: Strategic approaches towards workforce competencies around the globe* (pp. 99–116). Charlotte, NC: Information Age Publishing.

Wang, X., Dannenhoffer, J. F., Davidson, B. D., & Spector, J. M. (2005). Design issues in a cross-institutional collaboration on a distance education course. *Distance Education, 26*(3), 405–423. doi:10.1080/01587910500291546

Warschauer, M. (2000). The changing global economy and the future of English teaching. *TESOL Quarterly, 34,* 511–535. doi:10.2307/3587741

Warschauer. (2003). Technology and second language writing: Researching a moving target. *Journal of Second Language Writing*, 12, 151-179.

Waxman, H. C., Lin, M.-F., & Georgette, M. M. (2003). *A meta-analysis of the effectiveness of teaching and learning with technology on student outcomes*. Naperville, IL: North Central Regional Educational Laboratory.

WCET. (2006, May 20). *EduTools*. WCET: Partners for Change, Technologies in practice, Advances in education. Retrieved May 28, 2009, from http://www.wcet.info/2.0/

Wei, C. Y., Evans, M. B., Eliot, M., Barrick, J., Maust, B., & Spyridakis, J. H. (2005). Influencing web-browsing behavior with intriguing hyperlink wording. *Journal of Information Science*, *31*(5), 433–445. doi:10.1177/0165551505055703

Weibler, J., & Laaser, W. (2003). *From Balanced Score Card to Performance Measurement* [DVD]. Hagen: FernUniversität

Weibler, J., & Laaser, W. (2004). *Looking for Charisma* [DVD]. Hagen: FernUniversität

Weibler, J., & Laaser, W. (2009) *Conflict and Stress in Organisations* [DVD]. Hagen: FernUniversität

Weisbord, M. (2004). Productive Workplaces Revisited: Dignity, Meaning, and Community in the 21st Century (2nd Ed.). San Francisco, CA: Jossey-Bass (Wiley).

Wells, M. (2007, September 18). Quality Matters: Does Your Online Course Meet the Standards. *Magna Publications*. Madison WI, USA: Magna Publications. Retrieved from http://www.magnapubs.com/aboutus/history.html

Wenger, E. (1998). *Communities of practice. Learning, meaning and identity*. Cambridge, UK: Cambridge University Press.

Wenger, E. C., & Snyder, W. M. (2000). Communities of practice: the organizational frontier. *Harvard Business Review*, *78*(1), 139–145.

Wenger, E. C., McDermott, R., & Synder, W. M. (2002). *Cultivating Communities of Practice*. Boston: Harvard Business School Press.

White, C. J. (2005). *Research: A practical guide*. Pretoria, South Africa: Intuthuko Investments.

Whitebread, D., & Neilson, K. (1999). *Cognitive And Metacognitive Processes Underlying the Development Of Children's Pedestrian Skills* (Road Safety Report No. 6). London, UK: Department for Transport. Retrieved May 13, 2009 from http://www.dft.gov.uk/pgr/roadsafety/research/rsrr/theme1/cognitive-andmeta-cognitivepro4734

Wiesenberg, F. P. (2004). Designing and co-facilitating online graduate classes: Reflections and recommendations. *Canadian Journal of University of Continuing Education*, *30*(2), 41–59.

Wiesenberg, F., & Stacey, E. (2005). Reflections on teaching and learning online: Quality program design, delivery, and support issues from a cross-global perspective. *Distance Education*, *26*(3), 385–404. doi:10.1080/01587910500291496

Williams, J., & Fardon, M. (2007). Perpetual connectivity: Lecture recordings and portable media players ICT: Providing choices for learners and learning. *Proceedings of ASCILITE07*, December 2-5, Singapore: Nanyang Technological University. Retrieved March 23, 2009, from http://www.ascilite.org.au/conferences/singapore07/procs/williams-jo.pdf

Winkelen, C. V., & Ramsell, P. (2003). Why aligning value is key to designing communities. *KM Review*, *5*(6), 12–15.

Wlodkowski, R. (2008). *Enhancing Adult Motivation to Learn: A Comprehensive Guide for Teaching All Adults* (3rd ed.). San Francisco, CA: Jossey-Bass.

Wood, D., Bruner, J., & Ross, G. (1976). The role of tutoring in problem solving. *Journal of Child Psychology and Psychiatry, and Allied Disciplines*, *17*(2), 89–100. doi:10.1111/j.1469-7610.1976.tb00381.x

Woods, R., & Ebersole, S. (2003). Using non-subject-matter-specific discussion boards to build connectedness in online learning. *American Journal of Distance Education*, *17*(2), 99–118. doi:10.1207/S15389286AJDE1702_3

World Bank. (1986). Poverty and hunger: Issues and options for food security in developing countries. Washington, DC.

World Commission on Sustainable Development. (1987). *Our common future*. New York: Oxford University Press.

Wu, C. (2006). Blog in TEFL: A new promising vehicle. *US-China Education Review*, *3*(5), 69–73.

Wu, P. (1988). Why change is difficult? Lessons for staff development. *Journal of Staff Development*, *9*(2), 10–14.

Yang, D. P. (2005). China's education in 2003: From growth to reform. (J. Eagleton, Trans). [Original work published in 2003]. *Chinese Education & Society*, *38*(4), 11–45.

Yin, R. (1994). *Case Study Research: Design and Methods* (2nd ed.). Beverly Hills, CA: Sage Publishing.

Young, I. (2008). *Swinburne in 2015*. Retrieved from http://www.swinburne.edu.au/chance/vc/documents/opinionpieces/Swinburne2015.pdf

Zirkle, C. (2001). Access barriers in distance education. *Contemporary Education*, *72*(2), 39–42.

Zirkle, C. (2002). Identification of distance education barriers for trade and industrial teacher education. *Journal of Industrial Teacher Education, 40*(1), 20-44. Retrieved July 30, 2008 from http://scholar.lib.vt.edu/ejournals/JITE/v40n1/zirkle.html

Zirkle, C. (2004). Distance education programming barriers in career and technical teacher education in Ohio. *Journal of Vocational Education Research, 29*(1). Retrieved July 30, 2008 from http://scholar.lib.vt.edu/ejournals/JVER/v29n3/zirkle.html#zirkle2001

About the Contributors

Siran Mukerji is Jawahar Lal Nehru scholar for her doctorate in HRD and also has Masters in Distance Education and Public Administration. She has been International Research Fellow of Open University Business School (2009), Open University, UK. She was associated with Arab Open University Saudi Arabia Branch for three years as a faculty member in Business Administration and co edited teaching case books and contributed articles in standard national and international journals and also presented papers in national and international conferences. Her current research interests are Performance management and HRM in open and distance learning institutions. She is a member of review committees of a number of international conferences / journals. In her parent institution IGNOU, India, she is Assistant Director.

Purnendu Tripathi, an International Research Fellow of Open University Business School (2009), Open University, UK, is Ph.D. in Management, with Masters in Distance Education also. He was associated with Arab Open University Saudi Arabia Branch for three years as a faculty member in Business Administration. In his parent institution IGNOU, India, he is Assistant Director. He has co edited teaching case books and contributed articles in standard national and international journals and presented papers in national and international conferences. He is a member of review committees of a number of international conferences and journals. His current research interest is Academic Program Life Cycle (APLC) and Educational Marketing.

* * *

Payal Arora is an Assistant Professor in International Communication and Media at Erasmus University in the Netherlands. Her expertise lies in social computing, informatics, new media and international development. Her recent work has been published in several peer-reviewed scholarly journals including *Information Communication and Ethics in Society* (ICES), *International Journal of Cultural Studies* (IJCS), *Education Philosophy and Theory Journal* (EPTJ), *Association for Academic Computing and Education Journal* (AACE), *International Journal of Education & Development using ICT* and the like. Her upcoming book titled, "Dot Com Mantra: Social Computing in Central Himalayas" entails an ethnography of social practice with computers and the Net in Almora, India. She earned her Doctorate from Columbia University, Teachers College in *Language, Literacy and Technology*, a Masters degree in International Education Policy from Harvard University, and a Teaching Certificate from the University of Cambridge. For more information, check her website: www.payalarora.com

Francis Bangou is currently an assistant professor at the Faculty of Education at the University of Ottawa. His research focuses on both the implementation of technology in language education, and technological literacies. He is also interested in the experiences of language learners in European and North Americans educational systems.

Ian Benest graduated from the University of Essex with a BA in Computer and Communication Engineering in 1974 and completed an MSc by research and then a PhD in interactive computer-aided circuit design - all at the University of Essex. He then spent five years at the UK Science and Engineering Research Council's Rutherford Appleton Laboratory, latterly in the role of MMI coordinator. Dr. Benest is currently a lecturer in Computer Science at the University of York. He is a member of the Advisory Board for the Information and Computer Sciences network of the UK's Higher Education Academy (HEA-ICS). His research interests include user interfaces to hypermedia systems, with special attention to inclusive design (for those with aural, visual, cognitive and physical impairments); the work is applied to teaching and learning in electronic circuit design.

Getnet D. Bitew was a Teacher in High Schools, an Instructor in a Teachers' Training Institute, a Lecturer and an Assistant Professor at a University in Ethiopia for more than eleven years. He has been conducting several research studies on Ethiopian education system and particularly on the secondary education. He obtained his Bachelor of Arts in Pedagogical Sciences and his Master of Arts in Curriculum and Instruction at Addis Ababa University, Ethiopia. He did one of his PhDs in Curriculum Development at the University of Innsbruck, Austria and his second PhD in Learning and Education Development at the University of Melbourne, Australia. He has been working as a Research Supervisor at the University of Melbourne and as a Research Fellow at a Postdoctoral level in USA. His major research interests include Students' School/College Experiences; Curriculum Development; Technology and Education; Assessment; Institutional Research; Education of Immigrants; Multicultural Education; and Gender and Education.

Hamed Fazlollahtabar is a Dean of Technology at the Mazandaran University of Science and Technology, Babol, Iran. He received his doctorate awarded in Electronic Systems from the Gulf University of Science and Technology. His research interests are optimisation in electronic-learning and information technology. He has published more than 40 research papers in international journals and conferences.

Douglas Fleming is an Assistant Professor at the Faculty of Education at the University of Ottawa. His research interests focus on immigration, equity, citizenship and English as a Second Language methodology. He has over 20 years public school ESL teaching experience.

Emmanuel Fokides is an Adjunct lecturer at the Department of Education of the University of the Aegean where he teaches the educational utilization of multimedia and virtual reality applications. His basic studies are in primary school education. His PhD concerns the development of a virtual reality environment for teaching courses in the elementary school. Since 1994, he is involved in a number of funded research projects. Dr. Fokides has published a number of papers in journals and conference proceedings, a book on virtual reality in education and a number of chapters in books. His scientific interests include the usage of the Internet as an educational tool, the educational uses of virtual reality, distance education, the development and evaluation of educational multimedia applications and ICT applications in multigrade schools.

Ruth Gannon-Cook is Assistant Professor at the DePaul University in the School for New Learning has been teaching and designing online courses for 8 years. She has presented at numerous conferences and published works on semiotics, distance education, and adult learning. She earned an Ed.D. with major in Instructional Technology, University of Houston; a Certificate for Advanced Studies: Change Diffusion and Technology Integration, Queens College, Cambridge; an M. S. Ed. in Educational Administration, Loyola University, New Orleans. She has also taught at University of Houston-Clear Lake and the University of Houston. Her email is rgannonc@depaul.edu

Deryn Graham FHEA, C. Eng, FBCS, CITP, PhD, MSc, MA is an Associate Professor at Unitec, and a Visiting Fellow at the University of Greenwich. Background is in Computer Science, PhD from Brunel University in Artificial Intelligence. As a Lecturer at Brunel, began funded research projects into Education, and "Knowledge-Based Image Processing Systems", leading to a book. Visiting Professorship at Mid Sweden University then employed as a Senior Lecturer at Greenwich, successfully completing an EU FP5 project. Dr. Graham has also been an organiser/chair/editor of an annual workshop on e-Learning. A member/referee of programme committees/conferences reviewed numerous papers, books and bulletins for several publishers. She has well over 40 publications and she has given keynote papers and been an invited speaker. Her teaching and research interests, publications and grants are in diverse areas; Modelling, Networks, Information Visualisation, e-Learning, and HCI. Member of the HCI Disciplinary Commons in 2008. Institutional Nominee for the ILTHE National Fellowship Scheme in 2004.

Peter Haber is a graduated telecommunication engineer and is working now over 10 years as a faculty member at the School of Telecommunications Engineering at Salzburg University of Applied Sciences. In 2007 he was conferred the position as Assistant Professor at the department of signal processing and system theory. As a member of different national and international working groups and EU projects he has made valuable research experiences in Engineering as well in the field of Education and Qualification. As a coordinator of a Leonardo da Vinci project in the EU-Lifelong Learning Programme he established together with international partners a curriculum model for a master degree program. In 2009 he has been appointed into the scientific advisory board of the International Conference of Education, Research and Innovation.

Wallace Hannum is a faculty member in the educational psychology program at the University of North Carolina and Associate Director for Technology of the National Research Center on Rural Education Support. Dr. Hannum teaches graduate level courses on learning theories, instructional design, and the use of technology in education. Dr. Hannum's research focuses on instructional uses of technology, especially distance education. He has participated in the design and implementation of numerous technology-based programs and projects. He has worked extensively on education projects in Africa, Asia and Latin America. Dr. Hannum is author of five books and numerous articles on topics related to technology and instructional design.

Erich Herber is a senior specialist in ICT and technology based learning (e-Learning, blended learning), with over 15 years of experience. His experience in training and skills development includes expert consulting and coaching, curriculum and methodology development, knowledge management & learning content development, VET and adult training as well as the design and implementation of online learning and collaboration communities for universities, municipalities and government. This combines with experience in ICT skills training, design and project development as well as the establishment of business clusters and industrial networks. He has worked in a number of European transition economies and recent Member States, mostly on EU-funded projects.

Matthew Irvin is a research scientist at the National Research Center on Rural Education Support at the University of North Carolina at Chapel Hill. He is also an assistant clinical professor in the School of Education at the University of North Carolina at Chapel Hill. His research has involved experimental intervention work, cross-sectional and longitudinal correlational studies, and the use of large-scale databases. This work has focused on rural youth, distance education, risk and resilience, student engagement, school adjustment, peer relations, and academic success. He has developed online courses at the university level on child and adolescent development and has taught in university courses utilizing online platforms to support student learning.

Jill Jameson is Director of Research and Enterprise at the School of Education and Training, University of Greenwich. The author of four books and hundreds of other publications, Jill is a Fellow of the Institute for Learning (FIfL), with a PhD and MA (Distinction, King's College), MA (Goldsmith's), MA (University of Cambridge), PGCE (Distinction, Univ. Nottingham) and BA, PG Dip (UCT). Co-Chair of *ALT-C 2008*, National Convenor, SRHE HE-FE Research Network, Special Editor for *BJET* (2006) and *ALT-J* (2000), Dr. Jameson is a reviewer for *AACE, ALT-J, Studies in HE* and *JFHE* and Series Editor for *Continuum International*. With many years HE-FE senior management experience, she is co-author, with Professor Sara de Freitas, of a new *e-Learning Reader* (forthcoming). Director of the JISC eLIDA CAMEL and JISC eLISA projects.

Nicola Jayne BSc(Hons)(Massey), GradCertHE(L&T), PhD(Massey) has been a lecturer in the School of Commerce and Management at Southern Cross University, since 1993, she has taught a wide range of quantitative units both undergraduate and postgraduate. Dr. Jayne has been innovative and experimental in her teaching; developing self-paced units, introducing Minitab and later PaceXL projects for Statistics students and developing unit websites since 2000. Nicola is a co-author of the Australian adaptations of two US statistics textbooks and is currently the Coordinator of Bachelor of Business Course.

Aleric Josephs is a lecturer in History in the Department of History and Archaeology at the University of the West Indies, Mona campus in Kingston, Jamaica. She has been involved in distance education for over a decade, writing courses for online delivery and coordinating her department's involvement in the Bachelor of Education (Secondary) Distance Programme.

Karen Kaun is co-founder and Executive Director of Knowledge iTrust, a non-profit organization that partners with educational institutions, NGOs, and experts to design, develop, and facilitate digital and real-world literacy through applied learning projects. She has received acclaim in the news media (e.g. The New York Times *Education Life* magazine, Technology and Learning magazine), from public figures (e.g. President William J. Clinton) and school leaders. The book *Recapturing Technology for Education*, has described her work as "a shadow revolution" (p. 74) for anticipating how education will be shaped in the future by technology. Her current research is accessible through YouTube (keyword search: Karen Kaun). In the mid-1990s through early 2000s, Ms. Kaun consulted for and developed business plans and strategies for corporations that were launching Internet-related businesses including the BellSouth Corporation, Education Division, Encyclopaedia Britannica, Sierra Online and Hasbro.

Angelina Khoro holds the Masters' Degree certificates in both Education and Distance Learning from Bath and Durham Universities respectively and presently a Lecturer at Lesotho college of Education. Her work experiences include writing and reviewing distance learning modules, mentoring in-service teacher learners as well as organising, co-ordinating and supervising distance education activities at the site, cluster and regional levels. Having served in primary, secondary and tertiary levels of education, she has developed interest in researching on teaching and learning with specific focus on: learner support, learner recruitment and progression, classroom assessment practices, curriculum and programme reviews.

Daesang Kim, a Ph.D. in Curriculum, Instruction, & Media Technology, is Assistant Professor at Saint Mary-of-the-Woods College. He has numerous successful teaching experiences at the university level in online and in technology enhanced traditional classroom. Dr. Kim is one of the Adobe Acrobat Connect Pro, Atomic Learning, and Desire2Learn administrators and provides variable instructional services including course templates. Dr. Kim has co-authored several articles relating to transformation in online and multimedia learning. He is a member of the SMWC IT Users Group and is a member of the Quality Review Committee for Woods Online.

Wolfram Laaser, PhD in Economics, Consultant in FernUniversität Hagen, was Academic Director at FernUniversität, from 1976-2008. He was also Co-ordinator of the didactic sections, Centre for Distance Study Development at FernUniversität. He had teaching assignments at Universities of Paderborn and Frankfurt. Besides, he was Online Lecturer at UNED and University of Alcala in Spain, University of Cordoba, Argentina, and University of Joensuu, Finland. He has been actively involved in the development of interactive multimedia courseware (CD-ROM and WEB-based Training) and in managing training seminars for distance educators in Europe, Africa, Latin America and Asia. He has interest in producing educational Video and TV on Education and Humanities, Economics, Business Administration, Law and Electrical Engineering. He is presently Member of SETRAD (India), GMW (Germany), Scientific Borrad, RIED, Spain, Revista de Educación a Distancia (RED) (Spain), Apertura (Mexico). He has numerous publications on media design and evaluation in books, national and international journals.

Kathryn Ley is an Associate Professor of Instructional Technology at University of Houston - Clear Lake where she teaches graduate courses in research design, motivation in instruction, and instructional technologies. She has authored over 25 journal publications, presented at educational and distance learning conferences. She has held tenured positions at two universities and has taught human resource management and performance technology courses. She served as the program coordinator of a graduate program in instructional technology. She is currently investigating how training faculty to support self-regulation in online courses may reduce their extraneous cognitive load. She earned a PhD in instructional systems from Florida State University, an M.S. in Environmental Management with Human Resources concentration from the University of Texas at San Antonio, and an M.L.S. from the University of Texas.

Birgit Loch (PhD, Dipl.-Math., GradCertTertT&L) is a Senior Lecturer in mathematics education at Swinburne University of Technology. She was previously a Senior Lecturer in mathematics and computing at USQ where she held a fractional secondment with the Division of ICT Services as Principal Advisor (Learning & Teaching). Birgit has a strong interest in the area of technology enhanced learning, and undertook a USQ Senior Learning & Teaching Fellowship to trial tablet technology in all faculties of the universities. Building on experience gained during the web conferencing trial, she completed a trial of lecture recording software, which led to a new system being implemented at USQ. Her current main research interests are in innovative use of technology, for instance tablet PCs and screencasting, in mathematics education.

Ravisha Mathur, Ph.D., is an associate professor in the Connie L. Lurie College of Education at San José State University. She received her doctorate in psychology from Purdue University in 2003. Dr. Mathur's research interests are focused on the development of close, interpersonal relationships and building institutional partnerships. Her most recent work has been published in journals such as the *Online Journal of Distance Learning Administration* and *Electronic Magazine of Multicultural Education.* In addition, she has presented her work at several national and international conferences both educational and technological. She currently teaches several undergraduate and graduate courses within the college and serves as newsletter editor for the *Society for Cross-Cultural Research.*

Manfred Mayr is a graduated Professor for economics, business and IT Management and department head technical management in the degree programme: Information Technology & Systems Management (ITS) at Salzburg University of Applied Sciences. As a researcher, promoter and coordinator of Leonardo da Vinci projects in the EU Lifelong Learning Programme he made verifiable research findings and experiences in the fields of Engineering, Education, Certification and Assessment.

Christopher T. Miller is an Associate Professor of Education and coordinator of the online educational technology program at Morehead State University in Morehead, Kentucky, USA. He received his Ed.D in Instruction and Administration from the University of Kentucky in the instructional systems design program. Dr. Miller's doctoral focus was on web-based instructional design and testing of the person-centered model of instruction. His research interests include web-based instructional design, games and simulations in education, classroom technology integration, and multimedia. He recently edited the book *Game: Purpose and Potential in Education* (2008) and is also an active instructional designer, trainer, and consultant.

Jennie Mitchell, CPA, CMA, has a Ph.D. in Curriculum, Instruction, and Media Technology. She is Director of the new Woods Online Degree Program and Professor in the Business, Art & Media Department at Saint Mary-of-the-Woods College (SMWC). With 25 years teaching experience, she is an experienced faculty in online course technology and has won various awards for teaching excellence. Dr. Mitchell authored various chapters on learning objects, podcasts scripts and develops interactive excel and accounting software problems for various accounting textbooks. She presents regionally and nationally on topics ranging from virtual team play to learning object development. Dr. Mitchell is a member of the SMWC IT Users Group and chairs the Program Development Team and the Quality Review Committee.

Peter Nicholl graduated with a B.Eng. in Electronic Systems and Diploma in Industrial Studies in 1991, and D.Phil. in Computing Science in 1994, from University of Ulster. Thesis entitled: feature Directed Spiral Image Compression (A New Technique for Lossless Image Compression) He started his academic teaching career as a Lecturer, at the University of Ulster, and completed the Postgraduate Certificate in University Teaching in 1996. He was awarded the 1993 Proctor & Gamble Prize for the best Faculty of Informatics Research Paper published by a Research Student during 1992 and in 2006 was awarded the University Awards Scheme for Leadership in Teaching and Learning Support (Distinguished Learning Support Fellowship: Team Award). Currently, he is a Senior Lecturer and has 31 publications, continuing research into teaching in relation to the recent SENDO legislation and the dissemination of Disability Guidelines and Tools to support hearing and visually impaired students.

Lisa Oliver, Ph.D., is an associate professor in the Department of Counselor Education at San José State University. She received her doctorate in Counseling Psychology from Stanford University. Dr. Oliver's scholarship has focused upon youth and adults, and includes resilience, cultural relationships, career happenstance, international partnerships, blended learning approaches, and globalization in higher education. Her current areas of interest also include identity development, multicultural counseling, and community engagement. She teaches a variety of courses at San José State University, with an area of expertise in cultural psychology. Dr. Oliver is currently the Treasurer for the *Society for Cross-Cultural Research* and the Graduate Program Coordinator for the Department of Counselor Education.

Shirley Reushle (EdD, MEd, BEd, DipTeach), a Senior Lecturer in online pedagogies is currently on secondment to the USQ Australian Digital Futures Institute (ADFI) as the Manager of Technology-Enhanced Learning Projects. ADFI is a research and development section of the University of Southern Queensland. Dr. Reushle has worked in the Australian school and higher education sectors. She has taught online in the higher education sector for over ten years. Her teaching, research, publication and consultancy work focus on designing and facilitating online and flexible programs and creating professional development experiences with a focus on transformative learning.

Stephen Rowe CPA, MA, BBus has been lecturing auditing and accounting in the School of Commerce and Management at Southern Cross University since 1986. He began adopting online approaches in his delivery in 2000 and currently works exclusively online. Steve has been recognized at the institutional, national and international levels for his development of online approaches for learning and teaching. Central to his approaches has been the use of Elluminate and he is recognized as an expert user of the tool. He is currently undertaking his PhD writing up an autoethnography of how his lecturing career has moved online and presenting the model he has developed for leaning and teaching auditing to undergraduates.

Sibongile Simelane is an Instructional Designer at Tshwane University of Technology. She has obtained a Higher Diploma in Education (Computer Literacy) with distinction in 2000, then she completed BEd (HONS) in Computer Based Education in 2002 at University of Johannesburg. She has also obtained a Blackboard Certified Trainer with distinction in 2007. Besides, she has also completed online facilitating course and obtained the e-Moderation certificate in 2006 and Efficient Online Tutoring @ e-Learning Africa Certificate in 2007. She did her Masters in Educational Technology in 2008 from Tshwane University of Technology. The study was on the implementation of a professional development programme in educational technology in higher education. She has presented international and national papers in various conferences that involve the integration of e-learning in higher education, besides, publishing articles in accredited journal and conference proceedings.

Costas Tsolakidis is Assistant professor at the Department of Education of the University of the Aegean where he teaches the Information technology related subjects. Basic studies are electronic engineering at the University of Dundee, Scotland. He is involved in a number of EU and Greek state funded projects as coordinator or partner. He has published a number of papers in journals, conferences and chapters in books. Scientific interests are: Introduction of information technology in education, distance education, Information technology as tools for the development of remote and rural areas, use of IT in multi-grade schools, virtual reality as a teaching tool.

Claire de la Varre is a Ph.D. candidate in educational psychology at the University of North Carolina at Chapel Hill. She is currently a research assistant at the National Research Center on Rural Education Support and holds a master's degree in information science. She recently spent three years at the Learning Technology Section at Edinburgh University in Scotland, as an e-learning developer on the Edinburgh Electronic Medical Curriculum (EEMeC), which was awarded the Queen's Anniversary Prize for Higher Education in 2005. Her research interests include online learning, particularly asynchronous online discussion and how it contributes to student learning, as well as child development with a focus on special populations.

Elena Verezub (BEd., Candidate of Science in Ed. Psych., PhD in Education (Melb)) is a Language and Academic Skills Advisor at Swinburne University of Technology, Australia. She has over 15 years of teaching experience in TESOL, Education and Educational Psychology, both in Australia and Ukraine. Dr. Verezub's professional and research interests include E-learning and hypertext literacy; study expectations in TAFE and Higher Education environments; Language and Academic skills; psychological aspects of text memorisation. She could be contacted on everezub@swin.edu.au

Victor C. X. Wang, Ed.D., an associate professor, at California State University, Long Beach (CSULB) has published well over 80 journal articles, book chapters and books and has been a reviewer for four national and international journals. Currently he serves as the editor in chief of the International Journal of Adult Vocational Education and Technology. He has won many academic achievement awards from universities in China and in the United States, including the Distinguished Faculty Scholarly & Creative Achievement Award in 2009. Two of the books he has written and edited have been adopted as required textbooks by major universities in the United States and China. Numerous universities worldwide including UC-Berkley, University of Chicago, Rice University, Cornell University, Princeton University and Yale University have catalogued his books and journal articles.

Index